W9-AZM-687

CLB 1637

Printed and bound in Barcelona, Spain by Cronión, S.A.

1987 edition published by Portland House, distributed by Crown Publishers, Inc.
ISBN 0 517 62366 8
h g f e d c b a
Dep. Leg. B-9.354-87

Text by Denise Jarrett-Macauley, Maureen McCall, Judith Ferguson, Beverley Piper, Carolyn Garner, Alice King, Lalita Ahmed and Helen Walsh
Photography by Peter Barry
Designed by Philip Clucas
Produced by Ted Smart and David Gibbon

The Complete Book of GOURMET COOKING

A Course-by-Course Guide to the Perfect Meal

PORTLAND HOUSE

1982
GRAND VIN

CONTENTS

Section 3

HOME FARE

Section 4

SALADS AND VEGETABLES

Section 5

MEALS WITH FLAIR

Section 6
CAKES AND DESSERTS

Section 7
ENJOYING WINE

Section 1

SOUPS AND APPETIZERS

Hot Soups

Hot and Sour Seafood Soup

PREPARATION TIME: 20 minutes

COOKING TIME: 20 minutes

SERVES: 4 people

3 dried Chinese mushrooms, soaked in hot water for 20 minutes
1 cake fresh bean curd (tofu), diced
4oz shrimp, shelled and de-veined
2½ cups fish stock
2oz white fish fillet
1 tbsp oyster sauce
1 tbsp light soy sauce
1 tbsp lemon juice
½ tsp lemon rind, cut into slivers
1 tbsp vegetable oil
1 red chili pepper, seeds removed, and finely sliced
1 green chili pepper, seeds removed, and finely sliced
2 green onions, sliced
Salt
Pepper
1 tsp sesame oil

Garnish
Fresh coriander, if desired

Soak mushrooms in hot water and set aside. Heat vegetable oil, and add shrimp, chili peppers, lemon rind and green onions. Add stock, oyster sauce and light soy sauce and bring to the boil. Reduce heat and simmer for 5 minutes. Season to taste. Remove hard stalks from mushrooms and slice caps finely. Dice white fish fillets and add them with bean curd and Chinese mushrooms to the soup, cooking for a further 5 minutes. Stir in lemon juice and sesame oil. Adjust seasoning, and serve sprinkled with fresh coriander leaves if desired.

Egg and Lemon Soup

PREPARATION TIME: 15 minutes

COOKING TIME: 15 minutes

SERVES: 4 people

2⅔ cups chicken stock
1 tbsp small noodles/soup pasta
2 small eggs, separated
1 lemon
Salt
White pepper
Sugar, if desired

Garnish
Slivers of pared lemon rind

Bring stock to the boil and add the noodles. Cook for 10 minutes or until noodles are tender, stirring occasionally. Meanwhile, juice lemon, and beat the egg whites until stiff. Add the yolks and beat until light and creamy. Add lemon juice gradually, beating all the time. Add a cup of the soup to the egg mixture and whisk. Pour back into the soup, whisking continuously. Adjust seasoning to taste. Garnish with pared lemon rind. Serve immediately.

This page: Hot and Sour Seafood Soup.

Facing page: Egg and Lemon Soup (top) and Celery and Apple Soup (bottom).

French Onion Soup

PREPARATION TIME: 15 minutes

COOKING TIME: 1 hour

SERVES: 4 people

2½ cups onions, peeled and sliced thinly
4 tbsps butter or margarine
3 tbsps flour
5 cups boiling water
2 beef bouillon cubes
1 small French bread loaf
¼ cup Parmesan or Gruyère cheese, grated
Salt
Pepper

Melt butter in a thick saucepan. Add onions and cook gently over moderate heat until golden brown – about 15 minutes – being careful not to burn them. Stir occasionally. Meanwhile, dissolve bouillon cubes in boiling water and put aside to cool. Stir flour into onions and cook for 2 minutes. Add stock gradually, stirring continuously. Simmer for 30 minutes. Add salt and pepper to taste. Pre-heat oven or broiler. Slice bread thickly and place in bottom of ovenproof serving dish. Pour over soup. Sprinkle the bread with cheese and place under the broiler or in a hot oven until browned. Serve very hot.

Tomato Soup

PREPARATION TIME: 15 minutes

COOKING TIME: 45 minutes

SERVES: 4 people

1lb ripe tomatoes
1 carrot
1 onion
2½ cups water
1 chicken bouillon cube
2 tbsps butter or margarine
2 tbsps flour
Pinch of grated nutmeg
1 tsp basil
Salt
Pepper

Garnish
Chopped parsley

Peel and finely dice onion and

This page: Goulash Soup (top) and Curried Chicken Soup (bottom).

Facing page: Tomato Soup (top) and French Onion Soup (bottom).

carrot. Cut tomatoes into quarters and squeeze out seeds into a strainer. Strain seeds and retain the juice. Melt butter in a pan. Fry the onion and carrot gently until the onion is transparent. Draw off heat and stir in the flour, nutmeg and basil. Add tomatoes, juice and water, return to heat and stir until boiling. Add crumbled chicken bouillon cube and salt and pepper to taste. Cover and simmer for 30 minutes. Push the soup through a strainer and return to pan. Adjust seasoning and reheat. Garnish with chopped parsley.

Bumper Soup

PREPARATION TIME: 30 minutes
COOKING TIME: 1 hour 45 minutes
SERVES: 4 people

5 cups good beef stock
1lb spinach, stalks removed, and shredded
2 onions, peeled and diced
2 carrots, scraped and diced
2 potatoes, peeled and diced
3 sticks celery, sliced
1 tbsp chopped parsley
2 tbsps tomato paste
½ cup lentils
Salt
Pepper

Heat stock in pan. When hot, add vegetables, parsley, tomato paste and seasoning. Bring to boil and simmer for 1 hour. Add lentils and simmer for a further 30 minutes stirring occasionally. Adjust seasoning if necessary. Serve hot.

Red Pepper Soup

PREPARATION TIME: 15 minutes
COOKING TIME: 45 minutes
SERVES: 4 people

1 medium onion, peeled and finely chopped
3 tomatoes
3 red peppers
2 tbsps butter or margarine
5 cups chicken stock
Salt
Pepper

Garnish
Chopped parsley and sliced red pepper

Remove core and seeds from peppers. Slice a pepper for garnish and set aside. Chop remaining peppers and tomatoes into small pieces. Melt butter in a large saucepan and add onion, tomatoes and peppers and fry gently for 5 minutes, stirring continuously. Pour on chicken stock, add salt and pepper and bring to the boil. Simmer for 30 minutes. Push the soup through a strainer to remove skin and any seeds. Adjust seasoning. Add a pinch of sugar if desired. Serve hot or cold, sprinkled with parsley and garnished with a slice of red pepper.

Curried Chicken Soup

PREPARATION TIME: 10 minutes
COOKING TIME: 20 minutes
SERVES: 4 people

2 tbsps butter or margarine
2 tsps curry powder
1 tbsp flour
1 chicken bouillon cube
5 cups water
½ tsp paprika
2 tbsps tomato relish
⅓ cup cooked chicken, chopped
2 tbsps rice
Yolk of 1 egg
¼ cup light cream
Salt
Pepper

Garnish
Chopped parsley or coriander

Melt butter in pan. Stir in curry powder and flour. Cook gently for 2 minutes. Draw off heat. Gradually stir in bouillon cube dissolved in water. Add paprika and bring to the boil to thicken. Add relish, chicken, and rice and simmer for 12-15 minutes. Mix egg yolk with cream and gradually add to soup off the heat. Do not re-boil. Season to taste. Serve hot, garnished with chopped parsley or coriander.

Goulash Soup

PREPARATION TIME: 20 minutes
COOKING TIME: 2 hours 45 minutes
SERVES: 4 people

1½ lbs skirt or chuck steak, cut into 1" cubes
4 medium onions, peeled and chopped roughly or quartered
1 green pepper, cored, seeds removed, and chopped
4 tomatoes, skinned and quartered
4 tbsps tomato paste
2½ cups good beef stock
1 tbsp paprika
2 tbsps butter or margarine
1 tbsp oil
1lb potatoes, peeled and cut into bite-size pieces
1 tbsp flour
Salt
Pepper

Heat oil in pan. When hot, add steak in batches so as not to overcrowd, and sauté over a high heat until well browned all over. Remove and set aside. Add butter, onion and green pepper, and fry until onion is lightly browned. Stir in flour. Remove from heat. Add stock, return to heat and bring to the boil, stirring continuously. Add tomato, tomato paste, paprika and salt and pepper to taste. Reduce heat, return meat, cover and simmer for 2 hours, stirring occasionally and adding more stock or water if necessary. Add potatoes and cook gently for a further 20 minutes, or until potatoes are cooked through.

Celery and Apple Soup

PREPARATION TIME: 15 minutes
COOKING TIME: 45 minutes
SERVES: 4 people

1 onion, peeled and chopped
3 sticks celery, chopped
3 cooking apples, peeled and sliced
2 tbsps butter or margarine
1 chicken bouillon cube
5 cups water
1 bay leaf
1 tbsp cornstarch
Salt
Pepper

Garnish
Finely sliced celery

Melt butter in pan. Add onion and fry for 5 minutes, then add apple and a third of the celery, and fry a further 5 minutes. Heat water. Add to crumbled bouillon cube and pour onto onion/apple mixture. Add salt, pepper and bay leaf. Bring to the boil and simmer for ½ hour. Push through a strainer and then return to the pan. Blend cornstarch with a little water, and stir into the soup. Bring soup to the boil, and cook for 2-3 minutes, stirring continuously. Cook remaining celery in water until tender. Add to soup. Garnish with finely sliced celery. Serve immediately.

Minestrone

PREPARATION TIME: 30 minutes
COOKING TIME: 1 hour 15 minutes
SERVES: 4 people

1 carrot, cut into strips
1 leek, sliced
1 turnip, cut into strips
3 tomatoes, skinned and diced
1 stick celery, chopped
4 slices bacon, blanched and diced
¼ small cabbage, sliced
3 cloves garlic, crushed
1 onion, peeled and sliced
2 tbsps butter or margarine
5 cups good, fat-free chicken stock
¾ cup short-cut or elbow macaroni
Salt
Pepper

Red Pepper Soup (right) and Bumper Soup (bottom).

Accompaniment
Freshly grated Parmesan cheese, if desired

Melt butter in pan, and add garlic, onion, leek and celery. Cover and cook over a gentle heat for 15 minutes without coloring. Add carrot and turnip, stock, and salt and pepper to taste. Bring to the boil, cover and simmer for 30 minutes. Add cabbage and simmer a further 5 minutes. Add tomato and macaroni, and simmer gently, uncovered, for 15 minutes. Meanwhile, broil bacon until crisp. Serve on top of soup with a side serving of Parmesan cheese if desired.

Cream of Cauliflower Soup

PREPARATION TIME: 10 minutes

COOKING TIME: 45 minutes

SERVES: 4 people

1 cauliflower
4 tbsps butter or margarine
1½ tbsps flour
2½ cups chicken stock
1 onion, peeled and chopped
2 medium egg yolks
⅔ cup heavy cream
Cheese, grated
Nutmeg
Salt
Pepper

Garnish
Snipped chives

Trim and break cauliflower into flowerets. Cook in gently boiling salted water for 5 minutes. Drain and set aside. Melt butter in pan and stir in the flour. Cook for 1-2 minutes, stirring. Remove from heat and stir in chicken stock. Add onion, and return to heat. Bring to

This page: Cream of Cauliflower Soup (top) and Lettuce Soup (bottom).

Facing page: Minestrone.

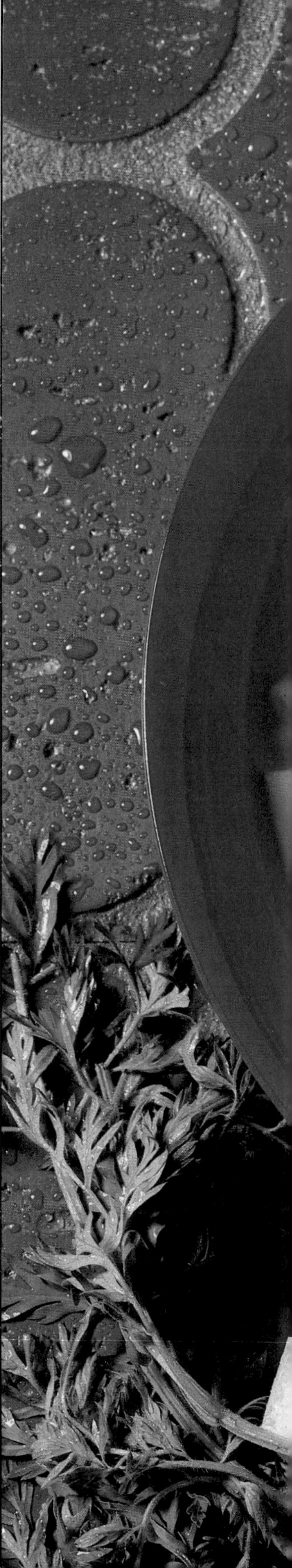

boil, stirring continuously, and simmer for 20 minutes. Allow to cool. Add cauliflower and blend. Push through a strainer. Return to pan, and re-heat. Lightly beat together egg yolks, cream and grated cheese. Stir in some soup, and then put all of the mixture back into the pan. Cook gently until thickened, but do not let it boil. Season with salt and pepper and grated nutmeg. Garnish with snipped chives.

Watercress Soup

PREPARATION TIME: 15 minutes
COOKING TIME: 45 minutes
SERVES: 4 people

4 bunches watercress, washed and trimmed
1 leek, cleaned and sliced thinly
8oz potatoes, peeled and sliced thinly
2 tbsps butter or margarine
2½ cups chicken stock
Pinch grated nutmeg
3 tbsps cream
Salt
Pepper

Garnish
Watercress

Heat butter and slowly soften leek. Add potatoes, stock and seasoning. Bring to the boil and simmer 15 minutes. Add watercress and simmer a further 10 minutes. Blend soup and push through a strainer. Adjust seasoning and add cream. Re-heat or chill as required. Garnish with watercress.

Carrot and Orange Soup

PREPARATION TIME: 15 minutes
COOKING TIME: 40 minutes
SERVES: 4 people

1 onion, peeled and chopped finely
2 carrots, grated
1 strip lemon rind
1 orange
2½ cups water
1 chicken bouillon cube
2 tbsps butter or margarine
2 tbsps flour
1 tbsp cream, if desired
Sugar, salt and pepper to taste
Pared orange rind, cut into fine shreds

Garnish
Carrot flowers

Melt half the butter in pan. Add onion, carrots and lemon rind. Cover and cook until onion is transparent. Push through a sieve and set aside. Pare and shred rind of orange. Squeeze orange. Blanch orange rind in boiling water. Drain and save. Melt remaining butter in the pan and stir in flour. Remove from heat and add water. Return to heat and bring to the boil, stirring continuously. Add crumbled bouillon cube, orange juice and vegetables. Simmer for 5 minutes, blend and return to pan. Add salt, pepper and sugar to taste. Add cream and orange rind, and stir. Serve garnished with carrot flowers. To make carrot flowers, slice strips out lengthwise to produce flower shape when cut across in rounds.

Pumpkin Soup

PREPARATION TIME: 10 minutes
COOKING TIME: 1 hour
SERVES: 4 people

1lb pumpkin, peeled, seeds removed and diced
2 tbsps butter or margarine
1 onion, peeled and chopped
5 cups beef stock
2 tbsps cream
Pinch of turmeric
Salt
Pepper

Garnish
Croûtons

Melt butter in pan. Add onion and cook over gentle heat until lightly colored. Add stock and pumpkin. Add salt and pepper and turmeric and bring to the boil. Reduce heat. Cover and simmer for 30 minutes. Purée and push through a strainer. Return to pan and bring to boil. Remove from heat, stir in cream, and serve garnished with croûtons. Serve immediately.

This page: Watercress Soup (top) and Pumpkin Soup (bottom).

Facing page: Pea and Ham Soup (top) and Carrot and Orange Soup (bottom).

To Make Croûtons
Take one slice of bread and cut into ¼" cubes. Fry in hot oil until browned well all over. Remove with a slotted spoon and drain on paper towels. Sprinkle with salt. Add to soup at last minute otherwise they will go soggy.

Mussel Soup

PREPARATION TIME: 15 minutes

COOKING TIME: 20 minutes

SERVES: 4 people

2 quarts live mussels, scrubbed clean
2 onions, peeled and chopped
2 cloves garlic, crushed
2 tbsps chopped parsley
2 tbsps butter or margarine
1¼ cups dry white wine
2 tbsps lemon juice
Salt
Pepper

Garnish
Chopped parsley

Place mussels, butter, garlic, onions, wine, parsley and a pinch of freshly ground black pepper in a pan, and cover. Place over a high heat and cook for a few minutes. Shake the pan to move the mussels and distribute the heat well. When mussels have all opened, transfer to serving dish and keep warm. Discard any that remain closed. Strain juices and return to pan. Reduce liquid by half over a high heat. Adjust seasoning. Whisk in lemon juice and pour hot soup over mussels. Serve immediately sprinkled with chopped parsley.

Cream of Spinach Soup (left), Vegetable Soup (below) and Mussel Soup (facing page).

Cream of Spinach Soup

PREPARATION TIME: 10 minutes
COOKING TIME: 30 minutes
SERVES: 4 people

1 11oz packet frozen chopped spinach
1 onion, peeled and chopped
2 tbsps butter or margarine
2 tbsps flour
2¾ cups milk
⅔ cup cream
Pinch of ground nutmeg
Salt
Pepper

Garnish
Cream

Allow spinach to thaw. Drain off excess liquid. Heat butter in pan and fry chopped onion until transparent. Stir in flour and gradually add milk, stirring all the time until thickened. Season with salt and pepper and nutmeg. Stir in spinach and cook for 10 minutes. Stir in all but 1 tbsp of cream. Re-heat carefully, do not re-boil. Garnish with remaining cream and serve.

Pea and Ham Soup

PREPARATION TIME: 1 hour
COOKING TIME: 1 hour
SERVES: 4 people

½ cup dried split peas
½ cup shoulder or leg ham, diced
2 tbsps butter or margarine
1 onion, peeled and chopped
2½ cups chicken stock
2 tbsps chopped mint
1 stick celery, diced
Salt
Pepper

Garnish
Sprig of mint

Cover peas with boiling water, and leave to soak for 30 minutes. Drain and repeat process, and leave for a further 30 minutes. Melt butter in a pan. Add onion and celery and fry gently for 5 minutes or until transparent. Add drained peas, stock, 1 tbsp mint, and salt and pepper, and simmer gently for 45 minutes. Strain the soup or blend until smooth. Return to pan. Add ham, and remaining mint, and cook for a further 5 minutes. Adjust seasoning. Serve immediately, garnished with a sprig of mint if desired.

Lobster Bisque

PREPARATION TIME: 20 minutes
COOKING TIME: 1 hour
SERVES: 4 people

1 cooked lobster
1 onion, peeled and diced
1 stick celery, cut into 1" slices
1 carrot, diced
5 cups fish stock or water
1 bay leaf
6 peppercorns
Parsley stalks
Salt
Pepper
2 tbsps butter or margarine
2 tbsps flour
1 tsp lemon juice
2 tbsps cream
3 tbsps white wine
2 tsps tomato paste

Garnish
Sour cream and chopped parsley

Remove meat from body, tail and claws of lobster. Put lobster shell, stock or water, onion, carrot, celery, herbs and seasoning into a pan. Bring to boil and simmer for 45 minutes. Allow to cool. Strain and reserve stock. Meanwhile, cut lobster meat into bite-size pieces. Melt butter in pan, stir in flour, and cook for 1 minute. Remove from heat and stir in reserved stock gradually. Return to heat. Bring to the boil, and simmer for 5 minutes, stirring continuously. Remove from heat and add lemon juice, tomato paste, wine and cream, and whisk in well. Adjust seasoning. Add lobster meat and garnish with soured cream and chopped parsley if desired. Serve immediately.

Lettuce Soup

PREPARATION TIME: 10 minutes
COOKING TIME: 30 minutes
SERVES: 4 people

½ head lettuce
1 small onion, peeled and diced
2 tbsps butter or margarine
1¼ cups chicken stock
½ cup milk
¼ cup light cream
½ tsp grated nutmeg
Salt
Pepper

Blanch lettuce leaves in boiling water for 30 seconds. Rinse under cold water and drain well. Chop roughly. Fry the onion in the butter for 5 minutes, or until it is soft. Add lettuce and stock, and bring to the boil. Simmer gently for 10 minutes. Season with nutmeg and salt and pepper. Blend the soup. Add milk and re-heat. Stir in cream and re-heat gently, being careful not to boil the soup. Serve immediately.

Corn and Bacon Soup

PREPARATION TIME: 10 minutes
COOKING TIME: 20 minutes
SERVES: 4 people

1 onion, peeled and chopped
2 tbsps butter or margarine
2 tbsps flour
½ cup water
1 cup milk
1½ cups canned corn
4 rashers bacon
Salt
Pepper

Garnish
Chopped chives

Heat butter in pan. Add onion, and fry until transparent. Stir in flour, remove from heat and add water and milk gradually. Return to heat, stirring until thickened. Add undrained sweetcorn to pan, and season to taste. Bring to the boil, and simmer for 10 minutes. Meanwhile, pre-heat broiler. Cut rashers in half lengthwise and form into rolls. Broil and serve in soup. Garnish with chopped chives.

Vegetable Soup

PREPARATION TIME: 20 minutes
COOKING TIME: 50 minutes
SERVES: 4 people

2 medium onions, peeled and finely chopped
1 carrot, finely diced
½ small turnip, finely diced
2¾ cups beef stock
2 tbsps butter or margarine
1 leek, cut into small rings
1 tbsp tomato paste
2 tbsps chopped parsley
Salt
Pepper

Garnish
Chopped parsley

Melt butter in a saucepan and add onions. Cook gently over a low heat for 5 minutes or until transparent. Add carrot and turnip, stock, seasoning and parsley. Bring to the boil and simmer gently for 15 minutes. Add leek, and tomato paste and simmer for a further 20 minutes. Garnish with chopped parsley. Serve hot.

Mushroom Soup

PREPARATION TIME: 10 minutes
COOKING TIME: 45 minutes
SERVES: 4 people

8oz mushrooms
1 small onion
3 tbsps butter or margarine
3 tbsps flour
2½ cups water
1 chicken bouillon cube
1 tbsp lemon juice
¾ cup milk
1 tbsp chopped parsley
1 tbsp chopped chives
Salt
Pepper

Garnish
Chopped parsley

Melt butter in a pan. Peel and chop onion and fry gently until transparent. Wash, trim and finely slice mushrooms. Add to pan and cook for 5 minutes, stirring often. Stir in flour and cook for 1 minute. Draw off heat and gradually add water. Return to heat and bring to boil, stirring continuously. Add crumbled chicken bouillon cube and stir until soup has thickened. Add lemon juice and milk. Cover and simmer for 15 minutes. Add chives and parsley and season with salt and pepper. Garnish with chopped parsley.

Facing page: Mushroom Soup (top) and Corn and Bacon Soup (bottom).

Fish Soup

PREPARATION TIME: 15 minutes

COOKING TIME: 40 minutes

SERVES: 4 people

2lbs of bass, whiting and monkfish, skin and bones removed, and cut into bite-size pieces
2 onions, peeled and chopped
3 cloves garlic, crushed
2 tomatoes, skinned and chopped
1 tbsp oil
Sprig of fresh thyme
1 bay leaf
2 pieces thinly pared orange rind
½ cup dry white wine
Salt
Pepper

Garnish
Chopped parsley

Make a court bouillon with the heads and trimmings of fish, one-third of the onion and 5 cups of water. Simmer 15 minutes, then strain. Put oil in a heavy pan and heat gently. Add garlic and remaining onion. Cover and fry gently for 5 minutes without coloring. Add fish, tomatoes, herbs, orange rind, wine, salt and pepper and court bouillon. Bring to boil and simmer for 10 minutes. Remove bay leaf, thyme and orange rind. Serve hot, sprinkled with parsley.

This page: Fish Soup (top) and Lobster Bisque (bottom).

Facing page: Avocado Cream Soup (top) and Tomato and Cucumber Soup (bottom).

Cold Soups

Tomato and Cucumber Soup

PREPARATION TIME:
20 minutes, plus chilling time

SERVES: 4 people

6 tomatoes, skinned
2 large cucumbers, peeled and cut into pieces, reserving 2" at end for garnish
3 tbsps lemon juice
⅔ cup sour cream
1 onion, peeled and grated
1 tsp tomato paste
Salt
Pepper

Garnish
Cucumber slices

Chop tomatoes. Remove seeds. Strain juice, and discard seeds. Put tomato flesh and juice, cucumber, onion, tomato paste and lemon juice into a blender. Blend at high speed for a few minutes until smooth. Stir in sour cream, and salt and pepper to taste. Serve chilled, garnished with cucumber slices.

Shrimp and Cucumber Soup

PREPARATION TIME:
20 minutes, plus chilling time

SERVES: 4 people

1lb shrimp, cooked, shelled and de-veined
2 3oz packages cream cheese
1 small cucumber
½ tsp dry mustard
Salt
White pepper
⅔ cup light cream
1¼ cups milk

Garnish
Finely sliced cucumber
Dill

Finely chop shrimp. Peel and slice cucumber. Place shrimp, cucumber, mustard, white pepper and a pinch of salt in a bowl. Beat cream cheese until soft and creamy, and gradually add cream and milk. Add cucumber and prawn mixture, and blend thoroughly. Cover and chill. If necessary, thin soup further with milk. Garnish with sliced cucumber and dill.

Blackberry and Apple Soup

PREPARATION TIME:
5 minutes, plus chilling time

COOKING TIME: 30 minutes

SERVES: 4 people

2 cups blackberries, fresh, or frozen and thawed
2 apples, peeled, cored and sliced
¼ cup sugar
2½ cups water
Crushed ice

Place apples and water in a pan and bring to the boil. Simmer covered for 15 minutes until apples are softened. Add sugar and blackberries, and simmer a further 15 minutes. Purée and push through a strainer. Chill. Serve with crushed ice.

Rhubarb Soup

PREPARATION TIME:
15 minutes, plus chilling time

COOKING TIME: 20 minutes

SERVES: 4 people

2 cups rhubarb, trimmed and cut into 1″ lengths
2 tbsps redcurrant jelly
¼ cup sugar
1¼ cups orange juice
1¼ cups water

Garnish
Slivered, pared rind of orange

Place rhubarb, redcurrant jelly, sugar and water in pan. Cover and heat gently for 10 minutes. Add orange juice and bring to the boil. Simmer uncovered for 5 minutes. Remove from heat, and allow to cool. Purée or push through a strainer, and chill. Serve garnished with slivered orange rind and crushed ice if desired.

Avocado Cream Soup

PREPARATION TIME:
10 minutes, plus chilling time

SERVES: 4 people

1¼ cups good, fat-free chicken stock
2 ripe avocados
1 tbsp lemon juice
⅔ cup milk
⅔ cup light cream
Salt and white pepper

Garnish
Snipped chives, if desired

Peel avocados, remove seeds, chop and put in blender with cream, lemon juice and milk, and blend until smooth. Put avocado mixture and chicken stock in a bowl, and stir until combined. Push through a strainer. Season with salt and white pepper. Chill in refrigerator. Garnish with chives, if desired.

Raspberry Soup

PREPARATION TIME:
5 minutes, plus chilling time

COOKING TIME: 20 minutes

SERVES: 4 people

1 cup raspberries, fresh, or frozen and thawed
2 tbsps lemon juice
3 tbsps sweet sherry
2 tbsps sugar
1¼ cups light cream
1¼ cups water
Crushed ice

Put sugar, raspberries, lemon juice, sherry and water in a pan, and heat gently for 10 minutes. Bring to the boil and simmer for 5 minutes. Remove from heat and push through a strainer, and allow to cool. Stir in cream. Chill. Serve with crushed ice.

Blackberry and Apple Soup (left), Rhubarb Soup (center), Raspberry Soup (bottom) and Shrimp and Cucumber Soup (facing page).

Vichyssoise (Leek and Potato Soup)

PREPARATION TIME: 15 minutes, plus chilling time

COOKING TIME: 30 minutes

SERVES: 4 people

3 large leeks
2 medium potatoes, peeled and sliced thinly
1 small onion, peeled and sliced
2 tbsps butter or margarine
1½ cups boiling water
½ chicken bouillon cube
⅔ cup light cream
Salt
White pepper

Garnish
Parsley or chives

Wash and trim leeks, discarding roots and any green part. Slice thinly. Melt butter in pan and add leek and onion. Cover, and allow to sweat gently over low heat for about 10 minutes. Dissolve ½ chicken bouillon cube in boiling water. Add potatoes to leek and pour over the stock. Season to taste. Cover and cook for a further 15 minutes, or until potatoes are soft. Push through a fine strainer. Cool. Stir in cream. Adjust seasoning. Chill well for at least 2 hours. Serve garnished with parsley or snipped chives.

Gazpacho

PREPARATION TIME: 20 minutes, plus chilling time

SERVES: 4 people

1lb ripe tomatoes, skinned and roughly chopped
1 onion, peeled and diced
1 green pepper, cored, seeds removed, and diced
Half a cucumber
2 tbsps stale white breadcrumbs
2 cloves garlic, crushed
2 tbsps red wine vinegar
1 large can tomato juice
Salt
Pepper

Accompaniments
Diced cucumber, onion, tomato and green pepper

Soak breadcrumbs in vinegar. Reserve tomato flesh, and half the onion and half the green pepper for garnish. Blend remaining onion and remaining green pepper with tomato juice, breadcrumbs, vinegar, and garlic, and season to taste. Push through a strainer. Chill well. Meanwhile, skin and chop cucumber. Serve with crushed ice and small bowls of cucumber, onion, tomato and green pepper.

Beet Soup

PREPARATION TIME: 10 minutes, plus chilling time

COOKING TIME: 1 hour 15 minutes

SERVES: 4 people

1lb raw beet
1 shallot, peeled and quartered
2 tbsps sugar
1 tbsp lemon juice
Bouquet garni
5 cups water
1 chicken bouillon cube
Salt
Pepper

Bring water to boil. Peel and dice beet. Add to water with crumbled bouillon cube, shallot, bouquet garni, sugar, lemon juice and salt and pepper. Bring to the boil. Reduce heat, and simmer, uncovered, for about an hour. Blend and push through strainer and leave to cool. When cool, put into refrigerator to chill.

Beet Soup (left) and Vichyssoise (Leek and Potato Soup) (bottom).

Dips and Pâtés

Tzatziki (Cucumber and Yogurt Salad)

PREPARATION TIME: 15 minutes

SERVES: 4 people

1 cucumber, peeled
1 clove garlic, crushed
1 medium-sized carton plain yogurt
2 tsps lemon juice
1 tsp chopped mint
Salt

Garnish
Cucumber slices
Sprig of mint

Grate the cucumber and drain off any excess liquid. Mix cucumber with garlic and yogurt. Stir in lemon juice and mint, and add salt to taste. Garnish with a few cucumber slices and a sprig of mint.

Taramasalata (Salmon Roe Salad)

PREPARATION TIME: 30 minutes

SERVES: 4 people

8oz smoked salmon roe
½ onion, peeled and grated
2 cloves garlic, crushed
4 slices white bread, crusts removed
¼ cup milk
⅓ cup olive oil
2 tbsps lemon juice
Pepper

Garnish
Lemon
Parsley

Crumble bread into a bowl, and add milk. Leave to soak. Scoop the roe out of its skin and break it down with a wooden spoon. Squeeze bread dry in a strainer. Add onion, garlic and bread to roe, and mix well. Very gradually add oil and

This page: Taramasalata (Salmon Roe Salad) (top) and Tzatziki (Cucumber and Yogurt Salad) (bottom).

Facing page: Gazpacho

lemon juice, alternating between the two. Beat until smooth and creamy. Add pepper to taste, and salt if necessary. Garnish with lemon and parsley, and serve with Melba toast (see recipe for Guacamole) or sliced French bread, and unsalted butter.

Crudités with Anchovy Dip, Oxford Dip, and Tomato and Chili Dip

Crudités
Half a cauliflower, broken into flowerets
Half a cucumber, cut into 2" sticks
4oz mushrooms, cleaned
3 carrots, scraped and cut into sticks
8 small radishes, cleaned
1 red pepper, cored, seeds removed, and cut into strips
8 green onions, trimmed
2 zucchini, cut into strips

Anchovy Dip
6-8 anchovies, drained and mashed
2 cloves garlic, crushed
2 tbsps butter or margarine
⅔ cup heavy cream, lightly whipped
1 tsp marjoram or oregano
1 tsp chopped fresh parsley
Pinch sugar or salt, to taste

Melt butter in pan, add garlic, and cook for 1 minute. Add anchovies, herbs and sugar or salt to taste. Cook for 10 minutes, stirring continuously. Set aside. When cool, fold in whipped cream. Chill.

Oxford Dip
Pared rind of 1 lemon
1 tsp lemon juice
1 tsp dry mustard
½ tsp grated ginger root
2 tbsps redcurrant jelly
¼ cup red wine
1 tsp arrowroot

Blanch rind in boiling water for 30 seconds. Remove and shred finely. Put all ingredients except wine and arrowroot into a pan, and bring to the boil, stirring continuously. When mixed, stir in wine and simmer, uncovered, for 15 minutes. Slake arrowroot in 1 tbsp of water and add to pan. Simmer a further 3 minutes, stirring continuously. Chill.

Tomato and Chili Dip
1 16oz can plum tomatoes, drained, reserving juice, and seeds removed
1 red chili pepper, seeds removed, sliced finely
1 clove garlic
1 onion, peeled and chopped finely
1 tbsp lemon juice or white wine vinegar
1 tbsp chopped fresh parsley
1 tbsp butter or margarine
Salt
Pepper

Melt butter in pan. Add garlic and fry until browned. Discard garlic. Add onion and cook gently till softened. Add chili pepper and cook a further 3 minutes. Add tomatoes, lemon juice or vinegar, reserved tomato juice and salt and pepper and simmer gently for 10 minutes. Remove from heat and set aside to cool. Push through a strainer, stir in parsley, and chill.

Pâté aux Herbes

PREPARATION TIME: 20 minutes
COOKING TIME: 1 hour
OVEN TEMPERATURE: 350°F (170°C)
SERVES: 4 people

1lb ground pork
1 11oz packet frozen spinach
8oz bacon
1 onion, peeled and chopped
2 cloves garlic, crushed
2 tbsps finely chopped fresh basil
2 tbsps chopped parsley
Freshly grated nutmeg
Freshly ground black pepper
½ tsp sage
1 small can ham
1 egg, lightly beaten
Pinch of cayenne pepper
⅔ cup heavy cream
Salt

Cook spinach in boiling salted water for 5 minutes. Drain and press between two plates to remove excess water. Chop finely and mix with pork. Combine onion, garlic, herbs and spices, cayenne pepper, cream, and salt and pepper. Cut ham into strips. Line bottom and sides of oven, roof tureen with rashers of bacon. Mix pork and spinach into cream mixture. Add egg and stir thoroughly. Press one-third mixture into tureen. Add half the ham strips. Repeat until all ham and mixture is used up. Cook in a slow oven for 45 minutes. Remove from oven, cool, and serve sliced.

Guacamole

PREPARATION TIME: 15 minutes
COOKING TIME: 5 minutes
SERVES: 4 people

2 ripe avocados
1 tbsp lemon juice
1 clove garlic, crushed
1 red chili pepper, seeds removed, sliced finely
1 shallot, very finely chopped, or grated
¼ tsp ground chili powder
Pinch of paprika
Salt

Garnish
Lemon slices and parsley
Serve with melba toast if desired

Blanch chili and shallot in boiling water for 2 minutes. Drain and set aside. Peel the avocados. Pierce the skin with the point of a sharp knife and run down from top to bottom of the avocado in quarters. Pull skin back off fruit and remove stone from center and any dark bits of flesh. Mash the flesh to a purée and mix in lemon juice. Stir in garlic and shallot. Add chili, chili powder, paprika and salt, a bit at a time, to desired taste. Garnish with lemon and parsley. Serve with Melba toast if desired.

Melba Toast
Pre-heat broiler. Put slices of bread in toaster and toast until golden brown. Remove crusts and cut horizontally through toast whilst still hot. Cut into triangles and toast untoasted side under the grill until golden brown. Keep inside a clean towel until ready to serve.

Crudités (right) with Anchovy Dip (bottom), Oxford Dip (far right) and Tomato and Chili Dip (below).

Tomato, Carrot and Spinach Slice

PREPARATION TIME: 30 minutes, plus chilling time

SERVES: 4 people

6 tomatoes, skinned, with seeds removed
1lb spinach, cooked
Pinch of nutmeg
3 carrots, finely grated
⅔ cup heavy cream, whipped
1 ¼oz envelope gelatine
¼ cup water
Salt
Pepper

Grease and line a loaf pan with wax paper. Blend tomato in a food processor until smooth. Add salt and pepper to taste. Set aside. Put water in a small bowl. Sprinkle over gelatine and leave 15 minutes to soak. Place bowl in a saucepan of hot water, so that water is part way up side of bowl. Heat gently until gelatine has dissolved. Meanwhile, chop spinach, squeeze out excess liquid and stir in half the cream. Add nutmeg, and salt and pepper to taste. Set aside. Stir one-third of gelatine into tomato mixture, and return bowl of gelatine to saucepan. Fill tomato into loaf pan. Level out, and put into freezer compartment. Leave 10 minutes. Meanwhile, stir carrot and remaining cream together. Stir half of remaining gelatine into carrot mixture, and pour over tomato mixture. Return tin to freezer for 10 minutes. Stir remaining gelatine into spinach mixture, and pour onto carrot layer. Smooth out and put into freezer for a further 10 minutes. Remove from freezer and chill in refrigerator overnight.

This page: Tomato, Carrot and Spinach Slice.

Facing page: Salmon, Watercress and Tomato Slice (top) and Pâté aux Herbes (bottom).

Salmon, Watercress and Tomato Slice

PREPARATION TIME: 30 minutes

SERVES: 4 people

6 tomatoes, skinned, and seeds removed
Half a bunch of watercress
1 8oz can red or pink salmon
⅔ cup heavy cream, whipped
1 ¼oz envelope gelatine
¼ cup water
Salt
Pepper

Garnish
Watercress

Grease and line a loaf pan with wax paper. Drain, and place salmon and one-third of the cream into a food processor, and process until smooth. Add salt and pepper to taste. Set aside. Put water in a small bowl, and sprinkle over gelatine. Leave 15 minutes to soak. Place bowl in a saucepan of hot water so that water is partway up side of bowl. Heat gently until gelatine has dissolved. Meanwhile, chop watercress, squeeze out excess liquid, and stir in half the remaining cream. Add salt and pepper to taste. Set aside. Place tomatoes and remaining cream in food processor, and process. Stir one-third of gelatine into tomato mixture and return bowl of gelatine to saucepan. Fill tomato into loaf pan. Level out, and put into freezer compartment for 10 minutes. Stir half the remaining gelatine into watercress mixture and pour over tomato mixture. Return pan to freezer for 10 minutes. Stir remaining gelatine into salmon mixture and pour onto watercress layer. Smooth out and put into freezer for 10 minutes. Remove from freezer and chill in refrigerator overnight. Garnish with watercress.

Salmon Pâté

PREPARATION TIME: 15 minutes

SERVES: 4 people

1 8oz can red or pink salmon, drained
½ cup cream cheese
2 tbsps butter
Pinch of ground mace or ground nutmeg
Few drops of lemon juice
¼ tsp tabasco sauce
2 tbsps heavy cream
Salt
Pepper

Garnish
Pickled gherkins (slice each pickle horizontally 4 or 5 times, and splay into a fan)

Remove any bones from salmon. Work into a paste with the back of a spoon. Cream the butter and cheese until smooth. Add salmon, lemon juice, seasonings and cream, and mix well. Put into a large dish or individual ramekins. Garnish dish with a pickle fan.

Chicken Liver Pâté

PREPARATION TIME: 15 minutes

COOKING TIME: 15 minutes

SERVES: 4 people

8oz chicken livers, trimmed
1 onion, peeled and diced finely
2 tbsps butter for frying
4 tbsps butter, creamed
1 clove garlic, crushed
1 tbsp brandy
1 tsp Worcestershire sauce
Salt
Pepper

Garnish
Dill

Heat butter in frying pan. Add garlic, onions, salt, and freshly ground black pepper, and fry gently until onions have softened. Increase heat, and sauté chicken livers in hot butter for about 2 minutes on each side, until just cooked through. Add Worcestershire sauce and stir. Blend contents of frying pan and push through a wire strainer with the back of a spoon into a bowl. Beat in creamed butter, brandy, and adjust seasoning. Place in one large dish or individual ramekin dishes. If not being eaten immediately, seal surface with clarified butter and refrigerate. Garnish with dill.

Kipper Pâté

PREPARATION TIME:
30 minutes, plus chilling time

SERVES: 4 people

8oz kipper fillets, skinned and bones removed
4 tbsps butter
Juice of half an orange
1 tsp tomato paste
1 tsp white wine vinegar
Black pepper, freshly ground
Salt, if desired

Garnish
1 can pimentos

Aspic
1¼ cups clear, strained chicken stock
1 ¼oz envelope gelatine
2 tbsps dry sherry
2 tbsps cold water
or
1 packet commercial aspic, used as directed

Cream butter. Place butter, kipper, orange juice, tomato paste, vinegar and black pepper in a blender. Blend until smooth. Add salt if necessary. Place in one dish or individual dishes. Cut pimentos into strips. Sprinkle gelatine over a small bowl with 1-2 tbsps of cold water in it and leave to soak for 15 minutes. Place bowl in a saucepan of simmering water, and leave until gelatine has dissolved. Heat stock in pan. Add gelatine. Allow to cool, and stir in sherry. Make a lattice of pimento on top of kipper pâté. Carefully pour over aspic to just cover pimento. Chill in refrigerator.

Smoked Kipper Pâté (right) and Salmon Pâté (bottom).

Vegetables and Fruit Appetizers

Stuffed Radicchio

PREPARATION TIME: 10 minutes
COOKING TIME: 5 minutes
SERVES: 4 people

1 radicchio, red or Italian endive (8 good whole leaves; the rest finely chopped)
¼ cup rice, cooked
1 tbsp chopped parsley
7oz can tuna fish, drained
2 tbsps capers
1 tsp lemon juice
2 tbsps heavy cream, whipped
2 tbsps vermouth or dry sherry
Salt
Pepper

Garnish
Lemon slices
Parsley

Flake tuna fish and mix with rice, chopped radicchio, parsley, lemon juice, capers, heavy cream and wine and salt and pepper to taste. Divide mixture evenly between 4 whole radicchio leaves and place remaining 4 on top. Serve garnished with lemon slices and parsley.

Asparagus with Hollandaise Sauce

PREPARATION TIME: 10 minutes
COOKING TIME: 30 minutes
SERVES: 4 people

20-32 asparagus spears
½ tbsp butter
Salt

Hollandaise Sauce
3 egg yolks
1 tsp lemon juice if desired
½ cup unsalted butter, diced
1 tbsp wine vinegar
Salt
White pepper

Wash and trim asparagus stalks, removing woody ends where necessary. Place in a large, shallow pan or large saucepan of boiling salted water. Add ½ tbsp of butter and allow to simmer gently until tender – about 10-15 minutes. If size of spears varies greatly, add thicker ones first so that they will all be ready together. Drain. Meanwhile, half-fill bottom half of double boiler with boiling water. Place egg yolks and wine vinegar in top half of double boiler. Whisk together until well mixed. Place over bottom of pan and heat gently, keeping water hot, but not boiling. Stir until yolks are smooth. Whisk in small pieces of butter, a few at a time, until all butter has been absorbed. Whisk sauce until thick and creamy. Season with salt and white pepper to taste and add lemon juice if desired. Serve asparagus spears with warm Hollandaise sauce.

This page: Stuffed Raddichio (top) and Asparagus with Hollandaise Sauce (bottom).

Facing page: Guacamole (top) and Chicken Liver Pâté (bottom).

Tomato and Pepper Frostie

PREPARATION TIME: 15 minutes, plus freezing time

SERVES: 4 people

¼ cup tomato juice
Juice of 1 lemon
6 ice cubes
1 tsp Worcestershire sauce
½ small green pepper
½ small red pepper

Garnish
4 tomato flowers

Crush ice. Put tomato juice, lemon juice, ice and Worcestershire sauce in blender. Blend together. Put into ice-trays and place in freezer for ½ hour or until half-frozen. Meanwhile, remove core and seeds from peppers and dice finely. Remove tomato ice from freezer and transfer to a bowl, breaking up with the back of a fork. Mix in peppers. Re-freeze for a further 2 hours, stirring occasionally. For a garnish, make tomato flowers. Peel tomatoes (drop into boiling water; count to ten slowly; then rinse in cold water; remove skins). Starting at one end, with a sharp knife slice a continuous strip around the tomato. Form into a rose shape. Serve on top of tomato and pepper frostie.

Pepper Appetizer (left), Eggplant Appetizer (bottom) and Tomato and Pepper Frostie (facing page).

Onion-Egg-Tomato Bake

PREPARATION TIME: 15 minutes
COOKING TIME: 20 minutes
OVEN TEMPERATURE: 400°F (200°C)
SERVES: 4 people

4 eggs, hard boiled
2 medium onions, peeled and sliced
4 tbsps butter or margarine
2 tbsps flour
⅔ cup milk
2 tomatoes, skinned and sliced thinly
1 tbsp breadcrumbs
1 tbsp freshly grated Parmesan cheese
Salt
Pepper

Garnish
Parsley

Melt butter in pan. Add onions and fry over gentle heat until softened but not colored. Remove with a slotted spoon and set aside. Stir in flour and cook for 1 minute. Remove from heat and gradually stir in milk. Beat well and return to heat. Cook for 3 minutes, stirring continuously. Add onions and plenty of salt and pepper to counteract the sweetness of the onions. Cut eggs in half. Remove yolks, strain and set aside. Rinse and slice egg whites. Place in the bottom of an ovenproof dish. Cover with onion mixture, then with a layer of sliced tomatoes. Mix together egg yolk, breadcrumbs and Parmesan cheese. Sprinkle over top and place in a hot oven until golden on top. Garnish with parsley.

Pepper Appetizer

PREPARATION TIME: 15 minutes
COOKING TIME: 1 hour 15 minutes
SERVES: 4 people

1 green pepper
1 red pepper
2 tomatoes
2 onions
¼ cup white vinegar
2 tbsps oil
Salt

Remove core and seeds from peppers and slice lengthwise. Peel and slice onions and tomatoes. Heat oil in a large suacepan. Add vegetables and salt to taste and simmer, covered, for 1 hour, stirring occasionally. Remove lid and add vinegar, and simmer for a further 15 minutes. Allow to cool, and chill in refrigerator.

Eggplant Appetizer

PREPARATION TIME: 15 minutes
COOKING TIME: 20 minutes
SERVES: 4 people

1 large eggplant
2 ripe tomatoes, peeled, seeds removed, and chopped
2 cloves garlic, crushed
¼ cup oil
1 tbsp tomato paste
¼ cup water
Salt
Pepper

Cut eggplant lengthwise into strips ¼" x 2½". Heat oil in pan until hot. Add eggplant and cook for 5 minutes or until cooked. Remove from pan with slotted spoon. Add extra oil as necessary and heat. Fry garlic for 30 seconds. Add tomatoes, tomato paste, salt and pepper, and water and cook for 10 minutes or until sauce is thick. Add eggplant and stir together. Adjust seasoning and cook for a further 5 minutes. Serve hot or cold.

Avocado Lemon Ring

PREPARATION TIME: 10 minutes, plus setting time
SERVES: 4 people

2 avocados
1 pkt lemon gelatine
⅔ cup hot water
1 lemon
2 tsps Worcestershire sauce
⅔ cup heavy cream
Salt

Garnish
Slices of lemon
Watercress

Dissolve the gelatine in hot water and leave to cool. Grate finely the rind of the lemon, and squeeze and strain the juice. Peel the avocados and remove the stones. Mash well with a fork. Pour on the cooled gelatine and whisk or blend. Add lemon juice, rind, Worcestershire sauce, a pinch of salt and cream, and mix well. Pour into dampened ring mold and leave to set. Turn out to serve and garnish with slices of lemon and watercress in center.

Grilled Grapefruit

PREPARATION TIME: 45 minutes
COOKING TIME: 10 minutes
SERVES: 4 people

2 grapefruit
¼ cup brown sugar
2 tbsps Grand Marnier or Cointreau liqueur
1 tbsp clear honey

Garnish
Fresh or maraschino cherries
Fresh mint leaf

Cut grapefruit in half around equators. With a grapefruit knife or sharp knife, cut around edge between flesh of fruit and pith. Then cut down between each segment, removing skin from flesh. Take core between finger and thumb and pull out, removing with skin. Remove any seeds. Pour excess juice into bowl. Sprinkle each grapefruit half with sugar and pour over liqueur. Leave to stand for 30 minutes. Meanwhile, mix together honey and grapefruit juice. Pre-heat broiler. Pour over honey/grapefruit juice mixture and broil until just browning on top. Trim away any burned skin and garnish with a cherry and mint leaf.

Broccoli Timbales

PREPARATION TIME: 10 minutes
COOKING TIME: 30 minutes
OVEN TEMPERATURE: 375°F (190°C)
SERVES: 4 people

4 broccoli flowerets
2 tbsps butter or margarine
2 tbsps flour
1¼ cups milk
1 tsp ground nutmeg
2 eggs, beaten
Salt
Pepper

Blanch broccoli in boiling salted water for 3 minutes. Drain and refresh under cold water. Drain and set aside. Melt butter in pan. Stir in flour and nutmeg and cook for 1 minute. Remove from heat and stir in milk gradually. Return to heat and bring to the boil, stirring continuously. Cook for 3 minutes. Add salt and white pepper to taste and beat well. Set aside to cool. Butter 4 ramekin dishes. Place a floweret of broccoli in each dish with stem pointing upwards. Beat eggs into cooled white sauce, and pour into each ramekin dish. Place ramekins in a shallow baking pan. Pour boiling water into pan to a depth of 1". Bake in a pre-heated oven for 15 minutes, or until just setting. Remove from oven and turn out onto individual plates. Serve immediately.

Onion-Egg-Tomato Bake (right) and Broccoli Timbales (bottom).

Fanned Avocado Salad with Shrimp and Tomato Dressing

PREPARATION TIME: 20 minutes

SERVES: 4 people

2 ripe avocados
Juice of ½ lemon or 1 lime
8oz shrimp, shelled and de-veined
3 tbsps mayonnaise
1 tbsp tomato paste
1 tbsp light cream
Salt
Pepper

Garnish
Lemon or lime rings
Lettuce leaves

Mix together mayonnaise, tomato paste, cream and salt and pepper to taste. Mix shrimp with 2 tbsps mayonnaise mixture and set aside. Cut avocados in half. Remove stones and peel back and remove skin. Slice down through flesh 5 or 6 times. Keep thin end intact. Place on lettuce leaves on serving dishes and press down so that avocado fans out. Sprinkle over lemon or lime juice to prevent flesh browning. Place shrimp at side of dish, around avocado. Garnish with lemon or lime rings.

Stuffed Mushrooms

PREPARATION TIME: 15 minutes

COOKING TIME: 20 minutes

OVEN TEMPERATURE: 400°F (200°C)

SERVES: 4 people

4 large or 8 medium mushrooms, stalks discarded
1 tbsp olive oil
2 medium onions, peeled and chopped finely
8oz spinach, trimmed, cooked and chopped finely
2 tbsps fresh white breadcrumbs
4 tbsps butter or margarine
4 cloves garlic, crushed
1 egg, beaten
½ tsp nutmeg
Salt
Pepper

Garnish
1 tbsp chopped parsley

Heat butter in pan. Add garlic, onion and nutmeg and fry gently until onion has softened. Remove from pan and set aside to cool. Meanwhile, heat oil in pan and sauté mushrooms on both sides until lightly browned. Place underside-up in a shallow oven-proof dish. Mix together onion mixture, spinach, breadcrumbs, and salt and freshly ground black pepper to taste. Stir in beaten egg. Cover each mushroom cap with the mixture, shaping neatly. Cover with aluminum foil and bake in a hot oven for 10 minutes. Serve immediately, garnished with chopped parsley.

This page: Grilled Grapefruit (top) and Avocado Lemon Ring (bottom).
Facing page: Stuffed Mushrooms (top) and Fanned Avocado Salad with Shrimp and Tomato Dressing (bottom).

Orange, Grapefruit and Mint Salad (right) and Melon Balls in Mulled Wine (inset below).

Melon Balls in Mulled Wine

PREPARATION TIME: 1 hour

COOKING TIME: 10 minutes

SERVES: 4 people

1 melon
½ bottle red wine
2 cinnamon sticks
4 cloves
3 blades mace
Juice and pared rind of 1 orange
1 tsp freshly grated nutmeg
4 tbsps sugar

Put wine, orange juice and rind, spices and sugar into a pan and heat gently. Do not allow to boil. When hot, remove from heat and leave to infuse for an hour. Strain. Meanwhile, cut melon in half and scrape out seeds. Then make melon balls with a melon-ball scoop, or cut into chunks. Place in individual serving dishes and pour over mulled wine.

Orange, Grapefruit and Mint Salad

PREPARATION TIME: 20 minutes, plus chilling time

SERVES: 4 people

2 grapefruit
3 oranges
1 tbsp sugar
4 sprigs of mint

Garnish
Mint sprig

Cut the peel and pith off the grapefruit and oranges. Cut carefully inside the skin of each segment to remove each section of flesh. When skin only is left, squeeze to extract juices over a pan. Repeat with all fruit. Add sugar to pan and set over a gentle heat until sugar dissolves. Cool. Meanwhile, arrange orange and grapefruit segments alternating in dish. Chop mint finely and add to fruit syrup. Carefully spoon syrup over fruit. Chill. Garnish with a sprig of mint.

Traditional Soups and Snacks

Nettle Soup

PREPARATION TIME: 15 minutes
COOKING TIME: 30 minutes
SERVES: 6-8 people

It has been established that nettle soup was part of the diet of the monks in Ireland as far back as the 6th century. It would often have been made with milk alone, or even milk and water, and you can vary the proportions of stock and milk used in this recipe.

3¾ cups stock
1¼ cups milk
2½ cups nettles
⅓ cup oatmeal
¼ cup butter

Wear gloves when you are collecting the nettles and only choose the young, bright green leaves. Remove any stalks and chop up the leaves. These days a food processor will do the job in a fraction of the time it takes to chop them by hand. Melt the butter in a large pan. Add the oatmeal and cook until the mixture is a golden brown. Remove the pan from the heat and add the stock. Bring it to the boil and add the milk. When it is boiling again, add the chopped nettles and cook for another few minutes. You may need more seasoning, depending how much seasoning there is in the stock.

Potato Soup

PREPARATION TIME: 20 minutes
COOKING TIMES: 1 hour 15 minutes
SERVES: 8-10 persons

Potato soup can be made with milk and water but its flavor is much improved if you use stock instead of the water. Boil down a chicken carcass with an onion, a carrot and some herbs. Strain off the stock and let it get cold. Remove any fat from the top and you will have a lovely, thick jelly which will keep for a week in the refrigerator or can be kept in the freezer for longer. The same can be done with all meat bones.

2lb potatoes
2 onions
1 small carrot
Bay leaf, parsley and thyme
Salt and pepper
5 cups stock
2½ cups milk
¼ cup butter

Peel and slice the potatoes, onions and carrot. Melt butter in a large

This page: Potato Soup (top) and Country Broth (bottom). Facing page: Nettle Soup (top) and Smoked Salmon Bisque (bottom).

saucepan and sweat onions in it until soft but not brown. Add potatoes and carrot. Stir in the stock and milk. Tie the bay leaf, thyme and parsley together and add with pepper and salt to taste. Simmer gently for about an hour then either liquidize or put through a sieve or vegetable mill. Add some cream or top of milk before serving and sprinkle with chopped chives.

Smoked Salmon Bisque

PREPARATION TIME: 30 minutes

COOKING TIME: 1 hour

SERVES: 6-8 persons

A side of smoked salmon is a rare gift these days, the price being what it is. If you should be the lucky recipient of one, be sure to save the skin and trimmings as they will make a delicious soup.

Skin and trimmings of a side of smoked salmon
1 onion, stuck with cloves
Bay leaf
1 tsp salt
Few peppercorns
1 carrot
1-2 stick of celery
¼ cup butter
½ cup flour
1 tbsp tomato paste
1 glass white wine
Cream and parsley to decorate

Put the skin and trimmings in a saucepan with the onion, stuck with 5-6 cloves, and the carrot and celery cut in chunks. Cover with cold water, add the bay leaf, salt and peppercorns. Cover the pan and simmer for about 30 minutes. Remove the bay leaf. Take out the onion, remove the cloves and return the onion to the pan. With a slotted spoon, take out the fish skin and scrape off any remaining flesh, which should also be returned to the pan. Strain half the liquid into a bowl.
In another large pan melt the butter, stir in the flour and make a roux. Stir in the tomato paste and gradually add the strained stock, stirring all the time until it thickens. Add a glass of white wine, or a glass of sherry will do very well! Put the rest of the stock, containing the fish and vegetables, in the blender and run it for half a minute. Add this to the soup. Test for seasoning. You can either stir in cream to the soup before serving or put a spoon of cream on top of each bowl of soup with a little chopped parsley sprinkled on top.

Sausage Pie

PREPARATION TIME: 15 minutes

COOKING TIME: 45 minutes

SERVES: 6 persons

This can be eaten hot or cold and is excellent for picnics.

¾lb frozen puff pastry
1lb lean sausage meat
1 small onion, minced
1 cup breadcrumbs
Level tsp dried sage
Salt and pepper
7oz can tomatoes
1 egg
1 tbsp milk

Cut defrosted pastry in two. Roll each half out into a 10 inch square and put it in the refrigerator while you mix the filling. Mix the onions and breadcrumbs, herbs and salt and pepper together and mix in with the sausage meat. Add the tomatoes and mix well. Break in the egg and stir that in well. Line a greased 10 inch pie dish with one layer of the pastry. Spread the sausage mixture over it to within 1 inch of the edge. Moisten the edge with milk and place the other piece of pastry on top. Trim the edges and crimp them together all around. Cut a cross in the center on top and use the pastry trimmings to make a leaf pattern in the center. Brush the top with milk and bake in a pre-heated oven, 400°F (200°C), for 45 minutes.

Country Broth

PREPARATION TIME: 20 minutes

COOKING TIME: 1 hour

SERVES: 8-10 persons

Home-made soups make a nourishing addition to a family meal and this one is almost a meal in itself. It is really made from what is available rather than from set ingredients. I always boil down chicken carcasses and meat bones, strain off the stock and keep it in the refrigerator. If I happen to have more than I need for the week I keep some in the freezer. Then, at the end of the week, I collect all the remaining vegetables and salad stuffs and use them to make this lovely soup. If you have a lot of leftover vegetables and the soup is very thick, it can be diluted with milk as you use it, or with the vegetable stock from the main course. Typical ingredients might be as follows:

1 onion
1 carrot
1 potato
¼ cucumber
½ green pepper
2 tomatoes
Some lettuce leaves
2 sticks celery
1 handful macaroni
1 handful pearl barley
1 handful lentils
Some chopped fresh herbs or
1 tsp dried herbs
2 tbsps oil and 1 tbsp butter
3¾ pints stock or stock made with bouillon cubes
Glass of sherry
2-3 tbsps cream

Prepare all the vegetables and salad stuffs and chop them roughly. Sweat them in the oil and butter, or in butter only, if you prefer. Add the pearl barley, macaroni and lentils then stir in the stock. Add the herbs and seasoning. Bring to the boil and simmer for half an hour. Test for seasoning. If you like it chunky, mash it down with a potato masher overwise put it through the coarse shredder of a vegetable mill or in the liquidizer. Return it to the pan, add the sherry and the cream or, if necessary, dilute with milk first. Bring back to simmering point and serve.

Stuffed Vine Leaves (right) and Sausage Pie (below).

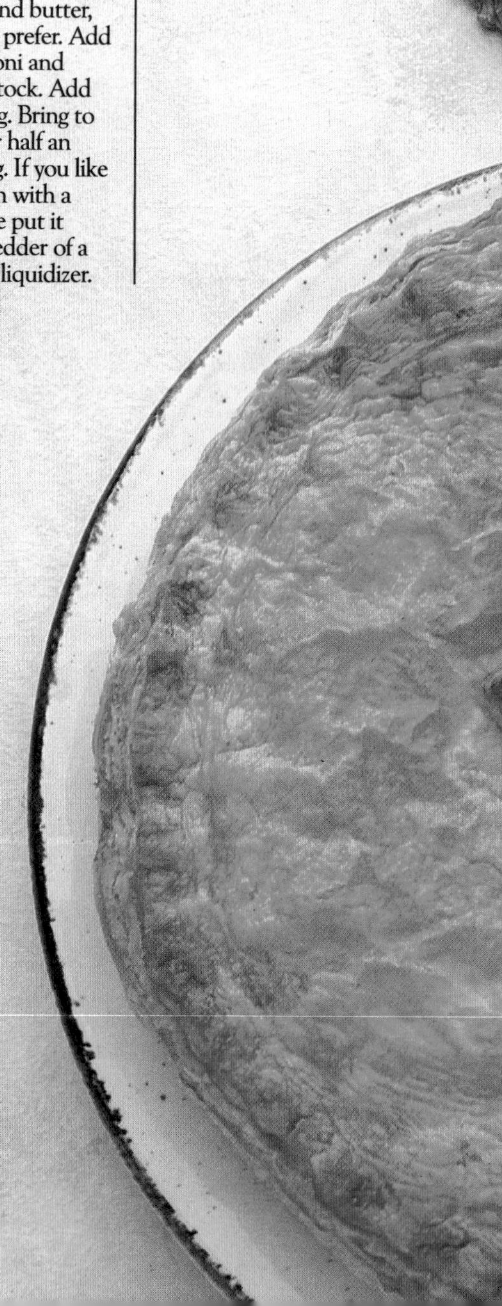

Stuffed Vine Leaves

PREPARATION TIME: 30 minutes

COOKING TIME: 30 minutes

SERVES: 8 persons

I have always been intrigued by the fact that so many Irish country houses have vines growing in their conservatories, or even against a south-facing wall. Although they seem to flourish in the mild climate, there is not enough sun to make the grapes suitable for wine making, or certainly not on a large scale. However, vine owners might like to try this recipe for stuffed vine leaves. The tangy flavor of the leaf goes well with the filling.

24 vine leaves
2-3 tbsps oil
8oz cooked rice
4oz cold lamb, ground
2-3 scallions, finely chopped
1 tbsp finely chopped walnuts
½ tsp marjoram
Salt and pepper
1¼ cups stock

Fry the scallions in the oil then add the lamb, rice, herbs and walnuts. Season with salt and pepper. Have ready a pan of boiling water and a bowl of iced water. Hold the vine leaves by their stalks and dip each one into the boiling water for about 10 seconds then plunge it into the iced water. Lay the leaves, underside up, on a board and put a tsp of the filling on each. Roll each one up into a sausage shape, tucking in the edges, and gently squeeze into shape in the palm of your hand. Pack the little parcels into a large pan in one layer. Pour the stock over them and cover with a plate to keep them in position. Simmer them for half an hour. Serve them with wedges of lemon.

Crubeens

PREPARATION TIME: 5 minutes

COOKING TIME: 3 hours

These could be called the "traditional Irish take-away," and are served in the pubs on a Saturday night to help mop up the alcohol! They may be eaten hot or cold. Taken straight from the pot they are eaten with brown soda bread and Guinness. If they are allowed to cool in the pot the meat will be firmer but they will be coated with a thick jelly. Either way, they are eaten in the fingers and much mopping up is required afterwards.

Some Irish restaurants now include them on the menu, but usually they are de-boned and rolled in well-seasoned egg and breadcrumbs, before being grilled. It is much less of a challenge to eat them when they are prepared in this way.

To cook Crubeens you need one pig's trotter (foot) per person and they say there is more meat on the hind ones. Put them in a pan with an onion, a carrot, salt, a few peppercorns, a bay leaf, some thyme and parsley. Cover with cold water, bring to the boil and simmer for three hours.

Drisheen

PREPARATION TIME: 40 minutes

COOKING TIME: 45 minutes

SERVES: 8 persons

Drisheen is a white pudding which is only found in County Cork. It is made from sheep's blood mixed with salt (which keeps it liquid), cream, oatmeal or breadcrumbs and seasoned with mace and tansy. It can be bought ready-made in Cork and in Dublin in the shape of thick sausages, as shown in the photograph, but the home-made sort was usually made in a wide, shallow pan and steamed or baked in the oven in a bain marie.

We used to love it for breakfast when we were children, but I'm sure we would not have even tasted it if we had been told how it was made. Just in case you can find some sheep's blood and are not too squeamish, here is the recipe.

4 cups sheep's blood
2 tsps salt
2½ cups creamy milk
Pinch tansy or thyme
2 cups breadcrumbs

Strain the blood into a mixing bowl, add all the other ingredients and mix well. Allow to stand for half an hour then pour mixture into a greased ovenproof dish, cover with foil and place in a roasting pan with water to come halfway up the sides of the dish. Cook in the oven at 350°F (180°C) for 45 minutes or until set.

Savory Pancakes

PREPARATION TIME: 1 hour 30 minutes

COOKING TIME: 45 minutes

SERVES: 6 persons

This is a very useful way of using up leftover cooked ground beef or lamb, or cold meat. In fact, it is a good idea to cook more than you need on some previous occasion and freeze some of it. If you are using cooked beef or lamb, put it through the grinder or in a food processor with a small onion and bind it with gravy or stock thickened with a little cornstarch.

8oz cooked ground beef or lamb
1 cup cooked rice
1 level tsp curry powder

Pancakes
1 cup plain flour
1 level tsp salt
1 egg
1¼ cups milk
Cooking oil

Sauce
3 tbsps butter
3 tbsps flour
Salt and pepper
2 cups milk
¾ cup grated cheese

Sift flour and salt into a mixing bowl, break in the egg and add the milk gradually, beating out any lumps and beating the batter with a whisk for several minutes. This can be done in an electric blender all at once in just one minute. The batter should be allowed to stand for at least an hour before making the pancakes. Grease a heavy frying pan with a tsp of cooking oil and heat it until it is very hot. Put in 2 tbsp batter mixture and quickly tilt the pan around until the batter covers the bottom. While it is cooking, loosen the edges with a spatula, ready to turn the pancake as soon as the bottom is done. Turn onto a plate. Add another tsp of oil to the pan and repeat the process until all the batter is used

Drisheen (top) and Crubeens (bottom).

up. Should make 10 or 12 thin pancakes.
Heat up the ground meat in a pan, stir in the curry powder and cook gently for a minute or two. Mix in the cooked rice. Grease an oblong ovenproof dish. Put a tablespoonful of filling into each pancake, roll them up and place them in one layer in the dish.

Sauce
Melt the butter in a saucepan, add the flour and make a roux. Very gradually add the milk, stirring all the time. When it comes to the boil continue cooking for a further minute then remove from heat and stir in grated cheese. Season with salt and pepper. Pour the sauce over the pancakes and bake in the oven, 375°F (190°C), for 45 minutes until just brown on top.

Creamed Mushrooms on Toast

PREPARATION TIME: 5 minutes
COOKING TIME: 20 minutes
SERVES: 4-6 persons

Cultivated mushrooms, so plentiful in the shops these days, bear no relation to the field mushrooms we used to gather in the fields in Ireland in the late summer. They were supposed to be gathered before breakfast, though, since there was no one else around who would be likely to take them, I could never understand why they wouldn't be there later in the day. However, my father would drag us out to search for them early in the morning, and it was worth it to savor the delicate flavor when they were cooked for breakfast.

8oz freshly gathered field mushrooms, or use the large, flat, cultivated mushrooms
2½ cups milk
¼ cup butter
¼ cup flour
Salt and pepper

Wipe mushrooms with damp paper towelling. Slice and place in a pan with the milk. Bring slowly to the boil and simmer gently for ten minutes. Meanwhile, melt butter in another pan, add flour and stir. Cook over very low heat for about a minute. Strain the milk in which the mushrooms were cooked into a jug and gradually add it to the roux, stirring all the time. When the sauce has thickened add the mushrooms, season with salt and pepper and serve on buttered toast. Serves 4-6 persons.

Irish Rarebit

PREPARATION TIME: 5 minutes
COOKING TIME: 20 minutes
SERVES: 4 persons

2 tbsps butter or margarine
2 tbsps flour
1 tsp Dijon mustard
1 tsp honey
½ cup milk
½ cup Guinness
1 cup Cheddar cheese, grated
Salt and pepper

Melt the butter in a heavy pan and stir in flour to make a roux. Cook on a low heat for a further minute without allowing it to brown. Remove pan from heat and gradually beat the milk into the roux. Return to heat and stir until the mixture thickens. Stir in mustard and honey and finally the Guinness. Cook this mixture fairly rapidly for 2-3 minutes then add grated cheese and stir over very low heat only until all the cheese has melted. Spread thickly on four slices of toast and brown under the grill.

Stuffed Marrow (Squash)

PREPARATION TIME: 15 minutes
COOKING TIME: 1 hour 15 minutes
SERVES: 4-6 persons

1 large marrow (squash)
6-8oz cooked lamb

This page: Creamed Mushrooms on Toast (top) and Irish Rarebit (bottom). Facing page: Savory Pancakes (top) and Stuffed Marrow (Squash) (bottom).

1 cup of gravy or stock made with bouillon cube
1 onion
1 carrot
3 large tomatoes or 7oz can of tomatoes, drained
½ tsp oregano plus chopped mixed garden herbs if available
1-2 cups of cooked rice, according to the size of the marrow
½ cup grated cheese

Put the lamb, onion and carrot through the grinder or chop in food processor. Mix in a bowl with the gravy or stock. Put tomatoes in boiling water and leave to stand for a few minutes then remove skins, chop and add to mixture. If using canned tomatoes, drain off liquid, chop up tomatoes and add to mixture. Add rice and herbs and season with salt and pepper to taste. Scrub squash well. Cut in half lengthwise, remove seeds and fill both halves with stuffing. Place side by side in a greased roasting pan with about half an inch of water in it. Cover pan with foil and bake at 400°F (200°C) for one hour. Remove from oven, take off foil, sprinkle grated cheese over squash and return to oven for a further ten minutes.

Bacon and Egg Pie

PREPARATION TIME: 15 minutes
COOKING TIME: 40-45 minutes
SERVES: 6 persons

During the summer months, most Irish families take off for the coast whenever the opportunity arises. There are miles of golden beaches where it is easy to find a secluded spot well out of earshot of other people's transistors. Inland, too, there are many beauty spots in the midst of mountain and lakeland scenery. I remember at Glendalough, in the Wicklow Mountains, some years ago, when one person brought a bacon and egg pie and it was very popular. It is such an easy dish to transport and very little trouble to make, which is especially important if you are on holiday. In fact, you can use frozen pastry and you should be able to find a shop which sells frozen food even in the most remote villages in Ireland.

2 cups all-purpose flour
1 level tsp salt
⅓ cup margarine
⅓ cup lard
3-4 tbsps cold water
6 rashers bacon
6 eggs

Sift flour and salt into a bowl. Cut up fats and rub into the flour. Gradually add the water, mixing it in with a knife until the mixture forms a ball and leaves the bowl clean. Lightly shape on a floured board and cut in two. Grease a 10-inch pie plate, roll out half the pastry and line the plate with this. Place the rashers like the spokes of a wheel and break an egg into each space. Roll out the other half of the pastry and carefully cover the filling with this. Crimp the edges all round, lightly mark segments with a knife so that each person gets a rasher and egg, and brush the top with milk. Place in a pre-heated oven 400°F (200°C) for 40-45 minutes.
The pie can be wrapped in layers of newspaper to keep it hot during a journey, or may be served cold with a salad.

Huntsman's Sandwich

PREPARATION TIME: 10 minutes
COOKING TIME: 6-8 minutes
SERVES: 2 persons

2½ inch thick fillet steaks
1 medium onion
2 tbsps vegetable oil
1 tbsp butter
Dijon mustard
Salt and pepper
2 round, crusty rolls

Peel onion and slice it finely. Heat oil and butter in a heavy frying pan. When sizzling hot put steaks in pan, turn immediately to seal and cook for 1-2 minutes on either side, according to how you like them done. Season with the salt and pepper. Slice rolls through the middle, spread mustard on the bottom half and put steaks on top of that. Add onion to the pan juices and cook until softened. Divide this between two steaks, cover with the top halves of the rolls. Eat hot or cold. Serves 2 persons (or one very hungry huntsman).

Potatoes

The potato was first introduced to Ireland by Sir Walter Raleigh in the sixteenth century. He lived in Youghal, County Cork and the house he lived in still stands today. Potatoes flourished so well that it wasn't long before they became the staple diet in Ireland because they were so cheap to grow and the majority of the population was extremely poor. It was the failure of the potato crop which was the main cause of the famine in Ireland. The potatoes I can remember as a child were best served bursting out of their skins – we used to be asked if we liked them laughing or smiling – and eaten with a generous

Huntsman's Sandwich (right) and Bacon and Egg Pie (below).

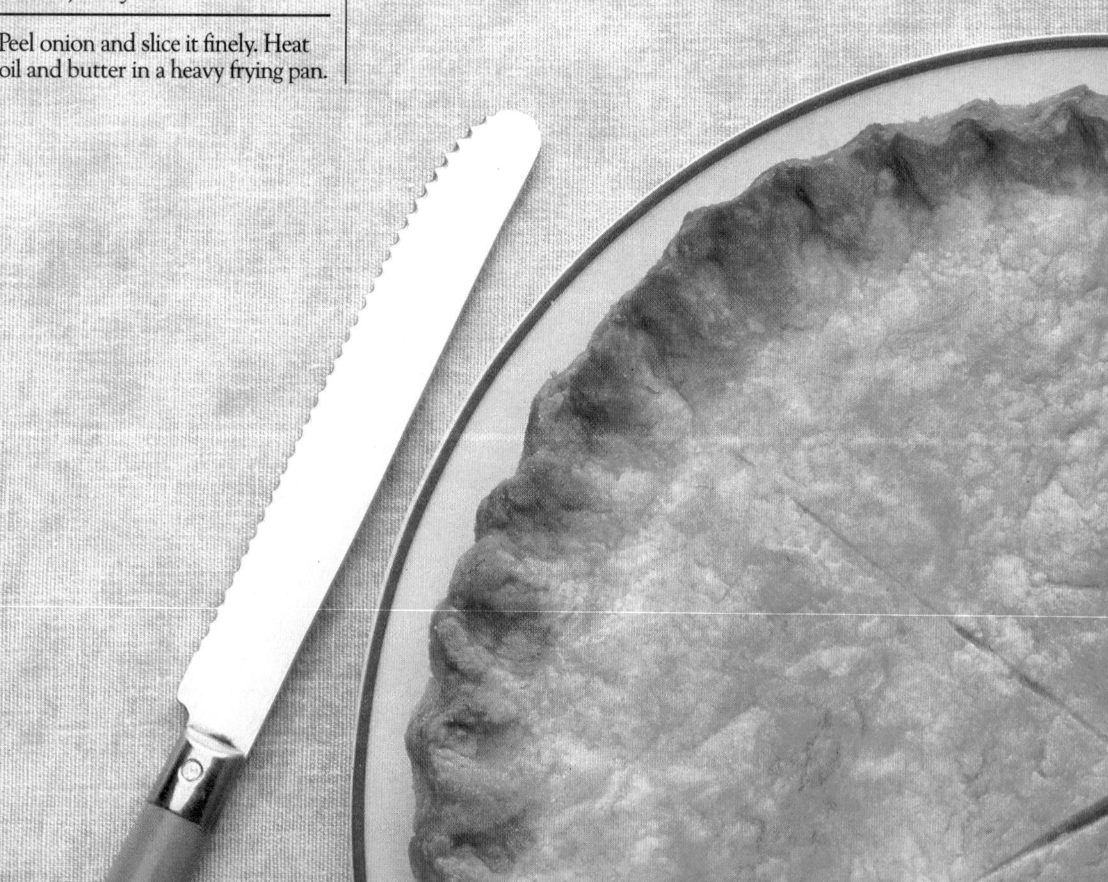

This page: Boxty Pancakes (top right), Flummery (center left) and Oaten Farls (bottom). Facing page: Colcannon (top) and Potato Cakes (bottom).

amount of home-made, salty, country butter. I suppose one reason for the marvelous flavor was the fact that they would be dug up from the garden the same day they were eaten, but there does not seem to be anything to compare with them in the shops today.
In the north they have many traditional potato recipes. A friend who grew up in Belfast tells me that when she was a child meat was a luxury which, in many households, was served only at weekends, and dishes such as Colcannon and Champ were the main dish for the main meal of the day.

Colcannon

PREPARATION TIME: 10 minutes
COOKING TIME: 20 minutes
SERVES: 4 persons

Colcannon is another traditional potato dish and it is always associated with Hallowe'en. It is a mixture of cabbage or kale and mashed potato which sometimes has leeks or green onions mixed in, as in Champ.
Being a dish to serve at Hallowe'en, with all its accompanying folklore, the tradition is to hide a ring for a bride, a bachelor's button, a sixpence for wealth and the thimble for a spinster in the Colcannon. When cold, it is very good fried in bacon fat and browned on both sides.

1lb (2 cups) cooked mashed potato
1½ cups cooked cabbage
¼ cup butter
¼ cup creamy milk
½ cup finely chopped onion, leek or scallion

Gently fry onion in melted butter until soft. Add creamy milk and the well-mashed potatoes and stir until heated through. Chop cabbage finely and beat into the mixture over a low heat until all the mixture is pale green and fluffy. It is an excellent accompaniment for boiled bacon.

Boxty Pancakes

PREPARATION TIME: 20 minutes
COOKING TIME: 15 minutes
SERVES: 6 persons

These are made with a mixture of cooked and raw potatoes, combined with flour and bound with potato starch and fat. Milk or buttermilk is added to make the mixture into a dropping consistency and the pancakes are cooked on a griddle.

8oz mashed potatoes
8oz raw potatoes
2 cups flour
1 level tsp baking soda
1 level tsp salt
Pepper
¼ cup butter, margarine or bacon fat
Milk

Peel and grate the raw potatoes. Wrap them tightly in a cloth and squeeze over a bowl to extract as

much of the starch liquid as possible. Mash the grated raw potato into the cooked mashed potato. Pour the liquid off the bowl of potato starch and scrape the starch into the potato mixture. Sift the salt and baking soda with the flour and mix this in and then add the melted fat. Add as much milk as necessary to make the mixture into a batter of dropping consistency and cook in spoonfuls on a greased griddle or heavy pan, turning until crispy and golden on both sides.

Potato Apple

PREPARATION TIME: 25 minutes
COOKING TIME: 12-15 minutes
SERVES: 6-8 persons

I have been told of two versions of Potato Apple. One is made by sandwiching sliced apple between two rounds of potato cake and cooking it on both sides on a

greased griddle or pan. When it is cooked through and the apple is soft, the lid is lifted and sugar, or sugar mixed with cinnamon, is sprinkled over the apple. Then the lid is replaced and the apple cake cut into wedges for serving.
But, as many of these traditional recipes were concocted to use up leftover ingredients for economy's sake, another method involves the use of cooked apple.
The potato mixture was rolled out into circles the size of a large saucer. Cooked apple was put on one half and the other half folded over and the edges sealed. Then it was cooked in the same way as in the previous recipe.

Potato Cakes

PREPARATION TIME: 20 minutes
COOKING TIME: 8-12 minutes
SERVES: 8 persons

These are a great favorite in the north of Ireland. They are eaten with lots of butter and go well with sausages and bacon and eggs.

2¾ cups mashed potato
1 cup flour
½ tsp salt
½ tsp baking powder
2 tbsps butter
Bacon fat or dripping

Sift flour, salt and baking powder. Rub in the butter. Mix in the potatoes and knead into a ball. Cut this in two and roll half out on a floured board or work surface into a circle ¼ inch thick. Divide into four farls or segments. Cook them for 2-3 minutes each side, on a very hot pan or griddle greased with bacon fat or dripping. Repeat the process with the other half.

Champ

PREPARATION TIME: 15 minutes
COOKING TIME: 45 minutes
SERVES: 4 persons

Champ is a traditional Irish dish more commonly found in northern counties. It is made of potatoes mixed with scallions or green onions. Each portion is served in a mound with an indentation on top with a pat of butter in it and the potato is dipped into the melted butter.

1½lbs cooked potatoes
4oz scallions (green onions)
½ cup milk
Salt and pepper
4 large pats butter

Peel the potatoes and boil them in salted water. Drain them well and allow to dry out completely. Meanwhile, trim and wash the scallions. Slice them finely, including the green part, and put them in a pan with the milk to simmer gently until soft. Drain the scallions, reserving the milk, and beat them into the potato, gradually adding the hot milk until you have a nice fluffy mixture. Season well with salt and pepper and divide between four bowls, shaping each serving into a mound with a dent in the top into which you put the butter. It is eaten by dipping the potato into the melted butter.

Oaten Farls

PREPARATION TIME: 20 minutes
COOKING TIME: 8-12 minutes
SERVES: 8 persons

In the north of Ireland, the nearer one gets to the coast of Scotland, the more the Scottish influence is noticed in the food, and many recipes in this part of Ireland contain oatmeal. Here is one for potato cakes mixed with oatmeal.

Make the potato cakes as in that recipe, but before rolling out knead a handful of oatmeal into each half. Sprinkle the board with more oatmeal and roll out the potato mixture, turning it over so that both sides are well coated with oatmeal. Divide into farls and cook in a little fat on a heavy frying pan or griddle.

Flummery

PREPARATION TIME: 24 hours
COOKING TIME: 30 minutes
SERVES: 4-6 persons

Oatmeal was sometimes used to make gruel – the thinnest imaginable mixture of oatmeal and water, or milk and water. There was just about enough nourishment in it to keep people alive during the famine. The lucky ones – that is! Flummery is a more substantial version of this, and it was given to children and to invalids.

2½ cups oatmeal
5 cups water
½ tsp salt

Soak the oatmeal in the water for at least 24 hours. Strain through muslin, and boil the liquid for 20-30 minutes, stirring all the time. Add salt and serve with milk or cream.

Champ (above left) and Potato Apple (left).

Elegant Pasta Appetizers

Chick-Pea Soup

PREPARATION TIME: Chick-peas soaked overnight plus 5 minutes

COOKING TIME: 1 hour 20 minutes

1 cup dried chick-peas
1 cup soup pasta
2 cloves garlic
3 tbsps olive oil
1 tsp basil
1½ cups plum tomatoes, chopped
3 cups water
1 chicken bouillon cube
2 tbsps Parmesan cheese, grated
Salt and pepper

Soak chick-peas overnight in enough water to cover by 1 inch. Discard water in which the chick-peas have soaked. Place the chick-peas in a large, heavy pan, and cover with 1 inch of water. Bring to the boil and simmer, covered, for about 1 hour until chick-peas are tender, ensuring that they do not boil dry. Heat olive oil in a heavy pan, and sauté garlic cloves. When browned, remove and discard garlic cloves. Add tomatoes and their juice, water and basil, and cook together for 20 minutes. Add drained chick-peas, crumbled bouillon cube, and salt and pepper to taste. Stir well; simmer a further 10 minutes. Bring back to boil. Add pasta, and cook, stirring frequently, for 10 minutes. Mix in half of the Parmesan cheese. Adjust seasoning, and serve immediately, with remaining Parmesan cheese sprinkled on top. Serves 4.
Note: Soup may be puréed before pasta is added, if desired.

Tagliatelle with Egg and Caviar

PREPARATION TIME: 5 minutes

COOKING TIME: 15 minutes

½ pound red tagliatelle
1 small jar red salmon caviar or lumpfish roe
4 small eggs, hard boiled
4 tbsps butter or margarine
Black pepper

Put eggs into boiling water and cook for 12 minutes. Rinse under cold water, to stop further cooking. Remove shells, cut in half, and scoop out yolks with a teaspoon. Push yolks through a strainer. Wash egg-whites, and cut into strips. Set aside. Cook tagliatelle in plenty of boiling salted water until *al dente.* Rinse in hot water, and drain well. Heat butter in pan, add freshly-ground black pepper and tagliatelle. Add egg whites, and toss well. Sprinkle caviar over, and top with egg-yolk. Serve immediately. Serves 4 as a starter.

Minestra

PREPARATION TIME: 15 minutes

COOKING TIME: 45 minutes

¾ cup short-cut/elbow macaroni
2 tbsps olive oil
1 onion
1 carrot
1 stick celery
1½ quarts water
½ pound fresh spinach
2 tomatoes
1 tsp rosemary
2 tbsps chopped parsley
2 cloves garlic, crushed
¼ cup Parmesan cheese, grated
Salt and pepper

Cut onion, carrot and celery into thick matchstick strips. Heat oil in a large, heavy pan, and fry vegetable strips until just browning, stirring occasionally. Pour on water, add salt and pepper, and let simmer for 20 minutes. Meanwhile, wash and cut spinach leaves into shreds, add to soup and cook for 10 minutes. Scald and skin tomatoes, and chop roughly, removing seeds. Add tomatoes, macaroni, garlic, parsley and rosemary to the soup, and simmer a further 10 minutes. Adjust seasoning. Serve with grated Parmesan cheese if desired.

Meatball Soup

PREPARATION TIME: 10 minutes

COOKING TIME: 1 hour 40 minutes

OVEN: 350°F (180°C)

½ pound ground minced beef
¼ cup breadcrumbs
1 egg, beaten
1 pound beef bones
1 stick celery
1 carrot
1 onion
1 tbsp oil
1 can tomato sauce
¾ cup soup pasta
1 tbsp chopped parsley
Salt and pepper

Place bones, peeled carrot, onion and celery in a large saucepan and cover with cold water. Bring to the boil: cover and simmer for one hour at least. Meanwhile, mix together lightly beaten egg with ground beef, breadcrumbs and plenty of seasoning. Roll a teaspoon amount into small balls and place on a roasting pan with the oil. Bake in a preheated oven for 45 minutes, turning occasionally. Strain stock into a saucepan. Add tomato sauce to the stock. Bring to the boil, and simmer for 15 minutes. Add pasta and cook for 10 minutes, stirring frequently. Add meatballs, adjust seasoning, and stir in chopped parsley. Serve hot.

This page: Tagliatelle with Egg and Caviar.

Facing page: Minestra (top), Meatball Soup (center right) and Chick-Pea Soup (bottom).

Tomato Soup

PREPARATION TIME: 15 minutes

COOKING TIME: 45 minutes

1 cup short-cut/elbow macaroni
2 tbsps butter or margarine
1 small onion, peeled and chopped
1 small green pepper, cored, seeds removed, and chopped
1 tbsp flour
1 quart brown stock, or water plus 2 beef bouillon cubes
1 pound tomatoes, chopped
2 tbsps tomato paste
1 tbsp grated horseradish
Salt and pepper

Garnish:
2 tbsps soured cream,
1 tbsp chopped parsley

Heat the butter in a pan. Cover and cook the onion and green pepper for 5 minutes. Add the flour and stir. Add stock, tomatoes and tomato paste. Simmer for 15 minutes. Purée soup and strain. Return to pan, and season with salt and pepper to taste. Add macaroni 10 minutes before serving. Simmer and stir occasionally. Add horseradish before serving. Garnish with soured cream and parsley. Serve immediately.

Tagliatelle with Smoked Salmon and Caviar

PREPARATION TIME: 5 minutes

COOKING TIME: 15 minutes

½ pound green tagliatelle
¼ pound smoked salmon, cut into strips
Juice of half a lemon
2 tbsps red salmon caviar or lumpfish roe
2 tbsps butter or margarine
2 tbsps heavy cream
Black pepper

Garnish:
Lemon slices

Cook tagliatelle in lots of boiling salted water for 10 minutes, or until tender but still firm. Rinse under hot water, and drain well. Heat butter in pan, and add lemon juice and freshly-ground black pepper. Return tagliatelle to pan, and add smoked salmon. Toss together. Serve topped with heavy cream and a sprinkling of red caviar. Garnish with lemon slices. Serve immediately. Serves 4 as a starter.

Tagliatelle with Smoked Salmon and Caviar (top left), Shell Pasta with Taramasalata (left). Top picture: Bean Soup (top) and Tomato Soup (bottom).

Shell Pasta with Taramasalata

PREPARATION TIME: 15 minutes

COOKING TIME: 15 minutes

1 9oz package shell pasta
1 cup taramasalata
2 tbsps lemon juice
10 black olives, pips removed, and chopped
1 tbsp black caviar or lumpfish roe

To Make Taramasalata:
½ cup smoked salmon roe
Half onion, grated
8 slices white bread, crusts removed
4 tbsps milk
⅓ cup olive oil
2 tsps lemon juice
Black pepper

Crumble bread into a bowl and add milk. Set aside to soak. Scoop the salmon roe out of its skin, and break it down with a wooden spoon. Squeeze the bread dry in a strainer. Add onion and bread to salmon roe, and mix well. Add oil and lemon juice very gradually, alternating between the two. Beat until smooth and creamy. Add pepper to taste, and salt if necessary. Cook pasta shells in lots of boiling salted water for 10 minutes or until *al dente*. Rinse in hot water, and drain well. Sprinkle over lemon juice; toss together with taramasalata, and garnish with caviar and black olives. Serve immediately. Serves 4 as a starter.

Bean Soup

PREPARATION TIME: 15 minutes

COOKING TIME: 1 hour 45 minutes

1 15oz can kidney beans
2 strips bacon, chopped
1 stick celery, chopped
1 small onion, peeled and chopped
1 clove garlic, crushed
½ cup plum tomatoes, chopped and seeds removed
4 cups water
1 chicken bouillon cube
1 tbsp chopped parsley
1 tsp basil
1 cup whole-wheat ring pasta
Salt and pepper

Place kidney beans, bacon, celery, onion, garlic, parsley, basil, tomatoes and water in a large pan. Bring to the boil and add bouillon cube and salt and pepper to taste. Cover and cook over a low heat for about 1½ hours. Raise heat and add pasta, stirring well. Stir frequently until pasta is cooked but still firm – about 10 minutes. Serve immediately.

Meat and Egg Appetizers

Cold Roast Beef and Horseradish Cream

PREPARATION TIME: 20 minutes

SERVES: 4 people

8 slices medium-rare roast beef
⅔ cup heavy cream
1 tbsp fresh grated horseradish
1 tsp lemon juice
1 tsp sugar
Pinch of salt and pepper

Garnish
Lettuce
Green onion flowers (trim and slice lengthwise, keep one end intact, and leave in cold water in refrigerator until curling)
Cucumber

Whip cream and salt together until stiff. Add horseradish, sugar and lemon juice. Check seasoning, and add more salt and pepper if desired. Place one-eighth of each mixture at end of each slice of beef. Roll up in a cornet shape and serve on a bed of lettuce. Garnish with green onion flowers and sliced cucumber.

Stuffed Eggs

PREPARATION TIME: 20 minutes

COOKING TIME: 15 minutes

SERVES: 4 people

6 medium eggs
1 tbsp vinegar
1 small can of pink salmon
Paprika
2 tbsps peas
4-5 mushrooms
1 8oz package cream cheese
Salt
Pepper

Garnish
Stuffed olive
Red pepper or tomato
Black olive

This page: Stuffed Eggs.

Facing page: Chicken Tongue Rolls (top) and Cold Roast Beef and Horseradish Cream (bottom).

Put eggs into a saucepan of gently boiling water with 1 tbsp of vinegar and boil gently for 12 minutes. Rinse immediately in cold water. Remove shells carefully and keep eggs in cold water until ready to use. Cut boiled eggs in half and carefully remove yolks. Rinse whites. Push yolks through a sieve and put aside for fillings. Soften cream cheese by beating. Drain and flake salmon. Mix carefully with one-third of cream cheese. Add a pinch of paprika and salt and pepper to taste. Pipe or spoon filling into 4 egg whites. Garnish with half a stuffed olive.
Wash and trim mushrooms. Chop very finely and add to one-third of cream cheese. Add salt or pepper to taste. Pipe or spoon filling into 4 egg whites. Garnish with red pepper or tomato.
Cook peas until tender. Push through a strainer. Add yolk of eggs and one-third of cream cheese. Pipe or spoon filling into remaining 4 egg whites and garnish with a slice of black olive.

Chicken Tongue Rolls

PREPARATION TIME: 15 minutes

COOKING TIME: 20 minutes

SERVES: 4 people

4 chicken legs
4 slices of smoked tongue
2 tbsps grated Parmesan cheese
1 tbsp grated Gruyère or Cheddar cheese
1 tbsp chopped parsley
1 tbsp oil
Salt
Pepper

Garnish
Parsley
Tomato

Remove bone carefully from chicken leg, keeping meat in one piece. Flatten out, and divide the tongue equally between each piece. Mix together grated cheeses, parsley and salt and pepper to taste. Place a tbsp of the mixture on each piece of chicken. Roll up chicken and tie each with string, 2 or 3 times. Heat oil in pan and fry chicken rolls gently for about 20 minutes, turning occasionally to cook evenly. Remove from heat and allow to cool. Cut off string and remove gently. Slice into rounds and serve garnished with parsley and tomato.

Egg Flower

PREPARATION TIME: 20 minutes

COOKING TIME: 15 minutes

SERVES: 4 people

6 eggs
1 tbsp vinegar
3 tbsps mayonnaise
1 tbsp light cream
1 tsp lemon juice (or to taste)
Salt
White pepper

Garnish
Watercress
Pinch of paprika

Fill a saucepan with water and 1 tbsp of vinegar and bring to the boil. Reduce heat and simmer. Gently add eggs and cook for 12 minutes. Rinse under cold water to stop cooking. Crack and peel off shells and set eggs aside in a bowl of cold water. Mix together mayonnaise, cream, lemon juice and salt and white pepper to taste. Cut 4 eggs in half. Place yolk-side down in a circle on a serving dish. Cut remaining eggs in half and separate yolks from whites. Rinse whites and cut into shreds. Push yolks through a strainer and set aside. Pour mayonnaise over eggs on serving dish. Sprinkle egg white around outside. Sprinkle yolk on top towards the center. Sprinkle with paprika. Finally garnish with a bunch of watercress in the center.

Eggs baked in Tarragon Cream

PREPARATION TIME: 5 minutes

COOKING TIME: 8 minutes

OVEN TEMPERATURE: 350°F (180°C)

SERVES: 4 people

4 large eggs
¼ tbsp of butter
¼ cup cream
1 tbsp chopped tarragon
Salt
Pepper

Butter individual oven-proof ramekin dishes. Break an egg into each dish. Add chopped tarragon, and salt and pepper to cream and mix well. Add 1 tbsp of cream mixture to each ramekin. Place ramekins on a baking sheet in a preheated oven until set, about 6-8 minutes. Serve hot.

Eggs baked in Tarragon Cream (left) and Egg Flower (below).

Fish Pâtés and Mousses

Smoked Trout Pâté

PREPARATION TIME: 20 minutes
SERVES: 4 people

4 lemons
2 fillets or 1 whole smoked trout
6 tbsps butter
8oz package cream cheese
Lemon juice
Tabasco
Ground nutmeg
Salt
Pepper

Garnish
Fresh bay leaves

Cut lemons in half and trim the ends so the shells sit upright. Scoop out the lemon flesh completely. Remove skin and bones from trout. Put fish into a food processor with the butter, cream cheese, seasoning, lemon juice, nutmeg and Tabasco. Work until smooth. Put the pâté into a pastry bag fitted with a rose tube and pipe into the lemon shells. Garnish each with a bay leaf. Serve with hot toast.

Pâté of Salmon and Scallops

PREPARATION TIME: 30 minutes
COOKING TIME: 1 hour
OVEN TEMPERATURE: 350°F (180°C)
SERVES: 4 people

¾lb salmon
1lb haddock or other white fish
5 scallops with roe attached
1¼ cups heavy cream
3 eggs
1 tbsp chopped parsley
1 tbsp chopped fresh tarragon
1 tbsp lemon juice
1 tbsp dry white wine
½ cup unsalted butter
Salt
Pepper
Pinch Cayenne pepper

Separate eggs and set aside yolks. Remove skin and bone from haddock and salmon. Put salmon into a food processor bowl with half the egg whites and half the cream. Season and process until smooth. Put into separate bowl, and repeat the process with the haddock. Lightly butter a 2lb loaf pan. Put half of haddock mixture into the bottom of the pan and smooth out. Cover with half of the salmon mixture. Clean scallops and separate roe from white part. Cut white part in half through the middle. Chop roe roughly and put it down the center of the salmon mixture. Place the rounds of white scallops on either side of the roe. Put another layer of salmon mixture over, and then the

This page: Pâté of Salmon and Scallops (top) and Kippered Fish Mousse (bottom). Facing page: Smoked Trout Pâté (top) and Crabmeat Mousse (bottom).

remaining haddock mixture on top and smooth out. Cover well with double thickness of buttered foil. Put into a roasting pan and fill it halfway up with hand-hot water. Bake pâté in oven for about 1 hour. Meanwhile, prepare a quick Bernaise sauce. Put reserved egg yolks into a food processor bowl or blender. Chop herbs roughly and add to egg yolks along with Cayenne pepper, pinch of salt, lemon juice and white wine. Process until mixed thoroughly and the herbs are chopped. Melt butter and, when foaming, turn on machine and pour the melted butter through feed tube very gradually. This will cook the egg yolks and the sauce will thicken. Keep warm in a double boiler. When pâté has finished cooking, allow to cool slightly in the pan. Gently turn fish pâté out and cut into 1" thick slices. Arrange on serving plates and pour over some of the Bernaise sauce. Serve the rest of the sauce separately.

Smoked Salmon Mousse

PREPARATION TIME: 20 minutes

COOKING TIME: 5 minutes

SERVES: 4 people

¾lb smoked salmon
2½ cups prepared mayonnaise
1 tbsp powdered gelatine
Lemon juice
¼ cup heavy cream
1 tbsp flour
1 tbsp butter
¾ cup milk
1 egg white
1 small cucumber
1 jar red caviar
1 bunch watercress
1 small head iceberg lettuce
Salt and pepper

Lightly oil ramekin dishes or small individual molds. Mix lemon juice with enough water to make 3 tbsps, and dissolve gelatine in the liquid. Warm gelatine through gently to melt. Prepare sauce by melting butter and, when foaming, adding flour. Stir together well and blend in the milk gradually. Put back on the heat and bring to the boil to thicken. Allow to cool slightly. Chop the smoked salmon roughly and put into a food processor bowl with half the prepared mayonnaise. Add seasonings and prepared sauce. Process until smooth and, with machine still running, pour in the melted gelatine. Pour in cream and process briefly. Set mixture over ice or in a cool place until thickening. When thickened, whisk egg white until stiff but not dry, and fold into salmon mousse mixture. Put mixture into individual molds and chill until firm. Meanwhile, prepare green mayonnaise. Pick over the watercress leaves, wash them well, remove thick stalks and the root ends. Chop roughly and put into food processor bowl. Add remaining prepared mayonnaise, seasonings and lemon juice to taste, and process until well blended and a good green color. Spread mayonnaise onto individual serving plates. When mousse is chilled and set, turn out on top of green mayonnaise. Garnish the plate with shredded lettuce. Garnish the top of each mousse with a thin slice of cucumber and a little red caviar.

Crabmeat Mousse

PREPARATION TIME: 30 minutes

SERVES: 4 people

1lb crabmeat, cooked and flaked
⅓ cup prepared mayonnaise
⅔ cup whipping cream
2 tbsps sherry
2 egg whites
2 tsps Dijon mustard
1 small bunch chives
1 tbsp commercial aspic powder
Juice of 1 lime or lemon
1 ripe avocado
1 tbsp gelatine
Salt and pepper

Dissolve gelatine in some of the lemon or lime juice. Warm gently to dissolve, and mix with mayonnaise, mustard, and salt and pepper to taste. Lightly whip the cream and fold into mayonnaise mixture along with crabmeat. Put over ice or in a cool place until thickened, then whisk the egg whites until stiff but not dry, and fold into mixture. Quickly pour into a bowl or soufflé dish, smooth the top and chill until set. Meanwhile, bring 1 cup water to boil. Stir in sherry, add 1 tbsp commercial aspic powder and stir until dissolved. Allow to cool slightly. Chop chives and add to aspic. When mousse mixture is set, chill aspic until it begins to thicken slightly. Pour about ¼" of the aspic over the top of the set mousse, and return to refrigerator to set the aspic. Cut avocado in half lengthwise and remove stone. Peel carefully and cut each half into thin slices. Brush with lemon juice and arrange slices on top of set aspic. Spoon over some of the aspic to set the avocado slices, and chill. When avocado is set, pour remaining aspic over to fill to the top of dish, and chill until set.

Kippered Fish Mousse

PREPARATION TIME: 20 minutes

SERVES: 4 people

6 small or 3 large kippered herrings
¾ cup heavy cream
⅔ cup prepared mayonnaise
1 tbsp brandy
1 tbsp grated horseradish
½ clove garlic
1 shallot, finely chopped
1 tbsp powdered gelatine
Salt
Pepper
Lemon juice
Vegetable oil

Garnish
Sliced cucumbers
Sliced lemon
Chives

Skin kippers and remove any bones. Mix lemon juice with water to make 3 tbsps. Dissolve gelatine in this liquid, and heat gently to melt gelatine. Put fillets into food processor with brandy, mayonnaise, salt, pepper, garlic, and finely chopped shallot. Work until smooth, then, with the machine running, pour the liquid gelatine through feed tube to blend. Put mixture over ice or in a cool place until it begins to thicken. Lightly whip cream and fold into thickened mousse mixture. Lightly oil a mold with vegetable oil. Pour in the mousse mixture. Smooth down and tap to remove any air bubbles. Chill overnight, or until set. Turn out onto a serving plate and surround with a garnish of thinly sliced cucumbers, and thinly sliced lemons. Chives may be used to decorate the mold if desired.

Tricolor Terrine

PREPARATION TIME: 25 minutes

COOKING TIME: 15 minutes

SERVES: 4 people

4oz smoked haddock (finnan haddie)
4oz fresh haddock or other white fish
1 large kippered herring
⅔ cup prepared mayonnaise
2 tbsps flour
2 tbsps butter
1¼ cups milk
1 tbsp chopped parsley
3 tbsps heavy cream
1 tbsp gelatine
1 egg white
Juice of 1 lemon
⅔ cup sour cream
1 tbsp grated horseradish
1 bunch dill, reserving 4 small sprigs
Iceberg lettuce
Watercress

Poach smoked haddock in water and half the milk to cover for 10 minutes. Skin and remove any bones. Cook fresh haddock separately, using fresh water and the remaining milk. Skin kippered herring. Mash the fish well, or work in a food processor, keeping each fish separate. Prepare the sauce by melting the butter, adding flour off the heat. Stir in the cooking liquid from the fish and put the sauce back onto the heat. Stir until boiling, then season well. Soak gelatine in 1 tbsp lemon juice plus enough water to make 3 tbsps. Melt over gentle heat until dissolved. Whip cream lightly until it just holds its shape. Put haddock, smoked haddock and kipper in separate bowls. Divide sauce, gelatine and mayonnaise equally between each bowl. Mix together

Smoked Salmon Mousse (right) and Tricolor Terrine (bottom).

together for the sauce, and season well. When the tureen is set, turn out of the pan and slice into ¾″ thick slices. Place on a serving plate with a garnish of lettuce, watercress and reserved dill, and a spoonful of the horseradish sauce. Serve the rest of the horseradish sauce separately.

well and fold in the heavy cream, similarly divided. Lightly oil a 1lb loaf pan. Set the mixtures in a cool place until thickening and, when starting to thicken, whip the egg white. Divide that equally into the fish mixtures. Put smoked haddock mixture into the bottom of the loaf pan and smooth out. Spoon the fresh haddock over the smoked haddock mixture and spread out on top. Spoon kipper mixture on top of that, and level out. Chill in the refrigerator until well set. Mix sour cream, horseradish, chopped dill, chopped parsley, and lemon

Crêpes and Pastries

Chicken Bouchées (Patty Shells)

PREPARATION TIME: 30 minutes
COOKING TIME: 30 minutes
OVEN TEMPERATURE: 425°F (210°C)
SERVES: 4 people

8oz frozen puff pastry, thawed
1 egg, beaten

Filling

4 tbsps butter or margarine
3 tbsps flour
1¼ cups milk
Salt
Pepper
4 chicken breasts, cooked and shredded
1 tbsp chopped parsley
6 peppercorns
2 parsley stalks
Slice of onion
Half a bay leaf

On a lightly floured board roll out pastry to about ¼″ thick. Using a 3″ fluted pastry-cutter, cut out pastry. With a 2″ fluted pastry-cutter mark center of each, being careful not to cut right through. Brush with beaten egg, being careful not to get any down sides or in groove made by 2″ cutter, as this will prevent rising. Place on a dampened baking sheet and chill in refrigerator for 15 minutes. Make pattern on outer edge with back of knife if desired. Bake in a hot oven until golden brown. Remove from oven and gently lift off center cap. Remove any soft pastry from inside. Return to oven for 1 minute to dry out. To help prevent pastry from toppling over, 4 wooden picks may be placed at equal intervals around outside circle and removed after cooking. Heat milk with peppercorns, parsley stalks, onion and ½ bay leaf until just simmering. Remove from heat, cover and leave to cool for 7 minutes. Strain. Melt butter in pan; stir in flour and cook for 1 minute. Remove from heat and gradually stir in infused milk. Return to heat, bring to the boil and cook for 3 minutes, stirring continuously. Add salt and pepper to taste. Stir in shredded chicken and parsley. Fill bouchées with hot chicken filling. Place lids on top at an angle. Serve hot.

Shrimp Bouchées (Patty Shells)

PREPARATION TIME: 30 minutes
COOKING TIME: 30 minutes
OVEN TEMPERATURE: 425°F (210°C)
SERVES: 4 people

8oz frozen puff pastry, thawed
1 egg, beaten

Filling

4 tbsps butter or margarine
3 tbsps flour
1¼ cups chicken stock
Salt
Pepper
8oz shrimp, shelled and de-veined
1 tbsp tarragon vinegar or lemon juice
1 tsp tomato paste
Pinch of sugar

On a lightly floured board, roll out pastry to about ¼″ thick. Using a 3″ fluted pastry-cutter, cut out pastry. With a 2″ fluted pastry-cutter mark the center of each, being careful not to cut right through. Brush with beaten egg, being careful not to get any down sides or in groove made by 2″ cutter, as this will prevent rising. Place on a dampened baking sheet and chill in refrigerator for 15

Roquefort Tarts (top) and Cheese Puffs (bottom).

Facing page: Chicken Bouchées (Patty Shells) (top) and Shrimp Bouchées (Patty Shells) (bottom).

minutes. Make pattern on outer circle with back of knife if desired. Bake in a hot oven until golden brown. Remove from oven and gently lift off center cap. Remove any soft pastry from inside and return to oven for 1 minute to dry out. To help prevent pastry from toppling over, 4 wooden picks may be placed at equal intervals around outside circle, and removed after cooking. Melt butter in pan. Stir in flour and cook for 1 minute. Remove from heat and gradually stir in chicken stock. Return to heat, bring to the boil, and cook for 3 minutes, stirring continuously. Stir in shrimp, tomato paste, tarragon vinegar or lemon juice, sugar and salt and pepper to taste. Simmer for a further 3 minutes. Fill bouchées with hot shrimp filling. Place lids on top at an angle. Serve hot.

Mushroom Bouchées (Patty Shells)

PREPARATION TIME: 30 minutes

COOKING TIME: 20 minutes

OVEN TEMPERATURE: 425°F (210°C)

SERVES: 4 people

8oz frozen puff pastry, thawed
1 egg, beaten

Filling
4 tbsps butter or margarine
3 tbsps flour
1¼ cups chicken stock
Salt
Pepper
8oz mushrooms
1 onion, peeled and chopped finely
2 tbsps cream
1 tsp chopped parsley

Garnish
Chopped parsley

On a lightly floured board roll out pastry to about ¼" thick. Using a 3" fluted pastry-cutter, cut out pastry. With a 2" fluted pastry-cutter mark center of each, being careful not to cut right through. Brush with beaten egg, being careful not to get any down sides or in groove made by 2" cutter, as this will prevent rising. Place on a dampened baking sheet and chill in refrigerator for 15 minutes. Make pattern on outer circle with back of knife if desired. Bake in a hot oven until golden brown. Remove from oven and gently lift off center cap. Remove any soft pastry from inside, and return to oven for 1 minute to dry out. To help prevent pastry from toppling over, 4 wooden picks may be placed at equal intervals around outside circle and removed after cooking. Wash mushrooms. Chop half of them very finely, the remainder roughly. Melt butter in pan. Add roughly-chopped mushrooms and cook for 3 minutes. Remove with slotted spoon and set aside. Add onion to pan and, after a minute, finely chopped mushrooms. Cook for 4 minutes. Stir in flour and cook for 1 minute. Remove from heat and gradually stir in chicken stock. Return to heat, bring to the boil and cook for 3 minutes, stirring continuously. Add cream, rough-chopped mushrooms, parsley and salt and pepper and simmer for 1 minute. Fill bouchées with hot mushroom filling. Sprinkle with parsley and place lids on top at an angle. Serve hot.

Quiche Lorraine

PREPARATION TIME: 30 minutes

COOKING TIME: 45 minutes

OVEN TEMPERATURE: 370°F (190°C)

SERVES: 6 people

Pastry
1 cup flour
Pinch of salt
⅓ cup butter or margarine
1 tbsp lard
Cold water

Filling
1 tbsp butter or margarine
2 eggs, beaten
¼ cup Gruyère or Cheddar cheese, grated
⅔ cup light cream
10 green onions, cut into 2" slices
½ tsp dried mustard
4 rashers bacon
Salt
Pepper

Sift flour and salt into a bowl. Cut cold fat into small pieces and drop into flour. Cut fat into flour. When well cut in, use fingers to rub in completely. Mix to a firm but pliable dough with cold water. Knead on a lightly floured board until smooth. Chill for 15 minutes in the refrigerator. Roll out on a lightly floured board and line a 9" flan ring. Melt butter in frying pan and add bacon and green onions, and fry gently until turning a light golden-brown color. Place in a bowl. Add beaten eggs, cheese, cream, mustard and salt and pepper to taste, and stir well. Pour into prepared pastry shell. Bake in oven for 20-25 minutes until golden brown. Serve hot or cold.

Cheese Puffs

PREPARATION TIME: 20 minutes

COOKING TIME: 20 minutes

OVEN TEMPERATURES: 375°F (190°C) 400°F (200°C)

SERVES: 4 people

Pastry
½ cup flour
Pinch of salt
5 tbsps butter or margarine
1 cup water
3 medium eggs, lightly beaten

Filling
½ cup Gruyère cheese, grated
½ cup Emmenthal cheese, grated
1 egg, beaten
2 tsps kirsch
1 egg yolk, beaten, for glaze

Pre-set oven to 375°F or equivalent. Sift flour and salt onto a sheet of wax paper. Place butter and water in pan over gentle heat. When butter has melted, bring to boil and straightaway add all flour. Beat well until mixture is smooth. Leave to cool. Add eggs gradually to mixture, beating well. Using a teaspoon or a pastry bag with a plain tube, shape mixture into balls about the size of golf balls onto a lightly greased baking sheet. Place in oven and increase heat to 400°F or equivalent. Bake for 10 minutes until firm on outside. Remove from oven and make a hole in bottom or side. Mix together cheese, egg and kirsch. Pipe in cheese mixture and brush tops with egg-yolk. Return to oven for 5 minutes. Serve immediately.

Roquefort Tarts

PREPARATION TIME: 30 minutes

COOKING TIME: 20 minutes

OVEN TEMPERATURE: 375°F (190°C)

SERVES: 4 people

Pastry
1 cup flour
Pinch of salt
⅓ cup butter or margarine
1 tbsp lard
Cold water

Filling
1 cup Roquefort cheese
1 cup cream cheese
2 tbsps light cream
2 eggs, lightly beaten

Sift salt and flour into a bowl. Cut cold fat into small pieces and drop into flour. Cut fat into flour. When well cut in, use fingers to rub in completely. Mix to a firm but pliable dough with cold water. Knead on a lightly floured board until smooth. Chill for 15 minutes in the refrigerator. Meanwhile, gently melt together Roquefort cheese and cream cheese in a pan, stirring continuously. When melted, set aside to cool. Mix together cream and beaten eggs, and add to cheese mixture, stirring well. Roll out dough on a lightly floured board. Using a 3" fluted pastry-cutter, cut out rounds of pastry. Line a muffin pan. Prick bottom of pastry shells with a fork. Spoon mixture into individual pastry shells and bake in the oven for about 15 minutes until golden brown.

Chicken and Ham Crêpes

PREPARATION TIME: 5 minutes

COOKING TIME: 30 minutes

OVEN TEMPERATURE: 400°F (200°C)

SERVES: 4-6 people

Crêpe Batter
1 cup flour
Pinch of salt
2 medium eggs
1 cup milk
1 tbsp olive oil or vegetable oil
Oil to grease pan

Filling
2 chicken breasts, cooked and shredded
2 slices ham, shredded
1 tsp Dijon mustard
2 tbsps grated Cheddar or Gruyère cheese

4 tbsps butter or margarine
3 tbsps flour
1¼ cups milk
Salt
Pepper

Garnish
Parsley

Sift flour and salt into a bowl. Make a well in the center and drop in eggs. Start to mix in eggs gradually, taking in flour around edges. When becoming stiff, add a little milk until all flour has been incorporated. Beat to a smooth batter, then add remaining milk. Stir in oil. Cover bowl, and leave in a cool place for 30 minutes. Heat small frying pan, or 7" crêpe pan. Wipe over with oil. When hot, add enough batter mixture to cover base of pan when rolled. Pour off any excess batter. When brown on underside, loosen and turn over with a spatula, and brown on other side. Pile on a plate and cover with a clean towel until needed. Melt butter in pan. Stir in flour and cook for 1 minute. Remove from heat and gradually stir in milk. Return to heat, bring to the boil, and cook for 3 minutes, stirring continuously. Add cheese, chicken, ham and Dijon mustard, and salt and pepper and stir until heated through. Do not re-boil. Divide the mixture evenly between the pancakes and roll up or fold into triangles. Place in a baking dish and cover with aluminum foil. Heat in a hot oven for 10 minutes. Garnish with parsley. Serve immediately.

Mushroom Bouchées (Patty Shells) (left) and Quiche Lorraine (bottom).

Seafood Crêpes

PREPARATION TIME: 45 minutes

COOKING TIME: 20 minutes

OVEN TEMPERATURE: 400°F (200°C)

SERVES: 4-6 people

Crêpe Batter

1 cup flour
Pinch of salt
2 medium eggs
1 cup milk
1 tbsp olive oil or vegetable oil
Oil to grease pan

Filling

4oz shrimp, peeled and de-veined
2 scallops, cleaned and sliced
4oz white fish fillets
Squeeze of lemon juice
1 tbsp lemon juice
8 green onions, sliced

4 tbsps butter or margarine
3 tbsps flour
1¼ cups milk
Salt
Pepper

Sift flour and salt into a bowl. Make a well in the center and drop in eggs. Start to mix in eggs gradually, taking in flour around edges. When becoming stiff, add a little milk until all flour has been incorporated. Beat to a smooth batter, then add remaining milk. Stir in oil. Cover bowl and leave in a cool place for 30 minutes. Heat small frying pan or 7" crêpe pan. Wipe over with oil. When hot, add enough batter mixture to cover base of pan when rolled. Pour off any excess batter. When brown on underside, loosen and turn over with a spatula and brown on other side. Pile on a plate and cover with a clean towel until needed. Poach scallops and fish in water with a squeeze of lemon juice for 4 minutes or until cooked through. Melt butter in pan. Add green onions and cook for 3 minutes. Remove with slotted spoon and set aside. Stir in the flour and cook for 1 minute. Remove from heat and gradually stir in milk. Return to heat, bring to the boil, and cook for 3 minutes, stirring continuously. Add green onions, seafood and lemon juice, and salt and pepper and stir well until heated through. Do not re-boil. Divide the mixture evenly between the pancakes and roll up or fold into triangles. Place in a baking dish and cover with aluminum foil. Heat in a hot oven for 10 minutes. Serve immediately.

This page: Egg and Fish Flan.

Facing page: Chicken and Ham Crêpes (top) and Seafood Crêpes (bottom).

Egg and Fish Flan

PREPARATION TIME: 30 minutes
COOKING TIME: 45 minutes
OVEN TEMPERATURE: 375°F (190°C)
SERVES: 6 people

Pastry
1 cup flour
Pinch of salt
⅓ cup butter or margarine
1 tbsp lard
Cold water

Filling
2 eggs, beaten
8oz white fish fillets
6-8 anchovies, drained
10 black olives, halved and stones removed
2 tbsps light cream
1 tbsp lemon juice
1 bay leaf
6 peppercorns
Parsley stalks
Slice of onion
1¼ cups cold water
1 onion peeled and chopped
4 tbsps butter
3 tbsps flour
Salt
Pepper

Poach fish in 1¼ cups water, with lemon juice, peppercorns, bay leaf, slice of onion and parsley stalks, for 10 minutes or until just cooked. Remove from poaching liquid. Strain, reserving liquid, and cool. Melt butter in pan. Add onion and fry gently until softened. Stir in flour and cook for 1 minute. Draw off heat and gradually stir in reserved liquid, stirring continuously. Add salt and pepper to taste. Return to heat and cook for 3 minutes. Set aside to cool. Sift salt and flour into a bowl. Cut cold fat into small pieces and drop into flour. Cut fat into flour. When well cut in, use fingers to rub in completely. Mix to a firm but pliable dough with cold water. Knead on a lightly floured board until smooth. Chill for 15 minutes in the refrigerator. Roll out on a lightly floured board and line a 9" flan ring. Flake fish and place in bottom of prepared pastry shell. Stir cream into lightly beaten egg. Add mixture to sauce gradually, and pour over fish. Arrange anchovies in a lattice over top, with a piece of olive in the center of each diamond. Bake in oven for 20-25 minutes until golden brown. Serve hot or cold.

Section 2

FISH AND SEAFOOD

Fish Soups and Appetizers

Chilled Shrimp, Avocado and Cucumber Soup

PREPARATION TIME: 15 minutes
COOKING TIME: 15 minutes
SERVES: 4 people

8oz unpeeled shrimp
1 large ripe avocado
1 small cucumber
1 small bunch dill
Juice of half a lemon
1¼ cups chicken stock
2½ cups plain yogurt
Salt and pepper

Peel all shrimp, reserving shells. Add shells to chicken stock and bring to boil. Allow to simmer for about 15 minutes. Cool and strain. Peel avocado and cut it into pieces. Cut 8 thin slices from the cucumber and peel the rest. Remove seeds and chop the cucumber roughly. Put avocado and cucumber into a food processor or blender and process until smooth. Add a squeeze of lemon juice, and strain on the cold chicken stock. Reserve a sprig of dill for garnish, and add the rest to the mixture in the processor and blend again. Add about 2 cups of yogurt to the processor and blend until smooth. Add salt and pepper. Stir in peeled shrimp by hand, reserving a few as garnish. Chill soup well. Serve in individual bowls, garnished with a spoonful of yogurt, a sprig of dill, and thinly sliced rounds of cucumber.

Matelote

PREPARATION TIME: 20 minutes
COOKING TIME: 20 minutes
SERVES: 4 people

1lb sole
1lb monkfish
1 small wing of skate
1 quart mussels
8oz unpeeled shrimp
3 onions
6 tbsps butter
1⅔ cups dry cider or white wine
2 tbsps flour
2 tbsps chopped parsley
Salt
Freshly ground black pepper
Lemon juice

Fillet and skin sole. Cut fillets into large pieces. Cut monkfish similarly. Chop wing of skate into 4 large pieces. Peel shrimp and set aside. Scrub mussels well, discarding any with broken shells. Chop onion finely and soften in half the butter. Add mussels and about 3-4 tbsps water. Cover the pan and shake over a high heat until all mussels have opened, discarding any that have not. Strain liquid into a bowl, allow mussels to cool, then shell them. Put cooking liquid back into pan. Add wine or cider, and the pieces of fish so that they are barely covered by the liquid. Simmer gently for about 8 minutes or until

This page: Chilled Shrimp, Avocado and Cucumber Soup (top) and Matelote (bottom).

Facing page: Devilled Stuffed Crab (top) and Soufflés St. Jacques (bottom).

fish is just cooked. Mix flour with remaining butter to a paste. Remove cooked fish from liquid and put into a serving dish to keep warm. Bring liquid back to boil.

Add flour and butter paste, a little at a time, whisking it in and allowing liquid to boil after each addition, until liquid is thickened. Add parsley, shelled prawns, shelled mussels, a little lemon juice, and seasoning. Heat for a few minutes to warm shellfish through. Pour over fish in serving dish and sprinkle with more chopped parsley if desired.

Devilled Stuffed Crab

PREPARATION TIME: 10-15 minutes

COOKING TIME: 20 minutes

OVEN TEMPERATURE: 375°F (190°C)

SERVES: 4 people

2 cooked crabs
¼ cup shelled pistachio nuts
2 hard-boiled eggs
1 tbsp flour
1 tbsp butter
1¼ cups milk
1 green pepper
1 medium onion
2 tbsps chili sauce or hamburger relish
2 tsps white wine vinegar
2 tsps chopped dill pickles
1 tsp Dijon mustard
½ tsp Worcestershire sauce
Tabasco
3 tbsps butter or margarine
4 tbsps dry breadcrumbs
Chopped parsley
Salt
Pepper

Garnish
Lemon wedges
Watercress

Buy the crabs already cleaned. If you wish to do it yourself, twist off all the legs, separate body from shell, and remove lungs and stomach. Cut body into 3 or 4 pieces with a sharp knife and pick out all the meat. Scrape brown meat from inside shell; crack large claws and remove meat, adding add all this meat to the body meat. Crab shells may be washed and used to bake in. Prepare cream sauce. Melt 1 tbsp butter in a small saucepan. When foaming, take it off the heat and stir in flour, then the milk, gradually. Mix well. Return to heat and bring to boil, allowing it to thicken. Set aside to cool slightly. Chop egg roughly, and green pepper and onion into small dice. Break up crabmeat roughly. Chop pistachio nuts, and add all other ingredients to the white sauce. Lightly butter the clean shell or individual baking dishes. Fill with crabmeat mixture and top with dry crumbs. Melt 3 tbsps butter and sprinkle over top of crumbs. Bake for 15 minutes, and brown under broiler if necessary. Sprinkle with chopped parsley and garnish with watercress and lemon wedges.

Soufflés St. Jacques

PREPARATION TIME: 20 minutes

COOKING TIME: 20 minutes

OVEN TEMPERATURE: 450°F (225°C)

SERVES: 4 people

8 large or 16 small scallops, with roe attached (if possible)
1¼ cups milk
2½ tbsps butter
2½ tbsps flour
2½ tbsps grated Cheddar cheese
4 eggs
Salt
Pepper
¼ tsp Dijon mustard

Tomato Sauce
1¾ cups canned tomatoes
1 small onion, finely chopped
Bay leaf
Pinch of thyme
Sugar
Half a clove of garlic, crushed
1 tbsp Worcestershire sauce
Salt
Pepper

First prepare tomato sauce. Combine onion with rest of the ingredients in a small, heavy saucepan. Bring to the boil, then lower heat, leaving to simmer, half-covered, for 20 minutes. Strain the sauce and set aside. Poach scallops in milk for about 5 minutes. Remove from milk and set aside. Melt butter in a small saucepan, and when foaming remove from heat, and stir in flour. Add milk in which scallops were poached. Bring to the boil, stirring constantly until thickened. Add salt and pepper, then stir in the grated cheese. Leave to cool slightly. Separate eggs, beat the yolks and add them to cheese sauce. Butter 4 deep scallop shells or porcelain baking dishes. Slice scallops through the middle, horizontally. Reserve 1 whole roe per serving. Place scallops in bottom of the shells. Beat egg whites until stiff but not dry, and fold into cheese mixture. Divide soufflé mixture between the scallop shells, and place them on a baking tray. Bake in a hot oven for about 10 minutes or until well risen. Meanwhile, re-heat tomato sauce and spoon some of it, when scallops are ready, into each dish. Serve remaining tomato sauce separately. Garnish each serving with the reserved whole roe.

Garlic Fried Scallops

PREPARATION TIME: 10 minutes

COOKING TIME: 6-8 minutes

SERVES: 4 people

16 scallops
1 large clove garlic, peeled and chopped finely
4 tbsps butter
3 tbsps chopped parsley
2 lemons
Seasoned flour

Rinse scallops and remove black veins. If scallops are large, cut in half horizontally. Squeeze the juice from 1 lemon. Sprinkle scallops lightly with seasoned flour. Heat butter in a frying pan and add chopped garlic and scallops. Fry until pale golden brown. Pour over lemon juice, and cook to reduce the amount of liquid. Toss in the chopped parsley. Pile scallops into individual scallop shells or porcelain baking dishes. Keep warm, and garnish with lemon wedges before serving.

Langoustine and Avocado Cocktail

PREPARATION TIME: 20 minutes

SERVES: 4 people

8oz cooked langoustines or large shrimp
2 oranges
2 large, ripe avocados
1 small red onion or 2 green onions
¼ cup whipping cream
2 tbsps ketchup
2 tbsps mayonnaise
2 tsps lemon juice
12 (approx) black olives, stoned and sliced
2 tsps brandy
Pinch of Cayenne pepper
Pinch sugar
Salt
Freshly ground pepper
Lettuce

Peel oranges over a bowl to reserve juice. Peel cooked langoustines and set aside. To prepare dressing, whip cream until thick, and mix with ketchup, mayonnaise, lemon juice, Cayenne, sugar, salt and pepper, brandy and some of the reserved orange juice to let down to the proper consistency – the dressing should be slightly thick. Chop onion finely. Cut avocados in half lengthwise and take out stones. Peel them carefully and cut each half into 4-6 long slices. Shred lettuce and put onto serving dishes. Arrange avocado slices in a fan shape on top of the lettuce. Brush each slice lightly with orange juice to keep green. Arrange an orange segment in between each slice. Pile langoustines up at the top of the avocado fan and coat with some of the dressing. Garnish with olives and sprinkle over chopped onion.

Quenelles au Beurre Blanc

PREPARATION TIME: 25 minutes

COOKING TIME: 20 minutes

SERVES: 4 people

1lb pike or other white fish
2 cups white breadcrumbs
4 tbsps milk
6 tbsps butter
2 eggs
Salt
Pepper
Nutmeg
Cayenne pepper

Beurre Blanc Sauce
½ cup unsalted butter
1 small onion, peeled and chopped finely
1 tbsp white wine vinegar
2 tbsps lemon juice
3 tbsps dry white wine
1 tsp snipped chives
Salt

Vegetable Garnish
1 medium zucchini, topped and tailed
1 leek, trimmed, with some green attached
1 carrot, peeled
1 stick celery, washed and trimmed

First prepare quenelle mixture. Skin and bone fish and cut into small pieces. Place in a food processor bowl. Soak the breadcrumbs in milk; drain away most of the liquid, and put into the food processor with the fish. Melt butter and pour into the fish mixture with the machine running. Work mixture to a smooth purée. Add eggs, continuing to mix until smooth. Add salt and pepper, cayenne pepper and nutmeg. Chill mixture in refrigerator for at least 1 hour, or overnight.

Garlic Fried Scallops (right) and Langoustine and Avocado Cocktail (below).

To cook quenelles, fill a sauté pan with salted water. Bring to the boil. Reduce heat until water is just simmering. With two spoons, shape quenelles into little ovals. Poach them in water for about 6 minutes, turning them over about half way through. Remove them with a slotted spoon. Drain and put them in a dish to keep warm in the oven, covered. To prepare beurre blanc sauce, put chopped onion into a small saucepan with the vinegar and wine. Bring to boil and allow to reduce by half. Remove pan from heat, and allow to cool a little. Cut butter into small pieces and add to onion mixture, a little at a time, whisking well to a creamy sauce. After 2-3 pieces have been added, place pan back over low heat and continue whisking until all butter has been added. Season the sauce, add lemon juice, strain, add the snipped chives and serve hot over quenelles.

To prepare garnish, cut all vegetables into 2" lengths, then cut those into thin strips. Bring water in a large saucepan to the boil, with a pinch of salt. Cook carrots for about 5 minutes. Then add celery strips and cook for another 5 minutes. Add zucchini and leek, and cook for 3 minutes more. Drain vegetables well, add them to the sauce and pour over the quenelles to serve.

This page: Cucumbers and Shrimp (top) and Quenelles au Beurre Blanc (bottom). Facing page: Marinated Smoked Fish (top) and Mussels in Lemon Cream (bottom).

Cucumbers and Shrimp

PREPARATION TIME: 20 minutes

SERVES: 4 people

1 large or 2 small cucumbers
8oz unpeeled shrimp
¼ cup heavy cream
¼ cup plain yogurt
½ tsp Dijon mustard
Juice of 1 lemon
1 tbsp chopped parsley
Pinch sugar
Large bunch of chervil, chopped, but reserving some whole for garnish
1 head of red chicory
1 head of Romaine lettuce
Salt and pepper

Peel cucumber and slice in half lengthwise. Scoop out seeds and cut each half into thin slices. Sprinkle slices with salt and leave to drain for about 1 hour. Peel shrimp, reserving 4 unpeeled for garnish. Whip cream lightly and fold together with yogurt, mustard, 1 tsp of the lemon juice, parsley and chervil. Add seasoning and sugar, and mix the dressing together with the shrimp. Wash salt from cucumber, and dry slices well. Divide lettuce and chicory between 4 serving plates and toss cucumber together with the shrimp. Peel shells from the tails of the reserved shrimp, and set aside. Pile cucumber and shrimp mixture onto lettuce leaves and garnish with reserved shrimp and whole sprigs of chervil.

Mussels in Lemon Cream

PREPARATION TIME: 10 minutes

COOKING TIME: 10 minutes

SERVES: 4 people

1 quart mussels
Grated rind and juice of 2 lemons
1 shallot, finely chopped
1¼ cups heavy cream
2 tbsps chopped parsley
Flour or oatmeal
2 tbsps butter

Scrub mussels well, discarding any with broken shells. Put into a bowl with clean, cold water, and add a handful of flour or oatmeal. Leave for ½ hour, then drain mussels under clean water. Put the butter and finely chopped shallot into a large pan and cook until shallot is soft, but not colored. Add lemon juice, then mussels. Cover and cook quickly, shaking the pan until mussel shells open. Discard any that do not open. Remove mussels and keep them warm. Strain the liquid and return it to the rinsed-out pan. Add the cream and bring to the boil. Allow to boil for 5 minutes to thicken slightly. Pour over the mussels, and sprinkle grated lemon rind and chopped parsley over.

Marinated Smoked Fish

PREPARATION TIME: 10 minutes, plus 1 hour to marinate

SERVES: 4 people

1 kippered herring
4oz smoked salmon
1 large fillet of smoked sable
1 large whole smoked trout
¼ cup vegetable oil
Juice of 1 large lemon

1 tbsp white wine vinegar
1 red onion, sliced
Lettuce
Parsley
Salt and pepper

Remove skin from kipper and sable, and cut each into 8 pieces. Fillet and skin the trout, and cut each fillet into 4 pieces. Shred the smoked salmon. Put fish into a large, shallow dish. Scatter onion slices on top of the fish. Mix oil, lemon juice and vinegar together. Add salt and pepper, and pour over fish. Leave to marinate for at least 1 hour. Serve on a bed of lettuce with some of the onions from the marinade, and chopped parsley. Other varieties of smoked fish may be substituted.

Solianka

PREPARATION TIME: 10 minutes
COOKING TIME: 1 hour 10 minutes
SERVES: 4 people

2lbs fish bones
1½lbs salmon or salmon trout
1¼ cups canned tomatoes
5 cups water
1 onion, roughly chopped
1 stick celery, roughly chopped
1 carrot, roughly chopped
1 small bunch green onions
4 small dill pickles
2 tbsps capers
1 tbsp chopped black olives
1 bay leaf
Salt and pepper
⅔ cup sour cream

Garnish
1 small jar black caviar

Cook fishbones in water with the carrot, celery and onion. Add bay leaf, and simmer for about 1 hour. Drain off stock and reserve. Add tomatoes to stock. Chop spring onions, pickles, olives and capers. Cut salmon into 1" cubes, add to stock, season and cover. Simmer for 10-12 minutes or until salmon is cooked. Put soup into warm serving dishes and top with sour cream and black caviar.

Oyster Bisque

PREPARATION TIME: 10 minutes
COOKING TIME: 27 minutes
SERVES: 4 people

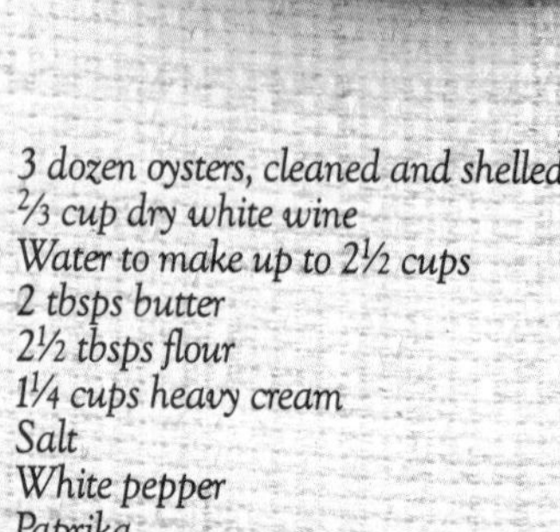

3 dozen oysters, cleaned and shelled
⅔ cup dry white wine
Water to make up to 2½ cups
2 tbsps butter
2½ tbsps flour
1¼ cups heavy cream
Salt
White pepper
Paprika
Squeeze of lemon juice

Chop oysters roughly, reserving 4 for garnish. Put chopped oysters and their liquid into a medium saucepan with the water and wine. Bring to boil and allow to simmer for 15 minutes. Blend, and measure the amount of liquid. Reduce, or add water, to make 1 pint. Melt 1½ tbsps butter in a saucepan and when foaming, remove from heat and add flour. Cook flour and butter together for about 1 minute until very pale brown. Add oyster liquid gradually.
Stir well, bring back to boil and simmer gently for about 10 minutes. Season with salt, a pinch of paprika and a good pinch of white pepper. Add heavy cream, return to heat and allow to boil for 1-2 minutes. Add lemon juice, if desired. Cook reserved oysters

quickly in remaining butter. Put soup into warm serving dishes. Top each with 1 oyster and a sprinkling of paprika.

Mussels alla Genovese

PREPARATION TIME: 15 minutes
COOKING TIME: 5-8 minutes
SERVES: 4 people

1 quart mussels
Lemon juice
1 shallot, finely chopped
1 handful fresh basil leaves
1 small bunch parsley
4-5 walnut halves
1 clove garlic
2 tbsps freshly grated Parmesan cheese
3-6 tbsps olive oil
2 tbsps butter

Solianka (above), Oyster Bisque (right) and Mussels alla Genovese.

Salt and pepper
Flour or oatmeal

Garnish
Fresh bay leaves or basil leaves

Scrub the mussels well and discard any with broken shells. Put mussels into a bowl of clean water with a handful of flour or oatmeal. Leave for ½ hour, then rinse under clear water. Chop shallot finely and put into a large saucepan with lemon juice. Cook until shallot softens. Add mussels and a pinch of salt and pepper. Cover the pan and cook the mussels quickly, shaking the pan. When mussel shells have opened, take mussels out of the pan, set aside and keep warm. Strain the cooking liquid for possible use later. To prepare Genovese sauce, wash the basil leaves and parsley, peel the garlic clove and chop roughly, and chop the walnuts roughly. Put the herbs, garlic, nuts, 1 tbsp grated cheese and salt and pepper into a food processor and work to chop roughly. Add butter and work again. Turn machine on and add oil gradually through the feed tube. If the sauce is still too thick, add the reserved liquid from cooking the mussels. Remove top shells from mussels and discard. Arrange mussels evenly in 4 shallow dishes, spoon some of the sauce into each, and sprinkle the top lightly with remaining Parmesan cheese. Garnish with bay or basil leaves and serve.

Broiled Oysters

PREPARATION TIME: 10 minutes
COOKING TIME: 2-3 minutes
SERVES: 4 people

2 doz oysters
4 tbsps butter
1¼ cups heavy cream
1 small jar red caviar
Salt
Pepper
Tabasco

Garnish
Watercress

Open oysters and leave them in their half-shells. Put a drop of Tabasco on each oyster, season, then 2 tsps of heavy cream. Melt butter and sprinkle it over oysters. Put them under a hot broiler for 2-3 minutes. When cooked, top each one with 1 tsp red caviar, and serve hot with bouquets of watercress as garnish.

Green Beans, Hazelnuts and Langoustines

PREPARATION TIME: 15 minutes
COOKING TIME: 19-21 minutes
OVEN TEMPERATURE: 350°F (180°C)
SERVES: 4 people

1lb green beans, trimmed
¾lb cooked langoustines or large shrimp
¼ cup whole hazelnuts, skinned
1 red pepper, stem and seeds removed, and sliced thinly
⅓ cup olive oil
3 tbsps white wine vinegar
1 tsp Dijon mustard
1 tbsp chopped parsley
1 small head iceberg lettuce, shredded
Salt
Pepper

Toast hazelnuts in moderate oven for about 15 minutes or until golden brown. Allow to cool. Chop roughly. Bring salted water to the boil in a saucepan, and cook beans in it for about 4-6 minutes – they should remain crisp. Drain, refresh under cold water, drain again and dry. Cook pepper slices in boiling water for about 1 minute. Drain and refresh under cold water, and allow to dry. Whisk oil, vinegar, Dijon mustard and seasonings together. Peel

This page: Devilled Whitebait (Smelts) (top) and Green Beans, Hazelnuts and Langoustines (bottom).
Facing page: Broiled Oysters (top) and Crab and Citrus (bottom).

langoustines, and mix together with beans, pepper, hazelnuts and dressing. Arrange lettuce on individual serving dishes, and pile remaining ingredients on top. Sprinkle parsley over the top to serve.

Smoked Salmon Stuffed Cucumbers

PREPARATION TIME: 15 minutes

SERVES: 4 people

4oz smoked salmon
1 8oz package cream cheese
1 large cucumber
1 head iceberg lettuce
1 bunch chives
1 bunch dill
⅔ cup plain yogurt
2 tbsps whipping cream
Squeeze of lemon juice
Salt
Pepper

Garnish
1 tsp red salmon caviar

Peel cucumber and trim off the ends. Cut in half lengthwise and scoop out the seeds. Sprinkle the surface with salt and leave on paper towels for 1 hour. Meanwhile, prepare the filling. Work the smoked salmon and the cream cheese in a food processor until smooth. Snip the chives and stir in by hand. Prepare the dressing by mixing the yogurt, whipping cream and finely chopped dill together with salt, pepper and lemon juice to taste. Rinse and dry the cucumber very well. Using a pastry bag fitted with a ½" plain tube, fill the bag with the smoked salmon mixture and pipe the filling into the hollow left in the cucumber. Put the other half on top, press together firmly, and wrap tightly in plastic wrap. Chill in the refrigerator for 1 hour. Separate the lettuce leaves, wash and dry well, and place on individual serving dishes. Unwrap the cucumber and slice into ½" slices. Place on top of lettuce. Spoon over some of the dressing and top with caviar. Serve the rest of the dressing separately.

Devilled Whitebait (Smelt)

PREPARATION TIME: 10 minutes

COOKING TIME: 5-6 minutes

SERVES: 4 people

1lb whitebait (smelt)
Flour
Salt
Pepper
¼ tsp Cayenne pepper
¼ tsp dry mustard
1 large pinch ground ginger
Paprika
Oil for deep frying

Garnish
Lemon wedges
Parsley

Pick over, but do not wash, fish. Mix flour with salt, pepper, Cayenne, ginger and mustard, and roll whitebait in mixture until lightly coated. Heat oil in deep-fat fryer to 350°F (180°C). Put small amount of floured fish into frying basket, lower into the fat, and fry for 2-3 minutes. Drain on crumpled paper towels. Sprinkle lightly with salt, and continue until all fish are fried. Re-heat fat, and add all fish. Fry for 1-2 minutes until crisp. Turn out onto hot serving dish. Sprinkle with salt and paprika. Serve at once with lemon wedges and bouquets of parsley.

Crab and Citrus

PREPARATION TIME: 20 minutes

SERVES: 4 people

8oz crabmeat, or 1 large crab
2 oranges
2 lemons
2 limes
1 pink grapefruit
1 small iceberg lettuce
⅔ cup plain yogurt
⅓ cup heavy cream
1 tbsp chili sauce
½ tbsp brandy
Pinch of Cayenne pepper
Salt
2 tbsps salad oil

Separate body from shell of whole crab, and remove and discard lungs and stomach sac. Chop body into 3 or 4 pieces with a very sharp knife and pick out the meat. Scrape brown meat from inside shell and add to body meat. Break off large claws and remove meat from legs; then crack the claws and remove claw meat. Mix all meat together and reserve legs for garnish. (If using canned or frozen crabmeat, pick over the meat to remove any bits of shell or cartilage.) Mix together yogurt, chili sauce, cream, brandy, Cayenne pepper and a pinch of salt, and toss with the crabmeat. Take a thin strip of peel from each of the citrus fruits, scraping off the bitter white pith. Cut each strip of peel into thin slivers. Put into boiling water and allow to boil for about 1 minute. Drain, refresh under cold water, and set aside. Peel each of the citrus fruits and cut into segments; do all this over a bowl to reserve juices. Add 2 tbsps salad oil to the juice in the bowl, and toss with citrus segments. Shred iceberg lettuce and arrange on plates. Put the crabmeat in its dressing on top of lettuce. Arrange citrus segments over and around crabmeat and sprinkle citrus peel over the top.

Lobster à la Creme

PREPARATION TIME: 10 minutes

COOKING TIME: 5 minutes

SERVES: 4 people

1 cold, boiled lobster
1¼ cups heavy cream
4 tbsps butter
¼ cup dry sherry or Madeira
Squeeze of lemon juice
Ground nutmeg
3 tbsps dry breadcrumbs
1 small bunch of tarragon, chopped
Salt and pepper

Cut lobster in half lengthwise with a sharp knife. Remove meat from tail. Crack claws and remove meat. Remove as much meat as possible from all the legs. Chop all meat roughly. Melt 3 tbsps of the butter in a sauté pan and sauté the lobster with the seasonings, lemon juice, nutmeg and tarragon. Flame the sherry or Madeira and pour over the lobster in the sauté pan. Shake the pan until flames die out. Pour over heavy cream and bring to the boil. Allow to boil for 5 minutes until cream begins to thicken. Spoon into individual serving dishes. Melt remaining butter in a small frying pan and brown the dry breadcrumbs. When golden brown and crisp, sprinkle over the top of lobster.

Shrimp and Watercress Bisque

PREPARATION TIME: 20 minutes

COOKING TIME: 25 minutes

SERVES: 4 people

2½ cups plain yogurt
2 medium potatoes
½ clove garlic
2 bunches watercress
butter
8oz cod or other white fish
16 (approx) unpeeled shrimp
Milk
Salt
White pepper

Shell all the shrimp, and reserve shells. Place cod in a pan with enough water to cover. Bring to boil, reduce heat and allow to simmer for about 5 minutes. Remove fish from pan and peel the skin away. Reserve the liquid. Return cod skin to pan with the shells from the shrimp. Cook for a few minutes and leave to cool. Meanwhile, peel and cook potatoes until tender, and mash with a little milk and the butter. Pick over watercress, discarding any yellow leaves and root ends. Reserve small sprigs of leaves for garnish and chop the rest roughly. Reserve 4 tbsps yogurt per serving for garnish. Put remaining yogurt, potatoes, salt, pepper, garlic and watercress into the bowl of a food processor. Add skinned cod and strain in fish liquid, discarding skin and shrimp shells. Work until to the consistency of thick cream, using as much milk as necessary. When soup is smooth and desired consistency is reached, put into a clean saucepan and warm gently – do not allow to boil. Put into warm soup bowls or tureen to serve. Garnish with a spoonful of yogurt, peeled shrimp and watercress leaves.

Chinese Crabmeat Soup

PREPARATION TIME: 10 minutes

COOKING TIME: 10 minutes

SERVES: 4 people

4oz crabmeat
Small piece fresh ginger
2 tbsps light soy sauce
2¾ cups light chicken stock
4 green onions
1 piece of to-fu or soy bean curd, well drained
2 tsps cornstarch
1 tsp sesame seed oil
1 tbsp dry sherry
Salt
Pepper

Smoked Salmon Stuffed Cucumbers (below) and Lobster à la Creme (bottom).

Heat oil in medium-sized saucepan, and fry crabmeat for about a minute. Peel and grate ginger, and add it to pan with sherry, salt and pepper and soy sauce. Stir together and add stock, reserving about 2 tbsps to mix with the cornstarch. Bring soup to boil. Add a little of the boiling liquid to the cornstarch mixture, then add to the soup. Stir until slightly thickened. Slice green onions on a slant and add to soup. Slice bean curd into ½" cubes, add to the soup, and heat through with the sesame seed oil. Serve.

Soupe de Poisson Provençal

PREPARATION TIME: 20 minutes

COOKING TIME: 30-40 minutes

SERVES: 4 people

Soup

3lbs white fish
8oz shrimp
1 large onion
2 leeks
5 cups canned tomatoes
2 cloves garlic
1 bay leaf
1 sprig thyme
1 small piece fennel or 2 parsley stalks
2 pinches saffron
Strip of orange rind
⅔ cup white wine
2 tbsps butter
2 tbsps flour
⅔ cup olive oil
5 cups water
Salt
Pepper
Tomato paste
Cream

Sauce Rouille

½ cup chopped red pepper or canned pimento
1 small chili pepper
3-4 tbsps fresh breadcrumbs
3 cloves garlic
1 egg yolk
⅔ cup olive oil
Salt
Pepper

Accompaniment

Grated Parmesan cheese
Croûtons

First prepare soup. Chop onion. Clean and chop leeks, and cook them slowly, with the onion, in the olive oil until tender, but not browned. Mash garlic cloves and add to leeks and onion, along with the canned tomatoes. Bring to the boil and cook for 5 minutes. Meanwhile, skin and bone fish, shell shrimp , and tie the bay leaf, thyme, fennel and orange peel together with a small piece of string. Put the water, wine, the bundle of herbs, the saffron, salt and pepper, fish and shellfish into the pan and cook, uncovered, on a moderate heat for 30-40 minutes. Meanwhile, prepare Sauce Rouille. Cut chili pepper in half and rinse out seeds. Use half or all, depending on desired hotness. Chop chili pepper together with sweet red pepper. Peel and chop garlic. Soak breadcrumbs in water and press them dry. Put peppers, breadcrumbs, garlic and egg yolk into a blender with a pinch of salt and pepper and blend to a smooth paste, or work together with mortar and pestle. Gradually add oil in a thin, steady stream. The consistency should be that of mayonnaise. Set aside. When soup is cooked, remove the bundle of herbs. Put contents of soup pan into the food processor and work to a smooth purée. Strain if necessary, correct seasoning, and add some tomato paste for color, if necessary. Return to saucepan. Mix butter and flour into a paste. Add about 1 tsp of the paste to the soup, whisking it in well, and bring the soup up to the boil. Add more paste as necessary to bring the soup to the consistency of thick cream. Stir in the cream. Serve soup with the rouille, cheese and croûtons.

This page: Soupe de Poisson Provençal.
Facing page: Chinese Crabmeat Soup (top) and Shrimp and Watercress Bisque (bottom).

Cold Dishes and Salads

Salad Niçoise

PREPARATION TIME: 20 minutes
COOKING TIME: 15-20 minutes
SERVES: 4 people

1 can tuna
4oz shrimp
6-8 anchovies
4 ripe tomatoes
4 hard-boiled eggs
1 red pepper
½ cup black olives, stoned
1 cup green beans
2 large potatoes, or 6 small new potatoes
2 tbsps white wine vinegar
6 tbsps olive oil
3 tbsps chopped mixed herbs
1 tbsp Dijon mustard
Salt and pepper

Peel and cook potatoes (skins may be left on new potatoes if desired) until tender. If using large potatoes, cut into ½" dice (new potatoes may be sliced into ¼" rounds). Trim beans, put into boiling salted water for about 3-4 minutes or until just barely cooked. Drain and rinse under cold water, then leave to drain dry. Cut the olives in half, lengthwise. Cut anchovies in half, lengthwise, then through the middle. Cut tomatoes into quarters (or eighths, if large) and remove the cores. Mix the vinegar and oil together for the vinaigrette dressing, and add seasoning, chopped herbs, and a little French mustard if desired. Drain oil from tuna fish. Cut red pepper into thin shreds. Mix together all the ingredients, including the shrimp, and toss in the dressing. Quarter the eggs and toss into the other ingredients very carefully – do not break up the eggs. Pile onto dishes and serve.

This page: Marinated Herring in Sour Cream with Beet Salad. Facing page: Salad Niçoise (top) and Spanish Rice and Sole Salad (bottom).

Spanish Rice and Sole Salad

PREPARATION TIME: 20 minutes
COOKING TIME: 8-10 minutes
OVEN TEMPERATURE: 350°F (180°C)
SERVES: 4 people

2 sole filleted and skinned
4-6 peppercorns
Slice of onion
Lemon juice
5 tbsps olive oil
1 cup long-grain rice
1 red pepper
1 shallot, finely chopped
1 small eggplant
1 green pepper
2 bunches watercress
1¼ cups prepared mayonnaise
1 clove garlic
1 level tsp tomato paste
1 level tsp paprika
1 tbsp chopped mixed herbs
Salt and pepper

Put sole fillets into a baking dish. Add onion, a squeeze of lemon

juice, peppercorns and enough water to cover. Sprinkle with salt, cover with buttered foil, and bake in a moderate oven for about 8-10 minutes. Allow fish to cool in the liquid, then cut into 1" pieces. Cook rice for about 12 minutes. Drain under hot water, then cold, and leave to drain completely dry. Chop green and red peppers into ¼" dice. Cut eggplant in half lengthwise, score each half, sprinkle with salt, and leave to sit for about ½ hour. Wash eggplant well, then dry it. Cut it into ½" cubes and fry very quickly in 2 tbsps olive oil.

Add salt and pepper, and toss with the cooked rice, and red and green pepper. Add a pinch of chopped herbs. Make a vinaigrette dressing with 1 tbsp lemon juice, 3 tbsps olive oil and shallot. Toss with the rice. Crush clove of garlic and work it together with the mayonnaise, tomato paste and paprika. Add salt, pepper and the rest of the chopped herbs. Thin with a little milk or hot water. Adjust seasoning. Arrange rice salad on one side of serving dish, and put sole fillets on the other. Spoon mayonnaise dressing over fillets. Divide the two sides with bunches of watercress.

Mussels à la Grecque (top left) and Fin and Feather (left).

Mussels à la Grecque

PREPARATION TIME: 15 minutes

COOKING TIME: 15 minutes

SERVES: 4 people

2 pints mussels
1 onion, chopped
¼ cup white wine
1½lb tomatoes (or the equivalent in canned tomatoes)
1 clove garlic
Lemon juice
Salt and pepper
Pinch Cayenne pepper
1 chopped shallot
1 tsp fennel seed
1 tsp coriander seeds
1 tsp crushed oregano
1 bay leaf
1 tbsp chopped fresh basil leaves
2 tbsps olive oil

Garnish
Chopped parsley
Black olives

Scrub mussels well, discarding any with broken shells. Put into a pan with chopped onion, white wine, squeeze of lemon juice, salt and pepper. Cover and cook quickly until mussels open, discarding any that do not. Remove mussels from shells and leave to cool. Heat olive oil in a saucepan and add crushed garlic and shallot. Cook until just lightly brown. Blend in the tomatoes, herbs, fennel and coriander seeds. Add seasoning and cooking liquid from the mussels and bring to the boil. Allow the sauce to boil rapidly until well reduced. Leave sauce to cool, then mix with mussels. Serve garnished with chopped parsley and black olives. Serve with green salad and French bread.

Fin and Feather

PREPARATION TIME: 20 minutes

COOKING TIME: 15-20 minutes

OVEN TEMPERATURE: 350°F (180°C)

SERVES: 4 people

4 chicken supremes (boned chicken breasts)
3oz fresh salmon, or canned red salmon
White wine
4 anchovies
⅔ cup olive oil
2 egg yolks
Salt and pepper
1½ tbsps lemon juice
1 tbsp chopped parsley

Garnish
4 small dill pickles
1 tbsp capers
Curly endive

Buy prepared chicken breasts. Put them on a sheet of foil and sprinkle over salt, pepper and a little white wine. Seal foil well. Put into a baking dish and bake in the oven for about 15 minutes, or until cooked through. Open foil packet and allow to cool. Reserve juices from the chicken. Poach the fresh salmon (or drain canned salmon) and remove bones. Put the salmon and anchovies into a food processor bowl or blender and work until broken up. Work in the egg yolks, and salt and pepper. With the machine running, add the oil gradually. Add lemon juice to taste and adjust seasoning. Stir in the cooking liquid from the chicken to give the sauce the consistency of thin cream: if it is too thick add a few drops of milk or water. Put cold chicken breasts onto a plate and coat with all the sauce. Before serving, garnish the dish with capers and pickles. Serve with a green salad or a cold rice salad.

Marinated Herring in Sour Cream with Beet Salad

PREPARATION TIME: 20 minutes

COOKING TIME: 30 minutes

SERVES: 4 people

4 fresh herrings

Marinade
1¼ cups dry white wine
¼ cup white wine vinegar
1 tsp sugar
1 shallot
1 bay leaf
6 black peppercorns
2 sprigs thyme
1 whole clove

Dressing
1¼ cups sour cream or yogurt
½ tsp dry mustard
Salt and pepper

Salad
1 tbsp chopped fennel or dillweed
4 green onions
8 even-sized cooked beets
¼ cup chopped walnuts
2 tbsps red wine vinegar
6 tbsps vegetable oil
Sugar
Salt
Pepper

Fillet the herring, removing heads and tails. Pick out as many of the bones as possible and separate the two fillets of each herring. Put all ingredients for the marinade into a saucepan, bring to the boil and cook for 20 minutes. Pour marinade over herring in a shallow sauté pan. Bring back to the boil and simmer, covered, for about 10 minutes. Leave fish to cool in marinade, then lift out and remove skin. Put herring into a shallow serving dish. Mix sour cream with 2 tbsps of strained marinade, and add mustard, salt and black pepper. Mix until smooth, and pour over fillets. Scatter over the chopped dill and half of the chopped green onions. Peel and slice beets into rounds about ¼" thick, and marinate in the oil, vinegar and sugar. Sprinkle with chopped walnuts and the remaining green onions, and arrange around the marinated herring fillets.

Seafood and Shell Salad

PREPARATION TIME: 20 minutes

COOKING TIME: 25 minutes

SERVES: 4 people

1lb halibut
8oz shrimp
6 Gulf shrimp
¼ pint mussels
1 red pepper
2 tbsps chopped tarragon, or a good pinch of dried tarragon
2 tbsps chopped parsley
4 green onions
Handful of black olives, pitted
8oz pasta shells, cooked
4oz sorrel or fresh spinach
1 bunch watercress
1 tbsp butter
1 tbsp flour
1¼ cups cream, or milk
⅔ cup whipping cream
Salt and pepper

Put halibut into a saucepan and just cover with cold water. Bring to the boil and poach gently till the fish is cooked. Remove pan from heat and allow fish to cool in the liquid. When cool, drain fish, remove all skin and bone, and break flesh into large flakes. Set aside. Scrub mussels. Cook them in their shells with 4 tbsps water or lemon juice. Cover the pan and cook them over the heat quickly until the shells open. Discard any mussels that do not open. Take

mussels out of shells and set aside. Shell all the shrimp. Cook pasta shells until just tender. Rinse under hot, then cold water, and leave to drain dry. Chop red pepper into small cubes, chop the olives and slice the green onions. Mix pasta with peppers, olives, tarragon, parsley and salt and pepper. Arrange in a large serving dish or small individual dishes, and pile mixed fish and seafood on top. Chill. Cook sorrel or spinach briefly in boiling water. Drain and refresh under cold water. Squeeze dry and chop to a fine purée. Pick over watercress leaves, removing discolored leaves and chopping off thick ends of stalks with the root hairs. Chop watercress very finely or work in a food processor. Melt butter in a small saucepan over a low heat. Stir in flour and cook over the heat for 2 minutes, stirring all the time. Pour on the milk or cream and stir until well blended. Simmer for about 3 minutes.

This page: Shrimp in Melons (top) and Red Snapper Niçoise (bottom).
Facing page: Seafood and Shell Salad (top) and Seviche (bottom).

Allow sauce to cool slightly, then blend with purée'd sorrel and watercress. Add chopped parsley and tarragon, salt and pepper. Cover top of sauce with a sheet of wax paper to prevent a skin from forming, and allow to cool completely. Whip the cream lightly and fold into the sauce. Pour some of the sauce over the fish, shellfish and pasta. Serve rest of the sauce separately. Garnish with a whole Gulf shrimp if desired.

Red Snapper Niçoise

PREPARATION TIME: 15 minutes
COOKING TIME: 15 minutes
SERVES: 4 people

4 small, whole red snapper
2 tbsps olive oil
Lemon juice
Small can anchovy fillets
½ cup pitted black olives
2 hard-boiled eggs
1 green pepper
1 chopped shallot
1 clove garlic, crushed
½ cup mushrooms
1lb ripe tomatoes
Salt
Pepper
Seasoned flour

Vinaigrette Dressing
2 tbsps red wine vinegar
6 tbsps olive oil
¼ tsp Dijon mustard
Handful of chopped mixed herbs (eg basil, oregano, thyme)

Scale and clean fish, trimming fins but leaving head and tail on. Cut tomatoes into quarters and remove cores. Cut eggs into quarters. Cut olives in half, lengthwise. If mushrooms are small, leave whole; if not, quarter them. Cut green pepper into thin slices, and cut anchovies in half, lengthwise. Prepare vinaigrette dressing and add chopped herbs, garlic and shallot. Put in the mushrooms and leave to marinate in the refrigerator for about 1 hour. Meanwhile, toss fish in seasoned flour to coat lightly. Heat 2 tbsps olive oil in a frying pan and fry fish on both sides until cooked through – about 2-3 minutes per side. When cooking the second side, sprinkle over some lemon juice. Season lightly, and leave to go cold. When ready to serve, add tomatoes, green peppers, eggs and olives to the mushrooms in their marinade, and toss. Pile the salad into a serving dish and arrange the cold, cooked red snapper on top. Garnish with anchovy fillet strips.

Seviche

PREPARATION TIME: 20 minutes
SERVES: 4 people

1lb codfish
⅔ cup lemon or lime juice
1 tbsp chopped shallot
1 green chili pepper
1 green pepper
2 tomatoes
1 tbsp chopped parsley
1 tbsp chopped fresh coriander
2 tbsps vegetable oil
1 small head iceberg lettuce
4 green onions
Salt
Pepper

Skin cod and remove any bones. Wash and pat dry, then cut across grain into slices approximately ½" thick and 2½" long. Put into a bowl and pour over lime or lemon juice. Put in shallot. Slice chili pepper and remove the seeds, then chop finely and add it to the fish. Add seasoning and put into the refrigerator for 24 hours, well covered. Stir occasionally. When ready to serve, chop green onions and herbs. Slice pepper into short, thin strips. Plunge tomatoes into boiling water for about 4 seconds, then into cold water, and peel. Cut tomatoes in half, squeeze out the seeds, and slice into fine strips. Drain off lemon or lime juice from fish, and stir in oil. Add herbs, peppers and tomatoes, and toss. Spoon onto lettuce leaves in a serving dish and sprinkle over spring onions.

Shrimp in Melons

PREPARATION TIME: 25 minutes
SERVES: 4 people

2 small melons
8oz peeled shrimp
Juice of half a lemon
1 small cucumber
4 medium tomatoes
⅓ cup toasted flaked almonds
1 orange
4 tbsps light vegetable oil
¼ cup heavy cream
Salt
Pepper
2 tbsps chopped mint, reserving 4 sprigs for garnish
Pinch of sugar
1 tsp chopped lemon thyme (optional)

Cut melons in half through the middle and scoop out flesh with a melon-baller or spoon, leaving a ¼" border of fruit on the inside of each shell. Cut a thin slice off the bottom of each shell so that they stand upright. Cut the melon into ½" cubes or leave in balls. Peel cucumber, cut in half lengthwise, then into ½" cubes. Peel and squeeze seeds from tomatoes and cut tomatoes into strips. Peel and segment orange. Mix lemon juice, oil and cream together for the dressing. Add chopped mint, and thyme (if desired), a pinch of sugar, and salt and pepper to taste. Toss fruit and vegetables together with the shrimp. Pile ingredients evenly into each melon shell. Chill well and garnish with a small sprig of mint leaves and the almonds.

Lobster and Smoked Chicken Salad

PREPARATION TIME: 25 minutes
SERVES: 4 people

Salad
1 small smoked chicken
1 large cooked lobster
4 sticks celery
4 green onions
4oz pea pods, trimmed
⅓ cup browned cashew nuts
1 head Chinese cabbage
1 head curly endive

Dressing
1¼ cups prepared mayonnaise
2 tbsps soy sauce
1 tsp honey
Sesame seed oil
½ tsp ground ginger
1 tbsp dry sherry, if desired

Garnish
1 red pepper, thinly sliced
2 tbsps chopped parsley

Twist off the claws and legs of lobster. Cut body in half, take out tail meat and set aside. Crack claws and remove meat. Remove as much meat as possible from all the legs. Cut breast meat from the smoked chicken into thin, even slices. Shred the rest of the chicken meat. Mix the shredded chicken and the meat from the lobster claws and legs together. Cut lobster tail meat lengthwise into 3-4 thin slices (depending on size of tail). Set sliced lobster tail and sliced chicken breast aside. Mix celery, cashew nuts and green onions together with the shredded lobster and chicken. Mix the dressing ingredients together – the mayonnaise, soy sauce, sesame oil and honey – and add some black pepper and salt if necessary. Add ground ginger and sherry, if desired. Mix dressing with shredded lobster and chicken. Slice red pepper into thin strips. Slice Chinese cabbage into thin shreds. Tear curly endive leaves into bite-sized pieces. Pile the greens and pea pods onto a large serving dish. Mound the shredded chicken and lobster salad in the middle. Arrange sliced chicken breast and lobster tail neatly over the top. Garnish with sliced red pepper and chopped parsley. Serve any remaining dressing separately.

Salade aux Fruits de Mer

PREPARATION TIME: 20 minutes
COOKING TIME: 10 minutes
SERVES: 4 people

Salad
8 scallops with roe attached
4oz langoustines, cooked and shelled
4oz shrimp, peeled
½ pint mussels
8oz monkfish
Lemon juice
1 head Romaine lettuce
2 heads Belgian endive (chicory)

Dressing
1 3oz package cream cheese
⅔ cup yogurt
Juice of 1 lemon
3 tbsps milk
1 tbsp Dijon mustard
1 tbsp chopped tarragon
1 tbsp chopped chives
1 tbsp chopped parsley
Salt and pepper

Poach scallops and monkfish in lemon juice and enough water to cover, for about 5 minutes and

leave to cool in the liquid. Scrub mussels well and put into a covered saucepan with 4 tbsps water. Shake pan over heat for about 5 minutes, or until the shells open. Discard mussels whose shells remain closed. Remove mussels from shells and set aside. When scallops and monkfish are cool cut scallops in half, horizontally, and cut monkfish into 1" pieces. Mix all fish and shellfish together. Remove core from Belgian endive; separate leaves and wash and dry well. Wash Romaine lettuce, remove core and shred finely. To make dressing, blend cheese and milk in a blender or food processor. Add lemon juice, salt and pepper to taste, and mustard, and stir in the chopped herbs. Arrange leaves of Belgian endive onto serving plates. Pile shredded lettuce on top, leaving points of endive leaves showing. Toss shellfish in half the dressing and pile on top of lettuce. Put another spoonful of dressing on top of each serving and serve any remaining dressing separately.

Salade aux Fruits de Mer (above) and Lobster and Smoked Chicken Salad (left).

Smoked Salmon Rolls with Shrimp Filling

PREPARATION TIME: 15 minutes

SERVES: 4 persons

8 slices of smoked salmon
8oz frozen shrimp
2 tbsps mayonnaise
1 tbsp whipped cream
2 tsps tomato paste
Squeeze lemon juice

Defrost shrimp and drain, or use fresh, shelled shrimp instead. Mix mayonnaise and cream, tomato paste and lemon juice in a bowl and fold in shrimp. Divide the mixture between the 8 slices of smoked salmon, placing it on top in a wedge shape and rolling the salmon around it in a cone shape. Allow two for each person. Garnish with lemon wedges and sliced cucumber and tomato. Serve with thinly sliced soda bread and butter. Serves 4 persons.

Poached Salmon Garni

PREPARATION TIME: 2-3 hours

COOKING TIME: 20-30 minutes

SERVES: 8-10 persons

A whole salmon, beautifully dressed, looks splendid at a buffet supper or a dinner party, but it is tricky to serve and, if people are helping themselves, looks rather mangled after the guests have attacked it. Also, you need to be the proud possessor of a fish-kettle in which to cook it and, of course, the preparation of salmon cooked in this way takes a lot of time and care. Here is a simple way to cook and serve fresh salmon.

1 fresh salmon, approx 2½lb
1 large lettuce
1 cucumber
5-6 hard boiled eggs
3-4 firm tomatoes
2 lemons

Have the fishmonger clean the fish and remove the head. Cut the fish in two, near the gills. Place each piece on a well buttered piece of foil and make a parcel, folding the join several times and folding in the ends. Place the two pieces in a saucepan large enough to hold them side by side, cover them with cold water, add a tbsp of vinegar and bring slowly to the boil. Gently turn the parcels over in the water. Turn off the heat, put on the lid, and leave to cool. Before the fish is completely cold put the parcels on a large plate, unwrap them and carefully skin the fish and remove the bones. Divide each section into serving-size pieces along the grain of the fish. Select large lettuce leaves, one for each portion of fish, and lay them in two rows, the

This page: Salmon Flan (top) and Poached Salmon Garni (bottom).
Facing page: Dublin Bay Prawn Cocktail (top) and Smoked Salmon Rolls with Shrimp Filling (bottom).

length of a large serving platter, with a piece of salmon on each. Place quarters of hard-boiled egg and lemon slices between them and, down the center of the dish, arrange two rows of alternating cucumber and tomato slices overlapping. Decorate the dish with parsley and serve mayonnaise separately and, of course, home-made brown soda bread.

Dublin Bay Prawn Cocktail

PREPARATION TIME: 15 minutes

SERVES: 4 persons

Dublin Bay Prawns are very large and rather expensive, so for prawn cocktail it is better to use ordinary prawns/shrimp and garnish the cocktail with king prawns/jumbo shrimp.

½lb cooked, shelled shrimp (frozen shrimp will do)
4 king prawns/jumbo shrimp
5-6 lettuce leaves
4 lemon wedges
A little chopped parsley

Cocktail sauce
4 heaped tbsps mayonnaise
2 level tbsps tomato paste
1 tsp Worcestershire sauce
2 tsps lemon juice
1 tbsp medium sherry
2 tbsps whipped cream

To make the sauce, add the tomato paste, Worcestershire sauce, lemon juice and sherry to the mayonnaise and mix well, then fold in the whipped cream. Shred the lettuce finely and divide between four glass goblets. If using frozen shrimp, drain them well and place equal amounts on top of the lettuce. Just before serving, coat the shrimp with the cocktail sauce and sprinkle a pinch of the chopped parsley on top of each. Garnish with a king prawn/jumbo shrimp and a lemon wedge on each glass. Serve with buttered brown soda bread.

Curried Shrimp Salad

PREPARATION TIME: 15 minutes

SERVES: 4 persons

Not so many years ago, in the West of Ireland, you could buy a lobster for a few shillings if you knew the right person, and on the quaysides where the fishing boats landed their catch, fish cost only a few pence, while crabs and shrimp were almost given away. It is a different story today, since fishing has become a major industry in Ireland, and almost all the shellfish is flown out to France almost as soon as it has left the water, or is ordered by the big hotels in Ireland.
If you should be fortunate enough to buy fresh shrimp, they need only butter and a little lemon juice to enhance their delicate flavor after they have been cooked in lightly salted water which has only just been allowed to come to the boil. However, frozen shrimp are easily available everywhere in Ireland and here is an easy supper dish to serve with brown soda bread and butter.

8oz frozen shrimp
¾ cup cooked rice
4 heaped tbsps mayonnaise
A squeeze of lemon juice
2 tsps of tomato purée
1 tsp curry powder

Thoroughly defrost the shrimp. Drain them well. Mix tomato purée, lemon juice and curry powder into the mayonnaise. Fold in rice and shrimp. Divide in two and serve on large lettuce leaves. Garnish with sliced, hard boiled egg, cucumber and tomato. This would be sufficient for a first course for four people.

Salmon Flan

PREPARATION TIME: 10 minutes

COOKING TIME: 40-45 minutes

SERVES: 4-6 persons

This would make an excellent luncheon or supper dish for four people. Serve it either with a tossed salad and brown bread and butter or with baked potatoes and petit pois.

¼lb frozen puff pastry
6oz cooked fresh salmon or 7½oz can of salmon
⅔ cup milk
2 tsps cornstarch
Salt and pepper
1 egg

Thaw pastry. Roll out into a square large enough to line a greased 8 inch quiche dish or flan dish. Trim pastry and crimp edges. Mix cornstarch with a tbsp of the milk, bring the rest to the boil, pour onto the cornstarch mix, stir well and return to the pan. Bring back to the boil and cook for 1 minute, stirring all the time. Season well with salt and pepper. If using canned salmon drain the liquid from the can into

Smoked Fish Pate (above right) and Curried Shrimp Salad (right).

the sauce. If using fresh salmon add a knob of butter. Remove the pan from the heat and break in the egg, beating it in thoroughly. Flake up the salmon, removing any bones and skin, fold it into the sauce and turn into the pastry case. Cook in the oven, 375°F (190°C), for 35-40 minutes.

Smoked Fish Pate

PREPARATION TIME: 10 minutes

SERVES: 4 persons.

8oz skinned, smoked mackerel fillets, or other smoked fish
⅓ cup softened butter
Juice of 1 lemon
Black pepper

This takes only seconds to make in a food processor or electric blender, but if you don't have access to either of these you can mash up the fish in a bowl and thoroughly mix in melted butter and lemon juice. Season with freshly ground black pepper and either divide between small individual ramekins or arrange it attractively in a serving dish, garnished with lemon slices and parsley. Serve with brown toast or brown soda bread.

Baked Stuffed Mackerel

PREPARATION TIME: 15 minutes

COOKING TIME: 30 minutes

SERVES: 4 persons

Mackerel should be eaten the day it is caught, so this is a recipe for people living near the sea. It is also very useful for people on self-catering holidays at the seaside because it is so easy to prepare.

4 mackerel which have been cleaned and washed thoroughly
¼ cup butter
1 small onion, finely chopped
1 tbsp oatmeal
1 heaped tsp fresh chopped lemon thyme
1 heaped tsp fresh chopped parsley or ½ tsp of each, dried
2 cups breadcrumbs
Salt and pepper
2-3 tbsps hot water

Fry the chopped onion in the butter to soften. Add oatmeal, breadcrumbs, herbs and seasoning. Mix well. Bind with the hot water. Fill the cavities of the fish with the stuffing and wrap each one separately in well-buttered foil. Place in a roasting pan or on a baking sheet and put in a pre-heated oven at 375°F (190°C) for half an hour.

Scallops au Gratin

PREPARATION TIME: 10 minutes

COOKING TIME: 15 minutes

SERVES: 4 people

4 scallops
2-3 tbsps finely chopped shallots (a small onion will do)
2 tbsps oil
¼ cup butter
A wineglass of white wine
2 egg yolks
¼ grated Cheddar cheese
4 tbsps white breadcrumbs
2 tbsps heavy cream

The fishmonger will prepare the scallops, removing the inedible bits and leaving you with what seems like a small amount of fish, but one each should be quite enough for a first course. Be sure to ask for the deeper section of the scallop shell to serve them in.
Heat the oil and butter in a heavy frying pan. Add the shallots and cook gently until they soften. Slice the white parts of the scallops. Increase the heat, stir in the white wine and then the sliced scallops and cook fairly briskly for 2-3 minutes. Slice the coral of the scallops and add to the pan, cooking the mixture for a further minute. Stir gently over a low heat until the mixture thickens, adding a sprinkling of salt and pepper. Divide between four scallop shells, making sure each one has its fair share of the coral. Place a tbsp of grated cheese and a tbsp of breadcrumbs on each and place under the heated grill until just beginning to brown on top. Serve immediately with brown bread.

Mackerel Rolls

PREPARATION TIME: 20 minutes

SERVES: 4 persons

The seas around Ireland are teeming with mackerel, the only problem about them is that, once out of the water, they don't stay fresh for very long. If you should be offered some freshly caught mackerel and you don't want to eat them that day, don't turn them down. Take them home and poach then in a little very lightly salted water, preferably with a dash of cider or white wine added. This will only take ten minutes. Cool them, put them in the refrigerator and next day you can have a delicious lunch or picnic of mackerel rolls.

4 long, crusty rolls or one loaf French bread
12oz skinned and filleted cooked mackerel
Small carton plain yogurt
Few chopped walnuts
1 medium apple
Thyme
Mint

Split rolls or loaf lengthwise. Scoop out some of the center. Chop up breadcrumbs on the breadboard with two knives. Put the breadcrumbs in a bowl and mix in finely chopped herbs and some freshly ground black pepper. Peel, core and quarter the apple; chop it up finely and fold it into the yogurt with the chopped walnuts. Flake up the mackerel, mix with the seasoned crumbs and bind with the yogurt mixture. Fill the scooped out rolls with the mixture and either serve as open sandwiches or put tops on and wrap in foil or plastic wrap if using for a picnic. Fill French bread in similar manner and cut into sections.

Grilled Trout with Almonds

PREPARATION TIME: 10 minutes

COOKING TIME: 15 minutes

SERVES: 4 persons

4 fresh trout
1 lemon
¼ cup butter
¼ cup flaked almonds

Clean the trout. Place a lemon wedge in the cavity of each. Line the broiler pan with buttered foil and carefully lay the fish on it. Smear a little butter on each. Preheat the broiler and cook the trout under it for 5 minutes. Turn them very carefully, put a little more butter on top and broil for another five minutes. Keep the fish warm on plates while you toss the almonds in the butter in the broiler pan and brown them under the broiler. Sprinkle them over the fish. Serve with a garnish of lemon slices and parsley. Eat with brown bread and butter.

Seafood Pancakes

PREPARATION TIME: Pancakes 1 hour 15 minutes
Filling 15 minutes

COOKING TIME: 45 minutes

SERVES: 6 persons

These are especially nice when made with sole and two or three scallops, but you can use 1½lb of any whitefish, filleted. Ask the fishmonger for the bones and trimmings for the fish stock. The pancake recipe is the same as the one for Savory Pancakes.

12 thin pancakes
1½lb fish
4oz shrimp (cooked)
4oz mushrooms
1 tbsp butter
1 tbsp lemon juice in 2 fl oz water
1 medium onion
Bay leaf
6 peppercorns
1 tsp salt
⅓ cup butter
¾ cup flour
Glass white wine
2½ cups fish stock
Grated nutmeg
⅔ cup whipped cream

Put washed fish trimmings in a pan with the bay leaf, peppercorns, salt and 1 pint water. Bring to the boil and simmer for half an hour. Strain. Cut the sole, or other fish, diagonally into 1 inch strips and poach in the fish stock for two minutes. Remove the fish from the stock with a slotted spoon and set aside. Melt the tbsp of butter in a pan, add the mushrooms sliced, the lemon juice and 2 fl oz water, bring to the boil, reduce heat and cook for 1 minute. Remove mushrooms with a slotted spoon.
Melt ⅓ cup butter in a pan, stir in the flour and cook over a low heat for a minute or two. Add the white wine and bring to the boil. Remove the pan from the heat and slowly add the fish and mushroom stocks, stirring all the time. Return to the heat and simmer for 2 minutes. Season with salt and pepper and a little grated nutmeg. Remove from heat and stir in the whipped cream. Use half the sauce to mix in with the fish, shrimp and mushrooms. Divide this mixture between the 12 pancakes, rolling each one up and placing them, side by side, in a large, shallow, greased ovenproof dish. Pour over the rest of the sauce and heat through in the oven, 350°F (180°C), for about half an hour or until the top begins to brown. Allow 2 pancakes per person for a main course, or one each as a first course.

Facing page: Baked Stuffed Mackerel (top) and Grilled Trout with Almonds (bottom).

This page: Scallops au Gratin (top right) and Sole Surprise (bottom left).
Facing page: Mackerel Rolls (top) and Seafood Pancakes (bottom).

Sole Surprise

PREPARATION TIME: 30 minutes
COOKING TIME: 30 minutes
SERVES: 4 persons

This consists of little puff pastry "boxes" filled with spinach, with the fillets of sole laid on top and coated with a cheese sauce. It makes an interesting luncheon for four people.

4 small or 2 large fillets of sole
8oz frozen puff pastry
8oz frozen spinach
¼ cup butter

Sauce
2 tbsps butter
2 tbsps flour
1¼ cups milk
Pinch fennel
Salt and pepper
½ cup grated cheese

Roll out the defrosted pastry into a rectangle 5x8 inches. Cut it down the center in both directions to make four rectangles 2½x4 inches. Carry out the following procedure with each one. Fold over, short sides together. Cut out the center with a sharp knife, leaving ½ inch all round. Roll out the center piece on a floured board until it is the same size as the ½ inch "frame." Brush the edges with milk and put the "frame" on the base. Brush the top with milk and put them on a greased baking sheet. Bake them in the oven, 425°F (220°C), for 10-15 minutes.
Meanwhile, put the spinach in a pan with ¼ inch water and a little salt. Cover and cook for 4-5 minutes. Drain and beat in half the butter. Skin the fillets and, if necessary, cut them in two. Use the rest of the butter to coat two plates and put the fillets on one and cover them with the other. Cook them over a pan of boiling water for twenty minutes.
For the sauce, melt 2 tbsps butter with the flour to make a roux. Gradually stir in the milk. Bring to the boil. Reduce heat and add fennel and salt and pepper; cook for another minute or two. Remove from the heat and stir in the grated cheese.
Divide the spinach between the four boxes. Lay the sole on top and and coat with the cheese sauce.

Seafood with Pasta

This page: Vermicelli Pescatore.

Facing page: Spaghetti Marinara (top) and Pasta Shells with Seafood (bottom).

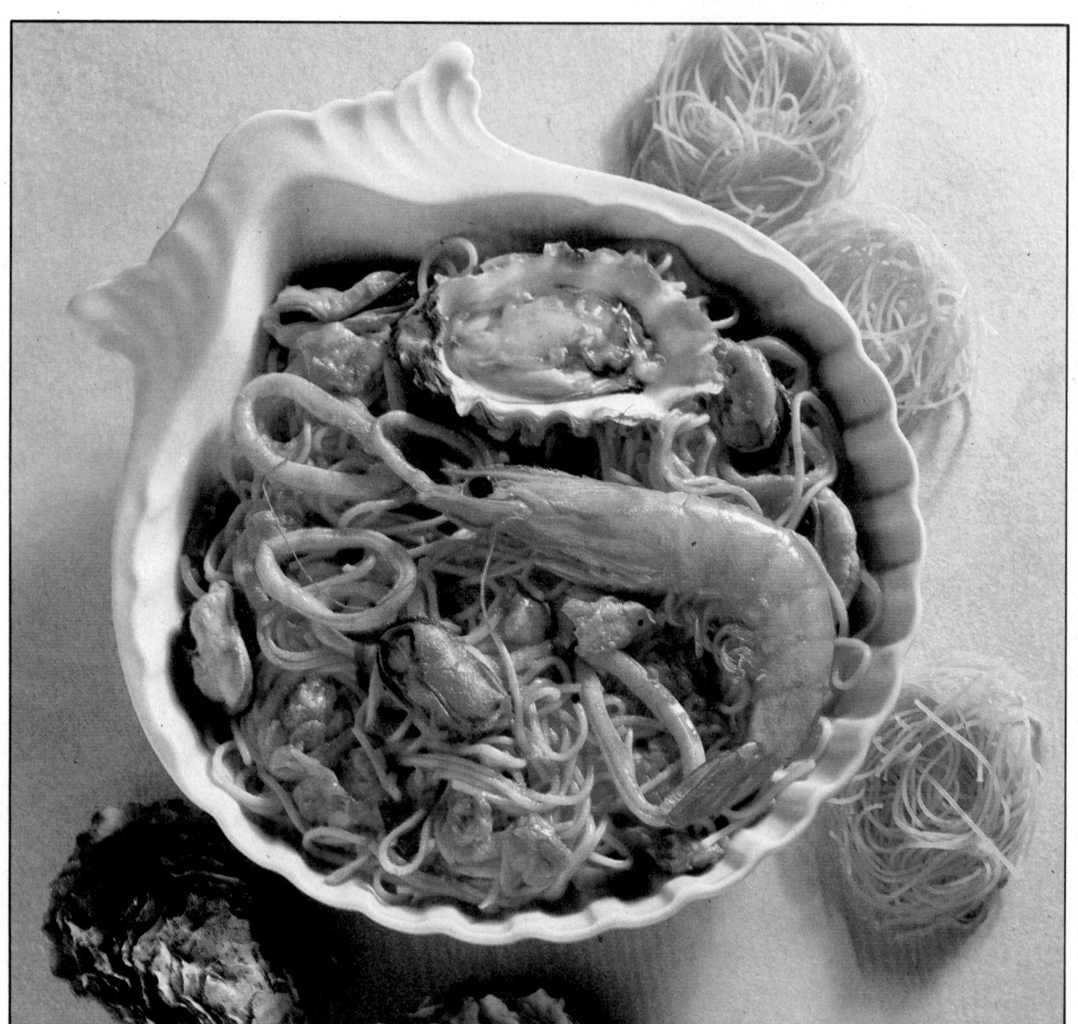

Spaghetti Marinara

PREPARATION TIME: 10 minutes

COOKING TIME: 20 minutes

1 9oz package spaghetti
1 pound shrimp, shelled and de-veined
½ pound scallops, cleaned and sliced
6-8 anchovies
1 large can (about 2 cups) plum tomatoes, seeded and chopped
½ cup dry white wine
½ cup water
1 bay leaf
4 peppercorns
2 tbsps olive oil
1 tsp basil
2 cloves garlic, crushed
1 tbsp tomato paste
1 tbsp chopped parsley
Salt and pepper

Drain anchovies and cut into small pieces. Place water, wine, bay leaf and peppercorns in a pan. Heat to a slow boil. Add scallops and cook for 2 minutes. Remove and drain. Heat the oil, add garlic and basil, and cook for 30 seconds. Add tomatoes, anchovies and tomato paste. Stir until combined. Cook for 10 minutes. Meanwhile, cook the spaghetti in a large pan of boiling salted water for 10 minutes, or until tender but still firm. Drain. Add seafood to sauce, and cook a further 1 minute. Add parsley and stir through. Season with salt and pepper to taste. Toss gently. Pour sauce over spaghetti and serve immediately, sprinkled with parsley.

Pasta Shells with Seafood

PREPARATION TIME: 5 minutes

COOKING TIME: 15 minutes

1 9oz package pasta shells
1 pound shrimp, shelled and de-veined
¼ pound scallops, cleaned and sliced
4 tbsps butter or margarine
2 cloves garlic, crushed
½ cup dry white wine
1 cup cream
2 tbsps water
1 tbsp cornstarch
1 tbsp lemon juice
1 tbsp chopped parsley
Salt and pepper

Melt butter in a pan. Add garlic, and cook for 1 minute. Add wine and cream, and bring back to boil, and cook 2 minutes. Slake cornstarch with the water, and pour into sauce. Stir until boiling. Add lemon juice and salt and pepper to taste. Meanwhile, cook the pasta in plenty of boiling salted water, until tender – about 10 minutes. Drain, shaking to remove excess water. Add shrimp and scallops to sauce and cook 3 minutes. Pour over pasta shells, toss, and garnish with parsley.

Vermicelli Pescatore

PREPARATION TIME: 15 minutes

COOKING TIME: 40 minutes

¼ pint mussels
¼ pint clams
½ pound cod fish fillets
¼ pound squid, cleaned
4 Gulf shrimp, cooked
4 fresh oysters, cooked
1 9oz package vermicelli
1 cup dry white wine
¼ cup olive oil
4 small cans (about 4 cups) tomato sauce
2 tbsps tomato paste
Half a green pepper, diced

Prepare seafood. If using fresh mussels, clean closed mussels, removing beard, and cook in boiling water for 3 minutes until they open. (Discard any that remain closed). Cool and remove from shells, keeping a few in shells for garnish if desired. Skin and bone fillets, and cut fish into ½ inch pieces. Clean squid and cut into rings. Heat 2 tbsps oil in a pan, and add the squid. Fry gently until golden brown, then add wine, tomato, green pepper, and salt and pepper to taste. Simmer for 20 minutes then add fish. Simmer for a further 10 minutes, stirring occasionally. Add clams and mussels and, when mixture reboils, adjust seasoning. Meanwhile, cook spaghetti in lots of boiling salted water for 10 minutes, or until tender but still firm. Drain well. Add seafood, and toss. Garnish with shrimp and fresh oysters.

Pasta and Smoked Salmon

PREPARATION TIME: 10 minutes

COOKING TIME: 18 minutes

SERVES: 4 people

3oz plain tagliatelle or fettuccine
3oz wholemeal tagliatelle or fettuccine
3oz spinach tagliatelle or fettuccine
8oz smoked salmon
¼ cup mushrooms
1 egg
⅔ cup heavy cream
1 tbsp chopped parsley
1 tsp chopped fresh basil
2 green onions, finely chopped
1 tbsp butter
1 jar red salmon caviar
Salt and pepper

Cook the pasta in boiling salted water until just tender. Drain under hot water and keep it warm. Slice and cook the mushrooms, with the onion, in the butter. Slice the smoked salmon into thin strips and set aside. Beat together the egg and heavy cream with the chopped herbs, salt and pepper. Add these to the onion and mushrooms, and heat through, stirring constantly. Do not allow mixture to boil. Toss with the pasta and the salmon. Top with red salmon caviar to serve.

Sole au Vin Rouge

PREPARATION TIME: 15 minutes

COOKING TIME: 25 minutes

OVEN TEMPERATURE: 325°F (160°C)

SERVES: 4 people

2 sole
⅔ cup red wine
¼ cup water
3-4 peppercorns
1 bay leaf
1 slice onion
1 tbsp butter
1 tbsp flour
⅔ cup light cream
1 small bunch purple grapes
Salt
Pepper

Fillet and skin the fish. Wash fillets and dry well, and fold the ends under to make small parcels. Put into an ovenproof dish and pour over the wine and water. Put in the onion slice, peppercorns and bay leaf. Add a pinch of salt, and cover with foil. Put into a pre-set oven and poach for about 10 minutes. Meanwhile, wash and seed the grapes, but leave whole unless very large, in which case halve them. Remove fish from baking dish, cover and keep fillets warm. Heat butter in a small saucepan. When foaming, add flour and cook for

This page: Sole au Vin Rouge (top) and Trout en Papillote (bottom).
Facing page: Pasta and Smoked Salmon (top) and Fritto Misto Mare (bottom).

about 2-3 minutes, until flour is lightly brown. Strain on the cooking liquid from the fish and stir until the sauce comes to the boil. Allow to continue boiling for about 2 minutes. Add cream and re-boil. Season to taste. Arrange fillets in a serving dish. Put the grapes into the sauce to heat them through, reserving a few to garnish. Coat the fish with the sauce to serve.

Spiced Salmon Steaks

PREPARATION TIME: 15 minutes

COOKING TIME: 12-15 minutes

SERVES: 4 people

4 salmon steaks, 1" thick
1 cup light brown sugar
1 tsp ground all-spice
1 tsp dry mustard
1 tsp grated fresh ginger
1 cucumber
1 bunch green onions
2 tsps chopped fresh dill or 1 tsp dry dill weed
1 tbsp chopped parsley
Salt
Pepper
Lemon juice
2 tbsps butter

Mix the sugar and spices together and rub into the surface of both sides of the salmon steaks. Set in a refrigerator for about 1 hour. Peel the cucumber and cut into quarters lengthwise, then remove seeds and cut each quarter into 1" strips. Trim roots of green onions; trim down the green part but leave some green attached. Put these and the cucumber into a saucepan with the butter, lemon juice, salt, pepper, parsley and dill, and cook over a gentle heat for about 10-15 minutes, or until tender. Place salmon steaks under a broiler and cook for about 5-6 minutes on each side. Serve with the cucumber and green onion accompaniment.

Fritto Misto Mare

PREPARATION TIME: 10 minutes

COOKING TIME: 5-6 minutes

SERVES: 4 people

4-8 scallops
8oz uncooked shrimp
1lb whitebait, smelts or sprats, or white fish such as sole or cod
½ pint shelled mussels
Vegetable oil for deep frying
Salt

Batter
1¼ cups water
2 tbsps olive oil
1 cup flour
1 tsp ground nutmeg
1 tsp ground oregano
Pinch salt
1 egg white

Garnish
Parsley sprigs
1 lemon

First make the batter so that it can rest for ½ hour while fish is being prepared. Blend oil with water, and gradually stir it into flour sifted with a pinch of salt. Beat batter until quite smooth, and add the nutmeg and oregano. Just before using, fold in stiffly-beaten egg white. If using smelts or sprats, cut heads off the fish; if using white fish, cut into chunks about 1" thick. Shell shrimp if necessary. If the scallops are large, cut them in half. Heat oil to 375°F (190°C). Dip fish and shellfish, one at a time, into batter, allowing surplus batter to drip off. Then put them into the frying basket and into the hot oil. Fry for 5-6 minutes, or until crisp and golden. Drain on crumpled paper towels. Sprinkle lightly with salt. Put fish on a heated dish. Garnish with parsley sprigs and lemon wedges. If desired, a tartare sauce may be served.

Trout en Papillote

PREPARATION TIME: 15 minutes

COOKING TIME: 10-15 minutes

OVEN TEMPERATURE: 350°F (180°C)

SERVES: 4 people

4 small trout, about 8oz each
2-3 shallots
Sprigs of rosemary
Lemon juice
½ cup butter
¾ cup flaked almonds
Salt
Pepper

Garnish
Slices of lemon

Clean fish well, trim the fins, wash and dry, then season insides. Place a sprig of rosemary inside each, reserving 1 tbsp of leaves for use later. Chop the shallots. Melt the butter. Cut 4 large rounds of foil or baking parchment, brush them with melted butter and place the fish on them. Cut 2-3 slashes on the side of each fish to help them cook quickly. Scatter over the chopped shallots, salt, pepper and some lemon juice, and pour over some of the melted butter. Fold the paper or foil over the fish and seal well. Place fish on a baking sheet and bake for about 10-15 minutes. Meanwhile, brown the almonds in the remaining melted butter and add salt, pepper and a good squeeze of lemon juice. Just before serving, add the reserved rosemary leaves to the hot butter and almonds. Pour over the fish when the parcels are opened, and garnish with lemon slices.

Paella

PREPARATION TIME: 20 minutes

COOKING TIME: 30 minutes

SERVES: 4 people

1lb Gulf shrimp
1 pint mussels in their shells
8oz shrimp in their shells
4oz chorizo (Spanish sausage), sliced
⅔ cup dry white wine
1 cup rice
1 small onion
1 clove garlic, crushed
4 tbsps olive oil
Lemon juice
Saffron
4 tomatoes
2 green peppers
Small bunch green onions, chopped
Salt and pepper

Wash all the shrimp and scrub mussels well, discarding any with broken shells. Cook mussels in the wine over a high heat until the shells open. Discard any that do not open. Strain the liquid for use in cooking the rice. Leave mussels in their shells. Peel half the washed shrimp. Chop the onion finely, heat the oil in a shallow, heatproof dish, and cook the onion and garlic until they become a pale brown. Add the chorizo and cook for 1-2 minutes, then add rice and cook till it looks clear. Add the shellfish liquid, lemon juice, a pinch of saffron and enough water to cover the rice. Cook for 20 minutes on a moderate heat. Remove cores from tomatoes and chop roughly. Slice the peppers and add to the rice during the last 5 minutes of cooking. Add the tomatoes and peeled shrimp to heat through, then add all the remaining shellfish. Adjust seasoning and sprinkle the chopped green onion over to serve.

Paella (left) and Spiced Salmon Steaks (below).

Put tomato sauce and remaining sauce ingredients into a pan and bring to the boil. Turn down the heat and allow to simmer for about 10-15 minutes, then set aside. Bring a large saucepan of salted water to the boil. Trim and wash the pea pods and put them in the boiling water to cook for about 1-2 minutes. Drain and refresh them under cold water. Heat the broiler and brush brochettes with oil. Broil for about 3-5 minutes on each side, basting occasionally with the sauce. Heat some butter in a saucepan and toss the pea pods over the heat with salt and pepper, and heat through. Serve brochettes on their skewers on a bed of cooked rice with almonds, garnished with the lemon wedges and pea pods. Reheat the remaining sauce to serve with the brochettes.

Shrimp Creole with Saffron Rice Ring

PREPARATION TIME: 15 minutes
COOKING TIME: 30 minutes
SERVES: 4 people

1lb shrimp
1 green pepper
1 red pepper
4oz mushrooms
1 medium onion
2 sticks celery
1 16oz can tomatoes
¼ cup butter
1 tsp sugar
1 bay leaf
½ tsp Tabasco
Pinch nutmeg
½ tsp chopped thyme
2 tbsps chopped parsley
1 cup long-grain rice
1 shallot, finely chopped
Good pinch saffron, or 1 pkt saffron powder
Salt
Pepper

Rinse the rice, put into a large saucepan of boiling salted water and cook for about 12 minutes.

Langoustine and Ham Brochettes

PREPARATION TIME: 20 minutes
COOKING TIME: 25 minutes
SERVES: 4 people

16 large raw langoustines or shrimp
8oz ham cut in a thick slice
1 small fresh pineapple
1 green pepper
Oil for basting

Sauce
8oz can tomato sauce
1 tbsp Worcestershire sauce
1 tbsp cider vinegar
1-2 tbsps soft brown sugar
1 clove garlic, crushed
½ tsp dry mustard
1 bay leaf

Garnish
8oz pea pods
2 cups hot, cooked rice, tossed in butter and black pepper
¼ cup toasted flaked almonds
2 tbsps butter
Salt and pepper

Cut most of the fat from the ham. Cut the ham into 1″ cubes. Peel langoustines or shrimp. Halve green pepper, remove the seeds, and cut into 1″ pieces. Peel and quarter the pineapple, remove the core, and cut each quarter into 1″ chunks. Thread a langoustine, pepper, gammon, and pineapple onto each of 4 skewers, continuing until all the ingredients are used.

This page: Shrimp Creole with Saffron Rice Ring.
Facing page: Tuna and Fennel (top) and Langoustine and Ham Brochettes (bottom).

Measure 3 tsps of the boiling water and soak the saffron in it. Melt half the butter and cook the shallot. Butter a 2 cup ring mold well, and set aside. Drain rice when cooked, and mix with cooked shallot, seasoning, 1 tbsp chopped parsley and saffron liquid. Stir well and ensure rice is evenly colored with the saffron. Put this mixture into the ring mold, pressing down well, and leave to keep warm. Melt the remaining butter, chop the onion and celery finely, slice peppers into fine shreds, and slice the mushrooms. Cook the onion in the butter until just lightly colored, then add peppers and mushrooms and cook gently for several minutes. Add celery and tomatoes and bring to the boil. Reduce heat and add the bay leaf, remaining parsley, thyme, Tabasco, sugar and seasoning. Allow to simmer for about 12 minutes, then add shrimp and heat through. Carefully unmold the rice ring onto a serving plate and pour the prawn creole into the center.

Herring and Apples

PREPARATION TIME: 15-20 minutes

COOKING TIME: 50 minutes

OVEN TEMPERATURES: 350°F (180°C) rising to 400°F (200°C)

SERVES: 4 people

4 herrings
1 onion
2 large apples
Dry breadcrumbs
4 large potatoes, peeled and sliced
⅔ cup dry cider or white wine
1 tsp sugar
4 tbsps butter
Salt
Pepper
1 tbsp chopped parsley

Cut heads and tails from herrings, split and bone them, but do not cut into separate fillets. Wash and dry them well. Peel, quarter, core and slice 1 apple. Slice the onion thinly. Butter a shallow baking dish well. Layer the potatoes, apple and onion, seasoning between each layer with salt and pepper, and neatly arranging the final layer of potato slices. Pour the cider or wine over the potatoes, cover the dish with foil and bake for about 40 minutes. Then take the dish from the oven and place herrings on top. Cook, uncovered, for 10 minutes, then sprinkle herrings lightly with breadcrumbs and dot with some of the butter. Increase heat and bake until herrings brown – about 5-10 minutes. Meanwhile, core remaining apple and slice into rounds, leaving peel on. Melt remaining butter in a saucepan and fry the apples in the butter. Sprinkle them lightly with sugar and continue to fry until a good brown. When herrings have browned, garnish with the apple slices and chopped parsley. Serve in the baking dish.

Tuna and Fennel

PREPARATION TIME: 15 minutes

COOKING TIME: 6-8 minutes

SERVES: 4 people

4 tuna steaks, cut (1") thick
4 tbsps olive oil
4 tbsps white wine
Crushed black pepper
1 clove garlic
Salt
1 head Florentine fennel

Peel garlic and cut into thin slivers. Push these into the tuna steaks with a sharp knife. Mix oil, wine and pepper and pour over steaks in a shallow dish. Leave to marinate in a refrigerator for 1 hour. Heat grill to high and grill fish for 3-4 minutes per side, basting frequently with the marinade. Reserve the green, feathery tops of the fennel. Cut the head in half and slice into ¼" pieces. Put into boiling salted water and cook for 5 minutes. Season with salt and pepper and keep warm. Garnish the tuna steaks with reserved fennel top and serve with the cooked, sliced fennel.

Buttered Perch

PREPARATION TIME: 10 minutes

COOKING TIME: 12-15 minutes

SERVES: 4 people

2lbs perch (or sole or other whitefish) fillets
½ cup butter
3 tbsps oil
Seasoned flour
2 eggs, beaten
Fine corn meal
Lemon juice
Salt

Garnish
Lemon wedges
Parsley sprigs

Skin, wash and dry the fillets well, cut each lengthwise into 4 strips and toss in seasoned flour. Beat the eggs, adding a pinch of salt, then coat the fish before tossing it in the corn meal. Shake off the excess. Heat oil in a large frying pan and add 1 tbsp butter. Shallow-fry the fish briskly for about 5-6 minutes, frying in 2 or 3 batches. Drain on paper towels and keep warm. Melt remaining butter and add lemon juice. Pour over the fish and serve with lemon wedges and sprigs of parsley.

Hazelnut Flounder

PREPARATION TIME: 15 minutes

COOKING TIME: 10 minutes

SERVES: 4 people

2 large flounder, filleted (sole or whitefish may be used)
2 eggs, lightly beaten, with a pinch of salt
½ cup dry breadcrumbs
½ cup ground browned hazelnuts
2 tbsps oil
4 tbsps butter
Salt
Pepper
Flour

Garnish
1 large bunch watercress
⅓ cup hazelnuts, crushed
Lemon wedges

Buttered Perch (left) and Herring and Apples (below).

Fillet the fish and coat lightly in flour. Dip fillets into the beaten eggs, then into a mixture of the crumbs and nuts. Sauté the fillets quickly in oil until browned on both sides. Add salt and pepper to taste. Remove fillets from pan and keep warm. Wipe out the pan and melt the butter in it. Add crushed hazelnuts to the butter and fry them until they are a nice golden brown. Serve the fillets with the hazelnuts on top, garnished with lemon wedges and a bunch of watercress.

Stuffed Salmon Trout

PREPARATION TIME: 10-15 minutes

COOKING TIME: 40-60 minutes

OVEN TEMPERATURE: 350°F (180°C)

SERVES: 4 people

1 fresh whole salmon trout weighing 2-2½lbs
1 head Florentine fennel
2lbs fresh spinach
¼ cup walnuts
1 shallot, chopped
1 cup fresh white breadcrumbs
1 tbsp chopped parsley
1 tbsp chopped thyme
4 tbsps butter, melted
Juice of 2 lemons
Grated nutmeg
Salt
Pepper

Garnish
Lemon slices

Have the fish boned for stuffing. The head and tail should be left on. Sprinkle the inside with some of the butter and all but 2 tbsps of the lemon juice. Place fish in the center of a large, lightly buttered square of foil, and set aside. Prepare the stuffing. Cut the head of fennel in half (or, if large, into quarters), then into ¼″ slices, and put in a pan of boiling water to cook for 2-3 minutes. Meanwhile, wash the spinach leaves well, and tear off any coarse stalks. Put into a large pan, sprinkled with salt. Cover and cook for about 3 minutes, then drain and chop finely. Chop the

shallot finely and soften in 1 tbsp of the remaining melted butter. Add to the spinach with the fennel slices, chopped walnuts, parsley, thyme, nutmeg, salt and pepper, 1 tbsp of the lemon juice, and the breadcrumbs. Fill the salmon with the stuffing, leaving a border of stuffing showing. Seal the foil over the top of the fish to enclose it, but do not wrap too tightly. Place in a roasting pan and bake for 40-60 minutes, depending on weight. To serve, unwrap and transfer to a large serving dish. Remove skin from one side, turn over carefully and remove skin from the other. Serve with remaining melted butter sharpened with remaining lemon juice, and garnish with sliced lemon.

Hazelnut Flounder (left), Salmon with Cucumber Cream (below) and Stuffed Salmon Trout (facing page).

Coulibiac

PREPARATION TIME: 30 minutes

COOKING TIME: 35-40 minutes

OVEN TEMPERATURE: 400°F (200°C)

SERVES: 4 people

Pastry

4 cups all-purpose flour
4 sticks butter
Salt
2/3 cup iced water
1 egg, beaten

Filling

1lb fresh salmon
4 small leeks
1/3 cup rice
2 hard-boiled eggs
4 tbsps butter or margarine
8oz mushrooms
2 tbsps chopped parsley
1 tbsp chopped thyme
Salt
Pepper

Sauce

1¼ cups sour cream
¼ tsp grated horseradish
1 small bunch chives
Salt and pepper

Skin, trim and bone the salmon, and cut into 4 equal-sized pieces. Cook rice until tender, rinse under hot water and set aside to cool. Slice mushrooms and clean leeks well, trimming their root ends. Cut leeks into lengths equal to those of the salmon, put them into a saucepan of cold water and bring to the boil. Cook until almost completely tender, drain and allow to cool. Cook mushrooms for a few minutes in the butter. Add rice, parsley, thyme and seasoning. Hard boil the eggs for about 10 minutes and leave to sit in cold water.
To prepare the pastry, cut the butter into ½" cubes. Sieve flour with a pinch of salt into a bowl and add cubed butter until it is well coated. Mix in the iced water, a little at a time, until the mixture just holds together. (The full quantity of water may not be needed.) Chill mixture for about 10 minutes in the refrigerator. Turn the dough out onto a well-floured surface and shape it into a rough square. Using a well-floured rolling pin, roll out to a rectangle 3 times as long as it is wide. Fold the bottom third of the dough up to the middle and the top third over it. Give the dough a half-turn, then roll out and fold again in the same way. Repeat the process once more, chilling the dough in between operations if the pastry gets too soft. Chill before using.
Roll out the pastry to a square ¼" thick and cut into 4 even-sized pieces approximately 6" square. Save the trimmings. Brush each square with water and put a layer of the rice and mushroom mixture onto each. Place the cut pieces of leek on top of the rice, then put on another layer of rice. Cut the hard-boiled eggs in half and put one half on the rice layer. Add another layer of rice and, finally, the salmon piece. Fold the pastry over the salmon like an envelope and seal the edges well. Turn the envelope over and put onto a lightly-greased baking sheet. Brush each parcel with lightly beaten egg and cut the pastry trimmings into shapes to decorate the top. Brush these decorations with egg. Make a small hole in the center of each parcel. Bake until pastry is brown and salmon has had time to cook – about 30 minutes. Meanwhile, prepare a sour cream sauce. Chop the chives and mix with the sour cream, horseradish and seasoning. Keep the sauce at room temperature, but just before serving heat it over a gentle heat. Do not allow to boil. Serve the sauce with the coulibiac and garnish with watercress if desired.

This page: Coulibiac (top) and Broiled Cod Steaks (bottom). Facing page: Sea Bass with Vegetables.

Broiled Cod Steaks

PREPARATION TIME: 10 minutes

COOKING TIME: 9 minutes

SERVES: 4 people

4 cod steaks, each about 1" thick
3 tbsps butter
Dry breadcrumbs
Pepper

Flavored Butters
½ cup unsalted butter
1 tbsp chopped parsley and 1 tbsp chopped thyme,
or 1 clove crushed garlic,
or 2 tsps anchovy paste, or 2 tsps tomato paste and 1 tbsp chopped chives and a few drops of Tabasco
Salt and pepper

Garnish
4 ripe tomatoes

Melt the 3 tbsps butter. Pre-heat broiler. Brush both sides of the cod steaks with some of the melted butter. Wash tomatoes, dry them well and cut them in half. Broil with the cod steaks for about 3 minutes. Turn the steaks, brush with more melted butter, and season with pepper. Dust with dry breadcrumbs. Broil for a further 6 minutes, basting well with the butter. To serve, top each steak with a slice of one of the flavored butters and the broiled tomato halves.
To prepare flavored butters, cream the unsalted butter until soft. Beat in either the herbs, or garlic, or anchovy paste, or tomato paste, chives and Tabasco. Add seasoning to taste and a squeeze of lemon juice if desired. When well mixed, pile onto a sheet of plastic wrap or wax paper and twist ends to shape the butter into a cylinder. Chill in the refrigerator until firm. The butter may also be frozen.

Broiled Red Snapper with Garlic Sauce

PREPARATION TIME: 15 minutes
COOKING TIME: 8-10 minutes
SERVES: 4 people

4 small red snapper
Olive oil
Lemon juice
Pepper

Garlic Sauce
2 egg yolks
½ tsp mustard powder
1¼ cups olive oil
2 tbsps lemon juice
1 or 2 cloves crushed garlic
Salt
White pepper

Garnish
Lemon wedges
Watercress

Put egg yolks, mustard, garlic, salt and pepper into a food processor or blender (an electric mixer can also be used). Beat ingredients together until yolks thicken slightly. Begin adding oil in a thin, steady stream while beating yolks. Be sure to use all the oil. When sauce has thickened, adjust seasoning, add lemon and set aside. Scale and clean the fish well, leaving heads and tails on. Cut 2-3 slashes on both sides of each fish, brush with oil, and sprinkle with pepper and some lemon juice. Put under a broiler for 4-5 minutes each side. Serve with lemon wedges and the garlic sauce. Garnish with watercress if desired.

Turbot in Lettuce Leaves

PREPARATION TIME: 15 minutes
COOKING TIME: 18 minutes
OVEN TEMPERATURE: 350°F (180°C)
SERVES: 4 people

2lbs turbot fillets
1 large Romaine lettuce
1 chopped shallot
⅔ cup dry Italian vermouth
⅔ cup heavy cream
4 tbsps butter
2 tbsps flour
1 tbsp chopped chervil or parsley
Salt and pepper
Lemon juice

Skin and wash the turbot fillets well. Trim into even-sized pieces. Trim and separate the lettuce leaves. Keep them whole and put the largest, best-looking ones into boiling water for less than 1 minute. Remove them with a slotted spoon, refresh in cold water and leave to drain. Cut remaining lettuce into thin strips and put into boiling water. Drain almost immediately and refresh them. Season the fillets and place on the whole lettuce leaves, hiding the fish trimmings underneath. Wrap the leaves securely round the fillets. Butter a large ovenproof dish and put in the wrapped fillets, folded side down. Pour over the wine. Sprinkle over the chopped shallot and poach for about 10-12 minutes. When cooked, take fillets out of the baking dish, leave them in their lettuce leaves and keep warm. Melt remaining butter in a saucepan and, when foaming, stir in the flour. Cook for 2-3 minutes or until flour is pale brown. Strain in the cooking liquid from the fish, stir well and bring to the boil. When sauce thickens, add cream and re-boil. Add the blanched lettuce shreds, adjust seasoning and add lemon juice if necessary. Stir in the chopped chervil or parsley just before serving and pour the sauce into the serving dish. Set the fish parcels on top of the sauce to serve.

Sea Bass with Vegetables

PREPARATION TIME: 30 minutes
COOKING TIME: 40-60 minutes
OVEN TEMPERATURE: 350°F (180°C)
SERVES: 4 people

1 sea bass, weighing 2-2½lbs
8oz broccoli or green beans
1lb new potatoes
4 zucchini
4 very small turnips
1 small bunch green onions
2 carrots
4 tbsps butter
2 tbsps flour
1¼ cups milk
1 small bunch fresh thyme
3 lemons
Paprika
Chopped parsley
Salt and pepper

Clean the bass, trim the fins, but leave the head and tail on. Put seasoning and thyme inside the fish. Put the fish in the center of a large square of buttered foil. Add the juice of 1 lemon, wrap fish loosely, and bake for 40-60 minutes, depending on weight. Cut broccoli into small flowerets (or trim beans, but leave whole). Scrub potatoes and turnips but do not peel. Trimp ends of zucchini and cut into 2" strips. Trim roots and tops from the green onions, leaving on some of the green. Peel carrots, and cut to same size as zucchini. Keeping the vegetables in separate piles, steam potatoes and turnips for 15-20 minutes, the carrots, broccoli or beans for 6 minutes, and the zucchini and green onions for 3 minutes. Arrange on a serving dish and keep warm.
Remove fish from wrapping and place in the middle of the vegetables, keep them warm while preparing the sauce. Melt the butter and cook the flour in it for 1-2 minutes until pale brown. Stir in the milk and allow sauce to boil for 1-2 minutes until thick. Strain in the cooking liquid from the fish. Peel and segment remaining lemons, working over a bowl to collect any juice. Chop the thyme and add to sauce along with lemon segments and juice. Sprinkle paprika on the potatoes, and chopped parsley on the carrots. Coat the fish with the lemon sauce and serve.

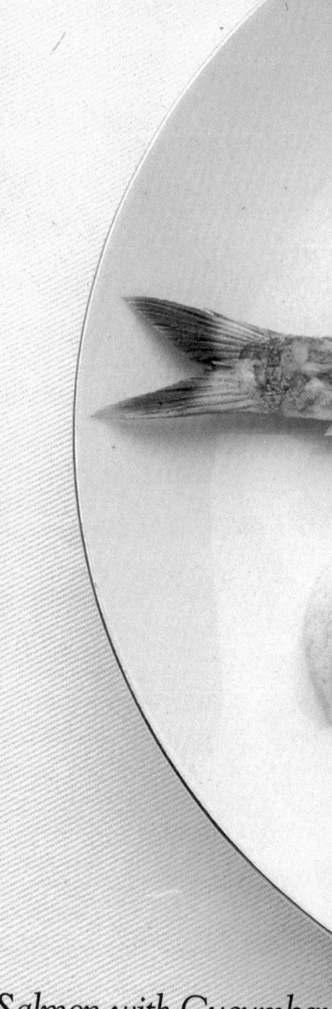

Salmon with Cucumber Cream

PREPARATION TIME: 15 minutes
COOKING TIME: 20 minutes
OVEN TEMPERATURE: 350°F (180°C)
SERVES: 4 people

4 salmon cutlets (tail pieces)
2 tbsps butter
1 small cucumber
2 tbsps light stock
⅔ cup milk
2 tbsps flour
Salt
Pepper
Lemon juice
Pinch sugar
Nutmeg
¼ cup heavy cream

Grate cucumber. Melt the butter in a saucepan, add half the cucumber and cook slowly for about 10 minutes. Add flour and stir to blend. Stir in the stock and milk, bring to boil, then allow to cook slowly until cucumber has softened. Put the contents of the pan into a blender or food processor and purée with the lemon juice, sugar, nutmeg, salt and pepper until smooth. Stir in remaining cucumber. Pour the cream over the top of the hot sauce and set aside in a saucepan while cooking the fish. Skin the cutlets and put into a baking dish with water and seasoning. Poach for 10 minutes, then remove from oven and keep warm. Re-heat cucumber sauce, stir in the cream and allow to boil for 1 minute. Spoon some of the sauce onto serving plates and put the salmon cutlets on top. Coat with more of the sauce.

Broiled Red Snapper with Garlic Sauce (left) and Turbot in Lettuce Leaves (below).

Lobster Newburg

PREPARATION TIME: 10 minutes

COOKING TIME: 12 minutes

SERVES: 4 people

1 large cooked lobster
1¼ cups heavy cream
2 egg yolks
2 tbsps butter
¼ cup dry sherry
Salt
Pepper
¼ tsp paprika
Cayenne pepper
1 tsp tomato paste

Heat the butter in a medium saucepan, add paprika and cook for 1 minute. Cut lobster in half. Take off tail and claws, remove the meat from these sections. Remove as much meat from the rest of the lobster as possible, add it to the pan, along with tail and claw meat. Put in the sherry and cook for 1 minute. Remove the tail and claw meat, and set aside for garnish. Mix egg yolks and cream together, and put in the pan with the lobster. Add the paprika, Cayenne, tomato paste and seasoning, and cook over a very low heat until the mixture begins to thicken. Serve with buttered rice, tossed with parsley. Garnish with the tail and claw meat.

Broiled Swordfish Steaks with Grapefruit

PREPARATION TIME: 10 minutes

COOKING TIME: 10 minutes

SERVES: 4 people

4 swordfish steaks, 1" thick
4 tbsps melted butter (or 4 tbsps oil)
2 grapefruit
1 tbsp sugar
Coarsely ground pepper

Melt butter, and brush fish steaks on both sides. Heat broiler to moderate. Season steaks with coarsely ground pepper. Broil on one side for about 5 minutes, turn, brush again with butter, then broil for about 3 minutes. Slice one grapefruit thinly, and peel and segment the other. Sprinkle the slices with sugar and brown under the broiler. Put the segments on top of the fish and heat through for 1 minute. Overlap the broiled grapefruit slices on serving plates and put the fish on top.

Shrimp Florentine

PREPARATION TIME: 15 minutes

COOKING TIME: 15-20 minutes

SERVES: 4 people

1lb cooked shrimp
2lbs fresh spinach
1 cup mushrooms
2 tomatoes, seeds removed
1 shallot
4 tbsps butter
1 tbsp flour
1¼ cups milk
½ cup grated Cheddar cheese
½ tsp Dijon mustard
Salt
Pepper
Nutmeg

Rinse spinach well, removing any thick stalks, and put it into a saucepan with a good pinch of salt. Cover and cook for about 3-5 minutes. In a small saucepan, heat half of the butter. Chop the shallot finely and cook it in the butter until soft. Wipe and slice the mushrooms and cook with the

This page: Shrimp Florentine (top) and Broiled Swordfish Steaks with Grapefruit (bottom).
Facing page: Lobster Newburg (top) and Skate with Capers, Olives and Shallots (bottom).

shallots: Drain the spinach well and chop finely. Mix the shallots, mushrooms and tomatoes with the spinach, add seasoning and a pinch of nutmeg, and put into an ovenproof dish. Melt half the remaining butter in a saucepan and

add the flour. Gradually stir in the milk, return the sauce to the heat and bring to the boil. Season with salt and pepper, and add mustard. Grate the cheese and add half to the sauce. Shell shrimp if necessary. Heat remaining butter and quickly toss shrimp in it over heat. Put shrimp on top of the spinach and cover with sauce. Sprinkle remaining cheese over, and brown quickly under a broiler. Serve immediately.

Skate with Capers, Olives and Shallots

PREPARATION TIME: 10 minutes

COOKING TIME: 15 minutes

OVEN TEMPERATURE: 350°F (180°C)

SERVES: 4 people

4 wings of skate
2 tbsps capers
2 shallots, chopped
½ cup stoned black olives, sliced
½ cup butter
1 tbsp chopped mixed herbs
1¼ cups white wine and water mixed
1 bay leaf
4 peppercorns
Salt
Lemon juice

Put the skate into a baking dish with the wine, water, bay leaf, salt and peppercorns. Cover and poach in the oven for 10 minutes. Drain well, removing any skin, and keep warm. Melt the butter and cook the shallots quickly, to brown both. Add capers and olives to heat through. Add herbs and lemon juice. Pour over the skate and serve immediately.

Monkfish Piperade

PREPARATION TIME: 20 minutes

COOKING TIME: 30 minutes

OVEN TEMPERATURE: 350°F (180°C)

SERVES: 4 people

1½lbs monkfish fillets
2 onions
1 yellow pepper
1 red pepper
1 green pepper
1-2 cloves garlic
1 8oz can tomatoes
Salt
Pepper
2-3 tbsps olive oil
1 small loaf French bread
Oil for deep frying

Slice onions thinly and soften in 1 tbsp olive oil in a saucepan. Slice all the peppers in half, remove seeds, and cut into ½" strips. Crush garlic and add to onions when tender, then cook gently for another 5 minutes. Add tomatoes and seasoning and let sauce simmer until liquid has reduced by about half. If the fish fillets are large, cut them in half again lengthwise. Heat remaining oil in a saucepan and cook the fish until it is lightly brown. Transfer fish to an ovenproof dish, and when the piperade is ready, spoon it over the top of the fillets, and heat through in the oven for about 10 minutes. Meanwhile, slice the French bread on the slant into ½" slices. Fry in enough oil to barely cover until golden brown, then drain on paper towels. Put the monkfish piperade into a serving dish and surround with the bread.

Halibut and Crab Hollandaise

PREPARATION TIME: 15 minutes

COOKING TIME: 20 minutes

OVEN TEMPERATURE: 325°F (160°C)

SERVES: 4 people

4 large fillets of halibut
¼ cup white wine
1 bay leaf
Slice of onion
8oz crabmeat
2 tbsps heavy cream
1 tbsp butter
1 tbsp flour
3 egg yolks
½ cup butter, melted
1 tbsp lemon juice
Salt and pepper
Cayenne pepper
Paprika

Poach the fish with the bay leaf, onion slice, wine and just enough water to cover. Cover the baking dish and cook for about 10 minutes in the oven. Put egg yolks, lemon juice, Cayenne and paprika into a blender or food processor. Turn on the machine, and gradually pour the melted butter through the feed tube. When the sauce has thickened, set it aside. Remove fish from baking dish, cover and keep warm. Put the remaining butter in a saucepan and add the flour, stirring well. Strain on the cooking liquid from the fish, stir well and bring to the boil. Add cream and bring back to the boil for 2-3 minutes. Adjust the seasoning of the sauce, mix it with the crab meat, and put into the bottom of an ovenproof dish that can also be used for serving. Put the fish on top of the crab meat and coat over with the Hollandaise sauce. Quickly brown the sauce under a broiler before serving.

Danish Sole and Shrimp

PREPARATION TIME: 15 minutes

COOKING TIME: 10-15 minutes

SERVES: 4 people

2 large sole
8oz shrimp
Seasoned flour
6 tbsps butter
2 tbsps oil
Salt
Pepper
Lemon juice

Garnish
Lemon wedges

Peel the tails, shells and legs from 4 whole shrimp and set aside. Fillet and skin the sole, rinse and dry well, and coat lightly in seasoned flour. Heat the oil in a large frying pan, then drop in 2 tbsps of the butter. Lay in the fish fillets and cook quickly to brown both sides. Transfer them to a serving dish and keep warm. Briefly cook the remaining peeled shrimp in the butter remaining in the pan and scatter them over the cooked fillets. Wipe out the pan, put in the remaining butter, and cook to a good nut brown colour. Add a squeeze of lemon juice. Adjust seasoning, then pour over the sole and shrimp. Garnish with the whole shrimp and lemon wedges.

Rock Salmon in Paprika Sauce

PREPARATION TIME: 20 minutes

COOKING TIME: 16 minutes

OVEN TEMPERATURE: 350°F (180°C)

SERVES: 4 people

1lb rock salmon fillets (other white fish may be substituted)
Lemon juice
Bay leaf
Slice of onion
6 peppercorns
2 tbsps butter
2 tbsps flour
¼ cup mushrooms
1 small red pepper
1¼ cups milk
2 tsps sweet paprika pepper
1 clove garlic, crushed
1 chopped shallot
1 tbsp chopped parsley
1 tsp chopped thyme
1 tsp tomato paste
8oz freshly cooked pasta
2 tbsps sour cream or yogurt
Salt
Pepper

Cut the fillets into 1" chunks. Put into an ovenproof dish with water to cover, lemon juice, bay leaf,

onion slice and peppercorns. Cover and poach for about 10 minutes. Slice mushrooms finely. Slice the red pepper in half, core and seed it, then slice into thin shreds. Melt the butter in a saucepan, add mushrooms and shallot and cook for about 1 minute. Add garlic, red peppers, and sweet paprika pepper and allow to cook for about 2-3 minutes. Add the flour. Stir in well, and pour on the milk and the poaching liquid from the fish. Bring the sauce to the boil and allow to cook for 2-3 minutes and add thyme, parsley and tomato paste. Add salt and pepper to taste. Arrange the freshly cooked pasta in a serving dish and place the chunks of fish on top of the pasta. Coat over with paprika sauce and spoon over the yogurt or sour cream to serve.

Danish Sole and Shrimp (left) and Monkfish Piperade (below).

Mackerel with Herb-Mustard Butter

PREPARATION TIME: 15 minutes
COOKING TIME: 12-20 minutes
SERVES: 4 people

4 mackerel
6 tbsps whole grain mustard
1 tbsp chopped parsley
1 tbsp snipped chives
1 tbsp chopped lemon thyme
1 tbsp chopped fresh basil
1 cup butter
Salt
Pepper
Lemon juice

Garnish
1 bunch watercress

Wash and trim the mackerel, leaving heads and tails on. Cut 3 slashes on each side and spread 1 tbsp mustard over each fish. Sprinkle with freshly ground pepper. Melt the butter and sprinkle about 1 tsp over each fish. Grill them for 6-10 minutes on each side, depending on their size. Mix remaining butter and mustard with the herbs, seasoning and lemon juice. When fish are cooked put them into a serving dish and pour over the herb-mustard butter. Garnish with the watercress.

Sardine and Tomato Gratinée

PREPARATION TIME: 20-25 minutes
COOKING TIME: 15 minutes
OVEN TEMPERATURE: 425°F (225°C)
SERVES: 4 people

2lbs large, fresh sardines
3 tbsps olive oil
⅔ cup dry white wine
8oz tomatoes
4 anchovies
2 tbsps dry breadcrumbs
¼ cup grated Parmesan cheese
2 tbsps chopped fresh herbs
2 leeks, cleaned and sliced
Salt and pepper

Scale and clean the sardines. Heat oil in a large frying pan, add the sardines and brown well on both sides. Remove from the pan and set aside. Add leeks and cook slowly in the oil from the sardines. When they are soft, pour in the wine and boil to reduce by about two-thirds. Add tomatoes, salt pepper and herbs, and continue to simmer for 1 minute. Pour into an ovenproof dish and put the sardines on top. Sprinkle with the cheese and breadcrumbs. Bake for about 5 minutes. If desired, cut anchovy fillets lengthwise into thinner strips and lay them on top of the gratinée before serving.

This page: Halibut and Crab Hollandaise (top) and Sardine and Tomato Gratinée (bottom). Facing page: Rock Salmon in Paprika Sauce (top) and Mackerel with Herb-Mustard Butter.

Fish Snacks

Strawberry Shrimp

PREPARATION TIME: 10 minutes

COOKING TIME: 3 minutes

SERVES: 4 people

¾lb shrimp, shelled and minced
1 small can water chestnuts, peeled and minced
½ cup ham, ground
1 tsp white wine
¼ tsp minced green onion
¼ tsp grated fresh ginger
1½ tbsps cornstarch
1 egg white
Sesame seeds
Pinch of salt
Oil for deep frying
4 tbsps hoisin (Chinese barbecue) sauce
1 tsp white or rice wine vinegar
1 tsp honey
2 tbsps water
1 tsp sesame oil

Mix prawns and water chestnuts with wine, green onion, ginger, egg white and a pinch of salt. Chill mixture for 30 minutes before using. Form mixture into strawberry-sized balls. Cover each ball with the finely ground ham. Fry in deep oil for about 3 minutes at 375°F (190°C). Drain, roll in sesame seeds to coat, and place on a plate. Mix hoisin sauce, honey, vinegar, water and sesame oil together, and serve with the shrimp balls. Garnish shrimp balls with parsley.

Fisherman's Pie

PREPARATION TIME: 20 minutes

COOKING TIME: 45 minutes

OVEN TEMPERATURE: 375°F (190°C)

SERVES: 4 people

1lb cod fillet
1lb smoked cod or haddock fillet
¼ pint clams
4oz peeled shrimp
1¼ cups milk
½ cup water
1 bay leaf
2 tbsps butter
2 tbsps flour
1 heaped tbsp chopped parsley
Squeeze of lemon juice
Salt
Freshly ground pepper

Topping
1½ lbs potatoes
1-2 tbsps milk
2 tbsps butter
Salt
Pepper

Skin fish and cut into pieces. Keep fresh cod and smoked fish separate. Put each into a separate saucepan with milk, water, and half a bay leaf in each. Bring to the boil; lower heat, and simmer, covered, for about 10 minutes. Meanwhile, peel potatoes and cut them into even-sized chunks. Add them to a pan of cold, salted water, bring up to the boil and cook for about 20 minutes, or until tender. Drain, return to the hot saucepan and shake over heat until they are dry. Mash them, and beat in 2 or 3 tbsps hot milk and half the butter. Season with salt and pepper and set aside. Take cooked fish from the milk and break it up, removing any bones. Strain cooking liquid from both saucepans – there should be 1¼ cups in all. Melt butter in a saucepan over a low heat. Stir in the flour, and cook gently for 1 minute. Gradually stir in the reserved fish liquid. Bring to boil. Stir well and simmer for 2-3 minutes. Take off the heat. Fold in

This page: Kedgeree. Facing page: Strawberry Shrimp (top) and Crab Toasts (bottom).

the fish and parsley, and add lemon juice, a seasoning of salt and pepper, clams and shrimp. Butter a 2½ cup ovenproof dish and put the fish mixture in it. Fill a pastry bag, fitted with a rosette tube, with the mashed potato mixture and pipe in a lattice over the surface of the fish. Pipe a border round its edge. Dot over the remaining butter in pieces, and put into the oven for about 20 minutes and brown under a broiler, with grated cheese sprinkled on top if desired.

Crab Ramekins

PREPARATION TIME: 10 minutes

COOKING TIME: 15 minutes

OVEN TEMPERATURE: 425°F (220°C)

SERVES: 4 people

¾ cup Cheddar cheese
¾ cup Parmesan cheese
1½ cups fresh white breadcrumbs
1¼ cups cream
1 cup crabmeat
3 eggs
1 tsp Worcestershire sauce
Cayenne pepper
Ground mace
Dry mustard
Salt and pepper

Separate the eggs and grate the cheese. Mix the breadcrumbs with the cream and grated cheese. Add the Worcestershire sauce, a pinch of mace, Cayenne, dry mustard and seasoning. Beat in the egg yolks. Whip the whites until stiff but not dry and fold into the cheese mixture along with the crabmeat. Pour into a large, buttered, ovenproof dish or smaller ramekin dishes. Bake until risen.

Smoked Haddock Lyonnaise

PREPARATION TIME: 15 minutes

COOKING TIME: 20 minutes

SERVES: 4 people

3 medium onions
1 tbsp unsalted butter
2 tbsps oil
3 medium-sized potatoes
1lb smoked haddock (finnan haddie)
Freshly ground pepper
2 tbsps white wine vinegar
Chopped parsley

Heat oil in a large frying pan and, when hot, drop in butter. Cut smoked fish into chunks and sauté. Remove from the pan and set aside. Slice onions and cook them slowly in the butter until they turn golden brown. Slice the potatoes and cook in boiling salted water until slightly softened. Add them just as onions are turning color, then sauté the mixture to brown lightly. Add the smoked fish, sauté for a few minutes, and adjust seasoning. Pile onto a serving platter. Add vinegar to the pan, bring rapidly to boil, add chopped parsley, and pour over potatoes and haddock.

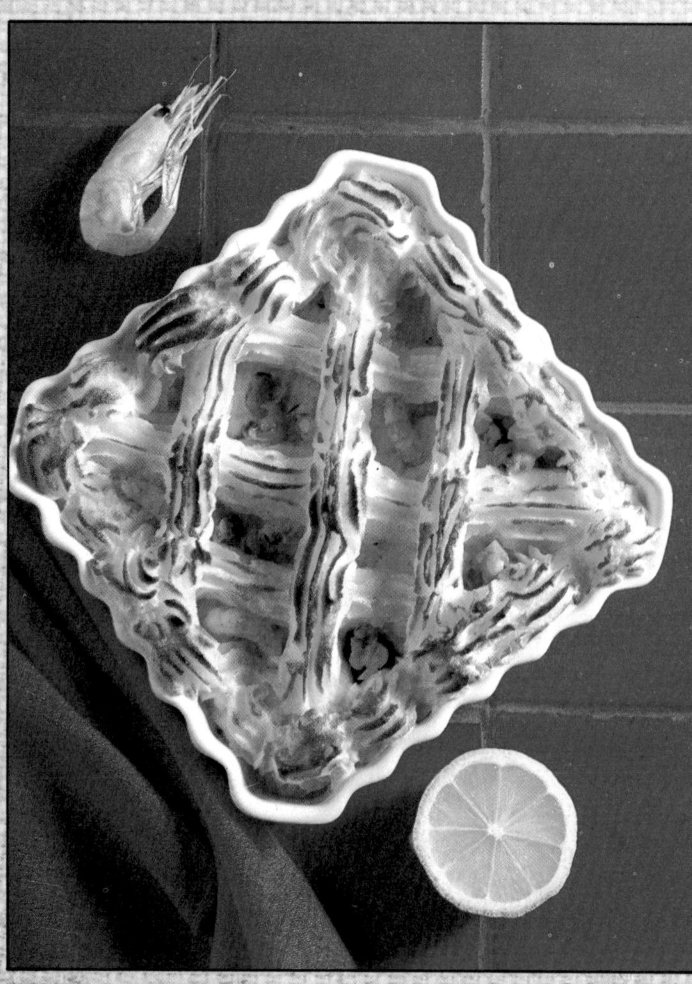

Crab and Spinach Roulade

PREPARATION TIME: 15 minutes

COOKING TIME: 18 minutes

OVEN TEMPERATURE: 400°F (200°C)

SERVES: 4 people

Roulade
1lb spinach, washed
1 tbsp butter
4 eggs, separated
Parmesan cheese, grated
Salt
Pepper

Filling
½ cup crabmeat
¼ cup mushrooms, thinly sliced
1 tbsp butter
1 tbsp flour
⅔ cup milk
Nutmeg
2-3 tbsps cream
Paprika
Cayenne pepper
Lemon juice

Cook the spinach in boiling salted water for about 5 minutes. Drain, rinse under cold water, and press well to remove excess liquid. Put the spinach into a food processor with the butter and egg yolks and process to a smooth purée. Whisk egg whites until they are stiff but not dry and fold into the spinach mixture. Line a 12" x 8" jelly roll pan with wax paper. Spread in the spinach mixture very quickly and dust lightly with Parmesan cheese. Bake in the top half of the oven for about 10 minutes or until mixture has risen and is firm to the touch. Meanwhile, prepare filling. Sauté sliced mushrooms in butter. Remove from heat, and add flour, paprika, Cayenne, lemon juice and seasoning to taste. Pour on the milk and bring to the boil, then simmer to a creamy consistency. Draw pan from heat and stir in nutmeg and cream (a dash of Tabasco and 1 tbsp dry sherry can also be used if desired). Once the pan is again off the heat, stir in the crabmeat. When the roulade is cooked, quickly turn it out onto a clean towel, cheese side down, and peel off the paper in which it was cooked. Spread it with the filling, roll up as for a jelly roll, starting at the short end, and serve sprinkled with more Parmesan cheese if desired.

Crab Toasts

PREPARATION TIME: 10 minutes

COOKING TIME: 4 minutes per piece

SERVES: 4 people

8 slices white bread
8oz crabmeat
3 tbsps minced water chestnuts
1 egg white
½ tsp white wine
½ tsp mustard powder
½ tsp salt
½ tsp minced green onion
¼ tsp grated ginger
1½ tsps cornstarch
1 tbsp minced parsley
Oil for deep frying

Remove crusts from the bread, and slice diagonally across each piece to form 2 triangles. Mix crabmeat and chestnuts together. Add egg white, wine, salt, green onion, ginger and cornstarch. Heap the mixture generously onto each triangle of bread. Sprinkle with parsley, pressing down firmly so that the mixture will not float off during frying. Heat oil to 350°F (180°C). Put a piece of the prepared bread, crabmeat side down, onto a slotted spoon, place it in the oil and gently remove spoon. Fry the pieces, a few at a time, until the bread side becomes a golden brown. Turn each piece over and fry again. Drain on paper towels and keep warm in the oven until all the pieces are finished.

Crab Ramekins (above right) and Smoked Haddock Lyonnaise (right) and Fisherman's Pie (inset above).

Oysters and Apples

PREPARATION TIME: 10 minutes

COOKING TIME: 2-3 minutes

SERVES: 4 people

1 3½oz can smoked oysters
1 large apple, unpeeled
4-5 strips bacon
1oz Cheddar cheese

Core and quarter the apple, and cut the quarters into 8-10 slices. Divide the cheese into 8-10 small pieces. Put 1 piece on each slice of apple and an oyster on top of the cheese. Cut each bacon strip in half. Wrap the bacon around the oysters and apples. Secure with a wooden pick and broil until the bacon is crisp, turning once.

Shrimp Pastry Puffs

PREPARATION TIME: 15 minutes

COOKING TIME: 25-30 minutes

OVEN TEMPERATURE: 400°F (200°C)

SERVES: 4 people

Choux Pastry
½ cup flour
⅓ cup butter
½ cup water
2-3 eggs
Salt

Filling
1¼ cups milk
2½ tbsps butter
2½ tbsps flour
2 tbsps white wine
¾ cup shrimp
2 hard-boiled eggs, quartered
Nutmeg
1 bay leaf
1 tsp chopped dill
Salt
Pepper

Prepare the pastry. Sift flour with a pinch of salt. Place butter and water in a pan over a gentle heat. When butter is melted, bring water to the boil. Take off the heat and immediately tip in all the flour. Beat until the mixture is smooth and leaves the sides of the pan. Leave to cool. Whisk the eggs lightly and add by degrees to the mixture, beating thoroughly between each addition. (This part of the recipe may be done with an electric mixer or in a food processor). When finished, the paste should be smooth and shiny and hold its shape when dropped from a spoon. Lightly grease a baking sheet and sprinkle it lightly with water. Place the pastry mixture by heaped teaspoonfuls onto the sheet. If desired, the puffs can be made slightly larger by using a tablespoon. Bake until the puffs are firm to the touch and a good golden brown. For the sauce, melt the butter over a gentle heat and blend in the flour. Stir in the milk gradually and add the bay leaf. Add the wine and bring the mixture to the boil, stirring constantly. Remove the bay leaf, add the shrimp, dill and eggs, and adjust the seasoning. Cut the pastry puffs almost in half through the middle and fill with the shrimp and egg mixture. Serve hot or cold.

This page: Crab and Spinach Roulade (top) and Shrimp Risotto (bottom).
Facing page: Shrimp Pastry Puffs (top) and Oysters and Apples (bottom).

shell fish, anchovies, olives and capers. Place cheese slices on top of the fish. Bake in a pre-set oven until cheese browns lightly and the crust is crisp.

Anchovy Pâté with Crudités

PREPARATION TIME: 15 minutes

SERVES: 4 people

8oz canned anchovies
¼ cup olive oil
1 3 oz package cream cheese
½ cup pitted black olives
2 tbsps capers
1 tbsp Dijon mustard
1 tsp ground pepper

Put all ingredients into the bowl of a blender or food processor and run the machine until well mixed. The mixture may have to be worked in 2 batches. Serve with French bread or toast, and raw vegetables of all kinds – tomatoes, mushrooms, celery, radishes, green beans, cauliflower, carrots, cucumber, peppers, spring onions, or quarters of hard boiled eggs.

Goujons

PREPARATION TIME: 20-30 minutes

COOKING TIME: 2-3 minutes

SERVES: 4 people

2 sole
Seasoned flour
1 egg
2 tsps olive oil
Dry breadcrumbs
Oil for deep frying
Pinch of salt

Tartare Sauce
2 tbsps mayonnaise
1 tbsp heavy cream
2 tsps chopped parsley
2 tsps chopped dill pickles
2 tsps chopped capers
1 tsp chopped onion

Pizza Marinara

PREPARATION TIME: 15 minutes

COOKING TIME: 25-30 minutes

OVEN TEMPERATURE: 425°F (220°C)

SERVES: 4 people

1 cup flour, sifted
1 tsp baking powder
½ tsp salt
⅓ cup milk
2 tbsp salad oil
½ cup canned tomatoes
1 tsp tomato paste
1 clove crushed garlic
½ tsp oregano
½ tsp basil
Fennel seeds
Salt
Pepper
¼ cup shrimp
4 anchovies
¼ cup clams
6-8 mussels
1 tsp capers
2-3 black olives
6 slices mozzarella cheese

Sift flour, baking powder and salt into a bowl and add milk and oil. Stir vigorously until mixture leaves the sides of the bowl. Press it into a ball and knead it in the bowl for about 2 minutes until smooth. Cover, and leave it to sit while preparing sauce. Put tomatoes, tomato paste, herbs, seasoning and garlic together in a small saucepan. Bring to the boil and reduce to thicken. Leave to cool. Roll out the pizza into a 12" circle. Spread the sauce evenly, leaving a ½" border around the edge. Scatter over the

This page: Anchovy Pâté with Crudités.
Facing page: Goujons (top) and Pizza Marinara (bottom).

Curry Sauce
2 tbsps mayonnaise
1 tbsp heavy cream
1 tsp curry powder
1½ tsps mango relish

Tomato Herb Sauce
2 tbsps mayonnaise
1 tbsp heavy cream
1 tsp chopped parsley
1 tsp chopped tarragon
1 tsp chopped chives
1 tsp tomato paste
Squeeze of lemon

Fillet the sole and skin the fillets. Rinse fillets in cold water and pat dry. Cut each fillet on the diagonal into pieces about ½" thick and 2½-3" long. Coat thoroughly with seasoned flour, shaking off any excess. Beat eggs lightly and mix in the olive oil. Dip fish pieces into the mixture and roll them in the breadcrumbs. Put fish aside in a cool place: do not coat the fish too soon before cooking. Mix ingredients for the various sauces together and set aside. Heat oil in a deep fryer to about 375°F (190°C). Put fish in the frying basket and lower into the hot oil. Fry for 2-3 minutes until crisp and golden brown. Fry in small batches. Drain fish on crumpled paper towels, sprinkle lightly with salt, and then pile the fish into a hot serving dish. Garnish with wedges of lemon and sprigs of parsley, if desired, and serve the sauces separately for dipping the fish.

Shrimp Risotto

PREPARATION TIME: 15 minutes
COOKING TIME: 25 minutes
SERVES: 4 people

1lb unpeeled shrimp
4 tomatoes
3 cloves garlic
1 large onion
3 tbsps olive oil
2 tbsps chopped parsley
1 glass white wine
1½ cups round Italian or risotto rice
1 tsp tomato paste
2 tbsps grated Parmesan cheese
Salt
Freshly ground pepper

Skin, seed and chop tomatoes, and peel and chop garlic and onion. Peel shrimp, leaving 4 unpeeled for garnish. Cook wine and shrimp shells together and leave to cool. Heat olive oil in a fairly wide pan or sauté pan. Soften onion in the oil without browning. Add garlic and parsley. Fry gently for a minute. Add rice and strain on the wine. Add tomato paste and more water to just barely cover rice. Season with salt and pepper, stirring the rice, adding more water as it becomes absorbed. The rice will take about 20 minutes to cook. When it is cooked, toss in the peeled shrimp and cheese to heat through. Pile risotto into a serving dish and top with unpeeled shrimp. Sprinkle over some chopped parsley.

Sardine Savories

PREPARATION TIME: 10-20 minutes
COOKING TIME: 20 minutes
OVEN TEMPERATURE: 375°F (190°C)
SERVES: 4 people

8oz pie or puff pastry
¼ cup fresh Parmesan or Cheddar cheese
4oz (approx) canned sardines
Cayenne pepper
Chopped chives or green onion
1 egg, beaten
Salt
Pepper

Prepare the pastry, or use ready-made. Roll it out and cut into 8 pieces large enough to fold up around the sardines. Remove bones from the sardines and put the fillets on top of one half of the pastry rectangles. Sprinkle over the grated cheese, Cayenne pepper, seasoning, and chives or onion, and fold the other half of the pastry over to cover the sardines. Seal the edges well and cut two slits in the top. Brush with the beaten egg and bake until golden brown and risen. Serve hot or cold.

Omelette of Clams and Mussels

PREPARATION TIME: 5 minutes
COOKING TIME: 7-10 minutes
SERVES: 4 people

½ pint shelled clams
½ pint shelled mussels
6-8 eggs
2½ tbsps butter
Drop of anchovy paste
Cayenne pepper
Salt
Pepper
Finely chopped parsley and chives

Poach mussels in boiling salted water for about 2 minutes. Add a bay leaf if desired. Rinse clams under cold water. Separate eggs and beat yolks with anchovy paste, Cayenne pepper and seasoning. Whisk whites until stiff but not dry and fold into yolks. Heat the butter in a large omelette pan and when foaming, pour in the egg mixture. Allow eggs to set on the bottom. Score the omelette down the middle. Add clams and mussels and fold in two. Heat through for 2 minutes to cook the inside of the omelette and to warm the shellfish. Serve immediately, sprinkled with finely chopped parsley and chives. (This dish can be adapted to make individual omelettes).

Kedgeree

PREPARATION TIME: 15 minutes
COOKING TIME: 20 minutes
SERVES: 4 people

¾lb smoked haddock (finnan haddie)
½ cup mushrooms
4oz peeled shrimp
Juice of half a lemon
¾ cup rice
1 small onion
2 cups milk
2 tbsps flour
4 tbsps butter
½ tsp curry powder
4 hard-boiled eggs
Fresh parsley
½ cup cream
Salt
Pepper

Cook rice for about 12 minutes. Drain under hot water to remove starch and leave to dry. Melt butter in a large pan. Slice the onion and fry until golden brown. Add mushrooms and fry for a few seconds before adding the flour. Add curry powder and cook for a minute or two. Gradually work in the cold milk until all is incorporated. Simmer for 5 minutes, stirring constantly, until thick. Skin smoked haddock, cut into small pieces, add to the sauce and continue to cook. Once cooked, add the lemon juice, shrimp and salt and pepper to taste. Stir in the rice. If sauce seems too thick, add cream. Mound kedgeree into a heated serving dish. Sprinkle on chopped parsley and garnish with slices or quarters of egg.

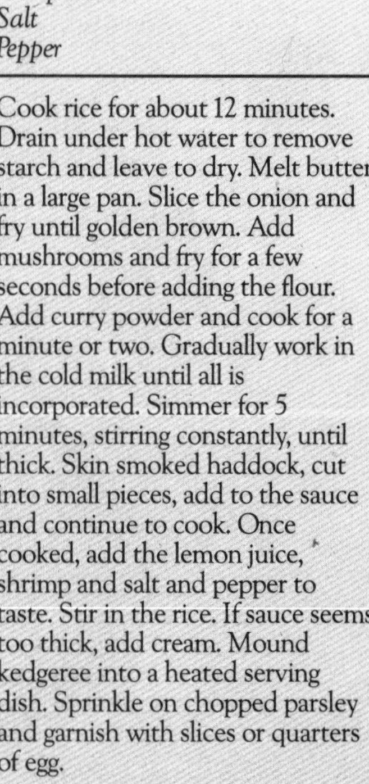

Omelette of Clams and Mussels (left) and Sardine Savories (below).

Section 3

HOME FARE

Family Recipes

Cod in White Sauce

1½lb cod fillet
Salt and pepper
⅔ cup milk
2 tblsp lemon juice
2 tblsp butter

White Sauce
2 tblsp margarine
¼ cup flour
Milk
Salt and pepper
Pinch of paprika

Wash and skin the fish and cut into four pieces. Place the fish in an ovenproof dish and season well. Pour the milk and lemon juice over the fish and dot with some of the butter. Cover the dish and cook for 20 minutes at 400°F. Melt the margarine and remaining butter in a pan, stir in the flour and cook for 1 minute. Drain the liquid from the fish and add enough milk to make up to 1¼ cups. Stir the liquid slowly into the roux, bring to the boil and cook for 1 minute, stirring continuously. Add seasoning and paprika. Serve with new potatoes and broccoli.
Serves four.

Beef Surprise

1 onion, peeled and chopped
3 tblsp fat
¼ cup flour
1¼ cups brown stock
Pinch of mixed herbs
1lb ground beef
Salt and pepper

Cook the onion in the fat until transparent. Add the flour and cook for 5 minutes. Add the stock, bring to the boil and cook until the sauce thickens. Add the herbs, ground beef and seasoning. Stir continuously, cook until the meat is browned. Lower the heat and simmer gently for 1 hour, stirring frequently. Arrange on a hot dish. Garnish with tomatoes and creamed potatoes, and serve.
Serves four.

Chicken Pie

Pastry
2 cups flour
Pinch of salt
¼ cup margarine
¼ cup lard
Beaten egg and milk mixed together to glaze top of pie

Chicken Sauce
⅔ cup milk
1 tblsp margarine
1 tblsp all-purpose flour
Salt and pepper
1 cup cooked chicken, chopped
3 tblsp white wine (optional)

First make the sauce by placing the milk, margarine and flour in a small pan. Bring to the boil, beating continuously. Simmer for 2 minutes until the sauce thickens. Add seasoning, stir in the chopped chicken and add the wine, if desired. Sift the flour and salt into a bowl and rub in the margarine and lard until it looks like breadcrumbs. Add enough water to form a dough. Use half the dough to line a large, flat plate. Add the chicken mixture then cover with the remaining pastry, sealing the edges. Cut slits in the top. Brush the top of the pie with the beaten egg and milk mixture. Cook in the oven for 25 minutes at 400°F, until golden brown. Serve with creamed potatoes and carrots.
Serves four.

Spaghetti Bolognese

2 tblsp butter
1 tblsp olive oil
¼ cup mushrooms, chopped
1 onion, peeled and chopped
1 carrot, peeled and chopped
½lb ground beef
½ cup tomato paste
1¼ cups brown stock
8oz spaghetti
Parmesan cheese, to serve

Heat the butter and oil in a pan and fry the mushrooms, onions and carrot. Stir in the meat, cook for a few minutes then add the tomato paste and stock and simmer gently. Cook for one hour, until the mixture thickens, stirring occasionally. Meanwhile, place the spaghetti in boiling, salted water and cook for 15 minutes. Drain. Serve together with the Bolognese sauce and sprinkle with Parmesan cheese.
Serves four.

Beef Bake

1½lb stewing steak
¼ cup flour
Salt and pepper
2 tblsp lard
2 onions, peeled and chopped
2½ cups brown stock
1 tblsp tomato paste
3 tblsp red wine (optional)
2 carrots, peeled and sliced
2 tsp dried mixed herbs

Topping
¼ cup white breadcrumbs
¼ cup butter
2 cups all-purpose flour
2 tsp baking powder
1 tsp salt
Pepper
1 tsp garlic salt
1 tsp Parmesan cheese
3 tblsp oil
⅔ cup milk

Cut the meat into cubes and toss in seasoned flour. Melt the lard in a pan and fry the onions. Add the meat and fry for 5 minutes or until the meat is brown. Remove from the heat and blend in the stock, tomato paste and red wine. Add the carrots and herbs. Return to the heat and bring to the boil. Turn the mixture into an ovenproof dish, cover and cook in the oven for 2 hours at 325°F. Fry the breadcrumbs in the butter until golden brown, then lift out on to a plate. Sieve together the flour, baking powder, salt, pepper, garlic salt and Parmesan cheese, add the oil and milk and gradually mix to a dough. Drop large spoonfuls of the dough into the fried breadcrumbs and roll into balls. Arrange on top of the meat mixture. Return the casserole uncovered to the oven and cook for a further hour, or until the top is golden brown. Serve with peas and new potatoes.
Serves four.

Sweet and Sour Pork Chops with Rice

4 large pork chops

Sauce
14oz can of tomatoes
1 large green pepper, cored, seeded and chopped
2 tblsp cornstarch
3 tblsp wine vinegar
2 tblsp brown sugar
2 tblsp soy sauce
Salt and pepper

To make the sauce place the tomatoes and ⅔ cup of their juice in a saucepan and break down with a fork. Add the green pepper, bring to the boil and simmer for 10 minutes. Blend the cornstarch and vinegar together to form a paste. Add the paste to the tomato mixture. Add the remaining sauce ingredients and cook for 15 minutes. Meanwhile, cook the pork chops under a moderately hot broiler. Place the chops on a flat, flameproof serving dish and pour over the sauce. Place under a hot broiler for 2-3 minutes to heat through.
Serves four.

Pork Chops with Brussels Sprouts and Corn (far left, top), Beef Surprise (far left, bottom) and Cod in White Sauce (left).

Pork Chops with Brussels Sprouts and Corn

1/3 cup butter
1 large onion, peeled and chopped
1lb Brussels sprouts
1/2 cup frozen corn
4 pork chops (large)
1 tsp salt
1 tsp cayenne pepper
1 tsp chopped parsley

Melt 2 tblsp of butter in a saucepan. Add the chopped onion and fry lightly. Cook the Brussels sprouts in boiling, salted water for about 8 minutes until cooked but still firm. Also cook the corn. Drain both vegetables. Melt 2 tblsp of the butter and add the drained Brussels sprouts and corn and cook very gently, shaking the pan frequently. Melt the remaining butter. Sprinkle the pork chops with the salt and the cayenne pepper and fry them in the butter over a medium heat for about 5-10 minutes on each side. Remove the chops to a serving dish. Add 2 tablespoons of water to the juices in the pan and bring to the boil, stirring continuously. Arrange the vegetables round the chops and pour over the sauce. Sprinkle with the chopped parsley and serve. Serves four.

Facing page: Spaghetti Bolognese (top), Chicken Pie (centre left) and Shepherd's Pie (bottom).

Chicken Casserole

2 tblsp lard
1/2 cup mushrooms, sliced
4 chicken joints
3/4 cup flour
2 large carrots, peeled and sliced
1 potato, peeled and sliced
1 1/4 cups chicken stock
1 1/4 cups white wine
Salt and pepper
6 tblsp peas

Melt half the lard, fry the mushrooms, then place them in an ovenproof dish. Coat the chicken in the flour and fry in the remaining lard until golden brown. Transfer to the ovenproof dish and add the sliced carrots and potato. Put the leftover flour in a pan and add the stock and wine, stirring all the time. Add the seasoning, bring to the boil and pour over the chicken and vegetables. Cover and cook in the oven for 1 hour 35 minutes at 350°F. Add the peas 10 minutes before the end of the cooking time. Serve with new potatoes.
Serves four.

Shepherd's Pie

2 tblsp fat
1 onion, peeled and chopped
1/4 cup mushrooms, chopped
2 tomatoes, skinned and chopped
12oz cooked beef or lamb, ground
Pinch of mixed herbs
Salt and pepper
1 1/4 cups brown stock
1lb mashed potato
1/4 cup butter

Heat the fat and fry the onion for 3 minutes. Add the mushrooms and fry for another minute. Add the tomatoes and the meat and cook for 3 minutes. Stir in the herbs and seasoning and finally add the stock. Put the mixture into a pie dish and cover with the mashed potato. Dot small pieces of butter over the mashed potato. Cook in the oven for 30-40 minutes at 400°F, until the top is crisp and brown. Serve with peas and leeks.
Serves four.

This page: Beef Bake (top left), Chicken Casserole (top right) and Sweet and Sour Pork Chops with Rice (bottom).

Country Chicken

4 chicken legs
Butter for frying
2 onions, peeled and chopped
2 tblsp cornstarch
A little milk
⅔ cup hot chicken stock
½ cup peas
½ cup corn

Fry the chicken legs in butter to seal. Set aside to drain on paper towels. Fry the onions until tender but not brown. Transfer the chicken and onions to an ovenproof dish. Blend the cornstarch with the milk. Add the chicken stock. Add the peas and corn to the casserole and pour the chicken stock over the vegetables but do not completely cover chicken. Cook in the oven, uncovered, for 20-30 minutes at 375°F. Serve with boiled potatoes. Serves four.

Liver With Oranges

12oz lambs' liver
¼ cup flour
Salt and pepper
Pinch of mustard
½ cup butter
1 tblsp olive oil
1 onion
1 tsp garlic salt
½ tsp brown ketchup sauce
⅔ cup brown stock
2 oranges, peeled and sliced, to garnish
Creamed potatoes, to serve

Trim the liver and cut into 3-4 slices. Season the flour with salt, pepper and the mustard. Dip the liver into the seasoned flour. Melt half the butter and 1 tsp of oil. Fry the liver in the butter and oil, cooking each side for 2-3 minutes. Remove the liver to a warmed dish and keep hot. Add the remaining butter to the pan and cook the onion until soft. Add the garlic salt and brown sauce. Stir in the stock. Simmer until the mixture thickens and add extra seasoning if desired. Place the liver on a serving dish, pour over the sauce and garnish with slices of orange. Pipe creamed potatoes round to make a border. Serves four.

Beef and Dumplings

1-1½lb chuck roast
Salt and pepper
¼ cup flour or
1½ tblsp cornstarch
2 tblsp fat
3¾ cups brown stock
Pinch of mixed herbs
2 onions, peeled and chopped
4 carrots, peeled and sliced

Dumplings
1 cup all-purpose flour
1 tsp baking powder
Pinch of salt
¼ cup suet
Water to mix

Wipe the meat and cut into small pieces. Remove excess fat. Coat the meat in seasoned flour or cornstarch and fry in the fat for a few minutes to seal. Add the stock, herbs and vegetables, and bring to the boil. Transfer to an ovenproof dish and cover. Cook in the oven for 2½ hours at 350°F. Meanwhile, make the dumplings. Sieve the flour, salt and baking powder into a basin. Add the suet and blend with a knife. Stir in enough water to bind. The dumpling mixture should be just soft enough to form into balls. Divide into 8 portions and roll into balls with lightly floured hands. If necessary thicken the casserole with extra cornstarch or flour, blended with a little cold water. Twenty minutes before the end of the cooking time put the dumplings into the simmering liquid. Leave uncovered, unless there is plenty of space between the dumplings and the lid to allow them to rise well. Serve with boiled potatoes.
Serves four-six.

Liver with Oranges (facing page), Beef and Dumplings (center) and Country Chicken (left).

Toad in the Hole

½lb sausages (pork or beef)
1 tblsp lard
1 cup all-purpose flour
½ level tsp salt
Pinch of garlic salt
1 egg
1¼ cups milk

Put the sausages into a large, shallow pan or dish. Add the lard and place in the oven at 450°F. Sieve the flour, salt and garlic salt into a bowl. Add the egg and a little milk and beat until smooth. Add the rest of the milk a little at a time, beating well, to make a batter. Pour the batter into the pan. Cook for 30-45 minutes. Serve with mixed vegetables and duchesse potatoes. Serves three.

Meat Loaf

2 slices of bread
1lb prime ground beef
1 onion, peeled and chopped
1 tsp Worcestershire sauce
Salt and pepper
1 egg, beaten

Grate the bread or place in a blender to produce crumbs. Mix the ground beef, onion, Worcestershire sauce, salt and pepper and breadcrumbs. Add the egg and bind the mixture together. Put the mixture into a greased loaf pan and cover with wax paper. Cook in the oven for 50-60 minutes at 390°F. When the meat loaf is cooked the juices should run clear when a skewer is inserted. Turn the loaf out onto a flat serving dish. Garnish with cooked vegetables such as carrots, runner beans, peas and Brussels sprouts. Serves four.

Black Pudding or Bratwurst with Apple

1lb potatoes, peeled
3 large tart apples
3 tblsp oil
2 tblsp butter
1lb black pudding or bratwurst, sliced
1 tsp chopped parsley

Boil and mash the potatoes and keep them warm. Peel and core the apples and cut each one into 8 segments. Heat half the oil and all the butter in a pan. Add the apple, cover and cook for 5 minutes on a low heat. Drain and keep warm. In another pan heat the remaining oil and add the sliced black pudding or bratwurst. Fry on both sides until it is slightly crisp and heated through. Remove and drain. Place the mashed potato in the center of a heated serving dish and surround it with alternate portions of black pudding or bratwurst and apple. Sprinkle the potato with the chopped parsley. Serve with a green vegetable and fresh tomatoes.
Serves four.

This page: Wine Coated Ham (top), Black Pudding or Bratwurst with Apple (center right), Gammon Rounds with Onion Sauce (bottom left). Facing page: Steak and Kidney Pudding (top left), Crunchy Lamb Pie (top right), Meat Loaf (center left) and Toad in the Hole (bottom right).

Wine Coated Ham

2lb ham
Salt and pepper
1 cup carrots, peeled and cut into sticks
1 cup turnips, peeled and cut into sticks
1 cup green beans
1 cup frozen peas
1 tblsp soft brown sugar
⅔ cup red wine
¼ cup butter

Cover the ham with cold water and soak for 4 hours, changing the water frequently. Place the ham in a large pan, cover with cold water and simmer for 40 minutes. Bring a large pan of salted water to the boil, add the vegetables and cook for about 10 minutes. When the vegetables are cooked drain them, rinse with cold water and drain them again. Lift the ham from the pan. Peel off the rind and place the ham in an ovenproof dish. Sprinkle the ham with sugar and place in the oven for 5 minutes at 375°F. Pour the wine over and return to the oven for 5 minutes, basting frequently. Melt the butter in a pan and add the drained vegetables, salt and pepper. Heat through, stirring continuously. Place the ham on a large serving dish with the vegetables and serve with the sauce from the cooking. Serve with new potatoes if required.
Serves four.

Gammon Rounds in Onion Sauce

4 gammon rounds
3 onions, peeled and sliced
¼ cup butter or margarine
½ cup flour
Salt and pepper
2½ cups milk

Broil the gammon rounds until tender. Boil the onions until soft, then drain. Melt the butter or margarine, remove from the heat and stir in the flour. Return to the heat and cook gently for a few minutes. Remove the pan from the heat and gradually stir in the milk. Bring to the boil and cook, stirring with a wooden spoon until smooth. Season well. If any small lumps have formed beat thoroughly. Stir in the boiled onions and serve with the gammon. Serve with potatoes in their jackets and green beans. Serves four.

Crunchy Lamb Pie

2 tblsp margarine
1 onion, peeled and chopped
½ packet parsley sauce mix
⅔ cup milk
1 tblsp half and half cream or top of the milk
¾ cup cold cooked lamb, minced
½ packet instant potato
2 tblsp Lancashire or Cheddar cheese, grated

Heat the margarine and fry the onion until soft. Make the parsley sauce as directed on the packet, using the milk, and stir in the cream, or top of the milk and the onion. Add the lamb to the sauce. Mix well and turn into a greased pie dish. Make the instant potato as directed on the packet and spread over the meat mixture. Sprinkle the cheese over the potato. Cook in the oven for 30 minutes at 400-425°F. Serve with a green vegetable or baked onions. Serves two.

Steak and Kidney Pudding

1½lb stewing steak
2 lambs' kidneys
1 tblsp flour
Salt and pepper
⅔ cup stock

Suet Crust Pastry
2 cups all-purpose flour
2½ tsp baking powder
½ tsp of salt
A pinch of pepper
½ cup shredded suet
⅔ cup water

To make the suet crust pastry, sift flour, baking powder and seasoning into a mixing basin. Add the suet and stir in enough water to mix to a firm dough. Turn out onto a floured board and use as required. Trim and cut the steak into strips. Cut the kidneys into small pieces. Mix the steak and kidney together. Put the flour and seasoning on a plate and use to coat the meat. To line a basin with the pastry, cut off ¼ of the dough and reserve for the lid. Roll out the rest of the pastry into a large, thin round. Lower into the basin. Add the meat and enough stock to come two-thirds of the way up the basin. Roll out pastry for the lid and place in position. Seal the edges. Cover with either wax paper or foil, or a muslin cloth dipped in boiled water and then floured. Fix securely round the basin rim with string. Put the pudding in a steamer, stand this over a saucepan of boiling water and steam for 4 hours. Add more boiling water when necessary. Serve with creamed potatoes and Brussels sprouts.
Serves four.

Breast of Lamb and Onion Stuffing

1½lb breast of lamb, boned
1 tblsp oil
1 tblsp butter
Salt and pepper
Lamb seasoning
⅔ cup chicken stock
1 tblsp cornstarch, blended in a little cold water

Stuffing
2 tblsp long grain rice
1 tblsp butter
2 onions, peeled and chopped
Salt and pepper
Pinch of mixed spice
½ tsp lamb seasoning

First make the stuffing. Cook the rice in boiling salted water, rinse and drain. Heat the butter and fry the onion. Mix the rice and onion together with the salt and pepper, mixed spice and the lamb seasoning. Spread the stuffing on the lamb; roll and tie. Brush with the oil and butter, season and sprinkle with lamb seasoning. Roast in the oven for 20 minutes at 400°F. Reduce the heat to 350°F. Pour the stock into the roasting pan and cover with foil. Cook for a further hour. Remove the meat from the pan and thicken the gravy with the cornstarch to accompany the meat. Serve with roast potatoes, turnips and mixed vegetables.
Serves four.

Peppered Mackerel with Gooseberry Sauce

8oz mackerel fillets, washed
¼ cup flour
¼ cup oil
2 tsp peppercorns

Marinade
3 tblsp oil
Grated rind and juice of 1 lemon
1 tblsp soy sauce
1 clove garlic, peeled and crushed
1 tblsp wine vinegar
1 tblsp sugar

Gooseberry Sauce
½lb gooseberries, topped and tailed
1 apple, peeled, cored and diced
¼ cup sugar
Sprig of mint
1¼ cups water
Pinch of salt
1½ tblsp arrowroot (optional)

To make the marinade, liquidize all the ingredients in a blender. Soak the fish fillets in the marinade for 15 minutes. Drain them and dry on kitchen paper, then dip them in the flour. Discard the marinade. Brush the fillets with the oil and place on a greased broiler rack. Broil for 3 minutes on each side, then remove and sprinkle with peppercorns. Arrange on a hot dish and keep warm. Place the gooseberries in a saucepan with the diced apple, sugar, mint and half the water. Boil for 8 minutes, then remove the mint. Work the gooseberry mixture in a blender or rub through a sieve to a purée. Add a pinch of salt. Reheat the purée in a saucepan and thicken, if liked, with the arrowroot mixed to a paste with a little cold water. Boil for 4 minutes until clear and thick. Serve the broiled mackerel with the gooseberry sauce. Serve with new potatoes and mushrooms.
Serves four.

Lamb Cobbler

¼ cup oil
1 onion, peeled and sliced
1½lb ground lamb
2 tblsp flour
2 tblsp tomato paste
1¼ cups brown stock
Salt and pepper
Pinch of rosemary
1 tsp dry mustard
2 tblsp Worcestershire sauce

Topping
2 cups all-purpose flour
Pinch of salt
2 tsp baking powder
¼ cup butter
¼ cup water
1 tblsp milk

Heat the oil in a pan and fry the onion until soft. Add the lamb and cook for 5 minutes. Stir in the flour and tomato paste and cook for 5 minutes. Then add the stock, seasoning, rosemary, mustard and Worcestershire sauce. Make the topping by sifting the flour and salt together, and cut in the butter. Add enough water to form a dough. Roll out the dough to ¼ inch thick. Cut into rounds to form small scones. Arrange the scones around the top of the dish. Brush the scones with milk. Bake in the oven for 30 minutes at 375°F, until the scones are browned. Serve with creamed potatoes and Brussels sprouts.
Serves four.

Peppered Mackerel with Gooseberry Sauce (top), Lamb Cobbler (center right) and Breast of Lamb and Onion Stuffing (bottom).

P
S

Farmhouse Meat and Game

Pheasant Braised in Red Wine

PREPARATION TIME: 15 minutes

COOKING TIME: 1 hour 15 minutes

SERVES: 4 persons

1 fairly large pheasant
2 tbsps oil
1 tbsp butter
1 heaped tbsp flour
1 onion
2 apples
Rind and juice of one orange
⅔ cup red wine
⅔ cup stock or water
Salt and pepper
Bay leaf, sprig of parsley and thyme, tied together
1 heaped tsp brown sugar

Melt oil and butter in a heavy pan. Put in pheasant, turning it to brown all over. Remove pheasant and place it in a casserole with the apples, quartered and cored but not peeled. Chop the onion and add it to the fat in the pan. Allow it to soften without browning. Stir in the flour then gradually add the stock and the wine and bring to the boil, stirring all the time. Add the grated orange rind and the orange juice and sugar. Season with pepper and pour the sauce over the pheasant. Add the herbs, cover the casserole and place in a preheated oven, 350°F (180°C), for one hour.

Limerick Ham

PREPARATION TIME: 12 hours

Limerick ham was smoked using a special recipe in which juniper berries were added to the fire to produce the distinctive flavor. It has been famous all over the world since the 18th century.

Smoked hams should be allowed to soak in cold water for at least twelve hours, then rinsed and covered with cold water to which a clove-studded onion, a few peppercorns and a tbsp of honey or brown sugar have been added. Bring slowly to the boil, skim, then simmer for 20 minutes to the pound and 20 minutes over. The ham is cooked when the thick skin peels back easily. Remove the ham from the water and peel off the skin. If it is to be served hot, coat the ham with browned bread-crumbs and put it in a roasting pan in the oven, 350°F (180°C), for 40 minutes. If it is to be eaten cold it should be replaced in the pot after the skin has been removed and allowed to cool in the liquor in which it was cooked. It can be

This page: Cold Chicken in Tarragon Sauce (top) and Beef Braised in Guinness. Facing page: Limerick Ham (top) and Pheasant Braised in Red Wine (bottom).

glazed by heating up equal quantities of brown sugar, vinegar and apricot jam and pouring this over the ham.

Beef Braised in Guinness

PREPARATION TIME: 15 minutes

COOKING TIME: 1 hour 30 minutes

SERVES: 4 persons

1½lb chuck or round steak
2 medium onions
½lb carrots
2 heaped tbsps flour
½ tsp basil
Salt and pepper
1 tsp honey
⅔ cup Guinness
⅔ cup stock or water
2-3 tbsps cooking oil

The beef should be about 1 inch thick and cut into about twelve pieces.
Peel the onions and chop them fairly small. Peel the carrots and slice them into pieces about the size of your little finger. Put the flour on a plate and mix in a tsp of salt and a good sprinkling of pepper. Heat the oil in the pan, add the onions and cook until soft. Transfer them with a slotted spoon to a large, shallow, greased, ovenproof dish. Dip the pieces of meat in the seasoned flour and brown them in the fat in the pan. Remove these as they are cooked and place in the dish on top of the onions, in a single layer. Arrange the carrots around them. If necessary, add a little more oil to the pan and stir in the remainder of the seasoned flour. Cook for a minute or two, stirring all the time, then add the basil and pour on the Guinness. Allow to boil for a minute or two then add the honey and the stock. Bring back to the boil and pour over the meat. Cover the dish either with a lid or with foil, and cook in the oven at 325°F (170°C) for 1½ hours. This dish tastes even better if you cook it the day before and heat it up again in the oven for about 45 minutes. If the gravy looks as though it needs to be a little thicker, mix a tsp of cornstarch with 2 tbsps of cold water and stir into the gravy 15 minutes before the cooking time is up.

Braised Liver and Bacon in Tomatoes and Red Wine

PREPARATION TIME: 15 minutes

COOKING TIME: 30 minutes

SERVES: 4 persons

8 slices of lambs' or calves' liver
4 rashers of bacon
14oz can of chopped tomatoes
1 large onion
3 tbsps oil
3 heaped tbsps flour seasoned with salt and pepper
1 wineglass of red wine
1 heaped tsp honey
½ tsp dried basil
3 cups pasta shells or macaroni

Peel and slice the onion. Heat oil in a frying pan and fry the onion until soft. Transfer onion with a slotted spoon to an ovenproof dish large enough to take all the liver in one layer. Toss liver in seasoned flour, brown lightly in remaining oil in frying pan and lay on top of onions. Mix remainder of seasoned flour with pan juices and mix to a paste over low heat. Add red wine and bring to the boil. Remove two tbsps of the chopped tomatoes and reserve, add the rest to the pan with the honey and basil. Bring mixture to the boil, stirring well. Pour around the liver in the dish. Slice rashers in half and place on top of liver. Put dish in a preheated oven at 375°F (190°C) for about 20 minutes.
Cook pasta shells or macaroni in boiling, salted water, following instructions on packet. Drain. Heat remaining tomatoes in a pan with a pinch of basil. Toss pasta in it and transfer to a serving dish to accompany the liver and bacon. Serves 4 persons.

Stuffed Breast of Lamb

PREPARATION TIME: 15 minutes

COOKING TIME: 1 hour 30 minutes

SERVES: 4 persons

Half breast of lamb
4 cups white breadcrumbs
¼ cup chopped suet
1 medium onion
½ level tsp marjoram
½ level tsp thyme
Grated rind of half a lemon
1 egg
Salt and pepper
1 tbsp flour

It is quite easy to remove the bones from the breast of lamb with a sharp knife. Put the bones in a saucepan with half the onion and some salt and pepper. Cover them with water, bring to the boil, skim, cover and simmer for half an hour. Mix the breadcrumbs, suet, herbs, lemon rind, a little salt and pepper and the other half of the onion, minced, and bind them with the egg. Add 2-3 tbsps of the bone stock and spread the stuffing on the breast of lamb. Roll up, starting at the wide end. Tie up firmly with string and place in a greased roasting pan. Bake in the oven, 400°F (200°C), for 1 hour.
Transfer the meat to a serving dish and keep hot while you make the gravy. Drain off any excess fat from the roasting pan, retaining about two tbsps. Stir in the flour and heat over the ring until mixture browns. Stir in about a cupful of the bone stock. Bring to the boil, stirring all the time. Boil for a few minutes then strain into a gravy boat and serve with the stuffed lamb. Serve with new potatoes and zucchini.

Cold Chicken in Tarragon Sauce

PREPARATION TIME: 45 minutes

COOKING TIME: 1 hour 20 minutes

SERVES: 6-8 persons

Although I use a fresh or frozen roasting chicken for this dish, I find the flesh is much more moist and goes further if the chicken is poached or steamed. It is very suitable for a summer lunch or supper party as it can be prepared well in advance and served with new potatoes and a tossed salad or with rice mixed with vegetables.

3½lb chicken
1 bay leaf
1 onion
1 carrot
1 stick celery
Tarragon
Salt and pepper

Sauce
¼ cup butter
½ cup flour
Glass white wine or cider
1¼ cups of the strained stock
3 heaped tbsps whipped cream
3 heaped tbsps mayonnaise
1 tsp chopped tarragon
2 tsps chopped parsley
Juice of ½ lemon

Generously sprinkle the inside of the chicken with salt, pepper and tarragon. Into a saucepan, just large enough to take the chicken snugly, put the onion, carrot and celery, all quartered, and the giblets and feet from the chicken. Place the chicken on top and pour the stock over it. Cover the pan tightly, bring to the boil then reduce heat and simmer for 1 hour. Remove the pan from the heat and carefully turn the chicken breast-side down in the

Stuffed Breast of Lamb (above right) and Braised Liver and Bacon in Tomatoes and Red Wine (below right).

stock, taking care not to break the skin. Cover again and allow to cool. This can be done the day before. Skin the chicken and remove all the flesh from the bones, slicing the meat from the legs into longish slivers and dividing the white parts up into similar sized pieces.
Melt the butter in a heavy pan. Stir in the flour and cook for a minute or two. Add the white wine, then gradually stir in the 1¼ cups of stock. Add the tarragon, parsley and lemon juice, bring the sauce to the boil and cook for a further 2 minutes, stirring all the time. Remove from the heat and allow to cool slightly before folding in the whipped cream and finally the mayonnaise. Toss the chicken pieces in about ¾ of the sauce and pile them into a large, shallow serving dish. Coat with the remainder of the sauce and garnish with a little chopped parsley, parsley sprigs and lemon slices before serving.

Irish Stew

PREPARATION TIME: 30 minutes
COOKING TIME: 2 hours-2 hours 30 minutes
SERVES: 4 persons

Either boned mutton, cut up and with most of the fat removed, or rib chops, trimmed but left on the bone, can be used. The most important points to remember are not to use too much liquid in the cooking and to cook the stew very slowly so that it doesn't dry out. A little more water may be added during the cooking, if necessary.

2lb boned mutton or 3lb rib chops
2lb potatoes
2 large onions
1 tbsp fresh, chopped thyme and parsley or 1 tsp dried thyme
Salt and pepper
1½ cups water

Trim the meat, leaving a little of the fat on. Peel and slice the potatoes and onions. Into a large saucepan – or casserole, if it is to be cooked in the oven – place layers of potato, meat and onion, seasoned with salt and pepper and herbs, starting and finishing with a layer of potatoes. Pour on the water and cover tightly. Either simmer on a very low heat on the top of the stove for 2-2½ hours or cook in a slow oven, 250°F (120°C), for the same length of time. The pot or casserole should be shaken occasionally to prevent the potatoes from sticking and you should check that the liquid has not dried out. The finished stew should not be too runny and the potatoes should thicken it sufficiently.

Boiled Ham and Cabbage

PREPARATION TIME: 2-3 hours
COOKING TIME: 1 hour 45 minutes
SERVES: 6-8 persons

Piece of uncooked ham about 3lb in weight
1½-2lb green cabbage
½ medium onion or one small onion cut in two

Parsley Sauce
1¼ cups milk
1¼ cups stock
½ cup chopped parsley
¼ cup butter or margarine
3 tbsps flour

Soak the ham for several hours, or cover it with cold water, bring to the boil, discard water and cover meat with more boiling water. Bring it back to the boil, skim and simmer for 20 minutes to the pound and 20 minutes more.
Meanwhile, cut the cabbage in two and cut out a V in the stalk end of both halves to remove the fibrous end of the stalk. Cut the two halves down through the V and put the quarters in salted water to clean them. Put them into a large saucepan with the cut onion (this miraculously seems to prevent the usual smell of cooked cabbage permeating the house). When the ham is cooked add 3-4 ladles of the stock to the cabbage, cover tightly and cook for about 20 minutes.
Meanwhile, skin the ham, if necessary, cut a lattice pattern in the fat, coat it with brown sugar and stud it with cloves. Brown it in a hot oven while the cabbage is cooking. Drain the cabbage and remove the onion.
Measure out 1¼ cups of the stock in which the cabbage was cooked to use for the parsley sauce. Melt butter or margarine in a pan, stir in the flour and make a roux. Cook without browning for a minute or two. Gradually add the stock and then the milk. Bring to the boil and stir for a few minutes. Add the chopped parsley. Test to see if it needs more seasoning – probably a little pepper. Serve with the ham and cabbage and potatoes boiled in their skins. Some people cook the cabbage in the pot with the ham, but I prefer to save some of the pure ham stock for other dishes.

Marinated Pork Chops

PREPARATION TIME: 3-4 hours
COOKING TIME: 1 hour
SERVES: 4 persons

4 pork chops
1 cup cider
½ tsp sage
½ tsp thyme
1 onion finely chopped
½ cup flour, seasoned with salt and pepper
2 tbsps oil
1 tbsp butter
1 or 2 apples, peeled, cored and sliced
1 tsp honey
1 tsp Dijon mustard
¾ cup stock

Put the chops into a shallow ovenproof dish just large enough to hold them. Chop the onion, add it with the herbs to the cider and pour over the chops. Leave for several hours, turning the chops occasionally. Heat oil and butter in a frying pan. Drain chops then dip them in the seasoned flour, lightly coating both sides. Seal them in the frying pan, browning them slightly. Strain the marinade liquid into a bowl, wash and grease the dish, place sliced apple on the bottom and chops on top. Add strained onion from the marinade to the fat in the frying pan; cook until soft and stir in remainder of the seasoned flour. Allow it to brown, stirring all the time, then gradually add liquid from the marinade and the stock. Stir in honey and mustard, bring to the boil and pour

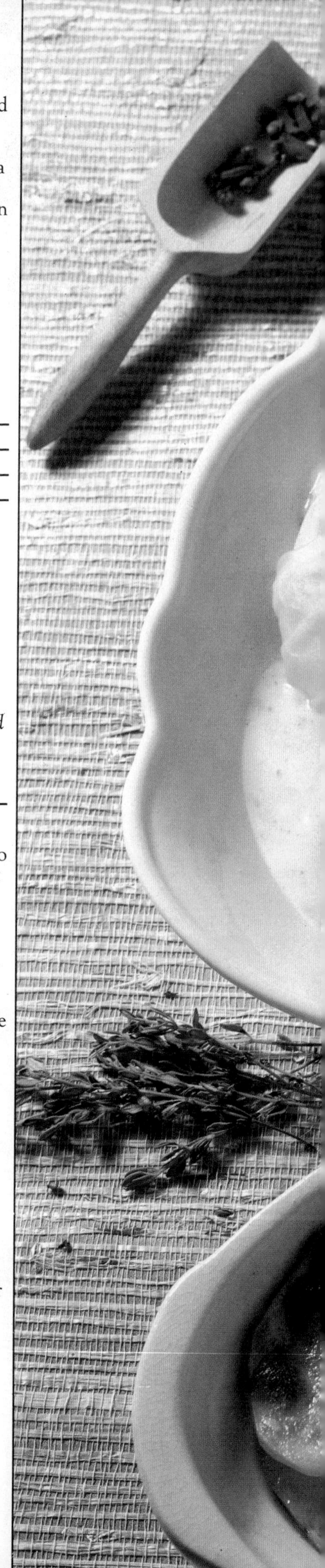

Boiled Bacon and Cabbage (top) and Irish Stew (bottom).

over the chops. Cover with foil and cook in a preheated oven, 350°F (180°C), for 45 minutes. Serve with peas and mashed potatoes.

Dublin Coddle

PREPARATION TIME: 30 minutes

COOKING TIME: 1 hour

SERVES: 4 persons

This was regarded as a Saturday night special in Dublin and it would always be served up with Guinness. I can always remember the sausages being boiled first, even if they were going to be fried or grilled later. I presume this was for reasons of hygiene, as sausages would be home made or made on nearby farms, where there would not necessarily be factory-like conditions of cleanliness.

1lb pork sausages
8oz thickly sliced bacon
1lb onions
1½lb potatoes
Salt and pepper to taste

Place the bacon and the sausages in a pan. Cover with boiling water. Return to the boil and simmer for 5 minutes. Drain off the liquid into a bowl and reserve. Peel and slice the potatoes and onions, and put them with the meat in a heavy pan or greased casserole. Cover with the stock, season with salt and pepper and cover with greaseproof paper before putting on the lid. Either simmer on top of the stove or in a moderate oven for about one hour.

Boiled Chicken and Parsley Sauce

PREPARATION TIME: 15 minutes

COOKING TIME: 3 hours 15 minutes

SERVES: 6-8 persons

In the days when most people living in the country in Ireland kept their own hens, if a letter was received announcing the imminent arrival of unexpected guests, the housewife didn't jump into the car and head for the supermarket – she went out and caught a hen which had finished laying, and wrung its neck. After plucking it and cleaning it, she would cook it slowly in a pot and serve it with parsley sauce. It would probably be accompanied by a piece of boiling bacon which, apart from helping the chicken to go further, provides an excellent contrast in flavor and color, and of course cabbage and lovely floury potatoes boiled in their skins.

1 large boiling fowl
1 onion
1 carrot
1 turnip
1 stick celery
A bouquet garni
Salt and Pepper

Parsley Sauce
¼ cup butter
½ cup plain flour
1¼ cups stock
1¼ cups milk
Cupful chopped parsley

Put 2-3ozs of dripping in a large pan. Wash and dry the bird, inside and out, and season well with salt and pepper. Turn it in the fat to brown slightly, remove the bird and add the vegetables, chopped into large pieces. Turn them in the fat for a few minutes then put in the bird and cover with boiling water. Add salt, pepper and bouquet garni. Bring back to the boil, skim, then cover the pot and simmer the contents slowly for about three hours or 40 minutes to the pound. When the bird is cooked remove it from the pot and keep hot on a serving dish. Melt the butter in a pan, stir in the flour and cook for a minute. Remove from heat and gradually stir in 1¼ cups of the strained chicken stock. Return to the heat and, when it has thickened, gradually add the milk and continue cooking until it boils up again. Lower heat and cook for a further 2 minutes; add parsley and season with salt and pepper. Serve separately in a sauce boat.

Spiced Beef

PREPARATION TIME: 1 week

COOKING TIME: 6 hours

At Christmas time in Ireland you will see spiced beef displayed in many butchers' shop windows. It will be attractively tied-up with red ribbons and decorated with holly to contrast with its dark and velvety exterior. The mixture of spices and saltpeter, which have been rubbed into it at regular intervals for a week or more, keep the beef inside its dark coating a spicy red. This, served cold and thinly sliced, is a great favorite in most Irish households at Christmas time. It is not difficult to prepare at home, although it does require quite a lot of time and care.

6lb piece of brisket, sirloin tip or eye of round

For the spicing:
3 bay leaves, finely chopped
1 tsp powdered mace
6 finely ground cloves
1 tsp crushed black peppercorns
Large clove garlic made into a paste with salt
1 tsp allspice
2 tbsps black treacle or molasses
2 heaped tbsps brown sugar
1lb cooking salt
2 tsps saltpeter

Mix all the spicing ingredients together. Place beef in a large dish and rub well all over with the mixture. Repeat this process every day for a week, turning the meat and rubbing in the spices which will now be mixed with the juices drawn from the meat.
Tie the meat up firmly and rub in a final tsp of ground cloves. Cover with water and simmer slowly for six hours. When cool, enough remove from the cooking liquid, place in a dish and cover with a weighted plate. Slice very thinly and serve.

Boiled Mutton

We rarely see mutton on sale these days, but it appeared regularly on the menu in Irish households in days gone by. The average leg of mutton weighed about 10lbs, which was not considered too large to boil for a typical household in the early part of this century. It was suggested that for a small family the leg could be divided into three parts; the shank for boiling, the fillet for roasting and the lap for Irish stew.
To boil a leg of mutton, or the shank end, allow 20 minutes to the pound and 20 minutes over. If using the whole leg, first skewer the lap into position then plunge the joint into enough boiling, salted water to cover it and boil for 4-5

Dublin Coddle (right) and Boiled Chicken and Parsley Sauce (below right).

GUINNESS

minutes, then reduce the heat and simmer gently for the remainder of the cooking time. Serve with caper sauce, pouring a little over the joint which has been kept hot on a serving dish, and serve the remainder separately.

Caper Sauce

COOKING TIME: 15 minutes

¼ cup butter or dripping
½ cup flour
1¼ cup milk
1¼ cup pot liquor
1 heaped tbsp capers and a little of their preserving liquid
Salt and pepper

The sauce for pouring over the mutton should be thicker than that served in the sauce boat so that it will nicely coat the meat. Good dripping can be used instead of butter. Melt the butter in a heavy pan, stir in the flour and cook for a minute but do not allow to brown. Remove from heat and stir in a little of the milk, then gradually add rest of the milk over gentle heat, stirring all the time. Gradually add 1 cup of the hot cooking liquor and bring to the boil. Boil for 2-3 minutes, stirring constantly. Test for flavor and season with pepper and more salt, if necessary. If it seems of a good coating consistency, add the capers and a little of the preserving liquid but do not bring the sauce back to the boil or it will curdle. Pour a little of the sauce over the mutton on the serving dish. Measure out the other ¼ cup of the hot stock and gradually add to the sauce in the pan. Pour into a sauce boat. Boiled white turnips and parsnips should be served around the meat and the dish garnished with parsley.

This page: Spiced Beef. Facing page: Marinated Pork Chops (top) and Boiled Mutton and Caper Sauce (bottom).

Chili Beef

PREPARATION TIME: 30 minutes
COOKING TIME: 2 hours

1½lb ground beef
3 tblsp fat
1 medium onion, peeled and chopped
1 clove garlic, crushed
1¼ cups stock
1 tblsp flour
2 tblsp chili powder
½ tsp oregano
1 bay leaf
Seasoning

Brown ground beef in hot fat. Remove to a casserole dish. Brown onion and garlic in remaining fat and add to meat. Pour in stock until just covered. Cover and cook in a slow oven, 325°F, for about 1 hour. Mix flour and chili powder smoothly with a little stock or water and stir into casserole. Add red kidney beans if required. Add oregano, bay leaf and seasoning and continue cooking for a further 30 minutes-1 hour.

Southseas Meatballs

PREPARATION TIME: 20 minutes
COOKING TIME: 10-20 minutes

1lb ground beef
1 egg, beaten
Seasoning
1 tblsp oil
3 small shallots, chopped
2 tblsp flour
1lb pineapple chunks
1 tblsp soy sauce
1 tsp wine vinegar
½ green pepper, finely chopped
2 tblsp blanched almonds

Blend the beef, egg and seasoning in a large bowl. Make the beef mixture into four flat balls, brush with oil and broil for 10-20 minutes. Keep warm. Heat the oil in a skillet. Fry the shallots gently for 3 minutes. Take out. Stir in the flour and cook the roux for 3 minutes. Pour in the juice from the canned pineapple and bring to the boil, stirring. Add the soy sauce and vinegar. Season. Add the shallots, pineapple chunks, green pepper and almonds. Place the meatballs in the pan and heat through, spooning the sauce over.

Steak Diane

PREPARATION TIME: 20 minutes
COOKING TIME: from 5-20 minutes

1 onion, finely chopped
4-6 tblsp butter
4 thin slices of sirloin steak
Worcestershire sauce
Brandy (optional)

Fry the onion in butter for a few minutes until soft. Add the steak and cook on both sides. Add Worcestershire sauce and the brandy to the butter. Ignite, if wished, and pour over the steaks. Garnish with chopped parsley.

Meat Roll

PREPARATION TIME: 30 minutes
COOKING TIME: 1 hour 30 minutes

1lb ground meat
½ cup suet, finely chopped
1 onion, finely chopped
¼ cup fresh breadcrumbs
Seasoning
2 tblsp fat
Meat stock

For Coating
Beaten egg
Dry breadcrumbs

Mix the meat, suet, onion, fresh breadcrumbs and seasoning. If necessary add a little egg to bind. Shape into a thick roll, molding out any cracks. Brush over with egg and coat with the dry breadcrumbs. Grease a piece of wax paper with the fat and wrap round the roll. Secure the ends an lay in a baking pan. Bake for 1¼-1½ hours at 425°F. Just before serving brush over with a little meat stock.

Beef Stroganoff

PREPARATION TIME: 30 minutes
COOKING TIME: 50 minutes

1½-2lb lean beef, cut into long strips
½ cup butter
1 tblsp oil
Flour
2-3 onions, chopped
½ cup sliced mushrooms
3 tblsp dry sherry
1¼-1¾ cups stock
Seasoning
¾ cup sour cream

Melt butter in an oiled skillet. Dip the strips of meat into seasoned flour and fry for several minutes. Transfer meat to a casserole dish. Fry onions for 7-10 minutes in the same fat. Spread over meat in the casserole. Fry mushrooms for a few minutes. Add to the casserole. Moisten with sherry and stock. Adjust seasoning to taste. Cover casserole and place in a slow oven, 325°F, for 30 minutes or until meat is tender. Add sour cream and cover again until heated through.

This page: Southseas Meatballs (top right), Chili Beef (center left) and Meat Roll (bottom).

Facing page: Steak Diane (top), Beef Stroganoff (center) and Steak and Kidney Pudding (bottom).

Roasted Standing Rib

PREPARATION TIME: 20 minutes

COOKING TIME: 15 minutes per 1lb, plus 15 minutes

Place meat in a roasting pan and spread with beef fat or cooking fat, and season. Place in the center of a preheated oven at 350°F. If a covered roasting pan is used, basting is not necessary, but if the joint is uncovered the meat should be basted every 20-30 minutes. The meat should be turned over using 2 metal spoons, halfway through the cooking. When the meat is cooked, transfer to a large carving dish. Keep hot.

Meat Roll in Pastry Case

PREPARATION TIME: 45 minutes

COOKING TIME: 30 minutes

1lb ground meat
1 onion, finely chopped
½ cup suet, finely chopped
Seasoning
8oz basic pastry
Egg or milk to glaze

Fry ground meat and onion till cooked. Remove from pan. Mix the meat, suet, onion and seasoning together. If necessary, add a little egg to bind to a pliable, slightly moist mixture. Shape into a thick roll, molding out any cracks. Roll out a piece of pastry large enough to cover the roll. Brush with egg or milk to glaze. Lay meat roll in a loaf pan and cook at 400°F for about 20 minutes until pastry is golden brown.

Bottom Round Roast (Salted)

PREPARATION TIME: soak overnight

COOKING TIME: 20 minutes per 1lb plus 20 minutes

To prepare meat for cooking, soak meat overnight in cold water to remove excess salt. Put the joint into a pan and cover with cold water. Bring to the boil, then pour off the liquor. Cover again with cold water and bring to the boil. After 5 minutes, reduce the heat and allow to simmer for the appropriate length of time.

Meat Roll in Pastry Case (far left), Curried Shepherd's Pie (top center), Roasted Standing Rib (bottom center) and Monday Beef Casserole (bottom right).

Curried Shepherd's Pie

PREPARATION TIME: 20 minutes

COOKING TIME: 45 minutes

12oz ground beef
2 onions, finely chopped
2 tblsp fat
2 tblsp flour
1 tblsp curry powder
1¼ cups stock or a small can of tomatoes and a little stock
Seasoning
1 tblsp chutney
1lb mashed potatoes

Fry onions in hot fat. Add flour and curry powder. Add stock, or tomatoes and stock. Bring to the boil and cook until thickened. Add the ground beef and cook gently, stirring from time to time. Break up any lumps in the mince. Add seasoning and chutney. When meat is tender put into a pie dish. Cover with the mashed potatoes. Brown in oven or under broiler until crisp.

Beef Cobbler

PREPARATION TIME: 45 minutes
COOKING TIME: 2 hours 15 minutes

Stew
¼ cup fat
2 large onions, sliced
1½lb chuck steak, diced
1 tblsp paprika
⅔ cup water
1 green pepper, seeded, cored and diced
4 tomatoes, skinned and quartered
Seasoning

Cobbler
1½ cups flour
2 tsp baking powder
Seasoning
3 tblsp margarine
Milk

Stew
Heat the fat and fry the onions and diced meat until brown. Stir in paprika, blended with water, and the rest of the ingredients. Put into a covered casserole dish and cook for 2¼ hours at 300-325°F.

Cobbler
Sieve dry ingredients, rub in margarine and mix to a soft dough with milk. Cut into small rounds and put on top of beef mixture. Glaze with a little milk. Turn oven up to 425°F, until cobbler mixture is golden brown.

Monday Beef Casserole

PREPARATION TIME: 25 minutes
COOKING TIME: 10-20 minutes

2 cups mashed potato
1 egg, beaten
¼ tsp salt
¾ cup cooked beef, chopped
½ cup celery, chopped
½ cup milk
Salt to taste
Dash nutmeg
Margarine or butter

Beat potatoes with egg and salt. Put half the potatoes in the bottom of a greased casserole dish. Blend and add remaining ingredients, except butter, to casserole. Cover with remaining potatoes. Dot with butter and bake in oven at 375°F until top is browned.

Round of Beef

PREPARATION TIME: 5 minutes
COOKING TIME: 15 minutes per 1lb plus 15 minutes

Place meat in a roasting pan and spread with beef fat or cooking fat and season. Place in the center of a preheated oven at 350°F. If a covered roasting pan is used basting is not necessary. If the joint is uncovered, the meat should be basted every 20-30 minutes. The meat should be turned over, using two metal spoons, halfway through the cooking. When the meat is cooked, transfer to a large carving dish and keep hot.

Steak and Kidney Pudding

PREPARATION TIME: 30 minutes
COOKING TIME: 4 hours

1½lb chuck steak
2 lamb's kidneys
1 tblsp flour
Seasoning
12oz suet crust pastry
⅔ cup stock

Cut steak and kidney into cubes and mix together. Put flour and seasoning onto a plate and toss meat in this. Line a pudding basin with the pastry. Put in meat, add enough stock to come two-thirds of the way up the basin. Roll out remaining pastry to make a lid and place on top of basin. Cover with greased paper. Fix firmly round the basin rim. Put the basin in a steamer. Stand this over a saucepan of boiling water. Steam for 4 hours. Allow water to boil rapidly for the first 2 hours; add more boiling water when necessary.

Steak Pie

PREPARATION TIME: 30 minutes
COOKING TIME: 2 hours 15 minutes

1½lb chuck steak
3 tblsp flour
Seasoning
¼ cup fat
2 onions, sliced and chopped
2½ cups brown stock
8oz Catherine's pastry

Prepare the steak, cutting it into pieces. Roll in seasoned flour and fry in hot fat for a few minutes in a saucepan. Add onions and turn in the fat for 2-3 minutes. Stir in the stock gradually; bring to the boil and cook until the sauce has thickened. Then lower the heat and simmer for 1½ hours. Put the steak into a pie pan. Roll out the pastry. Put a band of pastry round the moistened rim of the pie pan. Top with the rest of the pastry, seal the edges. Bake for 40-45 minutes at 450°F.

Swiss Steak

PREPARATION TIME: 25 minutes
COOKING TIME: 1 hour 30 minutes

1-1½lb thick slice of steak
1 tblsp flour
Seasoning
Beef fat or margarine
1 medium can peeled tomatoes
1 onion, peeled and grated

Mix flour and seasoning together and rub well into the surface of the meat. Melt fat in a saucepan and fry meat gently until brown. Rub tomatoes through a sieve and add to meat with grated onion. Place joint, onions and tomatoes in a casserole dish. Cover and simmer gently at 350°F for 1½ hours.

Top Chuck Roast

PREPARATION TIME: 25 minutes
COOKING TIME: 30 minutes per 1lb

¼ cup good beef fat
6 large onions, peeled
6 large carrots, peeled
3 large turnips, peeled
2-3lb piece of chuck roast, boned and rolled
Seasoning

Melt fat in a large pan and fry vegetables until a good brown color, then take out of pan. Fry meat on all sides over a fierce heat to seal in juices. Return vegetables to pan, with just enough water to give about 1½ inches in depth. Season well. Put meat on top of vegetables and cover pan. The vegetables should not be too small, otherwise they may break during cooking. Reduce heat so the liquid simmers gently. Carve the meat as you would a roast joint. The liquid from the pan can be used for the gravy.

Stew and Dumplings

PREPARATION TIME: 30 minutes
COOKING TIME: 2 hours 20 minutes

1-1½lb chuck steak
Seasoning
3 tblsp fat
2 onions, sliced
2 or 3 large carrots, sliced
1¾ cups water
½ bay leaf
Mixed herbs

For Dumplings
1 cup flour
1¼ tsp baking powder
Seasoning
¼ cup shredded suet
Water to mix

Cut the meat into cubes, season, then brown in the fat. Add onions, carrots, water and herbs. Cover pan and cook slowly for 2 hours.

For Dumplings
Sieve the dry ingredients together, add the suet and mix to a dough with the water. Roll into balls with lightly-floured hands. Check there is sufficient liquid in the stew, then drop in the dumplings and cook for 15-20 minutes.

Facing page: Steak Pie (top), Beef Cobbler (center left) and Stew and Dumplings (bottom right).

Peppered Steak

PREPARATION TIME: 15 minutes

COOKING TIME: from 5-25 minutes

4 shell or fillet steaks
Oil
2 tblsp black hot peppers for steak
¼ cup butter
Salt
4 tblsp brandy
3 tblsp light cream
Watercress

Brush the steaks on both sides with oil, then coat with black hot peppers and crush into the steak with a steak hammer. Melt butter in a skillet and cook steaks for about 1½ minutes on each side. Reduce heat and cook for about a further minute for rare steak, 3 minutes for medium steak or 7 minutes if a well-done steak is required. Season with salt. Warm brandy in a ladle near the heat. Set it alight and pour over steaks. Remove steaks and place on a warmed serving dish. Keep hot. Stir cream into the juices in the skillet. Heat gently for a few minutes. Pour sauce over steaks and garnish with watercress.

Steak Française

PREPARATION TIME: 30 minutes

COOKING TIME: 30-40 minutes

1-1¼lb club or shell steak
Seasoning
3 tblsp Pernod
2 onions, peeled and chopped
1lb tomatoes, skinned and chopped
2 tblsp butter
½ tsp marjoram

Cut steak into ½ inch strips with a sharp knife. Place in a shallow dish. Sprinkle with seasoning and Pernod. Cover and leave on one

Steak Française (left), Peppered Steak (center) and Beef in Cider (right).

side for 1 hour. Fry onions in melted butter until tender but not brown. Add tomatoes and stir well. Add onions and tomatoes to the steak mixture with the marjoram. Cook in an oven just above the center at 350°F for 30-40 minutes.

Beef in Cider

PREPARATION TIME: 30 minutes

COOKING TIME: 2 hours 30 minutes

1lb blade steak
2 tblsp fat
3 medium onions, quartered
4 carrots, quartered
1 clove garlic, crushed
8oz tomatoes, sliced
Seasoning
2½ cups dry cider

Cut beef into cubes and brown lightly in fat. Brown the onions and carrots. Put meat into an overproof dish with onions, carrots, garlic and tomatoes. Add seasoning to taste and cover with cider. Put on lid and cook at 325°F for 2½ hours.

Goulash

PREPARATION TIME: 25 minutes

COOKING TIME: 2 hours

1½lb chuck steak
2 tblsp fat
2 onions, peeled and chopped
2 carrots, peeled and chopped
¼ cup flour
1 beef stock cube
3 tblsp tomato paste
1¾ cups water
2 tsp paprika
3 tblsp yogurt

Cut meat into cubes and brown in hot fat. Remove to a casserole dish. Put onions and carrots into a pan and fry until lightly browned. Add to the meat. Put flour, crumbled stock cube and tomato paste into pan and add a little more fat if necessary. Cook for a few minutes, then add paprika and water and stir until boiling. Pour into casserole, cover and cook in a slow oven, 300°F, for about 2 hours. Just before serving, adjust seasoning and stir in yogurt.

Beefburgers

PREPARATION TIME: 25 minutes

COOKING TIME: 10-20 minutes

1 large onion, finely chopped
1lb ground beef
3 tblsp fresh breadcrumbs
4 tblsp milk
Salt
Paprika
1 tsp mustard powder
Oil
4 burger rolls, sliced horizontally
4 tomatoes, sliced (optional)
4 slices of Cheddar cheese (optional)

Preheat the broiler. Mix the onion, ground beef, breadcrumbs and milk in a large bowl. Season with salt, paprika and mustard. Leave for 10 minutes. Make four beefburgrs from the mixture. Brush with oil. Cook under the broiler for 5 minutes on each side. Remove from heat. Top the burgers with tomato and cheese, if desired. Put back under the broiler to melt cheese. Serve in warm rolls.

Broiled Fillet Steak

PREPARATION TIME: 10 minutes
COOKING TIME: from 5-20 minutes

Fillet steak
Butter or oil

Preheat broiler. Put steak on the grid of the broiling pan and brush with melted butter or oil. Cook on one side, then turn over with tongs. Brush second side with butter or oil. Minute steak – 1 minute cooking each side. Under-done steak (rare, ¾ inch thick), 3-4 minutes. Medium-done steak – cook as under-done, then cook under lower heat for a further 3 minutes. Well-done steak – cook as under-done, then cook under lower heat for further 5-6 minutes.

Sausage and Egg Pie

PREPARATION TIME: 20 minutes
COOKING TIME: 30-40 minutes

6oz basic pastry
1lb beef sausages
2 eggs
⅔ cup milk
¼ tsp made mustard

Roll out pastry to line a deep pie pan and prick the base. Fry sausages until cooked. Place in flan case. Beat eggs. Add milk and mustard. Pour beaten mixture over the sausages. Place pie in oven, 440°F, for 15 minutes. Reduce temperature to 325°F for a further 30 minutes, until pastry is cooked.

Cinnamon Roast

PREPARATION TIME: 30 minutes
COOKING TIME: 2 hours 30 minutes

3-4lb chuck roast
¼ cup flour
Seasoning
1 tsp powdered cinnamon
2 tblsp beef fat
3-4 carrots, peeled and chopped
1 bay leaf
1¾ cups stock
1 onion

Coat joint with flour, seasoning and cinnamon. Melt fat in a pan and brown joint all over. Transfer joint to a dish. Fry onion and carrot in the pan until soft. Replace joint on top of vegetables. Put in bay leaf and add stock. Cover and simmer gently for 2-2½ hours. Thicken liquor with flour and serve separately.

This page: Cinnamon Roast (top), Curried Chuck Steak (center left) and Swiss Steak (bottom right).

Facing page: Beefburgers (top left), Sliced Cold Beef and Bubble and Squeak (top right) and Broiled Fillet Steak (bottom).

Sausages in Tomato Sauce

PREPARATION TIME: 20 minutes

COOKING TIME: 25 minutes

1lb beef sausages
3 sticks celery, sliced
¼ cup salted peanuts

Tomato Sauce

1 tblsp margarine
2 onions, finely chopped
2 carrots, finely chopped
1 stick celery, finely chopped
2 tblsp flour
2 tblsp tomato paste
¼ cup chopped red pepper
1 chicken stock cube
1¼ cups boiling water
1 clove garlic, crushed
½ bay leaf
Sprig thyme
Seasoning
3 tblsp medium sherry

Tomato Sauce

Put the margarine in a saucepan, add the onions, carrots and celery and brown slightly. Add the flour, stir and brown slightly, until the flour is sandy in color. Add the tomato paste and red pepper. Stir well. Cool. Add the stock cube mixed with the boiling water, add garlic and herbs. Season and simmer for 1 hour, then check the seasoning. Sieve the sauce and stir in the sherry.

Sausages

Broil the sausages and keep them hot in a dish. Scald the celery sticks for 5 minutes in boiling water. Drain and add to the sausages. Pour the sauce over and keep hot. When ready to serve, garnish with salted peanuts.

Sliced Cold Beef and Bubble and Squeak

PREPARATION TIME: 20 minutes

COOKING TIME: 10-20 minutes

Sliced cold beef enough for 4 servings
½ medium cabbage
3 tblsp butter
1 small onion, finely chopped
Leftover mashed potato equal to the amount of cabbage

Bring a saucepan of water to the boil. Remove the core and any damaged leaves from the cabbage. Shred the cabbage. Put the cabbage into the water and cook for 6-7 minutes. Drain well. Heat the butter in a large skillet. Fry the

onion gently until softened. Add the cabbage and stir over a low heat for 2 minutes. Fold in the mashed potato until it is completely mixed with the cabbage. Press the mixture lightly into the skillet to form a large pancake. Cook for 5 minutes or until the underside is lightly browned. Turn and brown on the other side for 5 minutes. Serve very hot with the sliced cold meat.

Curried Chuck Steak

PREPARATION TIME: 35 minutes

COOKING TIME: 3 hours

1¼lb chuck steak, cut and diced
2 tblsp fat
1 large onion, chopped
1-2 tblsp curry powder
1 tblsp paprika
¼ cup walnuts
¼ cup blanched almonds
¼ cup flour
1¾ cups stock
Seasoning
¼ shredded coconut
¼ cup white raisins
1 tblsp redcurrant jelly
1 tblsp lemon juice
¼ cup mixed spice

Melt the fat and fry meat and onion until just brown. Add curry powder, paprika, walnuts and almonds, and cook for 3 minutes. Stir in flour and cook gently for several minutes. Gradually blend in stock. Bring to boil and cook until thickened. Season and add coconut, white raisins, redcurrant jelly and lemon juice. Transfer mixture to a casserole dish, cover and cook at 325°F, for 2½-3 hours.

Sausage and Egg Pie (far left), Sausages in Tomato Sauce (bottom center) and Goulash (top right).

This page: Roast Lamb with Rosemary (top right), Savory Pudding (top left) and Lamb Kebab (bottom).

Facing page: Country Lamb Casserole (top left), Wagon Wheel Lamb (top right) and Roast Herbed Leg of Mutton (bottom).

Festive Leg of Lamb

PREPARATION TIME: 30 minutes

COOKING TIME: 30-35 minutes per 1lb

1 leg of lamb
8oz pineapple rings
Candied cherries

Score the surface of the joint in a diamond pattern. Drain the pineapple and reserve the juice. Place the joint in a roasting pan and pour the pineapple juice over the scored surface. Roast at 350°F, basting occasionally. Cut pineapple rings in half. Garnish the joint with pieces of pineapple in a line down the length of the leg. Pin each piece in place with a cherry on a cocktail stick and serve.

Country Lamb Casserole

PREPARATION TIME: 30 minutes

COOKING TIME: 2 hours

2lb best end of neck of lamb
1 cup onions, peeled and chopped
1lb carrots, peeled and chopped
1½lb potatoes, peeled and thickly sliced
Seasoning
½ tsp dried thyme
3¾ cups boiling water
Chopped parsley

Cut neck into chops and season well. Put alternating layers of vegetables and meat in a large casserole dish. Season well between the layers and sprinkle the herbs at the same time. Finish with a layer of potatoes. Pour the water over the meat, cover and cook in a slow oven, 325°F, for about 2 hours. Just before serving, skim and sprinkle well with parsley.

Roast Herbed Leg of Mutton

PREPARATION TIME: 15 minutes

COOKING TIME: 30 minutes per 1lb plus 30 minutes

1 leg mutton
2-3 cloves garlic
2 bay leaves
½ cup soft butter
1 cup fresh breadcrumbs
1 tsp thyme
1 tsp rosemary
1 tblsp chopped parsley
Juice of ½ lemon
Seasoning

Prepare a sheet of foil to wrap meat completely. Slice 1 or 2 of the garlic

cloves and insert in small cuts on underside of meat. Place meat on foil, with bay leaves underneath. Cream butter with rest of the ingredients and crushed garlic cloves. Spread over the surface of the meat. Cover with foil and roast in the center of the oven at 400°F. Then uncover and baste with the butter that has run onto foil. Continue roasting, uncovered, for 30 minutes, until crust is brown and crisp.

Lancashire Hot Pot

PREPARATION TIME: 45 minutes

COOKING TIME: 2 hours 30 minutes

1lb middle or best end of neck, cut into cutlets
1 tblsp seasoned flour
4 medium onions, sliced
2 lamb's kidneys, skinned, cored and sliced
½lb mushrooms, sliced
1½lb potatoes, sliced
1¾ cups stock
Chopped parsley

Trim the lamb of any excess fat and coat with seasoned flour. Place layers of lamb, onion, kidney, mushrooms and potatoes in a large casserole, finishing with a layer of potatoes. Add the stock, cover and bake in a moderate oven, 350°F, for 2 hours. Remove the lid and cook for a further ½ hour to brown the potatoes. Sprinkle with chopped parsley.

Lemon and Ginger Chops

PREPARATION TIME: 3 hours

COOKING TIME: 15 minutes

4 chump lamb chops

Marinade
4 tblsp oil
Grated rind of 1 lemon
2 tblsp lemon juice
1 tblsp ground ginger
Seasoning

Mix all the marinade ingredients together. Place the chops in a shallow dish and pour the marinade over them. Leave for 2-3 hours, turning occasionally. Remove the chops and place under a hot broiler for 15 minutes, turning the chops occasionally and basting them with the marinade. Serve at once.

Wagon Wheel Lamb

PREPARATION TIME: 30 minutes

COOKING TIME: 20 minutes per 1lb

2-2½lb loin or best end of neck of lamb
2 tblsp fat
Small can pineapple rings, cut into halves
2-4 tsp brown sugar
Juice of ½ lemon

Garnish
¾ cup wagon wheel pasta
2 quarts water
Salt
2-4 tblsp butter

Place meat into a roasting pan and brush lightly with melted fat. Roast for 20 minutes per 1lb at 425°F. 30 minutes before end of cooking time, remove joint from oven and make six slits in the fat and skin. Press one pineapple half into each slit, brush with melted fat. Return to oven for rest of cooking time. When cooking time is finished, place the meat onto a hot dish and pour off all but 1 tblsp of the fat.

Garnish
Chop the rest of the pineapple, add to the fat with the pineapple syrup, sugar and lemon juice, and heat. Cook pasta in boiling, salted water, strain and toss in butter. Arrange pasta around the meat and serve the syrup in a sauceboat.

Roast Lamb with Rosemary

PREPARATION TIME: 20 minutes

COOKING TIME: 20 minutes per 1lb plus 20 minutes

½ leg lamb
¼ cup butter
Seasoning
Rosemary
1 clove garlic (optional)
2lb potatoes, peeled and cut into thick slices

Spread butter over lamb and season well. Stick rosemary leaves into the fat of the meat. Insert a clove of garlic near the bone. Place joint on a rack in a roasting pan. Roast in the center of the oven at 425°F. Place sliced potatoes under the meat after it has been cooking for 30 minutes. Baste joint from time to time.

Lamb Kebab

PREPARATION TIME: 15 minutes

COOKING TIME: 10-25 minutes

¾lb lean lamb, cut into bite-size pieces
1lb chipolata sausages, cut into halves
4 small tomatoes, halved or quartered

Thread a mixture of the lamb, tomatoes and sausages onto metal skewers. Brush with melted butter and cook under the broiler, turning the skewers to make sure that the food is well cooked.

Cutlets and Tomato Dip

PREPARATION TIME: 30 minutes

COOKING TIME: 30-45 minutes

4 large or 8 small cutlets
1 egg, beaten
3 tblsp crisp breadcrumbs
Fat for frying

For the Dip
1 medium onion, peeled and chopped
1 small apple, peeled and chopped
2 tblsp butter or margarine
Small can or tube tomato paste
1 tsp cornstarch
1¼ cups water
Seasoning
Pinch sugar
Pinch garlic salt

Coat cutlets with beaten egg and breadcrumbs. Fry onions and apple in the hot butter for several minutes. Add the tomato paste and cornstarch blended with the water. Bring the mixture to the boil and cook steadily, stirring well, until it comes to the boil and thickens slightly. Add the rest of the ingredients, lower the heat and contine cooking until a thick dip is made. Fry the cutlets in hot fat until golden brown and drain on kitchen paper. Serve with the tomato dip.

Lancashire Hot Pot (top right), and Cutlets and Tomato Dip (above right) and Lemon and Ginger Chops (bottom right).

Rolled and Stuffed Breast of Lamb

PREPARATION TIME: 15 minutes

COOKING TIME: 25 minutes per 1lb plus 25 minutes

2lb breast of lamb, boned
Sage and onion stuffing
A little oil or fat
Seasoning

Spread the breast of lamb with stuffing and roll. Brush the lamb with oil or melted fat. Season. Allow 25 minutes per 1lb + 25 minutes cooking time – weigh after stuffing the meat. Place in roasting pan and cook at 325°F.

Stuffed Lamb Chops

PREPARATION TIME: 40 minutes
COOKING TIME: 35 minutes

4 chump lamb chops

Stuffing
1 small onion, finely chopped
2 tblsp butter
2 lamb's kidneys, skinned, cored and chopped
¼ cup mushrooms, chopped
2 tblsp fresh breadcrumbs
1 tblsp sherry
1 tsp chopped parsley
Seasoning
2 tsp oil or melted fat

Garnish
¼ cup mushrooms
2 small tomatoes, halved
Triangle of bread
Parsley
A little oil or fat

Using a sharp knife, cut each chop horizontally through the fat and meat to make a small pocket for stuffing.

Stuffing
Fry the onion in butter, add the kidneys and mushrooms and continue cooking gently for 5 minutes. Add the rest of the ingredients and mix well. Press a spoonful of the stuffing into the pocket of the chops. Brush chops with oil. Broil the chops under a medium heat for 8-10 minutes on each side, turning once, until cooked.

Garnish
Fry the mushrooms, tomatoes and bread. Serve the chops on a hot dish garnished with the tomatoes, mushrooms and triangles of bread.

Lamb Chops and Mint Sauce

PREPARATION TIME: 10 minutes
COOKING TIME: 25 minutes

4 lamb chops

Mint Sauce
2 tblsp mint leaves
2 tsp sugar
2 tblsp vinegar
½ tblsp hot water

Broil chops until cooked and tender. Keep hot. Wash and dry the mint leaves. Place on a chopping board with 1 tsp sugar. Chop until fine, then put into a sauceboat. Add the rest of the sugar, stir in the hot water and leave for a few minutes to dissolve sugar. Add the vinegar. Serve with the chops.

Moussaka

PREPARATION TIME: 45 minutes
COOKING TIME: 1 hour 20 minutes

1lb eggplant, thinly sliced
1 tblsp oil
2 large onions, thinly sliced
1 clove garlic, crushed
1lb ground lamb
15oz can tomatoes
2 tblsp tomato paste
Seasoning
2 eggs
⅔ cup light cream
¼ cup Cheddar cheese, grated
2 tblsp Parmesan cheese, grated

Fry the eggplant in oil for 3-4 minutes. Remove and drain well. Fry the onions and garlic in 1 tblsp oil until golden brown. Add the lamb and cook for about 10 minutes, stirring occasionally. Add the tomatoes and tomato paste. Mix well. Bring to the boil and simmer for 20-25 minutes; season. Arrange alternate layers of eggplant and the lamb mixture in a large soufflé dish or shallow casserole dish. Bake in oven at 350°F for 35-40 minutes. Beat the eggs and cream together and stir in the cheese. Pour onto the moussaka and return to the oven for a further 15-20 minutes until the top is firm and golden brown.

Lamb and Kidney Pie

PREPARATION TIME: 50 minutes
COOKING TIME: 2 hours

1 large onion, thinly sliced
2 tblsp oil
1lb lamb from leg or shoulder, cubed
1 tblsp flour
8oz lamb's kidney, skinned, cored and chopped
½ cup mushrooms, sliced
⅔ cup beef stock or red wine
Few drops of soy sauce
Seasoning
7oz packet frozen pastry, thawed
Beaten egg to glaze

Fry the onion in oil until soft, but not brown. Toss the lamb in the flour with the kidney. Add to the onion and fry for 5-10 minutes, stirring occasionally. Add the mushrooms, stock, soy sauce and seasoning. Bring to the boil, stirring. Cover and simmer for 1 hour. Cool. Transfer the lamb mixture to a pie dish, then roll out the pastry. First make a collar of pastry round the dish and cover the pie. Seal edges but make a small hole in center to allow the steam to escape. Brush with beaten egg to glaze. Cook at 425°F for 10-15 minutes. Reduce the heat to 375°F for a further 25-30 minutes, until pastry is well risen and golden brown.

Noisettes Provençales

PREPARATION TIME: 40 minutes
COOKING TIME: 35 minutes

8 noisettes of lamb
¼ cup butter
1 tblsp oil

Provençale Sauce
¼ cup butter
1 tblsp oil
1 large onion, finely chopped
1 clove garlic, crushed
1lb tomatoes, skinned and chopped
1 tblsp tomato paste
⅔ cup dry white wine
Seasoning

Sauté the noisettes in the butter and oil for about 15 minutes, turning occasionally to brown the lamb on both sides.

This page: Stuffed Lamb Chops (top right), Lamb Chops and Mint Sauce (center left) and Lamb and Kidney Pie (bottom). Facing page: Moussaka (top), Rolled and Stuffed Breast of Lamb (center) and Noisettes Provençales (bottom).

Provençale Sauce
Meanwhile, heat the butter with the oil and add the onion and garlic. Fry gently until soft but not brown. Stir in tomatoes, tomato paste and white wine, and bring to the boil, stirring. Allow to cook uncovered over a fairly brisk heat for 10-15 minutes, stirring occasionally. Season to taste. Serve the sauce with the noisettes.

Risotto

PREPARATION TIME: 35 minutes

COOKING TIME: 1 hour

2 tblsp butter
2 tblsp oil
1 large onion, finely chopped
1 clove garlic, crushed
1 cup long grain rice
½ cup mushrooms, sliced
7oz can corn and peppers
½ cup frozen peas
1 whole green or red pepper, seeded, cored and chopped
12oz cooked lamb (leg or shoulder)
2½ cup chicken stock

Melt the butter with the oil. Add the onion and garlic and fry gently for 10-15 minutes until soft and golden brown. Stir in the rice and cook for a further 3-4 minutes, stirring continuously. Add the mushrooms, corn and peppers, peas and the chopped red or green peppers. Cut the lamb into small pieces, add to the saucepan and mix well. Add the stock and bring to the boil. Reduce heat, cover and simmer for 35-40 minutes, until the rice is cooked and the stock has been absorbed.

Winter Lamb

PREPARATION TIME: 35 minutes

COOKING TIME: 1 hour 55 minutes

2lb scrag or best end of neck of lamb
½ cup flour
¼ cup fat
2-3 onions, cut into rings
3 cups brown stock
4-6 carrots, peeled and sliced
Seasoning
½ tsp chopped mint
4 firm tomatoes, quartered
¼-½ cup mushrooms, sliced
Chopped parsley

Coat the lamb in the seasoned flour and fry for 2-3 minutes; add onions and continue cooking for a further 3 minutes. Stir in the stock gradually, bring to the boil and cook until thickened. Add carrots, seasoning and mint. Put lid on pan and simmer gently for 1½ hours. Add tomatoes and mushrooms and cook for 15 minutes. Garnish with chopped parsley.

Crown Roast of Lamb

PREPARATION TIME: 20 minutes

COOKING TIME: 25 minutes per 1lb plus 25 minutes

2 best ends of neck of lamb, chined
Stuffing (optional)
1 cup mushrooms
¼ cup butter
Cutlet frills

Trim the fat and skin from the ends of the rib bones, so that 1 inch of bone protrudes. Place the joints back-to-back and sew the ends together using fine string and a trussing needle, with the cutlet bones curving up and outwards. Most butchers will make the crown for you if given notice. If a stuffed joint is preferred, use your favorite stuffing to fill the crown roast. Cover the top of the crown of lamb with foil to keep the stuffing moist and to prevent the bones from burning during cooking. Roast at 350°F. Fry mushrooms in butter for 5-6 minutes. Remove the foil and top the stuffing with the mushrooms. Place a cutlet frill on each bone and serve.

Scandinavian Lamb

PREPARATION TIME: 50 minutes

COOKING TIME: 1 hour 20 minutes

1 breast of lamb, boned and cubed
1 tblsp oil
1 medium onion, sliced
1¼ cups stock
1 tsp rosemary
Seasoning
1 tblsp cornstarch
5oz carton sour cream
10 tblsp cooked peas

Fry the lamb in oil for 15-20 minutes. Remove from the pan and drain off most of the fat. Fry the onion in the remaining fat until soft. Return the lamb to the pan and add the stock, seasoning and rosemary. Bring to the boil, cover and simmer for 1 hour. Remove from the heat and add the sour cream and peas. This dish goes well with boiled rice.

Savory Pudding

PREPARATION TIME: 40 minutes

COOKING TIME: 2 hours 15 minutes

1 onion, finely chopped
1 tblsp oil
8oz ground lamb
1 tblsp tomato paste
½ tsp thyme
Seasoning
1¾ cups stock
1 large carrot, grated
12oz suet pastry
3 tblsp cornstarch
Soy sauce

Fry the onion and ground lamb in oil for 5 minutes, until the meat is brown. Stir in the tomato paste, thyme, seasoning and stock, and simmer for 10 minutes. Drain, reserving the stock. Add the carrot to the lamb mixture. Divide the pastry into three, and place one layer in the bottom of a greased 2½ pint basin. Place half the lamb mixture on top and repeat, finishing with a layer of suet pastry. Cover with buttered wax paper or foil and steam for 2 hours. Mix cornstarch with 2 tblsp of cold water and add to reserved stock with a few drops of soy sauce. Bring to the boil, stirring continuously, and serve with the pudding.

Lamb Chops in Wine Sauce

PREPARATION TIME: 40 minutes

COOKING TIME: 45 minutes

2 tblsp margarine or butter
4 loin chops
1 onion, sliced
1-2 tsp paprika
⅔ cup dry white wine
⅔ cup chicken stock
1 tblsp medium sherry
Seasoning
1 tsp cornstarch
¼ cup mushrooms, sliced
2 tomatoes, skinned
Chopped parsley

Heat fat and brown chops on both sides. Drain and leave on one side. Add onion to pan and cook, with the paprika, until soft. Allow to cool slightly then pour on wine, stock and sherry. Return chops to pan, season well, bring to the boil, reduce heat and simmer, covered, for about 30 minutes. Blend cornstarch with a little cold water and stir into wine and stock, stirring all the time. Add the mushrooms and tomatoes. Adjust seasoning and simmer for a further 15 minutes. Place chops on a serving dish, spoon over sauce and garnish with chopped parsley.

Crown Roast of Lamb (right), Festive Leg of Lamb (below) and Risotto (bottom).

Lamb Chops Reform

PREPARATION TIME: 35 minutes

COOKING TIME: 1 hour 10 minutes

8 lamb chops
¼ cup flour, seasoned
Beaten egg and breadcrumbs for coating
Oil for deep frying

Reform Sauce

¼ cup butter
¼ cup bacon rashers, chopped
1 small onion, chopped
1 large tomato, quartered
1 small carrot, sliced
½ cup flour
2½ cups brown stock
2 tsp mushroom ketchup (optional)
1 bouquet garni
Seasoning
1 tblsp redcurrant jelly
1 tblsp port

Trim and wipe chops. Dip them in seasoned flour and coat with egg and breadcrumbs.

Reform Sauce

Melt the butter in a saucepan. Add bacon and fry for 10 minutes. Add sliced vegetables until golden brown, stirring occasionally. Add flour and continue to fry slowly until a rich, brown color. Add stock, mushroom ketchup and bouquet garni and simmer, covered, for 40 minutes. Skim and sieve the sauce. Add the redcurrant jelly and heat gently until the jelly dissolves. Stir in the port and check seasoning.

To Fry the Crumbed Cutlets

Heat a pan of cooking oil until hot. Place chops in the hot oil and fry for 1 minute. Turn off heat and allow the chops to continue cooking in the oil for a further 5 minutes. Drain well and arrange on a serving dish. Serve with the reform sauce.

Lamb Provençale

PREPARATION TIME: 30 minutes

COOKING TIME: 1 hour

1lb lamb from a cooked leg
¼ cup butter
1 tblsp oil
2 medium onions, chopped
1 clove garlic, crushed
14oz can tomatoes
1 tblsp tomato paste
1¼ cups dry white wine
½ cup mushrooms, sliced
1 large green pepper, seeded and sliced
Seasoning

Cut lamb into small cubes. Melt the butter with the oil and add onions and garlic. Fry gently for about 10-15 minutes until soft, but not brown. Stir in the tomatoes, tomato paste and wine. Bring to the boil and add the lamb. Simmer, covered, for 25 minutes. Add the mushrooms and green peppers and cook for a further 15 minutes, stirring occasionally.

This page: Spareribs and Sweet and Sour Sauce (top), Lamb à l'Orange (center left), Lamb Provençale (center right) and Lamb Chops Reform (bottom). Facing page: Winter Lamb (top left), Scandinavian Lamb (top right), Irish Stew with Parsley Dumplings (center left) and Lamb Chops in Wine Sauce (bottom right).

Lamb à l'Orange

PREPARATION TIME: 20 minutes

COOKING TIME: 25 minutes

1 small onion, finely chopped
1 tblsp oil
1 large orange
1 tblsp redcurrant jelly
1¼ cups stock
½ tsp dry mustard
½ tsp sugar
Pinch cayenne pepper
1 tblsp cornstarch

12oz cooked lamb leg or shoulder

Fry onion gently in oil until soft, but not brown. Grate the orange rind. Cut three fine slices from the orange, trim the pith and reserve for garnish. Squeeze the juice from the remainder of the orange and add to the onion with the orange rind, redcurrant jelly and stock. Bring to the boil, reduce heat and cook, stirring, for 5 minutes. Blend the mustard, sugar, pepper and cornstarch together with 2 tblsp cold water and stir into the orange sauce. Slice the lamb, add to sauce and bring to the boil. Reduce heat and simmer for 15 minutes. When cooked, garnish with the reserved orange slices.

Irish Stew with Parsley Dumplings

PREPARATION TIME: 45 minutes

COOKING TIME: 2 hours 50 minutes

Irish Stew
3lb middle neck lamb chops
2 tblsp seasoned flour
2 tblsp dried onion flakes
1 tblsp pearl barley
2 tsp casserole seasoning
1 bay leaf
2½ cups boiling water
8oz potatoes, cut into chunks

Dumplings
1 cup flour
1¼ baking powder
½ tsp salt
¼ tsp ground black pepper
¼ cup suet, finely shredded
2 tsp chopped parsley
2 tblsp cold water

Coat the chops with seasoned flour and put them into a saucepan. Add the onion flakes and pearl barley. Sprinkle on the casserole seasoning and tuck in the bay leaf. Pour over the water and bring to the boil. Skim off any scum that rises to the surface. Reduce the heat, cover, simmer gently for 1 hour, add the potatoes and cook for a further 1½ hours.

Dumplings
Sift flour, baking powder and seasoning into a bowl. Stir in suet and parsley, then add enough water to bind to a dough. Divide the dough into 4 large portions and shape into balls. About 20 minutes before the lamb has finished cooking, check that the liquid is boiling and drop dumplings into the pan. Replace the lid and finish the cooking at boiling point. Discard the bay leaf, adjust the seasoning and serve.

Spareribs and Sweet and Sour Sauce

PREPARATION TIME: 30 minutes

COOKING TIME: 50 minutes

4-8 spareribs

Sauce
1½ tblsp cornstarch
⅔ cup water
2 tblsp vinegar from mixed pickles
Seasoning
1 tblsp Worcestershire sauce
2 tsp brown sugar

Garnish
Cooked rice
Lemon wedges

Put meat into roasting pan. Cook at 400°F for about 30 minutes. Pour off surplus fat and return to oven for a further 15-20 minutes, until chops are crisp and brown.

Sauce
Blend cornstarch with water, place all sauce ingredients in a pan and cook until thickened.

Garnish
Make a wide border of rice on a warm dish and arrange the spareribs on this. Pour sauce into center and place lemon wedges round the edge.

Meals with Pork

Facing page: Roast Leg of Pork (top), Roast Half Leg of Pork (center) and Savory Bacon (bottom).

Piquant Pork Chops

PREPARATION TIME: 30 minutes

COOKING TIME: 1 hour 10 minutes

4 pork chops
1 tblsp oil
1 small onion, peeled and chopped
1 tblsp brown sugar
1 tblsp dry mustard
2 tsp tomato paste
1 beef stock cube
1¼ cups water
1 tblsp Worcestershire sauce
2 tblsp lemon juice

Put the chops in a baking pan or a wide, shallow casserole and bake uncovered at 375°F, for about 20 minutes. Meanwhile, heat the oil, add the onion and fry until browned. Add the sugar, mustard, tomato paste and crumbled beef stock cube. Mix well, then add water and stir till boiling. Add the Worcestershire sauce and lemon juice and check seasoning. Pour off any excess fat from the chops and pour the sauce over them. Cover and continue cooking in the oven at 350°F, for about 40-45 minutes.

Piquant Pork Chops (top left), Pork Steaks and Apple Sauce (top right) and Pork Chops and Apple Chips (bottom).

Pork Steaks and Apple Sauce

PREPARATION TIME: 20 minutes

COOKING TIME: 25 minutes

4 pork steaks
Seasoning

Apple Sauce
1lb apples
⅔ cup water
1 tblsp sugar
1 tblsp butter or margarine

Season the pork steaks and fry or broil until cooked, turning often to ensure that they are cooked all the way through. Peel, core and thinly slice the apples. Put into a pan with the water, sugar and butter or margarine. Cook gently until soft, then rub through a sieve. Serve the apple sauce with the cooked pork steaks.

Roast Leg of Pork

PREPARATION TIME: 20 minutes

COOKING TIME: 30 minutes per 1lb plus 30 minutes

2½lb leg of pork
2 tblsp beef fat or cooking fat

Place meat in a roasting pan, season, and spread with beef fat or cooking fat. Place in the center of a preheated oven, 350°F. If a covered roasting pan is used, basting is not necessary, but if the joint is uncovered the meat should be basted every 20-30 minutes. The meat should be turned over, using two metal spoons, halfway through the cooking. When the meat is cooked, transfer to a large carving dish and keep hot.

Roast Half Leg of Pork

PREPARATION TIME: 15 minutes

COOKING TIME: 30 minutes per 1lb plus 30 minutes

Place meat in a roasting pan, season, and spread with beef fat or cooking fat. Place in the center of a preheated oven, 350°F. If a covered pan is used, basting is not necessary, but if the joint is uncovered the meat should be basted every 20-30 minutes. The meat should be turned over, using two metal spoons, halfway through the cooking. When the meat is cooked, transfer to a large carving dish and keep hot.

Savory Bacon

PREPARATION TIME: 30 minutes

COOKING TIME: 45 minutes

1 cup diced bacon (gammon or back) rashers
3 scallions, chopped
3 eggs
1¼ cups milk
½ tsp powdered sage
Seasoning
1½lb creamed potatoes
6 tblsp cheese, grated

P
S

Fry onion until crisp. Beat eggs and add milk, sage and onion, and season. Grease an ovenproof dish and shape creamed potatoes round the edge. Put the bacon in the center of dish and pour the egg mixture over the bacon. Sprinkle the top with cheese. Bake in the center of the oven at 375°F, for about 30 minutes until set, and the potato border has browned.

Spicy Pork Meatballs

PREPARATION TIME: 50 minutes

COOKING TIME: 40 minutes

1½lb ground pork
1 large onion, grated
Pinch garlic granules
¼ cup ground almonds
¼ cup fresh breadcrumbs
1 small egg, beaten
1 tsp chopped parsley
¼ tsp ground cinnamon
½ tsp salt
½ tsp black pepper
2 tblsp medium sherry
1 tblsp butter
4 tblsp oil

Sauce
1 small onion, finely chopped
Pinch garlic granules
1½ tsp soft brown sugar
4 tomatoes, skinned and chopped
½ green pepper, cored, seeded and sliced
½ red pepper, cored, seeded and sliced
¼ tsp crushed chilis
¼ tsp cayenne pepper
1 tsp paprika
1 tsp chopped parsley
1¼ cups beef stock
2 tsp cornstarch
4 tblsp medium sherry

Meatballs
Mix together the pork, onion, garlic granules, almonds, breadcrumbs, egg, parsley, cinnamon, seasoning and sherry. Combine well, then shape into about 40 walnut-sized balls. Melt the butter with half the oil in a skillet. Add the meatballs, in batches, and fry gently until browned on all sides, taking care not to break up the meatball shapes. Remove from the pan with a slotted spoon and drain on paper towels.

Sauce
Heat the remaining oil in a saucepan, add the onion, garlic granules and brown sugar to the pan and fry until the onion is soft. Stir in the tomatoes, green and red peppers, crushed chilis, cayenne pepper, paprika and parsley, and cook for a further 3 minutes. Add stock and bring to the boil, stirring occasionally. Dissolve the cornstarch in the sherry and add to the pan. Simmer, stirring, until thickened. Add the meatballs to the sauce and shake the pan to coat well. Cover the pan and cook gently for 20-25 minutes or until the meatballs are cooked through. Taste and adjust seasoning before serving.

Pork Chops and Apple Chips

PREPARATION TIME: 40 minutes

COOKING TIME: 30 minutes

4 pork chops
Fat for deep frying
2 large tart apples
A little flour

Broil or fry the chops for 15-20 minutes, turning frequently. Peel and core the apples and cut them into chips. Roll the chips in flour and fry in deep fat until cooked. Serve with the chops, at once.

Ground Pork Loaf

PREPARATION TIME: 45 minutes

COOKING TIME: 1 hour 45 minutes

½lb eggplant
1½lb ground pork
1 onion, chopped
¼ cup fresh breadcrumbs
1 tblsp chopped parsley
Seasoning
Pinch curry powder
Pinch garlic salt
1 egg, beaten

Preheat oven to 400°. Bake the eggplant in its skin for 15 minutes. Cut in two and scoop out the pulp. Mix in a bowl with the meat, onion, breadcrumbs, parsley, seasoning, curry powder and garlic salt. Blend in the beaten egg. Place the meat mixture in a greased, oblong bread pan. Stand the pan on a cooky tray half filled with water and bake for 1½ hours. Cool and turn out onto a dish.

Bacon and Onion Roll

PREPARATION TIME: 30 minutes

COOKING TIME: 2 hours 15 minutes

1 large onion, chopped
1 tsp powdered sage
Seasoning
1¼ cups fresh white breadcrumbs
2 tblsp margarine, melted
4 bacon rashers, trimmed

Spicy Pork Meatballs (above right), Bacon and Onion Roll (right) and Ground Pork Loaf (top right).

Suet Pastry
2 cups flour
2 tsp baking powder
½ tsp salt
Pinch of pepper
½ cup finely shredded suet
⅔ cup water

Mix together the onion, seasonings and breadcrumbs. Stir in the margarine. For the pastry: sift the flour, baking powder and seasonings into a mixing basin. Add suet and stir in enough water to mix to a firm dough. Turn out onto a floured board and roll out to an oblong. Arrange bacon rashers over surface and spread with stuffing to within 1 inch of edges. Moisten pastry edges and roll into a roly-poly about 8 inches long. Pinch edges to seal. Wrap in greased, double-thickness wax paper, folding into a large pleat the length of the roll to allow for expansion. Wrap loosely in kitchen foil. Steam briskly for 2 hours.

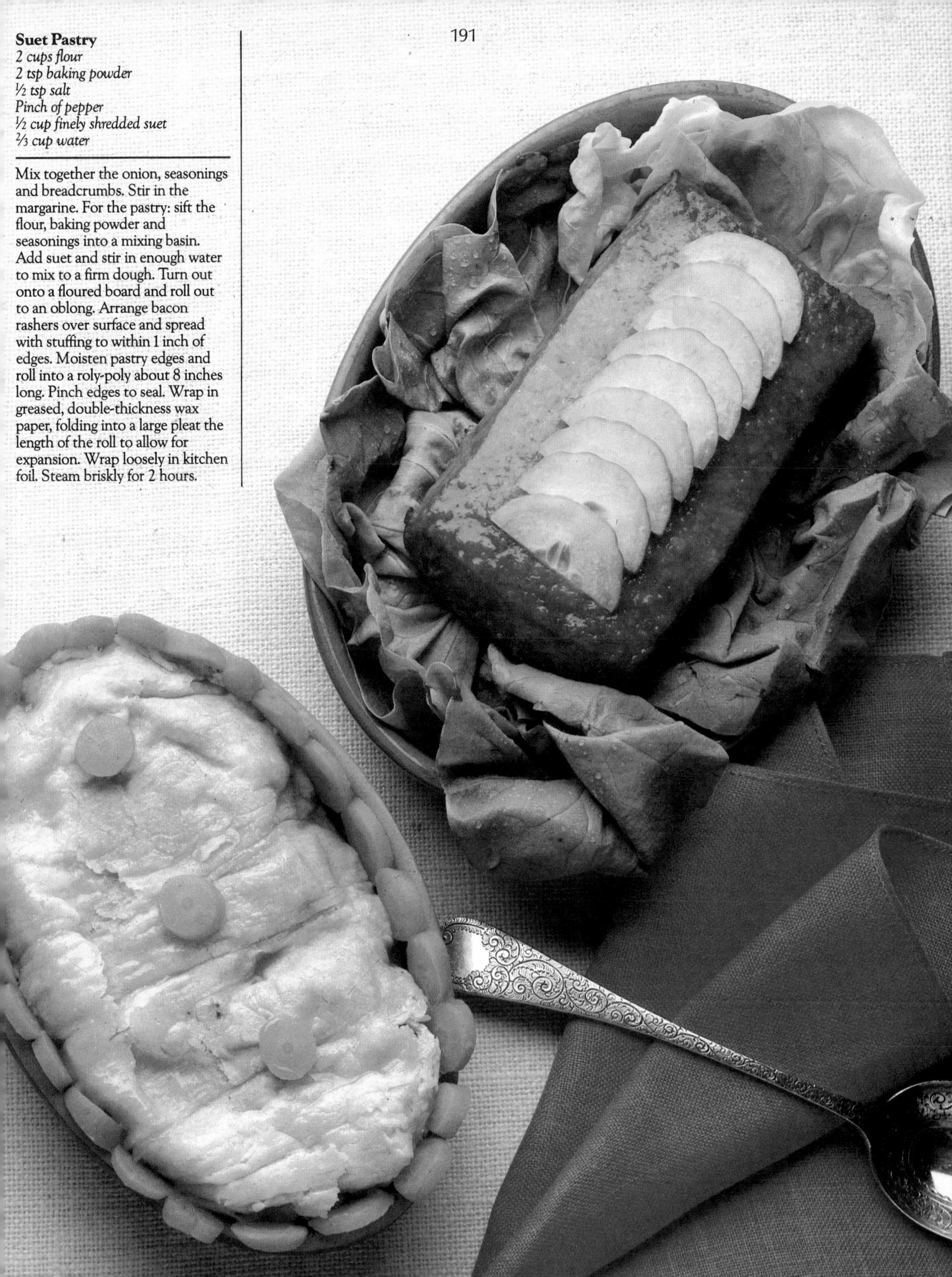

Curried Pork

PREPARATION TIME: 25 minutes
COOKING TIME: 40 minutes

¾ cup pasta (macaroni or shaped pasta)
Salt
1lb frozen mixed vegetables
1lb pork fillet, diced
2 tblsp oil
1 large onion, chopped
1 green pepper
1 tblsp dark molasses
1-2 tsp curry powder
Seasoning
Butter
1 onion, sliced into rings

Cook the pasta in 2 quarts of boiling, salted water until tender; strain and keep half on one side for a garnish. Cook the frozen vegetables in a little salted water until they begin to soften; strain. Toss the pork in the hot oil for 5 minutes, add the onion, green pepper, molasses, curry powder and seasoning, then lower heat and continue to cook for a further 5 minutes. Stir in the vegetables and half the pasta. Heat gently for 10 minutes. Serve in a border of pasta tossed in a little butter, and garnish with sliced, raw onion rings.

Pork Croquettes

PREPARATION TIME: 30 minutes
COOKING TIME: 15 minutes

12oz cooked pork, ground
2 tblsp butter or margarine
¼ cup flour
⅔ cup milk
2 tsp chopped parsley
2 tsp chopped gherkins
6 tblsp soft, fresh breadcrumbs
Seasoning
Oil or fat to fry

To Coat
1 egg, beaten
¼ cup crisp breadcrumbs

Make a thick sauce of the butter or margarine, flour and milk, and add the parsley, gherkins and meat. Blend well, then stir in the breadcrumbs and seasoning. Allow the mixture to cool, form into eight finger shapes, brush with egg and coat in breadcrumbs. Fry in hot fat or oil until crisp and brown. Drain well on kitchen paper. Serve hot.

Shepherd's Pie

PREPARATION TIME: 40 minutes
COOKING TIME: 30 minutes

8-12oz cooked ground pork
2 tblsp beef fat or fat
1 onion, finely chopped
2 tomatoes, skinned and chopped
Good pinch of mixed herbs
Seasoning
⅔-1¼ cups stock
1lb mashed potato
2 tblsp butter or margarine

Heat the fat and fry the onion for 3 minutes. Add the tomatoes and the meat and heat together for 2-3 minutes. Stir in the herbs, seasoning and stock. Put into a pie dish and cover with the mashed potato, forking this neatly over, or shape it using a pastry bag. Scatter pieces of butter on the potatoes to help the topping to brown. Bake in the center of the oven at 375°F until crisp and brown on top.

Pork Fillet with Apricots

PREPARATION TIME: 30 minutes
COOKING TIME: 40 minutes

1lb pork fillet, cut into bite-size pieces
2 tblsp seasoned flour
¼ cup butter
14oz can apricot halves, drained and juice retained
2 tblsp Worcestershire sauce
2 tblsp demerara sugar
2 tsp vinegar
2 tsp lemon juice
8 tblsp water
1 cup long grain rice

Toss the pork pieces in seasoned flour. Heat the butter and fry the pork until lightly browned. Chop all but three of the apricot halves. Mix 8 tblsp apricot juice with the Worcestershire sauce, sugar, vinegar, lemon juice and water. Add any remaining flour to the pork and pour in the apricot sauce and chopped fruit. Bring to the boil, stirring. Reduce heat, cover and simmer for about 15 minutes. Spoon pork and sauce onto a serving dish. Cook the rice in boiling, salted water and arrange in a border around the meat. Garnish with remaining apricot halves.

Cranberry Ham

PREPARATION TIME: 25 minutes
COOKING TIME: 15 minutes

4 thick slices cooked ham
2 tblsp fat
2 tblsp cranberry jelly or sauce

Heat the ham for 2-3 minutes in the hot fat or brush with melted fat and heat under the broiler. Spread with the sauce or jelly and leave under a hot broiler until the sauce bubbles; serve at once.

Bacon Pancakes

PREPARATION TIME: 20 minutes
COOKING TIME: 30 minutes

8 bacon rashers, de-rinded

Batter
1 cup flour, preferably all-purpose
Pinch of salt
1 egg
1¼ cups milk

Sieve the flour and salt into a large basin, big enough for beating in the liquid. Add the egg and about a quarter of the milk. Stir carefully with a wooden spoon until the flour is blended. Beat hard until smooth. Add the rest of the liquid. When the batter becomes thinner use a flat egg whisk to aerate the mixture. Cook pancakes in the usual way. Meanwhile, fry or broil the bacon rashers and cut into pieces. Sandwich the pancakes with really crisp bacon and serve hot.

This page: Stuffed Loin of Pork (top), Pork Fillet with Apricots (center left) and Curried Pork (bottom). Facing page: Bacon Pancakes (top), Pork Croquettes (center left), Shepherd's Pie (center right) and Cranberry Ham (bottom).

Stuffed Loin of Pork

PREPARATION TIME: 40 minutes

COOKING TIME: 25 minutes per 1lb plus 25 minutes

3lb loin of pork, boned

Stuffing

½ cup soft breadcrumbs
¼ cup suet, finely shredded
2 tblsp chopped parsley
1 tblsp chopped chives or scallions
Seasoning
1 egg
A little oil or fat

Score the fat on the meat with a knife. Blend the stuffing ingredients together and then spread the stuffing over the meat carefully and roll it up. Brush the scored fat with melted fat or oil and sprinkle lightly with salt. Weigh after stuffing meat. Cook in a roasting pan at 425°F. Remove the meat to a hot dish when cooked, pour off the surplus fat, leaving just 1 tblsp in the roasting pan and make a gravy with this.

Fluffy Baked Eggs and Bacon

PREPARATION TIME: 15 minutes

COOKING TIME: 15 minutes

4 slices of bread
Butter
4 eggs
Seasoning
8 bacon rashers, de-rinded

Toast the bread and spread with butter. Separate the egg yolks and whites. Whisk the whites until very stiff, seasoning well. Make the egg white into a ring on each slice of toast, drop a yolk in the center and bake in oven at 375°F until set. Serve with broiled bacon.

This page: Belly of Pork Casserole (top), Pork Chops and Frankfurters (center right) and Bacon and Sausage Plait (bottom left). Facing page: Bacon Chops with Pears (top), Pork with Sweet and Sour Sauce (center left), Bacon Casserole (center right) and Fluffy Baked Eggs and Bacon (bottom).

Bacon Casserole

PREPARATION TIME: 30 minutes

COOKING TIME: 40 minutes per 1lb plus 5 minutes to thicken

6-9oz bacon or ham per person
Ground black pepper or peppercorns
1lb mixed vegetables

Soak the bacon in cold water. Put into a casserole dish and cover with cold water. Add pepper or peppercorns and cover. Allow about 40 minutes per 1lb for a wide, thin joint; a little longer if a thick joint is used. Bake at 325°F. Add vegetables during cooking.

Belly of Pork Casserole

PREPARATION TIME: 40 minutes

COOKING TIME: 2 hours 15 minutes

1 large onion, sliced
1 large tart apple, peeled and sliced
1½lb belly of pork
2 tblsp tomato paste
1 chicken stock cube
1¾ cups boiling water
A pinch of freshly-ground black pepper
A pinch of sage

Put the onion and apple into a casserole and put the meat on top. Mix the tomato paste and stock cube together, add boiling water and stir till stock cube has dissolved. Pour over meat in casserole, add pepper and sage. Cover and bake at 325°F for about 2 hours.

Pork Kebabs

PREPARATION TIME: 25 minutes
COOKING TIME: 20 minutes

1lb lean pork, cut into bite-size pieces

Brush kebabs with melted butter and cook under the broiler, turning the skewers to make sure that the food is well cooked. The food can be slipped from the skewer easily onto serving plates.

This is a most attractive way of serving broiled foods. You can thread a mixture of foods – kidneys, bacon, sausages, diced pork, mushrooms, onions, tomato halves, etc. – onto metal skewers.

Bacon Chops with Pears

PREPARATION TIME: 25 minutes

COOKING TIME: 20 minutes

6 slices of gammon bacon
3 dessert pears
2 tblsp melted butter
2 tblsp flour
1 egg, beaten
½ cup breadcrumbs
Oil for deep frying

Brush the bacon with melted butter and broil for 4-5 minutes on both sides. Peel and core the pears and cut into halves. Coat pear halves with flour, then with egg and breadcrumbs. Fry in deep oil for 10 minutes until golden brown. Serve bacon with a pear half on each slice.

Bacon and Sausage Plait

PREPARATION TIME: 50 minutes

COOKING TIME: 30-40 minutes

¾lb basic puff pastry, frozen

Filling

8oz pork sausage meat
8oz cooked bacon, chopped
2 hard-boiled eggs, roughly chopped
1 tsp sage
Seasoning

Glaze

1 egg, beaten
A little salt

Roll the pastry out to a 10 inch square. Mix all the ingredients together and place down the center of the pastry, leaving equal sides of unfilled pastry. Cut the sides obliquely in ½ inch strips and brush with beaten egg. Lift alternate strips over the sausage mixture to form a roll resembling a plait. Brush with egg and sprinkle with salt. Bake at 400°F for about 15 minutes. Lower heat to 350°F for a further 15 minutes.

Ham in Cider and Raisin Sauce

PREPARATION TIME: 45 minutes

COOKING TIME: 30 minutes per 1lb plus 30 minutes

4lb forehock, ham or bacon
1 carrot, sliced
1 onion, sliced
Bouquet garni
3 whole cloves
2½ cups cider
2½ cups water

Cider and Raisin Sauce

½ cup seedless raisins
1¼ cups stock (from cooking bacon)
2 tblsp brown sugar
2-3 drops soy sauce
Juice of ½ lemon
2 tsp cornstarch
2 tblsp water

Put the ham, vegetables, herbs and cloves in the pan and add cider and water. Bring to the boil and cover. Simmer slowly, allowing 20 minutes per 1lb plus 20 minutes for ham, or 30 minutes per 1lb plus 30 minutes for forehock.

Cider and Raisin Sauce

Put all the sauce ingredients, except the cornstarch and water, into a saucepan. Cover and simmer for 10 minutes. Blend the cornstarch with 2 tblsp water. Stir into the sauce, simmer for a further 3 minutes. Serve sauce separately.

Pork Chops and Frankfurters

PREPARATION TIME: 30 minutes

COOKING TIME: 20 minutes

4 small pork chops (loin or spareribs)
Seasoning
4-6 tblsp melted butter
4-8 frankfurters
1 green pepper, cored and sliced
2 small eating apples, cored and sliced
12oz can sauerkraut
Parsley

Season pork chops. If they are lean, brush with a little melted butter and broil until tender, turning over and lowering the heat when browned on either side. Simmer the frankfurters in boiling water for 5 minutes; drain. Fry the green pepper and apples in the rest of the butter, add the sauerkraut and heat thoroughly. Put the apple mixture onto a hot dish, top with the chops and frankfurters and garnish with parsley.

Boiled Bacon and Pease Pudding

PREPARATION TIME: overnight plus 30 minutes

COOKING TIME: 2 hours

6-9oz bacon per person
Pepper

Pease Pudding

1 cup dried split yellow peas
1 onion
2 cloves
Seasoning
A stick of butter

Wash and soak salted bacon overnight, or for several hours, in cold water. Put soaked bacon into a saucepan, cover with cold water. Bring to the boil, skim, removing any greyish film floating on top. Add pepper, but no salt. Put a lid on the pan and cook slowly, allowing 30 minutes per 1lb for thinner joints, 35 minutes per 1lb for thicker joints.

Pease Pudding

Place split peas in a bowl, cover with cold water and soak for 3 hours. Rinse thoroughly. Peel the onion and press a clove into each end. Place the onion and split peas in boiling water. Do not salt. Simmer for ¾-1 hour or until peas are soft. Drain. Remove the cloves from the onion. Mash the peas and the onion together or pass them through a blender to form a smooth purée. Season well and beat in the butter.

Ham in Cider and Raisin Sauce (top left), Pork Kebabs (bottom left) and Boiled Bacon and Pease Pudding (left).

Ham and Egg Pie

PREPARATION TIME: 50 minutes
COOKING TIME: 20-30 minutes

8oz basic pastry
8oz lean cooked ham, finely chopped
6 eggs, lightly beaten
Seasoning
A little onion juice or minced onion
Beaten egg or milk to glaze

Line a pie plate with half the pastry. Mix the ham and eggs together, season and add the onion juice. Pour into the pastry case, damp the edges and cover with the remaining pastry, pressing edges well together. Brush with a little egg or milk and bake at 375°F, for 20 minutes, until pastry is golden brown.

Pork Pie

PREPARATION TIME: 50 minutes
COOKING TIME: 2 hour 30 minutes

Hot Water Crust Pastry
3 cups flour
Pinch of salt
10 tblsp lard
2/3 cup water

Filling
1/2 cup bacon rashers, diced
11/2lb pork fillet, diced
Seasoning
Pinch of powdered ginger
1 tblsp water

Jelly
21/2 cups water
1 pig's trotter
1 bay leaf
1 onion

Pastry
Sieve the flour and salt into a mixing bowl. Heat the lard and water, cool slightly, then pour over the flour and knead well until smooth. Roll out two-thirds of the pastry for lining a cake pan (with loose base) or a raised pie pan that unlocks. Line the pan. Keep the rest of the pastry warm.

Filling
Fill with the bacon, pork, seasoning, ginger and water. Roll out the rest of the pastry and make a lid. Seal the edges firmly and make a center slit. Brush the top with beaten egg to give a glaze.

Bake in the center of the oven at 350°F for about 2 hours, until golden brown and firm.

Jelly
Boil the pig's trotter in the water with the onion and bay leaf until tender, then remove the onion and bay leaf and boil rapidly to give about 5 tblsp strong liquid. Remove the pie from the pan, cool, allow stock to cool, then pour through center hole with a funnel. Leave to set for 1 hour in refrigerator.

Apricot Glazed Gammon

PREPARATION TIME: 1 hour
COOKING TIME: 2 hours

4lb gammon
2 bay leaves
Medium tin apricot halves
Watercress

Soak gammon for a few hours in cold water, then place in an ovenproof dish with the bay leaves. Pour over enough boiling water to half cover the gammon. Cover the dish with foil and bake for 11/4 hours in the center of the oven at 350°F. Remove from the oven and strain off the bacon stock. Remove the skin from the gammon and put the joint back into the ovenproof dish. Drain the juice from the apricots and pour it over gammon. Return the joint to the oven for another 45 minutes, basting frequently with the syrup. Remove the gammon from the oven and score diagonal designs on the fat with a sharp knife. Garnish with apricot halves and watercress.

Pork with Savory Rice

PREPARATION TIME: 35 minutes
COOKING TIME: 40 minutes

4 good-sized pork chops
1 large onion, thinly sliced
1/4 cup cooked long grain rice
3 large tomatoes, thickly sliced
Seasoning
11/4 cups canned or bottled tomato juice

Put the pork chops in an ovenproof dish and cook for 15 minutes at 375°F. Remove the dish from the oven and top with onion slices, then the rice, then the tomatoes. Season each layer well. Pour the tomato juice into the dish. Return to the oven for a further 20-25 minutes, lowering the heat slightly if the mixture on top of the chops is becoming too brown.

Spareribs with Barbecue Sauce

PREPARATION TIME: 25 minutes
COOKING TIME: 45 minutes

8 pork spareribs
2 tblsp melted butter
Seasoning

Barbecue Sauce
2 tblsp butter
2 onions, sliced
1 clove garlic, crushed
1/2 cup mushrooms, chopped
Medium can tomatoes
1 tsp Worcestershire sauce
1 tsp made mustard
1/2 tsp mixed herbs
1/2 tsp sugar
Seasoning

Garnish
Parsley

Brush chops with melted butter, season well. Broil for 15-20 minutes, turning once or twice, and lowering heat after 10 minutes.

Barbecue Sauce
Melt butter in pan. Gently fry onions and garlic, add mushrooms and fry for a few minutes. Add tomatoes, Worcestershire sauce, mustard, herbs, sugar and seasoning. Simmer for about 10 minutes.

Garnish
Arrange chops on serving dish. Pour sauce over chops and garnish with fresh parsley.

Pork Chops with Sweet and Sour Sauce

PREPARATION TIME: 25 minutes
COOKING TIME: 1 hour 10 minutes

4 pork chops

Sweet and Sour Sauce
11/2 tblsp cornstarch
2/3 cup water
2 tblsp wine vinegar
Seasoning

Bacon and Corn Quiche

PREPARATION TIME: 40 minutes

COOKING TIME: 50 minutes

Basic Pastry

1½ cups flour
Pinch of salt
6 tblsp mixed margarine and lard
1-2 tblsp cold water

Filling

1 tblsp margarine
6 bacon rashers, de-rinded and chopped
1 small onion, finely chopped
7oz can corn, drained
2 eggs
1 cup milk
1 tsp dried thyme
Seasoning

Pastry

Sift flour and salt into a mixing bowl. Add the lard and margarine and cut in until the mixture resembles breadcrumbs. Bind together with water to form a dough. Leave to rest for about 10 minutes. Roll out the dough to line a 9 inch loose-bottom quiche pan. Place a piece of wax paper over the pastry and fill with 'blind' baking beans. Bake in a preheated oven, 400°F, for 10 minutes. Remove paper and beans and bake for a further ten minutes. Allow to cool.

Filling

Melt the margarine in a skillet and fry bacon and onion until soft. Drain and place in the cooked quiche case. Cover with the corn. Beat the eggs and add the milk, herbs and seasoning to taste. Pour over the bacon and corn mixture. Cook in a hot oven at 400°F for 10 minutes. Reduce heat to 350°F, and bake for another 25 minutes.

1 tblsp Worcestershire sauce
2 tsp brown sugar

Put chops into a roasting pan and roast at 400°F for about 30 minutes. Pour off surplus fat and return to oven for a further 15-20 minutes until chops are crisp and brown.

Sweet and Sour Sauce

Blend cornstarch with water, then put all ingredients for the sauce into a pan and cook until thickened. Serve sauce with cooked chops.

Facing page: Spareribs with Barbecue Sauce (top), Pork with Savory Rice (center) and Bacon and Corn Quiche (bottom).

This page: Apricot Glazed Gammon (top), Pork Pie (center right) and Ham and Egg Pie (bottom).

Cooking with Veal

Veal Casserole

PREPARATION TIME: 30 minutes
COOKING TIME: 50 minutes

1½lb veal shoulder, cubed
Seasoning
¼ cup chicken stock
2 large carrots
2 sticks celery, chopped
1 tblsp quick tapioca
1 tblsp water
4 slices of bread
Margarine

Season the veal. Bring chicken stock to the boil, add the meat, carrots and celery, cover and let simmer for 45 minutes. Mix the tapioca with the water, stir into the meat and simmer until the sauce thickens. Transfer to a casserole dish. Spread the bread slices with margarine on both sides and place on top of the casserole. Put in a hot oven until bread is toasted.

Veal en Croûte

PREPARATION TIME: 30 minutes
COOKING TIME: 55 minutes

Basic Pastry
1¾ cups flour
Pinch of salt
7 tblsp fat
Water to mix

Filling
6 tblsp mushrooms, finely chopped
¼ cup butter
Seasoning
1-1½lb veal (in one piece)

Pastry
Sieve flour and salt together, cut in fat, bind with water and roll out to a large oblong.

Filling
Blend mushrooms with the butter and seasoning and spread over the center of the pastry, leaving the ends plain. Put the veal on top, season lightly and wrap pastry round this. Seal the edges with water. Cook on a greased cooky sheet for 20-25 minutes, in the center of the oven, at 425-450°F. Lower heat to 350-375°F for a further 30 minutes.

Veal Chops with Cheese

PREPARATION TIME: 35 minutes
COOKING TIME: 30 minutes

8 thick veal chops
½ cup butter
Seasoning
1¾ cups Gruyère cheese, grated
2 eggs
4 tblsp heavy cream
Grated nutmeg
½ cup white wine

Melt the butter in a large sauté pan with an ovenproof handle. Add the veal chops and sear them on both sides over a high heat. Reduce heat, season the chops, cover pan and cook gently for about 20 minutes, turning the chops once. In a bowl mix the cheese, eggs and cream. Season and add the nutmeg. Drain off the cooking butter from the pan and reserve it. Put some of the cheese mixture on each chop. Add the wine to the pan and place it, uncovered, in the oven, 375°F, for 10 minutes to finish the cooking. Baste the chops with the reserved cooking butter once or twice.

Fricassée of Veal

PREPARATION TIME: 25 minutes
COOKING TIME: 1 hour 20 minutes

1½lb veal cutlets
1 onion, stuck with cloves
Seasoning
Bouquet garni
2 tblsp butter
¼ cup flour

Garnish
Bacon rolls
Lemon slices

Cut meat into small pieces and put in a saucepan, together with the onion, seasoning and bouquet garni. Cover with water, bring to the boil and simmer until the meat is tender (about 1 hour). Melt the butter in a pan, add the flour and stir well. Do not brown. Remove the bouquet garni and the onion from the veal. Add the liquid to the flour and fat, then add this to the veal. Cook gently for a further 10 minutes. Garnish with bacon rolls and lemon slices.

Veal and Mushroom Pie

PREPARATION TIME: 50 minutes
COOKING TIME: 2 hours 50 minutes

1lb veal, cubed
Seasoned flour
Butter or oil for frying
1 small bay leaf
¾ cup mushrooms, peeled and sliced
1¼ cups stock
6oz basic pastry
1 egg, beaten

Dust veal in seasoned flour. Fry until lightly brown. Add bay leaf and stock and bring to simmering point. Cover and cook in oven at 350°F until tender (about 2 hours). Leave to cool. Roll pastry out to fit a large ovenproof plate. Put meat and mushrooms onto the plate, adding seasoning to taste. Cover with pastry. Brush with beaten egg to glaze, and bake at 450°F for about 30 minutes.

This page: Veal and Mushroom Pie (top), Fricassée of Veal (center left) and Veal en Croûte (bottom).

Facing page: Ragoût (top), Veal Chops with Mushrooms (center right) and Veal Chops with Cheese (bottom).

Rolled Breast of Veal

PREPARATION TIME: 30 minutes

COOKING TIME: 1 hour 20 minutes

3lb breast of veal, boned and trimmed
½ cup smoked ham streaked with fat, finely chopped
¼ cup lard
6 tblsp finely chopped parsley
1 garlic clove, crushed
Seasoning
1 cup dry white wine

Score the inside of the breast crossways, in lines ⅛ inch deep. Mix the smoked ham, 2 tblsp of the lard, 4 tblsp of the parsley, the garlic and 1 tsp seasoning to make a paste. Spread the paste over the cut surface of the veal. Beginning at one of the narrow sides, roll up the veal tightly and skewer or tie with string. Season the surface of the meat. In a heavy pan, slowly brown the veal on all sides in the rest of the lard. Add the wine, cover and simmer for 1 hour or until tender. Remove the veal to a carving board and allow to stand for 10 minutes before cutting into slices. Skim any excess fat off the pan juices. Taste the juices, adjust the seasoning to taste, then reheat, adding the remaining parsley, and use as a sauce for the veal.

Veal Chops with Mushrooms

PREPARATION TIME: 45 minutes

COOKING TIME: 1 hour 10 minutes

4 veal chops
Seasoning
2 tblsp oil
4 medium-sized carrots, sliced
½ cup mushrooms, sliced
1 small onion, sliced
4 tblsp white wine
2 tomatoes, peeled and sliced

Trim chops and season. Heat oil, brown chops on both sides, then transfer to a casserole dish. Add all other ingredients and cook in the oven at 325°F for about 1 hour.

Fried Veal with Rice

PREPARATION TIME: 30 minutes

COOKING TIME: 1 hour

4 neck cutlets
Seasoned flour
1 small onion
1 small green pepper
1 stick celery
1 tomato
6 tblsp fat or oil
⅔ cup stock
1 cup rice

Toss the cutlets in seasoned flour. Peel and chop the onion and chop other vegetables. Melt ¼ cup fat and fry the veal until brown on both sides. Add the stock; simmer the meat until it is tender (45 minutes). Boil the rice. Melt 2 tblsp fat and fry the onion, green pepper and celery. Stir in the cooked rice and add the tomato. Serve the cutlets on top of the rice mixture and pour over the juices from the skillet.

Veal Chops with Wine (above), Fried Veal with Rice (right) and Roast Best End of Neck (far right).

Roast Best End of Neck

PREPARATION TIME: 10 minutes

COOKING TIME: 25 minutes per 1lb plus 25 minutes

Place joint in a roasting pan, spread with cooking fat, and season. Place in the center of a preheated oven, 400°F. If a covered roasting pan is used, basting is not necessary, but if the joint is uncovered, the meat should be basted every 20-30 minutes. The meat should be turned over, using two metal spoons, halfway through the cooking. When the meat is cooked, transfer to a large carving dish and keep hot.

Veal Chops with Wine

PREPARATION TIME: 30 minutes

COOKING TIME: 1 hour 20 minutes

4 veal chops
6 tblsp flour
Seasoning
2 tblsp oil
1 onion, chopped
½ cup mushrooms, sliced
1¼ cups white wine

Trim chops and coat with seasoned flour. Heat oil and brown the chops on both sides, then transfer to a casserole dish. Add onion to remaining oil and cook till lightly brown. Add remaining flour and mix well. Add mushrooms and wine and bring to boiling point, stirring all the time. Pour sauce over chops in the casserole. Cover and cook for about 1 hour at 350°F.

Blanquette of Veal with Prunes

PREPARATION TIME: 20 minutes

COOKING TIME: 30 minutes

1lb veal, diced
2 onions, diced
1 sachet of bouquet garni
2½ cups white stock
¼ cup butter
½ cup flour
⅔ cup cream or evaporated milk
1-2 egg yolks
1 tblsp lemon juice

Garnish
Freshly cooked prunes
Freshly cooked vegetables

Put the veal, onions and herbs into a pan with the stock. Simmer gently until tender. Strain; keep the meat hot. Make a sauce with the butter, flour and stock; cook for 2 minutes. Add the cream or evaporated milk and reheat. Stir in the egg yolks and lemon juice. Reheat, but do not boil. Pour over the veal. Garnish with the prunes and vegetables.

Veal Roll with Prune and Apple Stuffing

PREPARATION TIME: 40 minutes
COOKING TIME: 1 hour 15 minutes

12oz basic pastry
1-1¼lb veal fillet

Stuffing
½ cup bacon, de-rinded and chopped
½ cup soft breadcrumbs
1 tsp mixed herbs
6oz soaked prunes, drained well
1 medium dessert apple
Seasoning
1 egg yolk

Glaze
1 egg white

Roll out pastry to an oblong about 8x6 inches. Flatten veal with a rolling pin into an oblong about ¼ inch thick. Fry bacon for about 5 minutes, then mix with other stuffing ingredients. Spread over veal, then roll. Lay onto the pastry, brush sides with water and roll. Seal edges firmly. Brush with leftover egg white to glaze. Cook on a cooky sheet for 20-25 minutes at 425°F, then lower the heat to 350-375°F for 45 minutes.

Veal Escalopes

PREPARATION TIME: 30 minutes
COOKING TIME: 15 minutes

4 thin slices veal, approx. 12oz each
1 egg, beaten
6 tblsp white breadcrumbs
6 tblsp Cheddar cheese, finely grated
Pinch of salt
Dash cayenne pepper
¼ cup vegetable shortening
¼ cup butter

Trim the veal slices to give neat shapes and dip them in the beaten egg. Mix the breadcrumbs and grated cheese together and season with salt and cayenne pepper. Use this to coat the veal. Fry the veal on both sides in hot vegetable shortening for about 10 minutes, till golden brown.

Veal Rolls

PREPARATION TIME: 30 minutes
COOKING TIME: 2 hours 15 minutes

4 veal escalopes
2 tblsp melted butter
Seasoning
2 tsp onion, finely chopped
1 tsp grated lemon rind
2 tsp parsley, finely chopped

Sauce
2 tblsp butter
1 small onion, grated or finely chopped
½ small apple, peeled and grated
2 tsp cornstarch
1 small can tomato paste
1 chicken stock cube
1¾ cups water

Brush the escalopes with a little butter and sprinkle with seasoning, onion, parsley and lemon, and roll up tightly. Secure with a small skewer or thin string. Put into a casserole dish. To make the sauce, heat the butter, add the onion and apple, and sauté for a few minutes without browning. Stir in the cornstarch, tomato paste and crumbled chicken stock cube and mix together well. Add the water and stir till boiling. Boil for 2 minutes, then pour over veal rolls. Cover and cook at 325°F for about 2 hours.

This page: Ginger Veal Chops (top), Rolled Breast of Veal (center left) and Veal Marengo (bottom right).

Facing page: Blanquette of Veal with Prunes (top right), Veal Rolls (center left), Veal Casserole (center right) and Veal Escalopes (bottom).

Veal Marengo

PREPARATION TIME: 30 minutes
COOKING TIME: 1 hour 20 minutes

1lb neck of veal
Seasoned flour
6 tblsp butter
2 onions, chopped
1¼ cups white stock
1 cup tomatoes, skinned and chopped
¼ cup mushrooms, chopped
Seasoning

Garnish
4 slices of bread, cut into croûtons
Fat for frying
Parsley
Lemon

Cut the veal into cubes. Coat with seasoned flour and fry in butter until golden brown. Add the onion and fry until transparent. Add the stock, tomatoes and mushrooms. Season well. Simmer gently for about 1 hour. Serve garnished with croûtons, parsley and lemon.

Ginger Veal Chops

PREPARATION TIME: 30 minutes
COOKING TIME: 30 minutes

4 veal chops
Meat tenderizer
2 tblsp margarine
1 can condensed cream of celery soup
1 small can peas or mixed vegetables
4 slices mild cheese
½ tsp ginger

Tenderize veal following package directions. In a covered pan slowly sauté veal in margarine, turning to brown on both sides. When meat is tender, add soup and vegetables to pan. When thoroughly heated, place a slice of cheese on each veal chop and sprinkle top with ginger. Place under broiler, or cover pan and cook, until cheese melts.

Ragoût

PREPARATION TIME: 30 minutes
COOKING TIME: 1 hour 5 minutes

1lb stewing veal and kidney, diced
½ cup fat
2 onions, sliced
¼ cup mushrooms or 2 sliced and seeded red or green peppers
1 large can cream of tomato soup
1 tsp paprika
1 cup water
Seasoning
Chopped parsley

Heat the fat in a pan and fry the veal and kidney, onions and peppers for a few minutes. Cover with the tomato soup and the paprika blended with water. Add seasoning to taste, cover, and simmer for about 1 hour. Garnish with chopped parsley, if desired.

Organ Meats

Calves' Brains

PREPARATION TIME: 10 minutes
COOKING TIME: 35 minutes

1lb calves' brains
1 tblsp vinegar

White Sauce
3 tblsp cornstarch
2½ cups milk
3 tblsp white wine

Soak brains in cold water for 1 hour. Remove skin and traces of blood. Place brains in fresh water to which 1 tblsp of vinegar has been added and boil for 15-20 minutes. Drain and put in cold water to cool. Dry and slice.

White Sauce
Put the cornstarch into a basin and blend to a thin cream with some of the milk, using a wooden spoon. Rinse a saucepan with cold water; this prevents milk from sticking to the pan. Heat the milk to boiling point and pour over the blended cornstarch, stirring all the time; add the white wine. Rinse the pan, return the mixture to the pan and boil for 3-5 minutes. Serve the brains with the white sauce, adding chopped carrot and runner beans if desired.

Liver and Onions

PREPARATION TIME: 15 minutes
COOKING TIME: 20 minutes

1½lb onions
6 slices of lamb's liver
Seasoning
3 tblsp flour
6 tblsp butter
2 tblsp chopped parsley (optional)

Peel and slice the onions. Trim and wipe the liver. Season the flour and use it to coat the liver. Melt the butter in a large skillet. Add the onions and fry till golden. Add the liver slices and fry for 3-10 minutes on each side. Stir in the parsley, if desired. Transfer to a warmed serving dish and top with fried onions. Spoon pan juices over.

Haggis

PREPARATION TIME: 50 minutes

COOKING TIME: 2 hours 40 minutes

8oz sheep's liver
½ cup beef suet
2 onions
1 breakfast cup oatmeal
Seasoning

Cover the liver with water and boil for 40 minutes. Drain and keep the liquid. Grind the liver finely. Parboil the onions, then chop them finely with the suet. Brown the oatmeal by tossing it quickly in a thick pan. Combine the ground liver, suet, onions and oatmeal and season. Moisten with the liquor in which the liver was boiled. Turn into a greased bowl, cover with wax paper and steam for 2 hours.

Calves' Brains (far left), Kidney and Sausage Casserole (center) and Haggis (above).

Liver and Bacon Kebabs

PREPARATION TIME: 20 minutes

COOKING TIME: 5-10 minutes

12oz piece of lamb's liver
6oz piece of bacon
½ cup mushrooms
¼ cup melted butter
¼ cup fine breadcrumbs
½ tsp paprika
Salt

Wipe and trim the liver. Cut it into 1 inch cubes. De-rind the bacon, cut it into thick rashers, then into squares. Wipe and trim mushrooms. Preheat the broiler. Line the broiling pan with foil. Thread the bacon, liver and mushrooms onto four skewers. Brush with melted butter. Mix the breadcrumbs, paprika and salt together on a plate. Turn the kebabs in the breadcrumbs till evenly coated. Arrange on the broiler pan and broil for about 5 minutes, turning the kebabs frequently and brushing them with the fat that runs from the bacon.

Piquant Kidneys

PREPARATION TIME: 10 minutes

COOKING TIME: 15 minutes

1lb calves' kidneys
1 onion, finely chopped
¼ cup butter
2 tblsp chopped parsley
1 tblsp wine vinegar
Seasoning

Prepare and wash the kidneys. Slice very thinly. Melt the butter in a skillet and cook the onion and parsley for 5 minutes. Add the kidneys and cook for a further 5-10 minutes, stirring occasionally. Stir in the vinegar and bring to the boil, then remove from heat immediately. Add seasoning to taste.

This page: Chicken Liver Omelette (top), Lambs' Hearts with Walnut Stuffing (bottom right) and Piquant Kidneys (bottom left).

Facing page: Liver and Bacon Kebabs (top), Sweetbread Fritters (center left) and Liver, Bacon and Onion (bottom right).

Tongue and Lentil Casserole

PREPARATION TIME: 4 hours 30 minutes

COOKING TIME: 2 hours 45 minutes

1 cup lentils, soaked overnight
4 sheep's tongues
2 tblsp fat
2 onions, chopped
1 cup carrots, chopped
Pinch of mixed herbs
Seasoning
1 clove garlic, crushed

Soak the sheep's tongues for 3-4 hours. Drain, cover with cold water and bring to the boil. Simmer for 10-15 minutes. Drain, cover with fresh, cold water and simmer for 1 hour. Pour off and retain water. Leave tongues to cool, then remove skin. Slice tongues and put into a casserole dish. Melt the fat, add the onions and fry till brown, then add to the tongues. Add the drained lentils and carrots to the fat and fry for a few minutes. Put into the casserole with the herbs, seasoning and garlic. Cover with stock. Cover the casserole and cook in oven at 325°F for 1½ hours.

Lambs' Hearts with Walnut Stuffing

PREPARATION TIME: 30 minutes

COOKING TIME: 1 hour 25 minutes

4 lambs' hearts
4 large onions
Stock
Butter or margarine

Walnut Stuffing
¼ cup fresh breadcrumbs
¼ cup chopped walnuts
¼ cup fat bacon
Seasoning
Pinch mace
Egg to bind
⅔ cup stock
2 tblsp butter or margarine
4 large onions

Put all the stuffing ingredients into a small basin and add sufficient egg to bind. Prepare the hearts by cutting away all tough skin, etc. Stuff the hearts and tie the ends with thread. Simmer gently for 1 hour in a little well-seasoned stock with the onions. Place in a fireproof dish, pour over the remainder of the stock, place a little butter or margarine on top of the hearts and onions, cover with a lid. Roast at 375°F for about 20 minutes. Cut away thread before serving.

Braised Oxtail

PREPARATION TIME: 30 minutes

COOKING TIME: 2 hours 45 minutes

1 oxtail
2 tblsp margarine
2 carrots
2 large onions
1 rasher bacon
1¼ cups stock
Seasoning

Wash the oxtail in cold water. Cut into sections. Fry the oxtail in melted margarine until browned. Prepare and slice the vegetables and arrange them in alternate layers with the meat, finishing with a layer of vegetables. Season each layer. Pour the stock into the dish and braise slowly for about 2-2½ hours at 325°F.

Pig's Trotters

PREPARATION TIME: 10 minutes

COOKING TIME: 30-45 minutes

Cook the trotters in water with a bouquet garni. Simmer until tender. Drain well. Brush with melted butter, season and broil until golden brown. Serve with mashed potatoes and vegetables.

Sweetbread Fritters

PREPARATION TIME: 30 minutes

COOKING TIME: 10 minutes

1lb prepared lamb's sweetbreads
Seasoning
4 tblsp flour
Oil for deep frying

Batter
2 egg whites
2 tblsp arrowroot
1 tsp chopped fresh chives
1 tsp chopped fresh tarragon

Cut the sweetbreads in half lengthwise. Season the flour and toss the sweetbreads in it till evenly coated. Shake off any excess flour. Heat the oil in a deep fryer to 340°F. Put the egg whites into a bowl and whisk till soft peaks form. Add the arrowroot and herbs and fold in gently with a metal spoon. Fold in the floured sweetbreads till coated with batter. Using two spoons, lift a few of the sweetbreads out of the batter and lower into the oil. Fry for 5-6 minutes till crisp and golden. Drain on kitchen paper, keep hot while you cook the rest, and serve.

Kidney and Sausage Casserole

PREPARATION TIME: 30 minutes

COOKING TIME: 2 hours 50 minutes

1½lb ox kidney
8oz pork sausages
¼ cup flour
Seasoning
¼ cup fat
1 medium onion, sliced
2 carrots, sliced
1 bay leaf
½ tsp sage, crushed
1¼ cups stock

Trim and core the kidneys. Cover with cold, salted water and leave for 15 minutes. Drain and dry. Cut the sausages into pieces. Season the flour and coat the kidneys and sausages well. Heat the fat and fry the meat till brown. Remove to a casserole dish. Add the onion and carrots to the fat and brown well, then place in the casserole. Add the bay leaf and sage. Put the remaining flour with the sediment left in pan, mix well, add the stock and stir till boiling. Pour over the meat in the casserole. Cover and cook at 325°F for about 2½ hours. Adjust seasoning before serving.

Kidney and Sausage Casserole (top), Pig's Trotters (center) and Tongue and Lentil Casserole (bottom).

Chicken Liver Omelette

PREPARATION TIME: 20 minutes

COOKING TIME: 30 minutes

4oz chicken livers
½ cup butter
2 sage leaves
Seasoning
3 tblsp sherry
8 eggs
Parsley

Trim, wipe and finely chop the livers. Melt 2 tblsp of the butter in a saucepan and add the livers. Stir fry for 5 minutes. Pour the sherry over and cook till it has almost evaporated. Remove pan from heat. Beat the eggs in a bowl with a little seasoning. Melt a quarter of the remaining butter in an omelette pan or small skillet. When it begins to foam, pour in a quarter of the egg mixture. Tilt the pan so that the mixture runs evenly over the bottom. As the omelette begins to set underneath, place a quarter of the liver mixture along the center and fold the sides of the mixture over the filling. Slide omelette onto a warmed serving dish and keep hot.

Braised Oxtail (top), Savory Sheeps' Hearts (center right) and Tripe and Onion Pie (bottom left).

Tripe and Onion Pie

PREPARATION TIME: 45 minutes

COOKING TIME: 1 hour

1lb tripe
3 large onions, chopped
1¼ cups water
¼ cup flour
2 tblsp milk
Seasoning
2 tblsp butter
8oz basic pastry

Place the chopped onion in a pan, cover with water, season and simmer until tender. Wash the tripe and cut it into small pieces. Strain the onions; reserve half of the liquid. Replace the onions and liquid in the pan. Add the tripe. Simmer for 15 minutes. Blend the flour with a little cold milk, add to the saucepan, stir continually; add remaining milk and butter. Cook for 5 minutes. Line a dish or pan with half the pastry, put in the filling, cover with the remaining pastry. Cook at 425°F for 25 minutes.

Savory Sheep's Hearts

PREPARATION TIME: 40 minutes

COOKING TIME: 2 hours 15 minutes

4 sheep's hearts

Stuffing

¼ cup butter
1 onion, chopped
1 stick celery, chopped
½ cup breadcrumbs
1 orange
Seasoning
1 egg, beaten
2 onions, cut into quarters or eighths
2 carrots, cut into quarters
1 beef stock cube
2½ cups boiling water

Prepare the hearts carefully, removing all the veins and arteries, and wash them well in cold water. Melt the butter, add the onion and celery and cook for a few minutes. Add the breadcrumbs, grated orange rind and juice, and seasoning. Bind with the egg. Fill the hearts with this stuffing and sew up with needle and thread. Put into a casserole dish with the onion and carrot pieces. Dissolve the stock cube in boiling water and pour over the hearts. Cover and cook at 325°F for 2 hours until tender. Remove thread before serving.

Poultry and Game

Turkey Fries

PREPARATION TIME: 45 minutes

COOKING TIME: 1 hour 10 minutes

4 tblsp oil
3 tblsp lemon juice
Salt
8x4oz slices of turkey breast
4 tsp Dijon mustard
2 eggs
1 cup fresh breadcrumbs
¼ cup butter

Garnish
Chopped parsley
Lemon wedges

In a shallow dish, mix half the oil with the lemon juice and a pinch of salt. Add the turkey, mix well and leave to marinate for 1 hour. Drain the turkey and pat dry on kitchen paper. Spread thinly with the mustard. Beat the eggs lightly on a plate and use to coat turkey. Dip the turkey slices into the breadcrumbs, pressing gently. Melt the butter and remaining oil in a skillet and gently fry the turkey for about 10 minutes on each side, till tender and golden brown. Drain. Garnish with chopped parsley and lemon wedges.

Roast Chicken Drumsticks

PREPARATION TIME: 10 minutes

COOKING TIME: 20-30 minutes

Place the chicken drumsticks in a roasting pan and spread with fat or oil. Season. Place in the oven at 350°F for about 20-30 minutes, until the juice runs clear and the skin is golden brown.

Turkey Roll (top) and Turkey Fries (bottom).

Roast Turkey

PREPARATION TIME: 10 minutes

COOKING TIME: 20 minutes per 1lb plus 20 minutes

Place the turkey in a roasting pan. Brush with melted fat or oil. Season. Lightly cover the bird with foil or double wax paper. The bird may be stuffed if desired but weigh it after stuffing to calculate cooking time. Place in the oven at 400°F for the first 15 minutes, then lower to 350°F for the remainder of the cooking time. Baste the turkey frequently. Remove covering for the last 20-30 minutes to allow the skin to brown. When the turkey is cooked, place it on a large carving dish and serve.

Chicken Casserole

PREPARATION TIME: 30 minutes

COOKING TIME: 2 hours 40 minutes

1 chicken, jointed
Seasoned flour
2 tblsp fat
1 carrot, sliced
1 turnip, sliced
1 onion, chopped
¼ cup flour
2½ cups stock
Bouquet garni
Seasoning

Toss the chicken joints in seasoned flour. Melt the fat, brown the vegetables and the joints. Remove them from the pan. Add the flour but do not brown. Remove from heat and add stock. Return to heat and bring to the boil. Season to taste. Put vegetables and chicken in a casserole dish, pour sauce over and add the bouquet garni. Cook at 325°F for about 2½ hours.

This page: Roast Guinea Fowl (bottom). Facing page: Roast Chicken Drumsticks (top right), Roast Turkey (center) and Chicken Casserole (bottom right).

Chicken Pieces in Breadcrumbs

PREPARATION TIME: 30 minutes

COOKING TIME: 35-40 minutes

4 chicken quarters
Seasoning
½ cup flour
1 egg
1¼ cups milk
¾ cup breadcrumbs
3 tblsp oil

Clean the chicken quarters and dredge in the seasoned flour. Beat the eggs in a bowl and mix in the milk. Dip the chicken pieces in the egg and milk and then coat with the breadcrumbs. Heat the oil in a skillet and fry the chicken for 10 minutes or until browned on both sides. Reduce the heat, cover the pan and continue cooking gently for 25-30 minutes until the chicken is tender.

Roast Turkey Legs

PREPARATION TIME: 10 minutes

COOKING TIME: 30-40 minutes

Place the turkey legs in a roasting pan and spread with fat or oil. Season. Cook in the oven at 375°F for about 30 minutes, until the juice runs clear and the skin is golden brown.

Roast Guinea Fowl

PREPARATION TIME: 10 minutes

COOKING TIME: 15 minutes per 1lb

Place the guinea fowl in a roasting pan and brush with melted fat or oil. Season. As guinea fowl can be very dry, be generous in the amount of fat used. Lightly cover the bird with foil or double wax paper and cook at 400°F. Baste frequently. Remove the covering for the last 20-30 minutes to allow the skin to brown. When the bird is cooked, place it on a warm carving dish and serve.

Roast Pheasant

PREPARATION TIME: 10 minutes

COOKING TIME: 40 minutes to 1 hour 30 minutes

Preheat the oven to 400°F. Stand prepared bird in a roasting pan, add a little fat or oil. Cover roasting pan or wrap bird in foil. Roast a young bird for 40-50 minutes, an older bird for 1-1½ hours. Reduce the oven temperature to 350°F after 10 minutes. If the bird is cooked in an open pan, baste frequently.

Game Pie

PREPARATION TIME: 40 minutes

COOKING TIME: 45 minutes

1 rabbit
4 bacon rashers, de-rinded
¼ cup fat
2 onions, sliced
Seasoning
1¼ cups stock
8oz flaky pastry
1 egg or milk to glaze

Soak the rabbit in warm water for about ½ hour. Wash well in cold water. Joint the rabbit into 6 pieces. Cut the bacon into large pieces. Melt the fat in a saucepan; first brown the onions, then the bacon and pieces of rabbit. Season well. Add the stock and simmer gently for 1 hour until tender. Leave to cool. When cool, fill a pie dish with the meat and onions, add the liquid, then cover with the flaky pastry. Bake at 400°F for ¾ hour. Brush with egg or milk during the last ½ hour.

Roast Turkey Legs (right), Chicken Pieces in Breadcrumbs (below).

S
P

Roast Stuffed Pigeons

PREPARATION TIME: 30 minutes
COOKING TIME: 35 minutes to 1 hour 15 minutes

4 small pigeons
3 tblsp lard

For the Stuffing
2 hard-boiled eggs
6 tblsp soft breadcrumbs
¼ cup suet
Seasoning
A little grated nutmeg
1 tblsp chopped parsley
1 egg

To make the stuffing, chop the hard-boiled eggs and blend with the breadcrumbs, suet, seasoning, nutmeg and parsley, and bind with the egg. Put the stuffing into each of the pigeons, then cover the birds with the lard. If very young, roast in a hot oven for about 35 minutes at 400°F. Note: pigeons tend to have a fairly firm flesh and so it is better to roast for about 1¼ hours in a moderate oven 350°F. Baste the pigeons well during cooking or, if preferred, wrap each pigeon in foil after covering with lard and roast for about 1 hour 25 minutes at 350°F, opening the foil for the last 10-15 minutes.

Fricassée of Guinea Fowl

PREPARATION TIME: 30 minutes
COOKING TIME: 1 hour 30 minutes

1 guinea fowl
4 slices bacon
2 tblsp flour
Seasoning
2 cups water

Clean the guinea fowl and joint into pieces. Fry the bacon, coat the pieces of fowl with seasoned flour and fry until brown. Remove the bacon and fowl from the pan, add the flour and stir, slowly adding the water. Bring to the boil. Replace the fowl and bacon, cover and simmer until tender (about 1½ hours).

Jugged Hare

PREPARATION TIME: 30 minutes
COOKING TIME: 3 hours 10 minutes

1 hare
1 onion, sliced
1 carrot, sliced
1 turnip, sliced
6 tblsp fat
¾ cup flour
Seasoning
2½ cups stock
1 tblsp port
Bouquet garni
Packet of sage and onion stuffing mix

Wash and joint hare. Fry the vegetables in fat. Remove vegetables from the pan, coat the hare in seasoned flour and fry. Add the stock and port, put into a casserole dish with the bouquet garni; cover and cook for about 3 hours at 350°F. Making stuffing as directed on packet and make into small balls. Add balls to casserole a quarter of an hour before serving.

This page: Jugged Hare (top) and Game Pie (bottom). Facing page: Roast Stuffed Pigeons (top right), Roast Pheasant (center left) and Fricasée of Guinea Fowl (bottom right).

Duck with Orange Sauce

PREPARATION TIME: 30 minutes

COOKING TIME: 15 minutes per 1lb plus 15 minutes; 20 minutes for the sauce

1 duck

Orange Sauce
1 orange
⅔ cup water
1¼ cups Espagnole sauce
1 tblsp lemon juice
2 tblsp port or claret

Place the duck in a roasting pan spread with fat. Season. Lightly cover the duck with foil or double wax paper and place in the oven at 400°F. The duck should be basted frequently and the covering removed 20-30 minutes before the end of cooking time. After removing the covering, prick the breast all over to allow extra fat to run out and leave the breast crisp and succulent.

Orange Sauce
Pare the rind from the orange, discarding any white pith. Cut into wafer-thin strips and simmer these in water for about 10 minutes. Strain the Espagnole sauce, reheat with the orange rind, orange juice, lemon juice and wine. Serve the sauce with the cooked duck.

Mild Fruity Chicken Curry

PREPARATION TIME: 2 hours 30 minutes

COOKING TIME: 1 hour 15 minutes

⅔ cup boiling water
⅔ cup milk
½ cup shredded coconut
4 tblsp oil
4 chicken pieces, skinned
2 tblsp curry powder
¼ cup flour
1¼ cups chicken stock
14oz can pineapple chunks
1 tblsp onion flakes
1 tsp salt
2 tblsp cream

Mix together the boiling water and milk in a bowl. Stir in the coconut and leave to infuse for about 2 hours. Strain liquid and discard the coconut. Heat half the oil in a large, heavy saucepan. Add the chicken pieces and fry until golden brown on all sides. Remove the chicken pieces from the pan with a slotted spoon. Heat the remaining oil in the pan. Stir the curry powder into the oil and fry for about ½ minute. Remove the pan from the heat and stir in the flour. Gradually stir in the stock, the strained coconut milk, the juice from the can of pineapple and the onion flakes. Return the chicken to the pan with the salt. Bring to the boil, stirring occasionally. Cover and simmer for 1 hour, stirring occasionally. Stir in the pineapple chunks and heat through, then remove from the heat and stir in the cream. Taste and adjust the seasoning and serve with boiled rice.

Roast Turkey Wings

PREPARATION TIME: 10 minutes

COOKING TIME: 20 minutes

Put turkey wings into a roasting pan, spread with fat or oil and season. Place in the oven at 350°F for about 20 minutes, until the juice runs clear and the skin is golden brown. Serve with a mixed salad, if desired.

This page: Duck with Orange Sauce (top left), Roast Duck (top right) and Roast Turkey Wings (bottom). Facing page: Chicken Pie (top left), Roast Poussin (center right) and Mild Fruity Chicken Curry (bottom).

Roast Duck

PREPARATION TIME: 10 minutes

COOKING TIME: 15 minutes per 1lb plus 15 minutes

Place the duck in a roasting pan, spread with fat and season. Lightly cover with foil or double wax paper and place in the oven at 400°F. The duck should be basted frequently and the covering removed 20-30 minutes before the end of the cooking time. After removing the covering, prick the breast all over to allow extra fat to run out and leave the breast crisp and succulent. When the duck is cooked, transfer to a carving dish and serve.

Roast Poussin

PREPARATION TIME: 20 minutes

COOKING TIME: 30-40 minutes

2 poussins
1 packet sage and onion stuffing
A little fat

Make the stuffing as directed on the packet and stuff the birds. Place the poussins in a roasting pan with melted fat. Cook in the oven at 350°F until tender.

Chicken Pie

PREPARATION TIME: 35 minutes

COOKING TIME: 45-50 minutes

1lb cooked chicken
¼ cup butter
¼-½ cup small mushrooms
½ cup flour
1¼ cups milk or ⅔ cup milk and ⅔ cup chicken stock
6oz basic pastry
1 egg or milk to glaze

Cut the chicken into neat pieces. Heat half the butter and fry the mushrooms for a few minutes. Heat the other half of the butter, stir in the flour and cook for 2-3 minutes. Add the milk or milk and stock. Season. Bring to the boil and cook until thickened; add the chicken and mushrooms. Put into an 8 inch pie plate. Cover with basic pastry, brush with egg or milk. Bake at 400°F for about 30 minutes or until the pastry is golden brown.

Chicken Liver Pâté

PREPARATION TIME: 30 minutes

COOKING TIME: 10 minutes

6 tblsp butter
8 chicken livers
3 tblsp cream
Good pinch of mixed herbs
Seasoning

Heat the butter in a skillet and cook the livers gently until just tender. If you have an electric blender put them into this with the cream, herbs and seasoning and blend until smooth. Put into a buttered dish and allow to cool. When making a pâté by hand, rub the cooked livers through a sieve and then add the hot butter from the pan, cream, seasoning and herbs. Put into a buttered dish to cool.

Roast Chicken

PREPARATION TIME: 15 minutes

COOKING TIME: 15 minutes per 1lb plus 15 minutes

Place the chicken in a roasting pan, brush with melted fat or oil. Season. Lightly cover the bird with foil or double wax paper The chicken may be stuffed, if desired, but weigh it after stuffing to determine cooking time. Cook at 400°F. Baste the chicken frequently. Remove the covering for the last 20-30 minutes to allow skin to brown. When the chicken is cooked, place it on a carving dish and serve.

Turkey Cutlets with Lemon Sauce

PREPARATION TIME: 30 minutes

COOKING TIME: 20 minutes

6 turkey cutlets
Seasoning
2 tblsp flour
2 thick rashers of lean bacon
1 tblsp butter
⅔ cup chicken stock
2 tblsp lemon juice
2 tblsp chopped parsley

Garnish
Lemon slices
Sprigs of parsley

Season flour and coat the turkey cutlets. De-rind the bacon and cut it into strips. Melt the butter in a skillet and cook the bacon for 5 minutes. Add the turkey pieces and fry for 3-5 minutes on each side. Remove the turkey and bacon and place on a warm plate. Keep hot. Add any remaining seasoned flour to the pan and stir well with a wooden spoon, scraping the sediment from the bottom of the pan. Gradually add the stock and bring to the boil; simmer for 5 minutes. Remove the skillet from the heat and stir in the lemon juice and chopped parsley. Taste and adjust seasoning. Pour the sauce over the turkey cutlets and garnish with lemon slices and sprigs of parsley.

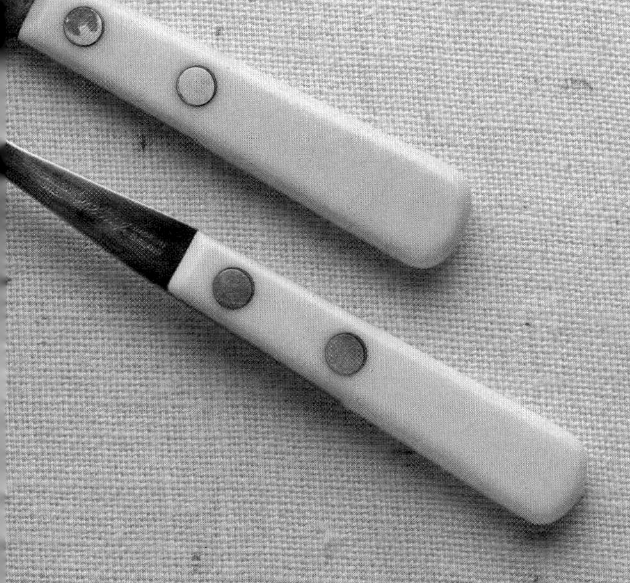

Turkey Cutlets with Lemon Sauce (top left), Chicken Liver Pâté (center) and Roast Chicken (bottom left).

Vegetarian Fare

Macaroni Cheese

6oz quick cooking macaroni
2 quarts water

Cheese Sauce
3 tblsp butter
6 tblsp flour
1¾ cups milk
Salt and pepper
½ cup Cheddar cheese, grated

Topping
2-4 tblsp Cheddar cheese, grated
2 tblsp dried breadcrumbs

Garnish
1 tomato
Parsley.

Boil the macaroni in salted water for about 7 minutes. Add a little pepper if desired. Melt the butter in a saucepan, stir in the flour and cook for 2 minutes. Cool. Gradually blend in the milk, bring to the boil and cook until thickened and smooth. Add seasoning, and the cheese. Strain the macaroni and blend with the sauce. Put into a 2½ pint dish, top with the cheese and breadcrumbs and brown under a hot broiler. Garnish with tomato and parsley.

Cheese and Potato Whirls

¼lb instant potato powder or 1lb of potatoes, cooked
2 tblsp butter and a little milk, if using cooked potatoes
2 cups grated cheese
1 egg
Salt and pepper
Mixed mustard
Egg, beaten to glaze

Basic Puff Pastry
2 cups all-purpose flour
½ tsp salt
¾ cup shortening
2 tsp wine vinegar or lemon juice
⅔ cup ice-cold water

First make the pastry. Sieve the flour and salt into a bowl. Cut shortening into ½" dice. Toss through the flour. Add vinegar or lemon juice to the water. Add to the flour and mix to a soft dough. Turn onto a floured board. Roll into a square. Fold the side edges to the middle, top and bottom to middle, then fold in half. Press gently together. Leave to rest in refrigerator for 15 minutes. Remove and roll the pastry once again into a square, fold the side edges to the middle, top and bottom to middle, then fold in half. Make the instant potato as directed on the can or packet or mash the cooked potato with the butter and milk. Add the cheese, egg, seasoning and mustard. Roll the pastry into a square, spread with the cheese and potato mixture. Roll up as for a jelly roll and brush with egg to glaze. Cut into the required number of slices and cook on a cooky sheet in the oven for 20-25 minutes at 440°F.

225 *Cheese Crust Vegetable Pie*

Cheese Pastry
1½ cups flour
Pinch of salt
½ cup shortening
6 tblsp Cheddar cheese, grated
2-3 tblsp cold water to mix

Filling
¼ cup butter
1 onion, peeled and sliced
7oz can corn
3 carrots, peeled and sliced
¼ cup mushrooms, sliced
2oz packet of leek soup
2 sticks celery, scrubbed and sliced
Pepper
1 egg, beaten to glaze

Sift the flour and salt into a mixing bowl. Cut the shortening into the flour and stir-in the cheese. Bind together with the water. Melt the butter in a pan and fry the vegetables for a few minutes. Drain on paper towels. Make up the packet of leek soup as directed, but using only 1¼ pints of water. Stir the vegetables into the leek soup, season with pepper and pour into a 3¾ cup pie dish. Roll out the pastry to top the pie. Trim and crimp the edges. Use any leftover pastry to decorate the pie top. Brush with beaten egg. Cook in the oven for 15 minutes at 400°F. Reduce the heat to 350°F and cook for a further 20 minutes. Serve with new potatoes.

Cheese Crust Vegetable Pie (top), Cheese and Potato Whirls (far left) and Macaroni Cheese (above left).

Corn Quiche

Pastry
1½ cups all-purpose flour
Pinch of salt
6 tblsp fat
2 tblsp water to mix

Filling
7oz can corn
2 eggs, beaten
1¼ cups milk
½-¾ cup cheese, grated
Salt and pepper

Garnish
Parsley
Tomato

Sieve the flour and salt into a bowl. Cut the fat into pieces and cut into the flour until it looks like breadcrumbs. Mix with enough water to make a dough. Roll out and use to line a pie pan. Drain the corn and mix with the eggs. Add the milk, cheese and seasoning. Pour into the pastry case. Cook in a hot oven for 15 minutes at 425°F. Reduce the heat to 375°F and cook for a further 10 minutes. Garnish with parsley and wedges of tomato. Serve hot or cold.

Cheese Crowns

2½ cups milk
½ wheatena
½ cup Parmesan cheese
2 tsp made mustard
1 tblsp Worcestershire sauce
Dash of cayenne pepper
Lettuce to garnish

Coating
1 eg, beaten
6 tblsp dried breadcrumbs
Fat for frying

Grease a cake pan and set aside. Heat the milk to near boiling point. Stir in the wheatena, bring to the boil and cook, stirring vigorously, for 3-4 minutes. Remove the pan from the heat, add the remaining ingredients and pour into the prepared cake pan. When the mixture is cold, turn onto a floured board, and divide into 8 wedges. Brush with beaten egg and coat with breadcrumbs. Heat the fat, carefully add the wedges and shallow fry on both sides until crisp and golden brown. Drain on paper towels. To serve, stand on end, top with cutlet frills and serve on a bed of lettuce.

Savory Egg Pie

Pastry
1½ cups all-purpose flour
Pinch of salt
6 tblsp fat
1½ tblsp water

Filling
1 onion, peeled and chopped
2 tblsp fat
1¾ cups milk
¼ cup soft, white breadcrumbs
3 large eggs, beaten
Few drops of Worcestershire sauce
Salt and pepper
Watercress to garnish

Sieve the flour and salt into a bowl. Cut the fat into pieces and cut into the flour until it looks like breadcrumbs. Mix with enough water to make a dough. Roll out the pastry and use to line a pie plate. Crimp the edges. Fry the onion in the fat, and spread over the pastry. Warm the milk, add the breadcrumbs and eggs. Stir in the Worcestershire sauce and seasoning. Pour the mixture into the pastry case. Cook in the oven for about 20-25 minutes at 400°F, until the pastry is crisp and the filling is set. Garnish with watercress and serve hot or cold with salad.

Cheese Loaf

2 cups all-purpose flour
2 tsp baking powder
Pinch of salt
Pinch of dry mustard
¼ cup shortening
6 tblsp cheese, grated
1 egg
7 tblsp milk

Grease a small loaf pan and line the bottom with wax paper. Sieve the flour, salt and mustard together and cut in the margarine. Add the cheese. Beat the egg and milk together and reserve a little to brush the top. Pour the rest into

Cheese Bread Pudding

4 large slices of buttered bread
½-¾ cup Cheddar cheese, grated
Salt and pepper
1 tsp Worcestershire sauce
Pinch of dry mustard
2 eggs
1¾ cups milk

Cut the crusts off the bread and cut each slice into 6 squares. Fill a greased, 3¾ cup pie dish with layers of bread, cheese, seasoning, Worcestershire sauce and mustard. Reserve a little cheese. Beat together the eggs and milk and pour over the layers. Sprinkle the top with the reserved cheese and cook in the oven for 40-45 minutes at 325°F. Serve with potato croquettes.

Cheese Hot Pot

1¼lb potatoes
6oz onions
6oz carrots
9oz grated cheese
Salt and pepper
⅔ cup water
Chopped parsley to garnish

Peel the potatoes, onions and carrots, and cut into thin slices. Put in layers into a deep dish with the cheese and a little seasoning between layers. Continue until all the vegetables are used, finishing with a layer of cheese. Pour the water into the dish to moisten. Cover with a greased lid and cook in the oven for 30 minutes at 450°F. Reduce to 375°F and cook for a further 1½ hours. Remove the lid and allow to brown for about 5 minutes. Garnish with chopped parsley.

the dry ingredients and mix to a soft dough. Shape into a loaf and put into the pan. Cook in the oven on a shelf above the center for about 35 minutes at 400°F, until well risen and golden brown. Cool on a wire tray. Serve, sliced and buttered, the same day. If kept to the next day, serve toasted and buttered.

Egg and Potato Omelette

¼ cup butter
2 small cooked potatoes, diced
4 eggs
½ tsp salt
Pinch of pepper

Heat the butter in a frying or omelette pan. Add the potatoes and cook until golden. Beat the eggs and season. Add the eggs to the potato and cook quickly until the mixture is set. Fold over and serve at once. Serve with a green vegetable.

Kedgeree Fish and Mushrooms

¾ cup cooked smoked haddock
1 hard-boiled egg, shelled
1 cup cooked, long grain rice
Pinch of cayenne pepper
Pinch of salt
½ cup mushrooms
A little butter
Chopped fresh parsley

Flake the fish coarsely with a fork. Chop the egg white, sieve the yolk and put the yolk to one side for garnishing. Using a fork mix the flaked fish, chopped egg white, cooked rice and seasoning in a saucepan over moderate heat until hot. Cook the mushrooms in a little butter. Pile the mixture into a hot dish and garnish with chopped parsley and sieved egg yolk. Serve at once with the cooked mushrooms.

Facing page: Cheese Hot Pot (top), Cheese Crowns (center left), Corn Quiche (center right) and Savory Egg Pie (bottom).

This page: Kedgeree Fish and Mushrooms (top), Cheese Bread Pudding (center left), Cheese Loaf (center right) and Egg and Potato Omelette (bottom).

Section 4

SALADS AND VEGETABLES

Meals with Salads

French Dressing

1 tblsp sugar
¼ tsp salt
¼ tsp dry mustard
⅔ cup vinegar
1¼ cups corn oil

Blend the sugar, salt and mustard with the vinegar. Gradually beat in the oil, a little at a time. Taste and adjust the seasoning if necessary. Pour the dressing into a screw-topped jar. Shake vigorously before using, as the oil and vinegar will separate if left to stand.

Cheese and Ham Pie

Packet white sauce mix
½ cup cheese, grated
½ cup cooked ham, finely chopped
A little milk or beaten egg

Basic Pastry
2 cups flour
½ cup shortening
1 tsp salt
2 tblsp cold water

First make the pastry. Sieve the flour and salt together in a bowl. Cut the fat into pieces and cut into the flour until it looks like breadcrumbs. Add the water to make a dough. Roll out enough pastry to line a shallow pie dish or pan. Make up the white sauce mix as directed on the packet. Mix the cheese and ham with the sauce and pour into the lined pie dish or pan. Roll out the remaining pastry to make a lid for the pie. Place on top, seal, and brush the top with milk or beaten egg. Place in the oven at 450°F for 15 minutes. Reduce the temperature to 350°F until cooked. Serve with a mixed salad.

Chunky Herrings

6-8 rollmop herrings
1lb small new potatoes, cooked
Small piece of cucumber, diced
Cooked peas
Sage or parsley to garnish

Vinaigrette Dressing
6 tblsp oil
3 tblsp wine vinegar
¼ tsp chopped fresh herbs, e.g. tarragon, chervil
4-5 capers, chopped
Salt and pepper
Pinch of dry mustard

Remove the herrings from their liquid, drain well. Arrange the herrings on a flat dish. Blend together all the ingredients for the vinaigrette dressing. Mix the potatoes, cucumber and peas and toss with the dressing. Put the mixture round the herrings and garnish with sage or chopped parsley. Serve with a mixed salad. Serves six

Mushroom Salad

Salt and pepper
Pinch of dry English mustard
9 tblsp oil
3 tblsp wine vinegar
1 tblsp chopped fresh parsley
1 garlic clove, peeled and crushed
12oz mushrooms, sliced

Put the salt, pepper, mustard, oil, vinegar, parsley and garlic into a screw-topped jar and shake well. Pour over the mushrooms in a bowl. Leave to stand for 1 hour then serve.

Egg and Cheese Pie (far left), Chunky Herrings (center) and Cheese and Ham Pie (above).

Egg and Cheese Open Pie

½ cup cheese, grated
2 eggs
⅔ cup milk
¼ tsp mixed mustard

Basic Pastry
2 cups flour
1 tsp salt
½ cup shortening
2 tblsp cold water

Make the basic pastry. Sieve the flour and salt together into a bowl. Add the fat cut into pieces and cut into the flour until it is like breadcrumbs. Add the water to make a dough. Roll out and use to line a pie pan. Prick the base. Sprinkle with the cheese. Beat the eggs, add the milk and mustard. Pour the egg mixture over the cheese. Cook the open pie in the oven for 15 minutes at 450°F. Reduce the temperature to 325°F and cook for about 30 minutes or until the open pie is cooked. Serve with a mixed salad.

Dressed Crab

1 large cooked crab
Parsley to garnish

Pull off all the crab claws and wipe the shell. Turn the crab onto its back and firmly pull the body from the main shell. Remove and discard the stomach bag which lies behind the head and gray feathered gills or 'fingers' as these must not be eaten. Take out all the meat with a skewer or small spoon, putting dark and white into separate basins, then crack the top of the shell and remove pieces so there is a flat cavity to fill. Scrub inside the shell thoroughly under cold water. Dry and brush with oil. Crack the claws and remove the meat, adding it to the light meat. Arrange dark and light meat alternately in the shell and garnish with parsley. Serve with a mixed salad.

Kidney Beans and Onion

Salt and pepper
Pinch of dry English mustard
½ tsp dried basil
1 garlic clove, peeled and crushed
3 tblsp olive or corn oil
1 tblsp wine vinegar
1 small onion, peeled and sliced
14oz can of red kidney beans, drained
Chopped parsley to garnish

Combine the salt, pepper, mustard, basil, garlic, oil and vinegar in a screw-topped jar. Lay the onion rings on a plate and sprinkle with salt. Leave for 30 minutes. Drain and rinse in cold water. Place the beans in a bowl, add the onion and toss in the dressing. Garnish with the chopped parsley and serve.

This page: Apple and Nut Salad (top), Kidney Beans and Onion (center right) and Mushroom Salad (bottom). Facing page: Dressed Crab (top), Chicken Legs in Breadcrumbs (center left), Tuna and Mackerel Loaf (center right) and Chicken and Tomato Salad (bottom).

Chicken Legs in Breadcrumbs

Chicken legs as required
1 beaten egg
Dried breadcrumbs
6 tblsp oil or butter

Coat the chicken legs with the beaten egg and breadcrumbs. Heat the oil or butter in a pan. Fry the chicken fairly quickly until brown all over, then lower heat and cook slowly to cook right through. When pierced with a skewer the juices should run clear. Drain on crumpled paper towels. Serve with fried tomatoes and mushrooms and a green salad or other cooked vegetables.

Cucumber and Tomato Salad

1lb tomatoes, chopped
½ cucumber, finely diced
2 tblsp French dressing
Watercress to garnish

Toss the cucumber and tomato in the French dressing. Garnish with watercress.

Tuna and Mackerel Loaf

2lb whole-wheat loaf bread, one day old, refrigerated for 24 hours
2oz powdered gelatin
1¼ cups white sauce
5oz canned tuna, drained
8oz mackerel fillets, drained
½ cup cooked potato, diced
¼ cup cooked peas
¼ cup green beans, diced
¼ cup corn
¼ cup cooked red peppers, diced
12 capers
2 tblsp small pickled cucumbers, diced
1oz chopped onion
Salt and pepper
Pinch of cayenne pepper
Juice and grated zest of ½ lemon
⅔ cup mayonnaise

Cut the crust off the loaf at one end and reserve. With a long bread knife cut round inside the crust and remove the bread from the center. Scoop out any remaining crumbs. Dissolve the gelatin in a cup of hot water. Bring the white sauce to the boil, add the gelatin and simmer gently for 10 minutes until thick. Blend the tuna and mackerel fillets to a smooth paste. Add the paste to the thickened sauce and blend well. Mix in the rest of the ingredients except the mayonnaise. Cool and then add the mayonnaise. Fill the crust shell with the mixture. Replace the reserved crust, stand the loaf on a plate, place in the refrigerator and leave overnight to set. Serve by cutting into slices with a bread knife dipped in hot water. This is ideal for picnics or served with a mixed salad.

Bean Salad

6oz can kidney beans, drained
14oz can sliced green beans, drained
1 small onion, peeled and chopped
1 stalk celery, peeled and chopped
3 tblsp wine vinegar
1 tblsp oil
Few drops of sugar substitute
Salt and pepper

Mix together the beans, chopped onion and chopped celery. Mix the vinegar, oil, sugar substitute and seasoning together and pour over the salad. Leave to marinate in the dressing for a few hours, stirring occasionally. Serve well chilled with cold, lean meat.

Pineapple, Cheese and Celery Salad

½ cup pineapple pieces
½ cup cheese, diced
¼ head of celery, coarsely sliced
Mayonnaise for dressing
Lettuce
Watercress to garnish

Drain the pineapple and cut into small cubes. Toss with the other ingredients. Serve on a bed of lettuce, garnished with watercress.

Rice Salad

½ cup patna rice
6 tblsp pineapple pieces
5oz corn
2 radishes, finely sliced
¼ red pepper, cored, seeded and finely sliced
¼ green pepper, cored, seeded and finely sliced
French dressing
Watercress or cucumber slices to garnish

Boil the rice in salted water for 15 minutes. Drain well and cool. Drain the pineapple thoroughly and cut into small cubes. Mix all the ingredients together in a bowl and toss in French dressing. Garnish with watercress or slices of cucumber.

Prawn Salad

6 tblsp thick mayonnaise
1 tblsp tomato paste
2 tblsp lemon juice
1 tblsp Worcestershire sauce
1 tsp grated lemon zest
1 tsp grated onion
2 tsp chopped fresh parsley
Salt and pepper
½ cup prawns

Mix the mayonnaise, tomato paste, lemon juice, Worcestershire sauce, lemon zest, onion, parsley and seasoning together thoroughly. Leave for 4 hours before using. Check the flavor before mixing the prawns with the sauce. Serve with a mixed salad.

Apple and Nut Salad

Salt and pepper
Pinch of dry mustard
3 tblsp corn or olive oil
1 tblsp wine vinegar
3 red eating apples, peeled and cored
8 sticks of celery, scrubbed and chopped
¼ cup chopped peanuts
Chopped fresh parsley to garnish

Put salt, pepper, mustard, oil and vinegar into a screw-topped jar and shake well. Put the apples and celery in a bowl with the chopped nuts. Pour the dressing over the apples and celery and toss well. Spoon into a serving dish and garnish with chopped parsley.

Chicken and Tomato Salad

1 lettuce, washed and cut into small pieces
2 cooked chicken breasts, sliced or ½ cup bought sliced chicken
2 tomatoes, peeled and quartered
¼ cup frozen corn, cooked and cooled
¼ cup frozen green beans, cooked and cooled

French Dressing
Salt and pepper
Pinch of dry English mustard
3 tblsp olive oil
1 tblsp wine vinegar

Make a French dressing by shaking together the salt, pepper, mustard, oil and vinegar in a screw-top jar. Place the lettuce pieces in a salad bowl, add the tomato, corn and beans. Toss with the French dressing. Serve the chicken with the salad.

Cucumber and Tomato Salad (left), Rice Salad (below) and Pineapple, Cheese and Celery Salad (bottom).

Spanish Pâté

1 cup chicken livers, ground
1lb pig's liver, ground
1 cup ground beef
1¼lb pork, ground
12oz bacon fat, ground
1 tblsp salt
Pepper
1 tsp ground mace
1 tblsp chopped, fresh mixed herbs
2 tblsp sherry
¼ cup brandy
3 garlic cloves, peeled and crushed
6 tblsp stuffed green olives

Mix together all the ingredients, except the olives, until well blended. Divide the patê mixture between two well-greased terrines or loaf pans, adding the olives throughout the páte, at different levels. Cover with foil and put in a roasting pan containing 2" water. Cook for 2 hours in the oven at 300°F. Leave to cool. Place the pâté in the refrigerator for 1-2 hours, then turn into a serving dish. Serve with a mixed salad.

Coleslaw

1 cup cabbage, finely shredded
2 radishes, finely sliced
¼ cucumber, finely diced
1 stick celery, finely diced
¼ green pepper, cored, seeded and finely sliced
¼ red pepper, cored, seeded and finely sliced
1 apple, peeled and finely sliced
1 large carrot, peeled and coarsely grated
Watercress
Mayonnaise for dressing

Mix the ingredients thoroughly together in a large bowl and dress with the mayonnaise. Garnish with watercress.

Pasta Salad

4oz spaghetti
1 tblsp of butter
2 carrots, peeled and coarsely grated
2 tblsp raisins
6 radishes, finely sliced
¼ green pepper, cored, seeded and finely sliced
¼ red pepper, cored, seeded and finely sliced
2 tblsp French dressing
Watercress to garnish

Boil the spaghetti in salted water for 10-15 minutes. Drain well, toss in the butter and leave to cool. Put all vegetables and raisins together in a bowl and mix well. Toss in the French dressing. Garnish with watercress.

Winter Salami Risotto

½lb salami, thinly sliced
4-6oz liver sausage, garlic sausage and luncheon meat, thinly sliced
2 green peppers
1 red pepper
4 large, ripe tomatoes
½ cup green beans, cooked
8 stuffed olives
8-10 tblsp medium or long grain rice, cooked
3-4 tblsp vinaigrette dressing

Chop some of the meats and roll the remainder. Chop most of the vegetables, leaving a few large pieces for garnish. Slice the stuffed olives. Blend the rice with the vinaigrette dressing, chopped meat, vegetables and olives and put in the bottom of a shallow dish. Top with the larger pieces of vegetables and rolls of meat. Serve with a green salad.

This page: Bean Salad (top right), Coleslaw (center left) and Pasta Salad (bottom). Facing page: Winter Salami Risotto (top), Prawn Salad (center left) and Spanish Pâté (bottom).

Sauté Potatoes

Peel potatoes and cut out any eyes and green parts. Cook in salted water until they are almost cooked, drain well and allow to cool slightly. Cut into slices. Fry the potato slices in hot fat, turning them until crisp and golden brown on both sides. Serve as required.

Duchesse Potatoes

1lb cooked potatoes
2 tblsp butter
1-2 egg yolks, beaten
A little hot milk if the egg yolks are small
2 tsp salt
Pinch of pepper
A little egg and water mixed together to glaze

Put the hot, cooked potato through a sieve. Melt the butter in a saucepan. Add the beaten egg yolks and hot milk, if used. Beat well and add seasoning. Allow to cool slightly. Put into a piping bag with a star vegetable nozzle. Pipe in crowns onto a greased cooky sheet. Brush with egg and water glaze. Cook in the top of the oven for about 15 minutes at 400-425°F, until brown and crisp on the edges. An alternative to duchesse potatoes is to make birds' nests. Pipe the potato into rings and cook the same as for duchesse potatoes. Fill with vegetables.

Baked Potatoes

Peel potatoes and cut out any eyes and green parts. Cut into slices. Melt fat in an ovenproof dish and place potatoes in the dish. Cook in the oven at 425°F, for about 1 hour. Serve as required.

Potato

Potatoes (Boiled)
New Potatoes

Scrub potatoes well, then scrape. Cook in salted water for 10-20 minutes according to size. Drain well, toss in butter and serve.

Creamed Potatoes

Peel potatoes and cut out any eyes and green parts. Cook in salted water for 15-20 minutes. When cooked, drain well. Using a potato masher or a fork, mash the potatoes in a pan until smooth and free of lumps. To each pound of potatoes add 2 tblsp butter, a little milk and seasoning. Beat the mixture until light and fluffy. Serve as required.

This page: Baked Potatoes (top left), Creamed Potatoes (center right) and Sauté Potatoes (bottom).

Facing page: Boiled Potatoes (top left), Duchesse Potatoes (top right), Birdsnest Potatoes (center) and Potato Croquettes (bottom).

Potato Croquettes

1lb cooked potato
2 tblsp butter
A little milk
2 tsp salt
Pepper to taste
1 beaten egg
Breadcrumbs

Mash the cooked potato with the butter and a little milk. Add seasoning and leave to cool. Divide the mixture into even-sized portions. Roll each portion into a ball, using a little flour on the hands to prevent sticking. Using a palette knife and the hand, shape the balls into cork shapes, with flat ends. Coat with beaten egg and breadcrumbs. Fry in deep, hot fat until golden.

Old Potatoes

Peel potatoes and cut out any eyes and green parts. Cook in salted water for 15-20 minutes until soft. Drain well and serve.

Bubble and Squeak

1½lb potatoes, peeled
A little milk
Knob of butter
1lb green cabbage, trimmed and roughly chopped
1 small onion, peeled and chopped
Salt and pepper
1 egg

Cook the potatoes in salted water until soft. Drain and mash with a little milk and butter. Plunge the cabbage into boiling, salted water. Cook for 5 minutes, drain well and chop finely. Mix the potato and cabbage with the onion, add seasoning and the egg. Put the mixture in a skillet and fry in a little fat until golden brown.

This page: Bubble and Squeak (top), Potatoes Normandie (center) and Jacket Potatoes (bottom).

Facing page: Brussels Sprouts (top), Mushrooms (center left) and Glazed Carrots (bottom right).

This page: Creamed Spinach (top left), Peas (fresh) (top right) and Green Beans (bottom).

Facing page: Cauliflower Cheese.

Glazed Carrots

¼ cup butter
1lb young carrots, scraped and quartered lengthwise
Salt and pepper
Pinch of sugar

Garnish
Knob of butter
Chopped fresh parsley

Melt the butter in a pan. Add the carrots, seasoning, sugar and enough water to cover. Cook slowly without a lid for about 15 minutes, until the carrots are soft and the water has evaporated, leaving the carrots with a slight glaze. Serve in a warm dish. Garnish with a knob of butter and chopped parsley.

Mushrooms

Baked
Remove the stalks and peel off the outer skin, beginning from the edge and pulling towards the center. Place in an ovenproof dish with a little butter, and cook for 10-15 minutes in the oven at 350°F.

Broiled
Prepare the mushrooms as above. Put a knob of butter the size of a pea on each mushroom in the hollow where the stalk was attached. Cook under a medium broiler for 7-10 minutes.

Fried
Prepare mushrooms as above. Fry in butter for about 7-10 minutes until tender.

Cauliflower Cheese

1 cauliflower, washed and trimmed
2 tblsp butter
¼ cup flour
1¼ cups milk
½ cup Cheddar cheese, finely grated
Salt and pepper
2 tblsp fresh white breadcrumbs

Cook the cauliflower in boiling, salted water for about 10 minutes. Drain and place in an ovenproof dish. Melt the butter in a pan, add the flour and cook for a few minutes. Allow to cool before gradually adding the milk. Bring to the boil. Stir in 6 tblsp of the cheese and season well. Pour the sauce over the cauliflower. Mix the remaining cheese and breadcrumbs together and sprinkle over the top. Brown in the oven for 5-10 minutes at 400°F and serve.

Green Beans

Top, tail and remove any tough strings. Shred the beans finely. Cook in boiling, salted water for 10-20 minutes until tender. When cooked, drain. Toss in butter and serve.

Creamed Spinach

3lb fresh spinach, washed and coarse stalks removed
2-4 tblsp butter
3 tblsp light cream
Salt and pepper
Pinch of powdered nutmeg

Put the washed spinach in a saucepan with a little water. Heat gently, turning the spinach occasionally. Bring to the boil and cook gently for 10-15 minutes until very soft. Drain thoroughly and pass through a sieve or use a blender. Add butter, cream, seasoning and nutmeg to the purée. Return to the pan and reheat. Serve in a warmed dish.

Jacket Potato

Scrub the potato until the skin is clean. Remove any eyes and discolored parts. Prick the skin, (this prevents the potato from bursting in the oven). Brush over with oil. Place on a cooky sheet in the middle of the oven. Cook for between 1-2 hours, according to size of potato, at 350-375°F, until tender.

Potatoes Normandie

3 tblsp butter
1½lb potatoes, peeled and thinly sliced
Salt and pepper
1¼ cups milk

Use a little of the butter to grease an ovenproof dish. Layer the slices of potato in the dish, seasoning between each layer. Pour the milk over the potatoes. Dot the remaining butter over the top. Cook in the oven for 1-1½ hours at 350°F, until the potatoes are soft. Serve with roast beef, lamb or pork.

Peas (Fresh)

Shell the peas. Cook in boiling, salted water with 1 tsp salt, 1 tsp sugar and a sprig of mint, for 10-15 minutes. Remove the mint, strain well and serve.

Beets (Boiled)

Boil beets in a saucepan for 1-1½ hours. Do not damage the skin before cooking. The skin will peel off easily once the beets are cooked.

Braised Celery

2 tblsp butter
2 medium-sized carrots, peeled and diced
8 sticks celery, scrubbed, trimmed and cut in half lengthwise
1¼ cups chicken stock
Salt and pepper
Chopped parsley to garnish

Heat the butter and fry the carrots for a few minutes. Add the celery and cook for a further 2 minutes. Place the vegetables in an ovenproof dish and pour on the stock. Season well. Cover and cook in the oven for about 1-1¼ hours at 350°F. Garnish with chopped parsley.

Collards or Greens

Wash well. Shred finely before cooking in boiling, salted water for 10-15 minutes. When cooked, drain well. Toss in butter, if liked, and serve.

Leeks

1½lb fresh leeks, washed, trimmed and halved
Butter
Pepper

Cook the prepared leeks in boiling, salted water for 10 minutes. Drain and toss in butter and add pepper.

Roast Parsnips

1lb parsnips, peeled, quartered and sliced

Garnish
Chopped fresh parsley

Cook the prepared parsnips in boiling, salted water for about 5 minutes. Drain well. Place in the fat around the joint and cook for about 45 minutes. Garnish with chopped parsley.

Brussels Sprouts

Cut a cross in the stalks and remove the outer leaves. Cook in boiling, salted water for between 7-15 minutes. When cooked, drain, toss in butter and serve.

Corn on the Cob

Strip off the husks and remove the silky threads. Cook the corn on the cob in boiling water for about 10-15 minutes, adding a little salt at the end of the cooking time. When cooked, drain. Serve with melted butter.

Broccoli

Thoroughly wash the broccoli and remove any withered leaves. Cook in boiling, salted water for 25-30 minutes. When cooked, drain and serve as required.

This page: Leeks (top), Roast Parsnips (center left), Boiled Beets (center right) and Broccoli (bottom).

Facing page: Braised Celery (top left), Collards or Greens (top right) and Corn on the Cob (bottom).

Pasta Salads

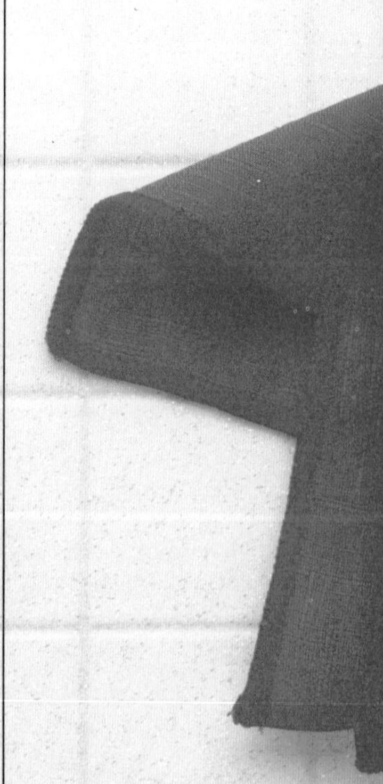

Bean Salad

PREPARATION TIME: 10 minutes

COOKING TIME: 15 minutes

SERVES: 4 people

3 cups macaroni
1 large can red kidney beans, drained
4 strips bacon, diced
1 onion, peeled and chopped
2 sticks celery, sliced diagonally
1-2 tbsps wine vinegar
3-4 tbsps olive oil
1 tsp chopped parsley
Salt
Pepper

Cook macaroni in plenty of salted boiling water for 10 minutes, or until tender but still firm. Rinse in cold water and drain well.
Heat frying pan, and sauté bacon in its own fat until crisp. Add onion, and cook until soft. Mix vinegar, oil and parsley, and season well. Add bacon, onion, kidney beans and celery to macaroni. Pour over dressing, and toss together.

Niçoise Salad

PREPARATION TIME: 15 minutes

COOKING TIME: 15 minutes

SERVES: 4 people

1½ cups penne
3 tomatoes, quartered
¼ pound green beans, cooked
½ cucumber, cut into batons
1 7oz can tuna fish, drained and flaked
12 black olives, halved, with stones removed
6-8 anchovy fillets, drained, and soaked in milk if desired
½ cup bottled oil and vinegar dressing

Nicoise Salad (far left), Bean Salad (left) and Tuna and Tomato Salad (below).

Cook penne in lots of boiling salted water until tender but still firm. Rinse in cold water; drain, and leave to dry. Put flaked tuna in the base of a salad dish. Toss pasta together with tomatoes, cucumber, green beans, olives, and anchovies, and then pour over oil and vinegar dressing. Mix together well.

Tuna and Tomato Salad

PREPARATION TIME: 10 minutes

COOKING TIME: 15 minutes

SERVES: 4 people

3 cups pasta shells
1 7oz can tuna fish, flaked
6 tomatoes
1 tbsp fresh chopped basil or marjoram, or 1 tsp dried basil or oregano
6 tbsps vinaigrette dressing

Mix herbs with vinaigrette dressing. Cook pasta shells in a large saucepan of boiling salted water until tender – about 10 minutes. Rinse with cold water, and drain, shaking off excess water. Toss with 3 tablespoons of vinaigrette dressing. Leave to cool. Meanwhile, slice enough of the tomatoes to arrange around the outside of the serving-dish. Chop the rest, and pour the remaining vinaigrette dressing over them, and place in the center of the dish. Add tuna to the pasta shells, and toss gently. Serve in the center of the dish over the chopped tomatoes.

Stuffed Eggplant

PREPARATION TIME: 15 minutes

COOKING TIME: 1 hour

OVEN: 350°F (180°C)
400°F (200°C)

4 small or 2 large eggplants
¾ cup macaroni
½ pound bacon, diced
1 green pepper, cored and diced
1 yellow pepper, cored and diced
2 tomatoes, skin removed, chopped and seeds removed
2 tbsps butter
½ tsp chili powder
1 tbsp tomato paste
1 small onion, peeled and chopped
1 clove garlic, crushed
¼ cup Gruyère or Cheddar cheese, grated
1 tbsp breadcrumbs
Salt and pepper

Cook macaroni in plenty of boiling, salted water for 10 minutes, or until tender but still firm. Rinse in cold water, and drain well. Wrap eggplants in baking foil, and bake in a moderate oven (350°F, 180°C) for 30 minutes. Cut eggplants in half lengthwise. Scoop out the pulp, leaving ½ inch of thickness on the skin. Chop pulp. Heat butter in a pan. Add onion and garlic, and cook until transparent. Add bacon and peppers and fry for 5 minutes. Then add eggplant pulp, tomato, tomato paste, chili powder, and salt and pepper. Cook a further 3 minutes. Stir in macaroni, and fill the scooped-out eggplant halves with the mixture. Top with grated cheese and breadcrumbs, and brown under a broiler or in a quick oven (400°F, 800°C). Serve immediately.

Gianfottere Salad

PREPARATION TIME: 40 minutes

COOKING TIME: 30 minutes

SERVES: 4 people

3 cups pasta spirals
1 eggplant
1 zucchini
1 sweet red pepper
1 green pepper
2 tomatoes
1 onion
4 tbsps olive oil
1 clove garlic
Salt
Pepper

Cut eggplant into ½″ slices. Sprinkle with salt and leave for 30

This page: Gianfottere Salad.

Facing page: Stuffed Eggplant.

minutes. Skin the tomatoes by putting them into boiling water for 20 seconds, and then rinsing in cold water, and peeling skins off. Chop roughly. Cut zucchini into ½" slices. Remove cores and seeds from peppers, and chop roughly. Peel and chop onion. Heat 3 tbsps olive oil in pan, and fry onion gently until transparent, but not colored. Meanwhile, rinse salt from eggplant, and pat dry with absorbent paper. Chop roughly. Add eggplant, zucchini, peppers, tomatoes and garlic to onion, and fry gently for 20 minutes. Season with salt and pepper. Allow to cool.
Meanwhile, cook pasta spirals in a lot of boiling salted water for 10 minutes, or until tender but still firm. Rinse in cold water and drain well, and toss in remaining 1 tbsp olive oil. Toss vegetables together with pasta spirals.

Stuffed Zucchini

PREPARATION TIME: 15 minutes
COOKING TIME: 30 minutes
OVEN: 400°F (200°C)

4 zucchini
¾ cup soup pasta
2 tomatoes, skin removed, chopped, and seeds removed
2 tbsps butter or margarine
¼ pound ground beef
1 small onion, peeled and chopped
2 cloves garlic, crushed
¼ cup Gruyère or Cheddar cheese, grated
1 tbsp breadcrumbs
1 tsp tomato paste
Salt and pepper

Cook pasta in lots of boiling salted water for 5 minutes or until tender. Rinse in cold water and drain well. Meanwhile, put zucchini in a pan and cover with cold water. Bring to the boil and cook gently for 3 minutes. Rinse under cold water. Cut zucchini in half lengthwise. Carefully scoop out the pulp, leaving ½ inch thickness on skin. Chop pulp. Heat butter in a frying-pan. Add garlic and onion, and fry gently until transparent. Increase heat and add ground beef. Cook for 5 minutes, turning often until meat is well browned. Stir in tomato paste and salt and pepper to taste. Add zucchini pulp, tomatoes and pasta, and cook for 2 minutes. Spoon into zucchini shells. Sprinkle top with grated cheese and breadcrumbs, and brown under a broiler or in a fast oven. Serve immediately.

Stuffed Tomatoes

PREPARATION TIME: 10 minutes
COOKING TIME: 20 minutes
OVEN: 350°F (180°C)

4 large ripe tomatoes
1 pound fresh spinach
¼ tsp grated nutmeg
2 tbsps butter, creamed
¾ cup soup pasta
1 tbsp heavy cream
1 clove garlic, crushed
1 tbsp Gruyère or Cheddar cheese, grated
4 anchovies, sliced
Salt and pepper

Cut tops off tomatoes, and carefully scoop out the insides with a teaspoon. Wash spinach well and remove stalks. Cook gently in a large saucepan, without added water, until spinach is soft. Chop very finely, or blend in a food processor. Meanwhile, cook pasta for 5 minutes, or until tender. Rinse and drain well. Mix with the spinach. Add butter, cream, nutmeg and garlic, and season well. Fill each tomato and top with cheese and anchovies. Bake in a moderate oven for 10 minutes. Serve immediately.

Mushroom Salad

PREPARATION TIME: 1 hour 10 minutes
COOKING TIME: 15 minutes
SERVES: 4 people

3 cups farfalle (pasta butterflies/bows)
1 cup mushrooms, sliced
5 tbsps olive oil
Juice of 2 lemons
1 tsp fresh chopped basil
1 tsp fresh chopped parsley
Salt
Pepper

Mix oil together with lemon juice and fresh herbs. Put the sliced mushrooms into a bowl, and pour over 4 tbsps of the dressing. Leave for 1 hour. Cook the pasta in a large saucepan of boiling salted water for 10 minutes, or until tender. Rinse in cold water, and drain. Toss with the rest of the dressing, and leave to cool. Fold mushrooms and pasta together gently, adding salt and freshly-ground black pepper to taste. Sprinkle with parsley.

Shrimp Salad

PREPARATION TIME: 10 minutes
COOKING TIME: 15 minutes
SERVES: 4 people

3 cups pasta shells
½ pound shrimp, shelled and de-veined
½ cup mayonnaise
Juice of 1 lemon
1 tsp paprika
Salt
Pepper
1 lettuce
1 cucumber, sliced

Cook the pasta in plenty of boiling salted water for 10 minutes, or until tender. Drain, and rinse under cold water. Shake off excess water; put into a bowl, and pour over lemon juice. Leave to cool. Mix paprika into mayonnaise. Add to shrimp, and toss. Arrange a bed of lettuce leaves and sliced cucumber in a dish, and pile pasta in center. Pile shrimp on top.
(This can also be made with flaked crab meat or salmon).

Stuffed Zucchini (above right) and Stuffed Tomatoes (top).

Shrimp Salad (left) and Mushroom Salad (far left).

Curried Shrimp Salad

PREPARATION TIME: 10 minutes
COOKING TIME: 20 minutes
SERVES: 4 people

1½ cups soup pasta
½ pound shrimp, shelled and de-veined
1 tsp paprika
Juice of ½ a lemon
1½ tsp curry powder
1 tsp tomato paste
2 tbsps olive oil
1 small onion, peeled and chopped
1 clove garlic, crushed
½ cup water
2 slices lemon
1 tsp apricot jam
1 cup mayonnaise
Salt
Pepper

Heat oil, and fry garlic and onion gently until soft but not colored. Add curry powder and paprika, and cook for 2 minutes. Stir in tomato paste and water. Add lemon slices, and salt and pepper to taste. Cook slowly for 10 minutes; stir in jam, and bring to the boil, simmering for 2 minutes. Strain and leave to cool. Add mayonnaise. Meanwhile, cook pasta in plenty of boiling salted water for 10 minutes, or until tender but still firm. Rinse under cold water and drain well. Toss in lemon juice, and put in serving-dish. Arrange shrimp on top, and pour over curry sauce. Toss well. Sprinkle with paprika.

Zucchini Salad

PREPARATION TIME: 15 minutes
COOKING TIME: 15 minutes
SERVES: 4 people

2 cups elbow macaroni
4 zucchini, sliced thinly
2 tomatoes, chopped
8 stuffed green olives, sliced
6 tbsps vinaigrette dressing

Cook pasta in lots of boiling salted water for 10 minutes, or until tender but still firm. Rinse in cold water, and drain well. Mix with 3 tablespoons vinaigrette dressing. Leave to cool. Meanwhile, cook the zucchini gently in boiling, lightly-salted water, until just tender but still crisp. Drain, and flush with cold water. Leave to cool. Mix together pasta, zucchini, tomatoes and stuffed olives, and 3 table-spoons vinaigrette dressing. Serve chilled.

Mexican Chicken Salad

PREPARATION TIME: 10 minutes
COOKING TIME: 15 minutes
SERVES: 4 people

1¼ cups soup pasta shells
½ pound or 1 cup cooked chicken, shredded
1 7oz can corn, drained
1 stick celery, sliced
1 sweet red pepper, cored, seeds removed, and diced
1 green pepper, cored, seeds removed, and diced

Dressing:
1 tbsp mayonnaise
2 tbsps vinegar
Salt
Pepper

Cook pasta in plenty of boiling salted water until just tender. Drain well, and leave to cool. Meanwhile, combine mayonnaise with vinegar and salt and pepper to taste. When the pasta is cool, add chicken, corn, celery and peppers. Toss well and serve with dressing.

This page: Mexican Chicken Salad.

Facing page: Curried Shrimp Salad (top) and Zucchini Salad (bottom).

Oriental Vegetables

Narangi Piyaz Salad
(ONION AND ORANGE SALAD)

PREPARATION TIME: 15 minutes
SERVES: 2-3 people

2 large seedless oranges
6 green onions, finely chopped
Salt
2 tsp lemon juice
1/4 tsp ground black pepper
1/2 tsp brown sugar
2 tsp salad or olive oil

Peel oranges and separate into segments. Cut each segment in half. Add onions, salt, lemon juice, pepper, sugar and oil. Gently toss to mix. Serve as a side salad.

Channa
(CHICKPEA)

PREPARATION TIME: soaking overnight
COOKING TIME: 20-30 minutes
SERVES: 4 people

8oz chickpeas
1 tsp baking soda
3 tblsp ghee or
3 tblsp salad or olive oil
1 onion, peeled and chopped
1 bay leaf
1 inch cinnamon stick
4 black cardamoms
1 tsp ginger paste
1 tsp garlic paste
1 tsp ground coriander
1 tsp chili powder
1/4 tsp ground turmeric
5 tomatoes, chopped or
1-2 green chilies, cut in half
Salt to taste
2 sprigs fresh green coriander leaves, chopped

Soak chickpeas overnight in 3 cups water with the baking soda. Drain chickpeas and boil in 2½ cups of water for 10-12 minutes in a pressure cooker. Strain and save the liquid. Heat ghee or oil and add onion, bay leaf, cinnamon and cardamoms. Fry for 1-2 minutes. Add ginger and garlic pastes. Fry for 1 minute. Sprinkle with coriander, chili and turmeric. Mix well and fry for half a minute. Add tomatoes, green chilies and chickpeas. Mix well and add 1 cup chickpea cooking liquid. Cover and simmer gently for 10-15 minutes. Add salt and green coriander. The chickpeas should disintegrate when pressed between thumb and index finger. If not fully tender, add extra water and continue cooking. Channa is a thick, moist dish. Serve with kulcha or nan.

Kassi Mooli
(GRATED MOOLI)

PREPARATION TIME: 10 minutes
SERVES: 4 people

8oz mooli
Salt to taste
Juice of 1 lemon
1 green chili, finely chopped
1 sprig fresh green coriander leaves, chopped

Wash and scrape mooli. Wash again and grate. Drain in a sieve and let some of the liquid run through. Press and squeeze gently. Put the drained grated mooli in a dish. Sprinkle with salt and lemon juice and mix in green chili and fresh coriander leaves. Serve with daal and roti. Note: mooli has a very strong smell; always store well wrapped in cling film, in the refrigerator.

Red Cabbage and Carrot Salad

PREPARATION TIME: 10 minutes
SERVES: 4 people

1/2 small red cabbage, finely chopped
2-3 carrots, peeled and grated
3 tblsp raisins
1 tsp brown sugar
1/4 tsp salt, or to taste
2/3 cup sour cream
2 tsp lemon juice

Mix cabbage, carrots and raisins. Sprinkle with sugar and salt and pour over the well-stirred sour cream. Sprinkle with lemon juice and mix well. Serve with any meal as a side salad. A thin mayonnaise may be used in place of sour cream.

Lobia Curry
(BLACK EYED LOBIA BEAN CURRY)

PREPARATION TIME: soak overnight and 10 minutes
COOKING TIME: 30-40 minutes
SERVES: 4 people

8oz lobia beans, washed and soaked overnight in water
1 onion, peeled and chopped
3 tblsp ghee or
3 tblsp salad or olive oil
1 bay leaf
1 inch cinnamon stick
1 tsp ginger paste
1 tsp garlic paste
1/4 tsp ground turmeric
1 tsp ground coriander
1 tsp chili powder
4 tomatoes, chopped
Salt to taste
2 green chilies, halved and chopped
2 sprigs fresh green coriander leaves, chopped

Boil drained lobia beans in 2½ cups water for 20 minutes. Cool. Fry onion in ghee or oil for 3-4 minutes. Add bay leaf, cinnamon, ginger and garlic pastes and fry for 2 minutes. Add turmeric, ground coriander, chili powder and stir the mixture well. Add drained boiled lobia beans and tomatoes. Add salt, chopped chili and fresh coriander leaves. Cover and cook for 10-15 minutes on gentle heat. The gravy should be thick. Serve with rice or rotis.

This page: Narangi Piyaz Salad (top) and Red Cabbage and Carrot Salad (bottom) with Kassi Mooli.

Facing page: Lobia Curry (top), Razma (center right) and Channa (bottom).

Aloo Methi
(POTATO AND FRESH FENUGREEK LEAVES)

PREPARATION TIME: 10 minutes
COOKING TIME: 10 minutes
SERVES: 3 people

3 tblsp ghee or
3 tblsp salad or olive oil
1 tsp cumin seed
1 pinch asafoetida (hing)
3 medium potatoes, peeled and cut into chunks
1 bunch fresh methi leaves, chopped
1 tsp chili powder
1 tsp ground coriander
Salt
¼ tsp ground turmeric
Juice of 1 lemon

Heat ghee or oil and add cumin seed and hing. When seeds begin to crackle, add potatoes. Fry and cook potatoes for 3-4 minutes then add methi leaves. Mix well and sprinkle with chili powder, coriander, salt and turmeric. Stir the mixture to distribute spices evenly. Cover and cook on low heat for 6-8 minutes. Add lemon juice before serving.

Kachhoomar
(SHREDDED ONION SALAD)

PREPARATION TIME: 20-25 minutes
SERVES: 4 people

1 large Spanish onion, finely sliced into rings
¼ tsp salt
¼ tsp chili powder
1 sprig fresh green coriander leaves, chopped

Aloo Gajjar (left), Toorai Tarkari (center) and Aloo Methi (right).

1 green chili, chopped
1 tblsp lemon juice
2 tomatoes, chopped (optional)

Put the onion slices into a dish with the salt, chili powder, fresh coriander, green chili and lemon juice. Mix well so as to release onion juice. Add tomatoes and mix well. Serve with meat or with kebabs.

Aloo Gajjar

PREPARATION TIME: 10 minutes

COOKING TIME: 10-15 minutes

SERVES: 2-3 people

3 tblsp ghee or
2 tblsp salad or olive oil
1 tsp cumin seeds
2 medium potatoes, peeled and cut into ½ inch cubes
3 medium carrots, scraped and cubed
1 tsp chili powder
1 tsp ground coriander
¼ tsp ground turmeric
Salt to taste
Juice of half a lemon

Heat ghee or oil and add cumin seeds. When they begin to crackle, add potatoes. Fry for 3-4 minutes then add carrots. Stir the mixture and sprinkle with chili, coriander, turmeric and salt. Stir fry the mixture for 1-2 minutes then cover and cook on low heat for 8-10 minutes. Sprinkle with a little water to help cook carrots. Sprinkle with lemon juice before serving.

Razma
(RED KIDNEY BEAN CURRY)

PREPARATION TIME: razma to be soaked overnight

COOKING TIME: 40-50 minutes

SERVES: 4 people

8oz red kidney beans, washed
1 tsp baking soda
3 tblsp ghee or
3 tblsp salad or olive oil
1 onion, peeled and chopped
1 inch cinnamon stick
1 bay leaf
3 black cardamoms
1 tsp ginger paste
1 tsp garlic paste
1 tsp chili powder
1 tsp ground coriander
1 tsp garam masala powder
¼ tsp ground turmeric
1 cup canned tomatoes, crushed
Salt to taste
2 green chilies, halved
2 sprigs fresh green coriander leaves, chopped

Soak kidney beans in 2½ cups water with baking soda overnight. Next day, pressure-cook the kidney beans in 2½ cups fresh water for 5-8 minutes. Cool and drain the beans, retaining the liquid. Heat ghee or oil and fry onion for 2-3 minutes. Add cinnamon, bay leaf, cardamoms, ginger and garlic pastes. Cook for 1 minute. Add chili powder, ground coriander, garam masala and turmeric. Stir the spices well. Add tomatoes and salt. Add kidney beans and cook the mixture for 2-3 minutes. Add 1 cup bean cooking liquid. Sprinkle with green chili and fresh coriander leaves. Simmer for 15-20 minutes. Add extra liquid if gravy is too thick. Remove from heat and serve.

Saag Bhaji
(BRUSSELS SPROUT BHAJI)

PREPARATION TIME: 6 minutes

COOKING TIME: 10 minutes

SERVES: 4 people

3 tblsp ghee or
3 tblsp salad or olive oil
1 tsp five spice mixture (panch-phoran)
1 bay leaf
1 inch cinnamon stick
1lb Brussels sprouts, cut in half
1 tsp chili powder
1½ tsp ground coriander
¼ tsp ground turmeric
Salt
1 tsp brown sugar
4 cloves, ground
Juice of 1 lemon

Heat ghee or oil and add five spice mixture. Add bay leaf and cinnamon stick and fry for half a minute. Add Brussels sprouts. Mix well and sprinkle with chili powder, coriander and turmeric. Add salt to taste and stir well to blend all the spices. Cover and cook on gentle heat for 8-10 minutes, stirring the mixture occasionally. Sprinkle with sugar and ground cloves. Mix well. Cover and cook for another 2-3 minutes. Sprinkle with lemon juice before serving.

Toorai Tarkari
(ZUCCHINI CURRY)

PREPARATION TIME: 10 minutes

COOKING TIME: 15 minutes

SERVES: 3 people

1½ tblsp salad or olive oil
1 tsp cumin seeds
½lb zucchini, peeled and sliced into ¼ inch thick rounds
½ tsp chili powder
1 tsp ground coriander
¼ tsp ground turmeric
3-4 tomatoes, chopped
Salt to taste
1 green chili, halved
1 sprig fresh green coriander leaves, chopped

Heat oil and add cumin seeds. When they crackle add zucchini slices. Stir and sprinkle with chili powder, coriander and turmeric. Mix well and add chopped tomatoes. Sprinkle with salt, green chili and fresh coriander. Cover and cook for 10-12 minutes.

Pochari Kosambri (top left), Kachhoomar (top right) and Phalon-Ka-Chaat (bottom).

Phalon-Ka-Chaat
(SWEET AND SOUR FRUIT SALAD)

PREPARATION TIME: 20-25 minutes

SERVES: 6 people

2 bananas, peeled and sliced
1 large guava, chopped
1 pear, peeled and chopped
2 ripe peaches, skinned, stoned and sliced
2 slices fresh pineapple, peeled and chopped
1 small fresh pawpaw, peeled, seeded and cut into chunks
A few grapes, seeded
1 apple, peeled, cored and chopped
2 tsp lemon juice
Salt
¼ tsp ground black pepper
¼ tsp chili powder
Pinch of black rock salt (kala namak)

Put all the fruits into a large bowl. Sprinkle with lemon juice, salt, pepper and chili. Mix well. Add pinch of ground black rock salt (kala namak). Mix and serve as a starter, side salad or snack. Note: many other fruits may be added i.e. mango, kiwi, plum, lychees, melons.

Baigan Dahivaley
(EGGPLANT SLICES IN YOGURT)

PREPARATION TIME: 10 minutes

COOKING TIME: 10-15 minutes

SERVES: 3 people

1 tsp chili powder
¼ tsp ground turmeric
1 large eggplant, cut into ¼ inch thick round slices
Salad or olive oil for deep frying
1¼ cups natural yogurt
1 tsp garam masala powder
¼ tsp salt
1 green chili, chopped
1 sprig fresh green coriander leaves, chopped

Rub chili and turmeric into eggplant slices. Deep fry eggplant slices, a few at a time, in oil for 2-3 minutes, and drain on kitchen paper. Beat yogurt and add garam masala powder, salt, green chili and fresh coriander. Mix well. Arrange eggplant slices on a flat serving plate or dish. Pour yogurt over evenly. Serve as a side dish.

Pachari Kosambri
(VEGETABLE, NUT AND COCONUT SALAD)

PREPARATION TIME: 20-25 minutes

SERVES: 4 people

4oz grated white cabbage
1 small onion, peeled and finely chopped
1 small apple, grated
1 firm mango, peeled and grated
Juice of 1 lemon
¼ tsp salt
2oz grated fresh coconut
1 green chili, chopped
2 sprigs fresh green coriander leaves, chopped
¾ cup bean sprouts
½ cucumber, grated
3 tblsp skinned unsalted peanuts, lightly roasted and coarsely ground

Put grated cabbage, onion, apple and mango into a bowl. Mix well, squeeze and discard excess juice. Drain well. Sprinkle with lemon juice, salt, coconut, green chili and fresh coriander. Add bean sprouts and cucumber and mix gently. Add lightly roasted and coarsely ground peanuts. Mix and serve. Note: other nuts, like cashews, chiroli, pecan, walnut and hazelnuts may be used. Grated carrots may also be included if desired.

Green Bean Bhaji

PREPARATION TIME: 10 minutes

COOKING TIME: 10-12 minutes

SERVES: 3-4 people

3 tblsp oil or melted ghee
1 tsp urid daal
2-3 green chilies
6-8 fresh curry leaves
12oz frozen sliced green beans, unthawed
Salt to taste
1 tblsp shredded coconut

Heat oil or ghee and add urid daal, green chilies and curry leaves. Stir fry for half a minute. Add beans and sprinkle with salt. Cover and cook for 6-8 minutes. Sprinkle with coconut and mix well. Cover and cook for 3-4 minutes. Serve with chapatis.

Mattar Paneer (top left), Saag Bhaji (top right) and Baigan Dahivaley (bottom).

Mushroom Aloo Bhaji
(POTATO AND MUSHROOM BHAJI)

PREPARATION TIME: 5-6 minutes
COOKING TIME: 10-12 minutes
SERVES: 4 people

3 tblsp ghee or
3 tblsp salad or olive oil
1 onion, peeled and chopped
1lb potatoes, peeled and cubed
½ tsp salt
2 tblsp garam masala powder
½lb button mushrooms, sliced
Lemon juice

Heat ghee or oil and fry onion until tender (2-3 minutes). Add potatoes and fry for 5-6 minutes. Sprinkle with salt and garam masala. Mix well and cover. Cook for 4-5 minutes until potatoes are tender. Add mushrooms. Stir well. Cover and cook for 2-3 minutes. Sprinkle with lemon juice to taste. Remove from heat and serve.

Mili-Juli Sabzi
(MIXED VEGETABLE BHAJI)

PREPARATION TIME: 15 minutes
COOKING TIME: 10-15 minutes
SERVES: 4 people

3 tblsp ghee or
3 tblsp salad or olive oil
1 onion, peeled and chopped
1 tsp cumin seeds
1 medium potato, peeled and chopped
3 cauliflower florets, cut into small pieces
1 small eggplant, cubed
1 medium green pepper, seeded and cubed
½lb mixed frozen vegetables
Salt to taste
1 tsp ground turmeric
1 tsp ground coriander
1 tsp chili powder
3-4 tomatoes, chopped
2 sprigs fresh green coriander leaves, chopped
1-2 green chilies, chopped

Heat ghee or oil and fry onion and cumin seeds for 2-3 minutes. Add potatoes and stir fry for 4-5 minutes. Add cauliflower, eggplant and green pepper and cook for 4 minutes. Add mixed vegetables. Stir to mix well. Sprinkle with salt, turmeric, coriander and chili powder. Add chopped tomatoes. Stir and cover. Cook on low heat for 5-6 minutes. Add fresh coriander and chopped chili. Mix and serve. To make a moist curry add ⅔ cup water after tomatoes are added.

Dum Aloo
(SPICED POTATO CURRY)

PREPARATION TIME: 10 minutes
COOKING TIME: 15 minutes
SERVES: 4 people

3 tbls ghee or
3 tblsp salad or olive oil
1 bay leaf
1 onion, minced finely
½ tsp ginger paste
½ tsp garlic paste
½ tsp whole mustard seed
½ tsp cumin seed
1lb small potatoes, with skins on, washed and dried
¼ tsp ground turmeric
2 tsp ground coriander
1½ tsp chili powder
⅔ cup natural yogurt
¼ tsp salt

Heat ghee or oil and add bay leaf and onion. Fry for 3-4 minutes. Add ginger and garlic and fry for 1 minute. Add mustard and cumin seed. Add potatoes, mix well and cook for 4-5 minutes, stirring continuously to avoid burning. Sprinkle with turmeric, coriander and chili powder. Add yogurt and salt to taste. Mix gently; cover and cook for 8-10 minutes until potatoes are tender and most of the liquid has evaporated. Sprinkle with a little water if potatoes are not quite tender. Dum aloo is a dry dish, with the potatoes coated with spices. Serve with puri.

Khata-Meetha Kaddu
(SWEET AND SOUR PUMPKIN)

PREPARATION TIME: 10 minutes

COOKING TIME: 15-20 minutes

SERVES: 4 people

3 tblsp ghee or
3 tblsp salad or olive oil
1 bay leaf
1 inch cinnamon stick
6 green cardamoms
6 cloves
1 tsp five spice mixture (panch-phoran)
2 medium potatoes, peeled and cut into chunks
1lb pumpkin, peeled and cut into chunks
1 tsp chili powder
1½ tsp ground coriander
¼ tsp ground turmeric
½ tsp salt
2 tsp brown sugar
1 tblsp tamarind pulp concentrate
3 tblsp water

Heat oil and add bay leaf, cinnamon, cardamom, cloves and five spice mixture and fry for half a minute. Add potatoes and fry for 4 minutes. Add pumpkin. Stir vegetables and cook for 3 minutes. Sprinkle with chili powder, coriander, turmeric, salt and sugar. Stir the mixture to blend the spices. Add tamarind pulp and water. Cover and cook on gentle heat for 8-10 minutes until potatoes are tender. This is a moist curry, without gravy. Serve with paratha or puri.

Palak Paneer
(PANEER AND SPINACH)

PREPARATION TIME: 20 minutes and overnight for paneer. Follow paneer making recipe.

COOKING TIME: 10 minutes

SERVES: 3-4 people

1lb fresh leaf spinach
3 tblsp ghee or
3 tblsp salad or olive oil
8oz paneer, cut into cubes
1 onion, peeled and finely chopped
1 inch root ginger, peeled and finely chopped
4 tomatoes, chopped
1 tsp chili powder – less if hot
1 tblsp lemon juice try commercial blend
1 tsp ground coriander
1½ tblsp unsalted butter
¼ tsp ground turmeric
¼ tsp salt

Boil fresh spinach in 2½ cups water for 5 minutes. Drain and save water. Mash or purée spinach and keep aside. Heat ghee or oil and fry paneer cubes until light brown. Remove. In the same oil fry onion and ginger for 3-4 minutes. Add tomatoes and sprinkle with chili, coriander, turmeric and salt to taste. Cover and cook for 2-3 minutes. Add paneer, puréed spinach and lemon juice. If too dry, use 2-3 tblsp spinach water to moisten the curry. Remove from heat and serve with knobs of butter on top. This is a thick, moist curry.

Daal Pulses

PREPARATION TIME: 5 minutes

COOKING TIME: 10 minutes

SERVES: 4 people

8oz split or dehusked moong daal, washed in 2-3 changes of water
2½ cups water
¼ tsp ground turmeric
1 tsp ground coriander
Salt to taste
1 small onion, peeled and chopped
3 tblsp unsalted butter, or clarified butter
1 green chili, chopped
2 cloves garlic, peeled and chopped

To garnish
1 sprig fresh green coriander leaves, chopped

Boil moong daal in water until tender and soft. Drain. Mash the daal with a potato masher or egg beater. Add turmeric, ground coriander and salt to taste. Simmer

This page: Khata-Meetha Kaddu (top), Palak Paneer (right), Dum Aloo (bottom).

Facing page: Green Bean Bhaji (top), Mili-Juli Sabzi (right) and Mushroom Aloo Bhaji (bottom).

until volume is reduced by ⅓rd. Fry onion in butter until golden brown and add chili and garlic. Fry until garlic is browned. Pour over daal. Garnish with chopped fresh coriander. Serve with rice or chapatis.

Khari Urid Daal
(DRY URID DAAL)

PREPARATION TIME: 5 minutes
COOKING TIME: 10-15 minutes
SERVES: 4 people

8oz white dehusked urid daal, washed in 3-4 changes of water
Salt to taste
¾ cup water

For garnish
1 onion, peeled and sliced
3 tblsp unsalted butter
1 green chili, chopped
1 inch root ginger, peeled and sliced
1 sprig fresh green coriander leaves, chopped

Cook drained urid daal covered with salted water, on a low heat, until the water has evaporated. Fry onion in butter until golden brown. Add chopped chili and ginger and fry for 2-3 minutes. Pour over dry daal. Garnish with chopped coriander. Serve with roti or paratha.

Masoor Daal
(RED LENTIL)

PREPARATION TIME: 6 minutes
COOKING TIME: 20-25 minutes
SERVES: 4 people

8oz red lentils
1 tsp chili powder
2 tsp ground coriander
¼ tsp ground turmeric
¼ tsp salt
1 sprig fresh green coriander leaves, chopped
4 tomatoes, chopped
1 onion, peeled and chopped
3 tblsp butter
1 green chili, halved and chopped

Wash lentils in 4-5 changes of water, until water is clear. Drain. Add 2½ cups water; cover and simmer gently, without stirring, for 10-15 minutes until lentils are thoroughly cooked. Blend with a masher or beat with an egg beater. Add chili powder, ground coriander, turmeric, salt, fresh coriander and tomatoes. Cover and simmer for 6-8 minutes. Remove from heat. Fry onion in butter, until brown; pour over daal. Garnish with chopped chili. Serve with rice or chapati.

Below: Sambhar (top), Masoor Daal (center) and Arhar Toor Daal (bottom).

Arhar Toor Daal
(YELLOW LENTIL)

PREPARATION TIME: 5-6 minutes
COOKING TIME: 20-25 minutes
SERVES: 4 people

8oz toor daal
¼ tsp ground turmeric
1 tsp ground coriander
¼ tsp salt
6 curry leaves
1 green chili, split in half
1 tblsp grated fresh coconut or shredded coconut
1 sprig fresh green coriander leaves, chopped
1 tsp mustard seed
3 tblsp butter

Wash toor daal in 4-5 changes of water. Drain. Add 2½ cups water, turmeric, salt and coriander. Cover and simmer gently for 10-15 minutes until daal is well cooked and soft. Blend with the aid of a masher or an egg beater. Add curry leaves, coconut, chili and coriander leaves. Cover and cook for further 8-10 minutes. Heat butter and fry mustard seed for half a minute. Pour over daal. Serve with rice or rotis. Toor daal should have a smooth, thick consistency.

Sabut Masoor
(WHOLE LENTIL)

PREPARATION TIME: 5 minutes
COOKING TIME: 20-25 minutes
SERVES: 4 people

3 tblsp butter
1 onion, peeled and chopped
1 bay leaf
1 inch cinnamon stick
1 tsp ginger paste
1 tsp garlic paste
8oz daal, washed in 3-4 changes of water
Water
1 tsp ground coriander
½ tsp chili powder
¼ tsp ground turmeric
3 tomatoes, chopped
1 green chili, chopped
1 sprig fresh green coriander leaves, chopped
Salt to taste

Heat butter and fry onion until golden brown. Add bay leaf, cinnamon stick, ginger and garlic pastes and fry for 1 minute. Add drained daal and water. Cover and simmer gently for 12-15 minutes. The daal should be well cooked. Beat with a potato masher or egg beater to blend. Sprinkle with coriander, chili and turmeric. Add tomatoes, green chili and fresh coriander leaves. Season with salt. Mix well; cover and cook gently for 7-10 minutes. Remove from heat and serve with rice or chapatis. The daal should have gravy of medium consistency. If too dry, add a little water and boil for 2-3 minutes.

Sambhar
(DAAL AND VEGETABLE)

PREPARATION TIME: 10 minutes
COOKING TIME: 20-30 minutes
SERVES: 4 people

8oz toor daal
1 carrot, peeled and sliced
1 potato, peeled and cubed
6-8 okra (bhindi), topped and tailed and cut into 1 inch pieces
1 small zucchini, sliced
1 small eggplant, halved and sliced

The following spices should be dry roasted and ground into a powder:
1 tsp coriander seed
1 tsp cumin seed
2 whole dry red chilies
2 tsp channa daal
¼ tsp fenugreek seed (methi)
6 curry leaves
2 tblsp tamarind pulp concentrate
1 green chili, slit in half
Salt to taste
1 sprig fesh green coriander leaves
1 tblsp salad or olive oil, for tempering
½ tsp mustard seed
¼ tsp asafoetida (hing)

Wash toor daal in 4-5 changes of water until water is clear. Drain. Add 1¼ cups water; cover and simmer gently for 6-10 minutes. Remove any froth that forms. When daal is soft, beat with a potato masher or whisk. In a separate pan, boil all the vegetables with the ground, roasted spice mixture and the 1¼ cups water, for 4-5 minutes. Mix daal and vegetables along with liquid and stir gently to give a smooth

Sabut Masoor (top), Khari Urid Daal (right) and Lal Mireh Aur Moong Phali (bottom).

mixture. Add curry leaves, tamarind pulp, salt, chopped chili and fresh coriander. Simmer for 10-15 minutes. Remove to a serving dish. For tempering, heat oil and fry mustard seed and asafoetida for half a minute and pour over sambhar. Serve with boiled rice.

Butter Beans and Green Capsicum

PREPARATION TIME: 10 minutes

COOKING TIME: 10 minutes

SERVES: 3 people

1 tblsp salad or olive oil
1 onion, peeled and chopped
8oz butter beans, soaked and partly cooked (or broad beans)
1 large green pepper, seeded and chopped
¼ tsp ground turmeric
½ tsp chili powder
1 tsp ground coriander
Salt to taste
4-5 tomatoes, chopped
1 green chili, chopped
1 sprig fresh green coriander leaves, chopped

Heat oil and fry onion for 3-4 minutes. Add beans and green pepper. Cook for 4-5 minutes. Sprinkle with turmeric, chili and ground coriander. Add salt and tomatoes. Mix well. Cover and cook for 5-6 minutes on low heat. Add green chili and fresh coriander. Cook covered for 2-3 minutes. If too dry, add 2 tblsp water. This is a dry dish.

Stuffed Peppers

PREPARATION TIME: 20 minutes

COOKING TIME: 30-35 minutes

SERVES: 4 people

3 tblsp ghee or
3 tblsp salad or olive oil
1 onion, peeled and finely chopped
1 potato, peeled and diced
8oz mixed frozen vegetables
1 tsp garam masala powder
½ tsp chili powder
2 tsp dried mango powder
Salt to taste
8 quite small green peppers
Salad or olive oil for frying peppers

Heat ghee or oil and fry onion until tender (3-4 minutes). Add potatoes and cook for 4-5 minutes. Add mixed vegetables, and sprinkle with garam masala, chili powder, mango powder and salt to taste. Cover and cook gently until potatoes are tender. Remove from heat and cool. Wash and dry the green peppers. Remove top by slicing across to form a lid. Remove center pith and seeds. Heat about 3 tblsp oil and fry peppers laid sideways, for 1-2 minutes; cook on all sides. Drain well. Fill each pepper with vegetable filling and arrange them on a baking tray. Bake in preheated oven, at 325°F for 20 minutes. Serve.

Aloo Gobi

PREPARATION TIME: 10 minutes

COOKING TIME: 10-12 minutes

SERVES: 3-4 people

1 large onion, peeled and chopped
4 tblsp ghee or
4 tblsp salad or olive oil
2 medium potatoes, peeled and cut into chunks
1 medium cauliflower, cut into small florets
2-3 green chilies, chopped
2 sprigs fresh green coriander leaves, chopped
1½ inch root ginger, peeled and finely chopped
Salt to taste
Juice of 1 lemon
2 tsp garam masala

Fry onion in ghee or oil until just tender (about 2-3 minutes). Add potatoes and fry for 2-3 minutes. Add cauliflower and stir fry for 4-5 minutes. Add green chilies, coriander, ginger and salt. Mix well. Cover and cook for 5-6 minutes on low heat, or until potatoes are tender. Sprinkle with lemon juice and garam masala before serving. Serve with parathas.

Nau-Rattan Chutney
(NINE JEWELED CHUTNEY)

PREPARATION TIME: 20 minutes
COOKING TIME: 20-30 minutes
MAKES: about 2½ cups

1 banana, peeled and sliced
1 apple, cored and chopped
1 large mango, peeled stoned and sliced
3 rings of canned pineapple, chopped
1 cup canned peach slices, chopped
4oz dates, pitted and sliced
2oz ginger root, peeled and chopped
3 tblsp raisins
1 cup soft brown sugar (or jaggery)
2-3 dry red chilies
¾ cup brown vinegar
1 tsp salt
½ tsp cumin seed
½ tsp coriander seed
½ tsp onion seed
½ tsp aniseed seed
4 tblsp chopped blanched almonds

Put all the fruits into a saucepan with the dates, ginger, raisins, sugar, chilies and vinegar. Add salt and simmer gently for 10-15 minutes. Roast and grind the cumin, coriander, onion seed, aniseed and almonds. Mix into the fruit mixture and cook for 5-6 minutes. Cool and bottle. Chutney should be thick and sticky.

Lal Mireh Aur Moong Phali Chutney
(RED-HOT CHUTNEY)

PREPARATION TIME: 5 minutes
MAKES: about 1 cup

1 large red pepper
3-4 whole dry red chilies
3 tblsp unsalted peanuts
½ inch root ginger, peeled and sliced
Juice of 3 lemons
Salt

Halve red pepper, remove pith and seeds. Blend red pepper, chilies, peanuts and ginger in the liquidizer. A few spoons of lemon juice may be needed to blend the mixture. Pour into a bowl. Add salt and the lemon juice. Mix well and serve. (Red-hot chutney can be frozen. Freeze in small tubs in small quantities.) Can be kept refrigerated in sealed bottles for up to 2 months.

Dahi-Podina Chutney
(YOGURT AND MINT CHUTNEY)

PREPARATION TIME: 5-6 minutes
MAKES: ⅔ cup

⅔ cup natural yogurt
4 tsp fine granulated sugar
2-3 sprigs mint leaves, chopped
Salt

Put yogurt, sugar and mint into a blender; liquidize for 1-2 minutes. Add salt and mix. Serve with kebabs, samosa and pakoras. Ready made concentrated mint sauce may be used in place of fresh mint leaves.

Inset illustration, far left: Meethi Tomatar Chutney (top), Tmali Ki Chutney (right) and Dahi-Podina Chutney (bottom).

Main illustration: Chutneys. Adrak Khajoor Ki Khati Mithi (top), Nau-Rattan (right), Coriander, Green Chili and Coconut (bottom), Coconut and Urid Daal (left) and Red Pepper and Peanut (center).

Tmali Ki Chutney
(TAMARIND CHUTNEY)

PREPARATION TIME: 6 minutes

COOKING TIME: 10-12 minutes

MAKES: about ½lb

½lb dry tamarind pods
¾ cup fine granulated sugar or jaggery
¼ tsp salt
1 tsp chili powder
1 tsp cumin seed, roasted and lightly ground
1 tsp coriander seed, roasted and lightly ground

Soak tamarind pods in ⅔ cup of boiling water for 5 minutes. Squeeze pods to remove soft pulp. Strain through sieve or squeeze by hand. Add a little fresh warm water to the pulp and repeat, taking 3 extracts. The first one is the thickest and subsequent ones will be lower in strength. Take 1 cup thick tamarind extract. Discard the pods. Add the sugar, salt, chili powder and ground, roasted cumin and coriander seeds to the tamarind extract. Mix well. Adjust sugar and salt if necessary. Serve with kebabs. Tamarind chutney can be kept refrigerated for up to 1 month.

Adrak Khajoor Ki Khati Mithi Chutney
(DATE AND GINGER CHUTNEY)

PREPARATION TIME: 20-30 minutes

MAKES: about 2 cups

4oz fresh dates, halved, stoned and sliced
2oz fresh root ginger, peeled and cut into matchstick-size strips
Flesh of 1 small, unripe mango, peeled and thinly sliced
3 tblsp raisins and currants mixed
2 tblsp chopped blanched almonds
¾ cup water
¾ cup fine granulated sugar (or grated jaggery)
¼ tsp salt
1 tsp red chili powder

Put dates, ginger, mango, raisins and currants, and almonds into a saucepan. Add water. Keep aside for 6-8 minutes. Add sugar (or grated jaggery), salt and chili powder and simmer gently. Cook for 15-20 minutes until chutney is thick and sticky. Remove, cool and serve. The chutney can be bottled and kept in or out of the refrigerator for up to 3 months.

Meethi Tomatar Chutney
(SWEET TOMATO CHUTNEY)

PREPARATION TIME: 5-6 minutes

COOKING TIME: 10-15 minutes

MAKES: 1¼lbs

1½ tblsp ghee or
1 tblsp salad or olive oil
1 inch cinnamon stick
1 bay leaf
6 cloves
1 tsp mustard seed
1 tsp chili powder
¼ tsp turmeric powder
¼ cup fine granulated sugar
1lb tomatoes, chopped
3 tblsp raisins
½ tsp salt

Heat ghee or oil and fry cinnamon, bay leaf and cloves for 1 minute. Add mustard seed. When they begin to crackle, add chili, turmeric and sugar. Mix well and add tomatoes. Mix well and add raisins and salt. Cover and simmer for 8-10 minutes. Add a little water if liquid thickens too much. Tomato chutney should have a medium thick consistency. Serve hot or cold. Once cooked it can be kept in refrigerator for 4-6 weeks.

Aloo-Mattar and Mirchi Bhaji
(POTATO, PEA AND GREEN PEPPER CURRY)

PREPARATION TIME: 15 minutes

COOKING TIME: 10 minutes

SERVES: 3-4 people

1 onion, peeled and chopped
3 tblsp ghee or
2 tblsp salad or olive oil
2 medium potatoes, peeled and cut into chunks
1 tsp ground coriander
1 tsp chili powder
¼ tsp ground turmeric
8oz frozen green peas
1 green pepper, seeded and cut into chunks
1⅓ cups canned tomatoes, crushed
Salt to taste
2 green chilies, cut into quarters
2 sprigs fresh green coriander leaves, chopped
½ cup water

Fry onion in ghee or oil until just tender (about 2-3 minutes). Add potatoes and fry for 5-6 minutes. Sprinkle with ground coriander, chili powder and turmeric. Mix well and add peas and green pepper. Stir and add tomatoes; season with salt. Add chopped green chilies and fresh coriander. Add water, cover and cook for 5-6 minutes until potatoes are tender. The dish should have a thick gravy.

Bharey Bhindi
(WHOLE STUFFED OKRA)

PREPARATION TIME: 20-30 minutes

COOKING TIME: 15-20 minutes

SERVES: 3 people

½lb bhindi (okra), washed, dried, topped and tailed
1 large onion, peeled and thickly sliced
4 tblsp ghee or
4 tblsp salad or olive oil
2 tsp ground coriander
2 tsp ground cumin
1 tsp ground turmeric
1 tsp chili powder
Salt to taste
1 tblsp dry mango powder
1 tblsp aniseed (sauf) powder

Split okra or bhindi halfway down. Fry onion for half a minute in 1 tablespoon of oil or ghee and remove. Mix coriander, cumin, turmeric and chili powder, and put a little of this spice mixture into each split okras. Heat the remaining oil in a skillet or wok. Add stuffed okras. Sprinkle with salt and stir well. Cover and cook on low heat for 5-6 minutes. Add fried onions, then sprinkle with mango and aniseed powder. Cover and cook for 3-4 minutes. Serve with roti.

Tendli Bhaji with Cashew Nuts

Tendli is an Asian vegetable that looks like a gooseberry and tastes like zucchini.

PREPARATION TIME: 10 minutes

COOKING TIME: 12-15 minutes

SERVES: 3 people

2 tblsp salad or olive oil
3 tblsp cashew nuts
3-4 cloves of garlic, peeled and crushed
½ tsp mustard seed
6-8 curry leaves
2-3 dry red chilies (or fresh green chilies)
½lb tendli, washed, dried and cut in half lengthways
Salt to taste
2 tsp shredded coconut
¼ tsp ground turmeric

Heat oil and fry cashew nuts until light brown. Remove the nuts and then fry the garlic until light brown. Add mustard seed, curry leaves and red or green chilies. Fry for half a minute. Add tendli, sprinkle with salt and stir the mixture. Sprinkle with shredded coconut, turmeric and fried cashew nuts. Cover and cook on low heat for 10-12 minutes, or until tendli is tender.

This page: Aloo-Mattar and Mirchi Bhaji (left), Bharey Bhindi (center) and Tendli Bhaji with Cashew Nuts (right).

Facing page: Butter Beans and Green Capsicum (top), Aloo Gobi (left) and Stuffed Peppers (bottom).

Section 5

MEALS WITH FLAIR

An Introduction to Wok Cooking

The wok is an ancient Chinese cooking utensil known for its versatility. It can be used for stir-frying, deep frying, steaming, boiling and braising a wide variety of food.

The traditional wok is made of heavy gauge carbon steel which conducts heat well, giving a quick high temperature. However, this medium will rust if not oiled and given proper care. Lengthy cooking in liquid may impart a metallic taste to the food or may cause the discolouration of white liquids or food. Aluminium and stainless steel woks are also available and are a good choice, particularly if steaming, braising, boiling, or cooking for a long time. These woks need no seasoning but do not heat as efficiently as carbon steel.

Cooking times in this book are only a guide, as actual times will vary with the kind of wok you use and the intensity of the heat source.

There are three types of wok: round-bottomed, for use on gas burners – with the use of a ring-base for stability; flat bottomed, for electric ranges; and electric woks, which can be used to cook at the table or anywhere there is a power point. Other equipment that may be needed includes a curved, long-handled spatula, and curved slotted spoon (which fit into the curved shape of the wok), a domed lid, a metal trivet or bamboo steamer and a deep fat frying thermometer.

Stir-frying, a fuel and timesaver. It is unique to wok cooking, where small pieces of food are toss-cooked in minutes over intense heat, in a very small amount of oil. The shape of the wok allows for tossing with abandon. Food is cooked in a matter of minutes and the flavours and juices are sealed in, resulting in succulent meat, poultry and seafood, and tender and crisp vegetables. Nutritional values are retained, as are the fresh and bright colours of vegetables.

A number of steps followed will lead to ease of cooking and best results:

☆ Heat wok before adding oil.

☆ Have all ingredients needed for the recipe prepared and to hand before beginning to cook. Care should be taken in the preparation of the food so that everything cooks in a short time and adds to the appearance of the final dish.

☆ Any sauces or seasonings should generally be prepared in advance.

☆ Slice meat and poultry very thinly and evenly (it will slice easier if partially frozen and a very sharp knife is used).

☆ Ingredients that take the longest to cook should be put into the wok first.

☆ Add a small amount of food at a time – in batches if necessary.

☆ Ensure everything is ready for serving, including family or guests, as the food must be eaten immediately it is cooked. It is not the sort of cooking that can be done ahead of time.

Deep frying. Points to note when cooking with oil:

☆ Care must be taken not to move or tilt the wok when it contains hot oil.

☆ Ensure wok is uncovered when heating oil.

☆ Ensure handles are not sticking over edge of stove.

☆ Be careful if adding moist food as it tends to spatter.

☆ After cooking, allow oil to cool before pouring out or returning to its container.

Steaming and Braising. Points to note when steaming and braising:

☆ During cooking some steam will condense and form drops of water under the domed lid. To shield the food, cover with a piece of greaseproof paper.

☆ Check the water level once in a while and top up as needed.

A few well-chosen ingredients, now readily available, will give you the authentic flavours for many a delicious Oriental dish, enabling you to savour the pleasures of exotic Eastern cuisine.

Though the wok is primarily an Oriental utensil, I have interspersed the Eastern dishes with a variety of Western-style recipes, since wok cooking adapts well to many types of cuisine.

Wok Soups and Appetizers

Wonton Soup

PREPARATION TIME: 15 minutes
COOKING TIME: 15 minutes
SERVES: 4 people

8oz ground pork
4 green onions, chopped finely
½ tsp finely chopped ginger root
1 tbsp light soy sauce
4oz wonton wrappers
1 tsp cornstarch
1 tsp sesame oil
1 tsp Chinese wine, or dry sherry
1 tsp sugar
Salt
Pepper
5 cups chicken stock
½ tsp sesame oil

Garnish
Coriander, or finely chopped green onion

Place in a bowl the ground pork, green onions, ginger, soy sauce, 1 tsp sesame oil, Chinese wine, sugar, cornstarch, salt and pepper. Mix together well and set aside. Heat stock in wok and bring to the boil. Season with salt and pepper. Wrap ½ teaspoon of pork mixture into each wonton wrapper. Close tightly and drop into stock. Cook for 5 minutes. Wontons will usually rise to the surface when cooked. Add ½ tsp sesame oil and stir in. Garnish with green onion or fresh coriander. Serve hot.

Chinese Combination Soup

PREPARATION TIME: 30 minutes
COOKING TIME: 20 minutes
SERVES: 4 people

4 dried Chinese mushrooms
8oz chicken
4oz fine/thread egg noodles
1 clove garlic, sliced thinly
1 tsp finely sliced root ginger
¼ small cabbage, shredded
2½ cups chicken stock
1 tbsp peanut oil
2 eggs, beaten
1 tbsp dark soy sauce
1 tbsp sherry
1 tbsp water
1 tsp cornstarch
2 shallots, peeled and sliced finely

Soak mushrooms in hot water for 20 minutes. Remove and discard stems. Slice mushroom caps thinly. Soak noodles in boiling salted water for 2 minutes. Rinse in cold water. Drain. Slice chicken finely. Heat wok and add peanut oil. Add garlic and ginger, and fry gently for 5 minutes, then discard. Add chicken, and fry for a few minutes until meat has turned white. Add mushrooms, shallots, cabbage and stock. Bring to the boil and simmer for 5 minutes. Gradually pour in eggs and stir so that they cook in shreds. Mix cornstarch with 1 tbsp of water, and pour into soup, stirring continuously. Cook for 2 minutes or until soup thickens. Add noodles, soy sauce and sherry. Serve immediately.

This page: Wonton Soup (top) and Curry Soup with Meatballs (bottom).

Facing page: Chinese Combination Soup (top) and Eggflower Soup (bottom).

Curry Soup with Meatballs

PREPARATION TIME: 30 minutes
COOKING TIME: 20 minutes
SERVES: 4 people

Meatballs
8oz lean ground beef
1 clove garlic, crushed
1 onion, peeled and chopped finely
½ tsp salt
½ tsp curry powder
½ tsp ground cinnamon
½ tsp ground cloves
½ tsp ground pepper
2 tbsps breadcrumbs
1 small egg, lightly beaten

Broth
1 tsp garam masala
1 tsp turmeric
2½ cups water
1 clove garlic, crushed
1 onion, peeled and finely chopped
1 tsp curry leaves
½ cup desiccated coconut, soaked in 1 cup hot water for 15 minutes
2 tbsps peanut oil

Mix together meatball ingredients, and form into small balls about the size of walnuts. Heat wok, add oil and, when hot, fry meatballs. When browned well all over, remove with a slotted spoon, and drain on paper towels. Carefully drain oil from wok. Add 1 tsp of oil, and fry spices for 30 seconds. Add onion, curry leaves, and garlic, and cook together for 3 minutes. Meanwhile, strain coconut in a strainer, press out as much liquid as possible, and discard the pulp. Add water and coconut milk to the wok and simmer together for 5 minutes. Adjust seasoning. Strain soup and return to wok. Add meatballs and simmer a further 5 minutes. Serve hot.

Hot and Sour Soup

PREPARATION TIME: 30 minutes
COOKING TIME: 30 minutes
SERVES: 4 people

4oz lean pork fillet
4 dried Chinese mushrooms
⅓ cup bamboo shoots, sliced
1 square beancurd, diced
2 tbsps sunflower or vegetable oil
5 cups light, clear stock, or hot water plus 2 chicken bouillon cubes
1 tsp cornstarch
2 tbsps cold water
1 tsp sesame oil

Marinade
1 tbsp light soy sauce
3 tbsps brown vinegar
2 tbsps water
1 tsp sesame oil
Salt
Pepper

Garnish
Fresh coriander

Soak Chinese mushrooms for 20 minutes in hot water. Meanwhile, slice pork into thin slivers. Make the marinade by combining light soy sauce, brown vinegar, water, sesame oil, and salt and pepper. Pour over pork and leave for 30 minutes. Drain mushrooms. Remove and discard stalks. Slice caps very finely. Remove pork from marinade, and reserve marinade. Heat wok, and add sunflower or vegetable oil. When hot, stir-fry pork, mushrooms and bamboo shoots for 2 minutes. Add stock and bring to the boil. Simmer for 10 minutes. Add beancurd, marinade, and salt and pepper to taste. Slake cornstarch in 2 tbsps of cold water. Add to soup and allow to simmer for 5 minutes. Add sesame oil and sprinkle with fresh coriander. Serve hot.

Chicken and Asparagus Soup

PREPARATION TIME: 10 minutes
COOKING TIME: 45 minutes
SERVES: 4 people

1lb chicken pieces
1 onion, peeled and chopped roughly
1 carrot, chopped roughly
1 stick celery, chopped roughly
4 peppercorns
10oz can asparagus pieces
5 cups water
Salt
Pepper

Garnish
Chopped parsley

Remove chicken meat from bones and cut into fine shreds. Put chicken bones, onion, carrot, celery, peppercorns and water in wok, and season with salt and pepper. Bring to the boil, reduce heat, and simmer for 30 minutes. Strain and return stock to wok. Add chicken shreds, and simmer until chicken is cooked. Add undrained asparagus pieces. Adjust seasoning. Serve sprinkled with chopped parsley.

Eggflower Soup

PREPARATION TIME: 10 minutes
COOKING TIME: 10 minutes
SERVES: 4 people

2½ cups chicken stock
2 eggs, lightly beaten
1 tbsp light soy sauce
1¼ cups canned plum tomatoes
2 green onions, chopped finely

Drain and chop tomatoes, removing seeds, and reserve juice. Bring soy sauce, tomato juice and stock to the boil in the wok. Add tomatoes and half the green onions, and cook for 2 minutes. Dribble beaten eggs in gradually, stirring continuously. Serve immediately, sprinkled with remaining green onions.

Chicken and Asparagus Soup (below) and Hot and Sour Soup (right).

Poppadums

COOKING TIME: 5 minutes

Poppadums
Oil for deep frying

Heat oil in wok. When oil is hot, deep fry 1 poppadum at a time for 2-3 seconds, holding edges apart with forks. They will puff up, and should be pale golden in color. If browning, reduce heat of oil. If not cooking quickly enough, increase heat. Remove, shaking off excess oil, and drain on paper towels. They may be eaten immediately, or when cool may be kept in an airtight container until needed.

Fried Bananas

PREPARATION TIME: 5 minutes
COOKING TIME: 10 minutes
SERVES: 4 people

3-4 bananas
1 tbsp lemon juice
2 tbsps oil
Salt

Peel bananas and slice diagonally. Heat wok and add oil. When hot, add bananas. Fry, turning carefully until browned well all over. Sprinkle with lemon juice and a pinch of salt, and serve as an accompaniment to a curry.

Shrimp Crisps/Crackers (Krupuk)

COOKING TIME: 5 minutes

Shrimp Crisps
Oil for deep frying

Heat oil in wok, and make sure the oil is hot, but not too hot. It should be hot enough to puff the shrimp crisps in 2-3 seconds: if they brown, the oil is too hot. If it is not hot enough, they will take too long to cook, and will be tough and chewy. A few can be fried together, but do not put too many in as they need to be removed quickly before overcooking. Use a slotted spoon to remove, and drain on paper towels. If necessary, store in an airtight container until needed.

Chicken Liver Pâté

PREPARATION TIME: 20 minutes
COOKING TIME: 20 minutes
SERVES: 4 people as a starter

8oz chicken livers, trimmed
1 cup butter
1 medium onion, peeled and chopped finely
1 bay leaf
1 clove garlic, crushed
1 tbsp brandy
1 tsp Worcestershire sauce
Salt
Pepper

Garnish
Sprig of parsley

Heat wok and add half of the butter. Add onion, garlic and bay leaf, and fry gently until onion is soft but not colored. Increase heat, and add chicken livers and salt and freshly-ground black pepper to taste, and fry for 5 minutes, turning regularly. Add Worcestershire sauce and stir well. Remove from heat, and set aside to cool. Meanwhile, cream remaining butter. Remove bay leaf and chop liver finely – this can be done in a blender. Push through a strainer; beat in creamed butter and stir in brandy. Fill into individual ramekin dishes or into a china dish. If keeping, smooth over surface and cover with clarified butter. Garnish with a sprig of parsley.

Cheese Nibbles

PREPARATION TIME: 20 minutes
COOKING TIME: 20 minutes
MAKES: 40 pieces

½ cup Gruyère cheese
½ cup Emmenthal cheese
1 egg, lightly beaten
2 tbsps milk
1 tsp dry mustard
1 clove garlic, crushed

This page: Shrimp Crisps/ Crackers (top left), Fried Bananas (center right) and Poppadums (bottom).

Facing page: Chicken Liver Pâté (top) and Cheese Nibbles (bottom).

2 tbsps flour
1 tsp baking powder
Salt
Pepper
10 slices stale whole-wheat bread
Oil for deep frying

Sift together flour, baking powder, mustard, and a pinch of salt and pepper. Grate cheese. Mix together cheese, egg, milk, garlic and flour mixture. Beat together well. Trim off bread-crusts, and cut each slice diagonally into 4 triangles. Spread one heaped teaspoon of mixture on each triangle of bread to cover well. Heat oil in wok. When hot, carefully fry in batches with bread side up first. Deep fry until golden brown on both sides. Remove and drain on paper towels. Keep hot until all frying is completed. Serve hot.

Seafood Hot and Sour Soup

PREPARATION TIME: 20 minutes
COOKING TIME: 20 minutes
SERVES: 4 people

2 dried Chinese mushrooms
1 cake fresh beancurd, diced
4oz shrimp, shelled and de-veined
2½ cups light stock, preferably fish stock
½ cup crab meat, or 2 crab-sticks, cut into ½" slices
1 tbsp oyster sauce
1 tbsp light soy sauce
1 tbsp lemon juice
½ tsp lemon rind, cut into slivers
1 tbsp vegetable oil
1 red chili pepper, seeds removed, and finely sliced
2 green onions, sliced
Salt
Pepper
1 tsp sesame oil

Garnish
Fresh coriander, if desired

Soak mushrooms in hot water and set aside for 20 minutes. Heat wok, add vegetable oil and, when hot, stir-fry shrimp, chili pepper, lemon rind and green onions. Add stock, oyster sauce and light soy sauce, and bring to the boil. Reduce heat and simmer for 5 minutes. Add salt and pepper to taste. Remove hard stalks from mushrooms and slice caps finely. Add crab meat, beancurd and Chinese mushrooms to wok, and cook a further 5 minutes. Stir in lemon juice and sesame oil. Adjust seasoning, and serve sprinkled with fresh coriander leaves if desired.

Spring Rolls (Egg Rolls)

PREPARATION TIME: 20 minutes
COOKING TIME: 30 minutes
MAKES: 12 rolls

8oz finely ground pork
1 red chili pepper, seeds removed, and sliced finely
10 canned water chestnuts, chopped
1 onion, peeled and chopped finely
1 clove garlic, crushed
½ tsp grated ginger root
1 tsp ground turmeric
2 tbsps peanut oil
12 spring roll (egg roll) wrappers
Salt
Pepper
Peanut or vegetable oil for deep frying

Heat wok, add 2 tbsps of peanut oil, and fry garlic, ginger, ground

Facing page: Seafood Hot and Sour Soup (top) and Corn and Chicken Soup (bottom).

This page: Shrimp Toast (top) and Spring Rolls (Egg Rolls) (right).

turmeric and onion for 3 minutes. Add pork, and stir-fry until pork is browning. Add water chestnuts and chili pepper, and salt and pepper to taste, and fry for a further 2 minutes. Remove from wok, and set aside to cool. Place spring roll wrapper with one corner pointing towards you. Spoon some of the mixture just in front of the center. Fold over the corner nearest to you, and roll to center. Fold the two side points into the center and finish rolling up. They may be sealed with a paste of water and flour if necessary. Refrigerate until needed. Heat oil for deep frying in wok, and deep fry spring rolls in batches just before needed. Drain on paper towels, and serve warm with chilli or sweet-and-sour sauce.

Shrimp Toast

PREPARATION TIME: 15 minutes
COOKING TIME: 15 minutes
MAKES: approximately 20 pieces

8oz shrimp, shelled and de-veined, and chopped finely
1 small egg, beaten
2 tsps sherry
2 tsps oyster sauce
½ tsp grated ginger root
2 tsp cornstarch
Salt
5 slices white bread
Oil for deep frying

Combine shrimp, beaten egg, sherry, oyster sauce, grated ginger, cornstarch and a pinch of salt. Using a 1½" round pastry cutter, cut out circles of bread. Spread mixture on each piece of bread to cover well. Heat oil in wok for deep frying. Fry in batches with bread side up first, until bread is golden brown. Remove and drain on paper towels. Keep hot until all frying is completed.

Corn and Chicken Soup

PREPARATION TIME: 15 minutes
COOKING TIME: 45 minutes
SERVES: 4 people

1 chicken, with giblets
1 8oz can cream style corn
1 onion, peeled and chopped roughly
1 carrot, scraped and chopped roughly

1 stick celery, chopped
6 peppercorns
Parsley stalks
1 bay leaf
5 cups water
Salt
Pepper

Garnish
Chopped parsley or chives

Clean chicken, and cut into quarters. Put into wok with giblets, chopped vegetables, peppercorns, bay leaf, parsley stalks, seasoning and water. Bring to the boil. Reduce heat and simmer for 30 minutes. Strain and return stock to wok. Remove meat from chicken and cut into fine shreds. Add undrained corn to stock, and bring to boil. Simmer for 5 minutes. Add chicken and cook for 1 minute. Sprinkle with chopped parsley or chives. Serve hot.

Rice Paper Shrimp Parcels

PREPARATION TIME: 15 minutes
COOKING TIME: 15 minutes
MAKES: about 20 parcels

8oz shrimp, shelled and de-veined
6 green onions, sliced finely
1 packet rice paper
1 egg white
½ tsp cornstarch
⅔ cup peanut oil
1 tsp Chinese wine, or 2 tsps dry sherry
1 tsp light soy sauce
1 tsp sugar
Salt
Pepper

Dry prepared shrimp on paper towels. Mix egg white, cornstarch, wine, sugar, soy sauce, green onions and seasoning together. Mix in shrimp. Heat peanut oil in wok until hot. Wrap five or six shrimp in each piece of rice paper. Gently drop in rice paper parcels and deep fry for about 5 minutes. Serve hot.

Crab Rolls

PREPARATION TIME: 20 minutes
COOKING TIME: 20 minutes
MAKES: 12 rolls

1 cup crab meat, fresh or canned
3 green onions, finely sliced
12 spring roll (egg roll) wrappers
1oz cellophane noodles
¼ tsp grated ginger root
1 tsp oyster sauce
2 tbsps finely chopped bamboo shoots
Salt
Vegetable or peanut oil for deep frying

Soak cellophane noodles in hot water for 8 minutes, or as directed, and drain. Flake crab meat, and drain if necessary. Combine crab meat with green onions, noodles, ginger, bamboo shoots, oyster sauce, and salt to taste. Place spring roll wrappers with one corner pointing towards you. Spoon some of the mixture just before the center. Fold over the corner nearest you and roll to center. Fold the two side points into the center, and roll up completely. They may be sealed with a paste of flour and water if necessary. Refrigerate until needed. Heat oil in wok and deep fry batches of spring rolls just before serving. Drain on paper towels. Serve warm with ginger sauce or sweet-and-sour sauce.

This page: Crab Rolls (top) and Rice Paper Shrimp Parcels (bottom).

Facing page: Ginger Scallops in Oyster Sauce (top) and Crispy Fish with Chili (bottom).

Wok Seafood Recipes

Crispy Fish with Chili

PREPARATION TIME: 40 minutes
COOKING TIME: 30 minutes
SERVES: 4 people

1lb fish fillets, skinned, bones removed, and cut into 1" cubes

Batter
4 tbsps flour
1 egg, separated
1 tbsp oil
5 tbsps milk
Salt

Sauce
1 tsp grated ginger root
¼ tsp chili powder
2 tbsps tomato paste
2 tbsps tomato relish
2 tbsps dark soy sauce
2 tbsps Chinese wine or dry sherry
2 tbsps water
1 tsp sugar
1 red chili pepper, seeds removed, and sliced finely
1 clove garlic, crushed
Salt
Pepper
Oil for deep frying

Sift the flour with a pinch of salt. Make a well in the center, and drop in the egg yolk and oil. Mix to a smooth batter with the milk, gradually incorporating the flour. Beat well. Cover and set aside in a cool place for 30 minutes. Whisk egg white until stiff, and fold into batter just before using. Heat oil in wok. Dip fish pieces into batter and coat completely. When oil is hot, carefully lower fish pieces in and cook until cooked through and golden brown – about 10 minutes. Remove with a slotted spoon. Reheat oil and refry each fish piece for 2 minutes. Remove with a slotted spoon and drain on paper towels. Carefully remove all but 1 tbsp of oil from wok. Heat oil, and add chili pepper, ginger, garlic, chili powder, tomato paste, tomato relish, soy sauce, sugar, wine and water, and salt and pepper to taste. Stir well over heat for 3 minutes. Increase heat and toss in fish pieces. Coat with sauce and, when heated through, serve immediately.

Squid with Broccoli and Cauliflower

PREPARATION TIME: 15 minutes

COOKING TIME: 20 minutes

SERVES: 4 people

1lb squid, cleaned
1 onion, peeled and chopped roughly
8oz fresh broccoli flowerets
8oz fresh cauliflower flowerets
2 sticks celery, sliced diagonally
½ tsp grated ginger root
1 tbsp cornstarch
2 tbsps water
2 tbsps light soy sauce
2 tbsps Chinese wine, or dry sherry
2 tbsps oyster sauce
½ tsp sesame oil
½ tsp sugar
⅔ cup oil, for deep frying
Salt
Pepper

Cut cleaned squid lengthwise down center. Flatten out with inside uppermost. With a sharp knife make a lattice design, cutting deep into squid flesh (to tenderize and make squid curl when cooking). Heat oil in wok. Add squid and cook until it curls. Remove from pan and drain on paper towels. Carefully pour off all but 1 tbsp of oil. Add onion, celery, broccoli, cauliflower and ginger, and stir-fry for 3 minutes. Slake cornstarch with water, and add soy sauce, wine, oyster sauce, sesame oil, sugar, and salt and pepper to taste. Mix well and add to wok. Bring to the boil and simmer for 3 minutes, stirring continuously. Return squid and cook until heated through. Place in a warm serving dish and serve hot with rice.

Ginger Scallops in Oyster Sauce

PREPARATION TIME: 10 minutes

COOKING TIME: 15 minutes

SERVES: 4 people

1lb scallops, cleaned, dried on absorbent paper, and sliced
10 green onions, sliced diagonally into 1" slices
1" green ginger, peeled and sliced very thinly
Salt
2 tbsps vegetable oil

Sauce

1 tbsp oyster sauce
1 tbsp light soy sauce
½ tsp sesame oil
1 tsp grated root ginger
1 tsp cornstarch
5 tbsps light stock, or 5 tbsps hot water and half a chicken bouillon cube
Pinch of sugar

Combine oyster sauce, soy sauce, sesame oil, cornstarch, sugar and grated ginger and set aside. Sprinkle the scallops with a pinch of salt. Heat wok, and add oil. Add sliced ginger and green onions, and stir-fry gently for 1 minute. Raise heat to high. Add scallops and stir-fry for 1 minute. Add sauce mixture and stir in. Remove from heat, and stir in stock gradually. Return to heat and bring to the boil, stirring continuously. Simmer gently for 3 minutes, until sauce is slightly thickened. Adjust seasoning. Serve immediately with boiled rice.

Steamed Fish with Black Beans

PREPARATION TIME: 15 minutes

COOKING TIME: 15 minutes

SERVES: 4 people

2lbs whole snapper, or bass, cleaned and scaled
1 tbsp salted black beans
2 cloves garlic, crushed
1 tbsp light soy sauce
1 tsp Chinese wine, or 2 tsps dry sherry
1 tsp sugar
½ tsp cornstarch
1 tsp sesame oil
½ can bamboo shoots, cut into shreds
Salt
Pepper

Facing page: Squid with Broccoli and Cauliflower.

This page: Singapore Fried Noodles (below) and Steamed Fish with Black Beans (bottom).

Wash and clean fish well and dry with paper towels. Make 3 or 4 diagonal cuts in flesh of fish on each side. Rub garlic into cuts and place fish on a heat-proof dish. Rinse black beans in cold water, then crush with the back of a spoon. Add cornstarch, sesame oil, soy sauce, sugar and wine, and salt and pepper and mix together well. Pour over fish. Sprinkle bamboo shoots on top of fish. Put plate on top of a bamboo steamer or metal trivet standing in wok. Add water, ensuring the level is below the level of the plate. Cover and bring to the boil. Steam for about 10 minutes after boiling point is reached. Ensure that the fish is cooked, but do not oversteam. Serve hot.

Stir-Fried Shrimp and Pea Pods

PREPARATION TIME: 5 minutes

COOKING TIME: 5 minutes

SERVES: 4 people

8oz shrimp, shelled and de-veined
4oz pea pods, trimmed
4 tbsps peanut oil
2 tbsps dry white wine
Juice of half a lemon
1 tbsp light soy sauce
Pinch of salt
Black pepper

Garnish
Parsley

Blanch pea pods in boiling salted water for 1 minute. Drain and set aside. Heat wok, add the peanut oil, and stir-fry shrimp for 30 seconds. Add pea pods, dry white wine, lemon juice, soy sauce, and salt and pepper, and toss together until heated through. Adjust seasoning and garnish with parsley. Serve immediately with boiled rice.

Seafood Combination

PREPARATION TIME: 20 minutes

COOKING TIME: 20 minutes

SERVES: 4 people

8oz shrimp, shelled and de-veined
4oz squid, cleaned, cut into 1" rings, opened up, and scored with lattice design
4oz pea pods, trimmed
4oz white fish fillets, cut into 1" cubes
1 stick celery, sliced diagonally
1 carrot, scraped and cut into matchstick strips
1 tsp grated ginger root
½ tsp salt
1 tbsp dry white wine
1 egg white
1 tsp cornstarch
Oil for deep frying

Combine wine, salt, egg white, grated ginger and cornstarch and mix well. Add shrimp and fish, and toss well. Drain shrimp and fish, reserving sauce. Blanch pea pods in boiling water for 1 minute. Drain. Heat oil in wok. Deep fry shrimp, fish and squid for 2 minutes. Remove from pan and drain on

This page: Seafood Combination.

Facing page: Mediterranean Fish Stew (top) and Stir-Fried Shrimp and Pea Pods (bottom).

paper towels. Carefully remove oil from wok, reserving 1 tbsp of oil in wok. Heat oil. Stir-fry carrot and celery for 3 minutes. Add pea pods and stir-fry a further 3 minutes. Add any remaining sauce and stir. Add seafood and toss well until heated through.

Honey Sesame Shrimp

PREPARATION TIME: 20 minutes

COOKING TIME: 20 minutes

SERVES: 4 people

1lb shrimp, shelled and de-veined
2 tbsps cornstarch
¾ cup flour
½ tsp baking powder
1 egg, lightly beaten
Pinch of salt
Pepper
⅔ cup water
Oil for deep frying
2 tbsps honey
1 tbsp sesame seeds
1 tbsp sesame oil

Sift flour, baking powder and salt and pepper into a bowl. Make a well in the center and add egg and water, gradually bringing in the flour. Beat to a smooth batter and set aside for 10 minutes. Meanwhile, toss shrimp in cornstarch and coat well. Shake off any excess cornstarch. Add shrimp to batter and coat well. Heat oil in wok, and add shrimp, a few at a time. Cook until batter is golden. Remove and drain on paper towels, and keep warm. Repeat until all shrimp have been fried. Carefully remove hot oil from wok. Gently heat sesame oil in pan. Add honey and stir until mixed well and heated through. Add shrimp to mixture and toss well. Sprinkle over sesame seeds and again toss well. Serve immediately.

Steamed Fish in Ginger

PREPARATION TIME: 20 minutes

COOKING TIME: 15 minutes

SERVES: 4 people

3lbs whole snapper, bass or bream, cleaned and scaled

Stuffing
½ cup cooked rice
1 tsp grated root ginger
3 green onions, sliced finely
2 tsps light soy sauce
6 green onions, cut into 2" lengths, then into fine shreds
3 pieces green ginger, cut into fine shreds

Garnish
Lemon slices and parsley, if desired

Mix together rice, grated ginger, sliced green onion and soy sauce. Stuff rice mixture into cleaned fish cavity, packing in well. Place fish on a heat-proof plate, and arrange strips of green onion and green ginger on top of fish. Put the plate on top of a bamboo steamer or metal trivet standing in wok. Add water, ensuring the water level is not up to the plate. Cover and bring to the boil. Steam for 10 minutes from boiling point. Ensure that the fish is cooked, but be sure not to oversteam the fish. Serve hot, garnished with lemon slices and parsley, if desired.

Singapore Fried Noodles

PREPARATION TIME: 20 minutes

COOKING TIME: 25 minutes

SERVES: 4 people

8oz packet egg noodles
8oz shrimp, shelled and de-veined
1 chicken breast, cut into shreds
1½ cups bean sprouts
2 cloves garlic, crushed
3 sticks celery, sliced diagonally
2 green onions, sliced
1 red chili pepper, seeds removed, and sliced
1 green chili pepper, seeds removed, and sliced
1 tsp chili powder
2 eggs, lightly beaten
3 tbsps oil
Salt
Pepper

Garnish
Chili flowers (carefully cut end of chili pepper into shreds, and soak in cold water until flower opens)

Soak noodles in boiling water for 8 minutes, or as directed. Drain noodles on paper towels and leave to dry. Heat wok, and add 1 tbsp of oil. Add lightly beaten eggs, and salt and pepper to taste. Stir gently and cook until set. Remove from wok, and cut into thin strips and keep warm. Add remaining oil to wok. When hot, add garlic and chili powder and fry for 30 seconds. Add chicken, celery, green onions and red and green chili peppers, and stir-fry for 8 minutes or until chicken has cooked through. Add noodles, shrimp and bean sprouts, and toss until well mixed and heated through. Serve with scrambled egg strips on top and garnish with chili flowers.

Mediterranean Fish Stew

PREPARATION TIME: 20 minutes

COOKING TIME: 30 minutes

SERVES: 4 people

1lb white fish fillets, cut into 2" cubes
2 tbsps olive oil
2 cloves garlic, crushed
1 onion, peeled and sliced finely
2 sticks celery, sliced
1 tbsp chopped parsley
1 tsp oregano
2 tbsps tomato paste
⅔ cup fish stock or water
2 tbsps sweet Italian vermouth, or sweet sherry
4oz squid (optional), cleaned
2 leeks, white parts sliced finely
1¾ cups canned plum tomatoes
½ cup flat mushrooms, sliced
Salt
Pepper

Garnish
Lemon slices
Parsley

Heat wok, and add oil. Add garlic, onion, celery, leeks, oregano, parsley and squid. Cover and cook gently for 10 minutes, stirring once or twice. Add tomato paste, stock or water, wine, undrained tomatoes, mushrooms, fish, and salt and pepper to taste. Bring to the boil, then cover and simmer gently for 15 minutes. Ensure fish is cooked through (it will be opaque all the way through, and will flake easily). Garnish with lemon slices and parsley. Serve immediately.

Honey Sesame Shrimp (top) and Steamed Fish in Ginger (right).

Wok Meat Dishes

Pork with Black Bean Sauce

PREPARATION TIME: 40 minutes
COOKING TIME: 45 minutes
SERVES: 4 people

8oz lean pork, cut into 1" cubes
1 tbsp oil
1 red pepper, cored, seeds removed, and sliced

Sauce
3 tbsps black beans, rinsed in cold water and crushed with back of a spoon
2 tbsps Chinese wine, or dry sherry
1 tsp grated ginger
2 tbsps light soy sauce
3 cloves garlic, crushed
1 tbsp cornstarch
⅔ cup water

Mix together black beans, wine, ginger, soy sauce and garlic. Blend cornstarch with 2 tbsps of water and add to mixture. Place pork in a bowl, and pour over sauce. Toss together well. Leave for at least 30 minutes. Heat wok, add oil and stir-fry red pepper for 3 minutes. Remove and set aside. Add pork, reserving marinade sauce. Stir-fry pork until browned well all over. Add marinade sauce and remaining water. Bring to the boil. Reduce heat, cover, and gently simmer for about 30 minutes, until pork is tender, stirring occasionally. Add more water if necessary. Just before serving, add red pepper and heat through. Serve with plain white rice.

Lamb Meatballs with Yogurt

PREPARATION TIME: 15 minutes
COOKING TIME: 30 minutes
SERVES: 4 people

1lb lean ground lamb
2 cloves garlic, crushed
1 small onion, peeled and grated
½ tsp chili powder
1 tsp garam masala
1 tbsp chopped mint
2 tbsps breadcrumbs
1 egg, lightly beaten
2 tbsps oil
½ cup plain yogurt
Small pinch of saffron strands, or ¼ tsp ground turmeric
2 tbsps boiling water
Salt
Pepper

Garnish
Fresh coriander or mint

This page: Beef and Oyster Sauce.
Facing page: Lamb Meatballs with Yogurt (top) and Pork with Black Bean Sauce (bottom).

In a bowl, mix together ground lamb, garlic, onion, chili powder, garam masala, mint and breadcrumbs. Add lightly beaten egg to bind ingredients together. Add salt and pepper to taste. Wet hands. Take a teaspoon of mixture, and roll between palms, forming small balls. Heat wok and add oil. Add meatballs, shake wok to make meatballs roll around, and fry until browned well all over. Add saffron or turmeric to 2 tbsps boiling water. Leave for 5 minutes. Add water to yogurt, and stir in until evenly mixed. Reheat meatballs and serve on yogurt. Garnish with mint or fresh coriander. Serve with rice.

Beef and Oyster Sauce

PREPARATION TIME: 30 minutes
COOKING TIME: 20 minutes
SERVES: 4 people

1lb sirloin or butt steak, sliced into thin strips
1½ cups bean sprouts
½ cup button mushrooms
1 red pepper, cored, seeds removed, and chopped roughly
2 sticks celery, sliced diagonally
2 onions, peeled and quartered
2 tbsps light soy sauce
2 tbsps peanut or vegetable oil

Oyster Sauce
3 tbsps oyster sauce
1 chicken bouillon cube dissolved in 2 tbsps boiling water
1 tbsp dark soy sauce
1 tbsp Chinese wine or dry sherry
1 tbsp cornstarch
2 tbsps cold water
Salt
Pepper

Place steak in a bowl and pour over 2 tbsps light soy sauce. Toss together well and set aside for at least 30 minutes. Meanwhile, mix together oyster sauce, chicken stock, dark soy sauce and wine. Blend together cornstarch and cold water, and set aside. Heat wok, and add oil. Add onion, celery, mushrooms and red pepper, and stir-fry for 5 minutes. Remove from wok and set aside. Reheat oil and, when hot, toss in steak. Brown well all over, then add sauce and fried vegetables. Add cornstarch mixture and bring to the boil, tossing continuously. Add salt and pepper to taste. Finally, add bean sprouts and simmer gently for 3 minutes. Serve hot with noodles or rice.

Sweet and Sour Pork with Peppers

PREPARATION TIME: 1 hour 15 minutes
COOKING TIME: 30 minutes
SERVES: 4 people

1lb pork tenderloin, cut into 1" cubes
1 large green pepper, cored, seeds removed, and chopped roughly
1 large yellow or red pepper, cored, seeds removed, and chopped roughly
1 small can or jar of Chinese mixed pickle
1 large onion, peeled and chopped finely
1¼ cups peanut oil

Batter
1 egg
1 tsp peanut oil
¼ cup cornstarch
¼ cup flour
¼ tsp baking powder
Water

Marinade
1 tbsp peanut oil
½ tsp light soy sauce
2 tsps Chinese wine, or 1 tbsp dry sherry
1 tsp cornstarch
1 tsp sugar
Pinch of salt
Pinch of pepper

Sauce
¼ cup sugar
⅓ cup wine vinegar
⅓ cup water
1 tbsp tomato paste
Pinch of salt
1 tsp cornstarch
Few drops of red food coloring (if desired)

Mix together marinade ingredients. Pour over pork pieces and leave for about 1 hour, turning occasionally. Mix together batter ingredients, with enough water to form batter. Add pork. Heat peanut oil in wok. When hot, deep-fry pork pieces in small batches, so that they do not stick together. Remove when golden brown, using a slotted spoon, and set aside. Continue until all battered pork pieces are cooked. Heat oil again and repeat process, cooking pork for 5 minutes to make batter nice and crisp. Keep warm. Carefully drain off all but 1 tbsp of oil. Heat, and add onion, peppers and Chinese mixed pickle. Cover and cook for 3 minutes. Remove and set aside. Heat vinegar, water, sugar, tomato paste, red food coloring and salt. Slake cornstarch with 1 tbsp of water. Stir into sauce. Bring to the boil and cook for 3 minutes. Add pork and vegetables to sauce. Serve hot with rice.

Beef Worcestershire

PREPARATION TIME: 40 minutes
COOKING TIME: 20 minutes
SERVES: 4 people

1lb sirloin or butt steak, cut into 1½" cubes
2oz wonton wrappers
⅔ cup oil for deep frying

Sauce
2 tbsps Worcestershire sauce
1 tbsp dark soy sauce
1 tbsp sugar
Pinch of salt
Pinch of pepper
½ tsp cornstarch

Mix together ingredients for sauce, and pour over steak. Toss well. Leave for at least 30 minutes, turning occasionally. Meanwhile, heat oil in wok. Fold wonton wrappers in half diagonally and sea open corners with water and press

Beef Worcestershire (top right) and Sweet and Sour Pork with Peppers (right).

together. Deep fry a few wonton wrappers at a time until golden brown. Remove with a slotted spoon and drain on paper towels. Repeat until there are enough wonton wrappers to go around the edge of the serving dish. Carefully remove all but 2 tbsps of oil from wok. Remove steak from sauce mixture and reserve. Heat wok, and when oil is hot, add steak and stir-fry until well browned. Pour over sauce and bring to the boil. Reduce heat and simmer, stirring continuously. When sauce thickens, and will coat steak well, place in warm serving dish and garnish with wonton wrappers. Serve immediately with boiled rice.

Pork with Plum Sauce

PREPARATION TIME: 40 minutes

COOKING TIME: 30 minutes

SERVES: 4 people

1lb pork tenderloin, cut into 1" cubes
1 tbsp cornstarch
1 tsp sesame oil

This page: Beef with Mango.

Facing page: Pork with Plum Sauce (top) and Stir-Fried Leeks and Lamb (bottom).

1 tbsp light soy sauce
1 tbsp sherry
1 tbsp brown sugar
½ tsp cinnamon
1 clove garlic, crushed
1 green onion, sliced finely
2 tbsps peanut oil
4 tbsps bottled plum sauce
¼ cup water
Salt
Pepper

Garnish
Green onion flowers

Mix together cornstarch, sesame oil, light soy sauce, sherry, brown sugar, cinnamon and salt. Pour over pork, and toss together. Leave for at least 30 minutes. Remove pork and reserve marinade. Heat wok and add peanut oil. Add pork, and stir-fry until golden brown all over. Add green onion, plum sauce and water to wok, and mix together well. Bring to boil, cover, and simmer gently for 15 minutes, or until pork is tender, stirring occasionally. Add marinade, and bring to boil. Simmer gently for a further 5 minutes. Garnish with green onion flowers. (To make these, cut green onion into 2" lengths. Carefully cut lengths into fine shreds, keeping one end intact, and then soak in cold water until curling.) Serve hot with boiled rice.

Guy's Curry (Hot)

PREPARATION TIME: 40 minutes

COOKING TIME: 2 hours 15 minutes

SERVES: 4 people

2lbs steak, skirt or rump, cut into ½" cubes
1½ cups coconut cream
1 onion, peeled and finely chopped
3 cloves garlic, chopped
2 tbsps golden raisins
1 tbsp curry leaves
1 dsp cumin
1 dsp coriander
1 tbsp vindaloo curry paste or powder (or milder if a curry less hot than vindaloo is desired)
1 carrot, grated
2 apples, chopped finely
1 banana, sliced finely
2 tomatoes, chopped finely
1 red pepper, cored, seeds removed, and chopped finely
6 small pieces lemon rind
2 tbsps desiccated coconut
2 tsps sugar
1 cup water
⅔ cup safflower or vegetable oil

Accompaniments
1 apple, chopped finely
1 banana, sliced
1 red pepper, cored, seeds removed, and chopped finely
1 carrot, grated
1 tomato, chopped finely
2 tbsps golden raisins
2 tbsps desiccated coconut
Half a cucumber, sliced, in 2 tbsps natural yogurt

Prepare fruit and vegetables. Heat wok, add oil and heat until warm. Add onion and garlic, and fry until golden brown. Remove garlic, and discard. Add steak and stir-fry until well browned all over. Add sultanas and stir in well. Add curry leaves, stir in, and cook for 5 minutes. Add cumin and coriander and stir. Cook a further 5 minutes. Add curry powder or paste and cook for 10 minutes. Add grated carrot, red pepper, apples, tomatoes, lemon rind and banana and mix in well. Add water. Cover and cook for 30 minutes. Stir in desiccated coconut and cook for a further 30 minutes. Add sugar and cook for another 20 minutes. Add more water as necessary. Add coconut cream and cook a further 20 minutes. Serve hot with boiled rice and accompaniments.

Stir-Fried Leeks and Lamb

PREPARATION TIME: 10 minutes

COOKING TIME: 30 minutes

SERVES: 4 people

1lb lamb, cut into 1" cubes
1lb leeks, cut into 1" slices
1 tsp rosemary
1 tsp redcurrant jelly
1 tbsp chopped mint
1 tsp basil
1 16oz can plum tomatoes
1 tbsp oil
Salt
Pepper

Garnish
Fresh mint

Heat wok, and add oil. Add rosemary, basil and leeks, and stir-fry gently for 3 minutes. Remove from wok, and increase heat. Add lamb and stir-fry until well-browned all over. Return leeks to wok. Add undrained tomatoes, redcurrant jelly, mint, and salt and pepper to taste. Cover and simmer for 20 minutes, adding water if necessary. Serve hot, garnished with fresh mint.

Right: Guy's Curry (Hot).

Devilled Kidneys

PREPARATION TIME: 1 hour 15 minutes

COOKING TIME: 20 minutes

SERVES: 4 people

1lb veal kidneys
1 tbsp Worcestershire sauce
1 tbsp dark soy sauce
2 tbsps butter
1 tsp cornstarch
1 tbsp water

Devilling Mixture
1 tsp salt
1 tsp sugar
½ tsp ground black pepper
½ tsp ground ginger
½ tsp dry mustard
¼ tsp curry powder

Garnish
Sprig of parsley

Skin the kidneys and cut in half lengthwise. Mix the dry devilling mixture together, and coat kidneys well. Leave for at least 1 hour. Heat wok and melt butter. Brown the kidneys quickly in the hot butter. Add Worcestershire sauce and soy sauce, and bring to the boil. Cover and simmer for 15 minutes thickening with cornstarch mixed with water if necessary. Garnish with parsley and serve with saffron rice.

Calves' Liver with Piquant Sauce

PREPARATION TIME: 10 minutes

COOKING TIME: 25 minutes

SERVES: 4 people

1lb calves' liver
1 onion, peeled and sliced
1 tbsp oil
2 tbsps butter
1 tbsp flour
1¼ cups brown stock, or 1¼ cups hot water and 1 beef bouillon cube
2 tbsps tomato, mango, or other fruit relish
1 tbsp tomato paste
1 clove garlic, crushed
1 tsp dry mustard, mixed with 2 tsps water
Salt
Pepper

Garnish
Chopped parsley

Heat wok and add butter. When melted, stir in flour and cook until lightly browned. Remove from heat and gradually stir in stock. Return to heat and add tomato paste and garlic. Stir until boiling. Add mustard and salt and pepper to taste, and let simmer for 5 minutes. Add relish and mix well. Remove from wok and set aside. Meanwhile, slice liver very thinly. Wash and drain on paper towels. Heat wok and add oil. When hot add onion. Fry gently over medium heat until just turning color. Add slices of liver in a single layer, and fry for about 3 minutes on each side, depending on thickness of slices. The liver should be cooked through and still tender. Do not overcook. Add piquant sauce to wok and toss together. Sprinkle with chopped parsley. Serve immediately on boiled rice.

This page: Devilled Kidneys (top) and Calves' Liver with Piquant Sauce (bottom).

Facing page: Sweet and Sour Pork and Pineapple.

Steak with Black Bean Sauce

PREPARATION TIME: 1 hour 15 minutes

COOKING TIME: 20 minutes

SERVES: 4 people

8oz sirloin or butt steak, thinly sliced
1 large onion, peeled and chopped
1 large green pepper, cored, seeds removed, and diced
3 cloves garlic, crushed
1 tsp grated ginger root
1 small can sliced bamboo shoots, drained
3 tsps black beans
2 tbsps light soy sauce
4 tbsps peanut oil
1 tsp Chinese wine, or 2 tsps dry sherry
3 tsps sugar
1 tsp cornstarch
1 tsp sesame oil
Pinch of baking soda
Salt
Pepper

Put sliced steak into a bowl, and sprinkle over baking soda. Add 1 tbsp of light soy sauce, 1 tsp of sugar, wine, sesame oil, salt and pepper, and leave to marinate for at least 1 hour. Heat wok and add 2 tbsps peanut oil. When hot, add steak and fry quickly. Remove from heat, and remove steak. Set aside. Add onion, green pepper, bamboo shoots, and a pinch of salt to wok. Cover and cook for 3 minutes. Remove and set aside. Make black bean sauce by crushing black beans and mixing with garlic, ginger, 1 tsp of sugar and 1 tbsp of peanut oil. Heat wok, add 1 tbsp of oil and pour in black bean mixture. Add steak and vegetables and mix well. Make seasoning sauce by mixing cornstarch with remaining 1 tbsp of light soy sauce, and adding 1 tsp of sugar. When well mixed, pour into wok and stir. Bring to the boil and cook for 3 minutes. Serve hot with rice.

Braised Pork with Spinach and Mushrooms

PREPARATION TIME: 20 minutes

COOKING TIME: 30 minutes

SERVES: 4 people

1lb pork tenderloin, cut into thin strips
8oz spinach leaves, washed, hard stalks removed, and shredded
4 dried Chinese mushrooms, soaked in hot water for 20 minutes, stems discarded, and caps sliced finely
½ tsp ground nutmeg
2 tbsps water
2 tbsps peanut oil
1 onion, peeled and quartered
1 clove garlic, crushed
1 tbsp flour
Salt
Pepper

Heat wok, add 1 tsp of oil, and roll it around to coat the surface. Put nutmeg and spinach in wok, and cook gently for 5 minutes. Remove from pan. Add remaining oil to wok and fry garlic and onion over gentle heat for 5 minutes. Remove from wok. Meanwhile, add a good pinch of salt and freshly-ground black pepper to the flour and toss in the pork, coating well. Fry pork until each piece is browned all over. Add water and mushrooms, and return onion mixture to wok. Cover and simmer gently for 10 minutes, stirring occasionally. Add spinach and salt and pepper to taste, and cook, uncovered, for 2 minutes. Serve hot with steamed rice.

This page: Braised Pork with Spinach and Mushrooms (top) and Steak with Black Bean Sauce (bottom).

Facing page: Steak Chinese Style (top) and Lamb Curry (Mild) (bottom).

Happys' Curry

PREPARATION TIME: 20 minutes

COOKING TIME: 30 minutes

SERVES: 4 people

1lb skirt or butt steak, cut into 1" cubes
8oz potatoes, peeled and diced
2 onions, peeled and chopped very finely
3 cloves garlic, crushed
1 tsp grated ginger root
1 tsp ground turmeric
½ tsp chili powder
1 tsp garam masala
½ tsp salt
1¼ cups water
¼ cup peanut oil

Garnish
Fresh coriander

Heat wok and add oil. Add ginger, garlic and onion, and fry gently for 5 minutes. Add turmeric, chili powder, garam masala and salt, and fry for 30 seconds. Add steak, and stir-fry until browned well all over. Add potatoes and water, and bring to the boil. Reduce heat, and cover. Simmer gently until meat is tender and potatoes are cooked. Garnish with fresh coriander and serve with rice if desired.

Pork with Chili

PREPARATION TIME: 1 hour

COOKING TIME: 20 minutes

SERVES: 4 people

10oz pork tenderloin, cut into 1" cubes
1 green pepper, cored, seeds removed, and sliced
1 red chili pepper, seeds removed, and sliced finely
4 green onions, chopped
1 clove garlic, crushed
1 tsp sugar
1 tsp cornstarch
1 tsp peanut oil
1 tsp Chinese wine, or dry sherry
⅔ cup peanut oil, for deep frying

Sauce
1 tsp chili powder
2 tbsps dark soy sauce
1 tsp Worcestershire sauce
½ tsp five-spice powder
Pinch of salt

Mix together garlic, sugar, 1 tsp peanut oil, wine and cornstarch, and pour over pork. Cover and leave for at least 1 hour, turning occasionally. Meanwhile, combine ingredients for sauce in a bowl. Mix well. Set aside. Heat oil in wok until hot. Toss in pork cubes, and cook until golden brown and cooked through – about 10 minutes. Drain and set aside. Carefully remove all but 1 tbsp of oil from wok. Heat oil and add green pepper, chili pepper and green onions. Stir-fry for 2 minutes. Add sauce and pork, and bring to boil, stirring continuously. Adjust seasoning. Serve immediately with rice or noodles.

Beef with Mango

PREPARATION TIME: 20 minutes

COOKING TIME: 15 minutes

SERVES: 4 people

1lb sirloin or butt steak, sliced thinly
1 can mangoes, drained, reserving ¼ cup mango juice
1 tsp sugar
½ tsp salt
1 tsp cornstarch
Pinch of pepper
2 tbsps mango chutney
1 tbsp plum sauce
1 tbsp oil

Combine 2 tbsps mango juice, sugar, cornstarch, salt and pepper, and pour over steak. Toss well and set aside for 15 minutes. Mix remaining mango juice with mango chutney and plum sauce, and set aside. Chop finely half of the mangoes and add to the sauce, retaining enough slices for decoration. Heat wok and add oil. Stir-fry steak for 5 minutes, tossing well, or until browned all over. Add mango-plum sauce and cook for a further 5 minutes. Decorate dish with reserved mango slices. Serve with rice.

Steak Chinese Style

PREPARATION TIME: 1 hour 15 minutes

COOKING TIME: 20 minutes

SERVES: 4 people

8oz sirloin or butt steak, cut into 1" pieces
1 can straw mushrooms, drained
2 green onions, sliced diagonally into ½" pieces
2 cloves garlic, crushed
1 can baby corn, drained
½ tsp crushed ginger
1 tbsp oyster sauce
1 tbsp light soy sauce
2 tbsps dark soy sauce
2 tsps sugar
1 tsp sesame oil
1 tsp Chinese wine, or 2 tsps dry sherry
1 tsp cornstarch
¼ cup water
Pinch of baking soda
3 tbsps peanut oil
Salt
Pepper

Garnish
Green onion flowers (cut green onions into 2" lengths. Carefully cut into fine shreds, keeping one end intact, and then soak in cold water until curling)

Put steak in a bowl and sprinkle over baking soda. Mix together light soy sauce, sesame oil, wine, half the sugar, half the cornstarch, and seasoning. Pour over the steak and leave for at least an hour, turning meat occasionally. Meanwhile, make sauce by mixing 2 tbsps of dark soy sauce, remaining sugar and cornstarch, and water. Mix together and set aside. Heat wok, add peanut oil and, when hot, fry steak for 4 minutes. Remove from wok and set aside. Add garlic, green onions, ginger, mushrooms, baby corn, and finally steak. Add oyster sauce, and mix well. Then add sauce mixture and bring to the boil. Cook for 3 minutes, stirring occasionally. Serve hot with rice, garnished with green onion flowers.

Sweet and Sour Pork and Pineapple

PREPARATION TIME: 20 minutes

COOKING TIME: 45 minutes

SERVES: 4 people

1lb pork tenderloin, cut into 1" cubes
1 clove garlic, crushed
1 tsp grated ginger root
2 tbsps light soy sauce
1 tbsp cornstarch
2 tbsps peanut oil
⅔ cup water
2 tbsps white wine vinegar
2 tbsps tomato paste
1 tbsp sugar
1 can pineapple chunks, drained

Garnish
Fresh coriander

Place pork in bowl. Pour over light soy sauce and toss together. Leave for 15 minutes. Make sauce. Mix together vinegar, tomato paste and sugar, and set aside. Heat wok and add oil. Remove pork from soy sauce, and add soy sauce to sauce mixture. Toss pork in cornstarch, coating well. When oil is hot, brown pork well all over. Remove

Pork with Chili (right) and Happys' Curry (below).

from pan and reduce heat. Fry garlic and ginger for 30 seconds. Add water. Bring to the boil, then return pork to wok. Reduce heat; cover and simmer for 15 minutes, stirring occasionally. Add sauce mixture and pineapple, and simmer for a further 15 minutes. Garnish with coriander. Serve hot with rice or noodles.

Lamb Curry (Mild)

PREPARATION TIME: 45 minutes
COOKING TIME: 1 hour
SERVES: 4 people

2lb leg of lamb
2 tbsps plain yogurt
1 tbsp sesame oil
2 tsps garam masala
4 cloves garlic, crushed
1 tsp grated ginger
2 tsps curry powder
½ tsp ground black pepper
2 tbsps desiccated coconut
1 onion, peeled and sliced finely
1 tsp curry leaves
3 ripe tomatoes, chopped roughly
2 tbsps golden raisins
1 potato, peeled and chopped into ½" cubes
1 tsp sambal oelek
3 cups lamb stock
1 tbsp peanut oil
Salt
Pepper

Garnish
1 tbsp desiccated coconut

Cut lamb into 1" cubes. Put bones in pan, cover with water, and bring to the boil. Simmer for 10 minutes. Strain and discard bones. Mix together yogurt, sesame oil, garam masala, garlic, ginger, curry powder, pepper and sambal oelek. Add lamb and toss well. Leave to marinate for 30 minutes. Heat wok, and add peanut oil. Fry onion and curry leaves. When softened, increase heat and add lamb and marinade. Brown lamb well. Add lamb stock, potato, tomatoes, desiccated coconut, raisins, and salt and pepper to taste. Bring to the boil. Reduce heat and cover, and cook gently for 20 minutes. Ensure potato is covered with liquid (add water if necessary). Remove cover, and cook for a further 15 minutes. Serve hot, sprinkled with desiccated coconut. Serve with boiled rice and poppadums.

Pork Chow Mein

PREPARATION TIME: 20 minutes
COOKING TIME: 20 minutes
SERVES: 4 people

10oz egg noodles
1lb pork, sliced thinly
1 tbsp Chinese wine, or dry sherry
1 tsp grated root ginger
1 leek, sliced
1 red pepper, cored, seeds removed, and cut into strips
1 stick celery, sliced diagonally
2 tbsps peas
⅔ cup chicken or light stock
1 tbsp light soy sauce
1 tsp sugar
1 tsp cornstarch
1 tbsp water
1 small can bamboo shoots, sliced
3 tbsps oil
Salt
Pepper

Soak noodles in hot water for 8 minutes, or as directed. Rinse in cold water, and drain. Combine wine, soy sauce and sugar, and pour over pork. Toss together and set aside for at least 15 minutes. Heat wok and add oil. Add ginger, celery and leek, and stir-fry for 2 minutes. Add red pepper and bamboo shoots, and stir-fry for a further 2 minutes. Remove from wok. Increase heat, and add pork, reserving marinade. Stir-fry over high heat for 4 minutes. Return vegetables to wok. Add chicken stock gradually and stir well. Add peas and cook for 2 minutes. Blend cornstarch with water. Mix into marinade sauce and stir well. Add noodles and sauce to wok and toss together, heating through as sauce thickens. Add salt and pepper to taste. Simmer for 3 minutes. Serve hot.

Pork Chow Mein (right).

Steak with Peanut Sauce

PREPARATION TIME: 45 minutes

COOKING TIME: 30 minutes

SERVES: 4 people

1lb sirloin or butt steak, cut into ½" cubes
1 tbsp oil

Marinade
½ tsp chili powder
Juice of half a lemon
2 tsps brown sugar
½ tsp salt
1 tsp ground coriander
1 tsp ground cumin

Peanut Sauce
2 tbsps peanut oil
⅔ cup raw shelled peanuts
2 red chili peppers, seeds removed, and chopped (or 1 tsp chili powder)
2 shallots, chopped
1 clove garlic, crushed
1 tsp brown sugar
Juice of half a lemon
Salt

Mix together marinade ingredients, and marinate steak for at least 30 minutes. Make sauce. Heat wok, add half peanut oil and heat gently. Stir-fry peanuts for 2-3 minutes. Remove from wok, and drain on paper towels. Crush chili peppers, shallots and garlic to a smooth paste or blend. Grind peanuts to fine powder. Heat remaining oil in wok over a medium heat. Fry chili paste for 1-2 minutes. Add ⅔ cup water. Bring to the boil. Add peanuts, brown sugar, lemon juice and salt to taste. Stir until sauce is thick – approximately 10 minutes. Put in bowl, and keep warm. Heat wok, and add oil. Stir-fry meat until well browned all over. Serve with peanut sauce and boiled rice.

Piquant Lambs' Livers

PREPARATION TIME: 15 minutes

COOKING TIME: 20 minutes

SERVES: 4 people

1lb lambs' livers, cut into thin strips
4 tbsps butter or margarine
2 tbsps wine vinegar
1 onion, peeled and sliced finely
⅓ cup white wine
1 tbsp chopped parsley
1 tbsp flour
Salt
Pepper

Garnish
Chopped parsley

Combine flour with a good pinch of salt and freshly-ground black pepper. Toss in liver and coat well. Heat wok and add half the butter over gentle heat. Add onion and fry gently until transparent. Add vinegar and cook over high heat until vinegar has evaporated. Add remaining butter and when hot add liver. Stir-fry briskly for about 3 minutes. Add wine, parsley, and salt and pepper to taste. Bring to the boil and simmer for 5 minutes. Sprinkle with chopped parsley and serve with saffron rice.

This page: Steak with Peanut Sauce (top) and Mee Goreng (bottom).

Facing page: Kidneys with Bacon (top) and Piquant Lambs' Livers (bottom).

Kidneys with Bacon

PREPARATION TIME: 20 minutes

COOKING TIME: 25 minutes

SERVES: 4 people

1lb lambs' kidneys
1 tbsp tomato relish
8 rashers bacon, diced
1 onion, peeled and quartered
3 cloves garlic, crushed
2 tbsps oil
1 tbsp light soy sauce
1 tbsp cornstarch
3 tbsps sherry
1 tbsp chopped parsley
2 tbsps water
Salt
Pepper

Garnish
Sprig of parsley

Cut kidneys in half and remove hard core with a sharp knife or scissors. Cut a lattice design on back of kidneys. Pour over sherry, and set aside for 15 minutes. Heat wok and add oil. Add bacon, onion and garlic, and stir-fry for 5 minutes. Remove from wok. Add kidneys, reserving sherry, and fry for 3 minutes. Stir in tomato relish. Add soy sauce and water to wok, and return bacon and onion mixture. Add salt and pepper to taste. Cover and simmer gently for 10 minutes. Meanwhile, blend cornstarch with sherry marinade. Add parsley and cornstarch mixture, and stir, cooking gently until sauce thickens. Garnish with parsley. Serve hot with rice.

Lamb with Cherries

PREPARATION TIME: 15 minutes

COOKING TIME: 1 hour 15 minutes

SERVES: 4 people

1lb boneless lamb from leg, cut into 1" cubes
2 tbsps butter or margarine
1 onion, peeled and chopped finely
½ tsp turmeric
½ tsp cinnamon
½ tsp ground nutmeg
1 tsp brown sugar
1 can black cherries, stoned
1 tbsp lemon juice
1 tbsp arrowroot or cornstarch
⅔ cup water
Salt
Pepper

Heat half butter in wok. Add lamb and fry quickly to brown well all over. Remove from wok and set aside. Add remaining butter and onion and fry for 2 minutes. Add turmeric, cinnamon, nutmeg and brown sugar, and fry for a further 1 minute. Add salt and pepper to taste. Return lamb to wok and add water. Cover and gently simmer for 45 minutes to 1 hour, until lamb is tender. And undrained cherries. Blend arrowroot or cornstarch with lemon juice and stir into mixture. Bring to boil and simmer for 4 minutes or until sauce has thickened. Serve hot with rice.

Mee Goreng

PREPARATION TIME: 20 minutes

COOKING TIME: 15 minutes

SERVES: 4 people

8oz fine egg noodles
¼ cup peanut oil
1 onion, peeled and chopped finely
4oz pork, finely sliced
4oz shrimp, shelled and de-veined
2 cloves garlic, crushed
1 tbsp light soy sauce
1 tsp sambal manis or sambal oelek
¼ cabbage, shredded
1 green chili pepper, seeds removed, and sliced
2 sticks celery, sliced
Salt
Pepper

Garnish
Sliced cucumber
Sliced green onions

Soak noodles in hot water for 8 minutes, or boil until cooked. Rinse in cold water. Drain in a colander. Set aside. Heat wok and add oil. Stir-fry onion, garlic and chili until onion starts to color. Add sambal manis or sambal oelek. Add pork, celery, cabbage and salt and pepper, and stir-fry for 3 minutes. Add soy sauce, noodles and shrimp, and toss mixture to heat through well. Place in a warm serving dish, surrounded with sliced cucumber and sprinkled with green onions on top.

Five-Spice Beef with Broccoli

PREPARATION TIME: 15 minutes

COOKING TIME: 15 minutes

SERVES: 4 people

8oz sirloin or butt steak
1 clove garlic, crushed
½ tsp finely grated ginger
½ tsp five-spice powder
½ cup broccoli flowerets
Bunch of chives, cut into 1" lengths
2 tbsps peanut oil
½ tsp salt
1 tbsp dark soy sauce
½ cup hot water
2 tsps cornstarch, slaked in 1 tbsp cold water

Cut steak into thin slices, then into narrow strips. Mix together with garlic, ginger, and five-spice powder. Heat wok, add 15ml (1 tbsp) of oil, and stir-fry broccoli for 8 minutes. Remove broccoli and add remaining oil. Add meat, and stir-fry for 3 minutes. Add broccoli, soy sauce, salt and water, and heat to simmering point. Mix cornstarch with cold water, and pour into wok, stirring continuously until liquid thickens. Toss in chives, stir, and serve immediately with boiled rice.

Lamb with Cherries (right), Five-Spice Beef with Broccoli (below right) and Boiled Rice (bottom right).

Beef with Pineapple and Peppers

PREPARATION TIME: 40 minutes

COOKING TIME: 15 minutes

SERVES: 4 people

1lb sirloin or butt steak, sliced thinly
1 can pineapple slices, drained and chopped
1 green pepper, cored, seeds removed, and chopped roughly
1 red pepper, cored, seeds removed, and chopped roughly
2 cloves garlic, crushed
1 tsp chopped ginger root

1 onion, peeled and chopped roughly
2 tbsps light soy sauce
1 tsp sugar
2 tsps cornstarch
2 tbsps water
1 tbsp peanut oil

Sauce
1 tbsp plum sauce
1 tbsp dark soy sauce
1 tsp sugar
1 tsp sesame oil
1 tsp cornstarch
¼ cup water
Salt
Pepper

Combine 2 tbsps of light soy sauce with 1 tsp of sugar, 2 tsps of cornstarch and 2 tbsps of water. Mix well and pour over steak. Toss together well, and put aside for at least 30 minutes, turning occasionally. Heat wok and add peanut oil. Add ginger, garlic, onion and peppers, and stir-fry for 3 minutes. Remove from wok and set aside. Add extra oil if necessary and stir-fry beef, well separated, for 2 minutes. Remove from wok. Mix together all sauce ingredients in wok, and heat until sauce begins to thicken. Add vegetables, beef and pineapple, and toss together over a high heat until heated through. Serve with boiled rice.

This page: Beef with Pineapple and Peppers.

Facing page: Duck with Orange.

Duck with Orange

PREPARATION TIME: 30 minutes
COOKING TIME: 50 minutes
SERVES: 4 people

1 small duck
1 tbsp butter or margarine
1 tbsp oil
3 oranges
1¼ cups light chicken stock
⅓ cup red wine
2 tbsps redcurrant jelly
1 tsp arrowroot
1 tbsp cold water
Salt
Pepper

Garnish
Watercress
Slivers of orange peel

Pare the rind of 2 oranges and cut into fine shreds. Blanch in hot water and set aside for garnish. Extract juice from 2 oranges. Cut peel and pith from 1 orange, and then slice into rounds, or cut flesh into sections if preferred. Wash duck and dry well with paper towels. Heat wok, and add oil and butter. When hot, add duck, and brown all over. Remove from wok and, using poultry shears or a chopper, cut duck in half lengthwise, and then cut each half into 1" strips. Return duck to wok, and add stock, red wine, redcurrant jelly, orange juice and rind, and salt and pepper to taste. Bring to boil, reduce heat, cover and simmer gently for 20 minutes. Add orange slices, and simmer a further 10 minutes, or until duck is cooked. If sauce needs to be thickened, mix arrowroot with cold water and add to sauce. Bring to the boil, and simmer for 3 minutes. Garnish with slivers of orange peel and watercress.

Chicken and Cashews

PREPARATION TIME: 15 minutes
COOKING TIME: 40 minutes
SERVES: 4 people

1lb chicken breasts, skinned, boned, and cut into shreds
4 tsps cornstarch
1 tbsp light soy sauce
¼ cup peanut oil
2 tbsps water
1 stick celery, sliced thinly
½ cup roasted cashews
½ cup green beans, trimmed and sliced
1 clove garlic, crushed
1 onion, peeled and sliced
1 carrot, cut into matchstick strips
2 green onions, sliced
½ cup chicken stock, made from chicken bones, or ½ cup of hot water plus 1 chicken bouillon cube
½ tsp five-spice powder
Salt
Pepper

Simmer chicken bones in a little water to make chicken stock, or dissolve chicken bouillon cube in hot water. Set aside to cool. Combine half the cornstarch, the five-spice powder, and a pinch of salt. Toss in chicken and mix well. Heat wok, add peanut oil and, when hot, add chicken pieces a few at a time, tossing well. Stir-fry until chicken just starts to change color – about 3 minutes. Lift out with a slotted spoon, and drain on paper towels. Repeat until all chicken is done. Carefully pour off all but 1 tbsp of oil. Add onion and garlic, and cook for 2 minutes. Add celery, beans, carrot, and green onions, and stir-fry for 2 minutes. Add strained chicken stock, and cook for 3 minutes until vegetables are tender but still crisp. Slake remaining cornstarch with 2 tbsps of water. Add soy sauce, and pour into wok. Adjust seasoning if necessary. Bring back to the boil and let simmer for 3 minutes. Add chicken and heat through. Remove from heat. Stir in cashews, and serve at once with noodles or rice.

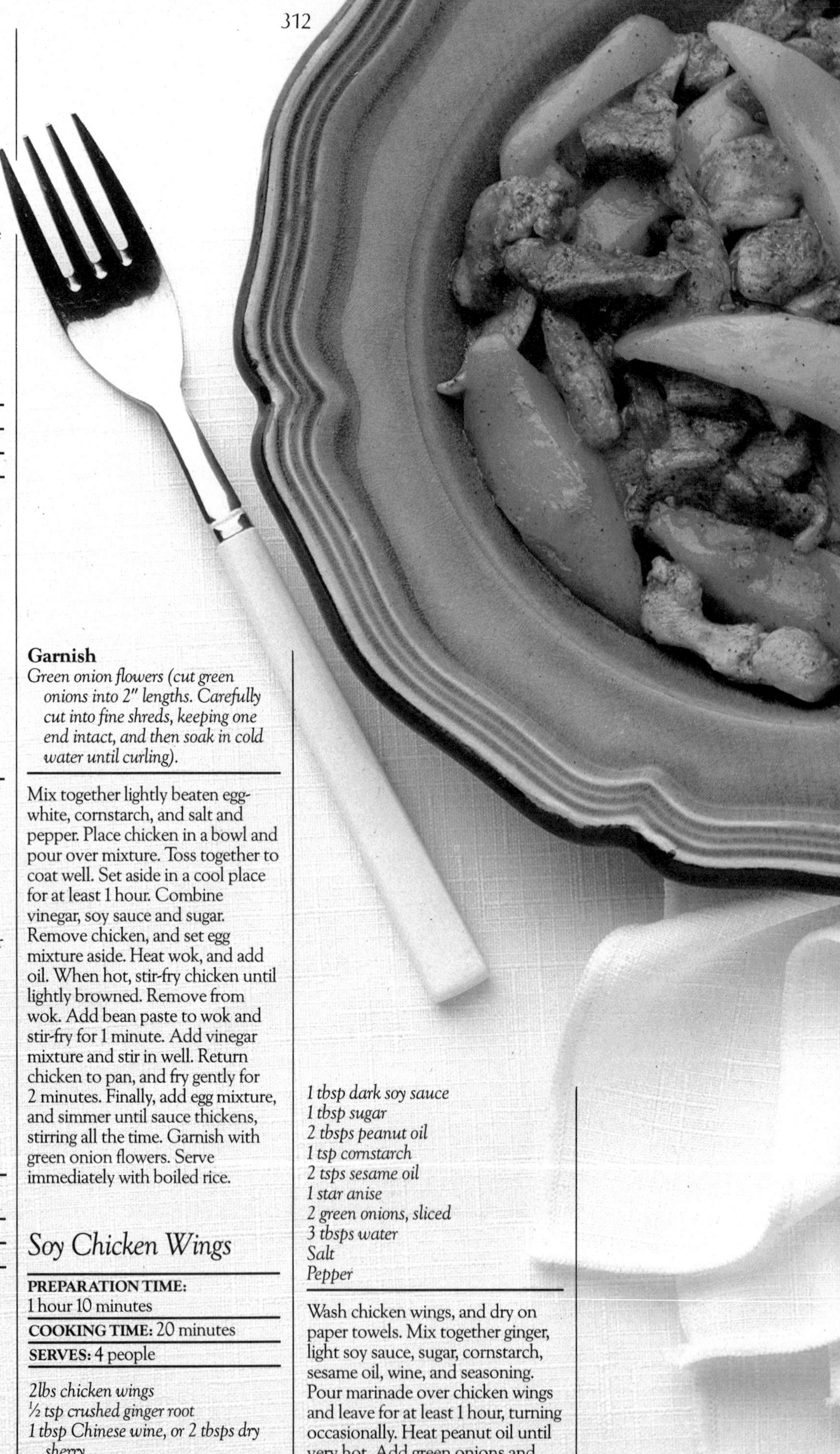

Chicken with Mango

PREPARATION TIME: 5 minutes

COOKING TIME: 30 minutes

SERVES: 4 people

4 chicken breasts, cut into shreds
2 ripe mangoes, sliced, or 1 can sliced mangoes, drained
4 green onions, sliced diagonally
½ tsp ground cinnamon
1 tsp grated ginger
1 tbsp light soy sauce
1 chicken bouillon cube
⅔ cup water
2 tbsps oil
2 tbsps sweet sherry
1 tsp sugar
Salt
Pepper

Heat wok and add oil. Add ginger and cinnamon, and fry for 30 seconds. Add chicken and green onions, and stir-fry for 5 minutes. Add light soy sauce, crumbled chicken bouillon cube, water and sugar, and bring to boil. Add salt and pepper to taste, and simmer for 15 minutes. Add mangoes and sherry, and simmer, uncovered, until sauce has reduced and thickened. Serve hot with boiled rice.

Stir-Fried Chicken with Yellow Bean Paste

PREPARATION TIME: 1 hour 10 minutes

COOKING TIME: 20 minutes

SERVES: 4 people

1lb chicken breasts, sliced thinly
2 tbsps oil
2 tbsps yellow bean paste
1 tsp sugar
1 egg white, lightly beaten
1 tbsp rice vinegar
1 tbsp light soy sauce
1 tbsp cornstarch
Salt
Pepper

Garnish

Green onion flowers (cut green onions into 2" lengths. Carefully cut into fine shreds, keeping one end intact, and then soak in cold water until curling).

Mix together lightly beaten egg-white, cornstarch, and salt and pepper. Place chicken in a bowl and pour over mixture. Toss together to coat well. Set aside in a cool place for at least 1 hour. Combine vinegar, soy sauce and sugar. Remove chicken, and set egg mixture aside. Heat wok, and add oil. When hot, stir-fry chicken until lightly browned. Remove from wok. Add bean paste to wok and stir-fry for 1 minute. Add vinegar mixture and stir in well. Return chicken to pan, and fry gently for 2 minutes. Finally, add egg mixture, and simmer until sauce thickens, stirring all the time. Garnish with green onion flowers. Serve immediately with boiled rice.

Soy Chicken Wings

PREPARATION TIME: 1 hour 10 minutes

COOKING TIME: 20 minutes

SERVES: 4 people

2lbs chicken wings
½ tsp crushed ginger root
1 tbsp Chinese wine, or 2 tbsps dry sherry
1 tbsp light soy sauce
1 tbsp dark soy sauce
1 tbsp sugar
2 tbsps peanut oil
1 tsp cornstarch
2 tsps sesame oil
1 star anise
2 green onions, sliced
3 tbsps water
Salt
Pepper

Wash chicken wings, and dry on paper towels. Mix together ginger, light soy sauce, sugar, cornstarch, sesame oil, wine, and seasoning. Pour marinade over chicken wings and leave for at least 1 hour, turning occasionally. Heat peanut oil until very hot. Add green onions and chicken wings, and fry until chicken

Chicken with Mango (left) and Stir-Fried Chicken with Yellow Bean Paste (below).

has browned well on all sides. Add dark soy sauce, star anise and water. Bring to the boil, and simmer for 15 minutes. Remove star anise. Serve hot or cold.

Chicken Livers with Peppers

PREPARATION TIME: 30 minutes

COOKING TIME: 15 minutes

SERVES: 4 people

1lb chicken livers
4 Chinese mushrooms
1 green pepper
1 red pepper
1 tbsp rice vinegar
2 tsps sugar
1oz fresh ginger
1 small leek
3 tbsps vegetable oil
1 onion

Garnish

2 green onion flowers (trim and slice lengthwise, keep one end intact, and leave in cold water in refrigerator until curling)

Soak mushrooms in hot water for 20 minutes. Clean and trim chicken livers, and blanch in boiling water for 3 minutes. Drain and slice. Peel and finely slice ginger. Mix vinegar and sugar, and add ginger, and set aside. Clean and trim leek and cut into thin rings. Peel and slice onion and cut into strips. Core and remove seeds from peppers, and cut into strips. Drain mushrooms, remove hard stalks, and cut caps into thin slices. Heat wok, add oil, and, when hot, add mushrooms, onion, leek and peppers, and stir-fry for 5 minutes. Remove and set aside. Add liver and ginger mixture. Stir-fry for a further 5 minutes, return vegetable mixture to wok and heat through. Serve garnished with green onion flowers.

This page: Chicken with Cashews (top) and Soy Chicken Wings (bottom), and Chicken Livers with Peppers (right).

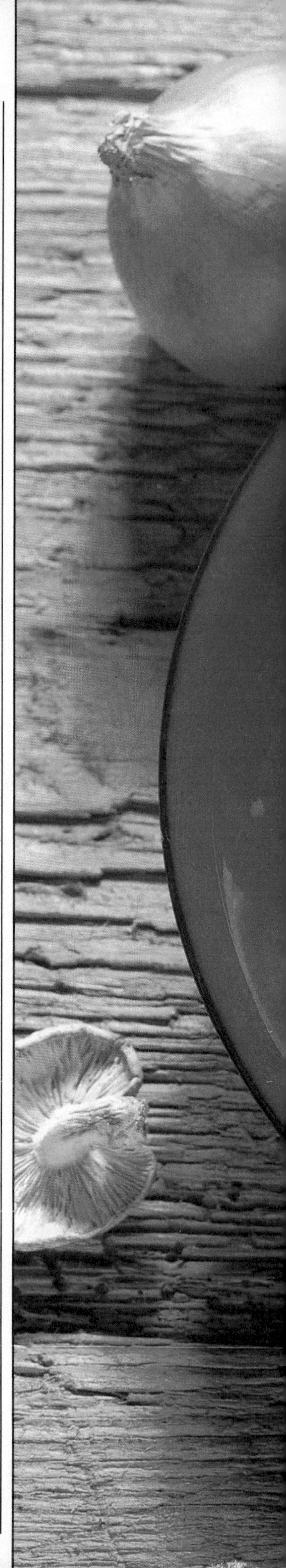

brown. Increase heat and add curry powder. Fry for 30 seconds. Add salt and vinegar, and cook for 1 minute. Add chicken, and turn so that mixture coats chicken well. Add coconut cream and milk, and simmer gently over a low heat for 20 minutes. Serve with boiled rice.

Honey Soy Chicken Wings

PREPARATION TIME: 5 minutes
COOKING TIME: 30 minutes
SERVES: 4 people

1lb chicken wings
½ tsp salt
2 tbsps peanut oil
¼ cup light soy sauce
2 tbsps clear honey
1 clove garlic, crushed
1 tsp ginger, freshly grated
1 tsp sesame seeds

Heat wok, add oil, and when hot, add chicken wings and fry for 10 minutes. Pour off excess oil carefully. Add soy sauce, honey, sesame seeds, garlic, grated ginger and salt. Reduce heat, and gently simmer for 20 minutes, turning occasionally. Serve hot or cold with rice.

Sesame Fried Chicken

PREPARATION TIME: 10 minutes
COOKING TIME: 30 minutes
SERVES: 4 people

1lb chicken breasts, or 4 good-sized pieces
¾ cup flour
1 tsp salt
1 tsp pepper
¼ cup sesame seeds
2 tsps paprika
1 egg, beaten, with 1 tbsp water
3 tbsps olive oil

Sift flour onto a sheet of wax paper and stir in salt, pepper, paprika and sesame seeds. Dip chicken breasts in egg and water mixture, then coat well in seasoned flour. Heat wok,

Chicken Curry (Mild)

PREPARATION TIME: 10 minutes
COOKING TIME: 40 minutes
SERVES: 4 people

3lbs chicken
1 tbsp peanut oil
1 onion, peeled and finely chopped
2 cloves garlic, crushed
½ tsp grated ginger
2 tsps curry powder
½ tsp salt
1 tbsp vinegar
⅔ cup milk
⅔ cup coconut cream

Cut chicken into small pieces: breast-meat into 4 pieces, thigh-meat into 2 pieces, and wings separated at joints. Heat oil until hot. Reduce heat. Add onion, garlic and ginger and cook gently, stirring continuously. Cook for 10 minutes, or until onion is soft and a golden

This page: Chili Sichuan Chicken (top) and Honey Soy Chicken Wings (bottom).

Facing page: Chicken Curry (Mild) (top) and Sesame Fried Chicken (bottom).

add oil and, when hot, fry the chicken breasts until golden brown on both sides. Turn heat down, and cook gently for 10 minutes on each side. Serve hot with rice.

Lemon Chicken

PREPARATION TIME: 5 minutes

COOKING TIME: 40 minutes

SERVES: 4 people

2lbs chicken pieces
⅓ cup oil

Lemon Sauce
Juice of 1 lemon
⅓ cup water
2 tsps cornstarch
2 tbsps sweet sherry
Pinch of sugar, if desired

Garnish
Lemon slices

Heat wok and add oil. When hot, add chicken pieces and toss in oil until well browned. Reduce heat and cover. Simmer for 30 minutes until chicken is cooked. Remove with a slotted spoon and drain on paper towels. Place chicken pieces in a serving dish and keep warm. Meanwhile, carefully drain oil from wok. Slake cornstarch in 2 tbsps of water. Put lemon juice and remaining water in wok, and bring to the boil. Add cornstarch, and stir until boiling. Simmer for 2 minutes until thickened. Add sherry and sugar, and simmer a further 2 minutes. Pour over chicken pieces and garnish with lemon slices. Serve with boiled rice.

Chili Sichuan Chicken

PREPARATION TIME: 40 minutes

COOKING TIME: 20 minutes

SERVES: 4 people

4 chicken breasts, sliced thinly
1 clove garlic, crushed
1 green pepper, cored, seeds removed, and diced
1 red pepper, cored, seeds removed, and diced
1 red chili pepper, seeds removed, and sliced finely
1 green chili pepper, seeds removed, and sliced finely
1 tsp chili sauce
1 tbsp light soy sauce
1 tsp Chinese wine, or dry sherry
½ tsp cornstarch
Salt
Pepper
⅔ cup peanut oil, for deep frying

Sauce
1¼ cups chicken stock
2 tsps cornstarch
1 tsp Chinese wine, or dry sherry

Mix together 1 tsp wine, ½ tsp cornstarch, light soy sauce, and a pinch of salt and pepper. Pour over chicken and mix well. Leave to marinate for at least 30 minutes. Heat oil for deep frying in wok. When hot, toss in sliced chicken and fry until just coloring and cooked through. Drain well. Carefully remove all but 1 tbsp of oil from wok. Heat, and when hot, add garlic, green and red peppers, green and red chili peppers, and chili sauce. Fry gently for 2 minutes. Stir 2 tbsps of chicken stock into cornstarch, then pour remaining chicken stock and wine into wok. Add cornstarch mixture and stir well, until sauce boils and thickens. Add chicken, and toss until heated through. Serve with rice.

Chicken Cacciatore

PREPARATION TIME: 15 minutes

COOKING TIME: 30 minutes

SERVES: 4 people

1lb chicken breasts, cut into bite-sized pieces
1 16oz can plum tomatoes
1 onion, peeled and sliced
1 green pepper, cored, seeds removed, and sliced
½ cup mushrooms, sliced
2 cloves garlic, crushed
1 tsp basil
1 tsp oregano
1 bay leaf
2 tsps tomato paste
⅔ cup dry white wine
3 tbsps olive oil
Salt
Pepper

Garnish
Parsley

Heat wok and add 1 tbsp oil. When hot, add chicken and stir-fry until chicken is opaque – about 8 minutes. Add more oil if necessary. Remove with slotted spoon and set aside. Heat remaining oil, and add basil, oregano and bay leaf, and fry for 1 minute. Add onion and garlic, and stir-fry until onion is soft but not colored. Add green pepper and mushrooms, and fry for a further 3 minutes. Add undrained tomatoes, tomato paste, wine, and salt and pepper to taste. Cook uncovered for 10 minutes. Return chicken to pan, and stir until heated through. Garnish with parsley and serve with spaghetti.

Chicken Cacciatore (left) and Lemon Chicken (below).

Wok Vegetables and Sauces

Sweet and Sour Cabbage

PREPARATION TIME: 5 minutes

COOKING TIME: 20 minutes

SERVES: 4 people as a vegetable

Half a small cabbage
2 tbsps butter or margarine
3 tbsps vinegar
2 tbsps sugar
3 tbsps water
Salt
Pepper

Slice cabbage into shreds. Melt butter in wok. Put cabbage into wok with other ingredients and set over a moderate heat. Stir until hot, then cover and simmer for 15 minutes. Adjust seasoning if necessary. Serve hot.

Gado Gado

PREPARATION TIME: 20 minutes

COOKING TIME: 30 minutes

SERVES: 4 people as a vegetable

1 cup bean-sprouts
1 cup Chinese cabbage, shredded
½ cup green beans, trimmed
Half a cucumber, cut into 2" strips
1 carrot, peeled and cut into thin strips
1 potato, peeled and cut into thin strips
1 tbsp peanut oil

Peanut Sauce
2 tbsps peanut oil
⅔ cup raw shelled peanuts
2 red chili peppers, seeds removed, and chopped finely, or 1 tsp chili powder
2 shallots, peeled and chopped finely
1 clove garlic, crushed
1 tsp brown sugar
Juice of half a lemon
¼ cup coconut milk
⅔ cup water
Salt

Garnish
Sliced hard-boiled eggs
Sliced cucumber

Heat wok and add 1 tbsp peanut oil. When hot, toss in carrot and potato. Stir-fry for 2 minutes and add green beans and cabbage. Cook for a further 3 minutes. Add bean-sprouts and cucumber, and stir-fry for 2 minutes. Place in a serving dish. Make peanut sauce. Heat wok, add 2 tbsps peanut oil, and fry peanuts for 2-3 minutes. Remove and drain on paper towels. Blend or pound chili peppers, shallots and garlic to a smooth paste. Grind or blend peanuts to a powder. Heat oil and fry chili paste for 2 minutes.

This page: Gado Gado with Peanut Sauce.

Facing page: Stir-Fried Vegetable Medley (top) and Sweet and Sour Cabbage (bottom).

Add water, and bring to the boil. Add peanuts, brown sugar, lemon juice, and salt to taste. Stir until sauce is thick – about 10 minutes – and add coconut milk. Garnish vegetable dish with slices of hard-boiled egg, and cucumber and serve with peanut sauce.

Sweet and Sour Sauce

PREPARATION TIME: 10 minutes

COOKING TIME: 10 minutes

Juice of 2 oranges
2 tbsps lemon juice
2 tbsps white wine vinegar
1 tbsp sugar
1 tbsp tomato paste
1 tbsp light soy sauce
½ tsp salt
1 tbsp cornstarch
2 tbsps water
Drop of red food coloring if desired

Combine orange and lemon juice, sugar, vinegar, tomato paste, soy sauce, salt, and red coloring (if desired). Place in wok and heat gently. Blend cornstarch with water, and stir into sauce. Bring to boil and simmer for 3 minutes, stirring continuously. Good with fish, pork, wontons and spring rolls (egg rolls).

Mango Chutney

PREPARATION TIME: 5 minutes

COOKING TIME: 20 minutes

1 can mango slices, drained and chopped
1 cup white wine vinegar
2 cloves garlic, crushed
1 tsp chopped ginger root
½ tsp five-spice powder
1 tsp salt
¼ cup sugar
2 tbsps golden raisins
Pinch chili powder (optional)

Place vinegar, salt, garlic, ginger, five-spice powder, chili powder and sugar in wok. Bring to boil, and simmer, uncovered, for 10 minutes. Add mango and raisins, and simmer gently until sauce is thick. Serve cool as an accompaniment to a curry.

Left: Sweet-and-Sour Sauce (top), Mango Sauce (center) and Chili Sauce (bottom). Tomato Chutney (right) and Mango Chutney (bottom).

Ginger Sauce

PREPARATION TIME: 5 minutes
COOKING TIME: 10 minutes

1 tbsp grated ginger root
2 tbsps light soy sauce
1 tbsp Chinese wine, or dry sherry
1 tsp sugar
1 tsp cornstarch
2 tbsps water
1 tbsp oil

Heat wok, add oil and gently fry ginger. Mix together soy sauce, wine and sugar. Blend cornstarch with water, and add to soy/wine mixture. Pour into wok and bring to the boil. Simmer for 3 minutes, stirring continuously. Push through strainer. Good with sea-food, pork, beef and crab rolls.

Brinjal Bhartha

PREPARATION TIME: 20 minutes
COOKING TIME: 30 minutes
SERVES: 4 people as a vegetable

2 large eggplants, cut into 1" slices
3 tbsps oil
⅔ cup water
1 onion, peeled and chopped finely
2 green chili peppers, seeds removed, and sliced very thinly
½ tsp ground cumin
Pinch of sugar
2 tsps lemon juice
Salt

Slice eggplants and sprinkle with salt. Set aside for 15 minutes. Rinse off salt and dry with paper towels. Heat wok and add 2 tbsps of oil. Fry eggplants in hot oil, browning lightly on both sides. When all oil has been absorbed, add water. Cover and simmer for 15 minutes, or until eggplants are soft. Remove from wok, and drain. Heat remaining oil in wok. Add onion, ground cumin and chili peppers, and cook gently for 5 minutes without coloring onion. Meanwhile skin eggplants, and push flesh through a strainer or blend. Add onion mixture to eggplants. Add sugar, lemon juice and salt to taste.

Special Fried Rice

PREPARATION TIME: 15 minutes
COOKING TIME: 20 minutes
SERVES: 4 people

2 cups boiled rice
4oz shrimp, shelled and de-veined
8oz Chinese barbecued pork, or cooked ham, diced or cut into small pieces
1 cup bean-sprouts
½ cup frozen peas
2 green onions, sliced diagonally
1 tbsp light soy sauce
1 tsp dark soy sauce
2 tbsps peanut oil
Salt
Pepper

Pancake
2 eggs, beaten
Salt

Garnish
2 green onion flowers (trim green onions, slice lengthwise, leaving one end intact and leave in cold water in refrigerator until curling).

Heat wok and add 1 tbsp of peanut oil. Roll oil around surface. Make pancake by mixing beaten eggs with a pinch of salt and 1 tsp of oil. Add egg mixture to wok, and move wok back and forth so that the mixture spreads over the surface. When lightly browned on the underside, turn over and cook on other side. Set aside to cool. Heat remaining oil in wok. When hot, add green

This page: Special Fried Rice (top) and Ginger Sauce (bottom).

Facing page: Brinjal Bhartha (top) and Okra and Tomatoes (bottom).

onions and peas and cook, covered, for 2 minutes. With a slotted spoon, remove and set aside. Re-heat oil and add rice. Stir continuously over a low heat until rice is heated through. Add soy sauces and mix well. Add peas, green onions, bean-sprouts, meat, shrimp, and salt and pepper to taste. Mix thoroughly. Serve hot, garnished with pancake and green onion flowers. The pancake may be sliced very finely and mixed in if desired.

Julienne of Vegetables

PREPARATION TIME: 20 minutes
COOKING TIME: 15 minutes
SERVES: 4 people as a vegetable

2 medium onions, peeled and cut into matchstick strips
2 carrots, scraped and cut into matchstick strips
1 parsnip, scraped and cut into matchstick strips
2 sticks celery, cut into matchstick strips
1 turnip, peeled and cut into matchstick strips
1 tbsp oil
2 tbsps water
1 tbsp butter
Salt
Pepper

Prepare vegetables. Heat wok and add oil. Stir-fry vegetable strips over gentle heat for 5 minutes. Add water and salt to taste, and increase heat. Cook for a further 5 minutes over high heat. Drain any liquid from wok. Add butter and freshly-ground black pepper, and toss to coat well.

Mango Sauce

PREPARATION TIME: 5 minutes
COOKING TIME: 20 minutes

1 can sliced mangoes
⅔ cup malt vinegar
½ tsp garam masala
1 tsp grated ginger root
1 tbsp sugar
1 tsp oil
Salt

Heat wok and add oil. Add garam masala and ginger, and cook for 1 minute. Add undrained mangoes, vinegar and sugar, and salt to taste. Simmer, uncovered, for 15 minutes. Blend and push through a strainer. Good with chicken, beef and spring rolls (egg rolls).

Stir-Fried Vegetable Medley

PREPARATION TIME: 20 minutes
COOKING TIME: 10 minutes
SERVES: 4 people as a vegetable

2 carrots, cut into flowers (slice strips out lengthwise to produce flowers when cut across into rounds)
1 can baby corn, drained
2 cups broccoli flowerets (slit stems to ensure quick cooking)
1 onion, peeled and sliced in julienne strips
2 sticks celery, with tough strings removed, sliced diagonally in half-moon shapes
1 zucchini, sliced diagonally
1 clove garlic, crushed
1 tbsp light soy sauce
¼ tsp finely-grated ginger
2 tbsps oil
Salt
Pepper

Prepare all ingredients before starting to cook. Heat wok and add oil. Add ginger, garlic, onion, carrots, broccoli and zucchini, and toss in oil for 2-3 minutes. Add celery and baby corn, and toss 1-2 minutes longer. Season with soy sauce, and salt and pepper if desired. Add cornstarch to thicken vegetable juices if necessary.

Ratatouille

PREPARATION TIME: 30 minutes
COOKING TIME: 30 minutes
SERVES: 4 people as a vegetable

1 eggplant, sliced into 1" slices
2 zucchini, sliced diagonally
4 tomatoes, chopped roughly
2 onions, peeled and quartered
1 red pepper, cored, seeds removed, and chopped roughly
1 green pepper, cored, seeds removed, and chopped roughly
3 cloves garlic, crushed
1 tsp dry basil
¼ cup olive oil
Salt
Pepper

Slice eggplant and sprinkle with salt. Leave for 20 minutes. Rinse in water, and dry on paper towels. Chop roughly. Heat wok and add oil. Add onions, garlic and basil. Cover and cook gently until onion is soft but not colored. Add peppers, zucchini and eggplant. Cover and fry gently for 15 minutes stirring occasionally. Add tomatoes and salt and pepper to taste and cook covered for a further 10 minutes. Serve hot or chilled.

Tomato Chutney

PREPARATION TIME: 5 minutes
COOKING TIME: 15 minutes

4-6 ripe tomatoes, chopped roughly
1 cup white wine vinegar
½ tsp garam masala
1 tsp salt
2 tbsps sugar
2 green chili peppers, seeds removed, and chopped finely
1 tsp chopped root ginger
Pinch chili powder (optional)

Place tomatoes, vinegar, salt, garam masala, chili powder, chili peppers, sugar and ginger in wok. Bring to boil, and simmer, uncovered, for 15 minutes or until thickened. Serve cool as an accompaniment to a curry.

Okra and Tomatoes

PREPARATION TIME: 15 minutes
COOKING TIME: 10 minutes
SERVES: 4 people as a vegetable

8oz okra, sliced into ½" pieces
1 onion, peeled and chopped
2 tomatoes, chopped
1 red chili pepper, seeds removed, and sliced finely
¼ tsp turmeric
¼ tsp chili powder
½ tsp garam masala
1 tbsp oil or ghee
⅔ cup water
Salt

Heat wok and add oil or ghee. When hot, add turmeric, chili powder and garam masala, and fry for 30 seconds. Add onion, okra and red chili pepper, and stir-fry for 3 minutes. Add tomatoes, water, and salt to taste, and cook uncovered for 5 minutes or until sauce thickens.

Chili Sauce

PREPARATION TIME: 5 minutes
COOKING TIME: 10 minutes

4 tbsps tomato paste
½ tsp chili powder
2 tbsps Chinese wine, or dry sherry
2 tbsps white wine vinegar
⅔ cup water
1 tsp cornstarch
2 cloves garlic, crushed
1 tsp grated ginger root
1 tbsp dark soy sauce
1 tbsp sesame oil

Heat wok and add oil. When hot, add garlic and ginger and fry for 1 minute. Mix together tomato paste, chili powder, wine, soy sauce and vinegar. Add to wok. Blend cornstarch with 1 tbsp of water and add to wok with remaining water. Bring to the boil and simmer for 3 minutes, stirring continuously. Good with sea-food, beef, vegetables and spring rolls (egg rolls).

Ratatouille (right) and Julienne of Vegetables (bottom right).

Indian Cuisine

Bhoona Gosht

PREPARATION TIME: 15 minutes
COOKING TIME: 1 hour
SERVES: 4 people

1 onion, peeled and chopped
3 tblsp salad or olive oil, or
2 tblsp ghee
1 inch cinnamon stick
6 small cardamoms
1 bay leaf
6 cloves
3 large cardamoms
1 tsp ginger paste
1 tsp garlic paste
1lb braising steak, lamb or beef, cubed
2 tsp ground coriander
2 tsp ground cumin
1 tsp chili powder
¼ tsp ground turmeric
4 large tomatoes or
⅔ cup canned tomatoes
1 cup water
Salt to taste
2 green chilies, chopped
2 sprigs fresh coriander, chopped

Fry onion in oil or ghee until light brown. Add cinnamon, cardamoms, cloves, bay leaf. Fry for one minute. Add ginger and garlic pastes and fry for further one minute. Add meat and sprinkle with coriander, cumin, chili and turmeric. Mix well and fry for 10 minutes. Add chopped fresh or canned tomatoes. Season with salt and add water. Cover and cook for 40-45 minutes on low heat, until meat is tender. Add chopped chilies and coriander.

Kofta Curry

PREPARATION TIME: 15 minutes
COOKING TIME: 30 minutes
SERVES: 4 people

1lb lean ground meat
½ tsp ginger paste
1 tsp garlic paste
1 egg
1 tsp ground garam masala
½ tsp chili powder

For sauce
1 onion, peeled and finely chopped about 1½oz ghee or
2-3 tblsp salad or olive oil
6 small cardamoms
1 inch cinnamon stick
6 cloves
1 bay leaf
1 tsp garlic paste
1 tsp ginger paste
1 tsp ground cumin
½ tsp chili powder
¼ tsp ground turmeric
2 tsp ground coriander
Salt to taste
⅔ cup natural yogurt
2 tblsp ketchup
2½ cups water

To garnish
2 green chilies, chopped
2 sprigs fresh coriander, finely chopped

Mix ground meat with ginger, garlic paste and egg. Add garam masala and chili powder. Mix well and make 16-20 even-sized balls. Keep in a cool place.

Sauce
Fry onion in oil or ghee for 4 minutes until light golden brown. Add cardamom, cinnamon, cloves and bay leaf. Stir fry for one minute. Add garlic and ginger pastes and fry for another minute. Sprinkle with cumin, chili, turmeric and coriander. Stir well and add yogurt and ketchup. Add water, cover and bring to boil. Add salt. Slide meat balls one at a time into the saucepan. Shake the saucepan to settle the meat balls; do not stir otherwise the balls will break. Cover and simmer gently for 20 minutes. Garnish with chopped chilies and coriander leaves. Serve with rice or chapatis.

Keema Methi

PREPARATION TIME: 30 minutes
COOKING TIME: 30 minutes
SERVES: 4 people

1 onion, peeled and chopped
1½ tblsp ghee or
2 tblsp olive oil or salad
4 small green cardamoms
1 inch cinnamon stick
1 bay leaf
6 cloves
1 tsp ginger paste
1 tsp garlic paste
1lb ground lamb or beef
1 tsp chili powder
2 tsp ground coriander
2 tsp ground cumin
¼ tsp ground turmeric
⅔ cup natural yogurt
Salt to taste
1 bunch fresh methi leaves, stemmed and chopped, or
1 tblsp dry kasuri methi leaves

Fry onion in oil till just tender. Add cardamoms, cinnamon stick, bay leaf, cloves and fry for one minute. Add ginger and garlic pastes and cook for one minute. Add ground meat. Stir the mixture and sprinkle with chili, coriander, cumin and turmeric. Mix well and cook for 5 minutes. Add well-stirred yogurt and fresh methi leaves or dry methi. Cover and cook till liquid is absorbed. Season with salt. Serve with chapati or rice.

Dam Ke Kebab
(BAKED KEBAB)

PREPARATION TIME: 30 minutes
COOKING TIME: 1 hour
SERVES: 4 people

1lb lean ground beef
1 tsp ginger paste
1 tsp garlic paste
2 green chilies, ground or finely chopped
2 tsp garam masala
⅔ cup natural yogurt
¼ tsp meat tenderizer
2 sprigs fresh coriander leaves, finely chopped
1 tsp chili powder
2 eggs, beaten
1 onion, peeled, thinly sliced, and fried until crisp
Salt to taste
2 green chilies, chopped
Juice of 1 lemon
Salad or olive oil

Mix together the ground beef, ginger and garlic pastes, ground chili, garam masala, yogurt, meat tenderizer, half the finely chopped coriander, chili powder, eggs and crisply fried onions. Mix well and season with salt. Spread the meat mixture to ½ inch thick in a well-greased baking tray. Brush with oil and bake in a preheated oven, 350°F for 20 minutes. Reduce temperature to 300°F for a further 20-30 minutes, or until liquid has evaporated. Cut into 2 inch squares. Garnish with chopped chihies and remaining fresh coriander leaves. Sprinkle with lemon juice before serving.

Boti-Kebab

PREPARATION TIME: 6 minutes plus 3-4 hours to marinate
COOKING TIME: 30 minutes
SERVES: 4 people

1lb shoulder or leg of lamb, cut into bite size pieces
1 tsp ginger paste
1 tsp garlic paste
1 tsp chili powder
¼ tsp salt
2 tblsp brown vinegar
Juice of ½ a lemon
Salad or olive oil for basting
1 green pepper, seeded and cut into 1 inch pieces
1 large onion, cut into 1 inch pieces
3-4 tomatoes, quartered

Mix meat with ginger, garlic, chili powder, salt and vinegar and leave to marinate for 3-4 hours. Sprinkle with lemon juice and rub spices well into meat; keep aside. Heat broiler. Thread pieces of meat onto skewers, alternating them with tomato, green pepper and onion. Brush with oil and broil for 3-4 minutes. Turn kebabs and continue cooking until meat is tender. Sprinkle with lemon juice and serve with mixed salad.

Facing page: Bhoona Gosht (top left), Kofta Curry (center right) and Keema Methi (bottom).

Rogan Josh (below).

Rogan Josh
(RICH LAMB WITH NUTS)

PREPARATION TIME: 20 minutes

COOKING TIME: 1 hour

SERVES: 4 people

1 onion, peeled and sliced
2½ tblsp ghee or
4 tblsp salad or olive oil
6 green cardamoms
4 large cardamoms
6 cloves
2 bay leaves
1 inch cinnamon stick
1 inch root ginger, crushed
3 cloves garlic, crushed
1lb boned lean lamb or beef, cut into cubes
1 tsp ground cumin
1 tsp chili powder
2 tsp paprika
1 tsp ground coriander
⅔ cup natural yogurt
1 tsp salt
2 tblsp chopped, blanched almonds
1 tblsp ground poppyseeds
1½ cups water
1 pinch saffron

Fry onion in ghee or oil until lightly browned. Stir fry cardamoms, cloves, bay leaf and cinnamon for 1 minute. Add ginger and garlic pastes, stir and add the meat. Sprinkle on, one at a time, the cumin, chili, paprika and coriander. Fry the mixture for 2 minutes. Add yogurt and salt; cover and cook for 5-7 minutes until dry, and oil separates. Add almonds and poppyseeds. Stir fry for 1-2 minutes and add water. Cover and cook for 40-50 minutes, simmering gently until meat is tender and the mixture is fairly dry. Sprinkle with saffron. Cover and cook gently for another 5-10 minutes, taking care not to burn the meat. Stir the mixture a few times to mix saffron. Rogan josh is a dry dish, with moist spices around the meat. Serve with pulao, nan or parathas.

Shami Kebab

PREPARATION TIME: 40 minutes

COOKING TIME: about 30 minutes

SERVES: 4 people

1lb leg of lamb, or beef, cubed
1¼ cups water
1 small onion, peeled and thickly sliced
1 inch root ginger, peeled and sliced
3 cloves of garlic, peeled and chopped
1 tblsp channa daal, washed, and presoaked in water for 10 minutes
1 inch cinnamon stick
1 bay leaf, finely crushed
1-2 eggs
Salt
6 cloves, ground
6 small cardamoms, ground
10 whole peppercorns, ground
1 tsp whole black cumin, ground
Salad or olive oil for frying

For filling
1 small onion, peeled and thinly sliced
2 tsp natural yogurt
Pinch of salt
1 sprig fresh coriander leaves, chopped

Pressure-cook meat with water, onion, ginger, garlic, channa daal, cinnamon and bay leaf for 15-20 minutes. Remove lid and evaporate remaining liquid. Remove cinnamon stick. Use an electric blender to mix the mixture to a sausage meat consistency. Add egg, season with salt, and sprinkle with ground spices. Mix well. Make 10-12 even portions. Mix onions, yogurt and coriander. Take a portion of meat, make a depression in the center, put a little of the onion yogurt filling in the center and pat the meat paste into a round, flat shape, to enclose the filling (about 2 inches in diameter). Continue to make the rest of the shamis in the same way. Heat oil in a skillet and fry the shamis light brown, for 2-3 minutes on each side. Serve with lemon wedges, onion salad and pitta bread.

Sheikh Kebab

PREPARATION TIME: 30 minutes

COOKING TIME: 20 minutes

SERVES: 4 people

1lb lean ground beef or lamb
1 onion, finely minced
1 green chili, ground to a paste
2 tsp kasuri methi
½ tsp chili powder
2 tsp garam masala powder
¼ tsp salt
2 sprigs fresh coriander leaves, chopped
1 tsp ginger paste
1 tsp garlic paste
2 eggs, beaten
Salad or olive oil
Lemon quarters

Picture below: Dum Ka Ran (top) and Masala Chops (bottom).

Mix the ground meat in a bowl with the onion, green chili, methi, chili powder, garam masala, salt, coriander, and ginger and garlic pastes; mix well. Add the beaten eggs and mix well. Let mixture stand for 10 minutes. Rub a skewer with a little oil. Take some of the mixture and spread it round the skewer to approximately 4 inches in length. Make the remaining sheikh kebabs. Cook them under the broiler, brushed with oil, for 3-4 minutes, turning frequently to cook all sides evenly. Serve piping hot with lemon quarters, tamarind pulp, or yogurt and mint chutney. A side salad of onions and plain roti goes well with sheikh kebab.

Tali-Kaleji/Gurda/Dil

PREPARATION TIME: 15 minutes

COOKING TIME: 40-45 minutes

SERVES: 4 people

½lb pig's liver, cut into half-inch cubes
4 lambs' kidneys, halved and cored
2 hearts, cored and cut into 1 inch pieces
1 tsp chili powder
2 tsp ground coriander
¼ tsp ground turmeric
2-3 cloves of garlic, or
1 tsp garlic paste
1 piece of root ginger or
1½ tsp ginger paste
2 tblsp ghee or
3 tblsp salad or olive oil
Salt to taste
Juice of 1 lemon

Rinse all the meats in lightly salted water and remove visible fats and sinew. Drain well and toss in chili powder, coriander, turmeric, ginger and garlic and set aside for 5 minutes. In a large saucepan, melt the oil or ghee and add the meat mixture. Cook gently for 40-45 minutes, stirring occasionally. Add salt to taste. The color will change to dark brown. When the mixture is dry and the oil separates, remove from heat and sprinkle with lemon juice. If the meats become too dry during cooking, add a little water or stock.

Masala Chops

PREPARATION TIME: 15 minutes

COOKING TIME: 20-30 minutes

SERVES: 4 people

4 lamb steaks
⅔ pint natural yogurt
1 tsp garlic paste
1 tsp ginger paste
1 tsp chili powder
1 tsp ground black pepper
1 tsp ground cumin
1 tsp salt
Salad or olive oil for basting

To garnish
Lemon wedges

Place lamb steaks in a bowl and add yogurt, garlic and ginger pastes, spices and salt. Mix spice mixture well into the lamb. Keep aside for 5-6 minutes. Pour on 2 tblsp oil and mix well. Spread aluminium baking foil over broiler tray. Arrange lamb steaks on top and broil for 5-6 minutes each side. Baste with oil if required. Alternatively, arrange lamb steaks on a baking tray and cook them in preheated oven, 350°F, for 30-35 minutes, turning them once. Serve hot with mixed salad and garnished with lemon wedges.

Dum Ka Ran

PREPARATION TIME: 24 hours to marinate

COOKING TIME: 2 hours

SERVES: 8 people

5-6lb whole leg of lamb
2 cups natural yogurt
3 tblsp brown vinegar
1 tsp salt
Juice of 2 lemons
2 tsp chili powder
¼ tsp red food coloring
2 tsp garlic paste
2 tsp ginger paste
¼ tsp fine granulated sugar
Salad or olive oil for basting
Aluminium foil

Put meat in a large container and make 3-4 half-inch-deep cuts. Mix yogurt, vinegar, salt, lemon juice, chili powder, food coloring, garlic paste, ginger paste and sugar. Mix well and pour over the meat. Press

well into the cuts and cover the container; refrigerate overnight to marinate. Turn once. Next day remove meat and discard marinade. Wrap in baking foil. Cook in a preheated oven at 375°F for 1-1¼ hours. Baste occasionally with oil and turn the meat to brown evenly. Reduce heat to 325°F, and cook for another 45 minutes. Serve with daal and pulao.

Karai Gosht

PREPARATION TIME: 15 minutes

COOKING TIME: 40-60 minutes

SERVES: 4 people

1lb lean beef, pork or lamb, cut into 1 inch pieces
1 tsp chili powder
1 tsp ground cumin
1 tsp ground coriander
1 tblsp aniseed powder
2 tsp kasuri dry methi leaves
⅔ cup natural yogurt
3 tblsp ghee or
4 tblsp salad or olive oil
1 large onion, peeled and sliced
2 bay leaves
2 inch cinnamon stick
6 cloves
6 small cardamoms
2 inch root ginger, peeled and crushed
4 cloves of garlic, peeled and crushed
¾ cup water
Salt to taste

In a bowl mix the meat with chili, cumin, coriander, aniseed powder, methi leaves and yogurt. Keep aside. Fry onion in oil until tender (4-5 minutes). Add bay leaves, cinnamon, cloves, small cardamoms, ginger and garlic and fry for 2 minutes. Add marinated meat, water and salt to taste. Cover the pan and cook for 30 minutes. Transfer the meat to a wok or large skillet and stir fry until the liquid has almost evaporated. Add extra water gradually, if needed, and keep stir frying until meat is tender. The oil should separate. This is a dry dish.

Meat Do Piaza

PREPARATION TIME: 15 minutes

COOKING TIME: 50-60 minutes

SERVES: 4 people

1 small onion, peeled and chopped
2½ tblsp ghee or
3 tblsp salad or olive oil
1lb shoulder or leg of lamb, cubed
1 tsp ginger paste
1 tsp garlic paste
1 inch cinnamon stick
6 cloves
6 small cardamoms
1 tsp chili powder
1 tsp ground coriander
2 tsp ground cumin
⅔ cup water
Salt to taste
2 large onions, peeled and cut into thin rings
Juice of 1 lemon
2 sprigs green fresh coriander leaves, chopped
1-2 green chilies
Extra oil if needed

Fry chopped onion in oil or ghee until just tender. Add meat, ginger, garlic, cinnamon, cloves, cardamoms, chili powder, coriander

This page: Tali Kaleji/Gurda/Dil (left), Meat Palak (center right) and Meat Madras (bottom right). Facing page: Meat Do Piaza (top), Korma (center right) and Karai Gosht (bottom).

and cumin. Fry for 5-6 minutes. Add water and salt to taste. Cook covered for 30-40 minutes on low heat until meat is cooked and liquid has evaporated. Add onion rings – they can be fried in a little extra oil if desired. Stir the meat; cover and cook for a further 10-15 minutes. The onions should be tender. Sprinkle with lemon juice and add green chilies and coriander. This is a dry dish. Serve with pulaos or puri.

Meat Palak

PREPARATION TIME: 30-45 minutes

COOKING TIME: 1 hour

SERVES: 4 people

4 tblsp ghee or
4 tblsp salad or olive oil
1 medium onion, peeled and chopped
1 bay leaf
1 inch cinnamon stick
4 small cardamoms
6 cloves
1 inch root ginger, crushed
3-4 cloves of garlic, crushed
1lb lean lamb or beef, cubed
⅔ cup natural yogurt
1 tsp chili powder
½ tsp ground turmeric
2 tsp ground coriander
2 green chilies, chopped
2 sprigs of fresh green coriander, chopped
1lb leaf spinach, boiled and puréed (or canned or frozen spinach purée)
Salt to taste

Heat the oil and fry the onion until light golden brown. Add bay leaf, cinnamon, cardamoms and cloves. Fry for one minute. Add ginger and garlic paste and fry for a further minute. Add meat and yogurt and sprinkle with chili, turmeric and coriander. Season with salt and cook with the lid on until moisture evaporates (30-40 minutes). Add puréed or canned spinach, mix well and cook for a further 15-20 minutes on a low heat until oil rises to the top. Garnish with chopped chili and coriander.

Chicken Masala

PREPARATION TIME: 10 minutes and marinate overnight

COOKING TIME: 40-50 minutes plus 10 minutes

SERVES: 8-10 people

3lb chicken, cut into 8-10 pieces
2 tblsp salad or olive oil
⅔ cup natural yogurt
1 tsp ground ginger
1 tsp garlic paste
2 tsp ground cumin
2 tsp garam masala
1 tsp salt
Juice of 1 lemon
2 tsp ground black pepper
2 tsp ground mango
1 tsp kasuri methi
1 tsp dry mint powder

Marinate chicken pieces overnight in a well-mixed marinade made from the oil, yogurt, ginger, garlic, cumin, garam masala, salt and lemon juice. Roast chicken with marinade, wrapped in baking foil, in a preheated oven 375°F, for 40-50 minutes. Save the liquid and mix with the black pepper, mango, methi and mint powder. Mix well and keep aside. Cool chicken slightly and cut into bite size pieces. Pour in the liquid mixture and mix well. Transfer onto baking tray and bake for further 10-15 minutes until the chicken pieces are dry. Serve as a snack, or with cocktails.

Meat Madras

PREPARATION TIME: 10 minutes

COOKING TIME: 1 hour

SERVES: 4 people

1 onion, peeled and chopped
2 tblsp ghee or
3 tblsp salad or olive oil
¾ inch cinnamon stick
4 small cardamoms
2 bay leaves
6 fresh curry leaves
6 cloves
1 tblsp grated fresh coconut, or shredded coconut
¼ tsp fenugreek seeds, crushed
3 cloves garlic, peeled and chopped
1 inch root ginger, peeled and sliced
1lb braising steak or lamb, cut into cubes
Salt to taste
1 tsp chili powder
2 tsp ground coriander
2 tsp ground cumin
¼ tsp ground turmeric
4 tomatoes, quartered
1 cup water
2 green chilies, quartered (optional)
2 sprigs fresh green coriander, chopped
Juice of 1 lemon

Fry onion in ghee or oil until just tender (2-3 minutes). Add cinnamon, cardamoms, bay leaves, curry leaves, cloves, coconut, fenugreek seeds, garlic and ginger and fry for 1-2 minutes. Add meat and fry for 3 minutes. Sprinkle with chili, coriander, cumin, and turmeric. Stir well and add water. Cover and cook for 20 minutes. Add salt, and cook for a further 15-20 minutes until liquid has evaporated. Add tomatoes, chili and coriander leaves. Cover and cook for 10 minutes on a low heat. Sprinkle with lemon juice. Serve with parathas.

Chicken Tomato

PREPARATION TIME: 30 minutes

COOKING TIME: 40-50 minutes

SERVES: 4-6 people

1 onion, peeled and chopped
3 tblsp salad or olive oil or
2 tblsp ghee
1 inch cinnamon stick
1 bay leaf
6 cloves
6 green cardamoms
1 inch root ginger, peeled and sliced
4 cloves garlic, peeled and chopped
3lb roasting chicken, cut into 8-10 pieces
1 tsp chili powder
1 tsp ground cumin
1 tsp ground coriander
2 cups canned tomatoes, crushed
1 tsp salt
2 sprigs fresh green coriander leaves, chopped
2 green chilies, halved

Fry onion for 2 minutes in oil or ghee. Add the cinnamon, bay leaf, cloves, and cardamoms; fry for 1 minute then add ginger and garlic. Fry for half a minute. Add chicken pieces. Sprinkle with chili powder, cumin, coriander. Fry for 2-3 minutes and add crushed tomatoes. Season with salt and add chopped green coriander and chilies. Stir chicken to mix well. Cover and cook for 40-45 minutes until chicken is tender.

Chicken Tandoori

Although the true taste of tandoori (clay oven) is not achieved, a very good result is obtained by baking in a conventional oven.

PREPARATION TIME: 10 minutes and marinate overnight

COOKING TIME: 30-40 minutes

SERVES: 4-6 people

3lb chicken, cut into 8-10 pieces
1 tsp garlic paste
1 tsp ginger paste
1 tsp ground black pepper
1 tsp paprika
¼ tsp red food coloring
1 tsp salt
3 tblsp brown vinegar
Juice of 1 lemon
⅔ cup natural yogurt
1 tsp dry mint powder
Salad or olive oil
1 lemon, cut into wedges

Mix all the ingredients together, apart from the lemon wedges and oil. Marinate chicken overnight. Arrange chicken pieces on baking tray. Brush with oil and bake in preheated oven 375°F for 40 minutes, turning them over so that they bake evenly. Bake until dry and well browned. Serve with lemon wedges.

Korma

PREPARATION TIME: 15 minutes

COOKING TIME: 40-50 minutes

SERVES: 4 people

2 tblsp ghee or
3 tblsp salad or olive oil
1 medium onion, peeled and thinly sliced
1 inch cinnamon stick
6 cloves
6 small cardamoms
1 bay leaf
1 tsp small whole black cumin seeds
2 tsp ginger paste
1 tsp garlic paste
1lb shoulder of lamb, cubed
1 tsp chili powder
1 tsp ground coriander
2tsp ground cumin
¼ tsp ground turmeric
⅔ cup natural yogurt
¾ cup water
Salt to taste
2 sprigs fresh coriander, chopped
2 green chilies, halved
1 tblsp ground almonds

Facing page: Chicken Tandoori (top), Chicken Tomato (center right) and Chicken Masala (bottom).

Fry onion in oil or ghee until golden brown. Add cinnamon, cloves, cardamoms, bay leaf and black cumin. Fry for 1 minute and add ginger and garlic paste. Stir for half a minute. Add meat and sprinkle with chili, coriander, cumin and turmeric. Mix well and add yogurt. Cover and cook for 10-15 minutes, stirring the mixture occasionally. Add water, salt to taste and cover. Cook on low temperature for 30-40 minutes, or until meat is tender. Korma should have a medium-thick gravy. Add ground almonds, green chilies and coriander leaves, and a little hot water if necessary. Serve with rice or chapatis.

Pork Vindaloo

PREPARATION TIME: 15 minutes
COOKING TIME: 1-1¼ hours
SERVES: 4 people

1 large onion, peeled and chopped
3 tblsp ghee or
3 tblsp salad or olive oil
1 inch cinnamon stick
6 cloves
6 green cardamoms
1 tsp ginger paste
1 tsp garlic paste
1lb lean pork, cut into cubes
3 tblsp brown vinegar
1 tsp chili powder
1 tsp ground cumin
2 tsp ground coriander
2 tblsp tamarind pulp concentrate
2 tsp ketchup
2 tsp brown sugar
Water
2 sprigs fresh green coriander leaves, chopped
1-2 green chilies, chopped
Salt to taste
1 tblsp salad or olive oil, for tempering
6-8 curry leaves

Fry onion in ghee or oil until light brown. Add cinnamon stick, cloves and cardamoms. Fry for half a minute. Add ginger and garlic pastes and pork and fry for 5 minutes, or until liquid from the pork has evaporated. Add vinegar, chili, cumin, coriander, tamarind pulp, ketchup and sugar. Cover and cook for 10-15 minutes. Add a little water if the mixture is too dry. Sprinkle with coriander leaves and chopped chili. Cook on a low heat for 30-40 minutes or until the pork is tender. The dish should have a rich gravy. Heat tempering oil and add the curry leaves. When leaves turn crisp and dark, pour the flavored oil and leaves over the curry. Mix well before serving. Serve with boiled rice.

Chicken Dhansak

PREPARATION TIME: 20 minutes
COOKING TIME: 40-50 minutes
SERVES: 6 people

3 tblsp ghee or
3 tblsp salad or olive oil
1 onion, peeled and chopped
4 cloves garlic, chopped
1 inch ginger paste
¼ tsp ground turmeric
1 tsp chili powder
2 tsp ground cumin
2 tsp ground coriander
4 green cardamoms, ground
8 peppercorns, ground
1 inch cinnamon stick, finely crumbled
2 tomatoes, quartered
3lb chicken cut into 10-12 pieces (ribcage discarded)
2½oz toor daal (yellow lentils), washed in a few changes of water
2½oz moong daal, washed in a few changes of water
2½oz masoor daal (red lentils) washed in a few changes of water
1 medium eggplant cut into ½ inch cubes
4oz red pumpkin, peeled and cut into 1 inch cubes
4 sprigs fresh methi leaves, chopped, or
4oz spinach leaves, chopped
2 sprigs fresh green coriander leaves, chopped
3¾ cups water
Salt to taste
1 tblsp brown sugar (or grated jaggery)
2 tblsp tamarind pulp concentrate
1 onion, sliced and fried until brown
1 lemon, sliced

Heat the ghee or oil in a deep skillet and fry chopped onion until light brown. Add garlic, ginger, turmeric, chili, cumin, coriander, ground cardamom, peppercorns and cinnamon stick; stir fry for 1 minute. Add tomatoes and cook for 2-3 minutes. Add chicken and cook until the juices have evaporated (10-15 minutes). Add the daals, eggplant, pumpkin, meth

This page: Chicken Makhani (left), Dum Ka Murgh (center) and Chicken Dhansak (right).

Facing page: Goan Curry (top) and Pork Vindaloo (bottom).

leaves and fresh coriander. Mix well and add the water. Add salt. Cover and cook on low heat until chicken is tender (20-30 minutes). Remove from heat and take chicken pieces out. Mash daal with the aid of a masher, or beat with an egg whisk, until the daal blends with the water to form a smooth, greenish gravy. Return chicken to skillet and sprinkle with sugar or jaggery and tamarind pulp. Cover and cook for 10 minutes. Before serving, a little extra water may be used to thin down the gravy if it is too thick. Garnish dhansak with onion rings and lemon slices and serve with rice.

Goan Curry

PREPARATION TIME: 20 minutes

COOKING TIME: 1 hour

SERVES: 4 people

3 tblsp ghee or
3 tblsp salad or olive oil
1 large onion, peeled and chopped
1 bay leaf
1 inch cinnamon stick
5 green cardamoms
6 cloves
1½ tsp garlic paste
1 tsp ginger paste
8 curry leaves
1lb lean pork, cut into cubes
1 tblsp tamarind pulp concentrate
⅔ cup natural yogurt
¼ tsp ground turmeric
1 tsp ground black pepper
1 tsp ground cumin
1 tsp ground coriander
½ tsp brown sugar
1 tblsp shredded coconut
Salt to taste
⅔ cup water
2 sprigs fresh green coriander leaves, chopped
2 green chilies, chopped

Heat oil or ghee and fry onion until golden brown. Add bay leaf, cinnamon, cardamoms, cloves, garlic, ginger and curry leaves and fry for 1-2 minutes. Add pork and fry for 5-7 minutes or until liquid from pork has evaporated. Add tamarind pulp, yogurt, turmeric, black pepper, cumin, coriander, sugar, coconut and salt to taste. Mix well; cover and cook for 20-30 minutes. Add a little water if the mixture is too dry. Add green coriander and chili. Cover and cook for 20-25 minutes or until pork is tender. The dish should have a smooth gravy. Serve with plain boiled rice.

Dum Ka Murgh
(WHOLE CHICKEN OR CHICKEN JOINTS)

The recipe can be used for both jointed and whole chicken.

PREPARATION TIME: 30 minutes

COOKING TIME: 1 hour

SERVES: 4-6 people

1 onion, finely minced
2 tsp ground coriander
1 tsp chili powder
¼ tsp ground turmeric
1 tblsp ketchup
1 tsp ginger paste
1 tsp garlic paste
½ tsp salt
⅔ cup natural yogurt
3lb chicken, cut into 8-10 pieces
Salad or olive oil

Mix onion, coriander, chili, turmeric, ketchup, ginger, garlic and salt with yogurt. Rub the mixture onto the chicken pieces. Brush with oil and bake in an oven at 375°F for 50 minutes to 1 hour, brushing frequently with oil until the liquid has evaporated and the chicken is cooked. For a whole chicken, bake with the above spices, wrapped in baking foil, for 1½ to 1¾ hours, then evaporate the liquid.

Chicken Makhani
(BUTTER CHICKEN)

PREPARATION TIME: 20 minutes

COOKING TIME: 1 hour

SERVES: 4-6 people

⅔ cup natural yogurt
1 tsp ginger paste
1 tsp salt
¼ tsp red or orange food coloring
3lb chicken, cut into 8-10 pieces, with skin removed
Salad or olive oil
¼ cup butter

1 inch cinnamon stick
6 cloves
6 green cardamoms
1 bay leaf
⅔ cup sour cream
¼ tsp saffron, crushed
⅔ cup pouring cream
Salt to taste
2 tsp ground almonds
¼ tsp cornstarch
1 tblsp water

Mix yogurt, ginger paste, salt and red coloring and rub into chicken. Let it marinate overnight. Place in an ovenproof dish and brush with oil. Bake in oven, 375°F, for 40-50 minutes. Save the liquid, if any. In a saucepan, melt butter and fry cinnamon, cloves, cardamoms and bay leaf for 1 minute. Add sour cream and chicken liquid. Add crushed saffron and pouring cream. Cover and simmer gently for 5-6 minutes. Add chicken pieces and adjust seasoning. Add ground almonds. Dissolve cornstarch in water and add to the chicken. Let it thicken. Cover and simmer for 3-4 minutes. Remove from heat. Serve with nan.

Malabari Chicken

PREPARATION TIME: 20 minutes
COOKING TIME: 40-50 minutes
SERVES: 6 people

1 large onion, peeled and chopped
3 tblsp ghee or
3 tblsp salad or olive oil
1 inch cinnamon stick
6 green cardamoms
6 cloves
1 bay leaf
1 tsp ginger paste
1 tsp garlic paste
3lb chicken, cut into 10-12 pieces
1 tsp chili powder
1 tsp ground cumin
1 tsp ground coriander
⅔ cup natural yogurt
1 tsp salt
1 tblsp coconut cream
1 tblsp flaked almonds
1 tblsp raisins
½ cup water
2 tblsp evaporated milk
2 sprigs fresh green coriander leaves, chopped (optional)
2 green chilies, chopped (optional)
1 cup canned pineapple chunks

Fry onion in ghee or oil until tender (3-4 minutes). Add cinnamon, cardamoms, cloves and bay leaf and fry for one minute. Then add ginger and garlic paste. Stir fry for half a minute. Add chicken. Stir and cook for 2-3 minutes. Sprinkle with chili, cumin and coriander. Stir and mix well. Add yogurt and salt. Cover and cook for 10 minutes or until yogurt is dry and oil separates. Add coconut cream, almonds, raisins and water. Cover and cook for 20-30 minutes. Add evaporated milk and cook for 5 minutes. Add coriander leaves, green chilies and pineapple chunks. Mix gently and cook for another 5 minutes. Malabari chicken is a moist curry with a thick, rich sauce. It is served with pulao rice.

Chicken Tikka

PREPARATION TIME: 10 minutes
COOKING TIME: 30 minutes
SERVES: 6 people

⅔ cup natural yogurt
1 tsp chili powder
2 tsp ginger paste
2 tsp garlic paste
2 tsp garam masala powder
½ tsp salt
¼ tsp red food coloring
3lb chicken, cut into 2½ inch pieces
Juice of 1 lemon
Salad or olive oil
1 lemon, cut into wedges

Mix yogurt with chili powder, ginger and garlic, garam masala, salt and red food coloring. Pour over chicken pieces and mix well. Sprinkle with lemon juice. Mix well. Line the broiler pan with baking foil. Arrange chicken pieces on top. Brush with oil and broil them for 4-5 minutes on each side. Brush with oil occasionally and continue cooking until chicken is tender. Serve with wedges of lemon and a crisp lettuce salad.

Maach Bhaja
(MACKEREL FRY)

PREPARATION TIME: 10 minutes
COOKING TIME: 15 minutes
SERVES: 4 people

2 large mackerel, gutted and cut into 1 inch thick slices
1 tsp chili powder
1 tsp ground turmeric
1 tsp salt
Salad or olive oil for frying
Lemon juice

Wash fish thoroughly. Drain and dry well. Sprinkle with chili powder, turmeric and salt. Rub in well. Heat oil and fry fish, a few pieces at a time, for 3-4 minutes on each side. Drain on kitchen paper. Serve with lemon juice sprinkled over fish.

Sprat Fry

PREPARATION TIME: 10 minutes
COOKING TIME: 15-20 minutes
SERVES: 2-3 people

8oz cleaned sprats, washed and dried
¼ tsp ground turmeric
1 tsp chili powder
1 tsp salt
Salad or olive oil for deep frying
Lemon juice

Rub sprats well with turmeric, chili powder and salt. Gently heat oil and fry fish, a few at a time, for 6-8 minutes, until crisp. Drain on kitchen paper. Sprinkle with lemon juice and serve.

Masala Fish
(WHOLE FRIED FISH)

PREPARATION TIME: 10 minutes
COOKING TIME: 15 minutes
SERVES: 6 people

1 tsp ginger paste
1 tsp garlic paste
1 tsp salt
3 sprigs fresh green coriander leaves, crushed
2 green chilies, crushed
1 tsp ground black pepper
¼ tsp ground turmeric
1 tblsp water
6 herring or rainbow trout, gutted, washed and dried
Salad or olive oil
Lemon slices

Make 3 diagonal slits on each fish. Mix together the ginger, garlic, salt, coriander, chili, ground pepper and turmeric. Add the water. Rub spices over fish, and inside the cuts. Broil for 10-15 minutes, brushing with oil and turning the fish occasionally, until cooked. Garnish with lemon slices.

This page: Malabari Chicken (top) and Chicken Tikka (bottom).

Facing page: Main dish – top to bottom – Masala Fish, Maach Bhaja, Sprat Fry and Cod Roe Fry.

Cod Curry

PREPARATION TIME: 15 minutes

COOKING TIME: 20 minutes

SERVES: 3-4 people

3 tblsp ghee or
3 tblsp salad or olive oil
1 large onion, peeled and chopped
1 inch cinnamon stick
1 bay leaf
1 tsp ginger paste
1 tsp garlic paste
1 tsp chili powder
1 tsp ground cumin
1 tsp ground coriander
¼ tsp ground turmeric
⅔ cup natural yogurt
1-2 green chilies, chopped
2 sprigs fresh green coriander leaves, chopped
1 tsp salt
1lb cod fillet, cut into 2 inch pieces

Melt ghee or oil and fry onion until golden brown. Add cinnamon, bay leaf, ginger and garlic pastes. Fry for 1 minute. Add chili, cumin, coriander and turmeric. Fry for 1 minute. Add yogurt, chopped green chilies and fresh coriander leaves. Add salt and cover. Simmer for 2-3 minutes. Add ⅔ cup water. Bring to boil. Add cod. Cover and cook gently for 15-18 minutes. Serve with rice.

Prawn Curry

PREPARATION TIME: 15 minutes

COOKING TIME: 20 minutes

SERVES: 4 people

1 large onion, peeled and chopped
3 tblsp ghee or
3 tblsp salad or olive oil
1 inch cinnamon stick
6 green cardamoms
6 cloves
1 bay leaf
1 tsp ginger paste
1 tsp garlic paste
1 tsp chili powder
1 tsp ground cumin
1 tsp ground coriander
½ tsp salt
1 green pepper, chopped into ½ inch pieces
1½ cups canned tomatoes, crushed
1lb large shrimps, peeled
2 green chilies, chopped
2 sprigs fresh green coriander leaves, chopped

Prawn Curry (left), Cod Curry (center), and Fish Kebab (right).

Fry onion in oil or ghee until just tender (3-4 minutes). Add cinnamon, cardamoms, cloves and bay leaf. Fry for 1 minute and then add ginger and garlic pastes. Add chili, cumin, coriander and salt. Fry for half a minute. Add chopped green pepper and tomatoes, then bring to the boil. Add prawns, cover and bring to boil. Cook for 10-15 minutes. Add chopped green coriander leaves and chopped chilies. Serve with plain boiled rice.

Cod Roe Fry

PREPARATION TIME: 5 minutes

COOKING TIME: 15 minutes

SERVES: 2-3 people

½lb soft cod roes
¼ tsp ground turmeric
1 tsp chili powder
½ tsp salt
1 tblsp all-purpose flour

For batter
1 cup baisen flour, sifted
¼ tsp salt
1 egg, beaten
Water
Salad or olive oil for deep frying

Put cod roes in a mixing bowl. Sprinkle with spices, one at a time, and add salt. Rub well so as to coat the roes thoroughly, then roll them in flour and keep aside. For the batter: mix the baisen flour, salt, egg and sufficient water to make a smooth coating batter. Heat oil gently. Fry the roes, a few at a time, well coated in batter, until crisp and golden. Drain on kitchen paper and serve hot.

Fish Kebab

PREPARATION TIME: 20 minutes

COOKING TIME: 15 minutes

SERVES: 3 people

10oz whiting or coley fillet (or other white fish)
1 onion, peeled and chopped
1 inch root ginger, peeled and finely chopped
1 green chili, finely chopped
2 sprigs fresh green coriander leaves, finely chopped
1 egg, beaten
2 tsp garam masala powder
Salt to taste
1 tsp ground black pepper
Juice of 1 lemon
Salad or olive oil

Boil fish in water for 8-10 minutes. Cool and drain. Remove skin and bones and mash fish flesh. Add choped onion, ginger, chili, coriander leaves, egg, garam masala, salt, black pepper and lemon juice. Beat or grind into a smooth paste. Devide into 10-12 equal-sized portions, and pat each portion into a flat burger shape. Heat oil in a skillet and shallow fry on each side for 3-4 minutes. Serve with onion salad.

Facing page: Farfalle with Beef, Mushroom and Soured Cream (top), Tagliatelle Carbonara (center left) and Pasta Spirals with Spinach and Bacon (bottom).

Tortiglioni alla Puttanesca

PREPARATION TIME: 10 minutes
COOKING TIME: 15 minutes
SERVES: 4 people

1 9oz package tortiglioni, spiral pasta
1 small can (about 1 cup) plum tomatoes, drained
6-8 anchovy fillets
2 tbsps olive oil
2 cloves garlic, crushed
½ tsp basil
Pinch chili powder
½ cup black olives, stoned and chopped
2 tbsps chopped parsley
Salt
Pepper

Chop tomatoes and remove seeds, and chop anchovies. Cook pasta in plenty of boiling salted water for 10 minutes, or until tender but still firm. Rinse in hot water, and drain. Pour into a warmed bowl. Meanwhile, heat oil in pan, add garlic, chili powder and basil, and cook for 1 minute. Add tomatoes, parsley, olives and anchovies, and cook for a few minutes. Season with salt and pepper. Pour sauce over pasta, and mix together thoroughly. Serve immediately.

Pasta Spirals with Spinach and Bacon

PREPARATION TIME: 15 minutes
COOKING TIME: 15 minutes

1 9oz package pasta spirals
½ pound spinach
¼ pound Canadian bacon
1 clove garlic, crushed
1 small red chili pepper
½ small sweet red pepper
1 small onion
3 tbsps olive oil
Salt and pepper

Wash spinach, remove stalks and cut into thin shreds. Core and seed pepper, and slice half finely. Peel onion and chop finely. Chop the bacon. Remove seeds from chili pepper, and slice thinly. Cook pasta spirals in plenty of boiling salted water for 10 minutes, or until tender but still firm. Drain. Meanwhile, heat oil in pan, and add garlic, onion, bacon, chili pepper and sweet red pepper. Fry for 2 minutes, add spinach, and fry for a further 2 minutes, stirring continuously. Season with salt and pepper to taste. Toss with pasta spirals. Serve immediately.

Tagliatelle Carbonara

PREPARATION TIME: 10 minutes
COOKING TIME: 15 minutes

1 9oz package tagliatelle
2 tbsps butter or margarine
8 strips bacon, shredded
1 tbsp olive oil
⅓ cup cream
Pinch of paprika
¼ cup Parmesan cheese, grated
2 eggs
Salt and pepper

This page: Tortiglioni alla Puttanesca.

Heat oil in a frying-pan, and cook bacon over a moderate heat until browning. Add paprika and cook for 1 minute. Add cream, and stir. Beat together eggs and grated cheese. Meanwhile, cook tagliatelle in lots of boiling salted water for 10 minutes, or until tender but still firm. Drain, return to pan with butter and black pepper, and toss. Add bacon mixture and egg mixture, and toss together. Add salt to taste. Serve immediately.

Farfalle with Beef, Mushroom and Soured Cream

PREPARATION TIME: 10 minutes
COOKING TIME: 15 minutes

1 9oz package farfalle (pasta butterflies – bows)
½ pound sirloin or butt steak, sliced
¾ cup mushrooms, sliced
¼ cup soured cream
10 green olives, stoned and chopped
1 onion, peeled and sliced
2 tbsps unsalted butter
1 tbsp flour
Salt and pepper

Garnish:
Soured cream
1 tbsp chopped parsley

With a very sharp knife, cut meat into narrow, short strips. Heat half the butter, and fry meat over a high heat until well browned. Set aside. Heat remaining butter in pan, and gently fry onion until soft and just beginning to color. Add mushrooms, and cook for 3 minutes. Stir in flour and continue frying for a further 3 minutes. Gradually stir in soured cream. When fully incorporated, add meat, olives, and salt and pepper to taste. Meanwhile, cook farfalle in plenty of boiling salted water for 10 minutes, or until tender but still firm. Drain well. Serve with beef and mushroom sauce on top. Garnish with a little extra soured cream and chopped parsley.

Penne with Anchovy Sauce

PREPARATION TIME: 5 minutes
COOKING TIME: 20 minutes

1 9oz package penne
6-8 anchovies
2 small cans (about 2 cups) tomato sauce
2 tbsps olive oil
3 tbsps chopped parsley
¼ cup Parmesan cheese, grated
2 tbsps butter or margarine
Pepper

Chop anchovies and cook them in the oil, stirring to a paste. Add tomato sauce to anchovies, with parsley and freshly-ground black pepper to taste. Bring to the boil and simmer, uncovered, for 10 minutes. Meanwhile, cook the penne in lots of boiling salted water for 10 minutes, or until tender but still firm. Rinse in hot water and drain well. Toss in butter. Combine sauce with the pasta, and sprinkle with parsley, and serve with Parmesan cheese. Serve immediately.

Whole-wheat Spaghetti with Peas and Bacon

PREPARATION TIME: 10 minutes
COOKING TIME: 15 minutes

1 9oz package whole-wheat spaghetti
1½ cups peas
1 tsp sugar
8 strips bacon, diced
4 tbsps butter or margarine
Salt and pepper

Garnish:
Parsley

Cook spaghetti in lots of boiling salted water for 10 minutes, or until tender but still firm. Drain. Meanwhile, cook peas in boiling water with a pinch of salt and a teaspoon of sugar. Melt butter in a pan, and fry bacon. When crisp, add peas, and salt and pepper to taste, and pour over spaghetti. Toss through, and serve immediately garnished with chopped parsley if desired.

Penne with Anchovy Sauce (left) and Whole-wheat Spaghetti with Peas and Bacon (below).

Spaghetti Neapolitana

PREPARATION TIME: 5 minutes
COOKING TIME: 30 minutes
SERVES: 4 people

1 pound spaghetti
2 small cans (about 2 cups tomato sauce)
2 tbsps olive oil
½ tsp oregano or marjoram
Salt
Pepper
2 tbsps chopped parsley
Parmesan cheese, grated

Heat oil in pan. Add oregano or marjoram, and cook for 30 seconds. Add tomato sauce, and salt and pepper. Bring to boil; reduce heat; simmer uncovered for 20-30 minutes. Meanwhile, cook spaghetti in lots of boiling salted water for about 10 minutes, or until tender but still firm. Rinse under hot water, and drain well. Pour tomato sauce over spaghetti, and toss gently. Sprinkle parsley over the top. Serve with Parmesan cheese. Serve immediately.

Spaghetti with Tomato, Salami and Green Olives

PREPARATION TIME: 15 minutes
COOKING TIME: 15 minutes

1 9oz package spaghetti
2 small cans (about 2 cups) tomato sauce
⅓ pound salami, sliced and shredded
1 cup green olives, stoned and chopped
1 clove garlic, crushed
2 tbsps olive oil
½ tbsp oregano
¼ cup pecorino cheese, grated
Salt and pepper

This page: Spaghetti with Tomato, Salami and Green Olives.

Facing page: Spaghetti Neapolitana (top) and Farfalle with Creamy Cheese Sauce (bottom).

Combine tomato sauce, oregano, salami and olives in a saucepan and heat gently. Add salt and pepper to taste. Meanwhile, cook spaghetti in plenty of boiling salted water for 10 minutes, or until tender but still firm. Drain well. Heat olive oil and freshly-ground black pepper in the pan used to cook the spaghetti. Add spaghetti, and pour the sauce over. Toss well. Serve immediately with pecorino cheese.

Farfalle with Creamy Cheese Sauce

PREPARATION TIME: 5 minutes

COOKING TIME: 15 minutes

SERVES: 4 people

1 9oz package farfalle (pasta butterflies /bows)
2 tbsps butter or margarine
2 tbsps flour
1 cup milk
¼ cup Gruyère or Cheddar cheese, grated
½ tsp Dijon mustard
1 tbsp grated Parmesan cheese

Heat butter in pan. Stir in flour and cook for 1 minute. Remove from heat and gradually stir in milk. Return to heat and stir continuously. Boil for 3 minutes. Stir in Gruyère or Cheddar cheese, and mustard; do not reboil. Meanwhile, cook the pasta in lots of boiling salted water for 10 minutes, or until tender but still firm. Rinse in hot water and drain well. Pour over cheese sauce, and toss. Top with a sprinkling of Parmesan cheese. Serve immediately.

Pasta with Tomato and Yogurt Sauce

PREPARATION TIME: 5 minutes

COOKING TIME: 40 minutes

1 9oz box pasta shells
⅓ cup plain yogurt
1 tbsp butter or margarine
1 tbsp flour
½ cup beef stock
2 small cans tomato sauce
1 bay leaf
Sprig of thyme
Parsley stalks
Salt and pepper

Melt butter in a pan. Stir in the flour, and pour in the stock gradually. Add tomato sauce, bay leaf, thyme and parsley stalks. Season with salt and pepper. Bring to the boil, and simmer for 30 minutes. Adjust seasoning. Meanwhile, cook pasta in plenty of boiling salted water for 10 minutes, or until tender but still firm. Rinse in hot water and drain well. Place in warmed serving dish; pour over tomato sauce, then yogurt. (Yogurt may be marbled through tomato sauce). Serve immediately.

Penne with Chili Sauce

PREPARATION TIME: 40 minutes

COOKING TIME: 20 minutes

1 9oz package penne
1 clove garlic, crushed
1 onion, peeled and chopped
1 pound ripe tomatoes
1 eggplant
1 red chili pepper
2 tbsps oil
¼ cup pecorino cheese, grated

Trim and cut eggplant into ½ inch slices, and salt lightly. Leave for 30 minutes. Rinse and wipe dry with absorbent paper. Meanwhile, heat oil in a frying-pan over a moderate heat, and fry garlic and onion until lightly colored. Peel and seed tomatoes, and chop roughly. Seed chili pepper, and chop finely. Cut eggplant roughly and add to onion. Fry together for 5 minutes. Add tomatoes and chili pepper, and mix well. Simmer sauce gently, uncovered, for 5 minutes, stirring occasionally. Meanwhile, cook pasta in lots of boiling salted water for 10 minutes, or until tender but still firm, stirring occasionally. Rinse in hot water, and drain well. Place in a warmed serving dish. Add hot sauce and toss well. Serve immediately with side dish of grated pecorino cheese.

Penne with Chili Sauce (above) and Pasta with Tomato and Yogurt Sauce (left).

browned all over. Add the tomato paste, salt and pepper to taste, and the stock, and simmer gently for about ¾ hour, until the mixture thickens, stirring occasionally. Add 2 tablespoons sherry, and cook for a further 5 minutes. Meanwhile, place the spaghetti in lots of boiling salted water, and cook for 10 minutes, or until tender but still firm. Drain. Serve with Bolognese sauce on top, and sprinkle with Parmesan cheese.

Fish Ravioli

PREPARATION TIME: 30 minutes
COOKING TIME: 30 minutes
OVEN: 350°F (180°C)
SERVES: 4 people

Dough:
1¼ cups bread flour
Pinch of salt
3 eggs

Filling:
½ pound sole fillets, or flounder, skinned and boned
2 tbsps breadcrumbs
2 eggs, beaten
1 green onion, finely chopped
1 slice of onion
1 slice of lemon
6 peppercorns
1 bay leaf
1 tbsp lemon juice
1 cup water

Lemon sauce:
2 tbsps butter or margarine
2 tbsps flour
1 cup strained cooking liquid from fish
2 tbsps heavy cream
2 tbsps lemon juice
Salt
Pepper

To make filling:
Pre-heat oven. Wash and dry fish. Place in oven-proof dish with slice of onion, slice of lemon, peppercorns, bay leaf, lemon juice and water. Cover and cook in oven for 20 minutes. Remove fish from liquid, and allow to drain. Strain liquid, and set aside. When fish is cool, beat with the back of a spoon to a pulp. Add eggs, breadcrumbs and green onion, and salt and pepper to taste. Mix well.

This page: Fish Ravioli.
Facing page: Spaghetti Bolognese (top) and Pasta Spirals with Creamy Parsley Sauce (bottom).

Pasta Spirals with Creamy Parsley Sauce

PREPARATION TIME: 5 minutes
COOKING TIME: 15 minutes

1 9oz package pasta spirals
2 tbsps butter or margarine
1 tbsp flour
1 cup milk
1 tbsp chopped parsley
1 tbsp lemon juice, or 1 tsp vinegar

Heat butter in pan; when melted, stir in flour. Cook for 1 minute. Remove from heat, and gradually stir in milk. Return to heat, and stir continuously until boiling. Cook for 2 minutes. Meanwhile, cook pasta spirals in lots of boiling salted water for 10 minutes, or until tender but still firm. Rinse in hot water, and drain well. Just before serving, add lemon juice and parsley to sauce, and pour over pasta. Serve immediately.

Spaghetti Bolognese

PREPARATION TIME: 10 minutes
COOKING TIME: 1 hour 15 minutes

1 9oz package spaghetti
2 tbsps butter or margarine
1 tbsp olive oil
2 onions, peeled and chopped finely
½ pound ground beef
1 carrot, scraped and chopped finely
¼ cup tomato paste
1 cup brown stock
2 tbsps sherry
Salt and pepper
Parmesan cheese, grated

Heat the butter and oil in a pan and fry the onions and carrot slowly until soft. Increase heat and add the ground beef. Fry for a few minutes, then stir, cooking until meat is

To make dough:
Sift flour into a bowl. Make a well in the center, and add the eggs. Work the flour and eggs together with a spoon, and then knead by hand, until a smooth dough is formed. Leave to rest for 15 minutes. Lightly flour board, and roll out dough thinly into a rectangle. Cut dough in half. Shape the filling into small balls, and set them about 1½" apart on one half of the dough. Place the other half on top, and cut with a ravioli cutter or small pastry cutter. Seal the edges. Cook in batches in a large, wide pan with plenty of boiling salted water until tender – about 8 minutes. Remove carefully with a perforated spoon. Meanwhile, make sauce.

To make sauce:
Melt butter in pan. Stir in flour, and cook for 30 seconds. Draw off heat, and gradually stir in liquid from cooked fish. Return to heat and bring to boil. Simmer for 4 minutes, stirring continuously. Add cream and mix well. Season to taste. Remove from heat, and gradually stir in lemon juice. Do not reboil.

Pour sauce over ravioli and serve immediately.

Ravioli with Ricotta Cheese

PREPARATION TIME: 30 minutes

COOKING TIME: 20 minutes

SERVES: 4 people

Dough:
1¼ cups bread flour
Pinch of salt
3 eggs

Filling:
2 tbsps butter or margarine
½ pound ricotta cheese
¼ cup Parmesan cheese, grated
1 egg yolk
2 tbsps chopped parsley
Salt
Pepper

Tomato sauce:
1 large can (about 2 cups) plum tomatoes
1 tsp basil
1 tbsp olive oil
2 strips bacon
1 tbsp heavy cream
1 small onion, peeled and chopped
1 bay leaf
1 tbsp flour
Salt
Pepper

To make filling:
Beat the butter to a cream, add egg yolk, and blend well. Beat ricotta cheese to a cream, and add butter-egg mixture gradually until smooth. Add Parmesan cheese and parsley, and salt and pepper to taste. Set aside.

To make dough:
Sift flour in a bowl. Make a well in the center, and add the eggs. Work flour and eggs together with a spoon, and then knead by hand, until a smooth dough is formed. Leave to rest for 15 minutes. Lightly flour board, and roll dough out thinly into a rectangle. Cut dough in half. Shape the filling into small balls and set them about 1½" apart on one half of the dough. Place the other half on top and cut with a ravioli cutter or small pastry cutter. Seal the edges. Cook in batches in a large, wide pan with plenty of boiling salted water until tender – about 8 minutes. Remove carefully with a perforated spoon. Meanwhile, make sauce.

To make sauce:
Heat oil, and fry bacon and onion until golden. Add bay leaf and basil, and stir in flour. Cook for 1 minute, draw off heat, and add tomatoes gradually, stirring continuously. Add salt and pepper to taste. Return to heat and bring to boil. Cook for 5 minutes, then push through a sieve. Stir in cream, and adjust seasoning.

Pour sauce over ravioli. Serve immediately.

Whole-wheat Spaghetti with Walnuts and Parsley

PREPARATION TIME: 10 minutes

COOKING TIME: 10 minutes

1 9oz package whole-wheat spaghetti
4 tbsps parsley
2 tbsps walnuts
¼ cup olive oil
2 cloves garlic, peeled
Salt and pepper
¼ cup grated Parmesan or pecorino cheese

Fry garlic gently in oil for 2 minutes. Set oil aside to cool. Wash parsley and remove stalks. Finely chop parsley, walnuts and garlic in a food processor with a metal blade, or in a blender. When chopped well, add cooled oil in a thin stream. Turn mixture into a bowl, mix in grated

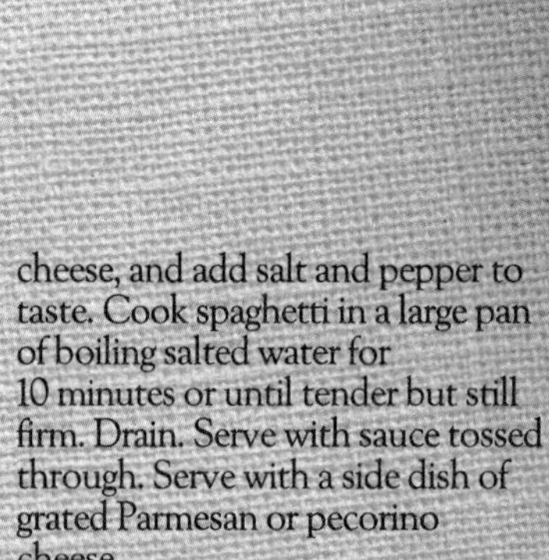

cheese, and add salt and pepper to taste. Cook spaghetti in a large pan of boiling salted water for 10 minutes or until tender but still firm. Drain. Serve with sauce tossed through. Serve with a side dish of grated Parmesan or pecorino cheese.

Tagliatelle with Bacon and Tomato Sauce

PREPARATION TIME: 15 minutes

COOKING TIME: 15 minutes

¾ pound red tagliatelle
1 onion, peeled and finely chopped
6 slices bacon, cut into strips

1 large can (about 2 cups) plum tomatoes, drained, seeds removed, and chopped roughly
2 tbsps chopped parsley
1 tbsp olive oil
1 tbsp dry basil
¼ cup pecorino cheese, grated
Salt and pepper

Heat oil in pan. Add onion and bacon, and cook over gentle heat until onion is transparent but not colored. Add parsley, basil and tomato. Simmer gently for 5 minutes, stirring occasionally. Add salt and pepper to taste. Meanwhile, cook tagliatelle in a large pan with plenty of boiling salted water. Cook for about 10 minutes, unil tender but still firm. Drain and return to the pan. Add sauce and toss through. Serve with grated pecorino cheese.

Tagliatelle with Bacon and Tomato Sauce (left) and Whole-wheat Spaghetti with Walnuts and Parsley (below).

Pasta Shells with Gorgonzola Cheese Sauce

PREPARATION TIME: 5 minutes

COOKING TIME: 15 minutes

⅓ pound gorgonzola cheese
⅓ cup milk
2 tbsps butter or margarine
3 tbsps heavy cream
1 9oz package pasta shells
Salt
Parmesan cheese, grated

Heat gorgonzola cheese, milk and butter gently in a pan. Stir to a sauce with a wooden spoon. Stir in cream. Add salt if necessary. Meanwhile, cook shells in plenty of boiling salted water for 10 minutes, or until shells are tender but still firm. Drain, shaking colander to remove excess water. Add shells to hot sauce and toss to coat well. Serve immediately with grated Parmesan cheese on the side.

Meat Ravioli

PREPARATION TIME: 30 minutes

COOKING TIME: 30 minutes

SERVES: 4 people

Dough:
1¼ cups of bread flour
Pinch of salt
3 eggs

Filling:
4 tbsps butter or margarine
½ pound ground beef
½ cup cooked spinach, chopped
2 tbsps breadcrumbs
2 eggs, beaten
½ cup red wine
1 onion, peeled and grated
1 clove garlic, crushed
Salt
Pepper

Sauce:
1 small can (about 1 cup) plum tomatoes
1 small onion, peeled and grated
1 small carrot, diced finely
1 bay leaf
3 parsley stalks
Salt
Pepper

Parmesan cheese, grated

To make filling:
Heat butter in pan. Add garlic and onion, and fry gently for 1 minute. Add ground beef, and fry until browned. Add red wine, and salt and pepper to taste, and cook uncovered for 15 minutes. Strain juices and reserve them for sauce. Allow to cool. Add breadcrumbs, chopped spinach, and beaten eggs to bind. Adjust salt and pepper to taste.

To make dough:
Sift flour in a bowl. Make a well in the center and add the eggs. Work flour and eggs together with a spoon, then knead by hand, until a smooth dough is formed. Leave dough to rest for 15 minutes. Lightly flour board, and roll out dough thinly into a rectangle. Cut dough in half. Shape the filling into small balls, and set them about 1½" apart on one half of the dough. Place the other half on top, and cut with a ravioli cutter or small pastry cutter. Seal the edges. Cook in batches in a large, wide pan with plenty of boiling salted water until

This page: Pasta Shells with Gorgonzola Cheese Sauce (top) and Spaghetti Amatriciana (bottom).

Facing page: Spinach Ravioli (top) and Meat Ravioli (bottom).

tender – about 8 minutes. Remove carefully with a perforated spoon. Meanwhile, make sauce.

To make sauce:
Put all ingredients in a saucepan. Add juice from cooked meat, and bring to boil. Simmer for 10 minutes. Strain, and return smooth sauce to pan. Adjust seasoning.

Put ravioli in a warm dish and cover with tomato sauce. Serve immediately, with grated Parmesan cheese.

Spaghetti Amatriciana

PREPARATION TIME: 10 minutes

COOKING TIME: 20 minutes

1 9oz package spaghetti
1 onion, peeled and chopped finely
6 slices bacon, cut into strips
1 large can (about 2 cups) plum tomatoes, drained, seeds removed, and chopped roughly
1 red chili pepper, seeds removed, and chopped finely
2 tbsps olive oil
¼ cup pecorino cheese, grated

Heat oil in pan. Add onion and bacon, and cook over gentle heat until onion is soft but not colored. Drain off surplus fat. Add tomato and chili. Stir. Simmer gently for 5 minutes, stirring occasionally. Meanwhile, cook spaghetti in lots of boiling salted water for about 10 minutes, or until tender but still firm. Drain and return to pan. Add sauce and stir through. Serve with grated pecorino cheese.

Carrettiera with Pasta Rings

PREPARATION TIME: 5 minutes

COOKING TIME: 15 minutes

SERVES: 4 people

1 9oz package pasta rings
1 7oz can tuna fish, flaked
¼ pound mushrooms, cleaned and sliced
2 tbsps butter or margarine

Heat butter in pan, and cook mushrooms. Add tuna to warm through. Meanwhile, cook pasta in plenty of boiling salted water for 10 minutes, or until tender but still firm. Rinse under hot water. Drain well. Pour over mushroom and tuna, and toss together. Serve immediately.

Hare Sauce with Whole-wheat Spaghetti

PREPARATION TIME: 10 minutes

COOKING TIME: 1 hour 15 minutes

SERVES: 4 people

1 pound whole-wheat spaghetti
½ pound hare or rabbit cut into small pieces
¼ pound bacon, diced
2 onions, peeled and sliced
1 clove garlic, crushed
2 tbsps olive oil
½ tsp oregano
1 tbsp flour
½ cup red wine

Heat oil in heavy pan. Lightly brown hare pieces. Remove hare pieces and put aside. Add onion, bacon, garlic and oregano to oil,

Ravioli with Ricotta Cheese (above), Brasciole with Tagliatelle (right) and Hare Sauce with Whole-wheat Spaghetti (top right).

and fry until lightly colored. Draw off heat, and stir in flour with a metal spoon. Return to heat and cook for 2 minutes. Remove from heat, and add wine, and return to heat, stirring until boiling. Add hare, cover pan, and simmer gently for about 1 hour, until hare is tender. Add salt and pepper to taste. When sauce is ready, cook spaghetti in lots of boiling salted water for about 10 minutes, or until tender but still firm. Rinse in hot water, and drain. Serve with hare sauce on top. Serve immediately.

Brasciole with Tagliatelle

PREPARATION TIME: 15 minutes

COOKING TIME: 25 minutes

SERVES: 4 people

½ pound tagliatelle
4 veal steaks, or cutlets
4 thin slices ham
4 tbsps grated Parmesan cheese
2 tbsps butter or margarine
2 small cans (about 2 cups) tomato sauce
Salt
Pepper

Pound veal steaks out thinly. Place a slice of ham on the top of each steak. Sprinkle a tablespoon of the Parmesan cheese over each steak, and freshly-ground black pepper. Roll up, and tie gently with string at each end and in the middle. Heat butter in a pan, and add veal rolls. Cook gently until lightly browned all over. Add tomato sauce, and cover. Cook for 15 minutes. Meanwhile, cook tagliatelle in plenty of boiling salted water for 10 minutes, or until tender but still firm. Rinse in hot water, and drain. Cut veal rolls into 1" rounds. Toss tagliatelle together with tomato sauce, and top with veal rolls and grated Parmesan cheese. Serve immediately.

Tagliatelle with Garlic and Oil

PREPARATION TIME: 5 minutes
COOKING TIME: 10 minutes

1 9oz package green tagliatelle
½ cup olive oil
3 cloves garlic, crushed
2 tbsps chopped parsley
Salt and pepper

Cook the tagliatelle in lots of boiling salted water for 10 minutes, or until tender but still firm, stirring occasionally. Meanwhile, make the sauce. Heat the oil in a pan and, when warm, add peeled, crushed garlic. Fry gently until golden brown. Add chopped parsley, and salt and pepper to taste. Drain tagliatelle. Add sauce, and toss to coat well. Serve hot.

Farfalle with Tomato Sauce

PREPARATION TIME: 10 minutes
COOKING TIME: 30 minutes

1 9oz package farfalle
4 small cans (about 4 cups) tomato sauce
1 tbsp olive oil
1 onion, peeled and sliced
2 cloves garlic, crushed
½ tsp dry basil
Salt and pepper
2 tbsps chopped fresh basil or chopped parsley
Parmesan cheese, grated

Heat oil in a deep pan. Add garlic and onion, and cook until softened. Add dry basil, and cook for 30 seconds. Add tomato sauce; season with salt and pepper. Bring to the boil, reduce heat, and simmer, uncovered, for about 20 minutes, or until sauce is reduced by half and stir in the fresh parsley or basil.

Meanwhile, cook the pasta in a large pan of boiling salted water, until tender but still firm – about 10 minutes. Rinse in hot water, and drain well. Toss sauce through pasta. Serve with grated Parmesan cheese. Serve immediately.

Pasta Shells with Mushroom Sauce

PREPARATION TIME: 5 minutes
COOKING TIME: 15 minutes

1 9oz package pasta shells
½ pound mushrooms
2 tbsps butter or margarine
1 tbsp flour
1 cup milk
Salt and pepper

Rinse the mushrooms and chop them roughly. Melt butter in a saucepan and add mushrooms. Fry for 5 minutes, stirring occasionally. Stir in the flour and cook for 1 minute. Draw off the heat, and add milk gradually, stirring continuously. Bring to the boil and cook for 3 minutes. Season with salt and pepper. Meanwhile, cook the pasta shells in lots of boiling salted water for 10 minutes, or until tender but still firm. Rinse in hot water and drain well. Place in a warmed serving dish, and pour over mushroom sauce. Serve immediately.

This page: Tagliatelle with Garlic and Oil (top) and Spaghetti with Basil Sauce (Pesto) (bottom).

Facing page: Pasta Shells with Mushroom Sauce (top) and Farfalle with Tomato Sauce (bottom).

CINNAMON
CINNAMON
PEPPER
PEPPER

Tortellini

PREPARATION TIME: 30 minutes

COOKING TIME: 15 minutes

SERVES: 4 people

Dough:

1¼ cups bread flour
Pinch of salt
3 eggs
1 tbsp water
1 tbsp oil

Filling:

1 cooked chicken breast, finely diced
2 spinach leaves, stalks removed, cooked and chopped finely
2 tbsps ham, finely diced
1 tbsp grated Parmesan cheese
2 tbsps cream cheese
1 egg, beaten
Salt
Pepper

Sauce:

1 cup cream
¼ pound mushrooms, cleaned and sliced
¼ cup Parmesan cheese, grated
1 tbsp chopped parsley
Salt
Pepper

To make filling:
Beat the cream cheese until soft and smooth. Add chicken, ham, spinach and Parmesan cheese, and mix well. Add egg gradually, and salt and pepper to taste. Set aside.

To make dough:
Sift flour and salt onto a board. Make a well in the center. Mix water, oil and lightly-beaten egg together, and gradually pour into well, working in the flour with the other hand, a little at a time. Continue until the mixture comes together in a firm ball of dough. Knead on a lightly-floured board for 5 minutes, or until smooth and elastic. Put into a bowl, cover with a cloth, and let stand for 15 minutes. Roll dough out on a lightly-floured board as thinly as possible. Using a 2" cutter, cut out rounds. Put ½ teaspoon of filling into the center of each round. Fold in half, pressing edges together firmly. Wrap around forefinger, and press ends together. Cook in batches in a large pan, in plenty of boiling salted water for about 10 minutes until tender, stirring occasionally.

To make sauce:
Meanwhile, gently heat cream in a pan. Add mushrooms, Parmesan cheese, parsley, and salt and pepper to taste. Gently cook for 3 minutes.

Toss sauce together with tortellini. Serve immediately, sprinkled with parsley.

Pasta Shells with Walnuts and Cream Cheese

PREPARATION TIME: 5 minutes

COOKING TIME: 15 minutes

1 9oz package pasta shells
1 tbsp olive oil
1 clove garlic, crushed
1 tbsp oregano
2 tbsps butter or margarine
⅓ cup milk
1 ¼ pound package cream cheese
½ cup walnuts, chopped very finely (keep a few aside to decorate)
⅓ cup cream
Parmesan cheese, grated
Salt and pepper

Heat oil in a pan. Add crushed garlic and oregano, and cook for 1 minute. Add butter, cream cheese, chopped walnuts, and salt and pepper to taste. Stir, and leave to simmer gently for 5 minutes. Meanwhile, cook pasta shells in plenty of boiling salted water for 10 minutes, or until shells are tender but still firm. Drain in a colander, shaking to remove any trapped water. Put into warmed serving dish. Remove sauce from heat; add cream, and stir. Pour over shells, and toss to coat evenly. Garnish with walnut halves. Serve immediately with grated Parmesan cheese.

Spinach Ravioli

PREPARATION TIME: 30 minutes

COOKING TIME: 20 minutes

SERVES: 4 people

Dough:

1¼ cups bread flour
Pinch of salt
3 eggs

Filling:

1 cup cooked spinach
2 tbsps butter or margarine
¼ cup Parmesan cheese, grated
Pinch of grated nutmeg
1 egg, beaten
Salt
Pepper

Cream cheese sauce:

2 tbsps butter or margarine
1 tbsp flour
1 cup milk
1 tsp Dijon mustard
2 tbsps grated Parmesan cheese

To make filling:
Chop spinach and heat in a pan. Beat butter into spinach. Add Parmesan cheese, nutmeg, and salt and freshly-ground black pepper to taste. Finally mix in the beaten egg well.

To make dough:
Sift flour in a bowl; make a well in the center, and add the eggs. Work flour and eggs together with a spoon, and then knead by hand, until a smooth dough is formed. Leave to rest for 15 minutes. Lightly flour board, and roll out dough thinly into a rectangle. Cut dough in half. Shape the filling into small balls, and set them about 1½" apart on one half of the dough. Place the other half on top, and cut with a ravioli cutter or small pastry cutter. Seal the edges. Cook in batches in a large, wide pan with plenty of boiling salted water until tender – about 8 minutes. Remove carefully with a perforated spoon. Meanwhile, make sauce.

To make sauce:
Heat butter in pan. Stir in flour and cook for 30 seconds. Draw off heat, and stir milk in gradually. Bring to boil and simmer for 3 minutes, stirring continuously. Add mustard, and half the cheese, and seasoning to taste.

Pour sauce over ravioli, and serve immediately with remaining cheese sprinkled over the top.

Spaghetti with Basil Sauce (Pesto)

PREPARATION TIME: 5 minutes

COOKING TIME: 15 minutes

1 9oz package spaghetti
2 cups fresh basil leaves

Tagliatelle with Butter and Cheese (top) and Pasta Shells with Walnuts and Cream Sauce (right).

2 tbsps pine nuts
¼ cup olive oil
2 cloves garlic, peeled
Salt and pepper
3 tbsps Parmesan or pecorino cheese, grated

Garnish:
Fresh basil

Wash basil and remove leaves, discarding stems. Heat 1 tablespoon of oil over a low temperature. Add garlic and pine nuts, and cook until pine nuts are a light golden brown. Drain. Finely chop basil leaves, pine nuts and garlic in a food processor with a metal blade, or in a blender. When smooth, add remaining oil in a thin stream, blending continuously. Turn mixture into a bowl; mix in grated cheese, and add salt and pepper to taste. Meanwhile, cook spaghetti in a large pan of boiling salted water for 10 minutes, or until just tender. Drain, and serve with basil sauce tossed through. Serve with side dish of grated cheese. Garnish with fresh basil.

Penne with Spicy Chili Sauce

PREPARATION TIME: 15 minutes
COOKING TIME: 40 minutes

1 9oz package penne
1 onion, peeled and chopped
1 large can (about 2 cups) plum tomatoes
2 red chili peppers, seeds removed, and chopped finely
2 cloves garlic, crushed
1 tbsp olive oil
4 strips bacon, diced
¼ cup pecorino cheese, grated
2 green onions, chopped
Salt and pepper

Garnish:
4 green onions (cut into 2 inch strips. Keeping one end intact, cut into strips. Soak in chilled water until the flower has opened).

Chop tomatoes, removing seeds by straining juice. Heat oil in a pan, and fry garlic, onion and bacon gently for 10 minutes. Add tomato, chili peppers and chopped green onions, and half the cheese, and salt and pepper to taste. Cook, uncovered, for 20 minutes.
10 minutes before sauce is ready, cook the penne in lots of boiling salted water for 10 minutes, or until tender but still firm. Rinse under hot water, and drain well. Put into a warmed serving dish, and toss together with half the sauce. Pour remaining sauce on top, and garnish with green onion flowers, and remaining cheese if desired. Serve at once.

Tagliatelle with Butter and Cheese

PREPARATION TIME: 5 minutes
COOKING TIME: 15 minutes

¾ pound tagliatelle – ¼ pound each yellow, green and red tagliatelle
3 tbsps butter
¼ cup Parmesan cheese, grated
⅓ cup heavy cream
Salt and pepper

Cook the tagliatelle in a large pan of boiling salted water for 10 minutes, or until just tender. Drain. Meanwhile, put the butter and cream in a pan, and stir over a low heat until butter has melted. Remove from heat, add half the grated cheese, and salt and pepper to taste. Stir into tagliatelle and serve immediately with remaining cheese on top.

Pasta Spirals with Peas and Tomatoes

PREPARATION TIME: 5 minutes
COOKING TIME: 15 minutes

1 9oz package pasta spirals
1½ cups peas
1 tsp sugar
1 large can (about 2 cups) plum tomatoes, chopped
1 tsp basil
2 tbsps butter or margarine
Salt and pepper

Cook pasta spirals in plenty of boiling salted water for 10 minutes or until tender. Drain. Meanwhile, cook peas in boiling water with a pinch of salt and a teaspoon of sugar. Melt butter in a pan. Add basil, and cook for 30 seconds. Add tomatoes and their juice. When hot, add pasta spirals and peas, and salt and pepper to taste. Toss together. Serve immediately.

Spaghetti with Egg, Bacon and Mushroom

PREPARATION TIME: 10 minutes
COOKING TIME: 15 minutes

1 9oz package spaghetti
1 cup mushrooms, sliced
4 strips bacon, diced
4 tbsps butter or margarine
¼ cup Parmesan cheese, grated
2 eggs, hard-boiled and chopped finely
1 tbsp chopped parsley
Salt and pepper

Melt half the butter in a frying-pan. Add mushrooms and bacon, and cook for 10 minutes over a moderate heat, until bacon is crisp. Meanwhile, cook the spaghetti in lots of boiling salted water until tender but still firm – about 10 minutes. Drain. Return to pan. Add rest of butter, salt and lots of freshly-ground black pepper, and the mushroom and bacon. Toss together. Serve with hard-boiled eggs sprinkled on top, and parsley if desired. Serve grated Parmesan cheese separately.

This page: Pasta Spirals with Peas and Tomatoes.

Facing page: Spaghetti with Egg, Bacon and Mushroom (top) and Penne with Spicy Chili Sauce (bottom).

Baked and Broiled Pasta

Cannelloni

PREPARATION TIME: 10 minutes
COOKING TIME: 1 hour
OVEN: 350°F (180°C)
SERVES: 4 people

12 cannelloni shells
2 tbsps Parmesan cheese, grated
1 tbsp oil

Filling:
1lb ground beef
1 tbsp olive oil
1 onion, peeled and chopped
2 cloves garlic, crushed
1 cup chopped, cooked spinach
½ tsp oregano
½ tsp basil
1 tsp tomato paste
4 tbsps cream
1 egg, lightly beaten
Salt and pepper to taste

Tomato sauce:
1 tbsp olive oil
1 onion, peeled and chopped
1 clove garlic, crushed
2 small cans (about 2 cups) tomato sauce
2 tbsps tomato paste
Salt
Pepper

Béchamel sauce:
1 slice of onion
3 peppercorns
1 small bay leaf
1 cup milk
2 tbsps butter or margarine
2 tbsps flour
Salt
Pepper

To make filling:
Heat oil in pan, and fry garlic and onion gently until soft and transparent. Add meat and cook, stirring continuously, until well browned. Drain off any fat, add tomato paste, basil and oregano, and cook gently for 15 minutes. Add spinach, egg and cream, and salt and pepper to taste. Cook cannelloni in a large pan of boiling salted water for 15-20 minutes, until tender. Rinse in hot water and drain. Fill carefully with meat mixture, using a pastry bag with a wide, plain tube, or a teaspoon.

To make tomato sauce:
Heat oil in pan. Add onion and garlic, and cook gently until transparent. Add tomato sauce to the pan with tomato paste and salt and pepper to taste. Bring to boil, and then simmer for 5 minutes. Set aside.

To make Béchamel sauce:
Put milk in pan with onion, peppercorns and bay leaf. Heat gently for 1 minute, taking care not to boil, and set aside to cool for 5 minutes. Strain. Melt butter in

This page: Shrimp Crespelle.

Facing page: Cannelloni with Tomato and Cheese (top) and Cannelloni (bottom).

Crespelle with Tuna (left) and Crespelle with Chicken and Tongue (below).

pan. Remove from heat and stir in flour. Gradually add cool milk, and bring to boil, stirring continuously, until sauce thickens. Add seasoning.

Spread tomato sauce on the base of an oven-proof dish. Lay cannelloni on top, and cover with Béchamel sauce. Sprinkle with grated cheese, and bake in a moderate oven for 30 minutes. Serve immediately.

Shrimp Crespelle

PREPARATION TIME: 40 minutes

COOKING TIME: 30 minutes

OVEN: 375°F (190°C)

SERVES: 4 people

12 crespelle:
3 eggs
¾ cup flour
Pinch of salt
1 cup water
½ tbsp olive oil
2 tbsps butter or margarine, melted

Filling:
1 cup shrimp, washed, peeled and deveined
2 tbsps butter or margarine
1 tbsp flour
1 cup milk
Juice of 1 lemon
Salt
Pepper

Garnish:
1 lemon, cut into slices

To make crespelle:
Sift flour with a pinch of salt. Break eggs into a bowl, and whisk. Add flour gradually, whisking all the time until the mixture is smooth. Add water, and stir in well. Add oil, and mix. Cover bowl with damp cloth, and leave in a cool place for 30 minutes.
Heat a crêpe pan or 7″ frying pan. Grease lightly with melted butter, and put a tablespoon of batter in the center. Roll the pan to coat the surface evenly. Fry until crespelle is brown on the underside. Loosen edge with a spatula; turn over and brown the other side. Stack and wrap in a clean cloth until needed.

To make filling:
Heat butter in pan; stir in flour, and cook for 1 minute. Remove from heat, and gradually stir in milk. Return to heat, and bring to the boil. Allow to simmer for 3 minutes. Stir in lemon juice and add salt and pepper to taste. Add half the sauce to shrimp. Place one crespelle in an oven-proof dish, and add a spoon of shrimp mixture. Cover with one crespelle, and repeat, finishing with a crespelle on top. Bake in a pre-heated oven for 10 minutes. When ready to serve, cover with remaining sauce. Garnish with lemon slices. Serve immediately.

Crespelle with Chicken and Tongue

PREPARATION TIME: 40 minutes

COOKING TIME: 20 minutes

OVEN: 450°F (230°C)

SERVES: 4 people

10 crespelle:
3 eggs
¾ cup flour
Pinch of salt
1 cup water
½ tsp olive oil
2 tbsps butter or margarine, melted

Filling:
¼ pound chicken, cooked and shredded
¼ pound tongue, cut into strips

Béchamel sauce:
2 tbsps butter or margarine
1 tbsp flour
1 cup milk
To infuse:
4 peppercorns
1 bay leaf
Slice of onion
Salt
Pepper

To make crespelle:
Sift flour with a pinch of salt. Break eggs into a bowl, and whisk. Add flour gradually, whisking all the time until the mixture is smooth. Add water and stir in well. Add oil, and mix. Cover bowl with a damp cloth, and leave in a cool place for 30 minutes.
Heat a crêpe pan, or 7″ frying pan. Grease lightly with melted butter, and put a good tablespoon of batter in the center. Roll the pan to coat the surface evenly. Fry until crespelle is brown on the underside. Loosen edge with a spatula; turn over and brown the other side. Stack and wrap in a clean cloth until needed.

To make Béchamel sauce:
Warm milk with peppercorns, bay leaf and slice of onion. Remove from heat, and let stand for 5 minutes. Strain. Heat butter in pan. Stir in flour and cook for 1 minute. Remove from heat, and gradually stir in two-thirds of the milk. Return to heat, and stir continuously until boiling. Simmer for 3 minutes. Add salt and pepper to taste. Put half of the sauce in a bowl, and add the chicken and tongue. Mix together. Beat remaining milk into remaining sauce.

Lay 1 crespelle on a plate, and top with a layer of chicken and tongue. Cover with another crespelle, and continue, finishing with a crespelle. Pour over sauce, and bake in pre-heated oven for 10 minutes. Serve immediately.

Crespelle with Tuna

PREPARATION TIME: 40 minutes

COOKING TIME: 30 minutes

SERVES: 4 people

12 crespelle:
3 eggs
¾ cup flour
Pinch of salt
1 cup water
½ tbsp olive oil
2 tbsps butter or margarine, melted

Filling:
1 cup tuna fish, drained
3 tbsps mayonnaise
1 tbsp tomato paste

Tomato sauce:
2 small cans (about 2 cups) tomato sauce
½ tsp basil
1 clove garlic, crushed
1 onion, peeled and chopped
1 tbsp butter or margarine
2 tbsps chopped parsley
Salt
Pepper

To make crespelle:
Sift the flour with a pinch of salt. Break eggs into a bowl, and whisk. Add flour gradually, whisking all the time, until the mixture is smooth. Stir in water, and mix oil in well. Cover bowl with a damp cloth, and leave in a cool place for 30 minutes.
Heat a crêpe pan, or 7″ frying pan. Grease lightly with melted butter, and put a good tablespoon of batter in the center. Roll the pan to coat the surface evenly. Fry until crespelle is brown on the underside. Loosen edge with a spatula; turn over and brown on the other side. Stack and wrap in a clean cloth until needed.

To make sauce:
Heat butter in pan, and gently fry garlic and basil for 30 seconds. Add onion, and fry until transparent. Add tomato sauce, and cook for 10 minutes. Add salt, and freshly-ground black pepper, to taste, and parsley if desired.

To make filling:
Flake tuna fish, and put into a bowl. Mix mayonnaise and tomato paste, and stir into tuna fish. Divide mixture equally between crespelle, placing mixture at one end, and rolling up. Place in an oven-proof dish. Pour over tomato sauce, and cook under a broiler for 5 minutes. Serve immediately.

Macaroni Cheese with Anchovies

PREPARATION TIME: 5 minutes
COOKING TIME: 15 minutes
SERVES: 4 people

1 9oz package macaroni
4 tbsps butter or margarine
3 tbsps flour
2 cups milk
½ tsp dry mustard
¾ cup Gruyère or Cheddar cheese, grated
6-8 anchovy fillets
Salt
Pepper

Drain anchovies, and set enough aside to slice to make a thin lattice over the dish. Chop the rest finely. Cook the macaroni in plenty of boiling salted water for 10 minutes, or until tender but still firm. Rinse in hot water and drain well. Meanwhile, melt the butter in a pan. Stir in the flour and cook for 1 minute. Remoye from heat, and gradually stir in the milk. Return to heat and bring to the boil. Simmer for 3 minutes, stirring continuously. Stir in the mustard, anchovies, and half the cheese. Season with salt and pepper to taste. Stir in the macaroni, and pour into an oven-proof dish. Sprinkle the remaining cheese over the top, and make a latticework with the remaining anchovies. Brown under a hot grill. Serve immediately.

Macaroni with Creamy Chicken Sauce

PREPARATION TIME: 5 minutes
COOKING TIME: 20 minutes
SERVES: 4 people

1 9oz package macaroni
4 tbsps butter or margarine
2 tbsps flour
2 cups milk
2 chicken breasts
1 tbsp olive oil
½ cup Cheddar cheese, grated
Salt
Pepper

Heat oil in a frying pan, and gently fry chicken for 10 minutes, or until cooked through. When cool, shred chicken. Cook macaroni in plenty of boiling salted water for 10 minutes, or until tender but still firm. Rinse in hot water. Drain well. Meanwhile, heat the butter in a pan, and stir in the flour, and cook for 1 minute. Draw off the heat and gradually add the milk, stirring all the time. Bring the sauce to the boil, stirring continuously, and cook for 3 minutes. Add the chicken, macaroni, and salt and pepper to taste, and mix well. Pour mixture into an oven-proof dish, and sprinkle with cheese on top. Cook under a broiler until golden brown. Serve immediately.

This page: Macaroni Cheese with Anchovies.

Facing page: Macaroni with Creamy Chicken Sauce (top) and Italian Casserole (bottom).

Italian Casserole

PREPARATION TIME: 15 minutes
COOKING TIME: 40 minutes
OVEN: 350°F (180°C)
SERVES: 4 people

1 cup small macaroni
2 tbsps butter or margarine
1 clove garlic, crushed
1 onion, peeled and chopped
1 large can (about 2 cups) plum tomatoes
1 tbsp tomato paste
1 sweet red pepper, cored, seeds removed, and chopped roughly
1 green pepper, cored, seeds removed, and chopped roughly
10 black olives, halved, and stones removed
¼ pound Mozzarella cheese, sliced thinly
½ pound salami, cut into chunks
Salt
Pepper

Cook the macaroni in plenty of boiling salted water for 10 minutes, or until tender but still firm. Rinse under hot water and drain well. Place in a shallow, oven-proof dish. Meanwhile, heat butter in pan, and fry onion and garlic gently until soft. Add undrained tomatoes, tomato paste, red and green peppers, salami and olives, and stir well. Simmer uncovered for 5 minutes. Season with salt and pepper. Pour over the macaroni, stir, and cover with the sliced cheese. Bake uncovered in a moderate oven for 20 minutes, until cheese has melted. Serve immediately.

Macaroni Cheese with Frankfurters

PREPARATION TIME: 10 minutes
COOKING TIME: 20 minutes
SERVES: 4 people

1 9oz package macaroni
4 tbsps butter or margarine
3 tbsps flour
2 cups milk
1 tsp dry mustard
⅓ cup Cheddar cheese, grated
8 Frankfurters
Salt
Pepper

Garnish:
1 pimento, cut into strips

Poach the Frankfurters for 5-8 minutes. Remove skins and, when cold, cut into diagonal slices. Cook macaroni in plenty of boiling salted water for about 10 minutes, or until tender but still firm. Rinse in hot water, and drain well. Meanwhile, melt the butter in a pan. Stir in the flour, and cook for 1 minute. Draw off heat, and gradually add milk, stirring all the time. Bring to the boil, stirring continuously, and cook for 3 minutes. Add Frankfurters, grated cheese, mustard, and salt and pepper to taste. Stir well. Add macaroni, and mix in well. Pour mixture into an oven-proof dish, and sprinkle the remaining cheese over the top. Make a lattice of pimento, and cook under a pre-heated grill until golden brown. Serve immediately.

Pastitsio

PREPARATION TIME: 10 minutes
COOKING TIME: 1 hour
OVEN: 375°F (190°C)
SERVES: 4 people

1 9oz package macaroni
4 tbsps butter or margarine
¼ cup Parmesan cheese, grated
Pinch of grated nutmeg
2 eggs, beaten
1 medium onion, peeled and chopped
1 clove garlic, crushed
1 pound ground beef
2 tbsps tomato paste
¼ cup red wine
½ cup beef stock
2 tbsps chopped parsley
2 tbsps plain flour
½ cup milk
Salt
Pepper

Set oven. Cook macaroni in plenty of boiling salted water for 10 minutes, or until tender but still firm. Rinse under hot water. Drain. Put one-third of the butter in the pan and return macaroni to it. Add half the cheese, nutmeg, and salt and pepper to taste. Leave to cool. Mix in half the beaten egg, and put aside. Melt half of the remaining butter in a pan, and fry onion and garlic gently until onion is soft. Increase temperature and add meat, and fry until browned. Add tomato paste, stock, parsley and wine, and season with salt and pepper. Simmer for 20 minutes. In a small pan, melt the rest of the butter. Stir in the flour and cook for 30 seconds. Remove from heat, and stir in milk. Bring to boil, stirring continuously, until the sauce thickens. Beat in the remaining egg and season to taste. Spoon half the macaroni into a serving-dish and cover with the meat sauce. Put on another layer of macaroni and smooth over. Pour over white sauce, and sprinkle with remaining cheese, and bake in the oven for 30 minutes until golden brown. Serve immediately.

Cannelloni with Tomato and Cheese

PREPARATION TIME: 10 minutes
COOKING TIME: 40 minutes
OVEN: 400°F (210°C)
SERVES: 4 people

12 cannelloni shells

Filling:
1 15oz can plum tomatoes
1 tbsp tomato paste
1 tbsp oregano or basil
½ cup ricotta cheese
½ cup Parmesan cheese, grated
Salt
Pepper

Sauce:
2 small cans (about 2 cups) tomato sauce
1 onion, peeled and chopped
1 tbsp olive oil
1 tbsp grated Parmesan cheese
1 tbsp cornstarch
Salt
Pepper

Cook cannelloni shells in a large pan of boiling salted water for 15-20 minutes until tender. Rinse in hot water and drain well.

Pastitsio (above) and Macaroni Cheese with Frankfurters (right).

To make filling:
Meanwhile, chop tomatoes and remove pips. Set juice aside for sauce. Beat ricotta cheese until smooth. Add tomato paste, oregano or basil, and Parmesan cheese, and beat well. Finally, stir in chopped tomato and salt and pepper to taste. With a teaspoon, or a pastry bag with a wide, plain tube, fill the cannelloni shells. Place in an oven-proof dish.

To make sauce:
Heat oil in a saucepan, and cook onion gently until transparent. Add tomato sauce to the saucepan. Mix the cornstarch with the reserved tomato juice and add to the pan. Bring to the boil and cook for 3 minutes, stirring continuously. Add salt and pepper to taste. Pour over the cannelloni, and sprinkle with cheese. Place in a hot oven, or under a broiler for 10 minutes or until heated through. Serve immediately.

Spinach Crespelle

PREPARATION TIME: 45 minutes

COOKING TIME: 30 minutes

SERVES: 4 people

12 crespelle:
3 eggs
¾ cup flour
Pinch of salt
1 cup water
½ tbsp olive oil
2 tbsps butter or margarine, melted

Filling:
1 8oz package cream cheese
1 8oz package frozen spinach, thawed
2 tbsps cream
¼ cup Parmesan cheese, grated
½ tsp grated nutmeg
2 tbsps butter or margarine
Salt
Pepper

To make crespelle:
Sift flour with a pinch of salt. Break eggs into a bowl, and whisk. Add flour gradually, whisking all the time until the mixture is smooth. Add water, and stir in well. Add oil, and mix in. Cover bowl with a damp cloth, and leave in a cool place for 30 minutes. Heat a crêpe pan, or 7″ frying pan. Grease lightly with melted butter, and put a good tablespoon batter in the center. Roll the pan to coat the surface evenly. Fry until crespelle is brown on the underside. Loosen edge with a spatula, and turn over and brown on the other side. Stack and wrap in a clean cloth until needed.

To make filling:
Cook spinach for 3 minutes in a pan of boiling water. Drain and chop, and set aside. Beat cream cheese and cream together until smooth. Add nutmeg and half the cheese, and salt and pepper to taste, and mix in well. Mix spinach into cream cheese mixture. Divide equally between 12 crespelle, placing mixture at one end, and rolling up. Place in an oven-proof dish, and dot with butter over the top. Sprinkle with Parmesan cheese, and place under a broiler for 5 minutes, or until browning lightly on top. Serve immediately.

Crespelle with Bolognese Sauce Filling

PREPARATION TIME: 45 minutes

COOKING TIME: 1 hour 15 minutes

SERVES: 4 people

12 crespelle:
3 eggs
¾ cup flour
Pinch of salt
1 cup water
1½ tsp olive oil
2 tbsps butter or margarine, melted

Bolognese Sauce:
2 tbsps butter or margarine
1 tbsp olive oil
2 onions, peeled and chopped finely
½ pound ground beef
1 carrot, scraped and chopped finely
4 tbsps tomato paste
1 cup brown stock
2 tbsps sherry
Salt
Pepper

Tomato Sauce:
1 large can (about 2 cups) plum tomatoes
½ tsp basil
1 clove garlic, crushed
1 onion, peeled and chopped
1 tbsp butter
Salt
Pepper

To make Bolognese sauce:
Heat the butter and oil in a pan, and fry the onions and carrot slowly until soft. Increase heat, and add the ground beef. Fry for a few minutes, then stir, cooking until meat is browned all over. Add the tomato paste, stock, and salt and pepper to taste, and simmer gently for about ¾ hour, until the mixture thickens, stirring occasionally. Add 2 tablespoons sherry, and cook for a further 5 minutes.

To make crespelle:
Sift the flour with a pinch of salt. Break the eggs into a bowl, and whisk. Add the flour gradually, whisking all the time until the mixture is smooth. Add water, and stir in well. Add oil, and mix. Cover bowl with a damp cloth, and leave in a cool place for 30 minutes.

Heat a crêpe pan, or 7″ frying pan. Grease lightly with the melted butter, and put a good tablespoon of batter in the center. Roll the pan to coat the surface evenly. Fry until crespelle is brown on the underside. Loosen edge with a spatula, and turn over and brown the other side. Stack and wrap in a clean cloth until needed.

To make tomato sauce:
Heat butter in pan, and gently fry garlic and basil for 30 seconds. Add onion, and fry until transparent. Add tomatoes, and cook for 10 minutes. Strain, and return to pan. Add salt and freshly-ground black pepper to taste.

Lay crespelle out, and put 2 heaped tablespoons Bolognese sauce filling at one end of each. Roll up, and place in an oven-proof dish. Repeat until all crespelle have been filled. Put into a hot oven or under a broiler for 5 minutes. Re-heat tomato sauce, and pour over just before serving. Serve immediately.

Spinach Lasagne

PREPARATION TIME: 10 minutes

COOKING TIME: 30 minutes

OVEN: 400°F (200°C)

SERVES: 4 people

8 green lasagne noodles

Spinach sauce:
4 tbsps butter or margarine
1½ cups frozen spinach, thawed and chopped finely
Pinch of ground nutmeg
3 tbsps flour
½ cup milk
Salt
Pepper

Mornay sauce:
2 tbsps butter or margarine
2 tbsps flour
1 cup milk
⅓ cup Parmesan cheese, grated
1 tsp Dijon mustard
Salt

To make spinach sauce:
Heat butter in pan, stir in flour and cook for 30 seconds. Draw off heat, and stir in milk gradually. Return to heat, and bring to the boil, stirring continuously. Cook for 3 minutes. Add spinach, nutmeg, and salt and pepper to taste. Set aside.

Cook spinach lasagne in lots of boiling salted water for 10 minutes, or until tender. Rinse in cold water, and drain carefully. Dry on a clean cloth.

To make Mornay sauce:
Heat butter in pan and stir in flour, cooking for 30 seconds. Remove from heat, and stir in milk. Return to heat, stirring continuously, until boiling. Continue stirring, and simmer for 3 minutes. Draw off heat, and add mustard and two-thirds of cheese, and salt to taste.

Grease an oven-proof baking dish. Line the base with a layer of lasagne, followed by some of the spinach mixture, and a layer of cheese sauce. Repeat the process, finishing with a layer of lasagne and with a covering of cheese sauce. Sprinkle with the remaining cheese. Bake in a hot oven until golden on top. Serve immediately.

Curried Tuna Cannelloni

PREPARATION TIME: 15 minutes

COOKING TIME: 45 minutes

OVEN: 350°F (180°C)

SERVES: 4 people

12 cannelloni shells

Filling:
2 tbsps butter or margarine
1 onion, peeled and chopped
1 stick of celery, chopped

Facing page: Crespelle with Bolognese Sauce Filling (top) and Spinach Crespelle (bottom).

½ cup mushrooms, cleaned and chopped
1 tbsp flour
1 tsp curry powder
½ cup milk
⅓ cup soured cream
⅓ cup mayonnaise
1 egg, lightly beaten
1 7oz can tuna fish
3 shallots, peeled and chopped
Salt
Pepper

Topping:
4 tbsps breadcrumbs
¼ cup Cheddar cheese, grated
2 tbsps butter or margarine

Cook cannelloni shells in a large pan of boiling salted water for 15-20 minutes until tender. Rinse in hot water and drain well. Meanwhile, melt butter in saucepan. Fry onion until transparent, add mushrooms and celery, and fry for 5 minutes. Add curry powder and flour, and fry until light golden brown. Draw off the heat, and gradually add milk, stirring continuously. Return to heat and bring to the boil. Cook for 3 minutes, stirring all the time. Add soured cream, mayonnaise, and undrained flaked tuna. Season with salt and pepper and stir until sauce boils. Simmer for 3 minutes. Add shallots and egg, and mix well. Spoon mixture into cannelloni shells, and place in an oven-proof dish. Sprinkle over a mixture of breadcrumbs and cheese, and dot with butter or margarine. Bake in a moderate oven for 20 minutes. Serve immediately.

Crab Cannelloni

PREPARATION TIME: 10 minutes
COOKING TIME: 40 minutes
OVEN: 400°F (200°C)
SERVES: 4 people

12 cannelloni shells

Filling:
½ pound fresh crab meat (or frozen crab meat, thawed)
2 tbsps butter or margarine
3 shallots, peeled and chopped

This page: Spinach Lasagne.

Facing page: Curried Tuna Cannelloni (top) and Crab Cannelloni (bottom).

½ tsp Worcestershire sauce
1 tsp Dijon mustard
Salt
Pepper

Mornay sauce:
2 tbsps butter or margarine
2 tbsps flour
1¼ cups milk
¼ cup Cheddar or Parmesan cheese, grated
Salt
Pepper

Cook cannelloni shells in a large pan of boiling salted water for 15-20 minutes until tender. Rinse in hot water and drain well. Meanwhile, heat butter in pan. Add shallots, crab meat, Worcestershire sauce, mustard, salt and pepper, and stir until heated through. Fill cannelloni shells with crab mixture, using a pastry bag with a wide, plain tube, or a teaspoon. Place in an oven-proof dish.

To make Mornay sauce:
Heat butter in pan, and stir in flour. Remove from heat and gradually add milk. Return to heat, and bring to boil. Cook for 3 minutes, stirring continuously. Stir in half the cheese until it melts. Do not reboil. Season with salt and pepper. Pour over the cannelloni and sprinkle with remaining cheese. Place in a hot oven, or under a broiler until golden brown. Serve immediately.

Lasagne Rolls

PREPARATION TIME: 5 minutes
COOKING TIME: 15 minutes
SERVES: 4 people

8 lasagne noodles
½ pound boned chicken breasts
2 tbsps butter or margarine
¼ cup Gruyère or Cheddar cheese, grated
1 tbsp flour
½ cup milk
¼ cup mushrooms, sliced
2 tsps oil
Salt
Pepper

In a large saucepan, fill two-thirds with boiling salted water and 2 teaspoons oil. Bring to the boil. Add 1 sheet of lasagne; wait about 2 minutes, and add another sheet. Only cook a few at a time. When tender, remove, and rinse under cold water, and leave to drain. Repeat until all the lasagne is cooked. Meanwhile, wash and slice mushrooms, and slice chicken. Put half the butter in a small frying pan, and fry the mushrooms and chicken. In a small saucepan, melt the rest of the butter. Add the flour, and cook for a minute. Remove from the heat, and add the milk. Mix well and bring to the boil. Cook for 3 minutes. Add sauce to chicken and mushrooms, and add half the cheese, mixing well. Add salt and pepper to taste. Spread out lasagne, and spread one-eighth mixture at one end of each. Roll up each piece of lasagne, and put into an oven-proof dish. Sprinkle with remaining cheese, and put under a broiler until golden brown. Serve immediately.

Lasagne

PREPARATION TIME: 10 minutes
COOKING TIME: 45 minutes
OVEN: 400°F (200°C)
SERVES: 4 people

8 lasagne noodles

Meat sauce:
4 tbsps butter or margarine
1 carrot, diced
1 celery stick, diced
1 onion, peeled and diced
¼ pound ground beef
1 tsp marjoram
1 tbsp flour
1 tbsp tomato paste
½ cup beef stock
Salt
Pepper

Béchamel sauce:
2 tbsps butter or margarine
2 tbsps flour
1 cup milk
6 peppercorns
1 bay leaf
Slice of onion
Parsley stalks

To make meat sauce:
Heat butter in pan and add onion, celery and carrot. Cook until golden. Add ground beef, and brown well. Stir in flour; add tomato paste, beef stock, marjoram, and salt and pepper. Cook for 15 minutes.

Meanwhile, cook the lasagne in lots of boiling salted water for 10 minutes, or until tender. Rinse in cold water and drain carefully. Lay out on a clean cloth to dry.

To make Béchamel sauce:
Heat milk in a saucepan with peppercorns, slice of onion, bay leaf and parsley stalks. Bring to simmering point and remove from heat. Allow to cool for 5 minutes. Strain. Melt butter in a saucepan. Stir in flour and cook for 30 seconds. Remove from heat and gradually add milk, stirring continuously. Cook for 3 minutes.

Grease an oven-proof baking dish. Line base with a layer of lasagne sheets. Cover with a layer of meat sauce, and a layer of Béchamel sauce. Place another layer of lasagne, repeating until all the ingredients are used, finishing with a layer of lasagne and a layer of Béchamel sauce. Bake in a hot oven until the top is golden. Serve immediately.

Lasagne Rolls (above right) and Lasagne (below right).

Section 6

CAKES AND DESSERTS

Springtime Desserts

Savarin Chantilly (top), Individual Banar Tarts (center) and Coffee Pecan Pie (bottom

Individual Banana Tarts

PREPARATION TIME: 30 minutes
COOKING TIME: 15 minutes
OVEN: 400°F

Pastry
1/3 cup butter
1½ cups flour
2 tablespoons sugar
1 egg yolk
1 tablespoon water

Filling
2 firm bananas
1 teaspoon lemon juice
2/3 cup heavy cream
Apricot jam to glaze

Pastry
Place the butter and flour into a bowl and rub to form a breadcrumb-like mixture. Stir in the sugar. Beat together the egg yolk and water and add to flour to form a stiff dough. Lightly knead and chill for ½ hour. Roll out pastry and cut using a 3 inch crimped cutter. Press into tartlet pans and bake until golden brown.

Filling
Slice the bananas and sprinkle with the lemon juice. Beat the cream and fill the pastry shells. Lay the sliced banana in a circle to cover the cream. Melt the apricot jam in a small saucepan and pour over tartlet pastry shells, making sure all the bananas are glazed. Serve cold.

Coffee Pecan Pie

PREPARATION TIME: 20 minutes plus chilling

6oz graham crackers
1/3 cup butter, melted
2 tablespoons soft brown sugar
3/4 cup pecan nut halves
8oz marshmallows
1¼ cups strong black coffee
½oz gelatin
3 tablespoons hot water
2/3 cup heavy cream
1 teaspoon ground coffee

Crush the cookies and mix together with the butter and sugar. Press the mixture onto the base and up the sides of a 7 inch spring-form cake pan. Chill. Reserve 8 halves of pecan nuts for decoration and chop the remainder. In a large saucepan dissolve the marshmallows in the coffee, heating gently and stirring frequently. Dissolve the gelatin in the hot water and stir into the marshmallow mixture. Leave to cool until almost set. Beat the cream until it peaks and fold into the coffee mixture. Add the chopped nuts. Pour onto the crushed cooky base and chill until set. Remove from the pan and decorate with the nut halves. Sprinkle with the ground coffee.

Savarin Chantilly

PREPARATION TIME: 35 minutes plus chilling
COOKING TIME: 30 minutes
OVEN: 400°F

Savarin
1½ cups strong white flour
½ teaspoon salt
6 tablespoons milk
2 level teaspoons dried yeast
1 level teaspoon sugar
2 eggs
1/3 cup butter

Syrup
3/4 cup sugar
1¼ cups water
Pared rind of ½ lemon and juice of 1 lemon
3 tablespoons rum

Filling
2/3 cup light cream
2/3 cup heavy cream
1lb canned or fresh fruit

Savarin
Butter and sprinkle with flour an 8 inch ring mold. Sift the flour and salt into a mixing bowl. Heat the milk in a small saucepan and add the dried yeast and sugar (do not boil the milk). Leave in a warm place for 20 minutes or until the mixture looks frothy. Mix the eggs into the yeast mixture and pour into the flour. Stir with a wooden spoon to form a smooth batter. Melt the butter and allow it to cool slightly. Pour into the batter and stir. Pour the batter into the ring mold and spread evenly. Put the mold into a polythene bag but leave room for the mixture to rise. Leave in a warm place. When the mixture has risen to the top of the pan bake in a preheated oven for half an hour until golden brown and firm to the touch.

Syrup
While the savarin is baking, add the sugar and water to a saucepan and finely pare the lemon rind. Stir over a low heat until the sugar has dissolved. Bring the mixture to the boil and simmer for 5 minutes. Remove from the heat and add the lemon juice and rum. When the savarin has cooled in the pan for five minutes remove it from the pan. Wash and dry the baking mold and pour the hot syrup evenly round the mold. Replace the savarin so that it floats in the syrup.

Filling
The savarin will soak up the syrup so that it can be turned out. Turn out the savarin and refrigerate overnight. Place savarin on a serving dish and whip the light and heavy cream. Spoon into the center and top with fruit (apricot, mango, oranges or stoned cherries make a suitable decoration).

Mont Blanc

PREPARATION TIME: 20 minutes plus chilling
COOKING TIME: 1¼ hours
OVEN: 250°F

2 egg whites
6oz sugar
1 teaspoon vanilla essence
1 cup heavy cream
1½ tablespoons confectioners' sugar
8oz can chestnut purée
1 tablespoon brandy
1oz semi-sweet chocolate, grated or chopped nuts to decorate

Beat the egg whites until they peak, adding the sugar and vanilla essence. Fill a pastry bag with the meringue mixture and fit a ½ inch plain tip. Draw six circles 3 inches in diameter on a cooky sheet lined with non-stick silicone paper and cover with the meringue. Bake in a very cool oven until firm but not brown. Cool. Whip the cream until it peaks and fold in the confectioners' sugar. Mix the chestnut purée with the brandy and spoon the mixture into a pastry bag fitted with an 1/8 inch tip and decorate round the edge of the meringue bases. Top with cream and chocolate or nuts to decorate. Serve chilled.

Mango Soufflé

PREPARATION TIME: 20 minutes plus chilling

1 tablespoon water
Juice of one lemon
1/3 cup sugar
½oz gelatin
3 eggs (separated)
1 mango peeled and stoned
2/3 cup heavy cream

To decorate
1/4 cup toasted chopped nuts
2/3 cup heavy cream, whipped
Caramel chips (see quick garnishes)

Prepare a 5 inch freezerproof soufflé dish. Cut a double strip of lightly oiled wax paper 20 x 5 inches and tie securely round the dish. Put the water and lemon juice in a small pan and sprinkle in the gelatin. Heat to dissolve the gelatin and cool. Beat the egg yolks and sugar until thick. Purée the mango and mix with the gelatin into the egg mixture. Fold in the stiffly beaten egg white with cream. Pour into the prepared dish and chill.

To decorate
Carefully remove the paper and press the nuts into the sides. Decorate with whipped cream. Another method of decoration is to use caramel chips.

Red Fruit Compote

PREPARATION TIME: 10 minutes plus chilling

½ cup granulated sugar
1¼ cups water
6oz redcurrants, stalks removed
8oz raspberries, hulled
8oz strawberries, hulled
2 tablespoons Cointreau or orange liqueur
Light cream

Boil the sugar and water in a pan till the sugar dissolves. This should take about 5 minutes. Remove from heat and cool. Put all the fruits in a serving dish and pour over the Cointreau and leave to stand for an hour and a half. Stir carefully from time to time. Pour the cold syrup over the fruits and serve chilled with cream.

Individual Fruit Salad

PREPARATION TIME: 20 minutes plus chilling

3 bananas
2 oranges
4oz strawberries
2oz redcurrants

Passion Fruit Sauce
3 passion fruits
3 tablespoons clear honey
Juice of one lime
2 tablespoons dark rum

Peel and slice horizontally the bananas and oranges. Hull and halve the strawberries and arrange on individual plates and chill.

Passion Fruit Sauce
Spoon out the seeds and flesh of the passion fruits and boil with the honey and lime juice. Add two tablespoons of dark rum and chill. Pour the passion fruit sauce over the fruit and serve. Decorate with the redcurrants.

Almond Cream Tart

PREPARATION TIME: 20 minutes
COOKING TIME: 35 minutes
OVEN: 400°F

Tart
¼ cup flour
¼ cup sugar
2 eggs

Filling
⅔ cup heavy cream
1 level tablespoon sieved confectioners' sugar
3 tablespoons ground almonds
12oz strawberries, hulled and sliced; keep one whole strawberry for decoration

Glaze
3 tablespoons water
⅓ cup superfine sugar
Whipped cream and strawberry leaves (optional)

Tart
Grease an 8 inch pie pan. Line the base with a circle of wax paper. Sieve the flour into a bowl. Put the sugar and eggs into another bowl and beat for 12 minutes over a saucepan of hot water, off the heat. The mixture should thicken and pale. Remove from the pan and beat for another 5 minutes. If using an electric beater, omit the beating over hot water. Sieve the flour a little at a time over the mixture and fold in with a metal spoon. Pour mixture into prepared pan and cook in a hot oven until firm. When cooked, leave to cool in the pan for a few minutes then turn onto a wire rack.

Filling
Whip the cream stiffly, adding the confectioners' sugar slowly. Fold in the almonds and spoon this mixture into the pie shell. Arrange the strawberries on top.

Glaze
Place water and sugar in a pan and slowly bring to the boil. The sugar should be dissolved. Stir the rapidly boiling mixture constantly. Boil for 2 minutes. Allow the glaze to cool and brush over the strawberries. Decorate with whipped cream and strawberry leaves if available.

Red Fruit Compote (far left), Individual Fruit Salad with Passion Fruit Sauce (center) and Almond Cream Tart (left).

Petits Pots de Café

PREPARATION TIME: 10 minutes plus cooling

3 tablespoons sugar
3 tablespoons butter
1½ tablespoons rum
3 teaspoons instant coffee powder (granules should be crushed)
3 eggs, separated
½ cup heavy cream, whipped
Walnut halves

Mix the sugar, butter, rum and coffee in a bowl over a pan of hot water, and stir until melted. Add the egg yolks and mix well. Leave to cook for 5 minutes over the hot water and remove from the heat. When the mixture has cooled, beat the egg whites until stiff and fold into the coffee mixture. Spoon into individual ramekins and decorate with whipped cream and nuts if available.

Fruit Coupelles with Dried Fruit Compote

PREPARATION TIME: 20 minutes
COOKING TIME: 7 minutes
OVEN: 400°F

¾ cup dried apricots
⅓ cup dried apple
¾ cup prunes
⅓ cup raisins
⅓ cup white raisins
⅓ cup currants
2½ cups strong black coffee

Coupelles
2 egg whites
5 tablespoons sugar
½ cup flour
¼ cup butter, melted and cooled

Place all the fruit ingredients in a saucepan and cover with the coffee. Boil rapidly then reduce heat to simmer for 3 minutes. Pour into a bowl and leave to cool for at least 10 hours. Beat the egg whites until frothy. Add the sugar slowly. The mixture should be very stiff. Fold in the flour and melted butter. Grease a cooky sheet. Drop the mixture onto the cooky sheet to form 4 inch rounds (the mixture makes 8). Cook in a preheated moderate oven until the edges are golden brown. Remove from the cooky sheet one at a time. Mold over an inverted ramekin to form a cup shape. When set remove from the dish and leave to cool on a wire rack. To serve fill the coupelles with the fruit compote.

Raspberry and Hazelnut Galette

PREPARATION TIME: 35 minutes
COOKING TIME: 20 minutes
OVEN: 375°F

1 cup hazelnuts, shelled
½ cup softened butter
⅓ cup sugar
1 egg yolk, lightly beaten
A few drops of vanilla essence
1½ cups flour
A pinch of salt
1¾ cups heavy cream
1 level tablespoon sugar
1lb raspberries, hulled

Lightly grease three cooky sheets and dust with flour. Roast the hazelnuts in a hot oven 425°F , or under the broiler until the skin is split. Rub off the skins using kitchen paper and chop the nuts finely. Beat the sugar and butter until fluffy and beat in the egg yolk and vanilla essence. Sieve the flour and salt and stir into the mixture adding the hazelnuts. Knead the mixture till it forms a smooth dough. Wrap in plastic wrap and chill for 30 minutes. Divide the dough into 3 pieces and roll on a lightly floured surface to form 7 inch rounds. Place each round onto the previously greased cooky sheet. Cook one at a time in a moderately heated oven until lightly golden. Cut one round into 8 equal portions while still hot and leave the remaining 2 to cool for 10 minutes. Whip the cream until thick and add the sugar. Put half the mixture into a pastry bag and save eight raspberries for decoration. Mix the remaining berries with the cream. Carefully position one galette on a serving plate. Cover with raspberry cream mixture and top with the remaining galette. Decorate eight swirls of cream on top and arrange the galette triangles on their edges supported by the cream swirls. Decorate with the reserved raspberries.

Pears in Wine

PREPARATION TIME: 15 minutes plus chilling
COOKING TIME: 30 minutes

1½ cups granulated sugar
⅔ cup water
6 large pears, peeled
1 cup dry red wine

Gently heat the sugar and water until the sugar has dissolved. Add the pears and cover. Then simmer for 15 minutes. Stir in the wine and continue to simmer uncovered for another 15 minutes. Remove the pears from the saucepan and arrange in a serving dish. Bring the wine syrup back to the boil until thick. Pour over the pears and allow to cool. Serve chilled.

Strawberry and Peach Heart

PREPARATION TIME: 20 minutes plus chilling

3 passion fruit
½ cup white wine
⅓ cup sugar
3 tablespoons Cointreau or orange liqueur
4oz strawberries, hulled
3 peaches, halved and stoned
3 tablespoons strawberry jam
3 kumquats
3 kiwi fruit
3 tablespoons clear honey
1 teaspoon lime juice

Poach the flesh with the seeds of the passion fruit in the white wine until just tender. Add the sugar and continue to poach for a further four minutes. Sieve the mixture. Add the Cointreau and the strawberries and leave to cool. In a large saucepan filled with boiling water quickly submerge the

This page: Mango Soufflé (top), Mont Blanc (center) and Petits Pots de Café (bottom).

Facing page: Raspberries and Hazelnut Galette (top), Fruit Coupelles with Dried Fruit Salad (center) and Pears in Wine (bottom).

peaches and halve, removing the stone. Sieve the strawberry jam and using a writing tip fill a pastry bag, and reserve in the refrigerator. Slice the kumquats. To make the kiwi fruit sauce, peel the kiwi fruit and purée them. Pass them through a sieve and stir in the honey and lime juice. Using the sieved strawberry jam reserved in pastry bag, make heart shapes on each of the individual plates making sure not to break the line of strawberry jam. Fill the outline with the fruit, placing the peach half to one side and fill the hole left by removing stone with the strawberries. Pour over the kiwi fruit sauce and decorate with leaves. Serve chilled.

Chocolate and Brandy Cheesecake

PREPARATION TIME: 30 minutes plus chilling

COOKING TIME: 1 hour

OVEN: 325°F

6oz chocolate graham crackers
⅓ cup butter, melted
6oz chocolate
2 tablespoons brandy
2 eggs, lightly beaten
½ cup soft brown sugar
1½ cups cream cheese
2 tablespoons cornstarch

To decorate
Confectioners' sugar

Crush the crackers and mix them with the melted butter. Butter the sides and base of a loose-bottomed 7 inch cake pan. Spoon the biscuit mixture into the cake pan, press onto the sides and base, and refrigerate for half an hour. Melt 4oz of the chocolate in a heatproof bowl over a pan of water and stir in the brandy. Beat together the eggs and sugar until thick. Add the cheese and continue to beat until the mixture is soft. Stir in the melted chocolate and cornstarch. Pour the mixture into the cake pan and stand it on a cooky sheet. Bake until it sets. Remove from the oven and cool, then chill for 4 hours before serving. To serve: remove the cheesecake from the cake pan and grate the remaining chocolate on top. Sift with a little confectioners' sugar and serve.

Peach Brûlée

PREPARATION TIME: 20 minutes

BROILER SETTING: high

8 egg yolks
⅓ cup sugar
2½ teaspoons vanilla essence
6 peach halves, canned or fresh
⅓ cup soft brown sugar
Heavy cream

Beat the egg yolks and sugar until smooth and thick. Beat in the cream and pour the mixture into a saucepan. Cook over a low heat. Stir frequently until the mixture is thick enough to coat the back of a wooden spoon. Beat for 2 minutes off the heat. Stir in the vanilla essence and pour the mixture into a heatproof serving dish. When cool, arrange the peach halves on top of the sauce (cut side down). Chill for 1 hour. Sprinkle the soft brown sugar over the peaches and place the dish under a hot broiler. When the sugar melts and starts to caramelize remove the dish from the broiler and serve at once.

This page: Summer Pudding (left) and Strawberry and Peach Heart (right).

Facing page: Apricot Cream Cheese Dessert (top left), Peach Brûlée (top right) and Chocolate Brandy Cheesecake (bottom).

Summer Pudding

PREPARATION TIME: 10 minutes plus chilling

1lb 8oz fresh soft fruit
¾ cup granulated sugar
9 slices of white bread (use thick slices and remove the crusts)
Whipped cream

Put all the fruit into a saucepan with the sugar and heat until the sugar is dissolved. Shake the pan so that the fruit will stay whole. Remove from heat and cool. Line the base and sides of a 1¾ pint pudding mold with the slices of bread, trying not to leave any gaps. Pour the fruit juice into the center of the pudding and cover the top completely with bread and press down firmly. Place a saucer or small plate on top of the pudding and weigh down. Chill in the fridge overnight. Turn out and decorate with whipped cream.

Almond Pear

PREPARATION TIME: 20 minutes plus chilling
COOKING TIME: 1 hour
OVEN: 300°F

2½ cups heavy cream
6 egg yolks
¼ cup sugar
½ teaspoon almond essence
½ cup granulated sugar
⅔ cup water
4 large pears peeled, stoned and sliced thinly
¾ cup soft brown sugar
Lemon juice to sprinkle on pears

Pour the cream into a saucepan and heat (do not allow the cream to boil). Put the egg yolks, sugar and almond essence into a bowl and stir well. Slowly pour into the heated cream. Pour the mixture into a 1¾ pint baking dish and stand the dish in a roasting pan half filled with water (this is known as a *bain marie*). Loosely cover with foil and bake until set. Remove the dish from the bain marie and leave until cold. Refrigerate overnight. Put the granulated sugar and water in a saucepan and heat gently until the sugar has dissolved. Bring to the boil until thick and golden in color. Oil a shallow cake pan and pour the caramelized sugar in. When the caramel has set, crack into small pieces with a rolling pin. Arrange the pear slices on top of the baked cream and sprinkle with soft brown sugar, and lemon juice. Broil until the sugar has dissolved and the juice is bubbling. Leave to cool and return to the fridge for half an hour. Sprinkle with caramel chips before serving.

Apricot Cream Cheese Dessert

PREPARATION TIME: 20 minutes plus chilling
BROILER SETTING: high

8oz crushed English rolled wafers
½ teaspoon ground ginger
½ cup butter, melted
2 cups cream cheese
¼ cup sugar
½ cup light cream
2 tablespoons lemon juice
1 tablespoon gelatin dissolved in 2 tablespoons hot water
1lb can of apricot halves, drained
2oz preserved stem ginger, drained and chopped
1¾ cups heavy cream
¼ cup soft brown sugar

Grease a 9 inch loose-bottomed cake pan with a little butter. In a large mixing bowl crush the English rolled wafers, ground ginger and butter and spoon into the base of the cake pan, pressing down with the back of a spoon. Place the cream cheese and sugar into a bowl and beat with a wooden spoon until the mixture is smooth. Stir in the light cream, lemon juice and dissolved gelatin. Beat well so that all the mixture is blended together. Spoon the mixture into the pan and refrigerate for 40 minutes. When the filling is set, remove the pan and arrange the apricot halves on top of the filling. Sprinkle over the preserved ginger and soft brown sugar. Broil for three minutes until the sugar has caramelized. Remove the dessert from the pan and serve.

Orange and Lemon Chiffon Tart

PREPARATION TIME: 45 minutes
COOKING TIME: 20 minutes
OVEN: 400°F

Pastry Shell
1½ cups flour
Pinch of salt
7 tablespoons butter
2 tablespoons sugar
1 egg yolk

Filling
3 eggs, separated
⅓ cup sugar
2 large oranges
1 large lemon
1 tablespoon gelatin
Warm water

For decoration
Sliced orange and lemon fan
⅔ whipped cream

Pastry Shell
Sieve the flour and salt into a bowl and cut in the fat. Add the sugar and mix well. Mix to a stiff paste with the egg yolk to form a pliable dough. Turn onto a floured board and roll out. Use to line an 8 inch pie ring. Cut a circle from non-stick silicone baking paper and lay on top of pastry. Sprinkle with baking beans or crusts of bread (baking blind). Bake for about 20 minutes at 400°F. Remove the baking beans and paper and return to the oven for 5 minutes.

Filling
Beat the egg yolks, sugar and grated rind of two oranges and one lemon until thick. Dissolve the gelatin in a little warm water and make up to 1¼ cups) with orange juice and water. Pour the gelatin mixture into the egg mixture and beat until it starts to thicken. Lightly fold in the stiffly beaten egg white, pile into the pie shell and leave to set. Decorate with whipped cream and slices of orange.

Gateau American

PREPARATION TIME: 10 minutes
COOKING TIME: 20 minutes
OVEN: 400°F

⅓ cup granulated sugar
1 tablespoon butter
⅓ cup breadcrumbs
3 eggs, beaten
¾lb stoned dates
⅓ cup walnuts, chopped
1¾ cups whipped cream
Nuts

Mix the sugar, butter and breadcrumbs with the beaten eggs, dates and walnuts. Cook in a shallow pan until cooked (20 minutes). When cold, crumble with a fork. Layer fruit mixture and stiffly whipped cream in tall glasses and top with a rosette of whipped cream. Decorate with a nut.

Facing page: Almond Pear (top), Gateau American (right) and Orange and Lemon Chiffon Tart (bottom).

Summer Desserts

Gooseberry Pie

PREPARATION TIME: 20 minutes

COOKING TIME: 1 hour

OVEN: 425°F for 30 minutes, then 350°F for 30 minutes

Pastry

2½ cups flour
Pinch of salt
5 tablespoons butter (cut into small pieces)
5 tablespoons lard (cut into small pieces)
2½ tablespoons cold water

Filling

2lb gooseberries, topped and tailed
1 cup granulated sugar
Milk to glaze or beaten egg
Light cream or custard

Pastry

Sift the flour with the salt. Add the fat and mix until it resembles breadcrumbs. Stir in the water and form into a firm dough. Roll out half the pastry on a lightly floured surface and use it to line an 8 inch quiche pan or pie pan.

Filling

Mix the gooseberries with the sugar and fill the lined pie pan. Roll out the remaining pastry and cover the pie. Dampen the edges and seal together. Any excess pastry can be used to make leaves to decorate. Make a small hole in the center of the pie and brush the pastry with milk or beaten egg. Place on cooky sheet and cook in a hot oven. Serve with light cream or custard.

Melons and Mangoes on Ice

PREPARATION TIME: 1¼ hours

1 medium size Ogen melon
2 large mangoes

Slice melon in half and scoop out flesh in balls. Peel mangoes and slice. Mix mango slices and melon balls together and arrange in a glass bowl. Chill for 1 hour.

Frozen Gooseberry Fool

PREPARATION TIME: 20 minutes plus freezing

COOKING TIME: 15 minutes

1½lb gooseberries
⅔ cup water
Sprig of mint
¾ cup sugar
A little green food coloring
⅔ cup heavy cream, lightly whipped

Top and tail gooseberries. Place in a pan with the water and mint. Cover and simmer for approximately 15 minutes or until soft. Take off the heat and stir in the sugar until dissolved, then add food coloring. Take out the sprig of mint. Sieve and ensure all pips are removed. Cool and blend with the cream. Place in container and freeze.

Brown Bread Ice Cream

PREPARATION TIME: 20 minutes plus freezing

2 cups plus 3 tablespoons vanilla ice cream
4 small slices brown bread
1 teaspoon ground cinnamon
½ cup water
⅓ cup sugar

Put the ice cream into a large mixing bowl and break it up, allowing it to soften. Cut the crusts from the bread and discard. Crumble the slices into a bowl, adding the ground cinnamon, reserve. Put the water and sugar into a small saucepan and stir until the sugar has dissolved. Boil until the mixture caramelizes and turns brown. Remove from the heat and stir in the breadcrumbs and cinnamon mixture. Blend the mixture into the ice cream, making sure the breadcrumbs do not form large lumps. Turn the mixture into a rigid container for freezing, (leave ½ inch space at the top of the container). Freeze the mixture and serve.

Brown Bread Ice Cream (top left), Melons and Mangoes on Ice (top right), Frozen Gooseberry Fool (bottom left) and Gooseberry Pie (bottom right).

Cherry 'Spoom'

PREPARATION TIME: 20 minutes plus freezing

1 cup plus 2 tablespoons sugar
1¼ cups water
Juice of 2 limes
2 fresh peppermint leaves
2½ cups Sauternes
3 egg whites
Cherry brandy

Boil ¼ cup of the sugar with the water, lime juice and peppermint leaves. Leave to cool and strain into the Sauternes. Freeze the sherbet. Beat the egg whites and add the remaining sugar until it peaks. Remove the sherbet from the freezer and beat in the meringue mixture. Serve in glasses and pour over the cherry brandy.

Apple and White Raisin and Brandy Ice

PREPARATION TIME: 10 minutes plus soaking and freezing time

2½ cups apple juice
¼ cup sugar
1¼oz packet dried apple flakes
¾ cup white raisins
A few drops green food color
1 egg white, stiffly beaten

Put the apple juice in a pan with sugar. Heat gently until the sugar has dissolved. Boil quickly for 5 minutes and remove from heat. Cool. Soak apple flakes and white raisins in brandy and add enough apple syrup to cover mixture. Soak for 4 hours. Then mix apple, white raisins and brandy adding a few drops of food color mixture with the remaining apple syrup in a shallow container and freeze. Mash with a fork and fold in egg whites. Return to the freezer. Serve frozen in glasses.

This page: Burgundy Granita (top), Apple and White Raisin and Brandy Ice (center) and Champagne Granita (bottom).

Facing page: Cherry 'Spoom' (top), Raspberry Malakoff (center) and Cherry Cinnamon Sherbet (bottom).

Burgundy Granita

PREPARATION TIME: 15 minutes plus freezing

⅓ cup sugar, plus 2 tablespoons
Juice of ½ lime and ½ orange
1 tablespoon water
Small bunch lemon balm leaves
½ bottle good Burgundy
½ cup heavy cream
Blackberries to decorate

Boil half the sugar with the lime and orange juice and water, and the balm leaves. Cool, strain and add to Burgundy. Freeze in a shallow container. To serve: whip the cream with the remaining sugar. Scrape the granita with a spoon to produce ice shavings and serve shavings into glasses, decorate with cream and blackberries.

Champagne Granita

PREPARATION TIME: 5 minutes plus freezing time

⅔ bottle champagne
Fresh blackcurrants and raspberries
Superfine sugar to dust

Freeze the champagne in a shallow container. When frozen, scrape off and serve into glasses. Decorate with blackcurrants and raspberries. Dust with superfine sugar.

Raspberry Malakoff

PREPARATION TIME: 35 minutes plus chilling

¾ cup sugar
¾ cup butter
1¼ cups heavy cream
¾ cup ground almonds
3 tablespoons kirsch
8oz fresh raspberries
1 packet ladyfingers
Whipped cream

Beat the sugar and butter until fluffy. Whip the cream until it peaks and fold in the ground almonds. Add the kirsch and raspberries. Mix the sugar and butter with the cream fruit mixture. Line a 7 inch cake pan with non-stick silicone paper. Stand the ladyfingers round the sides of the cake pan with the sugary side outermost. Spoon the malakoff mixture into the middle and press it down. Make sure the top is smooth. Refrigerate until the malakoff feels firm. With a sharp knife, trim the cookies to the same level as the malakoff mixture. Turn the malakoff out upside down. Decorate with whipped cream if desired. Serve chilled.

Cherry Cinnamon Sherbet

PREPARATION TIME: 25 minutes plus freezing

1¼ cups plus 1 tablespoon sugar
1¼ cups water
1 piece cinnamon stick
18oz fresh sour cherries
Juice of ½ lemon
1 cup heavy cream
Seeds of ¼ vanilla pod
Fresh cherries

Boil 1¼ cups of the sugar for 3 minutes in water and cinnamon and leave to cool. Remove the cinnamon sticks and stone the cherries. Purée the cherries and stir in the lemon juice. Mix with the sugar syrup and freeze. Flavor the cream with the tablespoon of sugar and vanilla. Whip until thick. Put the sherbet into individual glasses and decorate with cream and cherries.

Strawberry Alaska

PREPARATION TIME: 10 minutes
COOKING TIME: 2-3 minutes
OVEN: 275°F

1 shop-bought strawberry jam jelly-roll
Soft-scoop strawberry ice cream to cover

Meringue
2 egg whites
½ cup superfine sugar

Cover jelly-roll with ice cream. Return to freezer. Beat egg whites until they form stiff peaks. Beat in half the sugar. Then fold in the rest. Remove ice cream covered jelly-roll from freezer and cover with meringue mixture. Place in oven and cook meringue until just turning golden. (Approximately 2-3 minutes.) Serve immediately.

Strawberry Yogurt Ice

PREPARATION TIME: 20 minutes plus freezing

8oz fresh or thawed, frozen strawberries
1¼ cups plain low fat yogurt
2 teaspoons gelatin
2 tablespoons water
1 egg white
5 tablespoons superfine sugar
A few strawberries

Blend strawberries and yogurt until smooth. Sprinkle gelatin over the water in a small bowl. Place bowl in a pan of hot water until the gelatin is dissolved. Cool slightly and add to the strawberry mixture. Pour into the container and freeze until icy round the edges. Put mixture into bowl and beat until smooth. In another bowl beat the egg white stiffly, carefully adding the sugar, and fold into strawberry mixture. Pour back into container and freeze. To serve – scoop into glasses and decorate with strawberries.

Peach Melba

PREPARATION TIME: 10 minutes

1 large can peaches (2 halves per person)
2 scoops ice cream per person
Chocolate sauce or raspberry purée
Flaked almonds

Place 2 scoops of ice cream per serving in individual bowls. Place 2 peach halves on top. Serve with chocolate sauce or raspberry purée. Decorate with flaked almonds.

Lemon Sherbet

PREPARATION TIME: 15 minutes plus freezing

Grated rinds and juice of 2 lemons
Cold water
⅓ cup sugar
1 teaspoon gelatin
2 egg whites

Mix the lemon juice and rind with cold water to make 3 cups of fluid. Put the liquid in a saucepan with the sugar and boil. Remove from the heat and beat in the gelatin. Pour into a mixing bowl and place in the freezer until it begins to harden. Beat the egg whites until stiff and beat them into the lemon mixture. Return to the freezer, leaving a ½ inch head space in the container.

Pastel Coupé

PREPARATION TIME: 35 minutes plus freezing

Yellow
2½ cups water
2 level teaspoons gelatin
1¼ cups superfine sugar
3 lemons
2 egg whites

Green
2½ cups water
2 level teaspoons gelatin
1 cup sugar
2 lemons
2 egg whites
2 tablespoons crème de menthe

Yellow
Measure out two tablespoons of water and sprinkle with gelatin. Place the remaining water and sugar in a saucepan. Add pared lemon rinds and stir over the heat until the sugar has dissolved. Bring to the boil and simmer for 5 minutes. Remove from heat and add gelatin mixture. Dissolve completely and stir in the lemon juice. Leave to cool. Strain the mixture into a container and freeze until partially frozen. Place in chilled mixing bowl and beat with beaten egg whites until thick and snowy. Return to container and freeze.

Green
For the green pastel coupé use basic method and ingredients as listed. Add the crème de menthe with lemon juice. To serve: use an ice-cream scoop, take half the green and half the yellow into one scoop. Serve in meringue cases or glasses.

Facing page: Strawberry yogurt Ice (top), Peach Melba (center) and Strawberry Alaska (bottom).

Curaçao Granita with Champagne

PREPARATION TIME: 10 minutes plus freezing

⅓ cup sugar
⅔ cup water
Juice of 1 lime
Juice of 1 orange
3 tablespoons blue Curaçao
⅔ bottle champagne

Boil half the sugar with the water, lime and orange juice for two to three minutes. Cool, strain, add to the Curaçao and the champagne. Pour into a flat freezer-proof container and freeze. To serve: scrape with a spoon and serve in glasses.

Blackcurrant Sherbet

PREPARATION TIME: 20 minutes plus freezing

2lb fresh or thawed, frozen blackcurrants
1 cup plus 2 tablespoons sugar
1¼ cups water
2 egg whites

Put all the ingredients except the egg whites into a saucepan. Heat slowly and cook for 15 minutes. Rub the fruit mixture through a sieve and pour into a freezer-proof container with a lid. Freeze until mushy. Beat the egg whites until firm and fold into the mixture. Return to the freezer.

Inset illustration: (from top to bottom) Curaçao Granita with Champagne, Lemon Sherbet, Pastel Coupé and Blackcurrant Sherbet.

Ginger Syllabub

PREPARATION TIME: 15 minutes

4oz jar preserved ginger
2½ cups heavy cream, lightly whipped

Chop 2 pieces of the ginger and mix into the cream along with 2 tablespoons of the syrup. Serve in glasses or bowls and decorate with sliced ginger. Chill until ready to serve.

Apricot Ice Roll

PREPARATION TIME: 35 minutes plus freezing
COOKING TIME: 12 minutes
OVEN: 425°F

Sponge mixture
2 eggs
¼ cup sugar
½ cup flour

Filling and decorating
4 tablespoons apricot jam
2½ cups soft-scoop ice cream (vanilla)
Cream to decorate
Dried apricots, thinly sliced

Beat eggs and sugar until light and fluffy. Carefully fold in flour. Turn into a greased and floured jelly-roll pan and bake. Turn out onto a clean cloth and leave to cool. Spread sponge with apricot jam and softened ice cream. Roll up using clean cloth. Place in freezer until ice cream is hardened. Decorate with cream and sliced apricots.

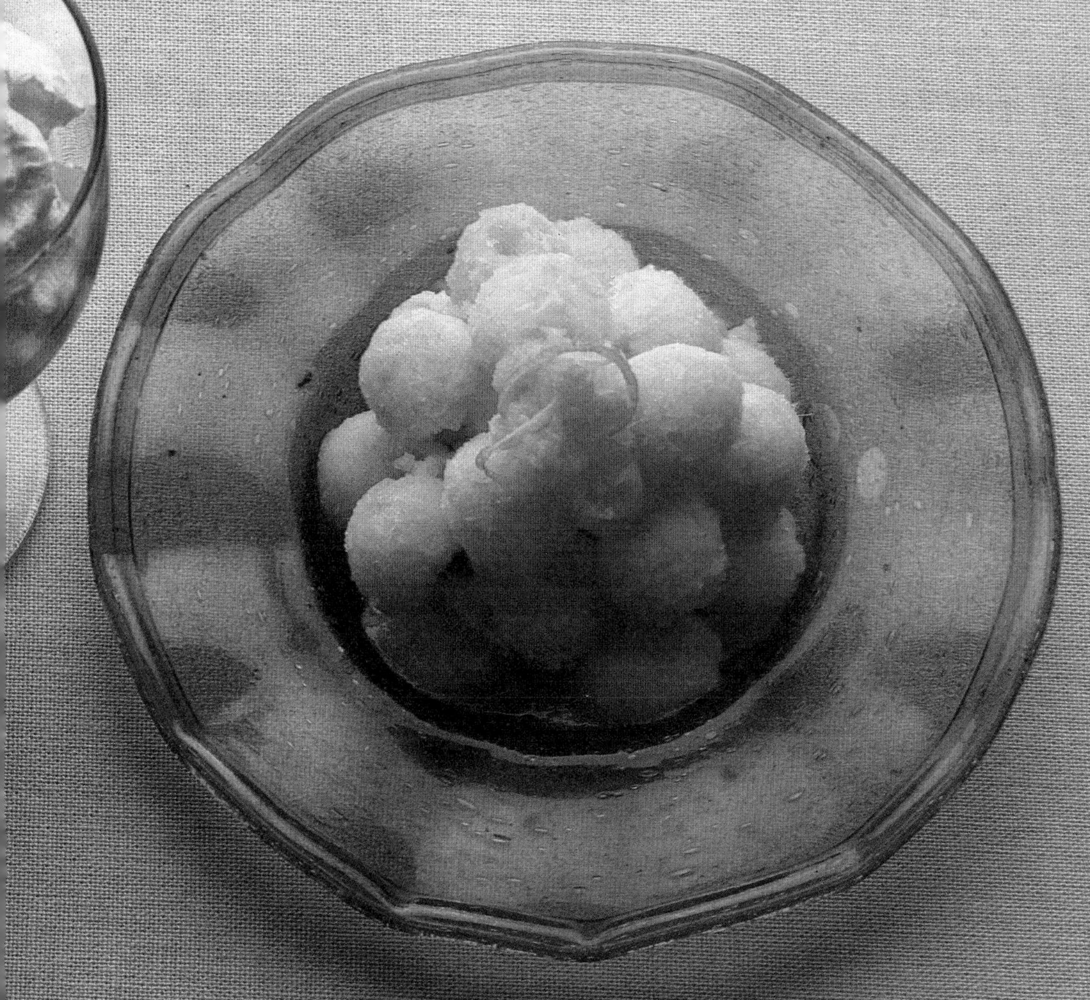

Mango Sherbet

PREPARATION TIME: 15 minutes plus freezing

1 cup mango purée
Juice of ½ lime
⅔ cup dry white wine
⅔ cup mineral water
1 egg white
¼ cup sugar

Mix the mango purée with the lime juice, white wine and mineral water. Beat the egg white until it peaks and slowly add the sugar. Fold the egg white into the mango mixture and freeze.

Apricot Ice Roll (far left), Ginger Syllabub (center) and Mango Sherbet (left).

Banana Ice Crêpes

PREPARATION TIME: 30 minutes

12 cooked crêpes
2 large bananas
12 scoops soft-scoop vanilla ice cream
Chocolate sauce

Mash one banana, and combine with ice cream. Fold the crêpes in half and place on individual plates. Fill crêpes with the mixture of banana and ice cream. Decorate with other sliced banana. Serve with chocolate sauce.

Mousse Glacée au Chocolat

PREPARATION TIME: 20 minutes plus freezing

4 egg yolks
2 tablespoons sugar
3 teaspoons vanilla essence
1¼ cups heavy cream
2 egg whites, stiffly whipped
Chocolate sauce

Beat egg yolks and sugar until light and creamy. Add vanilla essence. Add the cream and egg whites. Freeze the mixture. Serve with chocolate sauce.

Chocolate Banana Ice

PREPARATION TIME: 35 minutes plus freezing

⅔ cup milk
3 tablespoons sugar
3 tablespoons chocolate (broken into bits)
1 egg, beaten
1 teaspoon vanilla essence
⅔ heavy cream, whipped until soft peaking

Banana Cream
4 medium bananas
1 tablespoon lemon juice
3 tablespoons confectioners' sugar, sieved
⅔ cup heavy cream, beaten

Place the milk, sugar and chocolate in a saucepan and heat gently. Pour onto the beaten egg and stir constantly until mixed. Return the mixture to the saucepan and cook until the custard thickens. Strain the mixture, add the vanilla essence and allow to cool. Fold the cream into the custard mixture. Beat rapidly and turn into a metal freezing container.

Banana Cream
Peel and chop the bananas and sprinkle with lemon juice. Dust the fruit with confectioners' sugar and fold the whipped cream in with the bananas. Stir the chocolate mixture with banana cream and freeze. Remove from freezer to fridge 20 minutes before serving.

Refreshing Sherbet

PREPARATION TIME: 15 minutes plus freezing

⅓ cup sugar
1¾ cups water
3 ripe mangoes, peeled, stoned and mashed
Juice of 3 lemons
3 tablespoons white rum
3 egg whites, beaten

Over low heat, dissolve sugar in the water, boil for 10 minutes. Leave to cool. Blend mangoes with lemon juice and rum. Add the syrup. Pour into a container and freeze until just frozen. Turn into a bowl. Fold in the egg whites. Freeze.

Minted Lime Ice

PREPARATION TIME: 15 minutes plus freezing

¾ cup sugar
1½ cups water
Grated rind and juice of 6 limes
4 tablespoons fresh mint, finely chopped
⅔ cup heavy cream
3 tablespoons light cream

Place the sugar and water in a saucepan. Stir gently over a low heat. When the sugar has dissolved bring the mixture to the boil. Remove the pan from the heat. Stir in the grated rind of the limes. Add the juice and stir in the mint. Let the mixture cool and pour into ice trays. Freeze the mixture, covered with foil. When the mixture is frozen, crush it. Lightly whip the creams together. Stir the lime ice into the cream and re-freeze. Slightly thaw and spoon into small glasses to serve.

Lemon Ice Cream Sponge

PREPARATION TIME: 20 minutes plus freezing
COOKING TIME: 15 minutes
OVEN: 425°F

Sponge
3 large eggs
⅓ cup sugar
¾ cup flour, sieved
1 teaspoon baking powder

Filling
4 level teaspoons lemon curd
1 grated rind of lemon
6 scoops soft-scoop vanilla ice cream

To decorate
3 tablespoons heavy cream
Confectioners' sugar
Sugared lemon slices

Sponge
Beat eggs and sugar until light and fluffy. Sieve in flour and mix in carefully. Bake in a large 5 inch cooky sheet. Turn out and cool.

Filling
Slice the cake into three horizontally. On bottom and middle slices spread lemon curd. Mix together the lemon rind and vanilla ice cream. Spread on top of the lemon curd. Sandwich together and freeze.

To decorate
Whip cream until stiff; place in pastry bag with a star tip; decorate rosettes on top of the sponge. Dust with confectioners' sugar and add lemon slices.

Custard Ice Cream

PREPARATION TIME: 20 minutes

5 egg yolks
⅔ cup light cream
¾ cup sugar
1¼ cups heavy cream

Combine egg yolks, light cream and ½ cup of the sugar in a mold. Place over a pan of simmering water and stir until mixture coats the back of a spoon. Strain mixture into a bowl and leave to cool. Whip heavy cream lightly. Mix with custard carefully. Fold in remaining ¼ cup of sugar. Pour into a freezer-proof container. Cover and freeze.

Coconut Sherbet

PREPARATION TIME: 20 minutes plus freezing

1 cup canned coconut juice
⅔ cup mineral water
2 tablespoons dark rum
2 egg whites
½ cup sugar

To decorate
2 bananas, sliced
Chocolate sauce

Mix the coconut juice with the mineral water and rum. Beat the egg whites until stiff, gradually adding the sugar. Stir the egg whites into the coconut mixture with a balloon whisk and freeze until creamy. Serve with banana slices and chocolate sauce.

Honey Ice Cream

PREPARATION TIME: 15 minutes plus freezing

1lb raspberries
⅔ cup clear honey
⅔ cup heavy cream
2 tablespoons lemon juice
3 egg whites
½ cup water
⅔ cup light cream
4 tablespoons granulated sugar

Cook the raspberries in a saucepan with the honey and water. Add the sugar and cook for 5 minutes until dissolved. Leave to cool. Rub the mixture through a sieve and chill. Beat the heavy cream until thick and stir in the light cream. Fold the creams into the fruit mixture. Freeze until almost solid. Beat and re-freeze.

Facing page: Mocha Soufflé (top), Chocolate Banana Ice (center left), Banana Ice Crêpes (center right) and Mousse Glacée au Chocolat (bottom).

Fancy Ice

PREPARATION TIME: 15 minutes

COOKING TIME: 10 minutes

OVEN: 425°F

Sponge
2 eggs
¼ cup sugar
½ cup flour

Topping
1 cup confectioners' frosting
1 tablespoon lemon juice
A few drops yellow food color

Filling and decoration
Blackberry sherbet
Apricot purée
Blackberries

Sponge
Beat eggs and sugar until light and fluffy. Sieve in the flour, fold gently into mixture. Lightly grease and flour a muffin pan. Spoon into 12 portions and bake until golden brown. Turn out and cool on a wire rack.

Topping
Melt the confectioners' frosting. Add the lemon juice and food coloring. Spoon over the cakes, leave to harden and set.

Filling and decoration
Fit a star tip on a pastry bag and fill with blackberry sherbet. Cut sponges in half, swirl sherbet on top of the base then sandwich with the remaining half of sponge. Serve with a spoonful of apricot purée on the side and decorate with blackberries.

Mocha Soufflé

PREPARATION TIME: 30 minutes plus chilling

½oz gelatin
4 tablespoons warm water
3 tablespoons cocoa
1 teaspoon instant coffee
1¾ cups milk
4 eggs, separated
⅓ cup sugar
2 tablespoons rum
⅔ cup fresh heavy cream, whipped
Chocolate curls

Dissolve the gelatin in a small mold with the warm water. Mix the cocoa and coffee with the milk and bring to the boil in a saucepan. In a mixing bowl beat the egg yolks and sugar together until pale and fluffy. Gradually beat in the milk mixture. Place the bowl over a saucepan of hot water for 15 minutes. Stir gently. Remove from heat and stir in the rum and dissolved gelatin. Allow to cool. Beat the egg whites until they peak and fold into the mixture. Mix in half of the heavy cream. Pour into a prepared 2½ cups soufflé dish. Chill until set. Decorate with the remaining whipped cream and chocolate curls.

This page: Fancy Ice (top), Custard Ice-Cream (center) and Coconut Sherbet (bottom). Facing page: Refreshing Sherbet (top), Minted Lime Ice (center left), Honey Ice-Cream (center right) and Lemon Ice-Cream Sponge (bottom).

Desserts for Autumn

Illustrations below: Charlotte (left), Steamed Chocolate Pudding with Rum Sauce (center) and Viennoise Pudding with German Sauce (right).

Charlotte

PREPARATION TIME: 30 minutes
COOKING TIME: 40 minutes
OVEN: 350°F

1lb tart apples
½ cup white breadcrumbs
¼ cup shredded suet
⅓ cup brown sugar
1 lemon
Superfine sugar for topping
Custard or cream

Wash, peel, core and slice the apples. Mix together the breadcrumbs, suet, sugar and grated lemon rind. Sprinkle a little of this mixture in the bottom of a greased pie dish. Then add a layer of apple slices (sprinkled with juice from the lemon) and fill the dish with alternate layers of the breadcrumb mixture and sliced apples – finishing with a layer of breadcrumbs. Bake in the oven for 40 minutes. Turn out onto a hot dish and sprinkle lightly with superfine sugar. Serve with custard or cream.

Steamed Chocolate Pudding with Rum Sauce

PREPARATION TIME: 25 minutes

COOKING TIME: 1½ hours or until firm to touch

3oz cooking chocolate
Few drops of vanilla essence
⅓ cup butter
¾ cup sugar
3 eggs
2¼ cups flour
2 teaspoons baking powder
7½ tablespoons milk

Sauce

3 tablespoons cornstarch
1¾ cups milk
3 tablespoons sugar
3 tablespoons dark rum

Put the chocolate, vanilla and butter in a heatproof bowl placed over a pan of hot water. Heat gently, stirring to melt the chocolate and butter. When melted remove from the heat and cool. Stir the sugar into the chocolate mixture and beat in the eggs. Sift the flour and baking powder and mix in well. Stir in the milk. Grease a 2½ pint pudding mold. Pour the mixture into the pudding mold. Cover with a foil lid tied on securely with string. Steam pudding for 1½ hours.

Sauce

In a saucepan dissolve the cornstarch in the milk. Stir in the sugar and heat gently, stirring constantly. Bring the mixture to the boil and then reduce heat and simmer until it thickens and is smooth. Stir in the rum. Turn out the pudding and serve hot with sauce.

Viennoise Pudding with German Sauce

PREPARATION TIME: 60 minutes

COOKING TIME: 90 minutes

1oz sugar cubes
1 tablespoon water
1¼ cups milk
6oz bread
Grated rind of 1 lemon
⅔ cup white raisins
1½oz chopped candied peel
3 eggs
½ wineglass of sherry
⅓ cup superfine sugar

Sauce

2 egg yolks
⅔ cup sherry
1 tablespoon sugar
Strips of lemon rind

Using a thick pan, dissolve the sugar in a tablespoonful of water. Heat gently until dissolved, then bring to the boil and boil rapidly until the syrup turns brown. Heat the milk and pour over the syrup. Remove the crusts from the bread, then cut the bread into small cubes. Add the lemon rind, white raisins and candied peel. Beat the eggs and add the milk/syrup mixture to the eggs. Then add the sherry and superfine sugar. Pour the whole mixture over the bread and leave to soak for 30 minutes. Transfer to a greased mold, cover with greased foil and steam for 60-90 minutes until firm.

Sauce
Beat the egg yolks, warm the sherry and then mix together with the sugar and lemon rind. Sit the mold in a pan of hot water and beat thoroughly for 10 minutes. Do not over-heat the sauce or it will curdle. Serve immediately.

Crêpes

1 cup flour
Pinch of salt or sugar (for extra sweetness)
1 egg, lightly beaten
1¼ cups milk
1 teaspoon vegetable oil

Before doing any of the following pancake recipes, follow these instructions for making the crêpes. This mixture makes 12 crêpes. You can also buy them ready made.

Sieve the flour and salt into a bowl. Make a well in the center and break an egg into it with half the milk. Beat well, then when smooth add the remaining milk. Leave the mixture to stand for 40 minutes. Grease the skillet and heat it a little. Pour the batter into the skillet. Quickly tilt and rotate the skillet so the batter coats the bottom and pour off the excess batter. Cook over a moderate heat until the underside of the crêpe is gently brown. Turn crêpe over and brown the other side. Turn onto wax paper and keep warm.

"Sissi" Crêpes

PREPARATION TIME: 25 minutes
COOKING TIME: 20 minutes
OVEN: 400°F

6oz almond paste
3 tablespoons sugar syrup
3 tablespoons lemon juice
1½ tablespoons kirsch
2 tablespoons softened butter
6 tablespoons strawberry sauce
6 tablespoons Advocaat
6 scoops vanilla ice cream
Whipped cream

Mix the almond paste with the sugar syrup, lemon juice and kirsch and beat until fluffy. Divide the mixture between the crêpes and roll or fold them. Spread with butter, put in ovenproof dish and heat through at oven temperature 400°F for five minutes. Put them on small plates and pour over strawberry sauce and liqueur. Serve with whipped cream and vanilla ice cream.

Chocolate Crêpes

OVEN: 400°F

6oz cherry jam
10 tablespoons softened butter
⅔ cup water
10 tablespoons sugar
4 tablespoons cocoa powder
3 tablespoons rum
6oz semi-sweet chocolate, chopped
6 tablespoons whipped cream

Fill the crêpes with the jam and roll or fold them. Spread them on top with half of the butter. Heat the crêpes for 5 minutes.

Sauce
In a saucepan boil up the water, sugar and the rest of the butter. Remove the pan from the heat and stir in the rum and chocolate. If the sauce is too thick, thin with light cream. Pour the hot sauce over the crêpes. Decorate with whipped cream.

Crêpes Suzette

PREPARATION TIME: 40 minutes
COOKING TIME: 35 minutes

Rind of 1 orange
6 lumps sugar
5 tablespoons butter
½ cup more sugar
¾ cup fresh orange juice
5 tablespoons orange liqueur
3 tablespoons brandy

Cream the ½ cup sugar and the butter till fluffy. Beat in the orange juice and rub the sugar cubes onto the rind so they look orange, reserve. Add the orange liqueur gradually. Spoon a little of the mixture into each pancake and roll or fold. Put the remaining mixture into a large skillet and place the crêpes on top. Scatter the sugar cubes on the top. Gently heat the skillet and melt the butter. In another saucepan warm the brandy and pour over the pancakes. Ignite the brandy and serve.

Pear and Nut Crêpes

PREPARATION TIME: 25 minutes
COOKING TIME: 15 minutes
OVEN: 350°F

12 cooked crêpes
¾ cup butter
½ cup confectioners' sugar
½ cup ground almonds
Few drops of almond essence
Grated rind of 1 lemon
26oz of canned pears, drained and sliced

Cream the butter and sugar together till the mixture is fluffy. Beat the ground almonds, almond essence and lemon rind into the mixture. Fold the pears carefully into the mixture. Divide the mixture between the crêpes and roll or fold each one. Arrange the crêpes in an ovenproof dish and re-heat gently in a moderate oven. Serve hot.

Apple and Nut Tart

PREPARATION TIME: 20 minutes
COOKING TIME: 40 minutes
OVEN: 425°F

1¼ cups flour
10 tablespoons sugar
Salt
1 egg
9 tablespoons butter, cut into pieces

Filling
1lb dessert apples, peeled, cored and sliced
¼ cup ground hazelnuts
1 teaspoon ground cinnamon
Juice of 1 lemon
3 tablespoons apricot brandy (optional)
½ cup apricot jam
½ cup chopped nuts

Pastry
Sift the flour and sugar (reserving 2 tablespoons of sugar for filling) and a pinch of salt into a mixing bowl. Make a well in the center and add the egg. Mix in the butter pieces, rub the ingredients to make a soft smooth dough. Rest the dough by leaving it in the fridge for 30 minutes. Grease an 8 inch pie dish. Roll out the pastry, line the dish.

Filling
Layer the apple and hazelnuts. Sprinkle with cinnamon and sugar, lemon juice and apricot brandy. Put the apricot jam in a saucepan and heat until melted. Pour over filling. Sprinkle with the chopped nuts. Bake until golden and fruit is soft. Take tart out of oven and cool.

Treacle Tart

PREPARATION TIME: 25 minutes
COOKING TIME: 30 minutes
OVEN: 350°F

Pastry
1½ cups flour
Pinch of salt
3 tablespoons butter
3 tablespoons lard
Cold water to mix

Filling
1 cup corn syrup
¼ cup breadcrumbs
Lemon juice

Sieve the flour into a bowl. Add the salt and the lard to the flour. Chop the lard into small pieces with a knife and then rub into the flour with the fingertips. Add the water and mix to a stiff dough. Turn onto a lightly floured board and knead the dough until free from cracks. Roll out a little larger than a 9 inch pan. Line the edge of the pan with a strip of pastry (cut from the edge). Damp it well and then line the whole pan with the rolled out pastry. Seal the edges, trim off any excess pastry and decorate the edges.

Filling
Sprinkle the breadcrumbs into the lined pan and cover with corn syrup. Add a little lemon juice. Cut the remaining pastry trimmings into thin strips, twist, and lay across the tart. Bake for 30 minutes.

Facing page: Pear and Nut Crêpes (top left), Crêpes Suzette (top right), Chocolate Crêpes (center) and "Sissi" Crêpes (bottom).

Cherry Clafoutis

PREPARATION TIME: 15 minutes

COOKING TIME: 15 minutes

OVEN: 350°F

1½ cups milk
1 tablespoon dark rum
4 eggs
½ cup sugar
1 cup flour
Generous pinch of salt
14oz stoned cherries
Confectioners' sugar

Grease a shallow medium-sized baking dish. Place the milk, rum and eggs in a large mixing bowl and beat with a balloon whisk until smooth and frothy. Add the sugar a little at a time and beat till the sugar is dissolved. Add the flour, sift it a little at a time, mixing in the salt with the last spoonful. Pour half of the batter into the prepared dish and spread the cherries over the top, then pour the remaining batter over all the cherries. Bake until the pudding is firm in the center and sprinkle with a little confectioners' sugar. Serve hot.

Red Fruit Crumble

PREPARATION TIME: 15 minutes

COOKING TIME: 25 minutes with a further 15 minutes

OVEN: 375°F reduced to 350°F after 25 minutes

2 level teaspoons cornstarch
6 tablespoons granulated sugar
12oz raspberries, hulled
3 medium-sized ripe pears, peeled, quartered, cored and sliced.
1 cup flour
¼ cup margarine
¼ cup soft brown sugar
1 cup crunchy breakfast cereal, crushed
Custard or cream

In a large mixing bowl, mix the cornstarch and granulated sugar with the raspberries. Grease a 2½ pint ovenproof dish. Arrange the mixture alternately with the pears. Sieve into another bowl the flour and cut in the margarine. Crush the cereal and stir in with the soft brown sugar. Put all the mixture over the fruit and flatten, using the back of the spoon. Cook in a moderate oven, temperature 375°F for 25 minutes, then reduce the temperature to 350°F and cook for 15 minutes until crumble is golden. Serve hot with custard or cream.

Honey Plum Cobbler

PREPARATION TIME: 30 minutes

COOKING TIME: 15 minutes plus a further 30 minutes

OVEN: 400°F

2lb ripe plums, halved and stoned
4-6 tablespoons clear honey
2 cups flour
2 teaspoons baking powder
2 tablespoons sugar
¼ cup butter
5-6 tablespoons milk
1 egg, beaten
Cream

Place the plums in an ovenproof dish with the honey, cover with a sheet of foil. Cook in a preheated oven for 15 minutes at 400°F. While the plums are cooking mix the flour, baking powder and sugar and cut in the butter. Using a knife stir in the milk and egg so the mixture forms a soft dough. Lightly flour the work surface and roll out the dough. Cut with 2 inch cutter to form cobblers. Remove the plums from the oven and cool. Arrange the cobblers round the top of the dish overlapping slightly. Brush the top of each one with a little milk and sprinkle with sugar. Cook until golden. Serve hot with cream.

Les Bourdaines

(Apples Baked in Pastry)

PREPARATION TIME: 30 minutes

COOKING TIME: 20-25 minutes

OVEN: 325°F

3 cups flour
Pinch of salt
¾ cup butter
1½ tablespoons sugar
5-7 tablespoons iced water
6 large dessert apples, peeled and cored
6 tablespoons plum jam
1 egg, beaten, to glaze
Cream

Sift the flour and salt into a bowl. Rub in the butter until the mixture is like fine breadcrumbs. Stir in the sugar. Mix in enough water to give a smooth, pliable dough. Divide the dough into 6 pieces and roll out each square. Fill the centers of the apples with jam and place an apple on each pastry square. Brush the edges of the squares with water and wrap up the apples, sealing them well. Cut out some pastry leaves and decorate. Place on a cooky sheet. Brush the pastry with beaten egg, bake in a moderate preheated oven. Bake until golden brown. Serve hot with cream.

Alma Pudding with Wine Sauce

½ cup butter
2 tablespoons sugar
2 eggs
4 tablespoons flour
2 tablespoons orange marmalade
½ teaspoon bicarbonate of soda
⅓ cup milk

Wine Sauce
1 egg
⅔ cup sherry
1 tablespoon sugar

Beat butter and sugar until light. Add eggs and flour. Add the marmalade, bicarbonate of soda and milk. Place mixture in a pudding mold and cover with foil, tied in place with string. Place in a large pan, pour in hot water until it comes ¾ of the way up the mold. Bring water to the boil and steam for 1 hour. Remove and turn out into a serving plate and serve with wine sauce.

Wine Sauce
Combine ingredients. Place over a pan of boiling water. Beat until light and frothy. Serve.

This page: Red Fruit Crumble (top left), Cherry Clafoutis (top right) and Honey Plum Cobbler (bottom).

Facing page: Treacle Tart (top left), Les Bourdaines (top right), Apple and Nut Tart (center) and Alma Pudding (bottom).

Winter Desserts

Yorkshire Apple Tart

PREPARATION TIME: 30 minutes plus chilling

COOKING TIME: 25 minutes plus 15 minutes

OVEN: 375°F

10oz basic pastry
12oz tart apples, peeled, cored and sliced
2 tablespoons sugar
1 tablespoon water
Little milk and sugar to glaze
4oz strong cheese, sliced
Whipped cream

Roll out the pastry and use two-thirds to line an 8 inch pie ring. Fill the center with the sliced apples, sprinkle with sugar and water. Seal the edges, cover the tart with the remaining pastry, and brush the top with a little milk and sprinkle with sugar. Place in a preheated, moderately hot oven and bake for 20 to 25 minutes until the crust is firm and lightly browned. Leave to cool, then with care remove the crust with a sharp knife. Place the cheese on top of the apples. Replace the crust. Return to the oven and bake for 15 minutes until the cheese has melted. Serve hot with whipped cream. Serves 4 to 6.

Fruit Cobbler

PREPARATION TIME: 20 minutes

COOKING TIME: 20 minutes

OVEN: 450°F

2¼ cups flour
2 teaspoons baking powder
½ cup butter
⅔ cup milk
3 large tart apples
12oz can raspberries, drained
¼ cup granulated sugar
Cream
¼ cup granulated brown sugar

Sieve flour and baking powder into a mixing bowl. Rub in butter excluding 1 tablespoon, and work into a soft dough by adding milk. Knead the dough and roll out onto a floured board. Cut out the scones. Place the scones on a cooky sheet and bake at 450°F for 10-15 minutes. Peel the apples and slice them. Put the apples in a saucepan, and cook in a little water with granu lated sugar until soft. Drain the apples and add the raspberries. Cut the scones and sandwich together with butter. Put a circle of scones round the edge of the apple and raspberry mixture. Put some cream in the circle left by the scones. Sprinkle with a little granulated brown sugar and broil until the sugar begins to caramelize. Serve at once.

Snowballs

PREPARATION TIME: 20 minutes

COOKING TIME: 30 minutes then 3 minutes

OVEN: 375°F

6 medium tart apples
⅓ cup soft brown sugar
¾ teaspoon mixed spice
2 eggs
⅓ cup superfine sugar
Candied cherries and angelica (optional)

Wash and core the apples. Mix together soft brown sugar and all the spices and fill the center of the apples. Put the apples on a cooky sheet and bake. Beat the egg white until it peaks and fold in the superfine sugar. Coat the apples with meringue and then return to the oven for a few minutes. Decorate with candied cherries and angelica if desired.

Apple Betty

PREPARATION TIME: 30 minutes

COOKING TIME: 30 minutes

OVEN: 350°F

½ cup butter
½ cup fresh white breadcrumbs
½ cup soft brown sugar
½ level teaspoon ground cinnamon
Grated rind and juice of 1 lemon
2lb tart apples, peeled, cored and sliced
3 tablespoons water
Ice cream or cream

Melt the butter in a saucepan. Take the pan off the heat and mix in the breadcrumbs. In a bowl mix the sugar, cinnamon and grated lemon rind. Add the apple slices. Butter a 2½ pint pie dish. Sprinkle some of the crumbs in the dish, layer the apple slices with the crumb mixture, ending with the crumb mixture on top. Squeeze the lemon juice and spoon the water over the pudding. Cover the pudding with buttered foil and bake until apples are cooked. The topping should be crisp and golden. Serve with ice cream or cream.

Rainbow Tart

PREPARATION TIME: 15 minutes

COOKING TIME: 35 minutes

OVEN: 375°F

Pastry
2 cups flour
Pinch of salt
¼ cup butter
¼ cup lard
About 3 tablespoons water

Filling
1½ tablespoons strawberry jam
1½ tablespoons blackberry jam
1½ tablespoons bilberry jam
1½ tablespoons lemon curd
1½ tablespoons orange marmalade
1½ tablespoons gooseberry purée
1½ tablespoons mincemeat
Custard

Pastry
Sift flour and salt into a bowl. Cut the butter and lard into pieces and work into the flour with fingers until it looks like breadcrumbs. Stir the water into mixture and mix into a dough. Roll out the pastry on a lightly floured surface. Line a 9 inch pie plate, trim the edges and reserve trimmings for twists.

Filling
Mark the dough and fill in the sections with the jams, curd and mincemeat. Twist the excess dough into spirals and use it to separate the jam sections. Brush the ends with water and press onto the edge to seal. Crimp the edge of pastry case and bake. Remove from the oven and leave to cool for 10 minutes. Serve with pouring custard.

Apple Dumplings with Walnut Sauce

PREPARATION TIME: 30 minutes

COOKING TIME: 35 minutes

OVEN: 400°F

Dumplings
18oz basic pastry
6 large tart apples, cored
9 tablespoons mincemeat
1 egg, lightly beaten

Walnut Sauce
⅓ cup butter
⅓ cup light brown sugar
2½ tablespoons heavy cream
¾ cup chopped walnuts

Divide the dough into 6 portions. Roll out each portion into a round large enough to wrap up one apple. Place the apple in the center of the dough round and fill the cavity (left by removing the core) with mincemeat. Wrap the dough round the apple and moisten the edges with beaten egg. Press together to seal. Place the dumplings on a cooky sheet and brush all over with beaten egg. Bake in preheated, moderately hot oven for 35 minutes or until golden brown. Meanwhile make the sauce.

Walnut Sauce
Melt the butter in a saucepan and stir in all the sugar. When the sugar has dissolved, stir in the cream and walnuts. Heat gently. Serve the dumplings with the sauce; both should be hot.

Facing page: Fruit Cobbler (top), Apple Betty (center) and Yorkshire Apple Tart (bottom).

Winter Fruits

PREPARATION TIME: 15 minutes plus 1 hour soaking

COOKING TIME: 40 minutes

OVEN: 375°F

3/4 cup seedless raisins
3/4 cup currants
3/4 cup white raisins
1 cup chopped mixed candied peel
Finely grated rind and juice of an orange
6 thick slices of toast, crusts removed
About 1/4 cup butter
1/2 cup soft brown sugar
1 1/4 cups milk
2 eggs, lightly beaten
1/4 teaspoon ground cinnamon
Custard

Put all the dried fruit, candied peel, orange rind and juice into a bowl and mix well. Put half the fruit mixture in the bottom of a buttered baking dish. Spread the toast with the butter, then cut it into small squares. Cover the fruit with half the toast and sprinkle with 1/4 cup of the soft brown sugar. Repeat the layers again. Mix together the milk, eggs and cinnamon and pour over the layered pudding. Leave the pudding to soak for one hour. Bake in a preheated oven until crisp on top. Serve with thin pouring custard.

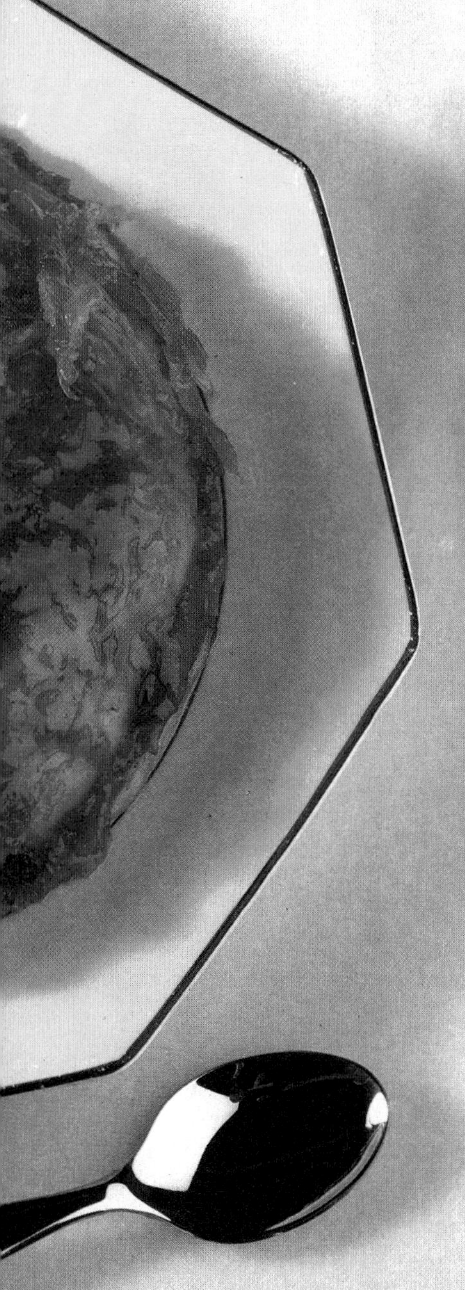

Apricot Pudding

PREPARATION TIME: 25 minutes

COOKING TIME: 2 hours

Pastry
1 1/2 cups flour
Pinch of salt
1/4 cup sugar
1/3 cup shredded suet
5 tablespoons milk

Filling
1 tart apple
6oz dried apricots, soaked overnight in cold water
1/3 cup seedless raisins
1/2 teaspoon ground mixed spice
3 tablespoons corn syrup
2-3 tablespoons granulated brown sugar, to finish
Custard or cream

Pastry
Sift the flour and salt into a bowl. Stir in the sugar and suet, add the milk gradually and knead lightly to form a firm dough. Wrap the dough in foil and chill in the fridge.

Filling
Peel and core the apples, then grate into a bowl. Drain the apricots and chop them very finely, then mix in with all the other ingredients for the filling. Roll out the dough on a lightly floured surface. Cut out a small circle large enough to fit the base of a well buttered 3 3/4 cups pudding mold. Put the dough in the mold. Layer with fruit and a circle of dough (4 layers of dough, 3 layers of filling). Cover the top of the pudding with a circle of buttered wax paper. Cover the mold with foil tied with string. Put the pudding mold in a steamer or in a pan half-filled with boiling water. Cover with a lid and steam. Keep the water level up. Remove the foil and wax disc and let the pudding stand for a few minutes. Turn out carefully on a warmed serving plate and sprinkle with granulated brown sugar. Serve hot with pouring custard or cream.

Rhubarb Tart

PREPARATION TIME: 30 minutes

COOKING TIME: 40 minutes, then another 25 minutes

OVEN: 350°F

Filling
2lb rhubarb, cut into 1 inch pieces.
2 1/3 cups sugar
1/2 cup butter
3 eggs
2 tablespoons white wine
2 1/4 cups flour
2 teaspoons baking powder

Topping
2/3 cup soured cream
1 teaspoon ground cinnamon
1/3 cup ground almonds
Confectioners' sugar

Put the rhubarb pieces into a bowl, sprinkle with sugar (reserve 10 tablespoons). Cover and allow the rhubarb to draw. Cream the butter and 6 tablespoons of the granulated sugar. Mix together until light and fluffy. Stir in one egg and the wine. Sift in the flour and baking powder. Stir into the other ingredients. Knead the ingredients together to make a smooth dough. Form into a ball, wrap with wax paper and allow to rest for 30 minutes in the fridge. Grease a 10 inch loose-based or spring-clip pie pan. Roll out pastry on a well floured surface. Line pie pan with pastry. Strain the rhubarb, arrange in pastry case and bake.

Topping
Beat the cream and remaining eggs together and stir in the remaining sugar, the cinnamon and ground almonds. Mix thoroughly until smooth. Take the tart out of the oven and pour the topping over the rhubarb. Return to the oven and bake for another 25 minutes. Remove from the oven, turn out and dust with confectioners' sugar, cool before serving.

Facing page: Rhubarb Tart (top), Winter Fruits (bottom left) and Apricot Pudding (bottom right).

Carrot Pudding

PREPARATION TIME: 15 minutes

COOKING TIME: 45 minutes

OVEN: 350°F

¼ cup butter
¼ cup sugar
2 eggs, separated
½ cup flour
1 teaspoon ground cinnamon
8oz carrots, peeled and grated
1 tablespoon chopped walnuts
4 tablespoons dry red wine
Grated rind, and juice of 1 lemon
Pinch of salt

Cream the butter with the sugar until the mixture is light and fluffy. Beat in the egg yolks. Sift in the flour and cinnamon, carrots, walnuts, wine, lemon rind, juice and salt. Beat the egg whites until stiff and fold into carrot mixture. Pour into a greased baking dish. Bake in a preheated moderate oven. Serve hot from the dish.

Orange Round

PREPARATION TIME: 30 minutes

COOKING TIME: 15 minutes for pastry 20 minutes for filled flan

OVEN: 350°F

10oz basic pastry
3 oranges, thinly sliced
2 eggs, beaten
½ cup ground almonds
3 tablespoons sugar
3 tablespoons clear honey

Roll out the pastry and line an 8 inch pie dish. Prick the base of the pie. Cut a piece of wax paper, line the pastry and sprinkle with baking beans (or any dried beans, to bake blind). Bake for 10 minutes at 375°F. While the shell is baking, prepare the orange filling. Put the oranges in a saucepan. Add enough water to cover the oranges and simmer for 20 minutes. Cook until the orange peel is soft and drain the water. Beat the egg, almonds and sugar until smooth. Spread the mixture in the pie shell. Arrange the poached orange slices on top of the mixture. Spoon the clear honey over all the slices. Cook the pie for 20 minutes.

Yuletide Pudding (Round)

PREPARATION TIME: 30 minutes

COOKING TIME: 5 hours plus 3 hours before serving

2¼ cups mixed dried fruit
1¼ cups stoned raisins
⅔ cup chopped mixed peel
1½ cups soft dark brown sugar
⅓ cup almonds, blanched and chopped
¾ cup fresh white breadcrumbs
¾ cup shredded suet
1½ cups flour
½ level teaspoon ground nutmeg
½ level teaspoon ground cinnamon
½ level teaspoon salt
1 carrot, grated
1 tart apple, peeled, cored and grated
Grated rind and juice of 1 lemon
3 tablespoons brandy
1 large egg

Put all ingredients in a large mixing bowl and blend together well. Grease 2 x 2½ pint pudding molds. Put the mixture into the pudding molds, dividing the mixture evenly between both. Fill the molds, but leave a gap of about 1 inch at the top. Cover both puddings with buttered round of wax paper. Make a foil pudding lid with a pleat and tie securely onto molds. Stand the puddings in pans and add enough water to keep the pans two-thirds full. Cover the pans and boil for 5 hours. Keep the pans topped up with hot water. Remove the molds from water and gently loosen one pudding from its mold, turn it out onto the other pudding. Press the puddings together to make one pudding. Press down on the top pudding. Leave to cool completely, then cover together with wax paper and foil. Before serving boil for three hours. Again make sure the water is topped up. Unwrap carefully and turn out of the bowl.

Pacific Pudding

8oz can pineapple rings
½ cup superfine sugar
½ cup soft margarine
Grated rind of 1 orange
2 eggs, beaten
¾ cup flour, sifted
½ teaspoon baking powder
¼ cup white breadcrumbs
2oz candied cherries, quartered
⅓ cup stoned raisins
1oz angelica
2 tablespoons corn syrup

Drain the pineapple and keep the juice. Cut 3 rings in half and reserve. Chop the remainder coarsely. Cream together the margarine and sugar, add the orange rind and beat in the eggs. Fold in the flour and breadcrumbs. Add the chopped pineapple, cherries, raisins and angelica, and mix well. Butter a 1¾ pint pudding mold. Put the syrup in the bottom and arrange the pineapple rings in a circle. Spoon in the sponge mixture on top and level it. Cover with buttered paper and foil. Put the pudding mold in a saucepan of boiling water two-thirds full. Boil for 1¾ hours. Serve with tangy butter.

This page: Rainbow Tart (top), Carrot Pudding (center) and Apple Dumplings with Walnut Sauce (bottom).

Facing page: Yuletide Pudding (top), Pacific Pudding (center left), Orange Round (center right) and Snowball (bottom).

Quick Puddings

Zabaglione

PREPARATION TIME: 5 minutes

COOKING TIME: 10 minutes

4 egg yolks
4 tablespoons sugar
4 tablespoons Marsala wine

Put all the ingredients into a large heatproof bowl. Beat with a wire whisk until light and frothy. Stand the bowl in a pan of water over a low heat and continue to beat. The mixture will froth and is now ready to serve. Pour into heatproof glasses and serve immediately with the sponge fingers. An instant Italian dessert. Note: Do not overheat or the mixture will curdle and not become frothy.

Raspberry Brioches

PREPARATION TIME: 15 minutes

12 small brioches (use either fresh or frozen brioches, or choux buns as illustrated).
¼ cup sugar
1 tablespoon lemon juice
2 tablespoons honey
⅔ cup water
1 teaspoon raspberry liqueur
1lb fresh raspberries
2 tablespoons toasted, flaked almonds

Let the sugar, lemon juice, honey and water boil for three minutes. Add the raspberry liqueur. Using some of the syrup, soak the brioches. Fill with the raspberries. Sprinkle over the rest of the syrup and add the flaked almonds. Serve.

This page: Poor Knights of Windsor (top left), Zabaglione (top right) and Coffee Liqueur Crêpes (bottom).

Facing page: Lemon Syllabub (top), Hot Fruit Brioches (center) and Raspberry Brioches (bottom).

Hot Fruit Brioches

PREPARATION TIME: 20 minutes

12 small brioches
1/3 cup sugar
2/3 cup water
10oz apricots, peeled and halved
6oz fresh blackberries
3 tablespoons brandy

Sabayon Sauce
6 egg yolks
1 cup sugar
1 cup very dry white wine

Heat the sugar and water in a saucepan. Add the apricots and poach until glossy. Meanwhile make up the sabayon sauce and reserve. Add the blackberries and brandy, leave for 4 minutes and reserve them. Cut the tops off the brioches and hollow them. Fill the hollowed brioches with the poached apricots and saturate the top with remaining syrup. Pour over sabayon sauce and put the lid on. A last minute alternative. They are delicious with hot stewed fruit, and the sabayon sauce adds a dash of extravagance.

Sabayon Sauce
Cream the egg yolks and sugar together. Place the bowl over warm water and add the wine. Stir continuously.

Poor Knights of Windsor

PREPARATION TIME and COOKING TIME:
15 minutes inclusive

1 egg
1 tablespoon of milk
2 tablespoons sugar
6 small slices of fruit or plain bread, crusts removed
1/4 cup butter
1 teaspoon ground cinnamon

To decorate
15oz can apricot halves in juice (drained)
Whipped cream
1 tablespoon toasted almonds

Beat the egg and mix with sugar and milk. Dip the bread into this mixture and fry. Sprinkle bread with ground cinnamon and decorate with apricot halves, whipped cream and toasted almonds. Serve hot.

Coffee Liqueur Crêpes

PREPARATION TIME: 35 minutes

Crêpes
1 cup flour
Pinch of salt
1 teaspoon sugar
1 cup cold milk
1 egg
4 tablespoons cold, strong black coffee
1 teaspoon vegetable oil
Oil for frying

Sauce
1 tablespoon butter
Grated rind and juice of 1/2 a lemon
2 tablespoons coffee liqueur

Crêpes
Sift the flour, salt and sugar into a bowl. Add the milk, egg, coffee and oil and beat until smooth. Lightly oil a frying pan and fry the crêpes until golden brown. Toss and cook on the other side. Keep the crêpes warm.

Sauce
Melt the butter in a large frying pan. Arrange the crêpes folded in the pan. Add the lemon rind and juice and coffee liqueur. Heat gently until hot. Serve immediately.

Syllabub

PREPARATION TIME: 10 minutes plus overnight soaking

Thinly pared rind of 1 lemon
6 tablespoons of lemon juice
9 tablespoons sweet white wine or sherry
3 tablespoons brandy
1/3 cup sugar
1 3/4 cups heavy cream
Grated nutmeg

Put the lemon rind and juice, brandy and wine or sherry in a bowl. Leave overnight. Remove the lemon rind and stir in the sugar. Gradually stir in the cream until it peaks. This will require beating. Spoon into glasses and sprinkle with grated nutmeg.

Caramel Oranges

PREPARATION TIME: 15 minutes

6 oranges (large and juicy)
3/4 cup sugar
1 3/4 cups water

Peel the oranges. Put the sugar and water in a heavy saucepan. Boil the mixture until it begins to caramelize. Place the oranges in a presentation dish and pour over the liquid caramel. Serve immediately.

Blackberry Fluff

PREPARATION TIME: 10 minutes

1lb blackberries, drained
1 1/4 cups heavy cream
1 egg white
1/4 cup sugar
Pieces of angelica to decorate
Ladyfinger confections

Sieve the blackberries. Beat the cream until thick and stir into the blackberry purée. Beat the egg white, adding the sugar slowly, until the mixture is stiff. Fold the egg white into the blackberry cream. Spoon into individual serving glasses and serve with ladyfinger confections. A quick and luscious dessert. Make it in advance but in individual glasses. Store in the refrigerator and serve chilled.

Spiced Pears

PREPARATION TIME: 20 minutes

1 1/2lb can of pear halves
1 1/2 cups red wine
3 teaspoons ground cinnamon
3oz stem ginger, chopped

Drain the pears, saving 2/3 cup of the juice. Put the pears in the wine with the juice and cinnamon. Boil for 10 minutes and reduce the heat. Simmer for ten minutes. Add the chopped ginger and leave to cool. Serve chilled.

Cherries Jubilee

PREPARATION TIME: 10 minutes

1 1/2lb canned black cherries
1 1/2 tablespoons grated lemon rind
3 tablespoons cornstarch
6 tablespoons brandy
Vanilla ice cream

Drain the cherries, reserving the juice. Put all except one tablespoon of juice into a saucepan, add the lemon rind and bring to the boil. Simmer for 2 minutes and strain the juice. Return the juice to the saucepan and add the cherries. In the reserved tablespoon of juice, dissolve the cornstarch. Add this to the saucepan and stir constantly until thick. Warm the brandy and set it alight. Pour it as it flames into the cherry mixture and stir until the flames die down. Serve immediately with ice cream.

Redcurrant and Blackcurrant Compote

PREPARATION TIME: 10 minutes plus chilling

1 1/2lb redcurrants or 12oz each of redcurrants and blackcurrants)
1 1/4 cups sugar
1 tablespoon water
2 tablespoons gin or brandy
Whipped cream
Sponge fingers

Put the fruit, sugar and water into a saucepan. Shake gently over the heat until sugar has dissolved. Remove from heat and stir in the gin or brandy. Cool. Spoon the compote into serving dishes. Chill for three hours before serving. Serve with the cream and sponge fingers.

Tarte Aux Fruits

PREPARATION TIME: 15 minutes

1 pie shell or sponge shell
1lb grapes, black and green (or 1lb fresh fruit or canned or bottled fruit)
2 1/2 cups vanilla sauce (optional)

Glaze
1 1/4 cups juice from the fruit after poaching
OR
drained syrup from can
OR
1 heaped tablespoon apricot jam
OR
sugar syrup

Facing page: Caramel Oranges (top), Blackberry Fluff (center left) and Cherries in Wine (bottom).

Halve and stone the grapes. Place them cut side down in alternate rings around a pie shell. Glaze with one heaped tablespoon of warmed apricot jam, poured and brushed over the fruit. Alternatively, spread the base of the tart with 2½ cups of made vanilla sauce before covering with fruit. Glaze with either apricot jam or sugar syrup.

Cherries in Wine

PREPARATION TIME: 5 minutes

COOKING TIME: 10 minutes

1lb cherries, stoned
½ teaspoon ground cinnamon
4 tablespoons sugar
1¼ cups light red wine
4 tablespoons redcurrant jelly
2 teaspoons cornstarch

Put the cherries, cinnamon, sugar and most of the wine into a heavy saucepan. Boil slowly. Mix the redcurrant jelly and cornstarch with the rest of the wine and form into a paste before stirring into the saucepan. Simmer for three minutes, then remove from heat. Leave covered for five minutes. Serve cold.

Brandy Bananas

PREPARATION TIME: 10 minutes

6 tablespoons butter
3 tablespoons soft brown sugar
3 tablespoons lemon juice
6 bananas
3 tablespoons brandy
Light cream

Put the butter, sugar and lemon juice in a frying pan. Add the bananas and fry gently, making sure they are coated with the mixture. Add the brandy and cook for a second to warm the brandy through. Ignite, and let the flames die naturally. Serve at once. Serve hot with light cream.

Raspberry Jelly Mold

PREPARATION TIME: 8-10 minutes plus setting

1 packet raspberry jelly
1¼ cups milk
⅔ cup water
8oz fresh or thawed, frozen raspberries
⅔ cup water to melt jelly
Cream

Put the jelly into a saucepan with ⅔ cup water and melt slowly. Stand until the jelly is tepid, then slowly stir in 1¼ cups of milk and ⅔ cup of water. Wet the jelly mold and fill with the fruit. Pour in the jelly and leave until set. To serve, decorate with any fruit, and cream.

Simple Trifles

PREPARATION TIME: 15 minutes

6 sponge fingers (2in x 3½ ins approx.)
3 tablespoons Cointreau or orange liqueur
3 oranges
4 tablespoons lemon curd
3 egg whites
6 lemon twists

Break sponge fingers into pieces and place in 6 individual dishes. Sprinkle each one with half a tablespoon of Cointreau. Peel the oranges. Chop them and remove all pith. Divide equally between the portions. Place the lemon curd in a bowl. Beat the egg whites until stiff and fold them into the lemon curd. Spoon this mixture over each serving and decorate with twists of lemon. Chill and serve.

This page: Brandy Bananas (top left), Cherries Jubilee (center right) and Spiced Pears (bottom).

Facing page: Simple Trifle (top left), Tarte Aux Fruits (top right), Redcurrant and Blackcurrant Compote (far right) and Raspberry Jelly Mold (bottom).

Stuffed Baked Peaches

PREPARATION TIME: 15 minutes
COOKING TIME: 30 minutes
OVEN: 350°F

6 large peaches, peeled, halved and stoned
3oz macaroons, crushed
4 tablespoons ground almonds
1 teaspoon finely grated orange rind
2 egg yolks
3 tablespoons butter, cut into small pieces
1 cup sweet white wine

Put the peaches on a baking dish, cut side up. In a small mixing bowl put the macaroons, almonds, orange rind and egg yolks. Mix together and use to fill the peaches. Put a knob of butter on top of each peach. Pour the wine into the baking dish and bake. Serve warm.

Fruit Salad with Cottage Cheese

PREPARATION TIME: 20 minutes

3oz cranberries
3oz raspberries
4 tablespoons orange juice
5 tablespoons granulated sugar
2 tablespoons brandy
1 ogen melon
3 kiwi fruit
3 tablespoons confectioners' sugar
1 cup cottage cheese

Raspberry Sauce
7oz raspberries
6 tablespoons sugar
⅓ cup red wine
Small piece of lemon rind
Walnut pieces to decorate

Boil the cranberries, raspberries and orange juice with the granulated sugar for five minutes. Strain the mixture through a sieve. Stir in the brandy and cool. Peel and slice the melon and kiwi fruit. Arrange the fruit on individual plates. Stir the confectioners' sugar into the cottage cheese and place a little on top of each plateful of fruit. Chill. Decorate using any of the fruit contained in the sauce.

Raspberry Sauce
Purée the raspberries. Boil for 5 minutes adding the sugar and wine and lemon rind. Continue to boil for three minutes. Serve hot or cold.

Baked Orange Rhubarb

PREPARATION TIME: 10 minutes
COOKING TIME: 45 minutes
OVEN: 325°F

2lb rhubarb, cut into 1 inch pieces
1 finely grated rind of, and juice of one orange
6 tablespoons clear honey

Place the rhubarb in a baking dish and sprinkle over the orange rind, juice and honey. Cover and bake in a moderate oven. Serve.

Plums Baked in Port

PREPARATION TIME: 5 minutes
COOKING TIME: 45 minutes
OVEN: 300°F

2lb plums, halved and stoned
½ cup brown sugar
⅔ cup port

Place the plums in a baking dish. Sprinkle over the sugar and port. Cover them and bake in a cool oven until the plums are tender. Serve warm or lightly chilled.

Pêches Carmen

PREPARATION TIME: 10 minutes

8 ripe peaches
1½lb raspberries
2 tablespoons kirsch
½ cup confectioners' sugar

Slice the peaches into a serving dish. Add the raspberries and kirsch. Leave to stand for an hour in a cool place. Spoon into individual dishes and sprinkle with confectioners' sugar. Chill and serve with cream.

Facing page: Highland Cream and Ginger Snaps (top), Stuffed Baked Peaches (center) and Fruit Salad with Cottage Cheese (bottom).

This page: (left picture) Pêches Carmen (top), Stuffed Oranges (center) and Plums in Port (bottom). (Right picture) Sour Cream Peaches (top), Ginger Roll (center) and Baked Orange Rhubarb (bottom).

Sour Cream Peaches

PREPARATION TIME: 10 minutes

COOKING TIME: 10 minutes

6 large peaches, peeled, sliced and stoned
3 tablespoons brown sugar
½ teaspoon ground cinnamon
1¼ cups sour cream
6 tablespoons granulated sugar

Divide the peach slices between 6 flameproof serving dishes. Mix together the brown sugar and cinnamon. Sprinkle this over the peaches. Spoon the sour cream over the top. Sprinkle a tablespoon of sugar over each portion. Broil quickly until the sugar melts and caramelizes.

Ginger Roll

PREPARATION TIME: This dish should be started the night before required, to allow the ginger cookies to absorb the rum.

36 ginger cookies
6 tablespoons rum
2½ cups heavy cream
2 teaspoons ground ginger
2 teaspoons soft brown sugar
2 tablespoons ginger syrup (from stem ginger)
Stem ginger slices

Put the cookies in a flat dish and sprinkle with rum. When the rum has been completely absorbed, beat the cream with the ground ginger and sugar and add the ginger syrup. Use some of the cream to sandwich together the cookies. Cover with the remaining cream and decorate with stem ginger slices. Serve.

Stuffed Oranges

PREPARATION TIME: 15 minutes

3 large oranges
2 dessert apples, peeled, cored and chopped
1½ tablespoons raisins
1½ tablespoons dates, chopped
1½ tablespoons nuts, toasted and chopped
1½ tablespoons soft brown sugar
¾ cup heavy cream
2 teaspoons confectioners' sugar
Orange twists

Halve the oranges and scoop out the flesh, keeping the shells intact. Chop the flesh, discarding all the pith, and put it in a bowl. Add to the orange flesh the brown sugar, apple, raisins, dates and nuts. Mix well. Scoop the mixture back into the orange halves. Whip the cream with the confectioners' sugar until it forms soft peaks. Spoon this cream on top of the orange mixture. Chill and serve. Decorate with twists of orange.

Highland Cream Served with Ginger Snaps

PREPARATION TIME: 15 minutes

4 tablespoons ginger marmalade
1½ cups heavy cream
4 tablespoons sugar
3 tablespoons whisky
3 tablespoons lemon juice
3 egg whites
Soft brown sugar
1 packet ginger cookies

Divide the marmalade between serving dishes. Whip the cream, adding the caster sugar gradually. Fold in the whisky and lemon juice. Beat the egg whites and fold into the cream. With a spoon, put a little of the cream mixture over the marmalade. Decorate with brown sugar and ginger cookies.

Orange Tart

PREPARATION TIME: 30 minutes

COOKING TIME: 25 minutes

OVEN: 375°F

1 cooked pie shell
2 navel oranges, boiled
2 egg yolks, beaten
¾ cup sugar

To decorate
3 navel oranges
Apricot jam, melted

Purée the boiled oranges. Stir in the egg yolks and sugar. Slice the remaining three oranges. Fill the pie shell with the orange purée and decorate with slices of orange. Bake in a moderate oven until bubbling. Remove from oven and brush on melted apricot jam. Return to oven and bake for a further 10 minutes.

Fraises Escoffier

PREPARATION TIME: 15 minutes plus chilling

2lb strawberries
2 oranges
2oz sugar cubes
⅓ cup Grand Marnier

Hull and slice the strawberries; peel and slice the oranges. Mash half the strawberries with the sugar cubes and Grand Marnier. Stir in the remaining fruit and chill for one hour. Serve in individual dishes.

Lemon Mousse

PREPARATION TIME: 6-10 minutes

¾ cup sugar
3 eggs, separated
5 lemons
1½ tablespoons gelatin
2 tablespoons warm water

Put the grated rind of the lemons in a basin with the egg yolks and sugar. Beat until stiff. Beat the egg whites until they peak. Dissolve the gelatin in the water and mix with the egg yolk mixture. Beat until the mixture begins to set. Fold in the egg whites. Fill the glasses with mousse. Serve chilled.

Fraises Escoffier (right), Orange Tart (center right) and Lemon Mousse (far right).

Strawberry Sauce

¼ cup sugar
1½ tablespoons lemon juice
1½ tablespoons brandy
9oz strawberries

Place sugar, lemon juice and brandy in a pan. Place over a low heat until sugar dissolves. Sieve strawberries to remove seeds and combine with syrup. Cool.

Caramel Chips

¼ cup superfine sugar

Put the sugar in a heavy saucepan and heat gently until the sugar liquifies and turns golden. Pour quickly onto foil and leave until cold. Break the chips with a rolling pin and use for decoration.

Apricot Purée

3 tablespoons sugar
1 tablespoon water
1 teaspoon lime juice
2 tablespoons apricot brandy
9oz well-ripened apricots

Combine sugar, water, lime juice and apricot brandy in pan. Dissolve sugar over low heat. Cool. Sieve or purée apricots in blender. Combine with syrup.

Chocolate Sauce

4oz dark chocolate
2 tablespoons milk
2 rounded tablespoons corn syrup.

Melt the chocolate in a bowl over a pan of simmering water. Beat in the milk and corn syrup until glossy.

Sugar Syrup *(medium syrup)*

6 tablespoons sugar (granulated)
⅔ cup water

Boiling sugar for dessert making can easily be done without a thermometer. Mix together water and sugar in a small saucepan and boil until the mixture begins to thicken.

Griddle Cakes

PREPARATION TIME: 20 minutes

COOKING TIME: 20 minutes

SERVES: 8 persons

2 cups flour
½ tsp baking soda
½ tsp cream of tartar
Pinch of salt
2 tbsps lard or margarine
1 tsp golden syrup
⅓ cup sour milk

If you are using fresh milk increase the cream of tartar to 1 tsp. Sieve the dry ingredients. Rub in the fat. Add the syrup to the milk and mix all ingredients together to form a soft dough.

I make these cakes in a heavy, cast iron frying pan. Heat the pan or griddle until very hot, then reduce heat and sprinkle with flour. Divide the dough into two and gently pat each portion into rounds ½ inch thick. Divide each into four triangular scones, lightly flour them and cook on the pan or griddle until golden brown on each side – about five minutes a side. Continue turning until they are cooked right through.

These are delicious with a brunch of bacon, egg and sausage.

Apple Purée

PREPARATION TIME: 45 minutes

If you have apple trees in your garden here is a quick and easy way to cook the fruit and store them for use all the year round. Cook them in batches of about 4lb. You can store the purée in the freezer in cottage cheese and yogurt cartons and use them as you need them.

4lb apples
⅔ cup water
Juice and rind of half a lemon
1 cup sugar

Wash apples, removing any bruised or discolored bits. Cut in quarters or eighths, depending on their size. You do not need to remove the seeds or cores. Place them in a large, heavy pan with the sugar, water and lemon rind and cook gently until soft. If you have a vegetable mouli, sieve the purée through this, otherwise sieve through a strainer. For variation you can put in 3 or 4 cloves or a tsp of cinnamon instead of the lemon. When cool, spoon the puxrée into the cartons allowing ½ inch room for expansion. Cover and put them in the freezer.

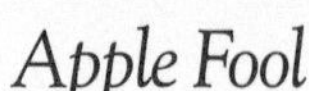

Apple Fool

PREPARATION TIME: 10 minutes

SERVES: 4 persons

Just fold in ⅔ cup whipped cream in 1 cup apple purée. Chill in individual glasses or double the quantities and pile into a glass serving dish.

This page: Apple Purée (top), Apple Fool (center left) and Rhubarb Fool (bottom). Facing page: Griddle Cakes (top right), Rock Cakes (center left) and Fruit Sponge (bottom).

Queen of Puddings

PREPARATION TIME: 20 minutes

COOKING TIME: 40 minutes

SERVES: 4-6 persons

This is a very attractive pudding which is, nevertheless, easy to make and requires only simple ingredients.

3 medium slices of white bread, crusts removed
1½ cups milk
1 heaped tbsp sugar
2 tbsps butter
Grated rind of 1 lemon
2 eggs
2 tbsps seedless red jam
Heaped tbsp sugar

Heat the milk with the butter. When simmering, remove the pan from the heat and add the bread, lemon rind and sugar. Allow to stand for 10-15 minutes then beat the mixture until no lumps remain. Separate the eggs and beat the yolks into the mixture.
Grease a 3-4 cup ovenproof glass dish and pour the mixture into it. Bake in a moderate oven, 350°F (180°C), until it is set – about 25 minutes. Spread the jam gently over the top, being careful not to break the surface. Whisk the egg whites until stiff, add the sugar and whisk again. Spoon the meringue over the pudding, making sure to cover the pudding right up to the edges and lifting the spoon to form little peaks. Return the dish to the oven for about 10 minutes until the 'peaks' are a golden brown.

Rhubarb Fool

PREPARATION TIME: 10 minutes

COOKING TIME: 40 minutes

SERVES: 6 persons

1lb rhubarb
¼ cup sugar
2-3 strips of lemon rind
1¼ cups whipped cream

Trim and scrub the rhubarb and cut into 1 inch lengths. Place in a buttered, ovenproof dish with a lid. Add sugar, lemon rind and about 3 tbsps water. Cover and cook in a slow oven, 300°F (150°C), for about 40 minutes or until rhubarb is soft. Liquidize and allow to cool before folding in the whipped cream. Chill before serving.

Fruit Sponge

PREPARATION TIME: 20 minutes

COOKING TIME: 40 minutes

SERVES: 6 persons

This is a quick and simple recipe that makes use of seasonal fruits. It can be served with cream or custard.

½ cup margarine
½ cup sugar
1 cup all-purpose flour
1 tsp baking powder
1 egg
4 tbsps milk
¼ tsp mixed spice
8oz fruit (either thinly sliced apples mixed with blackberries and sprinkled with ¼ cup sugar, or sliced apples only with a level tsp cinnamon mixed with the sugar, or rhubarb cut in 1 inch lengths and finely grated lemon rind sprinkled over the sugar).

Grease a 3-4 cup ovenproof dish and put the fruit in the bottom. Cover with the sugar and appropriate flavoring.

Sponge Topping
Beat sugar and margarine until creamy; add egg and continue beating. Sift flour and baking powder with mixed spice. Fold in half the flour, then add the milk and finally the rest of the flour. If you have a food processor this can be done in one operation. Spread sponge mixture carefully over fruit and bake for 40 minutes in center of oven at 350°F (180°C).

Bread and Butter Pudding

PREPARATION TIME: 20 minutes

COOKING TIME: 45 minutes

SERVES: 6 persons

This recipe is for a less frugal and much lighter version of bread pudding.

4-5 slices of bread from a medium-sliced loaf
Butter or margarine
¾ cup sugar with 1 tsp cinnamon mixed in
½ cup golden raisins
2 eggs
2 cups milk

Butter the bread and cut into triangles. Grease a 3-4 cup ovenproof dish and put in layers of bread, sugar and raisins. Heat up milk and pour over beaten eggs. Pour mixture over bread and fruit. Bake for 40-45 minutes at 350°F (180°C).

Irish Soda Bread

PREPARATION TIME: 15 minutes

COOKING TIME: 40-45 minutes

This is very easy to make, and it can also be bought almost anywhere in Ireland. I sometimes used to buy it in Bewleys, the famous Dublin coffee shop, and was intrigued by the fact that it was called a "brown square," despite the fact that it is a round shape which can be divided into triangular-shaped pieces. But, this is Ireland!

2 cups all-purpose flour
1 level tsp salt
1 level tsp sugar
1 heaped tsp cream of tartar
1 heaped tsp baking soda
4 cups whole-wheat flour
2 cups sour milk or fresh milk with 1 tbsp yogurt

Add salt, sugar, cream of tartar and baking soda to the all-purpose flour. Sift into a large mixing bowl. Add whole-wheat flour and mix thoroughly with a round-ended knife, using a lifting motion to aerate the mixture. Make a well in the center and add milk, mixing until the dough leaves the sides of the bowl clean. Knead into a ball, flatten slightly and place on a greased baking sheet. Cut a cross

Queen of Puddings (right) and Bread and Butter Pudding (below).

top of the loaf, deep but not right through. Brush the top with a little milk and place in the oven, 200°C, 400°F, Gas Mark 6, for 40 minutes. Remove from the oven, turn loaf upside down and return to the oven for a further five minutes. The loaf is done when it sounds hollow when tapped on the base. Wrap it in a slightly dampened cloth and stand on its side to cool. Cut into quarters, slice and butter generously.
Excellent with prawns, smoked salmon or fish pate, or at tea time with strawberry jam.

White Sultana Soda Bread

PREPARATION TIME: 15 minutes
COOKING TIME: 30 minutes

1lb (450g) plain white flour
1 level tsp (5ml) salt
1 level tsp (5ml) bicarbonate of soda
1 level tsp (5ml) cream of tartar
½ pint (300ml) sour milk or fresh milk with 1 tblsp (15ml) yogurt
3oz (85g) sultanas
1 level tblsp (15ml) sugar

Sift flour, salt, bicarbonate of soda and cream of tartar into a mixing bowl. Stir in sugar and sultanas then add the milk, mixing with a knife to form a firm, but not too stiff, dough. Knead lightly on a floured board and form into a slightly flattened round. Cut a deep cross on the top and brush the top with milk. Place on a greased and lightly floured baking sheet and bake in centre of the oven at 200°C, 400°F, Gas Mark 4 for 25 minutes. Turn the loaf upside down on the tray and return to oven for a further five minutes. The loaf is done when it sounds hollow when tapped on the base. Wrap in a damp cloth and place on its side to cool.

This page: Irish Soda Bread (top) and White Sultana Soda Bread (bottom).
Facing page: Raspberry Souffle (top) and Apple Cake (bottom).

Rock Cakes

PREPARATION TIME: 10 minutes

COOKING TIME: 10-15 minutes

MAKES: 16-18 cakes

2 cups all-purpose flour
2 tsps baking powder
¼ tsp salt
¼ tsp mixed spice
⅓ cup butter or margarine
⅓ cup sugar
1 egg
2 tbsps milk
A little turbinado sugar

Sift flour, salt and mixed spice into a bowl; add fat and rub into flour mixture. Add sugar and mix. This can be done in the electric mixer if you have one.
Lightly beat egg and milk and mix in with other ingredients with a fork. Grease a baking sheet and divide mixture into heaps, about a tablespoon each, spaced well apart on the baking sheet. Sprinkle a little turbinado sugar on each. Bake at 400°F (200°C) for 10-15 minutes. Remove from baking sheet and cool on a wire rack, placing a quarter candied cherry on each before cooling. Makes 16-18 cakes.

Apple Cake

PREPARATION TIME: 20 minutes

COOKING TIME: 45 minutes

¾ cup butter or margarine
¾ cup sugar
1½ cups all-purpose flour
1½ tsps baking powder
1 level tsp cinnamon
3 eggs
2 tbsps milk
2-3 apples

Add the cinnamon and baking powder to the flour and sift into a bowl. Cream butter and sugar until light and soft. Beat in one egg then add a tbsp of the flour and beat in another egg. Repeat this once more then fold in two-thirds of the remaining flour. Stir in the milk then fold in the last of the flour. This can all be done in an electric mixer if you have one.
Quarter, peel and core the apples. Slice them very thinly. The slicing attachment of a food processor does this in seconds. Grease either a lasagne dish or a roasting pan approx 11x8½ inches. Spread half the mixture in the bottom, distribute the apple slices over it and cover with the rest of the mixture. Bake in the oven at 350°F (180°C) for 15 minutes then at 325°F (170°C) for 30 minutes until golden brown and firm to the touch.

Raspberry Souffle

PREPARATION TIME: 1 hour

SERVES: 6 persons

Irish gardens produce bumper crops of raspberries because of the mild climate. Of course, the best way to eat them is just as they come, or served with cream and a sprinkling of sugar. However, when there is a glut of them a raspberry souffle makes an excellent dessert.

1lb raspberries (frozen raspberries, thawed, may also be used)
¼ confectioners' sugar
1 envelope gelatine dissolved in ½ cup hot water
4 eggs, separated
½ cup sugar
1¼ cups heavy cream, lightly whipped

Tie a sheet of wax paper round a 6 inch souffle dish to form a collar above the rim of the dish. Reserve a few of the raspberries and sieve the rest. Fold the confectioners' sugar into the purée. Heat the gelatine in the water over a pan of hot water until it has dissolved completely and allow it to cool a little. Whisk the egg yolks and sugar together over the hot water. Fold in the raspberry purée and the gelatine and cool. Fold-in half the cream. Whisk the egg whites until stiff, and fold into the mixture with a metal spoon. Turn into the prepared souffle dish and leave to set. When set, remove the collar carefully and decorate the souffle with the remaining whipped cream and raspberries.

Irish Coffee Cake

PREPARATION TIME: 3-4 hours

COOKING TIME: 35-40 minutes

½ cup butter or margarine
½ caster sugar
1 cup all-purpose flour
1 tsp baking powder
2 tsps instant coffee dissolved in 2 tbsps hot water
2 eggs

Syrup
⅔ cup strong coffee
½ cup sugar
3 tbsps Irish whiskey

Topping
⅔ cup whipped cream
1 heaped tbsp confectioners' sugar
1 tbsp Irish whiskey
Chopped hazelnuts

Butter an 8 inch ring pan and coat well with flour. In a bowl, cream together the butter and sugar, then add the eggs, one at a time. Sift the flour and baking powder and fold in ⅔ of it then add the 2 tbsps strong coffee. Fold in the remainder of the flour. Place in the prepared cake pan and bake in a pre-heated oven for 35-40 minutes at 350°F (180°C). Test with a skewer and when done turn out onto a wire rack to cool.
To make the syrup: heat sugar in coffee until it has all dissolved, then boil rapidly for 1 minute. Remove from heat and beat in the whiskey. Return the cooled cake to well-washed pan and pour the syrup over it. Leave it to soak for several hours. Beat up whipped cream with confectioners' sugar and whiskey. Turn the cake out onto a serving plate and decorate with cream and chopped hazelnuts. Chill before serving.

Tipsy Cake

PREPARATION TIME: 45 minutes

SERVES: 8 persons

Generally known as trifle, Tipsy Cake provided a way of using up left over sponge cakes. My old Irish cooking book says "take five or six penny sponge cakes" which proves just how old it is! Some recipes are well laced with Irish whiskey as well as with sherry.
My version is a great standby for unexpected guests as all the ingredients can be kept in the store cupboard, apart from the cream, which can be kept in the freezer.

6 trifle sponges or pound cake slices
Raspberry jam
14oz can fruit cocktail
2oz ratafia or amaretto biscuits
½ cup flaked almonds
¼ cup sherry

Custard
1¼ cups milk
2 tbsps vanilla sugar (or sugar and ½ tsp vanilla essence)
2 level tbsps cornstarch
1 egg
1 tbsp sherry
1¼ cups whipped cream, not too stiff
Few candied cherries

Drain fruit into a bowl. Measure out ¼ cup of the juice and add the sherry. Crumble the ratafias, saving some for decoration. Slice the cakes in half and spread them with raspberry jam. Cut each diagonally

Irish Coffee Cake (left) and Tipsy Cake (below).

This page: Bananas with Irish Mist (top), Dulse (center right) and Yellow Man (bottom). Facing page: Scrap Bread Pudding (top) and Carrigeen Moss Pudding (bottom).

and line the bottom of a glass serving bowl with the wedges. Place half the fruit on top and sprinkle with some ratafias and flaked almonds and ⅓ of the juice and sherry. Repeat this once, then cover with the final layer of cakes and add the rest of the juice.
I keep a vanilla pod in a screw-top jar of sugar and just top up with sugar as I use it. Put cornstarch and sugar in a small mixing bowl, mix with 2 tbsps of the milk and bring the rest of the milk to the boil. Pour it over the cornstarch mixture, stirring all the time. Return the pan to the heat and bring the custard back to the boil and simmer for 1 minute. Remove from heat and beat in the tablespoonful of sherry and the lightly beaten egg. Cool and, while luke-warm, pour over the trifle, allowing some to trickle down between the trifle and the bowl. When quite cold top with whipped cream and sprinkle on the remainder of the ratafias and almonds and a few pieces of chopped candied cherry.

Carrigeen Moss

PREPARATION TIME: 30 minutes
SERVES: 6 persons

It seems to be spelt "Carrigeen" in County Cork and "Carrageen" in the West of Ireland, but whichever way you spell it, it is a seaweed which grows on the rocks on the Atlantic coastline. It is picked at low tide in early summer and laid out to dry in the sun. It is washed once or twice in fresh water and spread out to dry again, after which it will keep for several years. It contains a rich jelly which is used as a thickening agent in cooking and also contains iron and other minerals.

Carrigeen Moss Pudding

Approx ¼oz Carrigeen moss
2 cups milk
Grated rind of ½ lemon
2 tbsps sugar

Take as much Carrigeen as will fit in your fist when almost clenched. Wash it in warm water for a few minutes, removing any grasses or other foreign bodies. Place the moss in a pan with the milk, grated lemon rind and sugar. Bring slowly to the boil and simmer gently for 15-20 minutes. Strain through a sieve, being sure to scrape all the jelly into the bowl. Stir well and transfer the mixture into a wet mold or serving bowl. Leave to set in a cool place overnight or for several hours before turning out onto a serving dish. Serve with cream and strawberry or raspberry jam.

Bananas with Irish Mist

COOKING TIME: 10 minutes
SERVES: 4 persons

4 bananas
¼ cup butter
1½ tbsps sugar
1½ tbsps Irish Mist

Melt the butter in a heavy frying pan. Peel the bananas and put them

in the pan, turning them carefully in the melted butter. Cook them over a low heat for about 3 minutes either side until they are heated through. Put them on individual plates and keep them warm while you make the sauce. Add the sugar to the remaining butter in the pan. Stir over a low heat until the granules have dissolved. Add the Irish Mist, stir well and bring the mixture to the boil. Spoon the sauce along the top of the hot bananas and serve.

Almond Tartlets

PREPARATION TIME: 10 minutes
COOKING TIME: 10 minutes
SERVES: 12 persons

Mrs. Myrtle Allen of Ballymaloe Hotel, County Cork, where the best of Irish food may be tasted, gave me the recipe for these little almond tartlets, which are one of the specialities of her sweet trolley.

⅓ cup butter
⅓ cup sugar
⅓ cup ground almonds

Beat the butter, sugar and almonds together to a cream. Put 1 tsp of the mixture into sixteen small muffin pans. Bake at 350°F (180°C) for about ten minutes or until golden brown. Cool in pans, but do not allow to set hard before removing to a wire rack. Fresh fruits such as raspberries, peaches or blackberries should be placed on these just before decorating with whipped cream and serving.

Barm Brack

PREPARATION TIME: 2-3 hours
COOKING TIME: 1 hour 10 minutes

4 cups flour
½ tsp cinnamon
½ tsp salt
Pinch grated nutmeg
¼ cup softened butter
⅓ cup caster sugar
1 cup tepid milk
1 package active dry yeast
1 egg
½ cup golden raisins
1 cup currants
½ cup cut mixed candied citrus peel

Add salt and spice to flour and sift into a large mixing bowl. Rub in the butter, this can be done in the electric mixer at low speed. Add a tsp of the sugar and a tsp of the milk to the yeast and mix well. Add the remainder of the sugar to the flour mixture and mix in. Lightly beat the egg, add the milk and pour this onto the yeast mixture. Add this to the flour and beat very well by hand, or in a mixer fitted with a dough hook, until the batter becomes stiff and elastic. Fold in the mixed fruit at this stage and cover the bowl with a lightly greased polythene bag. Leave bowl in a warm place for 1-2 hours, to allow the dough to rise. Divide the mixture between two greased loaf tins 8½"x4½" or two 7 inch cake pans. Cover again and allow to rise for half an hour. Bake for one hour in center of oven at 200°C. Dissolve a tbsp of sugar in a quarter cup of hot water and brush over brack, return it to the oven for five minutes with the heat turned off. Turn out onto a rack to cool. Slice and butter.

Barm brack is a delicious fruit loaf eaten all the year round in Ireland, but especially popular at Hallowe'en when, by tradition, a ring is hidden in the loaf and the one who finds it will be the next to wed.

Almond Tart

PREPARATION TIME: 25 minutes
COOKING TIME: 35 minutes
SERVES: 8-10 persons

6oz frozen puff pastry
¼ cup grated almond paste (left uncovered in the refrigerator to harden before grating)
Damson jam or plum jam
½ cup butter or margarine
½ cup sugar
2 eggs
1 cup all-purpose flour, sifted
1 tsp baking powder
1 egg-cup of milk
½ tsp almond essence

Take ⅔ of the puff pastry, roll it out thinly and line a greased 10 inch tart plate with it, allowing a 1 inch overlap all round. Roll out the remainder of the pastry slightly thicker, cut into strips ½ inch wide and set aside.
Cream slightly softened butter or margarine and sugar together, add eggs one at a time, beating well and beating in 1 tbsp of the sifted flour before adding the second egg. Mix the almond essence with the egg-cup of milk, add to the mixture then fold in the remainder of the flour. This can be done in the food processor if you have one.
Spread the jam on the pastry case to within 1 inch of the rim. Sprinkle the grated almond paste on top. Cover with the sponge mixture using a spatula and taking care not to disturb the filling. Make a lattice with the pastry strips over the top and crimp the edges, turning in the overlap of pastry to form a rim. Bake in the oven at 400°F (200°C), for 20 minutes, then 350°F (180°C) for a further 15 minutes.

Guinness Cake

PREPARATION TIME: 1 hour 30 minutes-2 hours
COOKING TIME: 2 hours

1 cup butter or margarine
1 cup brown sugar
1¼ cups Guinness
1½ cups raisins
1½ cups currants
1½ cups golden raisins
¾ cup mixed candied citrus peel
5 cups all-purpose flour
½ tsp baking soda
1 tsp mixed spice
1 tsp nutmeg
3 eggs

Butter and line a 9 inch cake pan with wax paper. Place the butter, sugar and the Guinness in a pan

This page: Barm Brack (top) and Guinness Cake (bottom). Facing page: Almond Tart (top) and Almond Tartlets (bottom).

and bring slowly to the boil, stirring all the time until the sugar and butter have melted. Mix in the dried fruit and peel and bring mixture back to the boil. Simmer for 5 minutes. Remove from heat and leave until cold. Sift flour, spices and baking soda into a large mixing bowl, stir in cooled fruit mixture and beaten eggs, turn into cake pan and bake in center of pre-heated oven, 325°F (160°C), for 2 hours. Test with a skewer. When done, cool in pan before turning out.

Baked Custard

PREPARATION TIME: 15 minutes

COOKING TIME: 45 minutes

SERVES: 4 persons

This used to be regarded as a nursery pudding but, if it is properly made and generously sprinkled with nutmeg, it can be delicious with stewed fruit or even canned fruit such as apricots or plums. Garden fruits like damsons or plums can be cooked in the oven with sugar and a little water at the same time as the custard.

2½ cups milk
2 tbsps sugar
2 eggs
Grated nutmeg

Beat the eggs with the sugar in a mixing bowl. Heat the milk but do not let it boil. Pour it slowly onto the egg and sugar mixture, stirring all the time. Pour the mixture into a greased ovenproof dish or casserole and grate nutmeg over the top. Place the dish in a roasting pan containing about 1 inch of warm water and bake in the oven for 45 minutes at 325°F (170°C).

Yellow Man

An Ulsterman recently described this to me as "a frothy, yellow sugar confectionary." It has been associated for centuries with "The Ould Lammas Fair" which takes place every year at Ballycastle, Co. Antrim.

4 cups golden syrup
1 cup brown sugar
1 heaped tbsp butter
1 tsp baking powder
2 tbsps vinegar

Melt the butter and coat the inside of the pan with it. Add the sugar and syrup and finally the vinegar. Stir over a low heat until the sugar and syrup have melted. Bring it to the boil and simmer without stirring. Test by dropping a little into a cup of cold water to see if it sets. Add the baking powder, which will make the mixture foam up. Stir well again, pour into a greased pan and cut into squares. It may also be turned out onto a slab after the boiling process, then pulled until it becomes pale yellow in color. When it hardens it is broken into pieces with a little hammer like toffee used to be.

Dulse

The Ulsterman sang me a song about "The Ould Lammas Fair" which goes:

Did you treat your Mary Anne
to dulse and Yellowman
at the Ould Lammas Fair, at
Ballycastle, O?

Dulse is a reddish-brown seaweed which grows on the rocks all around the Irish coast. It is dried like Carrigeen Moss, but is usually eaten raw. Sometimes it is cooked, in which case it must first be soaked for several hours. It is sometimes used instead of scallions to make Dulse Champ. It has a much stronger smell and flavor than Carrigeen Moss.

Hydropathic (Summer) Pudding

PREPARATION TIME: 30 minutes

SERVES: 8 persons

I have in my possession an Irish cookery book which must be almost 100 years old. It has lost its original cover but I know it was used as a text book by the young ladies who did a domestic economy course at the Munster Institute in Cork at the end of the last century. In my family it is always referred to as "Aunt Anna's cookbook," and it contains some very quaint recipes and household tips.
The recipe for trifle begins: "take 4 or 5 penny sponge cakes." Then there is a recipe for Hydropathic Pudding. On reading it through I realised that it was Summer Pudding and would love to know why it was called Hydropathic Pudding.

Here is the original recipe, but since no measurements are given I would suggest 1½lbs fruit (raspberries, redcurrants and blackberries are the best to produce the lovely ruby-red color, but other stewing fruits may be included), and ½ cup sugar. The pudding bowl should of 3 cup size.

Bread
Fruit
Sugar to taste

Line a pudding bowl with bread as follows. Cut some slices of bread about half an inch in thickness. From one of these cut a round to fit easily in the bottom of the bowl. For the sides cut the bread in finger pieces, the height of the bowl in length, and, in breadth, about one and a half inches at one end and one inch at the other. Pack these tightly around the sides of the bowl.
Stew the fruit, adding sugar to taste, and if not very juicy add a little water. Pour while hot into the lined bowl and cover the top with bread. Set it on a plate so as to catch any juice that may flow over. Place a small plate on top and over this a weight. When cold turn out and pour round it any juice that may have run into the plate. Serve with custard, cream or milk.

Scrap Bread Pudding

PREPARATION TIME: 40 minutes

COOKING TIME: 2 hours 30 minutes steaming or 1 hour 15 minutes baking

SERVES: 6-8 persons

6-8 bread scraps, crusts removed
¼ cup sugar
1 tsp mixed spice
1 tsp grated lemon rind
2 tbsps flour
¼ cup suet (chopped)
½ cup each of currants, raisins, golden raisins
¼ cup mixed cut candied citrus peel
1 egg, beaten
1 tsp baking powder
1¼ cups milk

Break up the bread and leave to soak in the milk for half an hour. Sift the flour, mixed spice and baking powder into a bowl. Add the chopped suet and lemon rind. Squeeze as much milk as possible out of the bread into a bowl. Beat all lumps out of the bread with a fork. Mix in the flour and suet and

Hydropathic (Summer) Pudding (above right) and Baked Custard (right).

the dried fruit. Add the beaten egg and the milk the bread was soaked in. This can either be turned out into a greased pudding bowl, covered with wax paper and steamed for 2½ hours, or spread into a greased ovenproof baking dish or pan and baked for 1¼ hours in the oven, 350°F (180°C). Serve hot with custard or the baked version can be allowed to cool before cutting into squares and serving like cake.

Vanilla Cream Melba

PREPARATION TIME: 15 minutes
COOKING TIME: 10 minutes
SERVES: 4 people

⅔ cup soup pasta
1½ cups milk
2½ tbsps brown sugar
½ cup cream, lightly whipped
Few drops vanilla extract
1 can peach halves
1 tsp cinnamon

Melba sauce:
1 cup raspberries
2 tbsps powdered sugar

Cook pasta in milk and sugar until soft. Stir regularly, being careful not to allow it to boil over. Draw off heat and stir in vanilla extract. Pour pasta into a bowl to cool. When cool, fold in cream. Chill. Meanwhile, make Melba sauce. Push raspberries through a strainer. Mix in powdered sugar to desired thickness and taste. Serve pasta with peach halves and Melba sauce. Dust with cinnamon if desired.

Black Cherry Ravioli with Soured Cream Sauce

PREPARATION TIME: 30 minutes
COOKING TIME: 15 minutes
SERVES: 4 people

Dough:
1¾ cups bread flour
1 tbsp sugar
3 eggs

Large can dark, sweet cherries, stoned
¼ cup sugar
1 tsp cornstarch
½ cup soured cream
½ cup heavy cream

Strain the cherries and reserve the juice. Make dough by sifting flour and sugar in a bowl. Make a well in the center and add lightly-beaten eggs. Work flour and eggs together with a spoon, and then by hand, until a smooth dough is formed. Knead gently. Lightly flour board, and roll dough out thinly into a rectangle. Cut dough in half. Put well-drained cherries about 1½" apart on the dough. Place the other half on top, and cut with a small glass or pastry cutter. Seal well around edges with the back of a fork. Boil plenty of water in a large saucepan, and drop in cherry pasta. Cook for about 10 minutes, or until they rise to the surface. Remove with a slotted spoon and keep warm. Keep 2 tablespoons cherry juice aside. Mix 1 tablespoon cherry

This page: Black Cherry Ravioli with Soured Cream Sauce.

Facing page: Vanilla Cream Melba (top) and Chocolate Cream Helène (bottom).

juice with cornstarch; mix remaining juice with sugar and set over heat. Add cornstarch mixture, and heat until it thickens. Meanwhile mix soured cream and heavy cream together, and marble 1 tablespoon of cherry juice through it. Pour hot, thickened cherry juice over cherry ravioli. Serve hot with cream sauce.

Chocolate Cream Helène

PREPARATION TIME: 15 minutes

COOKING TIME: 10 minutes

SERVES: 4 people

⅔ cup soup pasta
1½ cups milk
2½ tbsps sugar
½ cup cream, lightly whipped
1 tsp cocoa
1 tbsp hot water
1 large can pear halves

Garnish:
Chocolate, grated

Cook pasta in milk and sugar until soft. Stir regularly, being careful not to allow it to boil over. Meanwhile, dissolve cocoa in hot water, and stir into pasta. Pour pasta into a bowl to cool. When cool, fold in lightly-whipped cream. Chill. Serve with pear halves, and a sprinkling of grated chocolate.

Honey Vermicelli

PREPARATION TIME: 1 hour

COOKING TIME: 15 minutes

SERVES: 4 people

½ pound vermicelli
4 tbsps butter
3 tbsps clear honey
2 tsps sesame seeds
¼ tsp ground cinnamon

Sauce:
½ cup heavy cream
½ cup soured cream

Cook vermicelli in boiling salted water for 5 minutes or until tender, stirring regularly with a fork to separate noodles. Drain, and spread out to dry on a wire tray covered with absorbent paper or a tea-towel. Leave for about an hour. Make sauce by mixing soured cream and heavy cream together. Melt butter in frying pan. Add sesame seeds, and fry until lightly golden. Stir in honey, cinnamon and vermicelli, and heat through. Serve hot, topped with cream sauce.

Cream Cheese Margherita

PREPARATION TIME: 1 hour

COOKING TIME: 10 minutes

SERVES: 4 people

¾ cup soup pasta
½ cup light cream
8oz package cream cheese
½ tsp ground cinnamon
4 tbsps sugar
4 tbsps golden raisins
Juice and grated rind of ½ a lemon

Garnish:
1 tbsp sliced almonds
Lemon peel, cut into slivers

Soak raisins in lemon juice for about 1 hour. Meanwhile, cook the pasta in plenty of boiling, lightly-salted water until tender, stirring occasionally. Work the cream cheese, sugar and cream together until smooth. Beat in grated lemon rind and cinnamon. Fold in pasta and raisins. Divide between individual dessert glasses or small dishes, and cover top with sliced almond and slivers of lemon peel. Chill.

Honey Vermicelli (top right) and Cream Cheese Margherita (right).

Oriental Desserts

Bananas Cooked in Coconut Milk

PREPARATION TIME: 20 minutes
COOKING TIME: 20 minutes
SERVES: 4 people

4-6 large, ripe bananas, peeled and sliced diagonally into 3 or 4 pieces
1 tbsp brown sugar
1 cup desiccated coconut
⅔ cup milk

Garnish
Desiccated coconut

Put sugar, coconut and milk into wok, and bring to simmering point. Turn off heat and allow to cool for 15 minutes. Push through strainer or a piece of cheesecloth to squeeze out juices. Return to wok, and simmer for 10 minutes, or until creamy. Add bananas, and cook slowly until bananas are soft. Serve immediately sprinkled with desiccated coconut.

Steamed Custard

PREPARATION TIME: 10 minutes
COOKING TIME: 20 minutes

1⅔ cups milk
2 tbsps sugar
2 eggs, beaten
½ tsp vanilla extract
Sprinkling of ground nutmeg or cinnamon

Place sugar and milk in wok. Heat gently until the milk reaches a low simmer and the sugar has dissolved. Remove from wok and leave to cool for 5 minutes. Meanwhile, wash wok and place steaming rack inside, with 1½"-2" of hot water. Return to heat and bring water to simmering point. Pour milk and sugar mixture over beaten eggs. Beat again, and add the vanilla extract, stirring well. Pour mixture into a heat-proof dish or metal molds and sprinkle lightly with nutmeg or cinnamon. Place on rack and cover with waxed paper, so condensation does not drop into custard. Cover wok and steam for 10-15 minutes. To test if cooked, a knife inserted in center will come out clean, and custard will be set and gelatinous. Cover and cool for 1 hour, then place in refrigerator until needed.

Bananas Flambés

PREPARATION TIME: 5 minutes
COOKING TIME: 10 minutes
SERVES: 4 people

4 firm, ripe bananas, peeled and cut in half lengthwise
¼ cup unsalted butter
¼ cup brown sugar
3 tbsps brandy
Juice of 2 oranges

Heat wok, and add half the butter. When hot, add bananas, rounded edge down, and fry until golden on underside. Add remaining butter, and carefully turn the bananas over, so their flat sides are in contact with the wok surface. Sprinkle with sugar, 1 tbsp of brandy, and orange juice, and allow to simmer for 3 minutes. Heat remaining brandy, set alight, and pour over bananas. When flame is extinguished, serve immediately. (Flaming can be done in serving dish).

Sesame Toffee Apples

PREPARATION TIME: 45 minutes
COOKING TIME: 30 minutes
SERVES: 4 people

2 large, firm Granny Smith or Golden Delicious apples
1 tbsp flour

Batter
2 tbsps flour
2 tbsps cornstarch
1 large egg
2 tbsps water
1 tsp sesame oil

Oil for deep frying
⅓ cup peanut oil
2 tsps sesame oil
½ cup sugar
2 tbsps white sesame seeds

Peel, core and cut apples into 1" chunks. Toss in 1 tbsp of flour. Combine flour, cornstarch, egg and sesame oil in a small bowl. Mix to a batter with water and leave for ½ hour. Place oil for deep frying in wok, and heat to a moderate temperature (350°F; 180°C). Put fruit in batter and coat well. Deep fry several pieces at a time until they are golden. Remove with slotted spoon and drain on kitchen paper. Repeat until all fruit is fried. Repeat process to fry fruit a second time for a couple of minutes. Remove with slotted spoon and drain. When fat has cooled, carefully drain and clean wok. Fill a bowl with cold water and ice cubes, and put on side. Put peanut and sesame oil and sugar into wok, and heat until sugar melts. When it begins to caramelize stir and add sesame seeds and then add all of fruit. Toss around gently to coat in caramel. Take out quickly, and drop into iced water a few at a time, to prevent sticking together. Serve at once. (This can also be made with sliced bananas).

Facing page: Bananas Flambés (top) and Sesame Toffee Apples (bottom). Steamed Custard (right) and Bananas Cooked in Coconut Milk (below).

Cake Making and Frosting

Lining Cake Pans
All pans must be greased and lined unless you are using a non-stick cake pans, in which case follow the manufacturer's instructions.
If using a shallow pan, only the base needs to be lined for beaten sponges and the quick cake mixture.
If you are making a fruit cake, which will take longer to bake, then the sides as well as the base need lining using a double thickness of wax paper.

To Grease the Pan
Brush with melted lard, margarine or oil. Grease the wax paper with melted fat or oil; if you are using non-stick silicone paper do not grease it. In the preparation of pans, it is necessary to grease and dust them with flour if you are not lining them.

Round Pans
To line a deep, round pan, draw with a pencil round the edge of the cake pan on double thickness wax paper and cut the resulting shape out.
Using a piece of string, measure round the pan. Use another piece of string to measure the height plus 1 inch. Cut out one long strip or two shorter lengths of wax paper to the equivalent of these measurements. If making two lengths, add on a little extra for them to overlap. Make a fold ¼ inch deep along one edge and cut into the fold at regular intervals at a slight angle. Place one of the circles of paper in the bottom of the pan, followed by the side pieces and, finally, the second paper circle which will cover the slashed edges.

Square Pans
To line a deep, square pan follow the instructions above as for a round pan, but fold the long strips so they fit into the corners of the pan.

Rich Fruit Cake

CAKE SIZES	5in round 4in square	6in round 5in square	7in round 6in square	8in round 7in square	9in round 8in square	10in round 9in square
APPROX COOKING TIME:	2½ hours	2¾ hours	3¼ hours	3¼ hours	4 hours	4¼-4½ hours
OVEN:	275°F	275°F	275°F	275°F	275°F	275°F
	Note for all recipes: First ⅔ of cooking time at 300°F.					
Butter	¼ cup + 1 tblsp	6 tblsp	½ cup	½ cup + 2 tblsp	¾ cup + 2 tblsp	1 cup + 2 tblsp
Eggs	2	2	3	4	5	6
Flour	¾ cup	1 cup	1½ cups	1¾ cups	2¼ cups	2¾ cups
Dark soft brown sugar	⅓ cup	⅓ cup + 1 tblsp	10 tblsp	¾ cup	1 cup	1¼ cups
Molasses	½ tblsp	½ tblsp	1 tblsp	1 tblsp	1 tblsp	1 tblsp
Ground almonds	2 tblsp	2 tblsp	3 tblsp	¼ cup	5 tblsp	⅓ cup
Ground mixed spice	¾ tsp	¾ tsp	1 tsp	1¼ tsp	1½ tsp	1¾ tsp
Grated lemon rind	½ lemon	½ lemon	1 lemon	1 lemon	1 lemon	2 lemons
Grated orange rind	½ orange	½ orange	1 orange	1 orange	1 orange	2 oranges
Grated nutmeg	¼ tsp	¼ tsp	¼ tsp	½ tsp	½ tsp	¾ tsp
Chopped almonds	¼ cup	⅓ cup	½ cup	¾ cup	1 cup	1¼ cups
Currants	1 cup	1¼ cups	1⅔ cups	2 cups	2⅔ cups	3¼ cups
Raisins	¼ cup	½ cup	¾ cup	1 cup	1¼ cups	1½ cups
White raisins	⅔ cup	1 cup	1¼ cups	1¾ cups	2 cups	2⅓ cups
Chopped mixed candied fruits	1oz	1½oz	2oz	2½oz	3½oz	4oz
Candied cherries	1oz	1½oz	2oz	2½oz	3½oz	4oz
Orange juice	1¼ tblsp	1¼ tblsp	1¼ tblsp	1¼ tblsp	2¼ tblsp	2¼ tblsp
Brandy	1¼ tblsp	1¼ tblsp	1¼ tblsp	1¼ tblsp	2¼ tblsp	3¼ tblsp

Jelly Roll Pans (Long, Shallow Pans)
Grease and line a shallow pan so that the cake may be easily removed. Line the sides of the pan with paper at least 1½ inches longer than the pan, cutting into each corner.

Loaf Pans
When lining a loaf pan the method is again the same, but the paper should be 6 inches higher than the top of the pan.

11in round 10in square	12in round 11in square
5¼ hours	6 hours
275°F	275°F
1⅓ cups	1½ cups + 2 tblsp
7	8
3½ cups	4 cups
1½ cups	1¾ cups
1½ tblsp	2 tblsp
7 tblsp	½ cup
1¾ tsp	2½ tsp
2 lemons	2 lemons
2 oranges	2 oranges
¾ tsp	1 tsp
1½ cups	1¾ cups
3⅓ cups	3½ cups
1¾ cups	2 cups
2¾ cups	3 cups
5oz	6oz
5oz	6oz
2¼ tblsp	3¼ tblsp
3¼ tblsp	4¼ tblsp

Oiling and lining cake pans.

Rich Fruit Cake

This is a traditional recipe which cuts well and is rich, dark and moist. Traditional fruit cake improves with keeping and is used for celebration cakes – weddings, birthdays and Christmas – with almond paste and royal frosting. Prepacked dried fruit is ready washed, but if you are buying your fruit loose rinse it through with cold water and dry it well with kitchen paper or clean cloths. Then spread it out on a tea towel placed on a cooky sheet in a warm (not hot) place for 24 hours. Do not use wet fruit in a cake as the fruit will sink.

Mix the white raisins, currants and raisins together. Cut the glacé cherries into quarters, rinse in warm water and dry with kitchen paper. Add the cherries to the fruit together with mixed peel, almonds, and grated orange and lemon rind.

Sift the flour with a pinch of salt, ground cinnamon and mixed spice. Cream the butter until soft, then add the sugar and cream until light and fluffy (do not overbeat). Add the eggs one at a time, beat well and after each egg add a spoonful of flour. Add the dark molasses, orange juice and brandy, if desired. Add the remaining flour, then the fruit, and mix well. Spread the mixture evenly into a greased and double-lined pan. Use the back of a spoon to make a slight hollow in the center of the cake so it will be flat when cooked. Tie two thicknesses of brown paper round the pan then bake in the center of the oven at 300°F, (see chart for the suggested time).

With large cakes turn the oven down to 275°F, after two-thirds of the cooking time. To test the cake, push a toothpick into the center. It should come out clean if the cake is cooked. When the cake is cooked, remove the pan from the oven and leave the cake in the pan to cool. Turn the cake onto a wire rack and remove the lining paper. Spike the top of the cake with a skewer and spoon a few tablespoons of brandy or other spirit over the top. To store the cake, wrap it in cheesecloth and foil. If possible, repeat the spooning over of brandy or spirit every few weeks. The cake can be allowed to mature for 2-3 months.

Quick Mix Cake

This is a quick cake, which is ideal for novelty cakes, and the mixture is firm enough to cut into any shape; it is moist and crumbly and can be filled with cream, butter or jam.

Put the margarine, sugar, eggs, sifted flour and baking powder in a bowl. Mix together all the ingredients with either a wooden spoon or electric mixer. Beat for 1-2 minutes until the mixture is smooth and glossy. In a food processor this will take 30 seconds-1 minute. Put the mixture in a prepared pan. Level the top with the back of a spoon and bake in the center of the oven at 325°F (see chart for the suggested time). When baked, the cake will be firm to the touch and shrink away from the sides of the pan. Loosen the sides of the cake from the pan and leave it to cool on a wire rack. Turn the cake right way up onto another wire rack.

Beaten Sponge Cake

This cake mixture is ideal for afternoon tea and the cake may be filled with cream, butter frosting or fruit. It does not keep well and is best eaten the same day it is made, although it can be kept in the freezer for up to 2 months.

Put the eggs and sugar in a

heatproof bowl over a saucepan of hot, not boiling, water. The bowl must not touch the water. Beat the mixture until it becomes thick enough to leave a trail when lifted. Sift the flour and baking powder together and fold into the egg mixture with a metal spoon, taking care not to knock the air out. Pour the mixture into a prepared pan and gently shake the mixture level. Bake in the center of the oven (see chart for oven temperature and suggested time). Remove from the pan and cool on a wire rack. When making a jelly roll, turn out the cake onto a sheet of wax paper sprinkled with confectioners' sugar. Quickly peel off the lining paper and trim the cake edges. Fold and roll the cake up without cracking it. Let it cool a little, then unroll and remove the wax paper. Fill and reroll the cake.

Madeira Cake

Madeira cake is a moist cake that can be covered with almond paste and then frosted with royal frosting or any other frostings.

PREPARATION TIME: 15 minutes
COOKING TIME: 1 hour 15 minutes to 1 hour 30 minutes
OVEN TEMPERATURE: 325°F

¾ cup butter
¾ cup sugar
Grated rind of 1 lemon
3 eggs
2 cups flour
2 tsp baking powder
2 tblsp warm water

Cream the butter and sugar until they are light and fluffy. Beat the eggs in one at a time, adding a spoonful of flour after each egg. Sift in the remaining flour and fold it into the mixture with lemon rind and juice. Turn into a prepared cake pan and bake in the oven for 1¼-1½ hours. When cooked, the cake should be firm to the touch. Leave it in the pan to cool for 5-10 minutes, then turn onto a wire rack and remove the lining paper.

Beaten Sponge Cake

CAKE SIZES	2 x 7in cake pans	8in cake pan 7in square cake pan	11 x 7in jelly-roll pan	18 sponge drops	8in round cake pan	2 x 8in cake pans
APPROX COOKING TIME:	20-25 minutes	25-30 minutes	10-12 minutes	5-10 minutes	35-40 minutes	20-25 minutes
OVEN:	350°F	350°F	375°F	375°F	350°F	350°F
Eggs	2	2	2	2	3	3
Fine white sugar	⅓ cup	⅓ cup	⅓ cup	⅓ cup	½ cup	½ cup
Cake flour	½ cup	½ cup	½ cup	½ cup	¾ cup	¾ cup
Baking powder	¾ tsp	¾ tsp	¾ tsp	¾ tsp	¾ tsp	¾ tsp

Quick Mix Cake

CAKE SIZES	2 x 7in cake pans	18 paper cake cases or small tart tins	8in cake pan 8in ring mold 7in deep square cake pan	*1¾ pint pudding mold **add 3 tblsp cornstarch sifted with the flour*	About 26 paper cases of small tart tins	2 x 8in cake pans
APPROX COOKING TIME:	25-30 minutes	15-20 minutes	35-40 minutes	about 50 minutes	15-20 minutes	30-35 minutes
OVEN:	325°F	325°F	325°F	325°F	325°F	325°F
Shortening	½ cup	½ cup	½ cup	½ cup	¾ cup	¾ cup
Fine white sugar	⅔ cup	⅔ cup	⅔ cup	⅔ cup	1 cup	1 cup
Eggs	2	2	2	2	3	3
Flour	1 cup	1 cup	1 cup	1 cup	1½ cups	1½ cups
Baking powder	1¼ tsp	1¼ tsp	1¼ tsp	1¼ tsp	1½ tsp	1½ tsp
Vanilla essence	4 drops	4 drops	4 drops	4 drops	6 drops	6 drops

For Victoria Sponge see "Tea Time Treats."

Variations

Chocolate Victoria Sponge
Replace 1oz flour with 1oz sifted cocoa powder. Add this to the other flour.

Coffee Victoria Sponge
Replace the water with coffee essence, or dissolve 2 tsp instant coffee powder in 1 tblsp boiling water.

Lemon Victoria Sponge
Add the very finely grated rind of 1 lemon.

11 x 7 x 1½in cake square	12 x 9in jelly-roll pan
30-35 minutes	12-15 minutes
350°F	400°F
3	3
½ cup	½ cup
¾ cup	¾ cup
¾ tsp	¾ tsp

9in cake pan	11 x 7 x 1½in cake square 8in round cake pan 8in square cake pan	2½ pint pudding mold	11½ x 8½ x 1½in cake square	9in round cake pan 9in square cake pan	12 x 10 x 2in cake square
about 25 minutes	35-40 minutes	about 1 hour	about 40 minutes	about 1 hour	50-60 minutes
325°F	325°F	325°F	325°F	325°F	325°F
¾ cup	¾ cup	¾ cup	1 cup	1 cup	1¼ cups
1 cup	1 cup	1 cup	1⅓ cups	1⅓ cups	1⅔ cups
3	3	3	4	4	5
1½ cups	1½ cups	1½ cups	2 cups	2 cups	2½ cups
1½ tsp	1½ tsp	1½ tsp	2 tsp	2 tsp	2¼ tsp
6 drops	6 drops	6 drops	8 drops	8 drops	10 drops

Basic Frosting Recipes and Their Uses

Quick Frosting

This is an easy white frosting which is a quick version of the traditional American frosting. A sugar thermometer is not required for this recipe, but the frosting must be used very quickly before it sets.

PREPARATION TIME: 7-10 minutes

1 egg white
¾ cup confectioners' sugar
Pinch of salt
2 tblsp water
Pinch of cream of tartar

Put all the ingredients into a heatproof bowl and mix. Put the bowl over a pan of simmering water and beat the mixture. If possible, use an electric mixer until the frosting peaks. Remove the frosting from the heat and pour it over the cake, spreading it quickly. This will cover a 7 inch cake.

Chocolate Fudge Frosting

PREPARATION TIME: 10 minutes

This is a delicious chocolate frosting which is quick and easy to make.

¼ cup butter
3 tblsp milk
1 cup confectioners' sugar, well sifted
2 tblsp cocoa powder, sifted

Melt the butter in a small saucepan with the milk. Add the confectioners' sugar and cocoa and beat well until smooth and very glossy. Cool until lukewarm and pour over cake. This is enough to fill and frost the top of a 8 inch cake.
NB: if the frosting is too thick to pour, reheat gently to thin. This frosting can also be made in a small bowl over a pan of gently simmering water.

Sponges: Beaten Sponge, Madeira Cake.

Marzipan or Almond Paste

This is a paste which is made firm and rollable, and is traditionally used as a base cover for fruit cakes before coating with royal frosting or any other decorative frosting. Prepare the cake by levelling the top, if necessary. Dust a work surface with confectioners' sugar and roll out half the almond paste 1 inch larger than the top of the cake. Brush the top of the cake with the apricot glaze, or the egg white and brandy. Invert the cake onto the almond paste and, using a palette knife, draw up the top of the almond paste around the cake. Put the top of the cake down on a board and brush the sides of the cake with apricot glaze. Cut two pieces of string or thread, one the height of the cake and the other equal in length to the circumference. Roll out the remaining almond paste into a strip, equal in width and length to the circumference of the cake, using the strings as a guide, or cut two short strips of paste instead. Carefully wrap the almond paste round the cake, pressing firmly round the sides and joins. For a square cake, cut the string into four lengths, equal to the sides of the cake and cut the paste to match. Press lightly on the paste when it is placed round the cake in order to produce sharp corners. When covered, leave the cake for 24 hours to dry. Wedding cakes should be left for up to 1 week before frosting, otherwise almond oil will stain the frosting if the cake is kept after the wedding.

Guide to Almond Paste Quantities Required for Cakes

Square	Round	Almond Paste/ Marzipan
5 inch	6 inch	12oz
6 inch	7 inch	1lb 4oz
7 inch	8 inch	1½lb
8 inch	9 inch	1½lb
9 inch	10 inch	2lb
10 inch	11 inch	2¼lb
11 inch	12 inch	2½lb
12 inch		3lb

Marzipan or Almond Paste

PREPARATION TIME: 15 minutes

½ cup sugar
½ cup confectioners' sugar
1 cup ground almonds
1 tsp lemon juice
A few drops almond essence
1 or 2 egg yolks, beaten

Mix the sugars and the ground almonds in a bowl. Make a well in the center and add the lemon juice, almond essence and egg yolk or yolks to the mixture and form into a pliable dough. Lightly dust the work surface with confectioners' sugar and turn out the dough. Knead until smooth. The almond paste can be stored in a polythene bag or wrapped in foil for 2-3 days before use. Makes 1lb.

Apricot Glaze

PREPARATION TIME: 10 minutes

This glaze can be stored in an airtight container for up to 1 week, if kept in the refrigerator. Re-boil the glaze and cool before applying to the cake.

6-8oz apricot jam
2 tblsp water

Put the jam and water in a saucepan and heat until the jam has melted, stirring occasionally. Pour the jam through a sieve and return it to a clean saucepan. Re-boil and simmer until you have a slightly thickened consistency. Cool before applying to the cake.

How to Royal Frost

It does not matter whether you frost the top or the sides first, the important point to remember is that the frosting should be applied in several thin coats. Try frosting a section first, rather than doing all of it in one go. Your aim is to achieve a smooth surface and you must let each coat dry before applying another. Most cakes require 2 coats on the top and sides, with maybe 3 on the top for a very smooth finish. Wedding cakes require three coats all over and the bottom tiers need 4 coats. For a 2 or 3-tier cake apply 4 coats to the bottom tier; for a 4-tier cake apply 4 coats to the bottom 2 tiers.

Method for Frosting a Cake – Frosting the Sides of a Round Cake

A flat-sided scraper is essential for producing smooth sides. Put plenty of frosting on the side of the cake and, using a small palette knife, move it back and forth to get a relatively smooth surface and to remove little air pockets. For round cakes, put your arm round the back of the cake and move the scraper forwards on the cake as this will help you to get a smooth, sweeping movement without stopping. The scraper should be upright against the side of the cake. Move the scraper off the cake at an angle so the join is not noticeable. If you use a turntable, it will make frosting larger cakes easier. Hold the scraper to the side of the cake and use the other hand round the cake so the turntable moves round quickly and smoothly in one revolution. Scrape off any extra frosting with a small palette knife. Wipe the cake board and allow each coat to dry for 2-3 hours or overnight before frosting the top.

Frosting the Top

When frosting the base tier of a wedding cake, remember not to add glycerine. Spread the frosting on the cake and, using a metal, or firm plastic, ruler held at a 30° angle, draw it gently across the cake with a positive movement. Try not to press down too hard or the frosting will be too thin. Remove any surplus frosting from the sides of the cake with a clean palette knife. Leave the frosting to dry for at least a day. Remove any rough edges round the joins with clean, fine-graded sandpaper. If the coating is not enough, repeat this 2-3 times. Wait 24 hours before applying frosting decoration onto the cake.

Frosting a Square Cake

Ice 2 opposite sides first, then the other 2 sides to produce sharp corners. Hold the palette knife parallel with the side of the cake when frosting.

Royal Frosting

The consistency of royal frosting depends upon its use. For rosettes and flat frosting it should be quite firm, whereas for applying latticework and writing it should be a little thinner. When frosting is required for any flooding and runouts, it should be thin and smooth. Royal frosting can be made in any quantity in the proportion of 1 egg per cup of sieved confectioners' sugar. Keep the frosting bowl covered with a damp cloth to keep it moist. As an egg substitute, egg albumen (white) can be bought in specialist cake decoration shops and the instructions for use are given on the packet. The addition of glycerine will aid the softening of the frosting when it is dry. This makes it easier to cut.

Wedding Cakes

When frosting wedding cakes, do not add glycerine to the two top layers of frosting on the bottom tier, so the cake can support the other tiers. Made frosting can be stored in an airtight container in a cool atmosphere for 2 days. Before use the stored frosting should be stirred well.

Beat the egg whites with a wire whisk until frothy, making sure that the bowl is clean and dry first. Gradually beat in half the confectioners' sugar using a wooden spoon. Beat in the remaining half of the confectioners' sugar with the glycerine and, if using lemon juice, add it now. Beat the mixture thoroughly until smooth and white. Beat in enough icing sugar to give the mixture a consistency which is stiff and stands in peaks. Add the color, if required. Cover the bowl with a damp cloth and leave the frosting to stand for several hours. This allows any air bubbles to rise to the surface of the frosting and burst. Before using, stir well with a wooden spoon. Do not overbeat. Note: if you are using an electric mixer, use the slowest speed and leave the frosting for 24 hours as this will incorporate more air and will need longer to stand.

Facing page: covering with almond paste, and using apricot glaze.

Guide to Royal Frosting Quantities Required to Flat Frost in Two Thin Coats

Square	Round	Icing Sugar
5 inch	6 inch	1½lb
6 inch	7 inch	2lb
7 inch	8 inch	2½lb
8 inch	9 inch	3lb
9 inch	10 inch	3½lb
10 inch	11 inch	3½lb
11 inch	12 inch	4½lb
12 inch		4½lb

Molding Frosting

PREPARATION TIME: 20 minutes

This is also known as kneaded fondant. It is very easy to use and can be rolled out like pastry. It is ideal for covering novelty cakes and even rich fruit cake. The frosting sets and becomes firm. Molding frosting can be used to cover a cake directly or over almond paste. If using almond paste first, allow the paste to dry before covering with the frosting, which can also be used to make flowers and other decorations.

2 cups confectioners' sugar
1 egg white
¼ cup liquid glucose
Food coloring or flavoring, if desired

Sift the confectioners' sugar into a mixing bowl and add the egg white and the liquid glucose to the center of the sugar. Beat the ingredients with a wooden spoon, gradually incorporating the confectioners' sugar to result in a stiff mixture. Knead the frosting until you have a pliable paste. This icing can be stored by placing it into a bag, wrapping it in plastic wrap or sealing it in a plastic container and storing it in a cool place for up to 3 days. If adding a color, sprinkle with a little more sifted confectioners' sugar to keep the frosting the same consistency.

To Apply Molding or Gelatin Frosting
Brush either the cake with apricot glaze or the almond paste with egg white. Roll out the frosting on a surface dusted with confectioners' sugar or cornstarch, or between two sheets of dusted polythene. Roll out the frosting at least 3 inches larger than the top of the cake. Support the frosting on a rolling pin and drape it over the cake. Dust your hands with cornstarch or confectioners' sugar and rub the surface of the cake, working in circular movements with the palms of your hands to make the frosting thinner and ease it down the sides of the cake. Smooth out any folds in the frosting and cut off the excess. If frosting a square cake, mold the corners so that the square keeps it shape. Leave to dry.

Gelatin Frosting

PREPARATION TIME: 20 minutes

This frosting can be used in the same way as molding frosting, but when it dries it becomes quite brittle. The frosting can be used to make decorations such as flowers and leaves.

2 tsp gelatin powder
2 tblsp water to dissolve the gelatin
2 cups confectioners' sugar
1 egg white

Put the gelatin powder into the water, which is contained in a small, heatproof basin held over a saucepan of hot water. Stir until the gelatin has dissolved. Sift the confectioners' sugar into another bowl and add the dissolved gelatin and egg white. Stir well until firm, then knead with the fingers until smooth. Dust with extra confectioners' sugar, if necessary. If adding food coloring, sprinkle with more confectioners' sugar to keep the frosting to the same consistency. This frosting can be stored for 2 to 3 days before use. To do so, wrap it in plastic wrap or a polythene bag and keep it in a sealed container. If it begins to dry, place the frosting in its sealed polythene bag and dip briefly in hot water. Leave for 1 hour and knead well before use.

Glacé Frosting

PREPARATION TIME: 10 minutes

Probably the quickest frosting to make, it is used on sponges, small cakes and cookies. To keep the frosting liquid, place the bowl over a pan of hot water.

1 cup confectioners' sugar
2 tblsp warm water
Various flavorings and colorings

Sift the confectioners' sugar into a mixing bowl and gradually add the water. The frosting should be thick enough to coat the back of a spoon when it is withdrawn from the mixture. Add the flavoring and the coloring, if desired. This quantity will frost 18 small cakes and half the amount will frost the top of a 8 inch cake.

Variations

Coffee
Replace 1 tblsp warm water with 1 tblsp coffee essence.

Orange or Lemon
Replace 1 tblsp warm water with 1 tblsp orange or lemon juice. Add the grated rind of one orange or lemon and a few drops of food coloring.

Chocolate
Sift 3 tblsp cocoa powder with the confectioners' sugar.
NB: you must be careful not to keep the frosting in too hot a bowl of water, otherwise it will lose its gloss. Also, if a newly-frosted cake is moved around without being given a chance to set, the glacé frosting could crack and spoil the smooth surface.

Buttercream Frosting

This frosting is good for covering sponge and quick cake mixture cakes. Butter frosting is ideal for covering novelty cakes, as it can be flavored and colored easily and is no problem to use.

PREPARATION TIME: 10 minutes

½ cup butter
1 cup sifted confectioners' sugar
2 tblsp milk
Flavorings (see 'Variations')

Beat the butter and some of the confectioners' sugar until smooth. Add the remaining confectioners' sugar with the milk and flavoring. Beat until creamy. This frosting will cover and fill a 8 inch 2-layer cake. Store in an airtight container in the refrigerator, for several weeks if necessary.

Variations

Lemon or Orange
Add the grated rind of 1 lemon or orange to the butter. Replace the milk with lemon or orange juice. Add a few drops of orange or lemon coloring.

Molding frosting, Royal frosting, Butter frosting, American frosting and Buttercream frosting.

Chocolate
Blend 2 tblsp cocoa powder with 2 tblsp boiling water. Cool, then add to the mixture with 1 tblsp milk.

Coffee
Replace 1 tblsp milk with 1 tblsp coffee essence.

Crème au Beurre

PREPARATION TIME: 15 minutes

2 egg whites
½ cup confectioners' sugar, sifted
½ cup unsalted butter
Flavorings (see 'Variations')

Place the egg whites and confectioners' sugar in a bowl over a pan of simmering water. Beat until the mixture holds its shape. Cool. Cream the butter until soft then beat into the egg white mixture, a little at a time. Flavor or color as required.

Variations

Chocolate
Melt 2oz plain chocolate in a bowl over a pan of hot water. Cool and beat into the egg white mixture.

Coffee
Add 1 tblsp coffee essence to the egg white mixture.

Praline
Gently heat ¼ cup of both sugar and blanched almonds in a small pan until the sugar turns brown round the nuts. Turn the mixture onto an oiled cooky sheet, cool and crush with a rolling pin. Add the 3 tblsp of this crushed praline to the egg white mixture.
NB: this frosting can be stored in an airtight container in the refrigerator for several weeks.

Confectioners' Custard

PREPARATION TIME: 10-15 minutes

3 egg yolks
¼ cup sugar
¼ cup all-purpose flour
1¼ cups milk
2 tblsp butter
1 tblsp sherry

Put the egg yolks and sugar in a bowl and beat until smooth and creamy. Stir in flour and mix well. Heat the milk until hot, but not boiling, and stir into the egg mixture. Return the mixture to the pan and stir, bringing it gently to the boil. Remove from the heat and beat in the butter and the sherry. Pour into a bowl, stirring occasionally to prevent a skin forming. Makes 1¾ cups of custard.
NB: the custard can be stored in the refrigerator for up to 48 hours.

Basic Equipment and Practising Skills
You will probably have most of the basic pieces of equipment needed for decorating simple cakes: various-sized bowls and basins, measuring cups, measuring spoons, wooden spoons, spatula, pastry brush, rolling pin, kitchen scales, airtight containers, cocktail sticks, artist's brush and a wooden skewer, to name but a few. However, special frosting equipment is often required, so it is wise to invest in a good, basic selection. You can extend your range as the need

arises. Palette knives are ideal for smoothing and spreading frosting. They come in various sizes and one would prove most useful. A frosting ruler is essential for flat icing the tops of cakes. Choose a firm, not flexible, ruler – at least 12 inches long, but preferably 14 inches. A frosting rule is even better. A frosting turntable is invaluable for frosting and decorating large cakes. There are several types of frosting scraper and these are used for pulling round the sides of the cake until it is smooth. Frosting cones come into the same category and have serrated teeth of various sizes.

Decorating Tips
Decorating tips come in various forms, the metal types giving the best definition. Try to start with a few basic tips. The range available starts from size 00. A basic frosting tip kit should consist of a fine, a medium and a thick writing tip; a shell tip; a leaf and a scroll tip; a ribbon tip (which is also used for basketwork); a forget-me-not and an 8-point and 10-point star tip. Tips are available in two styles: plain or screw-on types. Screw-on tips are used in conjunction with nylon pastry bags and a screw connector. Plain tips can be used with paper or nylon pastry bags. With this type of tip remember that the frosting has to be removed in order to change a tip. You can either make your own, or use a nylon pastry bag or frosting pump. To make a paper pastry bag, cut a piece of good quality wax paper or non-stick silicone paper into a 10 inch square. Fold in half to form a triangle. Fold the triangle in half to make a yet smaller triangle. Open out the smaller triangle and re-shape into a cone. Turn over the points of the cone so that it stays conical. Secure the join with a little sticky tape. Cut about ½ inch off the tip of the bag and push in a tip.

Nylon Pastry Bags
Nylon bags are sold in various sizes and can be easily filled. These bags are used with a screw connector. The connector is pushed into the bag and protrudes through the hole at the tip of the bag. This allows the tip to be placed at the end and secured with a screw-on attachment, allowing the tip to be changed without emptying the pastry bag.
Nylon pastry bags are most useful for gâteaux as they can be filled with cream, and a meringue tip (a large decorative tip) can be attached to make rosettes.

Frosting Pumps
These are bought as part of a frosting set; some are made of metal and others of plastic. They consist of a tube with a screw attachment for the screw-on type of tip. The frosting is controlled with a plunger which is unscrewed to refill the tube. Unfortunately, pumps are difficult to use for delicate work as you cannot feel the movement of the frosting to help control it.

Decorations

Frosting Decorations

Stars
Stars can be made with various-shaped tips ranging from 5 to 8, or more, points. With the 5-point star, use a tip number 13 or 8. These are the most useful sizes. Place the star nozzle in the bag and fill with frosting. Hold the bag upright and push out enough frosting to form a star. Remove the tip from the surface of the star swiftly. Stars should be fairly flat without a point in the center.

Rosettes
These are made with a star tip, but using a circular movement. Start at one side of the circle and finish slightly higher than the surface of the frosting in the middle of the circle.

Shell
Use either a star tip or a special shell tip No. 12. Shell tips give fatter shells. Hold the pastry bag at an angle to the surface on which the shell is required and start pushing out frosting towards the center of where the shell will rest. First move the tip away from you and then towards you. Push out more frosting for the thicker parts of the shell. Link the shells together by starting the second shell over the tail of the first.

Leaves
Use a leaf tip, which is No. 10 and has a pointed tip, or sometimes an indentation in the center of the point. Leaves can be decorated straight onto the cake or on non-stick silicone paper, left to dry and then placed onto the cake for decoration. Two or three overlapping movements can be used to give the leaf some form.

Basket Weaving
See 'Tracy Rose Wedding Cake'.

Templates
These are patterns made of paper or card which are used to transfer the pattern onto the top of a cake. It is easy to create your own or, for simple decorations, i.e. circles and squares, draw round a saucepan lid or plastic storage container. On the 21st birthday cake we use a round template. Draw a circle of the required size onto a piece of wax paper and cut it out with a pair of scissors.
Fold the circle in half, into quarters and into eighths, ending with a flattened cone shape. Draw a line in a concave shape from one point to another and cut it out. When the circle is opened, the edge of it will be scallop shaped.

Frosted Flowers
Use a large, medium or fine petal tip, depending on the size of flower required, and a frosting nail, or a piece of waxed paper cut into squares and attached to a cork. Once made, leave the flowers to dry for at least 1 day before transferring them to a cake.

Rose
Hold the pastry bag with the thin part of the tip upright. Push out a cone of frosting, twisting the nail quickly through the fingers and thumb. Push out frosting to make three, four or five petals round the center of the rose by curving them outwards.

Forget-me-nots
Push out the frosting straight onto the cake, using a No. 2 writing tip for the petals, by joining five or six dots together round the edge of the frosting nail and frosting a curved petal in the center. Alternatively use a forget-me-not tip.

Holly Leaves
Color some almond paste green, roll out onto waxed paper and cut into rectangles. Using a frosting tip, cut each holly leaf into shape by cutting first two corners of the rectangle and working your way down the sides until you have a holly leaf shape. Mark the 'veins' with a knife point. Roll out a little more almond paste and color it red for the holly berries.

Christmas Roses
Cover the top of an essence bottle with a little foil and take a piece of molding frosting the size of a pea and dip it into cornstarch and roll it into a ball. Shape another piece into a petal (see 'Molded Roses'). Repeat until you have five petals. Place the small ball in the foil and surround it with the petals, overlapping them. Leave to dry. Remove from the foil and paint the center yellow with a little food coloring.

Mistletoe
Roll out a little molding frosting or almond paste colored green. Cut into tongue shapes and round the ends. Mark a definite vein down the middle of the leaf with a knife and leave it to dry. Make small, pea-sized balls out of either natural almond paste or white molding frosting.

Molded Roses
Make a cone with a little colored molding frosting and press it out at the base so that it stands. Place a piece of frosting the size of a pea in a little cornstarch and roll it into a ball. Using a hard-boiled egg, flatten the frosting in your hand with quick strokes into a petal shape. Use more cornstarch if it gets too sticky. Gently try to get the frosting very thin. Carefully wrap the petals round the cone and turn the edges outwards. Repeat the process until a fully shaped rose is achieved. Leave the rose to dry and cut off the base. It may be necessary to use a cocktail stick to curl the petals.

Chocolate Leaves
Break the chocolate into small pieces and place in a bowl over a pan of hot water. Gently heat until the chocolate melts. Do not overheat the chocolate or let any water dilute it. With an artist's small paintbrush, paint the underside of the freshly-picked, undamaged and washed rose leaf, making sure that the chocolate spreads evenly over the surface of the leaf. Allow the chocolate to set and, when hard, carefully peel the leaf away from the chocolate, starting from the tip.

Facing page: a variety of cake decorations.

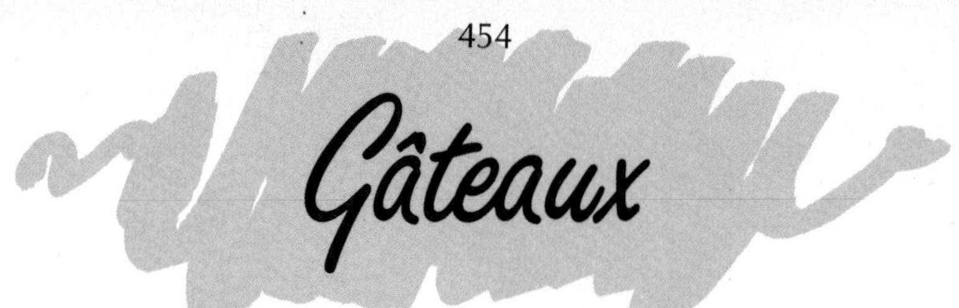

Gâteaux

Minted Lime Gâteau

PREPARATION TIME: 35 minutes
COOKING TIME: 20 minutes
OVEN TEMPERATURE: 375°F

½ cup sugar
3 eggs
¾ cup cake flour
3 tblsp melted butter
Grated rind of 1 lime
Flesh of 1 lime, de-pipped

Decoration
1¼ cups heavy cream
1 fresh lime
Grated chocolate (optional)

Beat the sugar and eggs together in a basin, over a saucepan of hot water, until the mixture is thick. Sieve the flour twice and fold into the beaten mixture. Mix in the lime flesh and grated rind. Grease and flour an 8 inch cake pan and fill with the mixture. Bake in the oven for 20 minutes. Cool on a wire rack.

To Decorate
Whip the cream and spread over the gâteau, reserving a little for decorating. Fill a nylon pastry bag with the remaining cream and, using a star tip, shape rosettes to decorate the gâteau. Sprinkle the sides with chocolate, if desired, and decorate with slices of lime.

Gâteau St Honoré

PREPARATION TIME: 1 hour 30 minutes
COOKING TIME: 30 minutes
OVEN TEMPERATURE: 325°F

This is a fantasy choux pastry dessert. Also known as a croquembouche, it can be built directly onto a serving stand or onto a meringue or basic pastry base, and is a French favorite for weddings. If making the choux pastry a day in advance, the buns can be crisped by heating in a preheated oven at 350°F for 5 minutes. Cool before filling and assembling.

Choux Pastry
6 tblsp butter
¾ cup water
1 cup flour
Pinch of salt
3 beaten eggs

Filling
2½ cups heavy cream
2 tblsp milk
2 tblsp sifted confectioners' sugar
2 tblsp raspberry liqueur

Caramel
1 cup granulated sugar
⅔ cup water

Sift the flour and salt together. Melt the butter in a heavy saucepan, with the water, and bring to the boil. Remove from heat. Add flour and salt mixture to the pan as soon as liquid has boiled. This should be carried out rapidly. Beat with a wooden spoon until glossy. The mixture should be the right consistency to form small balls at this stage. Turn out onto a plate and spread out to cool. Return it to the pan and gradually beat in the eggs. Fill a pastry bag with the choux paste. Attach a ¾ inch plain tip. Shape the choux paste into small balls onto a greased cooky sheet. Make sure they are well apart. Bake in the oven for 25 minutes until well risen and golden brown. They should be firm to touch. Pierce each bun to allow the steam to escape and return them to the oven for 2 minutes. Cool on a wire rack.

Filling
Whip half the cream with the milk, fold in the confectioners' sugar and the raspberry liqueur. Whip the remaining cream and use half to form a mound in the center of the serving plate or stand. With the other half, fill a pastry bag fitted with a star nozzle and reserve. Use the raspberry cream to fill another pastry bag fitted with a plain tip and fill each of the choux buns. Stick the choux buns round the cream mound so that it is completely covered and shape rosettes between each bun using the plain cream.

For the Caramel
Melt the sugar gently in a saucepan with the water and boil until it turns brown and caramelizes. Cool until the caramel begins to thicken but not set and pour quickly, but gently, over the gâteau. Leave to set and chill for ½ hour before serving.

Raspberry Gâteau

PREPARATION TIME: 40 minutes
COOKING TIME: 35 minutes
OVEN TEMPERATURE: 375°F

4 eggs
½ cup sugar
¾ cup flour
2 tblsp melted butter
3 tblsp cornstarch
Grated rind of ½ lemon

Filling
1lb raspberries, fresh (or drained, if tinned)
6 tblsp sherry
1¾ cups heavy cream, whipped
Finely-grated chocolate or chocolate vermicelli

Put the sugar, eggs and lemon rind in a basin over a pan of hot water and beat until pale and thick. Remove from the heat and continue to beat until cool. Sieve the flour and cornstarch together. Fold the flour and melted butter into the mixture using a metal spoon. Bottom line and grease an 8 inch square cake pan, fill with mixture and bake in the oven for 35 minutes. When cooked, turn out and cool on a wire rack. Cut the cake in half horizontally and sprinkle with sherry. Spread the bottom layer with whipped cream and reserve a little cream for decoration. Cover the cream with half the raspberries. Put the top layer of the sponge onto the raspberry filling and cover the sides of the cake with a thin layer of cream using a palette knife. Press the chocolate over the sides of the cake. Cover the top of the cake with a thin layer of cream and fill a nylon pastry bag fitted with a large tip with the remaining cream. Shape a cream border round the top of the cake. Fill the top with the remaining raspberries.

Apricot Meringue

PREPARATION TIME: 30 minutes
COOKING TIME: 1 hour to 1 hour 15 minutes
OVEN TEMPERATURE: 275°F

6 egg whites
1½ cups sugar
2 cups heavy cream, whipped
6 apricot halves, sliced

Line a cooky sheet with non-stick paper. Beat the egg whites in a clean, dry bowl until stiff. Continue to beat and add the sugar, 1 tblsp at a time, until the mixture is very stiff and glossy. Fit a large star tip to a pastry bag and pipe 8 swirls onto the cooky sheet. Bake in the oven for 1-1¼ hours until crisp and dry. Leave to cool and peel from the paper. Lay half the meringue swirls onto a presentation plate and fill a pastry bag, fitted with a star tip, with the whipped cream. Shape a line of cream onto each swirl and layer with slices of apricot. Shape with cream again. Stick together with another meringue swirl and shape with cream around the edge of the top meringue and decorate the cream with further slices of apricot.

Facing page: Gâteau St. Honoré (top left), Minted Lime Gâteau (top right) and Raspberry Gâteau (bottom).

Black Forest Gâteau

PREPARATION TIME: 35 minutes
COOKING TIME: 40 minutes
OVEN TEMPERATURE: 375°F

3 eggs
½ cup sugar
¾ cup flour
1 tblsp cocoa powder

Filling
15oz can black cherries, pitted
1 tblsp arrowroot
2 tblsp Kirsch
1¼ cups heavy cream
Grated chocolate or chocolate flakes to decorate

Place the eggs and sugar in a basin and beat over a saucepan of hot water until thick. Remove from the heat and continue to beat until cool. Sieve the cocoa powder and flour together and gently fold into the mixture using a metal spoon. Grease and line the bottom of an 8 inch cake pan. Pour the mixture into the pan and bake in the oven for 40 minutes. Turn out and cool on a wire rack.

Filling and Decoration
Drain the juice from the cherries into a pan and blend with a little arrowroot. Bring to boil and stir until it thickens. Add the cherries to the syrup and allow to cool. Cut the cake in half and sprinkle the base with a little kirsch. Whip the cream and use it to fill a nylon pastry bag fitted with a large star tip. Shape a circle of cream into the border edge of the base cake. Fill with half the cherry mixture. Sprinkle the top of the cake with a little kirsch and place on top of the filling. Spread a little cream on the sides of the gâteau and press the grated chocolate onto it using a palette knife. Shape swirls of cream on top of the gâteau and fill the center with the remaining cherries. Sprinkle with a little chocolate.

Walnut and Banana Galette

PREPARATION TIME: 45 minutes
COOKING TIME: 25 minutes
OVEN TEMPERATURE: 350°F

½ cup butter
1½ cups flour
½ cup sugar
½ cup chopped walnuts
Grated rind of ½ lemon

Filling and Decoration
1¼ cups heavy cream
2 tblsp confectioners' sugar
4 bananas

Cream the butter, sugar and lemon rind until fluffy. Fold the flour in and knead it until you have a soft dough. Put the dough in a polythene bag and chill for ½ hour in the refrigerator. Grease and flour 3 cooky sheets and mark a 7 inch circle on each. To make the circles, use a saucepan lid as a guide. Divide the dough into 3 and place a piece of dough on each circle. Press it out until it fills the circle. Sprinkle the top of each circle with chopped walnuts and bake in the oven for 25 minutes. When cooked, allow to cool before turning onto a wire rack.

Filling and Decoration
Whip the cream and fold in the confectioners' sugar. Slice the bananas and sprinkle them with a little lemon juice, which prevents them from discoloring. Stick the layers together with some cream sprinkled with banana slices. Using a nylon pastry bag filled with the remaining cream and fitted with a large star tip, shape the decoration around the top of the galette and decorate with slices of banana. Allow the galette to stand for 30 minutes before serving.

Brandied Chestnut Roll

PREPARATION TIME: 35 minutes
COOKING TIME: 12 minutes for the base, 10 minutes for the filling
OVEN TEMPERATURE: 425°F

3 eggs
½ cup sugar
2 tblsp brandy
1 cup flour

Filling
1 tblsp sugar
1¼ cups heavy cream
1 tblsp sugar
8¾oz can chestnut purée (crème de marron)
6oz plain chocolate
1 tblsp butter
2 tblsp brandy

Beat the eggs and sugar until thick. Gently fold in the sieved flour and the brandy with a metal spoon. Line and grease (bottom only) a 9x13 inch jelly roll pan. Pour the mixture into the pan and bake in the oven for 12 minutes. Cover a clean, damp cloth with a sheet of wax paper. Sprinkle the paper with 1 tblsp sugar. Turn the cake out onto the paper and remove the wax used to line the pan. The edges of the cake will be crisp, so trim with a sharp knife. Roll up the cake by putting a clean sheet of wax over the cake. Cool on a wire tray.

Filling
Whip the cream and sugar until stiff and stir half the cream into the chestnut purée. The chestnut purée mixture must be smooth before use. Gently unroll the cake and remove the wax paper rolled with it. Spread the chestnut cream on the inner side of the cake and re-roll. Melt the chocolate in a bowl over a pan of hot water, adding the butter and brandy. Cover the cake completely with the chocolate mixture. Mark the chocolate-coated cake with a fork when half set. Pipe the whipped cream with a large tip into whirls on top of the cake.

Ginger Ice Cream Gâteau

PREPARATION TIME: 1 hour
COOKING TIME: 25 minutes
OVEN TEMPERATURE: 325°F

Ice Cream
⅔ cup milk
1 egg
6 tblsp sugar
¼ cup green ginger wine
1¼ cups heavy cream

Almond Base
3 egg whites
10 tblsp sugar
6 tblsp cornstarch
½ cup ground almonds

Topping
⅔ cup heavy cream
4 tblsp apricot jam, sieved
3 pieces stem ginger, chopped
¼ cup whole or flaked almonds, toasted

Ice Cream
Put the milk, egg and sugar into a basin over a pan of hot water. Stir continuously until the custard mixture begins to thicken. When it will coat the back of the spoon, remove it and let it cool. Stir in the ginger wine and cream. Pour into a rigid, shallow freezer container and partially freeze. When the ice cream is partially frozen, remove from the freezer and pour into a bowl. Beat until smooth and creamy. Line an 8 inch cake pan with plastic wrap and pour in the ice cream. Return to the freezer until frozen.

Almond Base
Beat the egg whites in a clean bowl until they are stiff. Add the sugar and beat again. Gently fold in the cornstarch and ground almonds. Line the bottom of a cooky sheet. Fill a nylon pastry bag fitted with a ½ inch tip with some of the almond mixture. Spread the mixture in an 8 inch circle and smooth evenly. Bake in the oven for 25 minutes.
Place the almond base on a flat plate. Carefully lift the ice cream out of the pan and peel off the plastic wrap. Place the ice cream on the almond base.

For the Topping
Whip the cream, fold in the jam, stem ginger and almonds and spread over the ice cream.

Brandied Chestnut Roll (left), Walnut and Banana Galette (below) and Black Forest Gâteau (bottom).

Peach and Almond Gâteau

PREPARATION TIME: 60 minutes

COOKING TIME: 60 minutes for cake, 20 minutes for confectioners' custard

OVEN TEMPERATURE: 350°F

4 eggs, separated
½ cup sugar
1 cup cake flour
1¼ tsp baking powder
2 tblsp corn oil
3 tblsp boiling water
1 tsp almond essence

Filling
2 tblsp apricot jam, warmed

Confectioner's Custard
3 egg yolks
¼ cup sugar
¼ cup flour
1¼ cups milk
2 tblsp butter
1 tblsp sherry

To Decorate
1¼ cups heavy cream
¼ cup flaked almonds, toasted
14½oz can sliced peaches, drained

Grease and line an 8 inch loose-bottomed, deep cake pan. Place the egg yolks, sugar, flour, oil, water and almond essence in a bowl and beat for 2 minutes with a wooden spoon. Stiffly beat the egg whites and fold into the cake mixture using a metal spoon. Pour the mixture into a prepared pan and cook in the oven for about 60 minutes until well risen. Remove cake from pan and cool on a wire rack. Remove paper when cake is cold.

For the Confectioners' Custard
Put egg yolks in a bowl and beat until smooth and creamy. Stir in the flour and mix well. Heat the milk until hot, but not boiling, and stir into the egg mixture. Return the mixture to the pan and stir, bringing it gently to the boil. Remove from the heat and beat in the butter and the sherry. Pour into a bowl, stirring occasionally to prevent a skin forming.

Assembling the Gâteau
Cut the cake into 3 layers, placing the bottom layer on a serving plate. Spread the cake with 1 tblsp of jam and half the confectioners' custard. Place the second layer on top and spread with the remaining jam and custard. Put the top of the cake onto the filling. Spread the cake with half the cream and arrange the peaches on the top. Fit a pastry bag with a medium star tip and shape the remaining cream to decorate the gâteau. Sprinkle on the toasted almonds.

Chocolate Torte

PREPARATION TIME: 35 minutes

COOKING TIME: 1 hour 30 minutes

OVEN TEMPERATURE: 300°F

6oz plain chocolate
1 tblsp strong black coffee
¾ cup butter
¾ cup sugar
4 eggs, separated
1¼ cups cake flour
1½ tsp baking powder

Filling and Icing
Cherry jam
6oz plain chocolate
2 tblsp strong black coffee
¾ cup confectioners' sugar
⅔ cup heavy cream or
½ cup chocolate shavings
14½oz can black cherries, pitted

Melt the chocolate and coffee over a basin of hot water. Allow it to cool. Cream the butter and sugar together until light and fluffy. Slowly beat in the egg yolks and the cooled chocolate mixture. Fold in the flour using a metal spoon. Beat the egg whites in a clean, dry bowl until stiff, then fold into the mixture. Line and grease the base of an 8 inch cake pan and bake in the oven for 1½ hours. Allow the cake to cool in the pan for 10 minutes before turning onto a wire rack. Cut the cake horizontally and stick together with the cherry jam. Melt the chocolate and coffee for the frosting in a basin over a saucepan of hot water and remove from the heat. Beat in the confectioners' sugar. Pour the chocolate frosting over the cake, working it over the sides of the cake with a palette knife. When set, decorate with either the whipped cream or chocolate shavings and drained cherries.

Avocado Cheesecake

PREPARATION TIME: 30 minutes plus chilling

Crumb Base
8oz chocolate Graham crackers
6 tblsp butter, melted

Filling
2 ripe avocado pears
½ cup cream cheese
6 tblsp sugar
Juice of ½ a lemon
Grated rind of 1 lemon
2 tsp gelatin powder
2 egg whites
⅔ cup heavy cream, whipped

Decoration
⅔ cup heavy cream, whipped

Crush the crackers into fine crumbs and stir in the melted butter. Use the mixture to line a 7½ inch springform pan. Press it down to line the base and the sides. Chill well.

For the Filling
Peel and stone the avocados and save a few slices for decoration. Put the remainder into a basin and mash well. Mix in the lemon juice and grated rind, cream cheese and sugar. Beat until smooth. Dissolve the gelatin in 2 tblsp of hot water and stir into the mixture. Beat the egg whites in a clean, dry bowl and fold into the mixture with the whipped cream. Pour onto a prepared cracker base and chill thoroughly until set.

To Decorate
Carefully remove the cheesecake from the pan. Fill a nylon pastry bag, fitted with a star tip, with the cream reserved for decoration. Decorate a border of cream round the edge of the cake. Decorate with the avocado slices.
NB: sprinkle the avocado with lemon juice to prevent it from discoloring. This is useful when reserving the slices for decoration.

This page: Chocolate Torte (top) and Apricot Meringue (bottom).

Facing page: Avocado Cheesecake (top), Ginger Ice Cream Gâteau (center left) and Peach and Almond Gâteau (bottom).

Teatime Treats

Baking at home is not as difficult as some might expect and in very little time one can create some appetizing treats for the tea table. Here are lots of recipes which may tempt you to try them for yourself at picnics, birthdays and tea parties.

Biscuits

PREPARATION TIME: 15 minutes

COOKING TIME: 10-15 minutes

OVEN TEMPERATURE: 400°F

2 cups all-purpose flour
1 tsp cream of tartar
½ tsp bicarbonate of soda
Good pinch of salt
3 tblsp butter or margarine
6 tblsp superfine sugar
3 tblsp white raisins
1 tblsp sugared ginger pieces
1 tblsp sunflower seeds
2 eggs, plus a little milk if required
1 egg, beaten or a little milk for glazing

Sieve the dry ingredients twice. Cut in the fat, add sugar, white raisins, ginger pieces and sunflower seeds and mix to a soft dough with eggs. Knead lightly on floured surface. Roll out to approximately ½ inch thickness. Place on floured cooky sheet and brush the top with beaten egg or milk. Bake in the oven for 10-15 minutes.

Walnut Cake

PREPARATION TIME: 15 minutes

COOKING TIME: 35 minutes

OVEN TEMPERATURE: 350°F

4 eggs
¾ cup superfine sugar
1 cup all-purpose flour, sifted
1 tblsp oil
½ cup walnuts, finely chopped
Recipe butter cream
Walnut halves to decorate

Grease and line two 8 inch cake pans. Place the eggs and sugar in a heatproof bowl and beat over a pan of hot, but not boiling, water until thick (see beaten sponge method). Partially fold in the flour, add the oil and chopped walnuts and fold in gently. Divide the mixture between the prepared pans and bake in the oven for 35 minutes. When the cake is cooked it will spring back when touched. Turn onto a wire rack to cool. Split each cake in half and fill with butter cream. Swirl the remaining butter cream on top of the cake and decorate with walnut halves.

Welsh Cakes (above), Walnut Cake (right) and Biscuits (far right).

Welsh Cakes

PREPARATION TIME: 15 minutes

COOKING TIME: 8 minutes (4 minutes per side)

OVEN TEMPERATURE: 275°F

1 cup all-purpose flour
1 tsp baking powder
3 tblsp sugar
3 tblsp butter or margarine
½ tsp ground nutmeg
3 tblsp currants
1 egg, plus a little milk if required
Pinch of salt

Sieve the flour, baking powder and salt. Cut in the fat and stir in sugar, nutmeg and currants. Mix to a pastry consistency with egg. Roll out to ¼ inch thickness and cut with a ¼ inch small biscuit cutter. Cook on baking stone or large greased pan. Switch oven off for 15 minutes then grease and reheat for second batch. Dredge with superfine sugar and serve. Makes 10.

Flapjacks

PREPARATION TIME: 15 minutes
COOKING TIME: 30 minutes
OVEN TEMPERATURE: 350°F

½ cup margarine
½ cup soft brown sugar
6 tblsp corn syrup
1 cup rolled oats

Melt the margarine, sugar and syrup in a bowl over a pan of hot water. Stir in the rolled oats and mix thoroughly. Grease a shallow 8 inch square pan. Turn the mixture into the pan and smooth down the top. Bake in the oven for 30 minutes until golden. Cool in the pan for 3 minutes before cutting into fingers. Remove from pan when cool. Makes 16.

Coconut Specials

PREPARATION TIME: 20 minutes
COOKING TIME: 30 minutes
OVEN TEMPERATURE: 325°F

8oz puff pastry
A little jam, melted
4 tblsp melted butter
½ cup shredded coconut
½ cup sugar
2 eggs

Roll out the puff pastry. Using a round cooky cutter, cut rounds and use to line a patty pan. Using a pastry brush, coat the pastry with a little jam. Beat together the butter, coconut, sugar and eggs. Divide the coconut mixture between the patty pans. Bake in the oven for 30 minutes until golden brown. When cooked, remove from pan and cool on a wire rack. Makes 14.

Victoria Sponge

PREPARATION TIME: 30 minutes
COOKING TIME: 20-25 minutes
OVEN TEMPERATURE: 375°F

A stick of butter or margarine
½ cup sugar
2 eggs
1 cup cake flour, sifted with a pinch of salt
1¼ tsp baking powder
1 tblsp hot water
3 tblsp jam
⅔ cup heavy cream, whipped
Confectioners' sugar

Grease and line two 7 inch cake pans. Cream the fat and sugar until light and fluffy. Beat in the eggs singly and fold in 1 tblsp of flour with each egg. Fold in the remaining flour, then add the hot water. Divide the mixture between the pans and bake in the oven for 20-25 minutes until the cakes are golden. When the cakes are cooked they will spring back when lightly pressed. Turn the cakes onto a wire rack to cool. Stick the cakes together with jam and cream. Sprinkle the top with confectioners' sugar.

Chocolate Fudge Triangles

PREPARATION TIME: 25 minutes
COOKING TIME: 30 minutes for base, 10 minutes for topping
OVEN TEMPERATURE: 350°F

A stick of butter
¼ cup superfine sugar
1½ cups all-purpose flour

Fudge Topping
A stick of butter
¼ cup superfine sugar
2 tblsp corn syrup
⅔ cup condensed milk
4oz plain chocolate

Cream the butter and sugar together until fluffy. Add the flour and stir until the mixture binds. Knead until smooth. Roll out and press into a shallow 8 inch square pan. Prick with a fork and bake in the oven for 30 minutes. Cool in the pan. Put the ingredients for the topping in a heavy saucepan and stir until dissolved. Slowly boil and stir for 7 minutes. Cool the topping a little and spread over the cooky base. Leave it to set. When set, cut into squares, then cut diagonally to make triangles.

Lemon July Cake

PREPARATION TIME: 30 minutes
COOKING TIME: 25 minutes
OVEN TEMPERATURE: 375°F

Base
A stick of butter or margarine
½ cup sugar
1 egg, beaten
1½ cups flour
2 tsp baking powder

1st Topping
⅔ cup water
3 tblsp sugar
1 tblsp cornstarch
Juice of two lemons

2nd Topping
⅔ cup milk
1 tsp cornstarch
2 tblsp butter
6 tblsp sugar
Shredded coconut to sprinkle

Base
Cream the butter and sugar, add the egg and flour and pour into a pan and press down. Bake in the oven for 20 minutes.

1st Topping
Mix the water with the cornstarch to make a paste. Boil with the other ingredients until the mixture begins to thicken, stirring constantly. Spread on the cooked cake base while the mixture is still warm.

2nd Topping
Boil milk and cornstarch until it thickens. Add the the butter and sugar, creamed. Mix well and spread on top of the July. Sprinkle with the shredded coconut, cut into fingers and serve.

This page: Chocolate Brownies (top), Chocolate Fudge Triangles (bottom) and Flapjacks (center).

Facing page: Victoria Sponge (top right), Lemon July Cake (center left) and Coconut Specials (bottom).

Chocolate Brownies

PREPARATION TIME: 25 minutes
COOKING TIME: 35 minutes
OVEN TEMPERATURE: 350°F

1 cup all-purpose flour
½ tsp baking powder
4oz plain chocolate
¼ cup butter
½ cup soft brown sugar
2 eggs
6 tblsp walnuts
6 tblsp mixed fruit

Frosting
4oz plain chocolate
1 tblsp butter

Sift the flour and baking powder together in a bowl. Melt the chocolate in a bowl over a small saucepan of hot water. Cream the butter for the brownies with the sugar until light and fluffy. Beat in the eggs separately, adding the flour with the second egg. Beat the melted chocolate into the mixture, then fold in the walnuts and fruit. Grease and line a shallow 8 inch square pan and bake in the oven for 35 minutes. Cut into squares while still warm and cool in the pan.

Spiced Cookies

PREPARATION TIME: 20 minutes
COOKING TIME: 15 minutes
OVEN TEMPERATURE: 350°F

1 cup wholewheat flour
½ tsp bicarbonate of soda
1 tsp ground cinnamon
1 tsp mixed spice
¼ cup rolled oats
6 tblsp sugar
6 tblsp butter or margarine
1 tblsp corn syrup
1 tblsp milk

Put the flour, bicarbonate of soda, cinnamon, mixed spice, oats and sugar into a bowl. Melt the butter in a small saucepan with the syrup and milk. Pour the liquid into the dry ingredients and beat until smooth. Make the mixture into little balls and place them a little apart on a lightly-greased cooky sheet. Flatten each one. Bake in the oven for 15 minutes until golden, and cool on the cooky sheet.

Macaroons

PREPARATION TIME: 20 minutes
COOKING TIME: 20 minutes
OVEN TEMPERATURE: 350°F

1 cup superfine sugar
10 tblsp ground almonds
1 tblsp rice flour
2 egg whites
Rice paper
20 split almonds

Mix the sugar, almonds and rice flour together. In a separate bowl, beat the egg whites lightly and add the ready-mixed dry ingredients. Let the mixture stand for 5 minutes. Line a cooky sheet with rice paper. Mold the mixture into little balls and place them on the lined cooky sheet slightly apart. Gently flatten the macaroons and put an almond on each one. Bake in the oven for 20 minutes, then cool on cooky sheet. Makes 20.

Almond Slices

PREPARATION TIME: 20 minutes
COOKING TIME: 20 minutes
OVEN TEMPERATURE: 400°F

Pastry Base
2 cups all-purpose flour
½ cup butter
¼ tsp salt
Cold water to mix

Topping
4 tblsp jam
½ cup sugar
½ cup confectioners' sugar
¾ cup ground almonds
1 egg, plus 1 egg white
A few drops almond essence
2 tblsp flaked almonds to decorate

Sift the flour and salt into a bowl and cut in the butter until it resembles fine breadcrumbs. Add enough water to mix into a pliable dough. Roll out the dough onto a floured surface and use to line a greased or dampened shallow 10x6 inch baking pan. Pinch the long edges to form a border. Cover the base with jam. In a clean bowl, mix together the sugars and almonds. Beat well and then add the whole egg, egg white and almond essence. Use the almond mixture to cover the jam, spreading evenly with a knife. Sprinkle with almonds. Bake in the oven for 20 minutes until well risen and golden. When cooked, cut in the pan and leave to cool for 10 minutes. Then remove from pan and leave to finish cooling on a wire rack.

Viennese Fingers

PREPARATION TIME: 20 minutes
COOKING TIME: 15 minutes
OVEN TEMPERATURE: 350°F

¾ cup butter or margarine
¼ cup confectioners' sugar
Grated rind of 1 orange
1 cup all-purpose flour
6 tblsp cornstarch

Cream together the butter, sugar and orange rind until fluffy. Sieve the flour and cornstarch together and beat well into the mixture. Fill a pastry bag fitted with a 1 inch fluted tip and pipe 3 inch fingers, well separated, onto a sheet of non-stick silicone paper. Bake in the oven for 15 minutes and, when cooked, transfer to a wire rack to cool. If required, two fingers can be sandwiched together with a little apricot jam. Makes 12.

Chocolate Fudge Cake

PREPARATION TIME: 15 minutes
COOKING TIME: 45-50 minutes
OVEN TEMPERATURE: 325°F

1¾ cups all-purpose flour
1 tsp bicarbonate of soda
1 tsp baking powder
2 tblsp cocoa powder
10 tblsp soft brown sugar
2 tblsp corn syrup
2 eggs
¾ cup oil
1¼ cups milk

Chocolate Frosting
6oz plain chocolate
2 tblsp light cream

To Decorate
1 packet chocolate chips
6 tblsp whole nuts

Sift together the dry ingredients into a bowl and make a well in the center. Add the sugar, syrup, eggs, oil and milk and beat until smooth. Grease and line a 9 inch cake pan and pour in the cake mixture. Cook in the oven for 45-50 minutes; leave in the pan for a few minutes before turning out the cake onto a wire rack.

To Make the Chocolate Frosting
Put the chocolate and cream into a small, heavy pan and heat gently until melted. Cool the mixture slightly and pour over the cake. Decorate with chocolate chips, or nuts.

Harvest Crunchies

PREPARATION TIME: 20 minutes
COOKING TIME: 15 minutes
OVEN TEMPERATURE: 375°F

¾ cup all-purpose flour
½ tsp mixed spice
¾ cup wholewheat flour
2 tblsp oatmeal
½ cup butter or margarine
¼ cup soft brown sugar
2 tblsp white raisins
2 tblsp milk

Sift the flour and spice into a bowl. Stir in the wholewheat flour and oatmeal. Cut the fat into the mixture until it resembles breadcrumbs. Add the brown sugar and the white raisins, then add the milk, a little at a time, and mix until the consistency is that of stiff dough. Flour a work surface and turn the dough out onto it. Lightly knead the dough and roll it out until very thin. With a 3 inch fluted cooky cutter, cut out rounds and place them on a lightly-greased cooky sheet. Bake in the oven, then cool on a wire rack. Makes 20.

Facing page: Macaroons (top), Spiced Cookies (right) and Harvest Crunchies (bottom left). This page: Chocolate Fudge Cake (top), Viennese Fingers (left) and Almond Slices (bottom).

Festive Cakes

Special cakes are traditionally used for the celebration of religious festivals; the most popular being the traditional Christmas cake and the simnel cake at Easter. Not everybody enjoys rich cake, so there are sponge variations in this book for both Easter and Christmas.

Simnel Cake

PREPARATION TIME: 40 minutes

COOKING TIME: 3 hours

OVEN TEMPERATURE: 325°F reduced to 300°F

8 inch round, rich fruit cake mixture
1¾lb almond paste
2 tblsp apricot glaze
1 egg white, beaten
Ribbon to decorate

Place half the mixture in a prepared, deep cake pan. Roll out a quarter of the almond paste into a 8 inch circle and lay it on top of the mixture. Spread the remaining mixture on the top of the almond paste. Bake in the oven for 1 hour, lower the temperature and bake for a further 2½ hours. Leave in the pan for 5 minutes and turn onto a wire rack to cool. Roll out a third of the remaining almond paste into a 8 inch circle. Brush the top of the cake with apricot glaze. Press the almond paste circle on top of the cake and brush with beaten egg white. Shape the remaining almond paste into balls and place round the edge. Brown under a hot broiler and allow to cool. Decorate with ribbon.

This page: Daffodil Cake (top) and Simnel Cake (bottom).

Facing page: Easter Cake with Chicks (top) and Easter Nest (bottom).

Daffodil Cake

9 inch round Madeira cake
Recipe vanilla-flavored butter frosting
Molding frosting daffodil
3 tblsp apricot jam
1 tblsp cocoa powder

Slice the cake and spread with the jam. Use half of the butter frosting and sandwich the cake together. Spread the top of the cake with a ¼ of the remaining butter frosting. Smooth it with a palette knife. Fill a pastry bag with the remaining butter frosting and fit it with a 5-point star tip. Make shells round the edge of the cake. Put the daffodil on the cake. Mix a little butter frosting with cocoa powder. With a pastry bag fitted with a writing tip, write 'Easter' on the cake below the daffodil.

Easter Nest

8 inch round lemon sponge (beaten or Victoria)
1 box orange-flavored chocolate sticks
½ cup candy-coated chocolate speckled eggs
Recipe lemon-flavored butter frosting

Put the cake on a plate or cake board. Cover the cake with lemon-flavored butter frosting. Put a

ribbon round the side of the cake and make a bow. Lay the orange-flavored chocolate sticks at angles round the sides of the cake, leaving an uncovered area in the center of the cake. Fill the center with eggs.

Fruit Easter Cake with Chicks

PREPARATION TIME: 45 minutes

COOKING TIME: 1 hour 30 minutes to 1 hour 45 minutes

OVEN TEMPERATURE: 325°F

¾ cup butter
¾ cup sugar
3 eggs
1 cup flour
¾ cup mixed dried fruit
1¼ cups cake flour
1½ tsp baking powder
¼ cup chopped mixed candied fruit
¼ cup candied cherries, halved
Grated rind of 1 orange
5 tblsp orange juice
1 crushed sugar cube

To Decorate
Fluffy chicks
Yellow ribbon

Cream the butter and sugar together until light and fluffy. Beat in the eggs singly, adding a little flour after each. Toss the fruit in the remaining flour and add to the mixture with the orange rind and juice. Grease and line a 7 inch cake pan. Fill with the mixture and smooth with the back of a spoon. Sprinkle with some of the crushed sugar cube. Bake in the oven for 1½- 1¾ hours. Turn out and cool on a wire rack. Decorate with yellow ribbon, chicks and fresh or artificial flowers. Sprinkle top of cake with remaining sugar cube.

Festive Garland

If you prefer you can make edible decorations for this cake.

8 inch quick mix cake, baked in a ring mold
Recipe apricot glaze
Recipe butter frosting
1 round cake board
Holly leaves, berries, Christmas roses, mistletoe, candle and ribbon (color of your choice)

Split the cake and sandwich together with the glaze. Put the cake on the plate or cake board and cover with the frosting, peaking it as you go around. Press the roses, holly leaves, berries and mistletoe into the cake, leaving a gap for the bow. When the frosting is dry and hard, place a candle in the center of the ring and attach the bow in the space reserved.

Christmas Bells

7 inch or 8 inch square Christmas cake
Royal frosting, made with 2½lb confectioners' sugar
½ recipe white molding frosting
½ cup granulated sugar
4 sprigs of holly, real or artificial
1 yard narrow, white satin ribbon
Food coloring – pink

Put the cake on a silver cake board. Royal frost the cake and leave to dry between coats. Roll out the molding frosting and, using a bell shape cutter, cut 10 bells and leave them to dry on non-stick silicone paper. Mix the granulated sugar and pink food color well until the sugar becomes pink. Sprinkle over the bells and leave to dry. Fill a pastry bag, fitted with a medium-sized star tip, with the royal frosting. Make a row of shells round the bottom of the cake. Make a border of shells round the top of the cake and a line of shells up each of the 4 corners of the cake and allow the frosting to dry. Make 5 bows with the narrow, white ribbon. With a little frosting sugar secure two frosting bells on each side panel of the cake. The tops of the bells should be nearest to each of the 4 corners. Two of the bells should be placed in the center of the top of the cake, with the tops of the bells together. Put a ribbon bow above each of the bells. Position the sprigs of holly in each of the four corners on top of the cake.

Christmas Tree

8 inch square quick mix cake or rich fruit cake mix
Recipe apricot glaze
Recipe almond paste, if using fruit cake
Recipe butter frosting, if using quick mix cake
1lb molding frosting

To Decorate
1 cake board
Silver balls
Shredded coconut to sprinkle
Recipe royal frosting
8oz molding frosting, white
Chocolate sticks
Gold or silver non-toxic food coloring
Food coloring – red, blue, green, yellow
8oz molding frosting

Cut the cake diagonally and place the outer edges of the square next to one another, i.e. back-to-back to produce a triangular shape. If using a fruit cake, brush with apricot glaze and cover with almond paste. If using a butter frosting on a quick cake mixture, cover the cake with the butter frosting and leave on the cake board. Roll out the molding frosting and, using a fluted pastry cutter, cut circles and then cut each one in half and use to stick onto the butter frosting. Start at the bottom edge of the cake and overlap slightly until you reach the top. With the remaining frosting, make some small presents and a square tub for the tree. Cover the tree trunk with a little of the remaining butter frosting and lay the chocolate sticks vertically on the tree trunk. Use any remaining frosting to frost the leaves of the tree, or make the leaves if desired. Decorate with the silver balls and sprinkle with shredded coconut. With the white frosting to decorate, color small pinches in various colors and, with the white royal frosting, make strings around the various colored shapes to make more little parcels. Roll out the remaining white frosting and cut it into a star. Color with a little non-toxic gold or silver food coloring.

Traditional Christmas Cake with Holly and Roses

7 inch round Christmas cake
Recipe apricot glaze
1½lb almond paste
Royal frosting, made with 2lb confectioners' sugar

To Decorate
Silver balls
Christmas roses
Almond paste holly leaves and berries, small snowman or Santa, if available
Ribbon

Brush the cake with apricot glaze. Cover with the almond paste and leave to dry. Flat frost the top and sides of the cake with royal frosting and leave to dry again. Use a pastry bag fitted with a 5-star tip and make shells around the top edge of the cake and then on the top, round the sides of the cake and, finally, around the bottom edge of the cake. When dry, make a further row between the top 2 rows using the 5-star tip upright to make stars. Decorate the top of the cake with almond paste holly and frosted or molded Christmas roses and a small snowman or Father Christmas, if desired. Tie the ribbon round the cake and make a bow. Push a silver ball into the center of each of the stars.

Christmas Tree (right) and Festive Garland (below).

Frosted Mistletoe Cake

This is a quick and easy Christmas cake, which can be made either round or square. Any bought decorations can be used to complement the design.

7 inch or 8 inch square or round Christmas cake
Recipe apricot glaze
1½lb almond paste
2lb green molding frosting
12 mistletoe leaves and berries made from almond paste
2ft x 2 inch length of green ribbon
Food coloring – green

Put the cake on a silver cake board. To decorate, roll out the green molding frosting. With a small, sharp knife cut out several mistletoe leaves. Make them long and narrow with rounded ends and mark them with a knife to indicate the veins. With the uncolored molding frosting roll small, pea-sized balls of frosting to represent the berries. Use the mistletoe to decorate the top of the cake. With the ribbon, tie a large bow and attach it to the top of the cake with a little royal frosting. Fill a shaker with a little frosting sugar, or put it through a small sieve and shake it gently round the edge of the cake, dusting some of the mistletoe.

Christmas Candles

2 jam-filled jelly rolls
1lb green molding frosting
4oz white molding frosting
Recipe apricot glaze
Rectangular silver cake board
Food colorings – red, yellow, blue
Red ribbon
3 cocktail sticks

Cut one jelly roll ¾ of the way down. Brush the jelly rolls with apricot glaze. Roll out the green molding frosting and cover the jelly rolls. Stand them upright with something for support. In a small, heavy saucepan stir to dissolve half to three-quarters of the white molding frosting. Roll out the

This page: Christmas Bells Cake (top) and Traditional Christmas Cake with Holly and Roses (bottom).

Facing page: Frosted Mistletoe Cake.

remaining white frosting on a surface dusted with confectioners' sugar or cornstarch and cut out 3 flame shapes. Leave on non-stick silicone paper to dry. When dry, paint a blue dot near the bottom; surround by yellow and edge with red. Reserve to dry. Pour the liquid molding frosting over the candles in a drizzle so that it dries like wax. Stick a flame in to the top of each candle, using a cocktail stick to support them. Decorate with ribbons.

Postbox

This makes a quick and easy festive cake for those who do not like traditional Christmas cake.

1 chocolate jelly roll
8oz red molding frosting
Recipe royal frosting
Recipe apricot glaze

Roll out the molding frosting and cut out two circles to cover the ends of the jelly roll. Roll out the remaining frosting to cover the rest of the jelly roll. Brush the jelly roll with the apricot glaze and cover with molding frosting. Fit a pastry bag with a writing tip and fill with some royal frosting. Frost the detail onto the postbox and leave to dry. With the remaining frosting, spoon half on top of the postbox and the remainder at the bottom. Dust with a little confectioners' sugar.

Icicles with Holly

7 inch or 8 inch square or round, rich fruit cake
Recipe apricot glaze
1½lb almond paste
Royal frosting, made with 2lb confectioners' sugar
Blue ribbon
Almond paste holly leaves and berries

Brush the top and sides of the cake with apricot glaze and cover with almond paste; leave to dry. With a little frosting, attach the cake to the cake board and flat frost the top and sides. Leave it to dry between and after coats. Using a pastry bag fitted with a shell tip, make a circle of shells on the top edge of the cake and again round the bottom of the cake. Fit the pastry bag with a plain or fine-band tip. Place the ribbon round the sides of the cake. Make the icicles down and over the ribbon, varying them in length and width. Fit the pastry bag with a writing tip and go over to make smaller icicles, which should hang free of the cake. Use the remaining frosting to secure the holly in a pattern on top of the cake.

This page: Postbox and Christmas Candles. Facing page: Icicles with Holly.

BOUTEILLE
A LA
PROPRIETE

Section 7

ENJOYING WINE

Introduction

Although wine is today produced around the globe, it was in Europe that the distinctive varieties were developed. Below: three South Sea Islanders enjoy a bottle of New Zealand wine, and (inset bottom right) Cabernet Sauvignon grapes growing in California's Napa Valley. Right: the vineyards of Champagne, which have given their name to the dry, sparkling wine of the area, and (inset bottom left) a taster in Armagnac samples the spirit for which the region is so famous.

Wine is made to be enjoyed, and drinking it should be fun!

It doesn't matter if you know nothing at all about wine. The most important thing is to drink what you like – after all, why should you spend your cash on a wine you don't enjoy just because some 'expert' says it's good? The best way to find out about wines is by experimenting with different ones and, once you find one you like, to remember its name. Having got to this stage you can make life more interesting by trying other wines made from similar grapes or from the same region.

This section is a basic guide to the most widely available wines, their tastes and styles. It is not in any sense the last word as there are literally hundreds of wine books which go into far greater depth on specific wines and regions. I have tried to set the scene and highlight the value-for-money wines on the market. Just because a wine is expensive does not necessarily mean it will be the best value.

Don't be put off by people who sound as if they know a lot about wine. Your choice is just as valid as theirs, and they will buy what they like – why shouldn't you! In any case, a large number of people who talk a lot about wine don't necessarily know a lot about it.

By reading this section you'll have some idea about where to start, but the great thing about learning about wine is that you have to keep experimenting.

What Exactly is Wine?

Right: the Chardonnay grape, which is grown widely throughout the world, but which perhaps finds its finest expression in the strong, dry wine of Chablis Grand Cru (facing page), grown only in seven small vineyards around the French town of Chablis. Below: the firm Cabernet-Franc grape, often used in the production of rosé wines.

Apart from being a drink, wine is the naturally fermented juice of grapes.

After the grapes have been picked and crushed, the skins are taken away from the juice if making a white wine. You may be surprised to learn that most red grapes have white juice. So how is red wine made? The colour comes from the skins which are left in contact with the juice for varying lengths of time depending on whether a red or a rosé wine is being made. The skins add colour and tannin, a bitter substance also found in tea, which gives the wine body and helps it to age.

The wine ferments because of the natural sugars in the grapes. In a dry wine the natural sugar is totally fermented out, whereas in a sweet white wine some of the natural sugar is left in the wine.

Over the past 50 years wine-making technology has improved greatly and the vast majority of wines now available are well-made, if not always to everyone's taste.

The choice of wines on sale in Britain is enormous and increasing all the time, with wines from as far flung places as California and China.

MÉDAILLE D'ARGENT 1965
1976
Chablis Grand Cru
"Vaudésir"
APPELLATION CHABLIS GRAND CRU CONTRÔLÉE

Styles of Wine

Facing page: two similar bottles of Spanish wine, though the paler, dry variety contains 0.6 percent sugar and the sweet wine ten times as much.

Choosing a wine from the huge selection on offer can be a difficult task. However, some shops and supermarkets have now introduced a coding system which indicates the sweetness of the wine. The best of these is a rating of 1 to 9, when 1 is a very dry wine like Muscadet and 9 is a very sweet wine like Sauternes. A medium sweet wine like Liebfraumilch would be rated around 5. By this method, if you know what a particular wine tastes like but if you want something a little drier or sweeter, you simply select one up or down the scale.

This system is generally only used for white and rosé wines because reds, apart from Lambrusco, are normally dry. Reds are often coded according to their style e.g. light-, medium- or heavy-bodied.

Many wines have informative back labels which indicate the style of the wine, where it is produced, how to serve it, and what are the best foods to eat with it.

The following table is a general guide to some of the most widely available wines, divided into their different styles.

WHITE: dry; light- to medium-bodied
Alsace
Bordeaux (dry, e.g. Entre-deux-Mers)
Fino Sherry
Frascati
Luxembourg wines
Mâcon
Muscadet
New Zealand Müller Thurgau
Rioja (new style)
Sancerre
Sauvignon de Touraine
Sercial Madeira
Soave
Spanish (new style)
Sparkling wines (most brut ones)
Swiss wines
Trocken (Germany)
Vin de Pays
Vinho Verde

WHITE: dry; full-bodied
Chablis
Côte d'Or white Burgundies, e.g. Meursault, Chassagne,
Graves
Rhône, e.g. Châteauneuf-du-Pape
Rioja (old-style)
New World Chardonnay/Sauvignon (most)
Vouvray (can be semi-dry)

WHITE: medium sweet; light- to medium-bodied
Amontillado Sherry
Asti
Bual Madeira
German wines up to Kabinett quality
Laski Riesling
Liebfraumilch
Orvieto
Vouvray (demi-sec)

WHITE: sweet; full-bodied
Beerenauslese
Cream Sherry
Côteaux du Layon
Late-picked wines
Liqueur Muscats (Australian)
Malmsey Madeira
Moscatel de Setubal
Muscat de Beaumes de Venise
Sauternes/Barsac
Spätlese
Tokay Aszu
Trockenbeerenauslese
Vouvray Moelleux

RED: light-bodied
Alsace
Beaujolais
Bourgueil
Chinon
Claret (Generic)
German
New Zealand
Sancerre
Saumur Champigny
Valpolicella
Vin de Pays

RED: medium-bodied
Barbera
Chianti
Clarets (good vintage ones)
Côte d'Or Burgundy
Côte-du-Rhône
Dão
Navarra
Rioja
St. Emilion/Pomerol
Zinfandel (or full-bodied)

RED: heavy- to full-bodied
Barbaresco
Barolo
Bull's Blood
California Cabernet/Shiraz
Clarets (Good vintage ones)
Rhône (Better quality ones, e.g. Côte Rôtie, Hermitage, Châteauneuf-du-Pape)
Rioja
Roussillion

RED: sweet
Lambrusco (light)
Port (heavy)
Zinfandel (late-picked)

DON CORTEZ
GARANTIA DE ORIGEN LA MANCHA
PRODUCE OF SPAIN
Dry
WHITE WINE
1l e
SERVE LIGHTLY CHILLED
Grants of St James's
DON CORTEZ
GARANTIA DE ORIGEN LA MANCHA
PRODUCE OF SPAIN
Sweet
WHITE WINE
SERVE LIGHTLY CHILLED
Grants of St James's

Chenas
APPELLATION CONTROLEE
PONTANEVAUX

Bottle Shape

Many areas of Europe produce their wines in distinctive shapes of bottle, based upon traditional designs. Far left: the claret bottle, which is ideal for stacking and laying down and is used by many bottlers throughout the world. Left: the Burgundy, which is used for both the red and white wines of the region. Below: the bocksbeutel, based on an old drinking flagon, is popular in Franconia and Portugal. Right: the Alsace flute, a slightly elongated version of the German flute.

Reading the Label

In France the Chateau, where the vines are grown and the wine produced, is of vital importance. Above: the Chateau of Clos de Vouguet, which produces some of the finest wine on the magnificent Côte de Nuits.

The vast majority of wine made, sold and drunk throughout the world is table wine. The label will state the country of origin, but not the region of origin, and the wine can indeed be from several regions. In France the next stage up is Vin de Pays – literally 'country wine' – which states the area of origin. Then there is VDQS – Vin Delimité de Qualité Supérieur, VDQS wines will state on the label which region of France they are from.

Appellation Controlée (or AC) is the top quality designation in France, and refers to specific regions like Appellation Beaujolais Villages Controlée or Appellation Bordeaux Controlée. Many areas have several small ACs within them. For instance, in Bordeaux you also find AC Pauillac, AC Médoc, etc. In general, the more specific (or smaller) the Appellation is, the better the wine is likely to be. For example, AC Margaux will be better than AC Bordeaux.

In Italy the equivalent is DOC (Denominazione di Origine Controllata), and a few of the top quality regions have

FRANCE

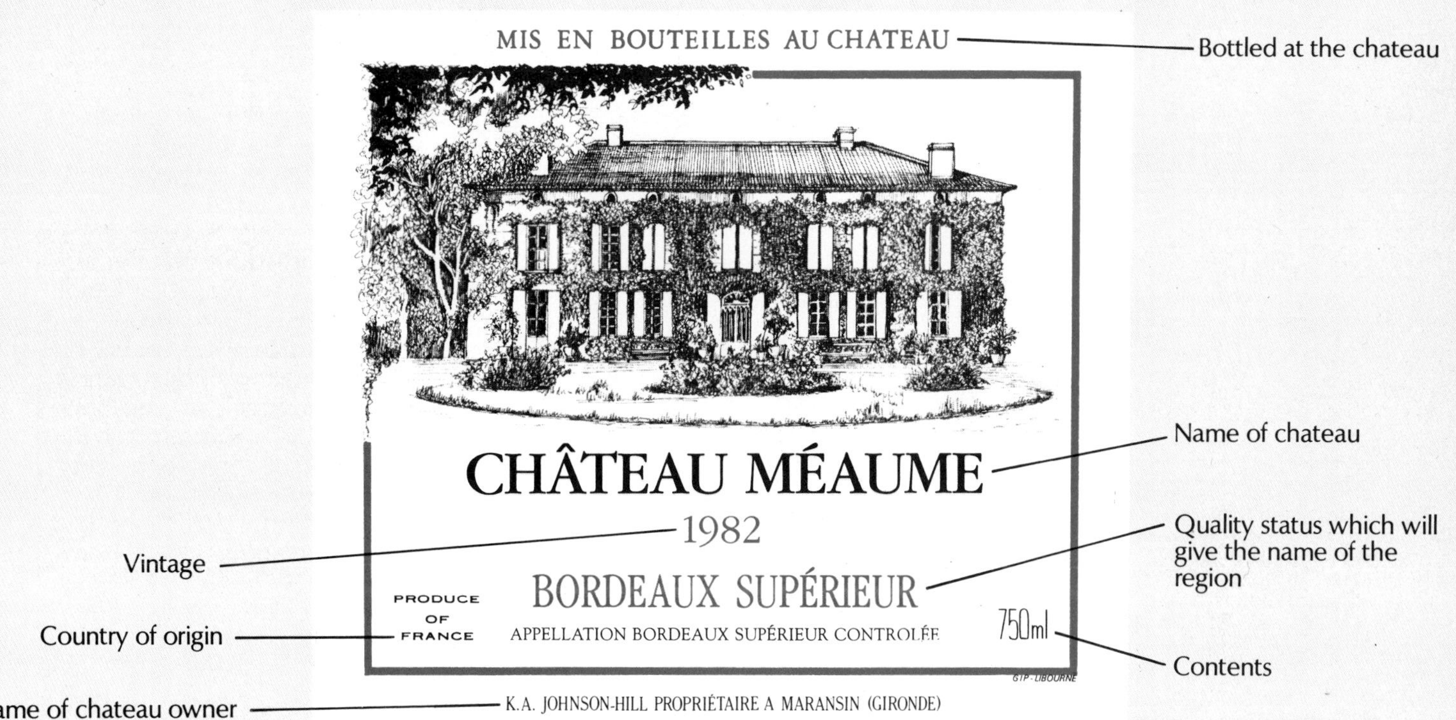

MIS EN BOUTEILLES AU CHATEAU
Bottled at the chateau
CHÂTEAU MÉAUME
Name of chateau
1982
Vintage
Quality status which will give the name of the region
PRODUCE OF FRANCE
BORDEAUX SUPÉRIEUR
APPELLATION BORDEAUX SUPÉRIEUR CONTROLÉE
750ml
Country of origin
Contents
Name of chateau owner
K.A. JOHNSON-HILL PROPRIÉTAIRE A MARANSIN (GIRONDE)

FRANCE

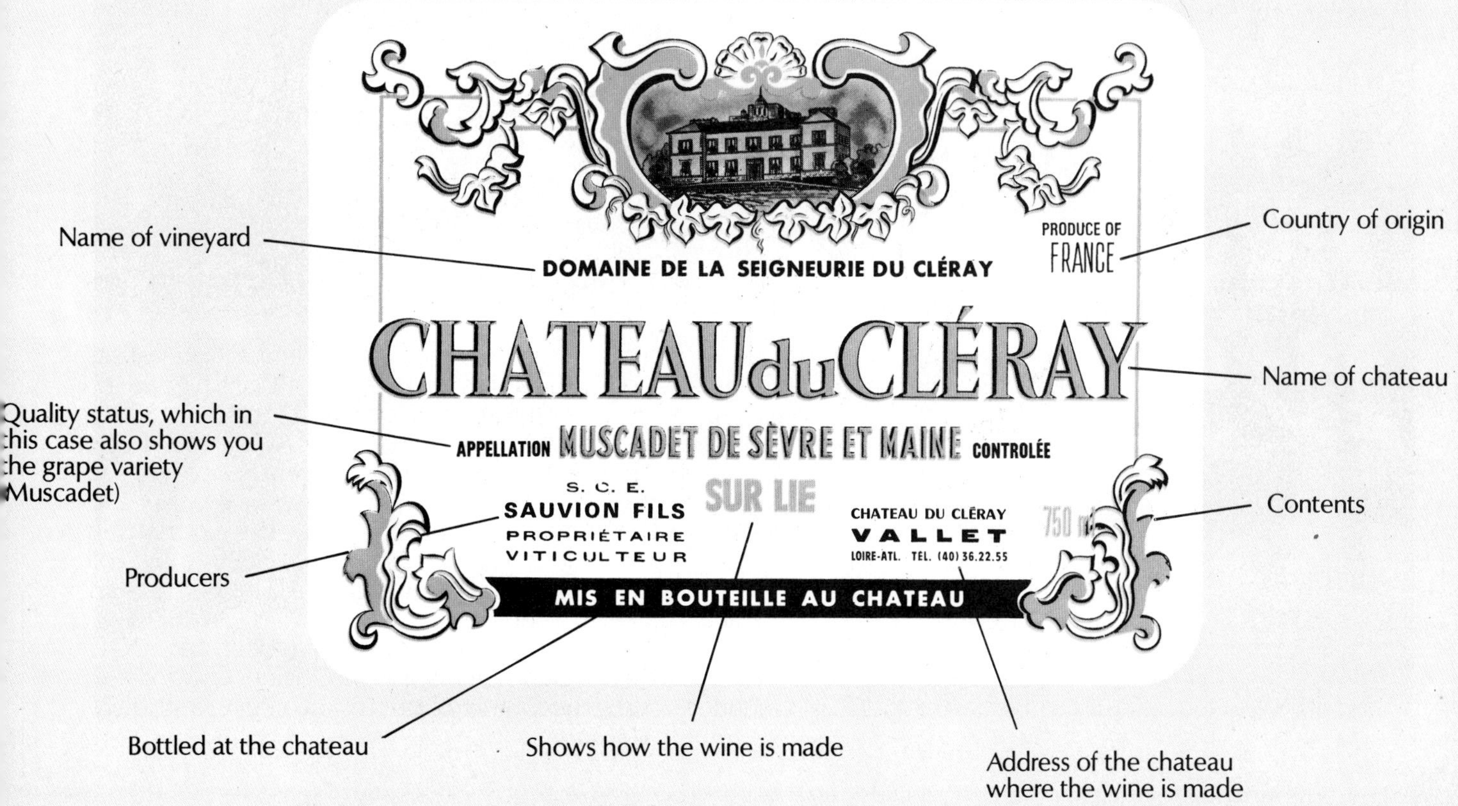
Name of vineyard
DOMAINE DE LA SEIGNEURIE DU CLÉRAY
PRODUCE OF FRANCE
Country of origin
CHATEAU du CLÉRAY
Name of chateau
Quality status, which in
his case also shows you
he grape variety
Muscadet)
APPELLATION MUSCADET DE SÈVRE ET MAINE CONTROLÉE
S. C. E.
SAUVION FILS
PROPRIÉTAIRE
VITICULTEUR
SUR LIE
CHATEAU DU CLÉRAY
VALLET
LOIRE-ATL. TEL. (40) 36.22.55
750 ml
Contents
Producers
MIS EN BOUTEILLE AU CHATEAU
Bottled at the chateau
Shows how the wine is made
Address of the chateau where the wine is made

now been granted a higher designation, DOCG, where the G stands for Garrantia (guaranteed).

Germanic-looking bottles are often, in fact, EEC wine – a Euroblend which, although Germanic in style, can come from any one or more EEC country.

Tafelwein (table wine) is Germany's basic wine quality, and above that comes Landwein – equivalent to Vin de Pays and coming from specific regions. However, the majority of German wine found in Britain is QbA (Qualitätswein bestimmte Anbaugebiete). Above this is the top classification, QmP (Qualitätswein mit Prädikat), with Prädikat refering to the sweetness levels. QmP wines are then classified according to the maturity of the grapes in ascending sweetness levels from Kabinett through Spätlese, Auslese, Beeranauslese to Trockenbeerenauslese which is the sweetest.

In Germany the area in which a wine is grown is important and village names often appear on the label. Right: the village of Punderich and surrounding vineyards. Below: an array of wines, on the pavement at Périgueux, France.

ITALY

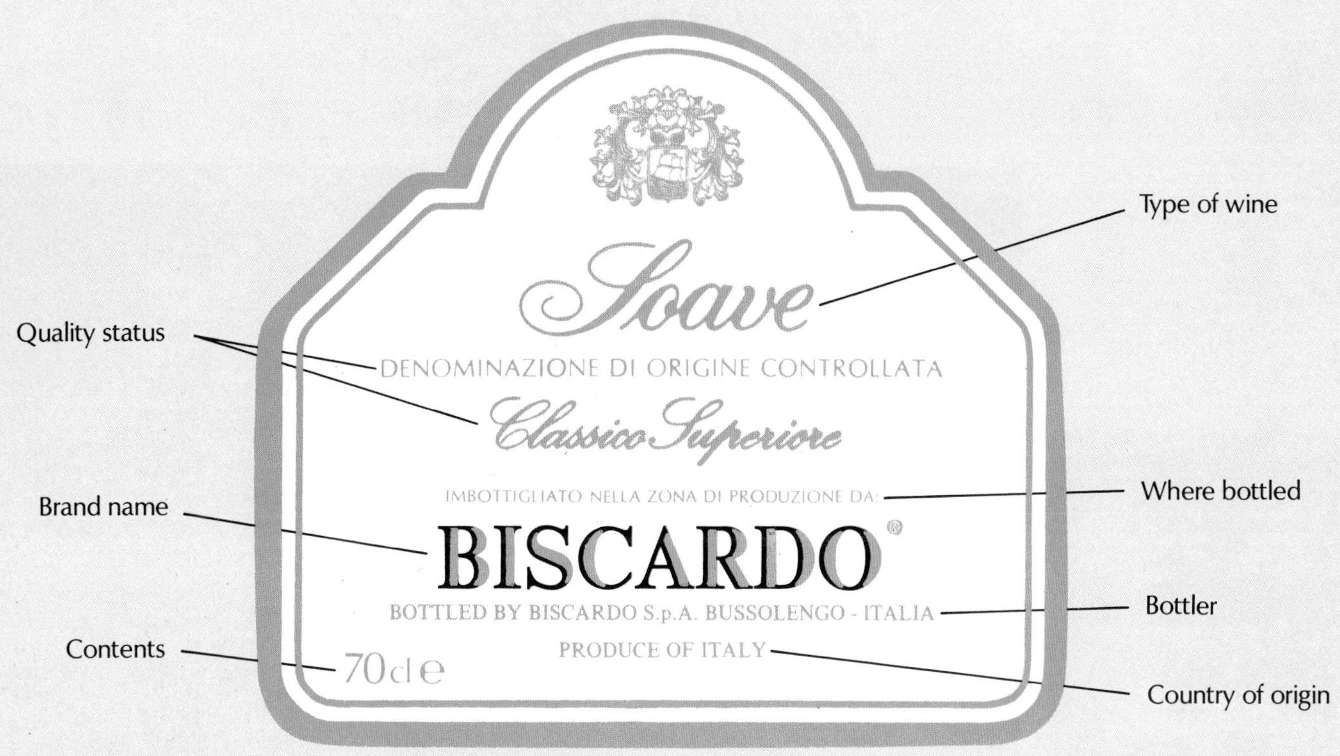

Soave
DENOMINAZIONE DI ORIGINE CONTROLLATA
Classico Superiore
IMBOTTIGLIATO NELLA ZONA DI PRODUZIONE DA:
BISCARDO®
BOTTLED BY BISCARDO S.p.A. BUSSOLENGO - ITALIA
PRODUCE OF ITALY
70cl e
Type of wine
Quality status
Brand name
Where bottled
Bottler
Contents
Country of origin

GERMANY

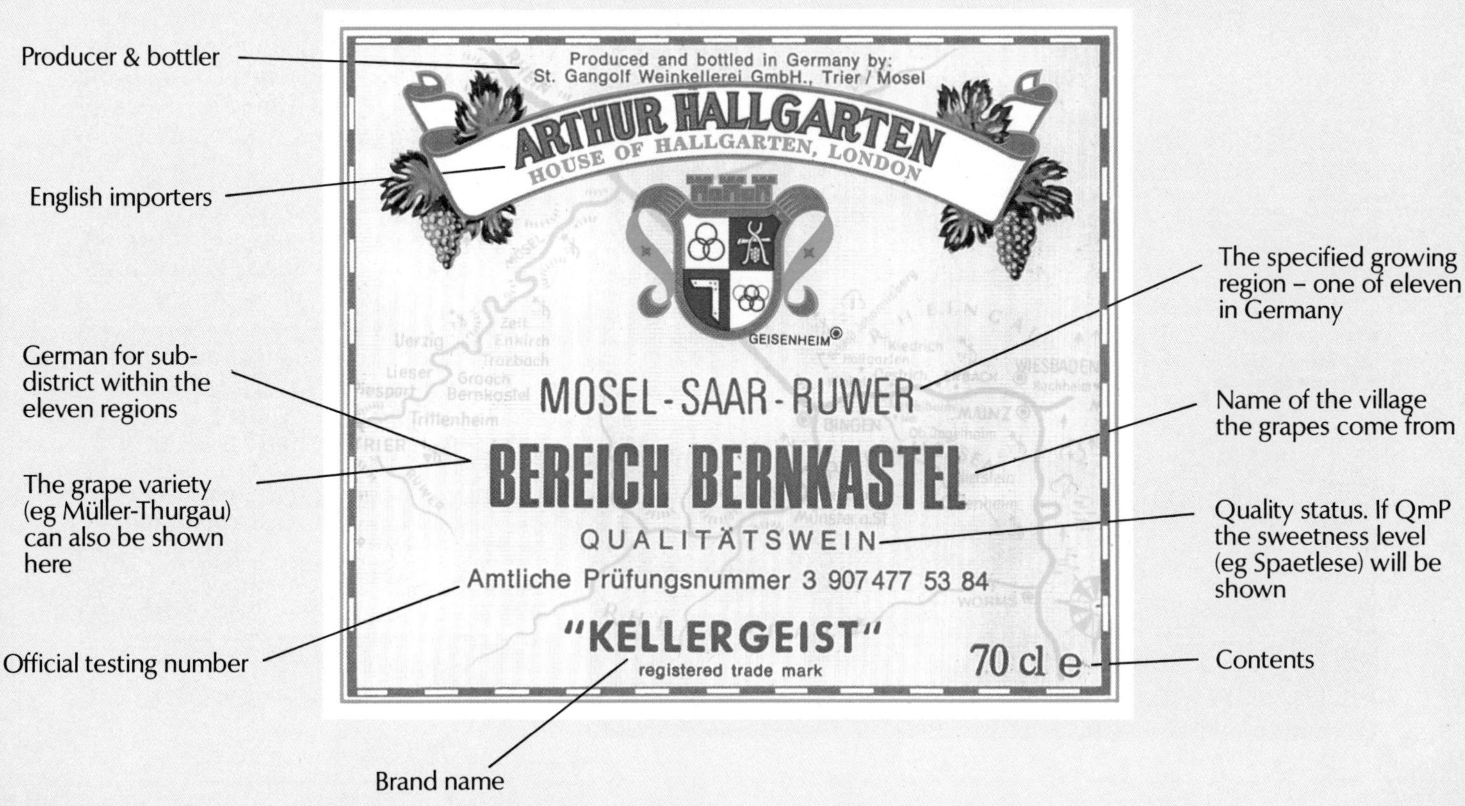

Produced and bottled in Germany by:
St. Gangolf Weinkellerei GmbH., Trier / Mosel
ARTHUR HALLGARTEN
HOUSE OF HALLGARTEN, LONDON
GEISENHEIM
MOSEL - SAAR - RUWER
BEREICH BERNKASTEL
QUALITÄTSWEIN
Amtliche Prüfungsnummer 3 907 477 53 84
"KELLERGEIST"
registered trade mark
70 cl e
Producer & bottler
English importers
The specified growing region – one of eleven in Germany
German for sub-district within the eleven regions
Name of the village the grapes come from
The grape variety (eg Müller-Thurgau) can also be shown here
Quality status. If QmP the sweetness level (eg Spaetlese) will be shown
Official testing number
Contents
Brand name

Vintage Guide

The year in which a wine is produced, known as the vintage, can be of crucial importance, being recorded on the label (below). In Champagne most wine is blended, but some outstanding vintages may be kept for years (remaining pictures).

If you've enjoyed a wine it's worth remembering the vintage on the label. A good vintage in one region is not necessarily good in another. The following is a general guide and should be used with care. There are always exceptions to the rule.

In good vintages Bordeaux can produce some of the greatest wines in the world. Due to modern vinification methods there has not been a really terrible vintage since 1968, and nowadays even poor vintages tend to produce very drinkable wines.
Excellent: 1983, 1982, 1978, 1975, 1970
Good: 1981, 1979, 1976, 1971
Average to poor: 1977, 1974, 1973, 1972

Burgundy is far less consistent than Bordeaux because of the large number of producers, the very varied wine-making techniques, and the climate. Thus it is very difficult to generalise and there are exceptions everywhere.
Excellent: 1983, 1978, 1971
Good: 1982, 1981, 1980, 1979, 1976, 1972, 1970

JEROBOAM 4 BT
SALMANAZAR 12 BT
Caves Museux
1 a 45
Galeries A.B.C.D.E.
Superficie-5527 m.46

Right: a junior cellarman in Champagne with a stack of jeroboams. Far right: snow carpets the ground in Burgundy. Although vines can survive temperatures of -18° centigrade, a late frost can kill young shoots and ruin that year's wine.

Average to poor: 1977, 1975, 1974, 1973

The best vintages in Germany are the ones which produce a very high level of natural sugar in the grapes, allowing the producer to make the great sweet wines like Beerenauslese.
Excellent: 1983, 1976, 1975, 1971
Good: 1981, 1979
Average: 1982, 1980, 1978, 1977, 1974, 1973, 1972

Vintage port is not made every year and so each year it is 'declared' the quality will be of a relatively high level to start with.
Excellent: 1983, 1982, 1977, 1963
Good: 1980, 1975, 1970, 1966, 1960, 1958, 1955

Vintage champagne, like vintage port, is only declared in certain years, the production of the other years going into non-vintage champagne.

The following vintages have been declared by many champagne houses in the last ten years:
1981, 1979, 1978, 1976, 1975

Tasting Wine

Far too much mystique is attached to wine tasting. The main reason for tasting is to determine if you like the wine, just as anyone cooking would taste a sauce to see if it is to their liking. Wine tasting is fun and enjoyable and one can learn a lot from it.

When you have ten or more wines to taste – and you want to remain standing and be able to remember what the first one tasted like – it's best to spit out the wine. Some people might think this is pretentious, but in fact it is very practical. If you have visited a wine fair where hundreds of wines are on show you will know that everything quickly starts to blur if you don't spit out!

Above: a shop sign in Chinon, France. Right: a professional wine taster with an array of wines and a spitoon. Facing page: the difference in colour between the slightly greenish Frascati from Rome and the deeper yellow Sauternes of Bordeaux indicates the greater sweetness of the latter.

How to Taste

Professionals who can tell you the name and vintage of a wine without seeing the label are not clairvoyants. They simply know what to look for in the colour, smell and taste of the wine.

1. Colour. First you look at the colour. To do this properly you need to use clear (not coloured or cut) glass. All wine should be bright – it is not a good sign if it is cloudy. A purpley-red colour usually indicates a fairly young wine; red wine that is a browny-orange colour is an older wine.

White wines with a green tinge are usually very young and, in general, the older the white wine the deeper its yellow colour becomes. Some dessert wines, such as Sauternes, generally have a much deeper colour, and are thicker in texture. If a wine is high in alcohol (for example Sauternes or port), the wine leaves glycerine – referred to as *legs* – down the sides of the glass when swirled around. From looking at the wine you can see if it is

The colour of wine is an important indicator of quality and is best seen against a light background. Above: (left) a rosé; (centre) a Beaujolais and (right) a Bordeaux. Facing page: (top) inspecting the colour prior to smelling (bottom left) and tasting (bottom right).

still, sparkling or pétillant (slightly sparkling).

2. Smelling the wine. This is just like smelling food to see if it's fresh, or whether the scent is pleasant. You should only fill the glass one third full to do this properly. Then, without spilling the wine, gently swirl it round in the glass. This allows the smell, or *bouquet*, to develop in the glass. Then take a good sniff. You can tell instantly if food is bad or has gone off by smelling it, and the same applies to wine.

In order to get a good sniff it is important not to serve the wine in too narrow a glass. If you've a big nose you'll have trouble tasting out of a tall, thin 'copita' shaped sherry glass!

3. Tasting the wine. After smelling the wine you should then take a sip and swirl it around your mouth so that it covers all parts of the taste buds on the tongue. Then, if you're tasting a number of wines, you spit it out. There are some people in the wine trade who can spit accurately up to 20 or 30 feet. However, be warned, this is not advisable unless you're outside in the garden or have had a lot of practice!

Many wines leave a lingering flavour in the mouth after swallowing or spitting. This is referred to as the *aftertaste*.

Tasting in a Restaurant

The procedure in a restaurant is slightly different – most proprietors are not too impressed if you spit wine all over their expensive carpets!

In a good restaurant the wine waiter will show you the bottle before he opens

Above: a wine from the complicated region of Pomerol, where nearly every family produces wine and generalisations are difficult. It is usual, in a restaurant, for the waiter to show the label to the customer before opening the wine. Facing page: a selection of cheeses and fruits which go well with white wine.

it. It is always worth checking that it is the same wine you ordered – in particular check that it's the same vintage. It's too late to discover it is the wrong wine when the bottle is practically finished.

In most restaurants the wine waiter will pour a little wine into the glass for you to taste. Inevitably they offer it to the male, but it should be offered to whoever ordered it, male, female or otherwise! You should look at the wine to check it isn't cloudy, smell it and taste it. If you think there is something wrong with it now is the time to say – once the bottle is half empty you won't have much success in complaining.

If you order the house wine (the restaurant's ordinary wine) it is usual not to be offered a taste. House wine is often a good choice if you are at a loss as to what to order, as it is usually relatively inexpensive. The main thing to remember in a restaurant is that you should drink what you want. Don't let the wine waiter frighten or bully you – it is quite possible that he knows less about wine than you do!

The following are some helpful questions (and answers) about faults in wine.

Q What does corked mean?
A This has nothing to do with bits of cork floating around in the wine. It is a mould which affects the cork and makes the wine taste and smell of cork. It can happen to any wine (at least all that are sealed with corks), from the cheapest to the most expensive. A good restaurant will change the bottle. Even if one bottle from a case is corked the other eleven may well be perfectly alright.

Bits of cork in the wine don't affect the taste, but it is best to fish them out as cork is not particularly digestible!

Q Should I send back a white wine with crystals in it?
A No. These are called *tartrates*, and do not in any way affect the flavour or taste of the wine. They are formed when the wine has undergone rapid changes in temperature.

Q I have noticed some older red wines which have had little bits in the bottom of the bottle. What causes this and how should one serve such a wine?
A This deposit is called the *sediment*, and is caused by the natural ageing of wine in the bottle. Vintage port (aged in bottle rather than cask) always has sediment in the bottle. The best thing to do with such wines is to decant them or, if that's not possible, to filter them. An easy way is to use a clean coffee filter. Young wines generally don't throw a sediment.

Sediment does not affect the taste of the wine and does not indicate a bad wine. Often, in fact, the contrary is the case.

Q What does the term 'drying out' mean?
A This is when a wine has passed its peak and the fruit is getting a little tired and dull, leaving a very bitter, dry flavour on the aftertaste. This should not be mistaken for tannin – the bitter substance (also found in tea) usually quite noticeable in young red wines.

Drinking Wine

Wine can be drunk out of almost anything, from the bottle itself to a glass slipper! As a rule of thumb, however, it is best to drink wine out of something which does not impair, or add anything to, its flavour. If you want to see the wine most clearly, glass is the ideal material. Glasses have been used for drinking wine ever since it was invented, and there are still some Roman glasses in existence.

To appreciate the exact colour of the wine to its full extent it is best to use clear, uncut and uncoloured glass.

Most wine glasses have stems. This helps you swirl the wine around the glass when tasting and also means that greasy fingerprints don't cover the glass. It is harder to swirl wine around in a tumbler – and a bottle wouldn't go very far if everyone drank out of tumblers.

There are many different shapes of glasses available, sold under various design names, many of which are largely unnecessary. Some shapes, however, are more complementary to certain types of wine.

Flutes (tall, relatively narrow glasses) are good for champagne or sparkling wine because the bubbles disappear less quickly than in a large glass, as they are not so exposed to the air. Saucer-shaped glasses are to be avoided as the wine loses its fizz quickly and if you try walking around with one in your hand you'll find you spill at least half!

In general, a tulip-shaped glass or a Paris goblet is the most versatile, and can be used for all types of wines. The size of the glass is optional, and although many restaurants serve the white wine in a

Above: the Savoy 90 cocktail, a mixture of lime juice, orangeflower water and champagne. Right: though attractive and tidy, keeping wine in the kitchen is less than ideal. The heat from cooking and washing impairs the flavour of reds and can destroy that of champagnes. Facing page: the modern way to maintain the temperature of wine.

DEPUIS
BOUTEILLE PAR HUGEL

Champagne flute. Although tricky to fill because the bubbles race to the top of the glass, the flute is ideal for champagne. The fizziness of the wine is released more slowly than in the saucer-shaped style and so the wine can be better enjoyed.

Small wine glass. A fairly standard shape which is not limited to any particular type of wine. However it is normal to serve chilled white wine in small glasses so that frequent replenishments from an ice-cooled bottle keep the wine cool and refreshing.

Large wine glass. Larger glasses are generally used for red wine, but they should not be more than a third-full at any time. This allows room for the wine to breathe, while the sloping sides capture the bouquet admirably.

Cheap pub glass. The glasses so often encountered in pubs and clubs are usually short-stemmed and made of thick glass. This makes them ideal for the rather rough treatment which they receive, but rather less than perfect for drinking wine.

Sherry copita. The copita is one of the finest wine glasses in the world. Its lines are simple and elegant, yet perfectly suited to the drinking of sherry. The long, thin shape funnels the scent of the wine into the nostrils, while it holds about the right amount for the average person.

Brandy bowl. A good quality brandy bowl should be made of the thinnest glass possible and contain little more than a splash of spirit. The bowl is then cupped in the palm of the hand and the brandy swilled around to be gently warmed. At the same time the inward-curving glass captures the heady fumes perfectly.

Although some fine Clarets, such as the bottle of Beau-Rivage (facing page), improve with careful handling, there is no point in being pretentious about wine: mixing white wine with mineral water and ice (right) produces spritzer, a cool and refreshing summer drink.

smaller glass than the red this is not essential.

However, if you are going to have several wines, it helps to know which wine is in which glass. The easiest way to do this is to have different shaped or sized glasses for each wine. Brandy or liqueur glasses are generally smaller, presumably because glass manufacturers don't think we should drink too much of these! The idea behind the balloon-shaped brandy glass is to allow the glass to be easily cupped in the hand and the brandy warmed up.

Keeping glasses spotlessly clean is extremely important. If you were to put some of the same bottle of wine in a clean and in a dirty glass you would be amazed at the difference in flavour.

However, getting the glasses clean can itself cause problems, since washing-up detergent can affect the taste of a wine quite considerably. When drunk from a glass which has not been properly rinsed, a sparkling wine will loss its fizz very quickly and a still wine will taste very unpleasant. It is always worth smelling the empty glass before you pour the wine into it. If it smells of dirty dishcloths or detergent you should rinse it again. After all, you want to enjoy the wine you've paid good money for!

Whatever glass designers would have us believe, it is important that you drink wine from a glass you like. It is often better to ignore the rules and simply enjoy the wine!

Decanters

Decanters can be used for any wine, although they are not advisable for sparkling wine as too much exposure to the air will make the fizz disappear rapidly.

There are two main reasons for using a decanter: to get rid of sediment and to aerate the wine. If there is sediment in the bottom of the bottle you can get rid of it by decanting the wine so that the deposit is left along the side of the bottle. You can then enjoy the wine without picking the bits from your teeth when you drink it.

When you decant a wine you allow air to get to it. Some heavy red wines like Italian Barolos benefit from this extra aeration, which can make the wine less hard and tannic. Equally, decanting some very special old wines could make them deteriorate because of too much aeration.

If you serve wine in a decanter most people will automatically assume it is an expensive wine. If you want to cheat you can serve bag-in-box wine in a decanter! It looks better, and most of your guests will think you have paid for a far better wine. Remember that the majority of people are very impressionable. You could even become a wine snob yourself!

When the wine has sediment, decanting should be done over a candle or torch so you can see through the wine. The bottle should be tilted slowly so as not to disturb the sediment. Before decanting, the bottle should be left upright so that the sediment has a chance to settle.

Serving Temperatures

All the rules about wine are there to be ignored, and the temperature at which you

RIVAGE
1982
GRAND VIN
BEAU-RIVAGE
BORDEAUX
APPELLATION BORDEAUX CONTROLÉE
BORIE - MANOUX
70 cl

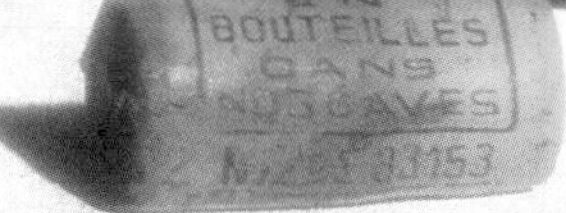

serve the wine is entirely up to you. If you like your white wines warm and all your red wines chilled – that's fine. If not, it is thought that white wines are at their best when slightly chilled, but beware – over-chilled white wines can lose much of their taste.

Red wines were traditionally served at room temperature, but a hundred years ago, before the advent of central heating, room temperature was very much lower than it is today.

Red wines today are often served so warm that the flavour of the wine is stewed. If a red wine is very cold and you want to warm it up quickly the best way to achieve this is to put it in a bucket of hot water. Putting it in the oven or, even worse, in the microwave, is definitely *not* recommended as it will destroy the wine.

Some red wines such as Beaujolais, Chinon or Bourgueil are traditionally drunk slightly chilled.

Sparkling wines generally taste fresher and crisper when chilled, and are more refreshing served that way. To chill a sparkling wine quickly you can put it briefly, for 15-30 minutes, in the freezer, but beware – if you forget about it it is likely to explode.

If you put a bottle of wine in an ice bucket it will chill more quickly if you add water to the ice. There are also a variety of coolers available: those that hold the wine at the same temperature and those which have detachable freezer packs which cool the wine very rapidly.

Right: a firm grip is often needed when pouring champagne as condensation on the cold bottle may cause it to slip. Facing page: a fine bottle of Alsace wine accompanies a prawn prepared in the fashionable *nouvelle cuisine* style.

If a wine served in a restaurant isn't cold enough for your liking (irrespective of what the wine waiter says), ask for an ice bucket. If a wine is too cold it's more difficult. You have to tell them not to give it three seconds in the microwave! However, if you cup a glass of wine in your hands it will soon warm up.

These are only suggestions, not necessities. Always remember that it is you who is going to drink the wine, and that you are the person who should determine the temperature at which it should be drunk.

Food and Wine

Good wine is best appreciated with fine, fresh food, but can also help the preparation of such food pass more quickly for the cook (right). Facing page: light red wine such as Chenas, which has long been considered one of the best Beaujolais, is ideal with smoked salmon and other delicate foods.

People get far too worried about choosing which wines to serve with which food, and often end up drinking something they don't enjoy just because some so-called 'expert' suggested it. Food and wine are made to go with each other in whatever combination you prefer. Like all rules, those traditionally relating to food and wine are there to be broken.

Red wine can be enjoyed with fish just as a white wine can go well with red meat. More important is to match the style of wine and food. Light wines go with light food and heavy, more full-bodied wines with rich, heavier foods. It is often worthwhile matching wine and food from the same region.

Because a dry wine can taste sour after a sweet wine it is best to serve dry wines first, or throughout a meal. The same applies to ordinary and fine wines – if you serve an ordinary wine after a particularly good one, the ordinary one will seem even worse because you subconsciously compare it with the better one.

Sweet wines should be at least as sweet as the pudding, if not sweeter, otherwise all that you will taste will be the acidity.

In France, the cheese is served before the pudding, so that if you haven't finished the red wine with the main course it can be finished with the cheese. Often the best red is served with the cheese.

1984
PRODUCT OF FRANCE
Chenas
APPELLATION CONTROLÉE
Mis en bouteille par

There are some foods, however, that don't go very well with wine because the flavour is so strong that it swamps the wine. These include highly spiced foods and curries, where lager is a sensible alternative to wine. Any food high in acidity (for example salad dressing) can make the wine taste odd.

Below are a few suggestions, but don't treat then as 'musts'. It is important to experiment to discover what you like best.

Many continental recipes call for wine as an ingredient, but it would be a great waste to use an *Appellation Contrôlée* wine for cooking. A VDQS, Vins Délimités de Qualité Supérieure, such as Minervois from the south of France, is more than adequate for such a purpose. For drinking with oysters (facing page) and other seafood, however, a good quality white, such as Chablis, is called for.

White fish and seafood – dry white wines/ light fruity reds
Pâté/foie gras – sweet whites/Sauternes/ full-bodied reds
Pheasant/game – strong, heavy reds
Chicken – medium to full dry whites and medium reds
Pasta – medium reds, especially Italian or Spanish
Stews – medium to full reds
Red meat – medium to full reds
Cheese – red/port
Pudding – Sweet wines or champagne/ fortified wines

It is often a good idea to match wines with foods from the same region, such as the French cheeses (this page) and combining Fitou with Cassoulet (facing page), both from Toulouse.

1981
Fitou
APPELLATION FITOU CONTRÔLÉE
Cuvée
Mme. Claude Parmentier
MIS EN BOUTEILLE A LA PROPRIÉTÉ
LES PRODUCTEURS RÉUNIS V.V.O. F 11100 NARBONNE
PRODUIT DE FRANCE

Avocado Cheese Balls (top), Celery Boats (above) and Shrimp Stuffed Eggs (right).

Snacks to accompany Wine

Avocado Cheese Balls

PREPARATION TIME: 30 minutes + 30 minutes to refrigerate

MAKES: 25 party snacks

1 medium size, ripe avocado
1-2 tbsps cream or yogurt
1 clove garlic, crushed (optional)
1 tsp lemon juice
⅓ cup finely grated low fat Cheddar cheese
1 tsp mustard
2 tbsps fresh breadcrumbs
½ small onion, finely chopped
Freshly ground black pepper to taste
2 tbsps freshly chopped parsley
4 tbsps toasted almond nibs

Halve the avocado and twist apart. Remove stone. Peel each half. Mash the avocado flesh in a medium size mixing bowl. Add the cream or yogurt, crushed garlic, lemon juice, grated cheese, mustard, breadcrumbs, onion and seasoning, mixing with a fork until a stiff paste results.

Using cold, damp hands, roll rounded teaspoons of the mixture into balls. Roll half in the finely chopped parsley to coat. Roll remaining balls in the cold, toasted nuts to coat.

Refrigerate for 30 minutes before serving.

Shrimp Stuffed Eggs

PREPARATION TIME: 15 minutes

MAKES: 12 party snacks

6 eggs
4 tbsps margarine or low fat spread
1 clove garlic, crushed
½ cup cooked, peeled shrimp, chopped
½ tsp finely chopped basil
Freshley ground black pepper to taste
Low fat milk if necessary

Garnish:
Tiny pieces of red pepper
Bed of lettuce

Hard boil the eggs, stirring as they come to the boil. Drain and plunge immediately into cold water. Allow to cool completely. Shell and cut each egg in half lengthwise. Remove yolks. Set aside.

Cream the margarine or low fat spread with the crushed clove of garlic. Beat in the egg yolks, shrimp, basil and black pepper to taste. Add a little milk if necessary until a soft consistency results.

Fill the egg whites with the prepared mixtures. Serve garnished with a tiny piece of red pepper.

Note: This snack may be prepared in the morning provided it is kept airtight in the refrigerator until just before serving.

Celery Boats

PREPARATION TIME: 15-20 minutes

MAKES: 100 party snacks

2 heads celery, cleaned

For the Fish Paté:
2 medium size kippered fish fillets
¼lb smoked salmon, chopped
Juice ½ lemon
4oz cream cheese
1 tsp tomato paste
1 tsp creamed horseradish
3 tbsps thick-set plain yogurt
Coarse black pepper
1 tbsp fresh parsley sprigs

Garnish:
Sprigs of fresh mint
Lumpfish caviar

Make the paté. Skin the mackerel and flake the fish into the bowl of a food processor, using the metal blade, or into a blender. Process to chop finely – 5-7 seconds. Add the roughly chopped smoked salmon, the lemon juice, cream cheese, tomato paste, creamed horseradish, yogurt, pepper, fresh parsley sprigs and seasoning. Process until smooth.

Cut the celery into boats and pipe or spread with the paté.

Garnish with the lumpfish caviar and sprigs of mint. Serve cold.

Note: This snack may be prepared in the morning provided it is kept airtight in the refrigerator until ready to serve.

Savory Eclairs

PREPARATION TIME: 20-30 minutes

COOKING TIME: 20 minutes

MAKES: 15 party snacks

1 recipe choux pastry (see recipe for Cheese Aigrettes)
Beaten egg to glaze
Salt and freshly ground black pepper to taste
6oz cream cheese, at room temperature
1 tsp tomato paste
1 tbsp chopped chives
¼lb cooked ham, chopped
2-4 tbsps almond nibs

To Garnish:
Finely chopped fresh parsley.

Make the choux pastry exactly as directed for Cheese Aigrettes, but do not add the grated cheese. Season. Allow to cool.

Using a large pastry bag and a ½ in plain tube, pipe fingers of the choux paste about 1 in long onto a greased baking sheet. Brush all over with the beaten egg. Sprinkle with the almond nibs. Bake on the top shelf of a pre-heated oven 400°F (200°C), for about 20 minutes, or until puffed up and golden.

Transfer to a cooling tray and immediately make a slit in the side of each with a sharp knife. This will allow the steam to escape. Allow to cool.

For the filling. Beat together the cream cheese, cream and tomato paste. Fold in the chives and ham. Season to taste.

Using a large pastry bag fitted with ½ in plain tube, or a teaspoon, fill the eclairs with the cream cheese mixture.

Serve immediately, sprinkled with the chopped parsley.

Note: The eclairs may be baked in the morning and left on the cooling tray until ready to fill.

Cheese Straws

PREPARATION TIME: 20-30 minutes

COOKING TIME: 15-20 minutes

MAKES: 18-20 party snacks

2 cups flour
1 tsp mustard powder
Salt and freshly ground black pepper to taste
Pinch of cayenne pepper
8 tbsps butter
4oz mature Cheddar cheese, finely grated
1 egg yolk
Cold water to mix } *mixed with*
A little beaten egg

Sieve the flour, mustard, seasoning and cayenne pepper.
Rub in the butter. Fork in the cheese. Mix to a stiff dough with the egg yolk and water.
Roll the pastry out to a thickness of ½ in. Cut into straws about 4 in long. Cut out a pastry ring, using two plain cutters.
Brush ring and straws with beaten egg.
Arrange on baking sheet and bake just above center of a preheated oven 400°F (200°C), for 15-20 minutes, or until golden.
Serve the cooled straws stacked in the ring.

Smoked Salmon Flowers (right), Savory Eclairs (center right) and Cheese Straws (far right).

Smoked Salmon Flowers

PREPARATION TIME: 20-30 minutes

MAKES: 12 party snacks

1½ cups flour
6 tbsps butter or margarine
½ tsp salt
Cold water to bind
2 eggs
2 tbsps milk
2 tbsps butter
Salt and freshly ground black pepper to taste
1 tbsp heavy cream
¼lb thin slices smoked salmon

To Garnish:
A few chopped chives.

Make the patties. Sieve flour and salt. Rub in margarine. Mix to a firm dough with the water. Roll out and cut 12 rounds using a fluted cutter. Line 12 muffin pans. Prick with a fork.

Bake blind on the second shelf of a pre-heated oven 400°F (200°C), for 10-15 minutes. Remove from pans and allow to cool.

Beat eggs and milk together, and season lightly. Melt butter in medium pan over low heat. Stir in egg mixture and cook over a low heat, stirring all the time until mixture scrambles. Remove from heat and allow to cool slightly, stirring. Stir in cream. Set aside to cool.

Cut smoked salmon into strips and line each pastry case. Top with a little of the cooled scrambled egg and garnish each salmon flower with a few chopped chives.

Sausage Toasties

PREPARATION TIME: 15-20 minutes

COOKING TIME: 20-30 minutes

MAKES: 24 party snacks

12 pork sausages, pricked
12 slices of bread
6 tbsps butter
2 tsp mustard

Cut the crusts off the bread and roll each slice out flat with a rolling pin.

Stirring continuously, melt the butter and mustard together over a low heat. Brush each slice of bread with the melted mustard butter.

Roll each piece of prepared bread round a sausage to enclose completely. Cut in half to give 24 rolls.

Arrange on a baking sheet, join-side down, and bake on the second shelf of a pre-heated oven 375°F (170°C), for 20-30 minutes, until golden brown.

Serve hot or cold.

Stuffed Mushrooms

PREPARATION TIME: 20 minutes

COOKING TIME: 20 minutes

MAKES: 28 party snacks

4 tbsps blue cheese mayonnaise
4 tbsps cooked bacon, chopped
1 clove garlic, crushed
2 tbsps fresh breadcrumbs
¾lb mushrooms, stalks removed
4 tbsps butter

To Serve:
Croutons of toast.

Put the mayonnaise into a mixing bowl. Fold in the bacon, garlic and the breadcrumbs.

Melt the butter in a 10 in flan dish in an oven preheated to 350°F (175°C). This will take about 7-10 minutes.

Fill the mushrooms, dark, gill side up, with the blue cheese mixture.

Arrange in the hot butter. Using a pastry brush, carefully brush the butter round sides of each stuffed mushroom.

Bake, uncovered, for 10-15 minutes, then increase temperature to 400°F (190°C), for 5 minutes.

Serve, hot or cold, on the circles of toasted bread.

Asparagus Peanut Rolls

PREPARATION TIME: 20 minutes

MAKES: 14 party snacks

1 whole-wheat loaf, uncut
4 tbsps butter, at room temperature
2 tsp smooth peanut butter
Few drops lemon juice
10oz package asparagus spears

Garnish:
Lemon butterflies
Chicory leaves

Cut the crusts off the loaf.

Beat the peanut butter and lemon juice into the butter. Cut the bread thinly and roll each slice out flat with a rolling pin. Spread the bread with the flavored butter and place a piece of drained asparagus on each piece of bread.

Roll bread round asparagus to enclose completely. Trim asparagus stem if necessary.

Serve garnished with the lemon butterflies and chicory leaves.

Salami Open Sandwiches

PREPARATION TIME: 20 minutes

MAKES: 6 party snacks

6 slices rye bread
3oz cream cheese
18 slices of salami
A few asparagus tips
1 small onion, ringed
Slices of cucumber
1 Iceberg lettuce, shredded

Remove crusts and cut each slice of bread into an attractive shape. Spread thickly with cream cheese. Top with salami and decorate as required – see picture.

Serve on a bed of Iceberg lettuce.

Note: It will be necessary to use a knife and fork for this snack.

Asparagus Peanut Rolls (left), Stuffed Mushrooms (below left) and Sausage Toasties (bottom).

Cauliflower and Zucchini Fritters

PREPARATION TIME: 30 minutes

COOKING TIME: 20-30 minutes

MAKES: 45 party snacks

6oz cauliflower flowerets
6oz baby zucchini

For the Fritter Batter:
1 cup flour
1 tsp baking powder
½ tsp salt
1 egg
1 cup cold water

Top and tail the zucchini and cut into bite-size pieces. Do not wash either the zucchini or cauliflower flowerets but wipe clean with a damp cloth if necessary.
Make the batter. Sieve the flour and salt into a mixing bowl. Make a well in the center. Separate the egg, putting the yolk into the well in the flour and the white into a clean, medium-sized mixing bowl. Adding the water gradually, mix the flour and egg yolk to a smooth batter with a wooden spoon.
Whisk the egg white until standing in soft peaks and fold into the batter with a metal spoon.
Meanwhile, heat the oil in a deep fat fryer to 375°F (190°C). Dip the prepared vegetables into the batter to coat and then, using a slotted spoon, lower each piece of battered vegetable into the hot oil. Fry until crisp and golden.
Do not try to fry more than 8 pieces of vegetable at a time so that the temperature of the oil is maintained.
Drain on paper towels and serve piping hot accompanied by Seafood Dip (see recipe).

Cheese Aigrettes

PREPARATION TIME: 20-30 minutes

COOKING TIME: 30 minutes

MAKES: 25-27 party snacks

For the Choux Pastry:
1 cup cold water
4 tbsps butter
5 tbsps flour
Salt and freshly ground pepper to taste
2 eggs, beaten

⅓ cup grated Cheddar cheese
1 tsp mustard
Pinch cayenne pepper
Oil to deep fry

Put the water and butter into a medium saucepan. Bring the water to the boil. Stir to ensure butter has melted.
Turn off heat and immediately add the sifted flour and seasoning, all at once. Beat well with a wooden spoon until a ball of shiny dough results which leaves the side of the pan clean. Set aside for 5-10 minutes to cool slightly.
Gradually beat in the beaten eggs, a little at a time, until a thick, glossy paste results. Beat cheese, mustard and cayenne pepper into prepared choux pastry.
Meanwhile, heat the oil in a deep fat fryer to 375°F (190°C).
Fry teaspoons of the mixture in the deep fat until puffed up and golden brown. Do not fry more than 8 teaspoons of choux paste at a time so that the temperature of the oil is maintained.
Drain on paper towels and serve immediately.

Breaded Shrimp

PREPARATION TIME: 20 minutes

COOKING TIME: 20-30 minutes

MAKES: 30 party snacks

1lb Gulf strimp
1 egg, beaten
½ cup fresh brown breadcrumbs
Oil to deep fry

Garnish:
Lemon wedges and fresh sprigs parsley

As an Accompaniment:
Tartare sauce

Pat the shrimp as dry as possible on plenty of paper towels. This is particularly important if frozen shrimp are used.
Put the beaten egg into a cereal bowl, and the breadcrumbs onto a dinner plate. Dip the shrimp into the beaten egg and then in the breadcrumbs to coat. Repeat until all the shrimp have been coated.
Meanwhile, heat the oil in the deep fat fryer to 375°F (190°C) and fry the prepared shrimp, no more than 10 at a time, so that the temperature of the oil is maintained, until golden brown (about 5 minutes).
Drain on paper towels and serve hot, garnished with the lemon and parsley. Pass a bowl of tartare sauce round separately.

Cheese Aigrettes (left), Cauliflower and Zucchini Fritters (below) and Breaded Shrimp (bottom).

Cocktail Sausage Rolls with Apple

PREPARATION TIME: 30 minutes
COOKING TIME: about 20 minutes
MAKES: 30 party snacks

12oz packet frozen puff pastry, defrosted
1lb pork sausage meat
1 apple peeled, cored and chopped
Salt and freshly ground black pepper to taste
Flour
1 beaten egg

Roll the pastry out to a thickness of about ¼ in and cut into 2 strips about 4 in wide.
Work the apple and seasoning into the sausage meat. Shape into two long rolls to fit the pastry. Dust sausage meat lightly with seasoned flour and arrange on each strip of pastry.
Brush the edges of each strip of pastry with beaten egg. Fold the pastry over and seal.
Using the back of a knife, knock up and then flute the edges.
Make two slits with a sharp knife on the top of each roll at ½ in intervals to allow the steam to escape.
Brush all over with beaten egg and cut into 1 in pieces.
Arrange on a dampened baking sheet and bake just above center in a pre-heated oven at 450°F (210°C), for about 20 minutes, or until golden brown.
Best served warm.

Spiced Chili Savories (above), Cocktail Sausage Rolls with Apple (right) and Salami Open Sandwiches (far right).

Spiced Chili Savories

PREPARATION TIME: 20 minutes
COOKING TIME: 10 minutes
MAKES: 30 party snacks

¾lb ground beef
4 tbsps fresh brown breadcrumbs
1 small onion, finely chopped
2 tsp finely chopped oregano
2 tsp chili powder
1 tbsp tomato paste
2 tsp mustard
Salt and freshly ground pepper to taste
½ a beaten egg
Seasoned flour for coating
2-4 tbsps garlic butter, melted

Put the beef into a large mixing bowl. Add the breadcrumbs, onion, oregano, chili powder, tomato paste, mustard and the seasoning.

Mix well. Bind the mixture together with the beaten egg.

Roll teaspoons of the mixture into small meatballs. Toss in the seasoned flour to coat.

Brush with the melted garlic butter and broil under a medium heat, turning occasionally until evenly browned.

Serve on wooden picks, accompanied by the mixed seafood dip (see recipe).

Note: This snack may be served hot or cold, but is best served within 2 hours of preparation.

Chinese Melon (top), Stuffed Vine Leaves (above) and Peach with Parma Ham (left).

Stuffed Vine Leaves

PREPARATION TIME: 20 minutes
COOKING TIME: 15 minutes
MAKES: 20-24 party snacks

8oz packet vine leaves
½ cup cooked chicken meat, ground
½ cup cooked lean lamb, ground
2 tbsps cooked brown rice
2 green onions, chopped
1 tsp tarragon, finely chopped
2 tbsps apple sauce
Salt and freshly ground black pepper to taste
2 tbsps grape seed oil or corn oil
1 medium onion, chopped
2 tbsps tomato paste
1 tbsp dry white wine

Carefully dip the vine leaves into a pan of boiling water. Drain well on paper towels.
Combine the ground chicken and lamb, the rice, green onions, the tarragon and apple sauce. Mix well. Season.
Put a small amount of the filling in the center of each drained vine leaf. Roll up.
Put the oil into a large, shallow frying pan. Heat for 1-2 minutes, then fry the onion until soft but not brown. Stir in the tomato paste and wine. Season.
Stir in 2 tbsps water. Lower the stuffed vine leaves carefully into the pan using a slotted spoon. Cover with a lid and simmer gently for 15 minutes, checking after 5 minutes that there is sufficient liquid.
Note: It will be necessary to use a knife and fork with this dish, which is delicious hot or cold.

Peach with Parma Ham

PREPARATION TIME: 20 minutes
MAKES: about 45 party snacks

2 large, ripe peaches
¼lb Parma ham
Wooden picks

Peel the peaches – this is much easier if the peaches are covered with boiling water for 1-2 minutes first.
Halve the peeled peaches and remove the stone. Cut each half into bite size pieces.
Cut the ham into thin strips and roll one strip round each peach piece. Secure with wooden picks. Serve chilled.
Note: When fresh peaches are not available, use drained, canned pineapple pieces or cubes of fresh melon.

Chinese Melon

PREPARATION TIME: 40 minutes
COOKING TIME: 10 minutes
SERVES: 8-10 people

¾lb pork tenderloin, cut into 1 in cubes
1 green or yellow melon, chilled
Oil for brushing
Salt and freshly ground black pepper to taste
15oz can pineapple pieces in natural juice, drained and juice reserved

For the Optional Dressing:
1 tsp soy sauce
2 tbsps pineapple juice
1 clove garlic, crushed
Pinch ground ginger
1 tbsp white wine vinegar
2 tbsps olive oil

Brush the cubes of pork with a little oil. Season and thread onto kebab sticks or meat skewers. Broil under a medium broiler, turning occasionally until well cooked. Set aside to cool.
Carefully cut the melon in half, horizontally. Remove seeds and discard. Remove melon flesh and dice. Serrate the melon shells.
Fill the serrated melon shells with the cooked pork cut into small pieces, the diced melon flesh and the pineapple pieces.
Put all the ingredients for the dressing into a screw-top jar. Screw on the lid. Shake to mix.
Arrange the filled melon on a serving dish and, just before serving, pour over the prepared dressing, if using. Serve immediately with wooden picks.

Fish Kebabs

PREPARATION TIME: 15 minutes
COOKING TIME: 10 minutes
MAKES: 6 party snacks

¾lb boneless cod, cubed
½lb Gulf shrimp, peeled
½lb lamb's liver, cut into pieces
8oz can pineapple rings drained and cut into pieces
4 tbsps butter
1 clove garlic, crushed
1 tsp finely chopped fresh parsley
6 finger rolls
Butter for spreading (optional)
6 metal meat skewers

Load each skewer with alternating pieces of the prepared food; that is, a cube of cod, a shrimp, a piece of lamb's liver and a piece of pineapple, until each skewer is full. Put the butter, garlic and parsley into a small pan and set over a low heat, stirring until the butter has melted. Brush the kebabs all over with the garlic butter, and broil, turning occasionally, until well cooked. Split the finger rolls and butter if required. Slip the food off the kebab sticks into the prepared rolls.
Serve immediately with a choice of relish.

Crab Rounds

PREPARATION TIME: 20 minutes
MAKES: 16 party snacks

2 cucumbers, ends removed
6oz can crab meat
3½oz can pink salmon, skin and bones removed
4 tbsps heavy cream, whipped
1 tsp tomato paste
1 tsp lemon juice
Salt and freshly ground black pepper to taste

Garnish:
Slices of pimento olives
Parsley

Cut both the cucumbers evenly into 8 large rings. Using a teaspoon, hollow out a boat in each ring, leaving a shell ¼ in thick. Sprinkle with salt and leave them to stand upside down while preparing filling.
In a mixing bowl combine the drained, chopped crab meat, the drained, flaked salmon, the cream, tomato paste, lemon juice and seasoning to taste. Rinse cucumber rings and pat dry.
Fill each prepared cucumber boat with the crab mixture.
Garnish with a slice of pimento olive and a tiny piece of parsley before serving.
Note: If liked, the cucumber boats may be crimped as in the picture, before hollowing out. This is rather time-consuming, however.

Mixed Seafood Dip

PREPARATION TIME: 15 minutes
SERVES: 8 people

¼lb Gulf shrimp, cooked
¼lb smoked salmon
¼lb lobster meat

For the Dip:
1 cup soured cream
¾ cup Stilton cheese, crumbled
1 tbsp plain yogurt
3 tbsps mayonnaise
1 tsp fresh basil, finely chopped
1 tsp lemon juice
1-2 cloves garlic, crushed (optional)
Salt and freshly ground black pepper to taste

To Accompany:
Strips of peeled carrot
Strips of cucumber, peel left on

Prepare the dip. Put the soured cream into a mixing bowl. Stir in the Stilton, yogurt, mayonnaise, basil, lemon juice, garlic if used, and seasoning to taste. Mix well. Transfer the dip to an attractive serving dish, set in the center of a large plate.
Put the seafood in groups around the dish of dip, leaving the shrimp whole, cutting the lobster meat into bite-sized pieces and making the smoked salmon into rolls, secured with wooden picks. Add the sticks of carrot and cucumber and serve immediately.
Note: This recipe may be prepared on the morning of the party, but keep covered with plastic wrap in the refrigerator until ready to serve.

Crab Rounds (right), Mixed Seafood Dip (below) and Fish Kebabs (bottom).

Parmesan New Potatoes (top), Bacon Mushrooms (above right) and Spiced Nuts (right).

MICROWAVE SNACKS

Parmesan New Potatoes

PREPARATION TIME: 10-15 minutes

COOKING TIME: about 10-18 minutes (depending on model)

MAKES: 15-16 party snacks

1lb tiny new potatoes, peeled, if required
4 tbsps butter
½ tsp salt (optional)
Grated Parmesan cheese
Finely chopped parsley

Put the potatoes into a roasta-bag. Dissolve the salt, if used, in 2 tbsps cold water and add to the bag. Seal the bag loosely with a rubber band and place in a casserole dish. Microwave on 100% (high) for
7 minutes (700W oven)
8-9 minutes (600W oven)
10-12 minutes (500W oven)
In each case, turn the bag over once, half-way through cooking time. Set aside for 10 minutes.
Put the butter in a large mixing bowl and microwave on defrost for
2-3 minutes (700W oven)
3-4 minutes (600W oven)
4-5 minutes (500W oven)
or until melted. Drain the potatoes and toss in the melted butter.
Sprinkle with parsley or Parmesan and serve hot or cold on wooden picks.

Bacon Mushrooms

PREPARATION TIME: 20-30 minutes

COOKING TIME: about 5-10 minutes (depending on model)

MAKES: 24 party snacks

12 slices bacon
24 small button mushrooms
2oz fine liver pate
Wooden picks

To Serve:
1 whole grapefruit
Wooden picks

Using the back of a knife, stretch each rasher of bacon out on a chopping board.
Arrange 6 of the bacon slices on a microwave rack or on 2 paper towels on a dinner plate. Cover with 2 paper towels. Microwave on 100% (high) for
2-3 minutes (700W oven)
4-5 minutes (600W oven)
5-7 minutes (500W oven)
Wipe the mushrooms clean and remove stalks. Stuff each mushroom with a little liver pate.
Cut each slice of partly cooked bacon in half, lengthwise, and wrap each half around a stuffed mushroom. Secure with wooden pick.
Arrange in a ring on the same dinner plate or roasting rack, standing on 2 paper towels if using the dinner plate. Do not cover.
Microwave on 100% (high) for about
3 minutes (700W oven)
4-4½ minutes (600W oven)
5-6 minutes (500W oven)
Repeat with remaining bacon rolls. Serve on wooden picks, pushed into the grapefruit.
Note: This snack is best served within two hours of preparation.

Spiced Nuts

PREPARATION TIME: 10 minutes

COOKING TIME: about 7-12 minutes (depending on model)

MAKES: ¾lb spiced nuts

¼lb shelled, husked peanuts
¼lb shelled, blanched almonds
¼lb shelled, husked cashew nuts
1 tbsp corn oil
1 tbsp butter
½ tsp ground ginger
½ tsp ground cinnamon
½ tsp cayenne pepper
Salt to taste

In a mixing bowl, combine the nuts.
Put the oil and butter in a 10 in flan dish and microwave on 100% (high) for 1-2½ minutes or until the butter melts.
Sprinkle the spices over the nuts (do not add salt at this stage). Pour on the butter and oil and toss to coat.
Transfer the nuts to the flan dish and microwave uncovered on 100% (high) for about
7-9 minutes (700W oven)
10-12 minutes (600W oven)
12-14 minutes (500W oven)
In all cases stir the nuts 2 or 3 times during the cooking time and remove when lightly golden as they will continue to color when removed from the microwave.
Allow to stand for 5 minutes.
Sprinkle with salt before serving hot or cold.
Note: When quite cold these nuts will keep well in an airtight container.

The World's Wine Producers

The Loire Valley produces some fine wines in the surroundings of its fairy-tale architecture. Facing page: the chateau of Luynes, where wine is bottled in the distinctive Loire bottle (above right), a more fluted version of the Burgundy.

France

The Loire Valley

The Loire Valley is one of the most attractive regions of France. Beautiful châteaux and gardens look out over France's longest river, which flows for about 635 miles, with vineyards on either side for the last 250 miles. Many of the châteaux have been converted into hotels, which are often very reasonably priced and are set in idyllic surroundings. A number of them have huge firework displays ('Feux d'artifice') on summer evenings.

The region's food is delicious, with lots of the fresh fish and shellfish which complement the wines of the Loire so well.

The Loire Valley produces some of the best value wines available in England. Starting from the Atlantic the first region you come to is the Pays Nantais, the home of Muscadet. This is a crisp, dry white wine, available in all wine shops in England. The actual grape is called Muscadet, or Melon de Bourgogne.

There are various types of Muscadet: straight AC Muscadet and AC Muscadet de Sèvre et Maine, referring to a more specific region. Of these wines the latter, with the addition of *Sur Lie* after its name, is the best quality Muscadet available and is, therefore, more expensive than ordinary Muscadet.

Sur Lie is a French expression referring to the way the wine is made, and means

quite simply that the wine is bottled directly off its lees (the dead bits of yeast etc which are left in the wine after fermentation). This technique gives the wine the maximum amount of flavour, and means it does not have to undergo any type of filtering. The basic theory about making wine is that the less it is moved during its vinification process, the better.

Muscadet is best drunk young – usually two years old at the maximum. If it is a lot older than this and still on the shelves the chances are, except in excep-

SANCERRE
APPELLATION SANCERRE CONTROLÉE
CLOS DE LA TERRE DES ANGES
RÉCOLTÉ PAR
RENÉ LAPORTE
PROPRIÉTAIRE-VITICULTEUR
FONTENAY-SAINT-SATUR (Cher)
MISE EN BOUTEILLES AU DOMAINE
SELECTED AND SHIPPED BY
Grants of St. James's Ltd.
LONDON S.W.1.
PRODUCE OF FRANCE
73 cl

Above: the labels of two wines from the upper Loire: Sancerre and Pouilly-Fumé. Both wines are slightly greenish in colour and smoky in flavour. Far right: the vineyards of Turckheim in Alsace.

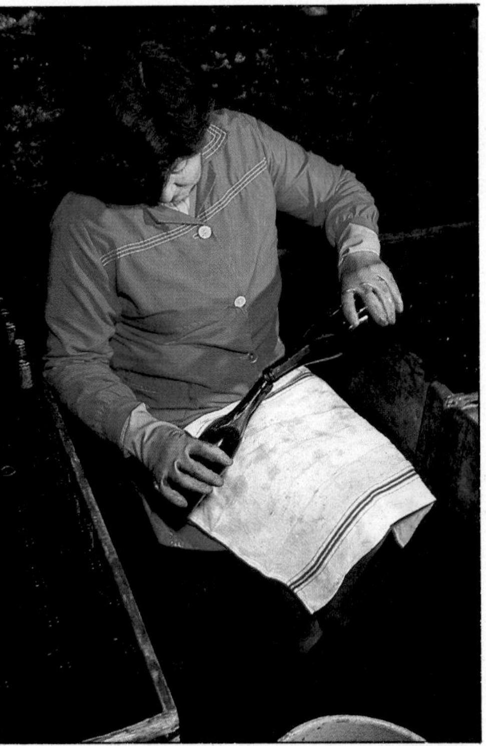

tional circumstances, that it will taste rather lifeless.

Another wine to look out for is Muscadet Nouveau, which is a very young wine, very crisp and dry, and usually first on sale between November and December following the vintage.

Also made in this region is Gros Plant, again the name of the grape. Similar in style, this dry white wine is generally slightly cheaper than Muscadet, but is not seen so widely in Britain.

Moving upstream along the Loire the next region you come to is Anjou Saumur. A huge quantity of Anjou Rosé, a fairly dry rosé wine, is made here. It is also the main

area for the sparkling, white Saumur wine made by the *méthode champenoise* and sold in a champagne-style bottle. This is a good, dry fizz, cheaper than champagne, but with the good, crisp flavour of the Chenin Blanc grape.

Of the red wines Saumur Champigny is probably the best known. This is a light, fruity dry wine which is a pleasant summer drink when slightly chilled.

The Loire produces a number of very sweet wines too, ideal for drinking with puddings. Names to look out for include Côteaux de Layon, Bonnezeaux, Savennières and Vouvray.

Vouvray comes from Touraine, the next region upriver. It can be sparkling (like Saumur), still, sweet or dry. The important words to look out for are *sec* (dry), *demi-sec* (medium dry/sweet) and *moelleux* (sweet). Some labels, however, give no description. In this instance, you can work it out if you can vaguely remember what the weather was like during the vintage. This might sound incredibly complicated but it isn't!

Below: one of many roadside signs in France proclaiming the pedigree of the local wine, which can usually be sampled nearby.

As a general rule, years with a lot of sunshine like 1976 or 1982 produce wines which will tend to be sweeter than those made after poor summers. Vouvray, unlike Muscadet, can keep for several years, and I've tasted some which were as much as 60 years old.

Red wines from Touraine include Chinon and Bourgueil; fruity, quite earthy in taste, dry wines which often smell and

taste of raspberries and strawberries.

The vineyards furthest up the Loire Valley are referred to as the central vineyards. This is where Sancerre and Pouilly-Fumé (not to be confused with Pouilly-Fuissé, a white burgundy) are made. Made from the Sauvignon grape, they are crisp, dry white wines with more depth than Muscadet, and generally rather more expensive. If you're visiting the region, Sancerre is a fascinating place to go to: an ancient, walled town, high on the top of a hill surrounded by vineyard slopes.

Below: a monument to the monk who became the father of champagne and one of the great figures in the history of wine. Right: a selection of champagne bottles and gift sets. Bottom: the tricky process of *dégorgement*, in which the sediment is removed from the bottle. Facing page: a map showing the first-class, and other, wine producing regions of France.

Champagne

Champagne, the drink everyone associates with success and happy occasions, is produced in one of France's most northerly vineyards.

Champagne has a long history, and many people attribute its invention to a monk named Dom Perignon. Legend has it that he was the man who discovered how to keep the bubbles in champagne.

The region of Champagne is relatively small (only 86,000 acres) and by law the only wine in the world that can legally carry the name 'champagne' is the sparkling wine made in this region by the *méthode champenoise*. Other sparkling wines, even those from France, California, Spain or anywhere else in the world made by the same method are not champagne.

Because the region is quite small and the process involved very complicated and labour-intensive, champagne has always been relatively expensive.

The bubbles in champagne are

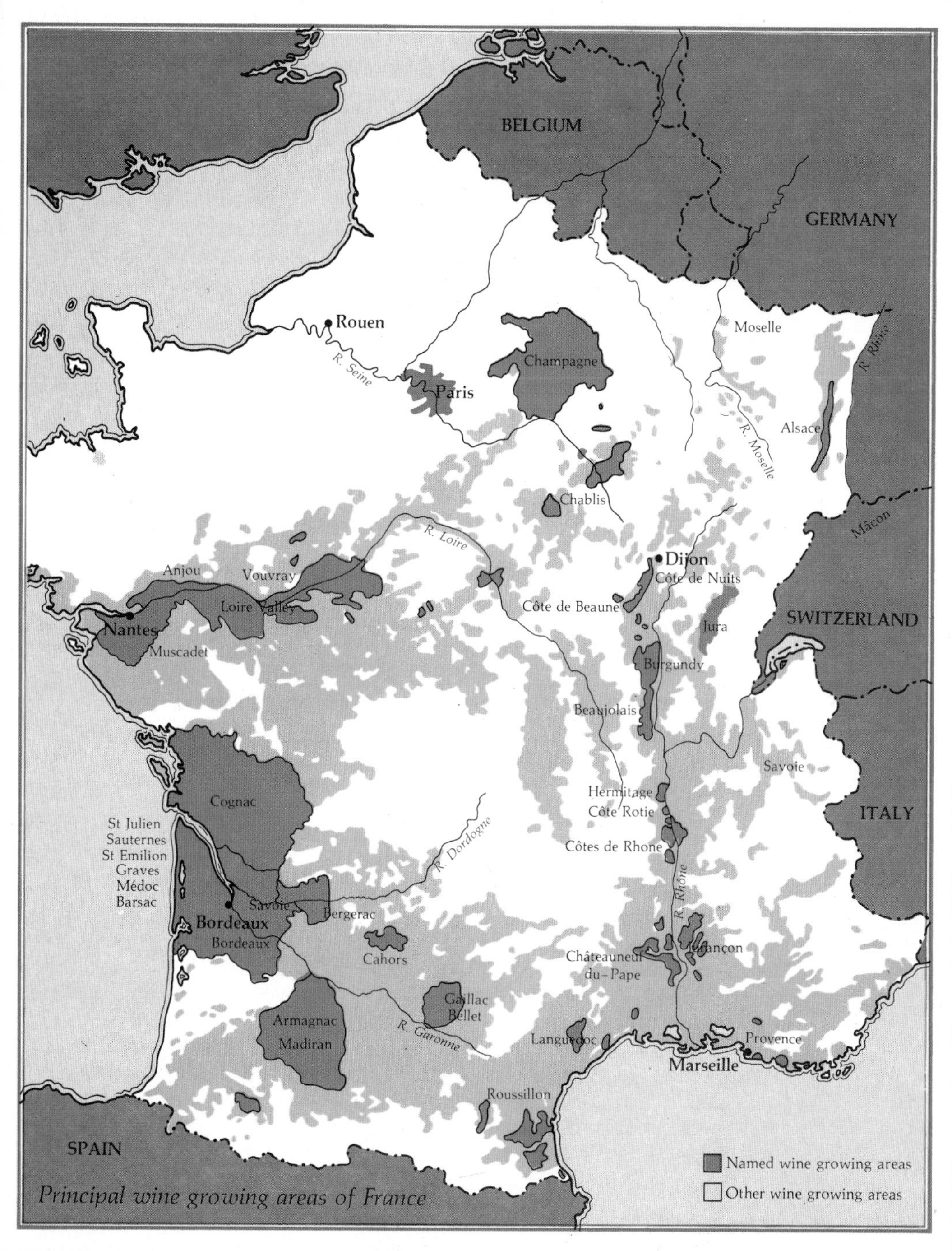

Principal wine growing areas of France

produced naturally, and the making process does not involve carbonating (inserting) bubbles into the wine. After a first fermentation in the vat, yeasts are added to the wine when it is in bottle. This causes a second fermentation in the bottle. As a result, the wine is sparkling but contains some sediment from the dead yeasts.

To get rid of this the bottles are tilted neck down and periodically shaken *(remuage)* so that the sediment collects near the neck. The neck of the bottle is then frozen, and the ice plug containing the sediment shot out of the bottle. Because of the pressure of gas inside the champagne bottle special corks are used, secured with wire. Care must be taken when opening champagne bottles, as they are likely to explode.

Champagne is made from three grapes: Chardonnay, a white grape, and two black grapes – Pinot Noir and Pinot Meunier. Although the last two are black grapes their juice is white, like that of most black grapes. To make rosé, champagne producers either leave the red skins together with the wine for between one and two days until they achieve the desired colour, or they add red wine.

Most non-vintage champagne is a blend of these grapes from different years, and is generally sold under a brand name such as Möet & Chandon, Bollinger or Lanson.

Vintage champagne, when a year is shown on the label, is the wine from one single year. It is more expensive than the blended non-vintage variety, and is only made in very good years. In general, a vintage champagne will keep far longer than a non-vintage one.

The words 'blanc de blancs' on the label means that the champagne is made from 100% white grapes. Most champagnes are 'Brut', meaning 'dry', and those called 'Ultra Brut' are extra dry, ideal for diabetics or slimmers (as they have less sugar added to them) although I've yet to see champagne included in any diet!

Burgundy

Burgundy, on the east side of France, is, like Bordeaux, one of France's classic great wine regions. It stretches from Chablis, in the north, to Beaujolais in the south. In between the two there are many different styles of wine. In Burgundy, more than any other wine region, the winemaker is very important.

Because the name Burgundy has become so famous internationally, prices have escalated and many Burgundies are now expensive. There are, however, some areas left which can offer value for money. These include (going north to south) St Bris, Haut Côte de Nuits, Haut Côte de Beaune, Côte Chalonnaise, Mâconnais and Beaujolais.

The red wines of Burgundy in general are fruitier, less tannic and lighter than the wines of Bordeaux or the Rhône. The whites (made from the Chardonnay grape) can be rich and are dry, but not as aggressively dry as most Loire whites.

Burgundy is divided up into hundreds of small vineyards. This means that in the village of Gevrey-Chambertin alone there are numerous different growers, all of whom make a different style of wine. If you enjoy a bottle of burgundy it's definitely worth remembering the grower's name.

Beaujolais red wines are made from the Gamay grape (all other Burgundy reds are made from Pinot Noir). Don't judge the region by Beaujolais Nouveau – there are in fact some delicious wines to be found, particularly from the nine Beaujolais villages listed in the Table.

Because Burgundy is such a confusing region with so many wines I have listed area by area, from north to south, the most commonly-found wines, together with their colour and style.

The Côtes-du-Rhône

The Côtes-du-Rhône region runs from Vienne in the north, downriver from Beaujolais, to Avignon in the south, just above Provence. It is split into two distinct regions, the Northern Rhône, going south as far as Valence, and the Southern Rhône, which starts at Montelimar and runs down to Avignon.

The Northern Rhône produces the fullest, heaviest wines, the best of which are now highly sought after and consequently not cheap! The best red wines include Côte-Rôtie, Hermitage, Crozes-Hermitage and Cornas and an excellent sparkling wine is made at St Peray. There are also two world-famous white wines, Condrieu and Château Grillet. The latter, which is owned by only

Facing page: rarely exported, but drunk in large quantities by locals, is the *Vin de Pays.* This classification ranks below VDQS but above Vin de Table and includes many very drinkable wines.

Vin de Pays
Côtes du Tarn
VINICOLE COOPÉRATIVE DU GAILLACOIS
81600 GAILLAC (TARN)

one proprietor, has the distinction of being the smallest Appellation in France.

AC Côtes-du-Rhône is the basic wine made in the region and is mainly produced in the Southern Rhône. It is a red wine (although you can find white Côtes-du-Rhône) which has a purpley red colour, and is fruity with a peppery flavour. It is not as dry as claret. The Southern Rhône produces somewhat lighter and jammier wines than the cooler Northern Rhône.

Three famous wine labels: (above and right) two of the finest wines from the Côte de Beaune and (above right) a fine wine from the banks of the Rhone. Facing page: pruning vines in Burgundy. Most of the prunings will be burnt, but some may later be used for grafting.

The best known of these is Châteauneuf-du-Pape, made from a mixture of up to thirteen different grape varieties. White Châteauneuf-du-Pape is also produced, but because of the hot climate the white wines tend to lack acidity. Apart from basic Côtes-du-Rhône, good value wines from the Southern Rhône include Gigondas, Vacqueyras, Côtes du Ventoux and Côteaux de Tricastin. There are also some very good dry, full-bodied rosés made in Lirac and Tavel.

My personal favourite from the Southern Rhône is a sweet dessert wine called Muscat de Beaumes-de-Venise. Made from the strongly-perfumed Muscat grape, this luscious wine is pinky-gold in colour, honeyed on the nose and

deliciously sweet and rich. It is high in alcohol and is classed as a 'fortified' wine meaning, that grape spirit has been added to the wine during its vinification. It goes especially well with raspberries and Christmas pudding. When served chilled it is easy to drink too much of it!

Bordeaux

For most connoisseurs bordeaux is the ultimate wine. In many ways that's because of tradition – in the 18th century *clairet*, now known as claret, was the gentleman's only drink. Many other countries have tried to imitate Bordeaux's wines by planting the same grape varieties, especially California and Australia. To this day, however, Bordeaux still leads the wine market, and arguably makes the finest wines in the world.

The main regions of Bordeaux are divided by two rivers, the Gironde and the Dordogne, whose confluence, the Garonne, runs into the Atlantic. On the left of the Gironde and Garonne are the Médoc and Graves, and on the right bank of the Dordogne are Saint Emilion and Pomerol.

In Bordeaux the wines are known by the name of the château (French for house or castle); these vary in size from huge castle-like buildings to tiny shack-like houses. The basic Appellation is AC Bordeaux, and the next one up AC Bordeaux Supérieur.

The top wines of Bordeaux are called *Crus Classés* (or Classed Growths) and are graded from First Growth through to Fifth Growth, following a classification in 1855. The First Growths are rated to be amongst the world's greatest wines, and this is reflected in their price.

There are only five First Growths – Châteaux Latour, Lafite-Rothschild, Margaux and Mouton-Rothschild in the Médoc and, in Graves, Château Haut-Brion. There are also two in St Emilion – Châteaux Ausone and Cheval-Blanc – and one in Pomerol – Château Petrus. Whilst delicious, these wines are very expensive and are often bought more because of the name on the label than for their taste. Below the Classed Growths are Cru Bourgeois wines – these often represent the best value for money in Bordeaux.

Claret, always red in colour, is a dry, fairly tannic wine. Many of the Classed Growths and the better Cru Bourgeois age their wines in oak barrels called *barriques*. The oak, together with the grape skins which are left in contact with the wine, produce the tannin, a bitter substance that makes the wines hard and unpleasant to taste when young, but enables them to last for a long time.

Three main grape varieties are used in claret: Cabernet Sauvignon, Cabernet Franc and Merlot. They are blended together in different proportions, determined by the winemaker and by how much of each grape variety the château has planted in its vineyards. In the Médoc the Cabernet Sauvignon is predominant, whilst Merlot is the main variety used across the river in Saint Emilion and Pomerol. This leads to different styles of wine. Médoc and Graves clarets tend to be more austere, powerful and longer lived than the more delicate, softer wines of Saint Emilion and Pomerol.

Many people don't realise how much white wine is produced in the Bordeaux region. This is where Entre-deux-Mers (the region between the rivers Dordogne and

Above left: the label of one of the finest wines of Bordeaux, the vineyards being located in the southern suburbs of the city. Above right: the label of an Alsace wine bottled for one of the more respected shippers. Facing page: an unusual bottle holder containing wine from Sancerre.

1977
1977
SANCERRE
SANCERRE CONTROLEE
RÉCOLTÉ PAR
LAPORTE
VITICULTEUR
(Cher)
AU DOMAINE
ncerre
CONTROLEE

Gironde) comes from, a crisp, dry white wine made mainly from a grape called Sauvignon.

The other white wine for which Bordeaux is famous is Sauternes. This is a rich, luscious, sweet wine, high in alcohol and often referred to as a dessert wine. Sauternes is a very difficult wine to make. The producer leaves the Sauvignon and Semillon grapes on the vines long after the grapes from the rest of the region have been picked. The grapes shrivel up, go a browny-yellow colour and are affected by a noble rot called *botrytis cinerea*. If successfully attacked by this rot, the shrivelled grapes are eventually harvested in October/November, the pickers often selecting individual grapes from the bunches. By this stage the grapes are very high in sugar levels and the resulting wine, deep gold in colour, is rich and sweet.

Making Sauternes is a risky business, because at any time whilst the grapes are left rotting they could be destroyed by bad weather. Because of this complicated process genuine Sauternes is expensive.

The wine industry of France preserves many traditional methods including: (left) horse-drawn transport, (top) hand picking and (above) wooden grape carriers.

1977
à la

1977
à la

Sancerre

DOMAINE DU ROCHO

Sancerre
APPELLATION SANCERRE CONTROLEE

Laporte

The Rest of France

Under this wide-ranging heading there are literally hundreds of wines from which to choose; almost every tiny village in France grows some vines. When on holiday in France it is always worth trying the local wine, even if you've never heard of it. Often the smaller or less known the village, the more eager the locals will be for you to try their wines.

Some areas of France that are becoming more and more popular in this country are in the south and south-west of France. Names to watch out for are Languedoc, Rousillon, Minervois, Cahors, Jurançon, Provence, Madiran and Buzet, amongst others. These are generally full-bodied, fruity red wines, and can be very good value for money.

Left: an array of better-known labels from the Sancerre region of the Loire Valley. Above: estate workers in Beaujolais sample the current year's *nouveau* before it is shipped to a waiting world.

For white wine drinkers Alsace is an important region. Once part of Germany, this region produces very spicy, dry white wines, in many ways more German than French in style, although heavier and more powerful in flavour. This is where the flowery, spicy Gewürztraminer grape is at its best. All Alsace wines (sometimes called Alsatian, although I always thought that was a dog!) are named after the grape variety from which they are made, and the majority of them are white. Seven basic grapes are used, of which Riesling is the most common, making a full-bodied dry wine.

Other grapes commonly used in Alsace include Pinot Gris, often, rather confusingly, called Tokay d'Alsace, again producing a dry wine. The sweet wines of Alsace are made from grapes which have been 'late-picked' *(Vendange Tardive)* and are, consequently, high in sugar content. Delicious though these wines are, they are generally quite expensive.

Another name you'll see quite often on labels is 'Edelzwicker', which means a blend of grape varieties.

Pinot Noir, the grape of Burgundy, is used to make both red and rosé wines in Alsace, although it is often difficult to tell the difference between the two! Reds and rosés from Alsace are not widely available in Britain.

Alsace wines are easily recognisable by their tall, thin, German-style bottles.

Germany

Most wine drinkers start by drinking German wines. This is probably because they are light, low-in-alcohol, fruity, flowery, often medium-sweet wines which are easy to drink, pleasant and rarely offensive.

Bottled in their distinctive, long-necked bottles, German wines are easily recognisable on a supermarket shelf. This is probably just as well because, apart from a few well-known brand names, the names on the labels are generally unpronounceable!

The labels may often look indecipherable, but don't be put off – they are generally quite logical, even if the ones written in flowery Gothic script are often impossible to read!

German wines come in two different coloured bottles, brown glass for hock, (Rhine wines) and green glass for wines from the Mosel.

Much wine that on initial appearances seems to be German is really an EEC blend – made in Germany but using a mixture of grapes from other countries (in particular Italy), and blended to produce a 'Germanic' style of wine.

The basic level of German wine is called *Tafelwein* (table wine), often prefixed by the word Deutscher, meaning German.

A fairly recent introduction is *Landwein* – similar to a French *vin de pays*. Above this are *QbA* wines *(Qualitätswein bestimmte Anbaugebiete)*, meaning quality wine from a designated region. These words cover a wide range of wines from the different regions.

In many ways it is surprising that vines prosper in Germany, as it is one of the most northerly vineyard regions in Europe. Much research has been done over the years to develop hardy grape varieties which can survive the low temperatures. The main variety used is the Riesling (pronounced Reece-ling), which has been crossed with another variety, the Sylvaner, to produce Müller-Thurgau. This is now the predominant grape variety in Germany and has the advantage of ripening early and producing a huge crop. Whilst Müller-Thurgau is used in the QbA wines such as Niersteiner or Liebfraumilch, the finest QmP wines are generally made from pure Riesling.

The top category is *QmP* wine – *Qualitätswein mit Prädikat* – meaning good quality wine with a special attribute. Within this section are various styles of wines grouped according to potential alcohol and sweetness, starting with the driest, *Kabinett*, then (in ascending order of sweetness) *Spätlese, Auslese, Beerenauslese* and *Trockenbeerenauslese*. In exceptional years *Eiswein* (literally, 'icewine') is produced. It is made from grapes which, once ripe, are left on the vine until December and are picked at sub-zero temperatures. Because Eiswein is so difficult to make, and because the mature grapes can be damaged by hail, excess rain, etc at any time, it is normally extremely expensive.

German wines are classified according to their region of origin – many by the names of rivers near which they are produced.

The Mosel is probably the best-known river. The wines are generally labelled as Mosel-Saar-Ruwer, thus including the Mosel's two tributaries. The top wines are made from the Riesling, grown on the best south-facing slopes, whilst the more well-known wines are made from blends using a lot of Müller-Thurgau. Amongst these are Moselblümchen, Bereich Bernkastel and

Facing page: Mannenburg, a typical wine-producing town on the Mosel, with its riverside buildings and vineyards climbing the hillside beyond.

Above: the massive castle of Cochem, which dominates the vineyards on this stretch of the lower Mosel. Right: the vine-crowded slopes of a side valley off the Rhine at Assmannshausen, in the Rheingau. Facing page: a map showing the principal wine regions of Germany.

Piesport – the name of the village the wine comes from. These wines are generally fairly low in alcohol.

The Rheingau produces some of Germany's best wines from the well-known villages along the right hand side of the Rhine, where the vines face due south. Generally, the sweeter QmP wines, where the grapes are picked late, are made in this area from the Riesling grape. The best wines come from individual villages such as Erbach, Oestrich and Rüdesheim.

The vast majority of Liebfraumilch comes from the Rheinhessen, although originally it was made in a tiny village called Worms. It is made mainly from the Müller-Thurgau, with other grapes blended-in to make soft, flowery, sometimes bland wines.

Niersteiner also comes from this area. A few years ago Liebfraumilch used to be medium-sweet in style, but has now changed due to the recent demand for slightly drier wines. However, even when

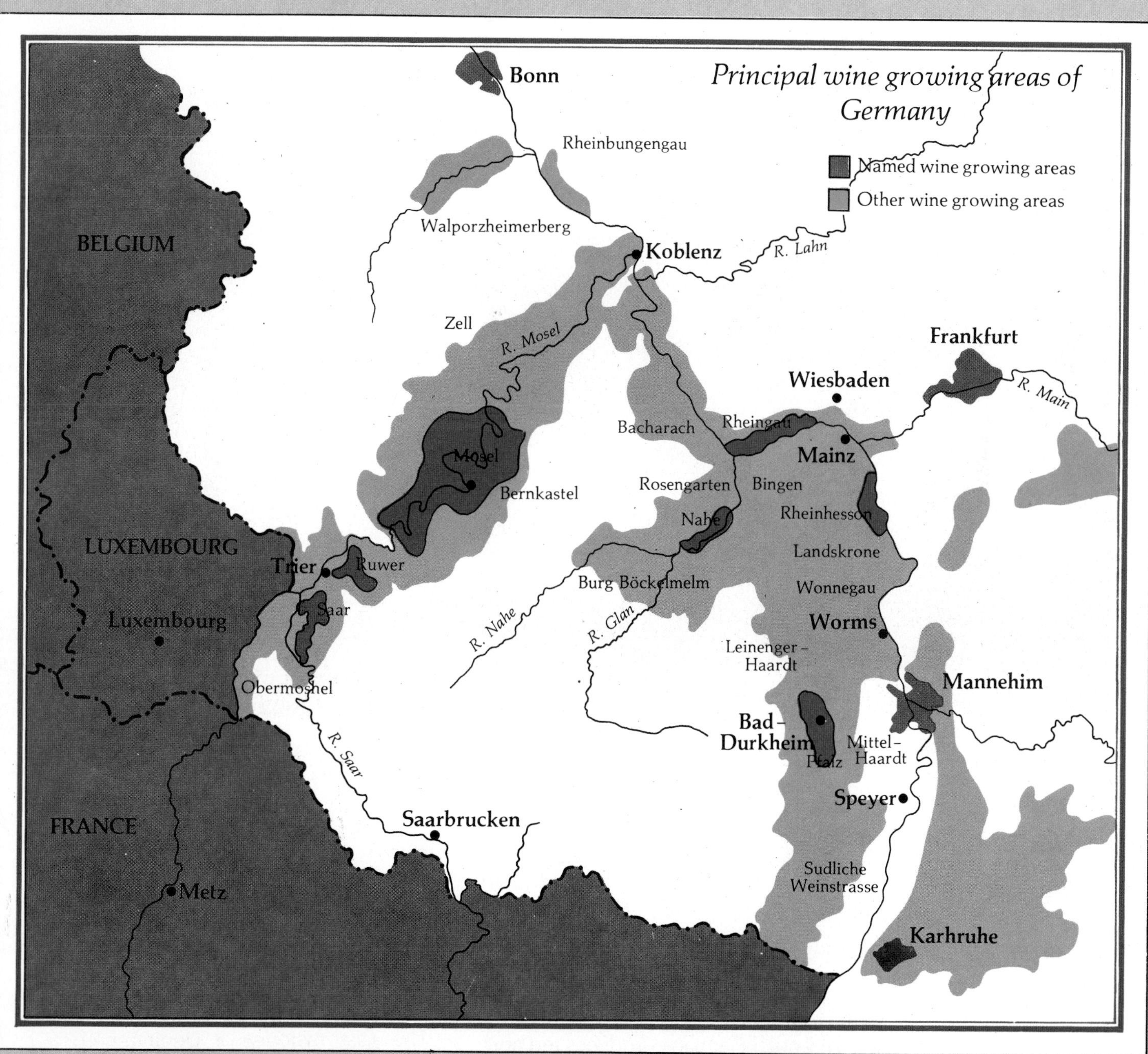
Principal wine growing areas of Germany
Named wine growing areas
Other wine growing areas
Bonn
Rheinbungengau
Walporzheimerberg
BELGIUM
Koblenz
R. Lahn
Zell
R. Mosel
Frankfurt
Wiesbaden
R. Main
Bacharach
Rheingau
Mainz
Mosel
Bernkastel
Rosengarten
Bingen
Nahe
Rheinhessen
LUXEMBOURG
Landskrone
Trier
Ruwer
Burg Böckelmelm
Wonnegau
Saar
R. Nahe
R. Glan
Worms
Luxembourg
Leinenger-Haardt
Mannehim
Obermoshel
Bad-Durkheim
Mittel-Haardt
Pfalz
R. Saar
Speyer
FRANCE
Saarbrucken
Sudliche Weinstrasse
Metz
Karhruhe

slightly dry, Liebfraumilch is nowhere near as acidic or as bone-dry as the white wines from the Loire.

Rheinpfalz (also known as the Palatinate) produces rich, flowery, spicy wines. This is not surprising when you realise it is really a continuation of Alsace, now in France, which produces wines with some of the same characteristics. Some fine German wines are made in this region.

Above: the delicate white wines of Germany are produced from such grapes as these. Right: the vine-covered slopes and traditional architecture of Beilstein, on the lower Mosel.

There are several other regions whose wines can only be found in specialist German wine shops because they are not exported in large quantities. The regions include Ahr, Franconia (the bottle is a distinctive flat flask shape), Württemberg and Baden.

Other words to look out for on German wine labels are *trocken* (meaning dry) or *halbtrocken* (meaning, literally, half dry). This tells you what style of wine to expect, but should not be confused with *Trockenbeerenauslese*, which is one of the best quality QmP wines and, far from being dry, is very rich and sweet.

Although Germany produces red and rosé wines they are not commonly seen, and are mainly interesting as a novelty rather than value-for-money. Often rather pale in colour, it's sometimes difficult to tell the difference between a red and a rosé. Unlike many red wines they are slightly sweet and without much body.

With Germany, as with any other country, it is only really by tasting different wines that you'll find what you like. Some

of the wines are commercial and, once you have acquired a taste for them, become a little bland. That's the time to experiment with a different wine. If you remember some of the words on the label, for example the region, sweetness (e.g. *Kabinett, Spätlese* etc), and/or the grape variety, you will get an idea of what is to your taste. At least that way you can eliminate those you don't like from the mass of labels and wines on offer.

Italy

Below: the monastery of St. Hidegard is surrounded by some of the highest-growing vines in the Rheingau. Facing page: an isolated chapel stands amid the vines which produce the famous Bernkastel Doktor wines of the middle Mosel.

In terms of production and per capita consumption, Italy produces and drinks the most wine per year. People tend to think of all Italian wine as cheap holiday plonk but, because of the sheer size and number of areas producing wine in Italy, this is far from the truth. There are several

hundred quality wines produced in Italy, generally found with the letters DOC and DOCG on the labels, the Italian equivalent of the French Appellation Controlée.

Wines from Italy can be rather confusing as they are allowed to take their name either from the region, the grape variety or the style of wine, and sometimes a mixture of all three! The same name often refers to both red and white wines. However, it is always worth considering Italy, as her finest wines are comparatively cheap by French standards.

Probably the most important quality wine-producing region is Piedmont in north-west Italy. It is a beautiful region to visit, and produces Barolo, often referred to as the king of all Italian wines. It is a deep-coloured, dry red wine which can last for many years and is often at its best after ten to fifteen years in bottle.

Barolo is aged in oak and, when young, like the young red wines of Bordeaux, is very tannic and leaves a bitter flavour in the mouth. It is this tannin, however, that enables the wine to last. Barolo is made from the Nebbiolo grape and is always a red wine.

Barbaresco also comes from Piedmont. Aged in wood, this is generally a slightly lighter wine, velvety and dry, and made from the same grape, the Nebbiolo. Another wine whose name begins with 'B', this time named after the grape variety, is Barbera. It is more pinky-red in colour and slightly lighter in style.

The best-known white wine made in this region is Italy's biggest-selling sparkler, Asti Spumante. Production is centred around the town of Asti, from which the wine takes its name. Made from the Moscato grape, Asti is usually sweet. It is made by a less expensive method than champagne, which does not involve the hours of work involved in the *remuage* (manually turning the bottles in their racks).

Another area producing some of Italy's best wines is Tuscany, the home of Chianti. This wine is made from a mixture of grapes, mainly the Sangiovese.

Amongst the white wines of Italy, apart from the sparkling Asti, Frascati (pronounced Frass-car-tee) and Soave (pronounced Swarvay) are probably the best known. They are both crisp, dry white wines, with lots of fruit, and the best examples are good value for money. Verdicchio (pronounced Ver-deek-eeo) is another wine made in the same style.

One of Italy's more recent success stories is Lambrusco. This is a sparkling wine made in Emilia-Romagna, south-east of Milan. When exported it is usually pink or red and is often *amabile* or semi-sweet. It is generally drunk chilled.

With such a wide range of Italian wines on the market the best thing to do is to buy them and taste them. Write down the names of the ones you like, noting the type of wine and district. Enjoy experimenting!

Right: an armed horseman guards the chalky vineyards around Jerez, Spain, from which sherry is produced. Below: a *barco rabelo* loaded with barrels of port for its journey down the Duoro to Oporto, Portugal.

Portugal

Portugal, a country famous for its beautiful beaches, is the home of one of Britain's oldest established 'gentleman's' drinks – port.

Port came into being almost by accident. After the British Government had fallen out with the French in the late 17th century they had to go elsewhere for their red wine supplies. Bringing the dry red wine of Portugal over to England meant a lengthy sea journey, and to help stabilise the wine some brandy was added. Reports went back to Portugal that the British approved of this style of wine, so the technique was developed one stage further and brandy was added to stop the fermentation of the wine, resulting in a fairly sweet, alcoholic wine similar to today's port. Port is therefore a 'fortified' wine, like sherry, with at least half as much alcohol again as wine.

There are many different types of port resulting from different grades of grape and the varied techniques used in its production. The most widely available

Above: in the more remote valleys of Portugal methods are more traditional than elsewhere in Europe.

type is Ruby Port, named after its colour, which is rich and sweet.

Tawny Port is made by leaving the wine a long time in cask so it loses the brilliant deep red colour of freshly pressed juice and turns a 'tawny' colour. Often the label shows an age, such as ten, twenty, thirty, or over forty years old. Generally speaking the older the wine the higher the price will be.

However, Tawny Port with an indication of age, for example 'over 40 years of age', should not be mistaken for Vintage Port. The latter is a wine made from the finest grapes from one selected year. Rather than being aged in cask, Vintage Port is bottled when two years old and then needs many years in bottle before it is ready to drink. Unlike Tawny Port, which is matured in cask, Vintage Port throws a sediment during its maturation in the bottle and consequently needs careful decanting.

Vintage Character Port is a good quality Ruby Port and is often good value for money.

Late-bottled vintage (LBV for short) is wine from one vintage, bottled four to six years after the harvest. These ports are ready for drinking much earlier than Vintage Ports and, because they spend more time in cask, they do not need decanting.

'Crusting Port' is a cheaper alternative to Vintage Port and is a blend of wines which is matured in bottle and deposits a 'crust' (or sediment) and, therefore, needs decanting.

White Port, drunk in large quantities in both Portugal and France, is golden yellow in colour, and can be dry or sweet. It is usually drunk as an aperitif.

Portugal's Other Wines

Much the biggest production in Portugal is of table wines. The best known in England is probably Vinho Verde (Vee-no ver-day). In general only the white Vinho Verdes find their way to England, but there are many reds produced in this area, which is in the north of Portugal.

The whites are easy-to-drink, crisp wines, slightly pétillant (fizzy) as a result of carbonation. There are various theories as to how Vinho Verde, meaning green wine, got its name. Maybe it was because of the luscious green area the grapes were grown in, or the acidic, or 'green', style of the wine. What is certain is that it does not refer to unripe grapes – the grapes are always fully ripe when picked.

Of Portugal's other wines, Dão (pronounced dow) wines are probably the best value. These are full-bodied, dry red wines which are excellent value for money and can last a long time. Portugal also produces a delicious, thick, sweet white wine from the Setubal Peninsula, called Moscatel, an alcoholic dessert wine.

Portugal's most famous wines, if not its most serious, are rosés like the well-known Mateus Rosé. These are generally medium-sweet in flavour and have a slight sparkle.

This page: *barco rabelos* on the upper Duoro. This method of transporting port to the sea has been largely replaced by rail.

Madeira

Madeira is a fascinating island to visit. Only 36 miles long and 14 miles wide, it has dramatically-steep cliffs, hot, terraced hillsides and cooler shaded valleys. Vines flourish everywhere. Halfway down steep cliff sides, which look extremely treacherous, small groups of vines grow on outcrops. In many ways the island of Madeira seems to have stood still in time and, because of the very steep, terraced vineyards, ploughing is still done manually.

Madeira, like port and sherry, is a fortified wine, which means grape spirit is added to the wine. Madeira, however, is made by an unusual method of heating the wine in an *estufa*, a large, heated store.

There are four distinctive styles of Madeira, varying from very full and sweet, to very dry wines. Named after grape varieties, these styles will be indicated on the label.

Sercial is the driest Madeira, often drunk chilled as an aperitif, and lighter in style than the sweeter Madeiras.

Verdelho is a slightly sweeter wine with a dry finish. This is the style of Madeira the Victorians used to drink with a slice of cake.

Bual is a much sweeter, richer wine for drinking with puddings.

Malmsey is the sweetest Madeira, a rich, luscious, very full wine which makes a welcome change from brandy or port after a meal.

Spain

Spain's 'plonk' image is gradually changing. It is true that much Spanish wine is very cheap but, fortunately for us, it is in many cases considerably better than plonk.

Long before the Costa Brava became popular as a holiday resort Britain had been importing a wine from Southern Spain – sherry. This is a fortified wine, which means its strength is increased by the addition of brandy or spirit. Many people are unclear as to what a fortified wine is – a recent example was a girl who worked for a brewery and listed all the 'châteaux' wines under the 'fortified' wine section.

Just as real champagne comes from the region of the same name in France, so real sherry comes from Jerez (pronounced Herr-eth) in Spain.

Because they are fortified, most sherries are half as strong again as wine. Sherry, which makes an excellent aperitif when chilled and is delicious with fish soups, comes in a variety of styles: *Fino,* generally pale in colour and dry; *Manzanilla,* slightly more bitter than Fino; *Amontillado,* amber in colour with a medium dry almondy taste; *Olorosso,* which can be sweet or dry, and *Cream Sherry,* which is rich and sweet.

Other countries, such as South Africa, Cyprus and California, produce wines similar in style to sherry. There is also 'British Sherry', not made from 'British' grapes, but from imported grape musts which are then made into 'Sherry' in Britain. None of these have quite the finesse of a true Spanish sherry.

One of the most enjoyable bi-products of sherry is sherry vinegar, delicious when used in salad dressings and always worth stocking up with when you're in Spain.

As well as sherry, Spain produces many excellent, non-fortified wines. Rioja (pronounced Ree-ock-a) has become very popular in Britain during the last ten years.

The red wines of Rioja are soft, round

Below: a typical small family holding in rural Portugal with its stone house and terraced fields.

Facing page: great stacks of wooden barrels containing maturing Californian wine.

wines, with a slightly woody taste. This taste, which adds to the complexity of the wine, giving it a vanilla-scented bouquet, is the result of ageing the wine in wooden barriques – 225 litre barrels. Rioja has many historical links with Bordeaux, and has the Bordelaise to thank for the introduction of wooden barrels.

Red Rioja is made from a variety of grapes, mainly Tempranillo, Garnacha, Mazuelo and Graciano, whilst the white is made from Viura, Malvasia and Garnacha.

The countryside in Rioja is impressive and the landscape quite severe. With its red-orange soil, it has a sunbaked, arid appearance. Grapes used in Rioja come from three areas: Rioja Baja, the hottest region producing wines high in alcohol, deep in colour and ideal for blending; Rioja Alta, wines with good fruit and consistent colour, and Rioja Alavesa, producing more delicate wines with more finesse. The best Riojas are made by blending wines from all three regions.

In Spain, the different companies are known as *bodegas* – the Spanish for cellars. The name of the bodega always features on the label. Most Riojas also have a back label, giving details about the wine's age. *Gran Reserve* is the oldest, then *Reserva*, followed by *Crianza*. *Sin Crianza* is a young wine.

Good Riojas can last for many years and, because they are continually moved from barrel to barrel during ageing and the lees (sediment) is left in the empty barrels, you don't need to decant them.

There are two distinct styles of white Rioja: *Reservas*, deep gold in colour, rich and dry with the smell and flavour of the oak in which they were aged, and wines with no classification, which are light, crisp, dry and fruity and which should be drunk within two years of the vintage on the label. The latter are a relatively modern development.

Now that Rioja has established itself as a good quality Spanish wine, a newcomer has recently come onto the market, hoping to repeat Rioja's success story. This is the region of Navarra, to the north of Rioja, which produces similar wines, although somewhat lighter and less concentrated.

Here, production is centred around the ancient town of Olite. It is a fascinating region to visit and you can even stay in the 15th century castle in Olite, which is a *parador* (government owned hotel, normally housed in a historic building) and is very reasonably priced and comfortable.

Navarra red and white wines are gradually finding their way into shops and supermarkets in Britain and are generally somewhat cheaper than Rioja wines. They are excellent value for money, far more so than many Spanish table wines which don't mention their region or origin.

La Mancha, a vast wine producing area in central Spain which used to produce fairly rough white wines, has recently been improving its wine making, and now produces crisp, dry white wines.

In Penedés, which is near the tourist track just south of Barcelona, many French grape varieties have been planted. The pioneer is Miguel Torres, whose wines, both red and white, are widely available in Britain and are of sound quality. Although more expensive than the average Spanish wine, they are well worth the extra money.

The Rest of Europe

England

Many people don't realise that vines have been grown in England since Roman times, when there were extensive plantings, nor that after this period the monasteries took over the upkeep of many of the vineyards. After the Dissolution of the monasteries, vines disappeared for a few hundred years until the early 1950s. However, since then there has been a resurgence of interest, and today over 1,000 acres are under vine, with vineyards planted as far north as Lincolnshire. The majority, however, are situated in the milder climate of the south of England, especially in the counties of Kent and Sussex.

It is important not to confuse English wine with British wine. The latter can be something of a consumer 'con', as the only connection it has with Britain is that imported grape musts, usually from Cyprus or Italy, are brought to this country and made into a wine which is often fortified. The commercial logic of this is that imported grape musts from countries with a warmer climate are much cheaper than home grown grapes. English wine, however, is made from grapes grown in England. Because of England's northerly position and relatively cool climate, vine cultivation is extremely difficult and

producing grapes of decent quality requires a lot of skill. When the weather is particularly bad English wine growers sometimes harvest no grapes at all.

English wine growers not only have to battle against the elements, they also have to contend with the high government taxation. English wine is taxed at exactly the same rate as imported European wines, where production costs are lower. It is not surprising, therefore, that English wines seem relatively expensive.

Those patriotic enough to drink them, however, will not be disappointed. Techniques have greatly improved over the last few years and, with the introduction of the E.V.A. (English Vineyards Association) seal, there are some excellent white wines being made. As yet English wines have no official classification (the EEC only allows them to be called table wine) but it is well worth looking out for the ones with the E.V.A. seal. Although a few brave producers have tried producing red wines, the results suggest that England is better off sticking to whites.

German grape varieties are usually favoured as they have to survive a similar type of climate. The Müller-Thurgau, Germany's most widely planted grape, seems to flourish in English vineyards, whilst experiments with French varieties such as Chardonnay have been far less successful.

The white wines produced are either fairly dry, similar to the crisp, dry wines of the Loire Valley, or medium sweet, and more Germanic in style.

Switzerland

Many people are surprised that Switzerland, with such a high snowfall, can grow vines. Vines are generally planted on south facing slopes to gain maximum sunlight.

The wines are usually quite light, dry and delicate, the whites being made mainly from the Chasselas grape. Reds, which are normally rather thin, are made from the Pinot or Gamay grape. Although some fine wines are produced, they are largely consumed in Switzerland and those that reach this country tend to be fairly expensive. Some of the best wines are produced around Dôle.

Right: the productive vineyards north of Stellenbosch in South Africa. Some grapes, such as those (facing page top) at Wentworth in Australia, are laid out in the sun to reduce their water content before pressing and fermentation. Facing page bottom: scenes from harvest time in France, when everyone available helps with the grape picking.

Austria

Austrian wines are similar to German wines, but with a little more depth and richness. The main white grape is the Grüner Veltliner which produces dry whites, whilst *Schluck*, produced near Austria's famous Danube River, is sweeter.

Though without the centuries of tradition of the European wineries, the vineyards of California (facing page) produce some excellent wines.

Another widely-grown grape is the Welschriesling.

Because Austria enjoys so much more sunshine than Germany, it produces mostly rich, sweet wines, expecially in Burgenland, where the weather encourages noble rot, producing wines with a high natural sugar content like Sauternes and Beerenauslese.

In the past, much of Austria's wine was drunk locally without being bottled, but now the producers realise its potential and more and more is being bottled and exported.

Eastern Europe

Hungary

Hungary's most famous wine is Tokay, a sweet wine matured in barrels called *gonci,* and sweetened by adding *puttonyos* (tubs) of concentrated grape juice called *aszu.* The more puttonyos added, the sweeter the wine. The best Tokay can last for centuries.

You can now find a Tokay also called *Szamorodni,* which tastes more like a dry sherry.

Hungary's most widely-known wine is Bull's Blood, a dry, deeply coloured red wine from the town of Eger. Although rarely left for long in bottle, Bull's Blood can keep for a considerable time.

Hungary is now developing more and more dry white wine, which is gradually becoming available in Britain.

Yugoslavia

Yugoslavia's best known wine is the Laski Riesling (pronounced Reece-ling) which is consumed in vast quantities in this country. The wine produced is similar in style to, but slightly sweeter than, Liebfraumilch, and is made in the area of Lutomer.

Yugoslavia's red wines are not seen very often in this country and are generally very hot, alcoholic wines. Recent plantings of Cabernet Sauvignon have, however, produced some decent wines.

Bulgaria

Bulgaria, a country which has been producing wine for centuries, has taken notice of wine drinking trends in Europe and has adapted its wines to follow consumer demand. Excellent 'varietal' wines are found in Bulgaria, made from Cabernet Sauvignon, Merlot and Chardonnay. Whilst not up to the standard of many French equivalents, these are sound wines which represent excellent value for money for everyday drinking.

The Rest of the World

Over the last ten years the choice of wines available has increased dramatically. In Britain you can buy wines from virtually all the wine producing countries, from China to the United States.

The most important countries are those known as "New World" countries, including Australia, the United States, New Zealand and South Africa.

California

California's wines have become popular through sales of carafe wine – offering the added bonus of re-using the carafe after you have drunk the wine.

However, there is more to California than re-usable carafes. Wine production in California is enormous, and huge amounts of 'jug' wines are drunk there. They often come from one of California's hottest regions, the San Joaquin Valley, and are similar in quality to French table wines.

The Californians are fortunate that their climate is so well suited to viticulture, although the climate does vary enormously across the state.

There is rarely a shortage of sunshine, in fact the weather is so consistently good that an 'off' vintage (as found in Europe) is virtually unheard of. However, this does create problems with water shortages. Fortunately, the Californian wine producers are allowed to irrigate their vineyards, whereas in most European wine producing areas irrigation is forbidden.

Many Californian wines are big, beefy, powerful wines, normally high in alcohol. They are not the kind of wines to drink at lunchtime if you intend doing any work in the afternoon. The best can rival Europe's top wines and, although their wines have always been rather larger than life, the more innovative producers are now trying to produce more elegant, European-style wines with more finesse.

The best Californian wines come from the Napa Valley and Sonoma County. If the

wine is of a good quality, the area as well as the individual estate and/or the name of the winery will be indicated on the label. Small wineries, which generally produce the top quality wines, are known as *boutique* wineries.

Californian wines are classed as *varietals*, a term which simply means they are mainly made from one grape variety. Amongst the red grapes grown are several of Bordeaux's leading varieties; particularly successful is the red Cabernet Sauvignon. Unlike wines from Bordeaux, where the varieties are blended, the Californians like to keep theirs pure.

Red Californian Wines

Zinfandel is California's most widely planted red grape, and produces a wine people either love or hate because of its highly individual flavour.

It can produce very full, heavy wines, often as high as 13% to 14% alcohol – an ordinary French table wine would be about 11% alcohol. They also make port-style wines from this grape. In contrast, it also produces lighter, Beaujolais-style wines.

Other red grape varieties are Merlot and some Pinot Noir.

White California Wines

The most widely planted white grape is Tompson's Seedless. However, this is not seen much on labels as it is mainly used for jug wines and for blending, and makes rather bland wines.

The Chardonnay grape of white burgundy fame produces deliciously rich, full, dry white wines, normally higher in alcohol and heavier than their European counterparts.

Other varieties to look out for on labels are Fumé Blanc (the Sauvignon of the Loire), Johannisberg or Rhine Riesling, Colombard, Chenin Blanc and Gewürztraminer.

Several other states in America produce wine; among the most important are New York State, Washington and Oregon.

Chile

Chile is probably the most interesting of the South American countries producing wine. Mainly made in large co-operatives, Chilean wines, particularly the reds, are good value for money. The reds are quite full, spicy wines with lots of flavour but without excesses of tannin (a bitter substance which comes from the grape skins). Cabernet Sauvignon is the most important red grape, followed by Merlot and Malbec. The white wines are generally not so interesting, often lacking the acidity to make them properly balanced.

Red Chilean bag-in-box wines are worth buying – the wine seems to have the ability to survive this type of packaging far more successfully than most of its European counterparts.

Chile has the potential to produce some very fine wines. Meanwhile, take advantage of the sound, good value reds already available in this country.

Australia

Australia has been shipping wine to England since the 1800s. Australians

Facing page: the contrast in style of Australian wine labels emphasises the many types of wine produced in that country. Around the town of Griffith in New South Wales is a vast area of irrigated land (this page), known as the Murrumbidgee, which produces a fair amount of Australia's wine.

Top: huge wooden presses with their solid columns and massive screws, in a German cellar. Bottom: grape juice lies in large wooden vats in a French winery, before being transferred to fermenting vessels.

themselves consume a large quantity of their wine, and there are a respectable number of serious producers, some of whose wineries have been producing wine for over a century. Many of the best wines are only made in very small quantities in *boutique* wineries, and examples of these now reach Britain. Probably the most important of these is Petaluma, whose wines are well worth searching out.

In the past, Australia produced quantities of fortified wine, often rather heavy and alcoholic, but lacking charm. Since then wine-making techniques have improved immeasurably, and excellent everyday table wines are now being made and have overtaken production of fortifed wines. Many of the best bag-in-box wines are Australian, which is not surprising since they pioneered the technique. Unlike most European bag-in-box producers, the Australians put good quality wines rather than the cheapest table wines in their boxes.

Australia's wines are divided into states and regions, of which the Hunter

River Valley, to the north of Sydney, is one of the best. Here the most widely planted red grape is the Shiraz, related to the Syrah grown in the Rhône, and the Semillon, known rather confusingly as the Hunter Riesling. Coonawara, in South Australia, bordering Victoria, produces big, rich red wines from the Shiraz and Cabernet Sauvignon grapes. Surprisingly, despite the flat, dusty plains, the region is now producing top quality wines made from the Riesling grape.

Across the board, Australian winemakers are amongst the best in the world. They grow and vinify a wide variety of grapes ranging from the German Riesling to the French Chenin Blanc. Few countries can compete with such a diverse range of grapes and fine wines.

New Zealand

Wines from New Zealand really started to become popular during the Second World War when, to keep up with the thirst of incoming American servicemen, more wine had to be produced.

New Zealand, although often classed along with Australia (it's over 1,000 miles away!) and California in wine terms, is very different because of its relatively temperate climate. As a result, the New Zealanders planted Müller-Thurgau to make dry and medium-dry white wines, light in style, and the light, spicy Gewüztraminer.

South Africa

Although it's only relatively recently that we have started to see South African wines in this country they have been produced for over 300 years. In the 18th century, for example, South Africa produced a famous sweet wine called Constantia.

In 1973, South Africa's Wine of Origin legislation was passed and the vineyards were divided into fourteen main areas. All the wines have to pass strict controls and only the very best are allowed the word *Superior* on their quality seal. South African labels have a series of coloured seals on them: the blue stripe states the region of origin, the red the vintage year and the green the grape variety used. Wines can only carry the word *Estate* if they are bottled at the vineyard from which they are produced.

In general, the best wines are produced near to the coast and are less 'cooked' than those made inland. Many of the country's finest wines are fortified dessert wines and sherries, although single varietal wines are getting better and better. Grapes most frequently used include Cabernet Sauvignon, Cabernet Franc, Shiraz and Pinotage for the reds, and, for the whites, Chenin Blanc (also known as Steen), Kerner and Riesling. The Chenin Blanc, when grown in South Africa, produces a much crisper and drier wine than the wines of the Loire Valley. Many South African white wines are slightly pétillant (fizzy), which helps keep them on the light side, while the red wines are characteristically round and soft and, although far from sweet, have an underlying rich, ripe fruit flavour.

Below: the ordered verdancy of the vineyards around the South African university town of Stellenbosch.

Much of South Africa's wine is made by large groups, KWV, Stellenbosch Farmers' Winery and The Bergkelder (who make the Fleur de Cap range), all of whom produce wine of respectable quality. Although South Africa is not as advanced as California or Australia, she is beginning to produce good quality wines.

Exclusive Meals for Fine Wine

The recipes on the following pages have all been selected for the way in which they complement fine wine. The ingredients and the suggested wine (and it is only a suggestion) may be expensive, but I think you will find the end result to be something rather special.

Faisan aux Marrons

Remove the legs from two pheasants. Skin the breasts, detach them from the carcase and season with salt and pepper. Place in a heavy saucepan and let them cook slowly with a knob of butter for about 8 minutes on each side. Remove from the pan and add a wineglass of sherry and one of cognac. Add ½ pint veal stock with 2 ounces of foie gras or foie gras purée diced small. Let the sauce reduce by half. Add 4 soup spoons of double cream and 2 ounces of butter mixing well. Pipe round the edge of the dish a purée of chestnuts, you may also place around the breasts some whole peeled and cooked chestnuts. Arrange the breasts on the dish and pour the sauce over.

You could use the legs, but naturally they will take longer to cook.

Corton-Grancey 1969
or Corton-Grancey 1973

Château Beychevelle is one of the anomalies of the claret business. Officially classified in 1855 as a 4th Growth, it is rated by most of those who know to be well worth the company of 2nd Growths.

It is a wine of character, one of the best St Juliens I know. Its name has a curious origin — if the story is to be believed. The property was at one time owned by the Duc d'Eperon, Grand Admiral of France. It overlooks the estuary of the Gironde, and ships sailing past the Château were ordered "baissez les voiles" (strike sail). Hence the corruption to Beychevelle. Well, it's a nice story . . .

DOMAINE
LOUIS LATOUR
Château
Année
Corton

Carré d'Agneau en Croûte

This really is a delicacy and so well worth doing. It can all be prepared two or three days in advance and kept in the refrigerator for cooking when required.

Skin and bone some best end of lamb. Cut away the fat so that only a thin layer remains and keep the fat as intact as possible. Spread the veal stuffing. Then fold the fat over the whole joint spread with the veal mixture and tie it up. Cook for three minutes on each side, in a heavy pan and on maximum heat on top of the cooker. Never give more than 6 minutes in total and do not even try to roast this dish in the oven. Remove the meat and leave it on one side to cool. Roll out puff pastry and envelop the carré completely. It looks best if you can trace fancy designs on the pastry, like hearts or diamonds. Glaze the pastry and bake for anything from 25 to 45 minutes according to whether or not you like pink lamb. Serve with madeira or perigourdine sauce. (Allow 1 best end of lamb for 2 persons).

For the stuffing, mince $\frac{1}{2}$ pound of veal and mix with purée of mushroom, tarragon, seasoning, a dessert spoon or two of brandy and about $\frac{1}{2}$ cup of double cream, to a stiff consistency.

Chevalier-Montrachet

Imagine a relatively small sports stadium: a football pitch or a baseball diamond, plus a few extras like a tennis court or two and a pitch-and-putt fun course. Tilt it sharply, so that walking up it becomes an effort as strenuous as playing ball would be on the level. Cover the surface with stones, expose it to hail in early spring and hot sun in August, and then you have a simulacrum of the Burgundian vineyard of *Chevalier-Montrachet*.

In a very good year this 18-acre vineyard produces not much more than 1,000 cases; and in a very good year this white wine is so superbly dry, so magnificently reminiscent of the stony soil from which it has perversely come that one feels privileged to taste it.

LOUIS JADOT

Grouse à la Crème Aigre

Take a grouse and put it in a hot pan with a stick of chopped celery and a sprig of thyme, and cook on each side for 9 minutes in a hot oven. Take out of the saucepan, cut off the breast and legs and keep warm. Chop the bones and put them in a saucepan with 2 tablespoons of vinegar and a glass of dry white wine. Add $\frac{1}{3}$ pint of double cream, salt and pepper and let reduce until it has thickened. You may add sliced button mushrooms after you have strained the sauce. Serve with a purée of celery.

Ch. Lynch-Bages 1969

Château Lynch-Bages is another of those excellent wines of Pauillac which most people feel ought to be a classified 2nd Growth rather than its official 5th Growth. Certainly the market would seem to uphold this view, for Lynch-Bages costs more than many 3rd or 4th Growths.

It is a rounded wine, perhaps with a tendency to fade a little with advancing years, a tendency not at all noticeable in the 1969 vintage.

Perdreaux aux Olives

Roast a young partridge with about 4 ounces of small stoned green olives in a heavy pan, turning it after 10 minutes and basting. The partridge should take 20 minutes to cook. Take the partridge out of the pan and keep it warm. Put in the pan 3 ounces of finely minced green olives, ½ wine glass of dry white wine and ½ glass of veal stock. Let it reduce for about 10 minutes on a fast fire. Add about 2 ounces of butter and pour the sauce over the partridge.

Corton-Grancey 1969
Louis Latour

Any wine with the name Corton as part of its label is worthy of respect, for here you have the finest wines of Beaune, firm and fruity. *Corton-Grancey* is a fine specimen. It is not, in fact, the name of a vineyard, that second half of the title, but the name of the château in Aloxe-Corton where it is bottled by a first-class merchant and vineyard owner, Louis Latour.

Sauté de Veau Provençale

Use trimmings of veal from a leg that is to be roasted, or cut an escalope in strips, which will cost a little more. The strips should be about ¼-inch thick by a ½-inch wide. To each portion add two large or three medium tomatoes skinned and chopped (even pipped but that is not essential), one onion and half a clove of pressed garlic. Sauté the veal on a hot stove with hot butter and a bayleaf, stirring all the time but never allowing the butter to burn. It will need 5 minutes at the very most and would become tough if it ever boils or is overcooked.

Remove the veal and add to the chopped tomato-and-onion mixture a tablespoon of vinegar, some white wine and a few stoned, green olives. Two or three anchovy fillets are very good but for those who dislike anchovies they can be left out. Add a little meat stock, season, and put the veal strips back on the mixture. Serve with chopped parsley and some of the curly leaves to decorate. This tastes and looks very well on rice.

Moulin à Vent 1973
Groffier-Léger

The presence or absence of anchovy in the Mirabelle Sauté de Veau Provençale is crucial in determining which wine one should offer one's guests: indeed, this apparently small ingredient is almost a touchstone for the host who wishes to present just the right wine for the right dish at the right moment.

So, with anchovy, I recommend one of the great white wines of Burgundy. There are other wines which include the vineyard name Montrachet on their labels, and there will always be argument about which is supreme. Let the disputants dispute: suffice it for our purposes to say that the pale gold of *Puligny-Montrachet*, with its extraordinary scent coming up to one as the glass is swirled, represents a very good wine indeed, something for which we should be prepared to give silent thanks to whichever gods there may be.

What a difference a taste makes! For Sauté de Veau without anchovy I suggest another Beaujolais: this time, to blend with the subtlety of the sauce, I commend *Moulin à Vent 1973*.

Strawberry Gâteau

You will need 4 eggs, 4 ounces of caster sugar and 4 ounces of plain flour. Never have self-raising flour in the kitchen if you want to acquire the Robinson touch. It robs you of complete control — even plain flours vary but nothing like to the same degree of their self-raising counterparts. Whip the eggs and sugar in a bowl standing in a double pan until the mixture makes a strong thread from the end of the whisk, then fold in the flour and transfer immediately to pre-greased moulds, preferably of the type with a base that slides out. When cooked — which will take about 10-15 minutes at 220 degrees Centigrade, allow to cool slightly.

Turn out on to a wire tray and slice in half when cold. Prepare in advance a little syrup made from sugar and water and add Kirsch in the proportion of one part Kirsch to two parts syrup. Pour into a bottle with a sprinkler cork, or a cork with a 'V'-shaped cut, and shake the Kirsch syrup all over the sponge to moisten it whilst keeping it firm and whole. Spread a thick layer of cream over the bottom half and arrange large strawberries that have been halved to cover the cream. Cover the strawberries with a further thin layer of whipped cream, then add the top half of the sponge. Add a further layer of cream then more strawberries, leaving a rim of half an inch around the edge.

The gâteau can be made with other fruits. With raspberries, it is delicious. It is equally excellent with apricots and sliced peaches but these are apt to look pale and need the addition of some fresh or glacé cherries for colour.

This can be made in advance for an evening dinner party and will keep firmly in the refrigerator all day. Do remember, however, to take it out at least 40 minutes before serving if you want its full taste.

Champagne G.H. Mumm
Cordon Rouge NV

Like several of the other great champagne houses of Reims, Epernay and Ay that grew up on the banks of the Marne, the House of G. H. Mumm was founded by a German. The first Herr Mumm came from a distinguished family of wine-makers at Rudesheim on the Rhine, and

BRUT
REIMS
G.H.MUMM &
REIMS
BRUT
CHAMPAGNE

started making champagne in Reims in 1827. His grandson, G. H. Mumm himself, joined the firm in 1838, and gave it his initials in 1853, and the firm continued to be family-owned and family-run up to the outbreak of the First World War. Alas, no Mumm had thought to take out French citizenship. The family were treated as enemy aliens, their property sequestered; the firm put up for public auction in 1920. Through it all, somehow, the champagne maintained its high quality.

Mumm's Cordon Rouge is now one of the largest of the grande marque champagne houses, and its famous red stripe, and the designation Cordon Rouge, on its bottles have undoubtedly helped to make it recognisable on both sides of the Atlantic.

Soufflé Roquefort

This is another of those dishes which leaves everybody guessing—once you have tried this you will scorn a plain cheese soufflé.

For liberal helpings for four people you need ½ pint of milk, 1 ounce of butter, 4 whole eggs, 1 heaped dessertspoon of plain flour and 4 ounces of Roquefort cheese. Have a greased mould ready and beat the egg yolks well, cover them and put aside. Melt the butter and add the flour, stirring to keep it smooth. Add the boiling milk while still stirring. To this roux add the beaten egg yolks, continuing to stir, then the Roquefort, seasoning and a dash of cayenne pepper. Set away from the stove to cool, while whipping the egg whites quickly to stiffen. Fold the whites into the cheese roux and pour all into the mould, making sure to leave about ½ inch from the top otherwise the soufflé will overflow and spoil. Bake for 15-20 minutes at 220 degrees Centigrade. Ambrosial with a glass of port.

Croft
Vintage 1963

As with champagne, so with vintage port. People settle on their favourites, and will be tempted away to no other, however distinguished the name. So the Taylor man will barely tolerate a Sandeman or a Cockburn, and he who has been weaned on Fonseca will scarcely nod in the direction of Warre or Dow.

Nonetheless, for the Soufflé Roquefort, I bravely commend a *Croft 1963*. It was John Croft who, in 1788, declared: 'An Englishman of a certain standing cannot do without a glass of port after a good dinner'. So let it be.

Coquilles St Jacques

Choose fresh scallops by the brightness and deep colour of the red parts. If that is dull they are not fresh enough. Some of the more exclusive frozen food firms sell good frozen scallops, although eaten beside the fresh ones, you will notice the difference.

Allowing four scallops per portion, this recipe will be sufficient for three persons. Put the scallops in a pan with three ounces of shrimps, 3 ounces of sliced mushrooms, a knob of butter, salt and pepper to taste and just cover with half dry white wine and half fish stock. Bring to the boil then let it simmer for about 6 minutes. Strain the stock; let it reduce to about two thirds. Add ½ pint of double cream and let it thicken. Put the scallops back in the sauce and pipe mashed potato around the edge of the shell. Place the scallops in the shells, keeping a drop of the sauce back. Add to the sauce ⅓ pint of double cream whipped with 2 egg yolks. Pour over the scallops, sprinkle some grated cheese on top and put under the grill to colour.

Pouilly Fumé de
Ladoucette 1973

A combination of the Sauvignon Blanc grape and the climate along the Loire near Nevers in the centre of France produces *Pouilly Fumé*, a pale white wine that has much more character than its colour might suggest. It accompanies most shellfish dishes perfectly.

Filets de Sole Marseillaise

Drees serves about 3 fillets per person, but 2 might well satisfy most people. Poach the fillets of sole in white wine and fish stock which just covers the fish and to which a pinch or two of the expensive shredded, not powdered, saffron has been added. In a maximum of 10 minutes, according to the size of the fillets, rest the sole on a pre-cooked pilaff of rice which should have been strained in cold water to separate grains if there is the slightest sign of stickiness when the rice has cooked. Put the dish with rice and fillets into a warm oven. Quickly make a sauce with reduced stock, double cream, seasoning and a tiny knob of butter. The sauce should look pale golden yellow. Strain the sauce over the dish and

serve. This looks very good garnished with little pink pieces of lobster or salmon, with prawns or with baby button mushrooms. Once covered with sauce, it can keep for a very short while as your guests finish their pre-dinner drink but do not let it overcook and do not let the sauce solidify, so time it well.

Gewurtztraminer — Hugel

Gewurtztraminer is a grape that produces a slightly spicy wine which is instantly recognisable both to palate and to nose. Certainly, the best of its product comes from Alsace in those distinctive slender green flutes, and the House of Hugel is rightly proud of this example.

Croustade de Saumon

Now here is a way of using salmon tails. I happen to love the tail, not only because it is always cheaper but because I like its firmness.

Put the boned fish into a pan with some melted butter and seasoning. Cook it gently for 5 to 6 minutes per side (rather less for leftover, cooked fish). Add chopped, cooked leaf spinach or cooked sorrel, double cream and more seasoning if needed. Lay the spinach or sorrel in the middle of some rolled, flat puff pastry and, on top, spread the salmon. Sprinkle with a little nutmeg and add a knob of butter. Fold the pastry edges to cover the filling. Glaze the top with milk or beaten egg yolk and then bake for 25 minutes or until nicely brown. Serve with melted butter mixed with a drop of lemon juice. Never make in advance and rewarm — prepare the raw materials and serve as soon as it is baked.

Sparkling Vin Fou
Brut Renaissance —
Henri Maire

No fashionable wine comes from the Jura, which is a pity, because the vineyards along the foothills of the mountain range yield wines which are always interesting, if some way from the first-class.

Vin Fou is, really, a fun wine: easy on the palate and something to talk about other than the excellence of the Croustade de Saumon.

Apples or Pears in Wine

Choose a William Pear or a Cox's Orange Pippin apple. Peel the fruit and add white wine to some syrup of Grand Marnier. Poach the fruit in a close-fitting dish for 15 minutes with the wine syrup halfway up the sides. Then cook for a further 7-8 minutes, ladling wine over the fruit but do not let the fruit break and fall apart.

You will need very little syrup as the fruits are sweet and should be ever so slightly acid when served. You can keep any unused wine in the fridge and use over and over again with fruit.

Graves

Crêpes Farcies

These are pancakes filled with a soufflé mixture (without egg whites), flavoured with any liqueur, for example Grand Marnier, Cointreau or Drambuie to name my favourites. Warm the mixture and add the liqueur. Fill the pancakes and place on a buttered dish in the oven for 5 to 6 minutes, at 218 degrees Centigrade.

An excellent alternative is apple, although many fillings can be used. Peel, core and chop 2 or 3 large Bramley cooking apples. Melt 1 ounce of butter in a pan, tip in the apples and stir in 3 ounces of caster sugar. Cook on a high gas to keep the apples white, stirring all the time with a wooden spoon. Take them from the heat before they become purée, and place in a strainer to drain away the surplus juice. Place a tablespoonful of apple in each pancake and fold over. Arrange on the dish and return to the oven for 5 minutes.

Ch. Climens 1970

Everybody knows Château d'Yquem, that king of sweet white wine from Sauternes. Not so many know its nearest rival from Barsac. *Château Climens,* like Yquem in many ways, is unlike it in that it is better comparatively young. The 1970 is just right: the wine is light, with a subtle sweetness that never cloys: a fantastic dessert wine, which has made a wonderful recovery from frost devastation in 1956.

LIQVOR
Triple Orange
Triple Orange
Grand Marnier
LIQVOR

INDEX